W9-AAX-195

Hiking in the
USA

Marisa Gierlich
John Mock & Kimberley O'Neil
Clem Lindenmayer
Jennifer Snarski
Diane Bair & Pamela Wright
Susy Raleigh & Daniel Frideger

LONELY PLANET PUBLICATIONS
Melbourne • Oakland • London • Paris

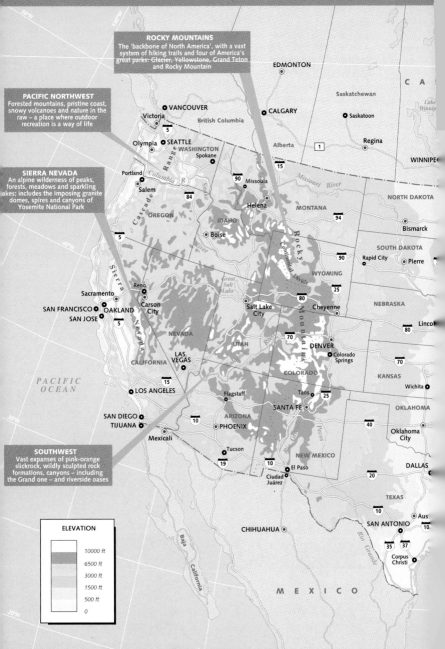

USA

ROCKY MOUNTAINS
The 'backbone of North America', with a vast system of hiking trails and four of America's great parks: Glacier, Yellowstone, Grand Teton and Rocky Mountain

PACIFIC NORTHWEST
Forested mountains, pristine coast, snowy volcanoes and nature in the raw – a place where outdoor recreation is a way of life

SIERRA NEVADA
An alpine wilderness of peaks, forests, meadows and sparkling lakes; includes the imposing granite domes, spires and canyons of Yosemite National Park

SOUTHWEST
Vast expanses of pink-orange slickrock, wildly sculpted rock formations, canyons – including the Grand one – and riverside oases

EDMONTON

CA

Saskatchewan

VANCOUVER
Victoria
British Columbia
Olympia
SEATTLE
WASHINGTON
Portland
Spokane
Salem
OREGON
Boise
IDAHO

CALGARY
Saskatoon

Alberta
Regina

Missoula
Helena
MONTANA

Continental Divide

NORTH DAKOTA
Bismarck

SOUTH DAKOTA
Rapid City
Pierre

WYOMING
Cheyenne

NEBRASKA
Lincoln

WINNIPEG

Reno
Sacramento
Carson City
SAN FRANCISCO
OAKLAND
SAN JOSE
NEVADA

Great Salt Lake
Salt Lake City
UTAH

Rocky Mountains

DENVER
Colorado Springs
COLORADO

KANSAS
Wichita

LAS VEGAS
CALIFORNIA

PACIFIC
OCEAN

LOS ANGELES

Flagstaff
ARIZONA
PHOENIX
SAN DIEGO
TIJUANA
Mexicali
Tucson

Taos
SANTA FE
NEW MEXICO
El Paso
Ciudad Juárez

OKLAHOMA
Oklahoma City

DALLAS

Rio Grande
Pecos

TEXAS

CHIHUAHUA

Rio Grande

MEXICO

Baja California

San Antonio
Aus
Corpus Christi

ELEVATION

10000 ft
6500 ft
3000 ft
1500 ft
500 ft
0

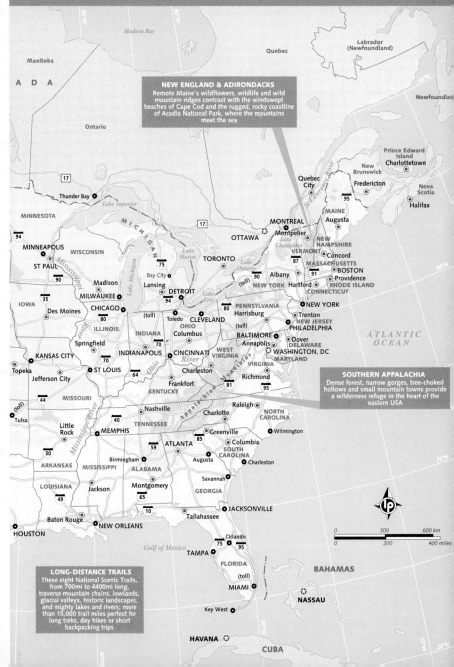

USA

NEW ENGLAND & ADIRONDACKS
Remote Maine's wildflowers, wildlife and wild
mountain ridges contrast with the windswept
beaches of Cape Cod and the rugged, rocky coastline
of Acadia National Park, where the mountains
meet the sea

SOUTHERN APPALACHIA
Dense forest, narrow gorges, tree-choked
hollows and small mountain towns provide
a wilderness refuge in the heart of the
eastern USA

LONG-DISTANCE TRAILS
These eight National Scenic Trails,
from 700mi to 4400mi long,
traverse mountain chains, lowlands,
glacial valleys, historic landscapes,
and mighty lakes and rivers; more
than 15,000 trail miles perfect for
long treks, day hikes or short
backpacking trips

Hudson Bay

Quebec

Labrador
(Newfoundland)

Manitoba

Newfoundla

CANADA

Ontario

Prince Edward
Island
Charlottetown

New
Brunswick
Fredericton

Nova
Scotia
Halifax

Thunder Bay

Lake Superior

17

MINNESOTA

MICHIGAN

17

Quebec
City

St Lawrence River

MAINE
Augusta

94

MINNEAPOLIS

WISCONSIN

Lake
Huron

MONTREAL

OTTAWA

Montpelier

VERMONT

NEW
HAMPSHIRE
Concord

ST PAUL

Mississippi River

75

TORONTO

Lake
Champlain

87

MASSACHUSETTS

BOSTON

90

Madison

Bay City

Lansing

DETROIT

Lake
Ontario

90
(toll)

Albany

91

Providence
RHODE ISLAND

MILWAUKEE

94

NEW YORK

Hartford

CONNECTICUT

IOWA

35

CHICAGO

Lake
Erie

PENNSYLVANIA

NEW YORK

Des Moines

80

Toledo

CLEVELAND

Harrisburg

Trenton
NEW JERSEY

ILLINOIS

INDIANA

OHIO
Columbus

(toll)

PHILADELPHIA

ATLANTIC
OCEAN

Springfield

70

INDIANAPOLIS

CINCINNATI

BALTIMORE

Annapolis
Dover
DELAWARE

KANSAS CITY

70

Ohio River

WEST
VIRGINIA

WASHINGTON, DC
MARYLAND

Topeka

ST LOUIS

64

Charleston

Jefferson City

Frankfort

VIRGINIA

Richmond

(toll)

44

MISSOURI

KENTUCKY

81

95

Appalachian Mountains

Tulsa

Nashville

Raleigh

Little
Rock

40

Charlotte

NORTH
CAROLINA

MEMPHIS

TENNESSEE

Greenville

Wilmington

30

59

ATLANTA

85

Columbia

Birmingham

Augusta

SOUTH
CAROLINA

ARKANSAS

MISSISSIPPI

ALABAMA

Charleston

Mississippi River

LOUISIANA

Jackson

Montgomery

65

Savannah

GEORGIA

49

10

Baton Rouge

NEW ORLEANS

Tallahassee

JACKSONVILLE

HOUSTON

Gulf of Mexico

75

Orlando

95

BAHAMAS

TAMPA

FLORIDA

(toll)

MIAMI

NASSAU

Key West

CUBA

HAVANA

0   300   600 km
0   200   400 miles

Hiking in the USA
1st edition – July 2000

Published by
Lonely Planet Publications Pty Ltd A.C.N. 005 607 983
192 Burwood Rd, Hawthorn, Victoria 3122, Australia

Lonely Planet Offices
Australia PO Box 617, Hawthorn, Victoria 3122
USA 150 Linden St, Oakland, CA 94607
UK 10a Spring Place, London NW5 3BH
France 1 rue du Dahomey, 75011 Paris

Photographs
All of the images in this guide are available for licensing from
Lonely Planet Images.
email: lpi@lonelyplanet.com.au

Main front cover photograph
Sunset over granite hills near Mono Lake, Sierra Nevada (Marisa Gierlich)

Small front cover photograph
Hiking the kelso dunes, Mojave Desert, California (Stuart Wasserman)

ISBN 0 86442 600 3

Printed by Colorcraft Ltd, Hong Kong

Although the authors
and Lonely Planet try
to make the informa-
tion as accurate as
possible, we accept
no responsibility for
any loss, injury or
inconvenience sus-
tained by anyone
using this book.

Contents – Text

TABLE OF HIKES   4

MAP INDEX   8

THE AUTHORS   9

THIS BOOK   12

FOREWORD   13

INTRODUCTION   15

FACTS ABOUT THE USA   17

History 17
Geography 22
Geology 24
Climate 24
Ecology & Environment 26
Flora & Fauna Guide 29
National Parks & Reserves 47
Population & People 49
Society & Conduct 50
Language 50

FACTS FOR THE HIKER   52

Suggested Itineraries 52
Planning 53
Hikes In This Book 60
Guided Hikes 61
Responsible Hiking 62
Women Hikers 63
Hiking With Children 64
Useful Organizations 65
Tourist Offices 66
Visas & Documents 67
Embassies & Consulates 70
Customs 71
Money 72
Post & Communications 74
Internet Resources 77
Books 77
Magazines 79
Weather Information 79
Photography 79
Time 80
Electricity 80
Weights & Measures 80
Laundry 81
Business Hours 81
Public Holidays & Special
Events 82
Accommodations 83
Food 85
Drinks 87

HEALTH & SAFETY   89

Predeparture Planning 89
Health Insurance 89
Immunizations 89
First Aid 89
Other Preparations 89
Online Resources 90
Staying Healthy 91
Hygiene 91
Nutrition 91
Food 91
Water 91
Common Ailments 92
Medical Problems &
Treatment 93
Environmental Hazards 93
Infectious Diseases 95
Insect-Borne Diseases 97
Traumatic Injuries 97
Cuts & Scratches 99
Bites & Stings 99
Women's Health 100
Safety On The Hike 100
Bears 100
Crossing Rivers 101
Hunting Season 101
Lightning 102
Rescue & Evacuation 102

GETTING THERE & AWAY   103

Air 103
Land 110
Sea 110

GETTING AROUND   111

Air 111
Bus 113
Train 115
Car 117
Motorcycle 121
Bicycle 121
Hitching 121
Local Transport 121

2 Contents – Text

NEW ENGLAND & ADIRONDACKS 122

100 Mile Wilderness 124
Appalachian Trail to Mt
Katahdin 124
Acadia National Park 132
Champlain Mountain 134
Cadillac Mountain 135

White Mountains 136
Presidential Traverse 136
Baldface & Carter Ranges ..143
Adirondack State Park 147
Adirondacks High Peaks 149
Mt Marcy 151

Green Mountains 152
Long Trail Loop 152
Cape Cod National
Seashore 156
Thoreau's Walk 156
Other Hikes 160

SOUTHERN APPALACHIA 162

Great Smoky Mountains 165
Gregory Bald 168
Little Cataloochee Church ..170
Alum Cave Trail 173
Blue Ridge Mountains 177
Roan Mountain 177

Three Ridges 181
Mt Rogers National
Recreation Area 184
Mt Rogers 184
Allegheny Mountains 189
Spruce Knob Loop 190

Blackbird Knob Loop 192
Shenandoah National Park 195
Cedar Run–Whiteoak Canyon
Loop 196
Old Rag Loop 198
Other Hikes 201

ROCKY MOUNTAINS 202

Glacier National Park 207
Swiftcurrent Mountain
Lookout 209
Highline Trail/Ptarmigan
Tunnel Loop 212
Grinnell Glacier 216
Gunsight Pass 217
Bob Marshall Wilderness ...219
Chinese Wall Loop 219
Absaroka-Beartooth
Wilderness 225
Beartooth High Lakes 226

Yellowstone National Park ..229
Mt Washburn & Sevenmile
Hole 234
Heart Lake 236
Bechler River 238
Grand Teton National Park ..240
Paintbrush Divide Loop 243
Teton Crest Trail..................245
Wind River Range 247
Cirque of the Towers 248
Rocky Mountain National
Park 251

Odessa Lake 253
Flattop Mountain 255
Glacier Gorge & Loch Vale 258
Longs Peak 259
Indian Peaks Wilderness 260
Pawnee Pass 261
Arapaho Pass & Arapaho
Glacier Trail 264
Maroon Bells–Snowmass
Wilderness 265
Maroon Bells Loop 266
Other Hikes 269

SOUTHWEST 278

Grand Canyon 281
Kaibab Trail 286
Thunder River Trail 289
Bryce Canyon National
Park 293
Under the Rim Trail 296
Zion National Park 300

Zion Narrows 303
Across Zion 305
Capitol Reef National Park...309
Upper Muley Twist
Canyon 311
Lower Muley Twist
Canyon 314

Navajo Knobs 315
Grand Staircase–Escalante
National Monument 317
Boulder Mail Trail 319
Paria Canyon 322
Paria Canyon 323

SIERRA NEVADA 330

Lake Tahoe Region 335
Tahoe Rim Trail 338
Mt Rose 339
Tahoe Meadows to
Spooner Summit 340
Desolation Traverse 342
Tahoe To Yosemite 345
Tahoe-Yosemite Trail 347

Echo Summit to Carson
Pass 348
Fourth of July Lake 349
Emigrant Wilderness 350
Sawtooth Ridge 353
Yosemite National
Park 355
Half Dome 360

Yosemite Falls 364
Tenaya Lake to Yosemite
Valley 367
Cathedral Lakes 368
Lyell Canyon 369
Mt Dana 370
Sequoia & Kings Canyon
National Parks 372

Franklin & Sawtooth
Passes 377
High Sierra
Trail 380
Rae Lakes Loop 382
Eastern Sierra **386**
Mt Whitney 389
John Muir Trail 391
Humphreys & Evolution
Basins 392
Minarets 396
Other Hikes **398**

PACIFIC NORTHWEST   402

Columbia Gorge **411**
Eagle Creek Trail 411
Dog Mountain 413
Mt Hood **416**
McNeil Point 416
Eagle Cap Wilderness **418**
Lakes Basin 418
Three Sisters Wilderness ...**422**
Green Lakes 423
Obsidian Cliffs 425
Belknap Crater 427
Southern Oregon Coast **429**
Oregon Dunes 429
Boardman State Park 431
Wild Rogue Wilderness **433**
Rogue River Trail 433
Alpine Lakes Wilderness ...**440**
Enchantment Lakes 441
Snoqualmie Pass North 444
Mt Rainier National Park ...**447**
Indian Henry's Hunting
Ground 448
Skyline Trail 451
Burroughs Mountain 453
Olympic National Park **455**
Cape Alava–Sand Point
Loop 456
Mt Baker **458**
Chain Lakes 459
**North Cascades National
Park** **462**
Cascade Pass 463
Other Hikes **465**

LONG-DISTANCE TRAILS   468

Appalachian National
Scenic Trail 470
Continental Divide National
Scenic Trail 474
Pacific Crest National
Scenic Trail 477
Florida National Scenic
Trail 480
Natchez Trace National
Scenic Trail 483
Potomac Heritage National
Scenic Trail 485
Ice Age National Scenic
Trail 487
North Country National
Scenic Trail 490

GLOSSARY   494

INDEX

Text 500
Boxed Text..........................511

MAP LEGEND   back page

METRIC CONVERSION   inside back cover

The Hikes	Duration	Standard	Transport
New England & Adirondacks			
Appalachian Trail to Mt Katahdin	6 days	medium-hard	no
Champlain Mountain	2½–4 hours	medium-hard	no
Cadillac Mountain	4–5 hours	medium	yes
Presidential Traverse	4 days	hard	yes
Baldface & Carter Ranges	3 days	medium-hard	yes
Adirondacks High Peaks	3 days	medium	no
Mt Marcy	7½–9 hours	hard	no
Long Trail Loop	2 days	medium	no
Thoreau's Walk	6 hours	easy	yes
Southern Appalachia			
Gregory Bald	5–6 hours	medium	no
Little Cataloochee Church	5–6 hours	medium	no
Alum Cave Trail	6–8 hours	medium-hard	no
Roan Mountain	7 hours	medium	no
Three Ridges	3 days	medium-hard	no
Mt Rogers	4 days	medium	no
Spruce Knob Loop	2 days	medium-hard	no
Blackbird Knob Loop	5–6 hours	easy-medium	no
Cedar Run–Whiteoak Canyon Loop	5–6 hours	medium	no
Old Rag Loop	4–6 hours	medium-hard	no
Rocky Mountains			
Swiftcurrent Mountain Lookout	7½–10 hours	medium-hard	yes
Highline Trail/Ptarmigan Tunnel Loop	5–7 days	medium-hard	yes
Grinnell Glacier	4½–5 hours	easy-medium	yes
Gunsight Pass	1–2 days	medium-hard	yes
Chinese Wall Loop	5–7 days	medium	no
Beartooth High Lakes	4 days	easy-medium	no
Mt Washburn & Sevenmile Hole	1 or 2 days	easy-medium	no
Heart Lake	2 or 3 days	easy or medium	no
Bechler River	4 days	medium	no
Paintbrush Divide Loop	2–3 days	medium	no
Teton Crest Trail	4 days	medium-hard	no
Cirque of the Towers	3 days	medium-hard	no
Odessa Lake	1–2 days	easy-medium	yes
Flattop Mountain	2–3 days	medium-hard	yes
Glacier Gorge & Loch Vale	1–2 days	easy-medium	yes
Longs Peak	1–3 days	hard	yes
Pawnee Pass	1–2 days	medium	no
Arapaho Pass & Arapaho Glacier Trail	2 days	medium-hard	no
Maroon Bells Loop	4 days	medium	yes
Southwest			
Kaibab Trail	3 days	hard	yes
Thunder River Trail	4 days	hard	no
Under the Rim Trail	3 days	easy-medium	no
Zion Narrows	1 or 2 days	medium-hard	yes
Across Zion	4 days	medium	no
Upper Muley Twist Canyon	1–2 days	medium	no

Season	Features	Page
June-Sept	Deep woods, remote lakes, and an ascent of a famous peak	124
May-Oct	Short, steep hike up ladders; Atlantic Ocean views	134
May-Oct	Tallest peak on Atlantic coast; mountain and ocean views	135
June-Sept	Traverse of northern New Hampshire; Mt Washington	136
June-Sept	Rivers, pools, and hiking on open ridgelines	143
May-Oct	Lakes, waterfalls, a gorge, and a scenic mountain pass	149
May-Oct	Open-summit views from New York's highest peak	151
June-Sept	Views of the Green Mountains, woodsy scenery and solitude	152
April-Oct	Sea cliffs, salt marshes, sand dunes and windswept beaches	156
May-Jun	Wildflowers, old-growth forest and a classic Smokies bald	168
year-round	Historic buildings set in the heart of a forest	170
year-round	A climb through forest to the Smokies' second-highest peak	173
June	A hike over three balds in beautiful surroundings	177
year-round	Steeply along part of the AT past waterfalls and along ridges	181
May-Oct	Wild ponies, rhododendrons, crags and pinnacles	184
May-Oct	Downhill hike visiting forest, waterfalls and swimming holes	190
May-Oct	Abundant wildlife, solitude and a windswept plateau	192
May-Oct	Follow a stream to a canyon and severeal waterfalls	196
year-round	A scramble through granite boulders to a bare peak	198
June-Sept	Scenic hike to one of the Rockies' most spectacular lookouts	209
July-Sept	Longer hike through varied scenery in the Lewis Range	212
July-Sept	Efficient, scenic route to Glacier National Park's largest glacier	216
July-Sept	Glaciers, snow fields, alpine lakes and a scenic pass	217
Apr-Jun, Sept-Oct	A circumnavigation of a 1000ft-high limestone escarpment	219
July-Sept	Traverse of a high-alpine wilderness with lakes and glaciers	226
May-Oct	Hot springs, wildlife and the Grand Canyon of the Yellowstone	234
July-Sept	Rich wildlife and and extensive geothermal field	236
Aug-Oct	Downhill past waterfalls and wetlands to a hot-spring bath	238
June-Oct	Traverse of a high shelf with extensive alpine views	243
June-Oct	An exhilerating and spectacular traverse of the Tetons	245
Aug-Sept	A steady climb into one of the Rockies' finest amphitheaters	248
June-Oct	Hiking through forest past many subalpine lakes	253
June-Sept	A high-level crossing of the Continental Divide; wildlife	255
June-Oct	Climb into raw glacial cirques with gem-like alpine lakes	258
July-Sept	A strenuous climb to the top of a landmark 14-thousander	259
July-Sept	Cross the divide on one of the region's most beautiful hikes	261
July-Oct	Another scenic high pass with lakes, peaks and mine ruins	264
July-Sept	Very high loop over four passes with views of Maroon Bells	266
May-Oct	The only maintained traverse of the famous Grand Canyon	286
Mar-June, Sept-Nov	Steep, primitive route to Colorado River through green oases	289
May-Oct	Quiet trail skirting Bryce Canyon's famous hoodoos	296
June-July, Sept	As close to canyoneering as you can get without ropes	303
May-Oct	Variety of scenery and terrain, but few people	305
April-June, Sept-Oct	Ridge-top views, natural arches and a narrow canyon	311

The Hikes *continued*	Duration	Standard	Transport
Southwest *continued*			
Lower Muley Twist Canyon	1–2 days	medium	no
Navajo Knobs	4–6 hours	medium-hard	no
Boulder Mail Trail	2–3 days	hard	no
Paria Canyon	5 days	medium-hard	no
Sierra Nevada			
Tahoe Rim Trail	14–17 days	medium	no
Mt Rose	6–8 hours	medium-hard	no
Tahoe Meadows to Spooner Summit	2 days	easy-medium	no
Desolation Traverse	4 days	medium	no
Tahoe-Yosemite Trail	19–23 days	hard	yes
Echo Summit to Carson Pass	2 days	easy-medium	no
Fourth of July Lake	2 days	easy-medium	no
Emigrant Wilderness	6 days	medium	no
Sawtooth Ridge	6 days	medium-hard	no
Half Dome	2 days	hard	yes
Yosemite Falls	6–8 hours	medium–hard	yes
Tenaya Lake to Yosemite Valley	3 days	medium	yes
Cathedral Lakes	4–5 hours	easy-medium	yes
Lyell Canyon	2 days	easy-medium	yes
Mt Dana	6–7 hours	hard	yes
Franklin & Sawtooth Passes	4 days	medium-hard	no
High Sierra Trail	8 days	hard	no
Rae Lakes Loop	5 days	medium	no
Mt Whitney	3 days	hard	yes
John Muir Trail	19–20 days	hard	yes
Humphreys & Evolution Basins	7 days	hard	no
Minarets	3 or 4 days	hard	yes
Pacific Northwest			
Eagle Creek Trail	1 or 2 days	medium-hard	no
Dog Mountain	5–6 hours	medium-hard	no
McNeil Point	5–6 hours	medium	no
Lakes Basin	4–5 days	medium	no
Green Lakes	1 or 2 days	medium	no
Obsidian Trail	6–7½ hours	medium-hard	no
Belknap Crater	2½–3 hours	easy-medium	no
Oregon Dunes	2½–3 hours	easy	yes
Boardman State Park	3–4 hours	easy-medium	no
Rogue River Trail	5 days	medium	no
Enchantment Lakes	3–4 days	hard	no
Snoqualmie Pass North	4 days	medium	yes
Indian Henry's Hunting Ground	1 or 2 days	hard	no
Skyline Trail	3–4½ hours	medium	yes
Burroughs Mountain	3½–4 hours	medium	no
Cape Alava–Sand Point Loop	4–5½ hours	medium	no
Chain Lakes	4–5 hours	medium	no
Cascade Pass	2 days	medium	no

Long-Distance Trails See table on pages 470–471

Season	Features	Page
April-June, Sept-Oct	A loop through a high-walled canyon and colorful Strike Valley	314
April-June, Sept-Nov	Climb to one of the Southwest's best viewpoints	315
April-June	Historic route through remote and rugged country	319
April-June, Sept-Oct	Traverse a deep river canyon with narrows and history galore	323
June-Oct	Ridge-top trail circling the spectacular Lake Tahoe	338
July-Sept	Incomparable views from Tahoe's third-highest peak	339
June-Oct	Fine views from the crest of the Carson Range	340
July-Oct	High passes, forests and lake-studded alpine wilderness	342
June-Oct	Seven high passes link two jewels in the region's crown	347
June-Oct	Lonely hiking along a section of the Pacific Crest Trail	348
June-Oct	Circuit of Round Mountain with a night at a beautiful lake	349
June-Oct	Gentle hiking through alpine meadows with fine fishing lakes	350
July-Sept	Follow forested rivers to high passes and glaciated peaks	353
June-Oct	A steep climb, finishing on ladders, to a landmark summit	360
May-June	Climb to the top of an amazing waterfall past towering cliffs	364
June-Sept	Largely downhill, this is a scenic approach to Yosemite Valley	367
June-Oct	Striking granite pinnacles fringe alluring alpine lakes	368
July-Sept	Traverse alpine meadows to Yosemite's highest peak	369
July-Sept	Steep hike to the area's second-highest peak with great views	370
June-Oct	Scenic passes, forested canyons and good fishing lakes	377
July-Sept	Classic route across Sequoia National Park to Mt Whitney	380
July-Oct	A waterfall, forests, meadows, a pass and a chain of lakes	382
July-Sept	Popular trail to the summit of the highest peak in the Lower 48	389
July-Aug	Perhaps the USA's finest mountain hiking	391
July-Sept	Demanding but beautiful hike through the High Sierra	392
Aug-Sept	Visit the knife-edged Minarets ridge; breathtaking lakes	396
May-Oct	Passes 11 waterfalls in a cliff-lined canyon	411
April-June	Steep climb to a grassy bluff famed for spring wildflower	413
June-Oct	Spectacular ridgeline hike with terrific views of Mt Hood	416
August-Oct	Moderate climb to a popular cluster of alpine lakes	418
July-Oct	Through forest to an arid meadow, snow-heaped volcanoes	423
July-Oct	Alpine scenery in a volcanic area near McKenzie Pass	425
July-Oct	A short hike across a lava flow in central Oregon's Cascades	427
year-round	High sand dunes and a lonely ocean beach	429
year-round	Dramatic seascapes and rocky headlands	431
May-June, Sept-Oct	Lonesome, rugged river canyon; historic homesteads	433
July-Oct	A grueling climb to a legendary granite basin full of lakes	441
July-Oct	Follow the Pacific Crest Trail along exposed mountain ridges	444
July-Sept	Long day hike to a famous wildflower meadow on Mt Rainier	448
July-Sept	Diverse alpine scenery on the Northwest's highest mountain	451
Aug-Sept	High tundra overlooking the largest glacier in the Lower 48	453
year-round	Flat loop through temperate rainforest to a wilderness beach	456
July-Oct	Climb to a wildflower-rimmed lake basin on Mt Baker	459
July-Oct	A night at a glacier-cut passage in the North Cascades.	463

8 Contents – Maps

MAP INDEX

New England & Adirondacks p123

Mt Katahdin	p127
Acadia National Park	p135
Presidential Traverse	p139
Baldface & Carter Ranges	p145
Adirondacks High Peaks & Mt Marcy	p150
Long Trail Loop	p154
Thoreau's Walk	p159

Southern Appalachia p163

Gregory Bald	p169
Little Cataloochee Church	p172
Alum Cave Trail	p175
Roan Mountain	p180
Three Ridges	p183
Mt Rogers	p186
Spruce Knob	p191
Blackbird Knob Loop	p194
Shenandoah Hikes	p198

Rocky Mountains p203

Glacier National Park	p210
Chinese Wall Loop	p222
Beartooth High Lakes	p227
Mt Washburn & Sevenmile Hole	p235
Heart Lake	p237
Bechler River	p239
Grand Teton National Park	p244
Cirque of the Towers	p250

Rocky Mountains Continued

Rocky Mountain National Park	p254
Indian Peaks Wilderness	p263
Maroon Bells Loop	p267

Southwest p279

Kaibab Trail	p287
Thunder River Trail	p291
Under the Rim Trail	p297
Zion Narrows	p304
Across Zion	p306
Upper & Lower Muley Twist Canyon	p313
Navajo Knobs	p316
Boulder Mail Trail	p321
Paria Canyon	p325

Sierra Nevada p331

Mt Rose	p339
Tahoe Meadows to Spooner Summit	p341
Desolation Traverse	p344
Echo Summit to Carson Pass	p349
Fourth of July Lake	p350
Emigrant Wilderness	p352
Sawtooth Ridge	p354
Yosemite National Park	p356
Yosemite Valley	p361
Tenaya Lake to Yosemite Valley	p368
Cathedral Lakes	p369
Lyell Canyon & Mt Dana	p371

Sierra Nevada Continued

Sequoia & Kings Canyon National Parks	p373
Franklin & Sawtooth Passes	p379
High Sierra Trail	p382
Rae Lakes Loop	p384
Mt Whitney	p390
Humphreys & Evolution Basins	p394
Minarets	p397

Pacific Northwest p403

Eagle Creek Trail	p413
Dog Mountain	p415
McNeil Point	p417
Lakes Basin	p420
Green Lakes	p424
Obsidian Cliffs	p426
Belknap Crater	p428
Oregon Dunes	p430
Boardman State Park	p432
Rogue River Trail	p438
Enchantment Lakes	p443
Snoqualmie Pass North	p446
Indian Henry's Hunting Ground	p450
Skyline Trail	p452
Burroughs Mountain	p455
Cape Alava–Sand Point Loop	p458
Chain Lakes	p462
Cascade Pass	p465

Long-distance Trails p469

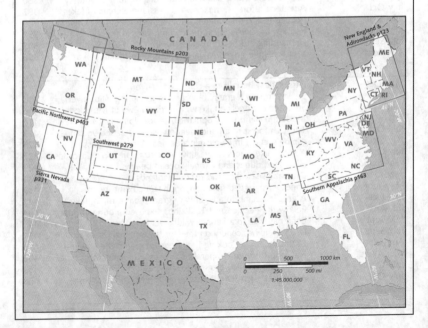

The Authors

Marisa Gierlich

Thanks to adventurous parents Marisa started her travels at a young age. The backpacking bug didn't get her, though, until her third year at UC Berkeley when she embarked on a laugh-filled trip to the 'Desperation' Wilderness with buddies Heather and Joanne. Since then, she's hiked most of the western USA, trekked in the Nepal Himalaya, traveled hut-to-hut in the Swiss Alps and climbed Mont Blanc (from the French side). If she's not hiking, she's probably running, cooking, reading about mountaineering or surfing with husband Paul in La Jolla, California. She's proud to be an *Angelena* – native of Los Angeles – and will defend her home town against slurs of misconception at any time.

John Mock & Kimberley O'Neil

John's summers as a youth were spent along the Appalachian National Scenic Trail, and Kimberley's were spent in Wisconsin's Northwoods. After college, both migrated independently to California where they have been living and hiking ever since. They divide their time between their northern California home and the mountains of South Asia, and were married in Kathmandu, Nepal, in 1991. With John's academic background in South Asian language and literature and Kimberley's background in the adventure-travel industry, they have worked as joint consultants on ecotourism for the World Conservation Union (IUCN); John has also worked as a consultant for the World Wide Fund for Nature (WWF) and the National Geographic Society.

John and Kimberley are co-authors of Lonely Planet's *Trekking in the Karakoram & Hinudkush* and have also contributed to *Pakistan* and *Rocky Mountains*.

Clem Lindenmayer

Clem has spent much of the past two decades exploring the earth's wildest mountain regions – pursuing a particular interest in alpine flora – on trips that have taken him to *almost* every continent (he still intends to trek across the Transantarctic Mountains at some stage). Clem authored Lonely Planet's *Walking in Switzerland* and *Trekking in the Patagonian Andes*, and has worked on sections of *Scandinavian & Baltic Europe*, *Europe on a shoestring*, *South-East Asia on a shoestring* and *Malaysia, Singapore & Brunei*. He divides his off-the-road time between the world's great cultural centers: Melbourne, Australia, and Winterthur, Switzerland.

Jennifer Snarski

After spending most of her life in a small timber town on the southern Oregon coast, Jennifer set off for India, Sri Lanka and

Thailand during her college years with no other goals than to blow her mind and learn to like vegetables. She achieved both, and upon returning put her degree in religious studies to use by writing for a cultural guide to India. She is an avid hiker and the co-author of Lonely Planet's *Pacific Northwest*. In the corresponding chapter in this book she writes about her all-time favorite adventure destination – the diverse wilderness areas of Oregon and Washington.

Jennifer lives in Portland, Oregon, where she works as a freelance writer, desktop publisher, research consultant and folkdance instructor. When not communing with nature she's either out riding a bicycle or dancing jigs and reels at an Irish céilí.

Diane Bair & Pamela Wright

Diane Bair and Pamela Wright, co-authors of 16 books, are avid outdoor adventurers. The duo has hiked, climbed, sailed, skied, caved, kayaked – even hot-air ballooned – over much of the United States' East Coast. One of their books, *Adventure New England*, chronicled 75 of their hair-raising escapades.

Their love of wildlife and the outdoors has taken them to bear camp on a remote Alaskan peninsula, to the gray whale breeding grounds in Baja, Mexico, and in the murky waters of a Florida river to snorkel with one-ton West Indian manatees. These experiences led to another book project, *Wild Encounters*, featuring their favorite animal adventures, as well as a series of wildlife guides for kids.

When they're not lurking behind animal blinds or tracking wolves, Diane and Pamela are busy writing travel and outdoor stories for national magazines. Bair lives on Massachusetts' North Shore, Wright resides in Durham, New Hampshire, and they meet in the middle at their office, a 200-year-old brownstone in the seaport town of Newburyport, Massachusetts.

Long-time admirers of Lonely Planet guidebooks, *Hiking in the USA* is their first project for LP.

Susy Raleigh & Daniel Frideger

For the past decade, Susy Raleigh and Daniel Frideger have been fulfilling their desire to travel, speak in foreign tongues, and meet the need for a bit of spare change by creating hiking- and biking-trip itineraries on four continents. From the Pyrenees to the Andes, the High Atlas to the Appalachians, they have walked, pedaled, grunted and sweated through some of the most beautiful mountains on earth. Finally succumbing to the 'there is no place like home' urge, they now spend most of their time with their young son Dominique in Durango, Colorado, nestled between high desert and lofty Rocky Mountain peaks.

FROM THE AUTHORS

Marisa Gierlich I am incredibly grateful to all those who offered me comfort during my frigid research session through the Southwest: Kate Worster for her naturalist knowledge; Val Brenneis and Leah Stein; John Flahrety, Fernando Barrios, Adrian Palomino, Leslie Hunt, Michael (Vandy) Vanderhurst and Jill Lewis; and Bobby Black and the rest of the 'Clipped Wings-does-Mancos' crew. I'd especially like to thank Kristin, Kate and Ashley; Joanne; Jeremy Frye; and the crew from the Thunder River Trail. 'Cheech' Calienete, of the University of Arizona, was an invaluable Grand Canyon resource, as was the geologist at Phantom Ranch. Thanks to the Burgins for housing and humoring me during hours of computer-sitting, and the Lands for being such terrific people. My parents, family and husband Paul get extra-special kudos for their unfailing optimism and support.

John Mock & Kimberley O'Neil We are grateful for the hospitality of family and friends – Tom O'Neil, Jeff O'Neil, Mary Carlson and Kelly Rich – who shared their homes between our many hikes, and to the rangers who shared their knowledge and expertise. We would especially like to acknowledge Bill Menke of the National Park Service for his help with national scenic trails; Steve Elkinton of the NPS; Shannon Raborn of the Tahoe Rim Trail Association; and Heidi Anderson of Inyo National Forest's White Mountain ranger station.

Clem Lindenmayer Special thanks to the NPS and USFS staff for their consistent help and advice during my research.

Jennifer Snarski Special thanks to Leo Sudnik, Laurie McLain and my father, Eugene Snarski, who endured endless stops for note-taking, map-checking and photographs as they hiked with me. NPS and USFS rangers all over the region patiently took time to answer questions. The knowledgeable staff at Nature of the Northwest visitor center provided valuable guidance regarding maps and information sources. Thanks to Stevyn Travillian for reading the manuscript, and to friends, family and colleagues who contributed good ideas, provided support and put up with long absences.

Diane Bair & Pamela Wright Thanks to everyone who made our treks in the woods that much more enjoyable: Charlotte Bair-Cucchiaro, Connor Bair-Cucchiaro, Carolyn Hintlian, Carroll Jones, Greg Nikas, Chuck Ward, Sadie Wright-Ward and Jared Wright-Ward.

Susy Raleigh & Daniel Frideger Thanks to Noel at Smoky Mountains National Park, for his invaluable advice; Frank and Worth MacMurray for their warm hospitality (and pool); Jacquie and Bryan Dear for their cookie-making and editing; and Andrea Avantaggio and Peter Schertz for epic tales of the Appalachian Trail (and their son Evan for keeping Domi out of trouble while Mom typed).

This Book

Material from the 1st edition of Lonely Planet's *USA* guide and the 2nd editions of *Southwest*, *Pacific Northwest*, *California & Nevada*, *New England* and *Rocky Mountains* was used for parts of this book. Marisa Gierlich was the coordinating author and wrote the introductory chapters and the Southwest chapter. John Mock & Kimberley O'Neil wrote the Sierra Nevada and Long-Distance Trails chapters. Clem Lindenmayer wrote the Rocky Mountains chapter. Jennifer Snarski wrote the Pacific Northwest chapter. Diane Bair & Pamela Wright wrote the New England & Adirondacks chapter. Susy Raleigh & Daniel Frideger wrote the Southern Appalachia chapter.

From the Publisher

This book was edited by David Burnett and designed and laid out by Glenn van der Knijff in Lonely Planet's Melbourne office. Glenn, Maree Styles (who also helped with the color sections), Paul Piaia, Katie Butterworth, Chris Klep and Jim Miller drew the maps and John Hinman, Mary Harber, Evan Jones, Emily Coles and Sally Dillon assisted David with editing and proofing. Thanks to Senior Editor Lindsay Brown and Vicki Beale for final proofing; Senior Designer Teresa Donnellan, Matt King and Ann Jeffree for helping us with illustrations; Tim Uden for his layout wisdom; Susan Rimerman, Molly Green, Alex Guilbert and Scott Summers of the Oakland office for intercontinental logistics; the good people of Lonely Planet Images for help with the photographs; and Jamieson Gross for the design of the cover.

Foreword

ABOUT LONELY PLANET GUIDEBOOKS

The story begins with a classic travel adventure: Tony and Maureen Wheeler's 1972 journey across Europe and Asia to Australia. Useful information about the overland trail did not exist at that time, so Tony and Maureen published the first Lonely Planet guidebook to meet a growing need.

From a kitchen table, then from a tiny office in Melbourne (Australia), Lonely Planet has become the largest independent travel publisher in the world, an international company with offices in Melbourne, Oakland (USA), London (UK) and Paris (France).

Today Lonely Planet guidebooks cover the globe. There is an ever-growing list of books and there's information in a variety of forms and media. Some things haven't changed. The main aim is still to help make it possible for adventurous travellers to get out there – to explore and better understand the world.

At Lonely Planet we believe travellers can make a positive contribution to the countries they visit – if they respect their host communities and spend their money wisely. Since 1986 a percentage of the income from each book has been donated to aid projects and human rights campaigns.

Updates Lonely Planet thoroughly updates each guidebook as often as possible. This usually means there are around two years between editions, although for more unusual or more stable destinations the gap can be longer. Check the imprint page (following the colour map at the beginning of the book) for publication dates.

Between editions up-to-date information is available in two free newsletters – the paper *Planet Talk* and email *Comet* (to subscribe, contact any Lonely Planet office) – and on our Web site at www.lonelyplanet.com. The *Upgrades* section of the Web site covers a number of important and volatile destinations and is regularly updated by Lonely Planet authors. *Scoop* covers news and current affairs relevant to travellers. And, lastly, the *Thorn Tree* bulletin board and *Postcards* section of the site carry unverified, but fascinating, reports from travellers.

Correspondence The process of creating new editions begins with the letters, postcards and emails received from travellers. This correspondence often includes suggestions, criticisms and comments about the current editions. Interesting excerpts are immediately passed on via newsletters and the Web site, and everything goes to our authors to be verified when they're researching on the road. We're keen to get more feedback from organisations or individuals who represent communities visited by travellers.

Lonely Planet gathers information for everyone who's curious about the planet – and especially for those who explore it first-hand. Through guidebooks, phrasebooks, activity guides, maps, literature, newsletters, image library, TV series and Web site we act as an information exchange for a worldwide community of travellers.

Research Authors aim to gather sufficient practical information to enable travellers to make informed choices and to make the mechanics of a journey run smoothly. They also research historical and cultural background to help enrich the travel experience and allow travellers to understand and respond appropriately to cultural and environmental issues.

Authors don't stay in every hotel because that would mean spending a couple of months in each medium-sized city and, no, they don't eat at every restaurant because that would mean stretching belts beyond capacity. They do visit hotels and restaurants to check standards and prices, but feedback based on readers' direct experiences can be very helpful.

Many of our authors work undercover, others aren't so secretive. None of them accept freebies in exchange for positive write-ups. And none of our guidebooks contain any advertising.

Production Authors submit their raw manuscripts and maps to offices in Australia, USA, UK or France. Editors and cartographers – all experienced travellers themselves – then begin the process of assembling the pieces. When the book finally hits the shops, some things are already out of date, we start getting feedback from readers and the process begins again …

WARNING & REQUEST

Things change – prices go up, schedules change, good places go bad and bad places go bankrupt – nothing stays the same. So, if you find things better or worse, recently opened or long since closed, please tell us and help make the next edition even more accurate and useful. We genuinely value all the feedback we receive. Julie Young coordinates a well travelled team that reads and acknowledges every letter, postcard and email and ensures that every morsel of information finds its way to the appropriate authors, editors and cartographers for verification.

Everyone who writes to us will find their name in the next edition of the appropriate guidebook. They will also receive the latest issue of *Planet Talk*, our quarterly printed newsletter, or *Comet*, our monthly email newsletter. Subscriptions to both newsletters are free. The very best contributions will be rewarded with a free guidebook.

Excerpts from your correspondence may appear in new editions of Lonely Planet guidebooks, the Lonely Planet Web site, *Planet Talk* or *Comet*, so please let us know if you *don't* want your letter published or your name acknowledged.

Send all correspondence to the Lonely Planet office closest to you:

Australia: PO Box 617, Hawthorn, Victoria 3122
USA: 150 Linden St, Oakland, CA 94607
UK: 10A Spring Place, London NW5 3BH
France: 1 rue du Dahomey, 75011 Paris

Or email us at: talk2us@lonelyplanet.com.au

For news, views and updates see our Web site: www.lonelyplanet.com

Introduction

While most USA-bound visitors tend to think of the obvious attractions – Disneyland, the Statue of Liberty, Las Vegas – as American 'must sees', they forget that in between lies some of the vastest, wildest and most untouched terrain within easy access of the developed world. The USA doesn't traditionally 'sell' it's outdoor spaces the way it does Hollywood or its skyscrapers, but its mountains and forests are certainly alluring destinations, especially for those who want to explore them on foot.

The USA's hikeable terrain is widely dispersed and extremely varied. The Pacific Northwest, Appalachians and desert Southwest may fall within the same geo-political boundaries, but going from one to the other is the equivalent of going from Japan to the French Jura to the Australian Outback. This is undoubtedly one of the most attractive aspects of hiking in the USA for people who have plenty of time – travel between regions is easy (if not exactly quick, due to the long distances) and the variety of landscapes is immense.

The nation's birthplace, New England, is known for the sumptuous hues of its falltime forests, where moose and bear roam and wildflowers dot the meadows with colorful sparks. Southern Appalachia contains the highest peak in the eastern USA and boasts a long and amenable hiking season; the Blue Ridge and Smoky Mountains evoke images of leafy forests and hazy days on the trail.

The spires of the Rocky Mountains form the country's most formidable mountain barrier, and shelter glaciers, alpine tundra and

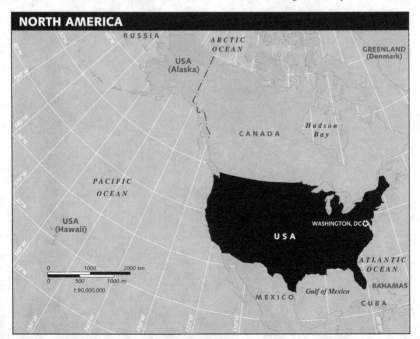

the famous hot springs and geysers of Yellowstone, the world's first national park. An unusual hiking destination, the mesas and canyons of the Southwest surround the hiker with lurid desert colors, layer after layer of rock laid bare like weather-polished bones. Also conspicuously shaped by nature's elements are the granite domes and cirques of the Sierra Nevada, where some of the world's tallest trees grow and hikers and tourists alike flock to the inspirational landscapes of Yosemite Valley, Lake Tahoe, and the Sequoia and Kings Canyon National Parks. The Pacific Northwest offers the chance to traverse slumbering volcanoes, windswept shores and wild, densely forested mountains where Bigfoot supposedly treads!

Snaking through the USA's scenic backcountry is one of the most extensive and well-maintained hiking-trail networks in the world, supported by hundreds of ranger stations, information centers and other facilities, most within easy reach of both backwoods towns and large cities.

For hikers without the luxury of unlimited time, the USA's appeal lies in the rapidity with which they can get from airport to trailhead. Land in San Francisco at 8 am, pick up a rental car, stop for gear and provisions and you can still make it to any number of trailheads in the Sierra Nevada by 1 pm.

Each hiker has their own preference of terrain, scenery and remoteness, and it's likely that any combination of steep, flat, forested or desert hikes to beaches, rock formations, swimming holes, peaks, passes or panoramas can be achieved in hiking the USA. The only thing that most hikers find lacking is their own opportunity to spend as long as they'd like on the trails!

Facts about the USA

HISTORY

While a relatively young country, the USA has a complex history. The most significant events are listed in the Chronology of US History on pages 18 and 19. For an in-depth understanding, refer to a book such as the *Penguin History of the USA* by Hugh Brogan (1990), the well-illustrated and thoughtful *Alistair Cooke's America* (1973), or Howard Zinn's *A People's History of the United States, 1492–Present* (1995).

Here, we cover those aspects of US history related to hiking, which in many ways reflect the greater historical picture. See the Conservation section under Ecology & Environment later in this chapter for the history of that movement.

Native Americans & Europeans

Before the Spanish introduced horses in the 16th century, the native population traveled by foot. While social organization differed from tribe to tribe and material culture depended on the local environment, migration patterns were similar throughout the USA: summer was spent in cooler, higher places and in winter people traveled to protected camps at lower elevations. Most travel routes, especially in areas with dense vegetation, followed trails cleared by bison and deer.

Trading was important to most tribes, enabling the supplementation of local materials with items from other regions. The Hopewell culture, for example, arose in the Ohio and Mississippi Valleys from around 500 BC and had extensive trading links which reached from Lake Huron to the Rocky Mountains and south to Mexico. These trade routes formed a blueprint for subsequent European exploration.

Columbus landed in the Caribbean in AD 1492 while in search of a route to the spice islands of Asia. Believing that he had landed in the East Indies, he called the native people Indians, creating a lasting linguistic confusion. The Spanish, who had sponsored his expedition, continued to build their American empire with Cortés' conquest of Mexico in 1519–20.

Continuing the search for spices and cities of gold, Francisco de Coronado wandered for two years (1540–41) in what is now Arizona, New Mexico and Colorado. English explorers such as John Cabot (in 1497) and Walter Raleigh (in 1584), also seeking a shortcut to Asia, probed the eastern coast of North America and claimed the Atlantic coast for England. Around the same period, French Bretons, who had fished off Novia Scotia from the early 16th century, began trading metal axes, pots and other implements for Native American furs. Dutch settlers formed the colony of New Amsterdam (later renamed New York) along the Hudson River in 1624, furthering the interest in the fur trade. As the Europeans navigated the trails laid by native North Americans, they documented the routes for use by future settlers.

Westward Expansion

In 1803 Thomas Jefferson obtained $2500 from Congress to explore the territory west of the newly formed United States. He hoped to find the 'great Western River' thought to flow from the Atlantic Ocean to the Pacific Ocean. To make the journey, Jefferson enlisted his personal secretary, Merriweather Lewis, who in turn sought the company of his friend William Clark, an army veteran and frontiersman. The Lewis and Clark expedition left St Louis, Missouri, in 1804 and covered around 8000mi in two years, recording everything they came across and naming some 120 species of animal and 170 types of plant. (See the boxed text on page 20.)

As knowledge of the West (the term for land west of the Mississippi River) grew, so did interest in its exploitable resources. Legendary 'mountain men' such as John Colter, Kit Carson, Jim Bridger and David Thompson found routes across the Rocky Mountains, opening the way for fur traders and

continued on page 21

Chronology of US History

Before 10,000 BC - migration from Asia to North America across Bering Strait

9000 BC - stone butchering tools made in Clovis, New Mexico

1000 BC - earliest rock art in California

500 BC - first moundbuilding cultures, Mississippi Valley

AD 300 - Hohokam people develop irrigation in the Southwest

450 - cliff dwellings built at Mesa Verde, Colorado

1000 - Norse seafarers land along northeast coasts; temporary settlements in Newfoundland area

1492 - Columbus 'discovers America,' making landfall in the Bahamas

1497 - John Cabot claims New England for his patron, Henry VII

1534 - Jacques Cartier sails up the St Lawrence River

1540 - Francisco de Coronado expedition wanders through the Southwest

1542 - Juan Rodríguez de Cabrillo's ships enter San Diego harbor while charting the west coast and the Channel Islands

1565 - Spanish settlement at Saint Augustine, Florida

1579 - Francis Drake lands on northern California coast and claims land for England

1584 - Walter Raleigh claims the Atlantic coast for England

1585 - Walter Raleigh founds the 'lost colony' of Roanoke

1607 - first English settlement at Jamestown, Virginia

1608 - first French settlements in Quebec

1619 - first black slaves sold in Virginia

1620 - *Mayflower* lands in Cape Cod with 102 English 'Pilgrims'

1624 - first Dutch settlement along Hudson River

1664 - English take over Dutch colonies in the northeast; New Amsterdam renamed New York

1682 - La Salle travels the length of the Mississippi, claims the region for France

1759 - British defeat French in Battle of Quebec, crucial victory in French & Indian War

1763 - Peace of Paris gives Britain control of Canada and all land east of the Mississippi

1769 - Padre Jun'pero Serra establishes California's first mission in San Diego

1773 - 'Boston Tea Party' protests against British taxation

1775 - Revolutionary War starts with battles at Lexington and Concord, near Boston

1776 - American colonies sign Declaration of Independence on July 4

1778 - France recognizes US independence

1778 - Captain James Cook lands in Hawaiian Islands

1781 - British surrender at Yorktown

1783 - Treaty of Paris; US independence from Britain

1787 - Constitutional Convention in Philadelphia draws up the US Constitution

1788 - constitution ratified by nine states; George Washington elected first president of the USA

1791 - Bill of Rights adopted as constitutional amendments

1794 - Battle of Fallen Timbers ends Indian resistance in Ohio

1800 - Washington, DC, becomes national capital

1803 - Louisiana Purchase from France doubles the area of US territory

1804–6 - Lewis and Clark expedition explores the new territory from the Mississippi to the Pacific

1810 - USA annexes West Florida (the Gulf Coast panhandle west to New Orleans)

1811 - Battle of Tippecanoe ends Indian resistance in Indiana

1812 - War of 1812 starts; ends with Treaty of Ghent in 1814

1812 - Russians build Fort Ross, north of San Francisco Bay

1819 - Spain cedes Florida to the USA

1821 - Mexico becomes independent of Spain after 10-year struggle

1823 - Monroe Doctrine warns European countries against interference in the Americas

1827 - Jedediah Smith arrives in southern California after overland journey from the Midwest

Chronology of US History

1830 - Indian Removal Act begins final forced exodus of Indians from East

1841 - first wagons follow new immigrant trails to California

1845 - annexation of Texas

1846 - Oregon territory acquired from Britain; USA declares war on Mexico

1848 - Treaty of Guadalupe Hidalgo cedes present-day California, Arizona, Nevada and New Mexico and parts of Wyoming, Utah and Colorado to the USA

1849 - California gold rush; 80,000 immigrants arrive

1856 - first railroad bridge over the Mississippi, at Moline, Illinois

1861 - Abraham Lincoln becomes president, Southern states secede, attack on Fort Sumter starts Civil War

1863 - emancipation of slaves

1865 - Southern forces surrender; Lincoln assassinated

1867 - Alaska purchased from Russia

1869 - completion of first transcontinental railway enables travel from New York to San Francisco in four days

1871 - Great Chicago Fire

1872 - Yellowstone becomes the first national park

1876 - Custer's Last Stand

1880 - New York City population exceeds one million

1881 - gunfight at OK Corral

1883 - USA adopts four standard time zones

1883 - Brooklyn Bridge opens

1886 - Statue of Liberty unveiled

1886 - Geronimo surrenders; American Federation of Labor formed

1889 - first movie made in New Jersey

1889 - Oklahoma land rush

1894 - Pullman Railroad strike

1897 - Klondike gold rush

1898 - victory in Spanish-American War gives USA control of Philippines, Puerto Rico and Guam; annexation of Hawaii

1906 - San Francisco earthquake and fire

1914 - Panama Canal opens

1917–18 - US involvement in WWI

1920 - 18th amendment bans alcohol, Prohibition starts; 19th amendment gives women the vote

1924 - Native Americans granted American citizenship

1929 - stock market crash starts the Great Depression

1932 - Olympic Games in Los Angeles

1933 - President Franklin D Roosevelt introduces New Deal economic initiatives; Prohibition ends

1937 - Golden Gate Bridge opens in San Francisco

1941 - Pearl Harbor bombed; USA enters WWII

1945 - end of WWII, US drops atomic bombs on Japan

1950 - start of Korean War

1954 - Supreme Court rules racial segregation unconstitutional

1955 - Disneyland opens

1957 - nine black students enroll in Little Rock Central High School under military protection

1961 - first US forces in Vietnam

1962 - Cuban missile crisis

1963 - President John F Kennedy assassinated in Dallas

1963 - California becomes the most populous state in the USA

1965 - race riots in Los Angeles; 34 killed

1967 - 'Summer of Love,' San Francisco

1968 - Martin Luther King Jr assassinated in Memphis

1968 - Robert Kennedy assassinated in Los Angeles

1969 - US astronauts land on moon

1973 - last US forces leave Vietnam

1974 - President Nixon resigns over Watergate

1979 - nuclear accident at Three Mile Island

1979–80 - US hostages held in Iran

1983 - President Reagan announces 'Star Wars' strategic defense initiative

1984 - Olympic Games in Los Angeles

1986 - space shuttle *Challenger* disaster

1987 - October stock market crash

1989 - Exxon Valdez oil spill

1991 - USA leads Gulf War coalition against Iraq

1996 - Olympic Games in Atlanta

1999 - President Clinton escapes impeachment over Lewinsky scandal

The Lewis & Clark Expedition

William Clark

Meriwether Lewis

When Jefferson made the decision in 1803 to explore the western part of the country to find a water passage to the Pacific, he enlisted his young protege and personal secretary, Meriwether Lewis, to lead an expedition. Lewis, then 29, had no expertise in botany, cartography or Native American languages and was known to have bouts of 'hypochondriac affections' – a euphemism for schizophrenia – but he couldn't resist the opportunity. Lewis in turn asked his good friend William Clark, already an experienced frontiersman and army veteran at the age of 33, to join him. In 1804, they left St Louis, Missouri, and headed west with an entourage of 40 including 27 bachelors, a dog and Clark's African-American servant, York.

They traveled some 8000mi in about two years, documenting everything they came across in their journals with such bad spelling that it must have taken historians a few extra years just to sort out what they wrote. In an almost biblical fashion they named some 120 animals and 170 plants, including the grizzly bear and the prairie dog. While Clark's entries are the more scientific, Lewis was known to explore alone and write pensive, almost romantic, accounts of the journey.

Despite encountering hostilities from local tribes, the group faired quite well, in part because they were accompanied by Sacagawea, a young Shoshone woman who had been married off to a French trapper. Her presence, along with that of her child, and her ability to liaise between the explorers and the local people eased many potential conflicts. York also eased tensions between the explorers and the locals: his color and stature – six feet and 200 pounds – being both fascinating and quite intimidating.

Lewis and Clark returned to a heroes' welcome in St Louis in 1806 and were soon appointed to high offices. In 1808 Lewis was appointed governor of the Louisiana Territory, but died a year later, purportedly during a 'fit' in which he either committed suicide or was murdered. Clark dealt with his new fame a bit better, and was appointed superintendent of Indian Affairs in the Louisiana Territory and governor of the Missouri Territory. He died at the age of 68.

continued from page 17

prospectors and paving the way for later emigrants. Even into the 20th century, hundreds of thousands of emigrants followed the Oregon Trail up the Missouri River to the North Platte and across the Continental Divide to South Pass, where they diverged to various destinations including Oregon, California and Utah.

Following the Mexican-American war, New Mexico, Arizona and California became US territories under the 1848 Treaty of Guadalupe Hidalgo. The annexation of Oregon, Idaho and Utah followed, and in 1849 word of gold discoveries in California reached the east coast. These events 'opened' the West, and soon people were traveling long-distance routes across the USA.

By this time the numbers of the indigenous population had shrunk drastically due to diseases (mainly smallpox) incurred from European contact. In a series of ad hoc treaties, individual chiefs were bribed to give away the lands of their people. Treaties that provided for land rights were soon disregarded and tribal members were forced onto reservations. With the 'Indian problem' secured, westward expansion accelerated. The federal government sent surveyors to find trade routes and potential railroad corridors, the Pony Express and Butterfield & Butterfield companies established overland mail routes, Mormon missionaries fleeing religious persecution established the Mormon Trail and thousands of prospectors traveled various paths to the goldfields of California.

Into the 20th Century

A sense of ownership and desire for protection of the land grew as more people began inhabiting every corner of the USA.

In 1875, the lobbying efforts of local residents convinced Congress to set aside the Yellowstone area as a 'National Park', the beginning of a movement that established the world's first national park system. Fifteen years later, the Grant Grove of giant sequoias, three other sequoia groves and Yosemite Valley, joined Yellowstone as national parks (see National Parks & Reserves

later in this chapter). Railroad companies saw these new parks as big tourism magnets – the means by which to sell seats on their passenger trains. At the end of the railroad lines the companies constructed lodges, formulated tourism circuits and built trails to entertain visitors who typically came for several weeks at a time. Mt Rainier and Glacier National Parks are prime examples of parks created almost solely by the efforts of railroad companies like Great Northern and Union Pacific. When Theodore (Teddy) Roosevelt, an ardent conservationist and avid outdoorsman, became president in 1901, the national awareness of 'out-of-doors' recreation was further elevated.

In New England and the Sierra Nevada, outdoor enthusiasts constructed footpaths to gain access to scenic, mountainous terrain. Hiking devotees in New England talked of a 'super trail' which was eventually given life by Benton MacKaye, a Massachusetts resident who saw the need for society 'to cope with nature directly – unshielded by the weakening wall of civilization'. He gained the support of existing hiking clubs, spurred the formation of new clubs and saw the nation's first interstate trail, the Appalachian Trail, begun in 1937 (delayed by WWII, it

President Theodore Roosevelt, a great advocate for the outdoors.

HUGH D'ANDRADE

was completed and opened in 1951). On the west coast, teams of YMCA workers explored a border-to-border trail corridor. Clinton Clarke formed the Pacific Crest Trail Conference in 1932, and by 1948 the Pacific Crest Trail was complete.

In 1968, in order to provide federal assistance to the upkeep of the Appalachian Trail and to establish a national system of trails, Congress passed the National Trails System Act 'in order to provide for the ever-increasing outdoor recreation needs of an expanding population and in order to promote the preservation of, public access to, travel within, and enjoyment and appreciation of the open-air, outdoor areas and historic resources of the Nation'. The Appalachian and Pacific Crest Trails were named as the first two National Scenic Trails; see the Long-Distance Trails chapter for more.

This act has been amended several times, generally with a positive slant towards hiking interests. In 1998, the Clinton administration appropriated $4 million for a Millennium Trails Program to fund the creation of 2000 new trails throughout the USA. The intention is to bring government, industry and grassroots groups together to create a new trail in each state, plus '12 nationally significant trails on public lands'.

The most recent major trail-related legislation reached Congress in March 1999, when Senator Frank Murkowski (Chairman of the Senate Energy and Natural Resources Committee) introduced legislation to create the American Discovery Trail. As the nation's first coast-to-coast, multi-use trail, it would link the Pacific Crest Trail to the Appalachian Trail and take in the urban communities in between. According to the senator, 'more than 100 organizations along the trail's 6000 miles support the effort.'

GEOGRAPHY

The continental US – referred to as the 48 contiguous states, or the 'Lower 48', and which does not include the huge state of Alaska or the volcanic Pacific islands of Hawaii – stretches 2600mi across North America in a band 1250mi from north to south. Mexico and Canada are on its southern and northern borders, respectively; the Pacific Ocean lies to the west and the Atlantic to the east.

John Wesley Powell, a one-armed Civil War veteran and explorer (a prominent figure in the Southwest chapter later in this book), was the first to attempt dividing North America into regions based on physical features. Powell's work laid ground for geologists and geographers who later divided North America into 40 provinces based on geologic history, vegetation, soil and climate. These provinces are further grouped, by the National Geographic Society and Dr Edwin H Colbert (Curator Emeritus, American Museum of Natural History) into seven large physiogeographic regions.

The *Canadian Shield*, a wide area of mineral-rich Precambrian rock, extends from the Great Lakes and Adirondack Mountains north to Canada's Queen Elizabeth Islands. Its complex vegetation cover includes boreal forests, swamps, rivers, lakes and tundra.

Adjacent to the coastal plain that spans Florida, Alabama, Louisiana and southeast Texas are the long ridges and valleys of the *Appalachian Highlands* which cover a vast region – from Newfoundland in the north to Alabama in the south. Natural communities range from subarctic to swamp and bayou, but for hikers the highlight is the rich, broadleaf forests of Southern Appalachia. Subsidiary ranges include the Great Smoky Mountains, Blue Ridge Mountains, Allegheny Mountains, the Catskills and the Green Mountains.

West of the Appalachians, the *Great Plains and Central Lowland* is drained by the extensive Mississippi-Missouri-Ohio river system. Once covered by a vast inland sea, the 'cotton belt' in the south and 'corn belt' in the north are the nation's agricultural heartland. There's not much hiking here, except at the extreme western edge where the plains rise to meet the eastern foothills of the Rocky Mountains.

Part of the complex North American Cordillera (which runs roughly north to south from Alaska to Mexico's Sierra Madre), the *Rocky Mountains and Columbia*

Where Do Mountains Come From?

Four primary geologic forces account for the formation of the worlds' mountain ranges. **Folded mountains** (A) such as the Appalachians rise – like a ripple in a rug – when parts of the earth's surface are pushed together by the shifting of continental plates. **Fault-block mountains** (B) such as the Sierra Nevada are formed when underground pressure from the same plate movements forces a mass of rock to break cleanly from another along a fault; generally, one mass is thrust up while the other subsides.

A **volcano** or **volcanic range** (C) such as the Cascades forms when a rush of molten material from deep within the earth pushes through a fault and deposits a pile of lava or cinders on the earth's surface. Often the lava intrusion remains behind as a round plug or linear wall after softer rock around it has eroded away. Surging molten rock is also the underlying force of the mountain-building process which results in **dome mountains** (D), the most famous of which is probably Yosemite's Half Dome. When molten magma rushes into a crack whose opening does not extend to the earth's surface, it can push the surrounding rock up into a bulge and slowly cool within its heart. When the material above the intrusion is eroded away, a dome-shaped mountain of granite is left.

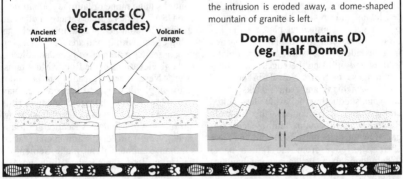

Folded Mountains (A)
(eg, Appalachians)

Fault-block Mountains (B)
(eg, Sierra Nevada)

Volcanos (C)
(eg, Cascades)
Ancient volcano Volcanic range

Dome Mountains (D)
(eg, Half Dome)

Plateau spans more than 1900mi from the Liard River (in Canada) to New Mexico. The subsidiary ranges of the Rocky Mountains – the Sawtooth, Teton, Bitteroot, Wind River, Bighorn, Medicine Bow and San Juan Mountains – exhibit just about every mountain-building force known to exist (for details, see the boxed text). Together they encompass 69 summits which are higher than 14,000ft in elevation and more than 4500 plant species.

In the Southwest, the Colorado River and its tributaries have eroded canyons, cliffs, mesas, buttes and arches into the high desert tableland of the *Colorado Plateau*. Hiking here is limited by lack of water and rough terrain, but the routes that do exist are unique.

West and south of the Four Corners area (where Utah, Colorado, New Mexico and Arizona meet), the *Basin and Range* province covers much of the western US and northern Mexico. Its four desert regions – the Great Basin, Mojave, Sonoran and Chihuahuan – are more hospitable to sagebrush, cacti and other water-storing plants than to hikers.

To the west of the Basin and Range lies the *West Coast* province. Here, the Coastal Range follows the full length of the nation's edge, becoming part of the Baja Peninsula in the south and the Coastal Mountains of Canada and Alaska in the north. Inland, the relatively young and undeniably magnificent Sierra Nevada range runs from southern California to where it meets the volcanic Cascade Range in the north. These ranges support some of the largest trees on earth and, on the Olympic Peninsula, the northern hemisphere's only temperate rainforest (see the Pacific Northwest chapter).

GEOLOGY

The geology of the USA is a result of three basic processes: plate tectonics, changing sea levels and erosion. Over the past two billion years, continental plates – the Pacific, Europe and Africa plates – mashed into the sides of the North American plate, folding and uplifting the edges into mountain ranges (the Sierra Nevada in the west, the Appalachians and Adirondacks in the east) and subducting rock which has melted and erupted as volcanoes (the Cascade Range). The two major fault systems engaged by the plate movement were the Lake Char (shortened from the Indian name 'Chargoggogoggmanchuaugagoggchaubungungamaug') Fault, which cuts a series of cracks from Newfoundland to Massachusetts, and the still very active San Andreas Fault, which stretches from mainland Mexico to the Alaska panhandle.

Superimposed on these tectonic forces were a series of sea-level rises that flooded North America, depositing thick sequences of limestone, sandstone and shale that make up the horizontal strata dominant throughout the continent. In areas of uplift and erosion, this layering sequence has been exposed: a close look at the limestones reveals marine flora and invertebrate fauna (clams, corals and the doughnut-shaped stems of ancient aquatic plants), while sandstones and shales bear dinosaur bones and footprints. The Grand Canyon is a good place to view the full spectrum of rocks laid down from two billion years ago.

Successive glaciations also altered the face of the land. As recently as 15,000 years ago the Laurentide Ice Sheet covered most of eastern North America and swept over much of the Great Plains, leaving deep sediments as it receded into the Arctic. A separate system of glaciers formed at higher altitudes in the Rockies and Sierra Nevada, scouring U-shaped valleys (such as Yosemite Valley) and carving the dramatic cirques, glacial horns and ridges in places such as Glacier, Grand Teton and Rocky Mountain National Parks. (See the boxed text 'Glaciers & Glacial Landforms' in the Rocky Mountains chapter.)

CLIMATE

With its huge range of latitude and altitude, the USA includes a great variety of climatic zones. The continental land mass itself has a big effect, with inland areas experiencing much greater extremes of heat and cold.

High elevations in the Rocky Mountains, Sierra Nevada and Cascades can be under snow until mid-July and temperatures may dip below freezing by mid-September (it is possible to wake to six inches of fresh snow on July 4th in Montana's Beartooth Mountains). That said, dry, warm spells (called 'Indian Summers') can make September feel more like summer than July and August, during which there are frequent (often daily) afternoon thunderstorms. Forest fires are common in late August.

The Southwest is dry year-round, hot in summer and cold in winter. Flash-flood season lasts from July through September, during which afternoon downpours are common.

For more detail, see the climate charts in this chapter, When to Hike under Planning in the Facts for the Hiker chapter, and the Planning sections of individual regions and hikes.

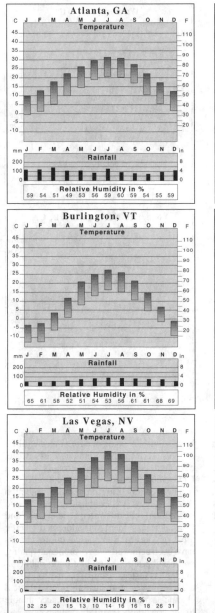

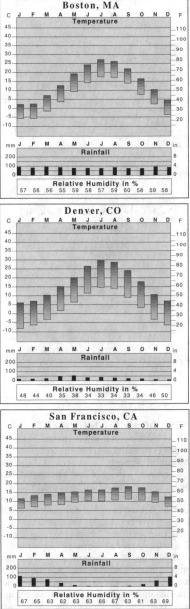

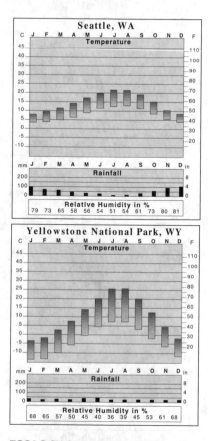

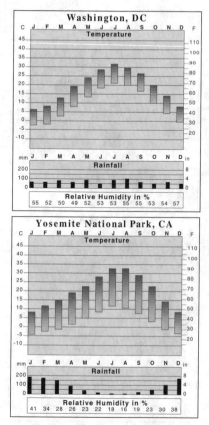

ECOLOGY & ENVIRONMENT

The USA's natural environment has been much exploited and greatly altered since European settlement. There remain, however, vast areas in a more-or-less-natural state that seem remote and wild when compared with European equivalents. But most 'wild' places in the USA are designated as such by one or more government agencies and come with their own set of regulations, intended to minimize the impact of a growing population.

While the USA remains absolutely committed to consumption and growth, there is a strong attachment to the ideal of 'America the Beautiful' and an awareness of the tragic environmental damage of the recent past.

Typically, Americans try to have it all – to have suburban expansion *and* more wildlife refuges, convenience items *and* less waste, cars that don't pollute, aerosols without CFCs and industries without acid rain.

The federal Environmental Protection Agency (EPA) was established in 1970, and subsequent Clean Water, Clean Air and Coastal Management Acts addressed specific areas of concern. Remarkable improvements have been achieved in environmental quality, not least because the revolution in public attitudes has fostered campaigns to protect natural resources and has, through political channels, made large industry accountable for its potentially harmful practices.

Agriculture

The 'Dust Bowl disaster' in the 1930s, affecting much of Kansas, Oakalhoma, Texas, New Mexico and Colorado, was caused by a combination of drought and high winds on land that had recently been cultivated and grazed. Thousands of tons of topsoil were stripped away in giant dust clouds, farms were ruined and Dust Bowl refugees went west. From 1935, state and federal governments helped farmers to develop contour plowing, crop diversification and other techniques to conserve soil. Nevertheless, erosion remains a big problem.

Individual farms and ranches can cover hundreds of thousands of acres of land and thus are managed with tools intended to achieve large-scale efficiency. The use of chemical fertilizers and pesticides has long been the normal mode of operation and has caused great damage to water and wildlife (see Endangered Species in the Flora & Fauna special section). A more recently discovered problem – dubbed 'environmental racism' – is the damage, including birth defects and several types of cancer, incurred disproportionately by laborers (most of whom have been immigrants) who handle the chemicals. Some of the most damaging chemicals, such as DDT, are now banned.

Logging

More than 80% of the nation's old-growth forests (defined as more than 200 years old and never altered by humans) from Northern California to British Columbia have been cut down. This timber brings the highest market price, but is home to species such as the northern spotted owl which face extinction as their habitat diminishes.

Clear-cutting, where a parcel of trees is cut down in a giant swath, is another devastating practice. Besides eliminating natural habitats, clear-cutting requires roads to be built in forested areas, promotes erosion and takes away shade from rivers and streams, causing water temperatures to rise to a point where fish cannot reproduce (salmon and trout are most threatened by this).

Central to both issues is the role of the US Forest Service: is it supposed to protect or to develop the land it regulates? In recent years the service has tried to sell land to timber and energy firms and is often caught between business interests and vocal, politically active environmental groups.

Air Pollution

The USA uses a quarter of the world's energy and is the largest emitter of carbon dioxide from the burning of fossil fuels. It is therefore the greatest single contributor to the greenhouse effect and global warming.

Nitrogen oxide and sulfur dioxide emissions from US factories are a major cause of acid rain, which has killed aquatic life in many lakes in the northeastern USA and Canada and damaged large areas of forest. Federal regulations and international agreements are pegging back emission levels.

Air pollution, caused mainly by motor vehicles, is a problem in many cities. While it rarely reaches the backcountry, hikers in the East, the lower Sierra Nevada foothills and on trails near Denver, Colorado, have reported heavy lungs after a day of exercise when conditions are smoggy. More often hikers view haze from above in areas where the topography favors temperature inversions. Stringent exhaust-emission controls have reduced the problem to some extent.

Water

This is probably the issue that most tangibly affects hikers in the USA: while the tap-water supply is clean and plentiful in most of the country, *nowhere* can you drink from a stream without the risk of contracting giardia (see the Health & Safety chapter).

Since the 1970s, new laws and clean-up programs have greatly reduced water pollution, revitalizing many aquatic habitats that had been damaged by years of unchecked waste disposal. But the USA still faces grave water issues. The damming of rivers (including the Tennessee, Missouri, Snake, Columbia and Colorado) for hydroelectric power and the diversion of waterways to support development are the two most talked-about problems.

In California natural river systems have been altered beyond recognition to bring water to the arid lands around Los Angeles and San Diego. In the rapidly growing Southwest, water is drawn from natural underground reservoirs, called aquifers, that are being used up faster than rainfall is replenishing them. Unfortunately, the economics of development often sweep these issues under the carpet.

Agricultural run-off and sewage has affected the coastal environment in Chesapeake and Delaware Bays, and all along the Pacific Coast, but active environmental groups have helped limit the damage.

Domestic Waste
The USA is the world's leading producer of garbage. In the densely populated Northeast, dump sites are becoming scarce and big cities like New York incur increasing costs to take out the trash. Recycling of glass, aluminum, paper products and some plastics is becoming more widespread, due to a combination of public support and government regulation. You'll find garbage cans at every trailhead and, often, a separate container for depositing glass and/or aluminum to be recycled; recycling bins are also found at most campgrounds and outside supermarkets.

Toxic Wastes & Chemicals
The high level of industrial development in the USA has led to a large volume of toxic and hazardous by-products that have caused some hideous instances of environmental damage. The Cuyahoga River in Cleveland was so polluted with chemicals in the 1950s and 1960s that it caught fire; leakage of toxic waste at Love Canal in upstate New York forced the evacuation of a neighborhood and caused national outrage. Numerous unsafe toxic waste dumps have been identified across the country. Decontaminating these sites and developing satisfactory methods of toxic waste disposal are major environmental problems.

Coal mining (in the Appalachians) and open-pit copper mining (in the Rocky Mountains) have left toxic bodies of water and piles of tailings (by-product) which pollute the local soil and water supply. The Berkeley Pit in Butte, Montana, yielded 290 million tons of copper ore from 1955 to 1980 but is now an 800ft deep pool that is the USA's deepest and most toxic body of water.

Nuclear Industry
About 20% of the USA's energy supply is generated by nuclear power plants. The accident at the Three Mile Island plant in 1979 dispelled much complacency in the nuclear power industry and led to much stricter standards – indeed, compliance with new standards made many new nuclear plants unprofitable. There is no permanent nuclear waste storage facility in the country and no reprocessing plant, so for years all radioactive waste has been placed in 'temporary' storage. A site in Nevada has been chosen for nuclear waste storage, but many local people regard it as a bad gamble.

Conservation
The first rumblings of a conservation ethic in the USA came during the nation's rapid westward expansion. People were flooding to the untouched valleys, mountains and coasts of the West, using native timber to build homes and railroads, and using local water sources for drinking, washing and powering small industry. At a time when the new nation's natural resources seemed unlimited, John Muir – perhaps the country's most famous environmental advocate – gave voice to the radical idea of preserving land for the sake of its beauty and aesthetic value instead of for economic purpose. Through articles in *Century Magazine* Muir exposed people in the East (where the bulk of the American population resided) to the 'boundless affluence of sublime mountain beauty' that lay in the Sierra Nevada. He criticized the timber industry, writing as early as 1860 that 'waste far exceeds use', and lobbied Congress (successfully) to preserve the giant sequoia groves in and around Yosemite Valley as public (now national) parks. In 1892, he created the Sierra Club, still one of the USA's most influential environmental organizations.

continued on page 46

FLORA & FAUNA
OF THE USA

The massive expanse of land that is the USA has just about every combination of latitude, elevation, precipitation and soil composition possible. From the northern hemisphere's only temperate rainforest (in the Pacific Northwest), to tundra-like landscapes atop the Rocky Mountains, to rich deciduous forests in Southern Appalachia, the USA's flora and fauna is one that defies generalization.

According to botanists, ornithologists and zoologists, North America belongs in the Nearctic (new north) Zoogeographical Realm which encircles the northern part of the globe in a broad band. Plants and wildlife found here are thus similar to those in parts of Europe and Asia. Further influences to North America's natural history have been the migration of species west to east across the Bering Strait and south to north across the Central American isthmus, both of which have been passable intermittently, depending on the level of the oceans, over the past several million years.

Title page: A bristlecone pine, White Mountains, California. These trees are reputedly among the world's oldest living things, some more than 4000 years old.

Flora

TREES

The USA has the tallest trees (redwoods), most massive trees (giant sequoias) and oldest trees (bristlecone pines) on earth. As recently as 300 years ago, most of the modern USA was covered with forests. But in the first hundred years of the nation's rapid growth, many of the forests were cut for timber, cleared for agriculture and used for construction, energy and trade. Still, there are more than 750 species of trees – at least 60 kinds of oak, 35 sorts of pine and a dozen types of maple – north of the Mexican border.

All hikers will spend a lot of time surrounded by trees, but by which trees is a question of latitude as well as elevation. Western forests are largely coniferous (dominated by pine and fir) while eastern forests are famous for their thick cover of broadleaf trees (mostly oak and hickory). Foresters and botanists divide the North American forests into distinct regions, but there is not one scheme that is agreed upon by all. For more information, see *Trees of North America* by Frank Brockman and the Reader's Digest *North American Wildlife Guide*.

The world's largest living organism, a giant sequoia called General Sherman, Sequoia National Park, Sierra Nevada, California.

JOHN ELK III

The White Mountains, California, are home to what is considered the oldest living thing on earth: a Great Basin bristlecone pine estimated to be more than 4000 years old. Bristlecone pines (their distinctive cones are illustrated here) are found on dry, rocky slopes and ridges. At low elevations they grow to 40ft, but at treeline the gnarled trees, with their wide-reaching limbs, reach a maximum height of 10ft.

Pines

North America has 36 native species of pine (*Pinus* spp) which foresters divide into two groups: white pines have softer wood, smooth cones (except the **bristlecone pine**, *Pinus aristata*) and needles that grow in clusters of five; yellow pines have very hard wood, cones with prickly barbs and needles in clusters of two and three.

The most common pines in the USA are the **western white pine** *(P. monticola)* and the longer-needled **eastern white pine** *(P. strobus)*, both of which grow in a wide range of climatic and soil conditions. Both have two white lines on the surface of each needle, cones that are flaky and slightly curved and smooth green-gray bark that becomes brown and deeply cracked as the tree matures. The western white can grow up to 175ft, while the eastern white only reaches 80ft to 100ft.

Western USA In the western half of the USA, the majestic **ponderosa pine** *(P. ponderosa)* grows to 180ft and is found on dry mountain slopes. The large, flat plates of its golden-brown bark resemble pieces of a jigsaw puzzle and its cones are recognizable for the way the barbed ends flare away from the stalk. Its long needles (four to seven inches) are clustered in twos or threes. In the same region but in moist environments (including near beaches), the **lodgepole pine** *(P. contorta)* has dark-gray, scaly bark and small, teardrop-shaped cones that remain closed until exposed to extreme heat. Lodgepoles are generally from 70ft to 80ft tall, though much shorter near the ocean, and have short, stiff needles that grow in twos.

Only found west of the Rocky Mountains, the magnificent **sugar pine** *(P. lambertiana)* has the longest cones (10 to 26 inches) of any North American conifer and can grow to be 200ft high, the tallest of pines. Its needles grow in clusters of five and are long and twisted. The bark of mature trees has deep, horizontal ridges and is a lovely purplish-brown color. Other pines found in limited areas of the west (mostly California) are the **limber pine** *(P. flexilis)*, **Jeffrey pine** *(P. jeffreyi)* and **Coulter pine** *(P. coulteri)*.

Eastern USA The eastern half of the USA is dominated by the **shortleaf pine** *(P. echinata)*, an important timber crop that grows from 80ft to 100ft tall in dry, gravelly soil. Its very dark, reddish-brown bark is scaly and separated into large plates (not dissimilar to the ponderosa) and its long, flexible, dark-green needles grow in clusters of two. Cones have a prickle at the end of each scale. The **loblolly pine** *(P. taeda)*, another important timber tree, grows to the same size and is found in the same region. Its needles are stiff, yellow-green and grow in threes, and its reddish-brown conical cones are covered with triangular-shaped prickles.

The northern reaches of the eastern USA are home to **pitch pine** *(P. rigida)*, **Scotch pine** *(P. sylvestris)* and, to a lesser extent, **jack pine** *(P. banksiana)*. In the southeast are the **Virginia pine** *(P. virginiana)*, the larger but closely related **Table-mountain pine** *(P. pungens)*, and the **longleaf pine** *(P. palustris)*.

Spruces

Of the 40 species of spruce *(Picea* spp) in the northern hemisphere, seven are native to the USA. As a rule they like moist soil, have cones that are composed of light-brown, woody scales, and have short, rigid needles that grow close together (so when you stroke a branch in the direction the needles grow it feels soft).

White spruce *(P. glauca)* and **black spruce** *(P. mariana)*, both found in the extreme Northeast, have four-sided needles, scaly, auburn-brown bark and cones with wavy (almost W-shaped) edges on the scales. The **Engelmann spruce** *(P. engelmannii)* resembles these two, but has plump, prickly needles and grows to 125ft (nearly twice the size of the white and black); Engelmanns are abundant in the Rocky Mountains and northern Cascades. Limited to the low elevations and moist climate along the coast of the Pacific Northwest, the awe-inspiring **sitka spruce** *(P. sitchensis)* grows to 200ft and can reach 6ft in diameter. Its needles are flat, silvery and very prickly, cones are flexible with wavy-edged scales, and its bark is purplish-gray.

Firs

Two genera are called 'fir' in the USA: Douglas firs *(Pseudotsuga* spp), which grow in the west, and true firs *(Abies* spp), of which all but two – the **balsam fir** *(A. balsamea)* and **Fraser fir** *(A. fraseri)* – also occur only in the western half of the USA.

CLEM LINDENMAYER

A grove of battered spruce trees shelter a lone tent high up in the southern Rockies, South San Juan Mountains, Rocky Mountains, Colorado.

CLEM LINDENMAYER

LEE FOSTER

ROB BLAKERS

JOHN ELK III

CLEM LINDENMAYER

CLEM LINDENMAYER

MARISA GIERLICH

Clockwise from Top Left: The globeflower grows in moist areas throughout the Rocky Mountains; the distinctive snowplant, Sierra Nevada; dogwood flowers, Sequoia National Park; the brilliant, desert flower of the cholla cactus, Southwest; silky lupine, Rockies; shoots of the Indian hellebore emerge from the melting snow, Rockies; an ancient bristlecone pine, White Mountains, California.

Clockwise from Top Left: The striking bald eagle; a lumbering moose can be more than 5ft tall at the shoulder; the peregrine falcon, an endangered predator whose numbers are now recovering; a marmot surveys its territory, high Sierra Nevada; black-tailed deer, Rocky Mountains; elk lock antlers in the snow, Jackson Hole, Wyoming.

LEE FOSTER

LEE FOSTER

LEE FOSTER

LEE FOSTER

CHRIS MELLOR

MICK ELMORE

Douglas firs are among the largest conifers, growing to 250ft. Scales on their cones have three-pointed bracts that grow longer than the scales themselves (giving the cones a shaggy appearance). Needles are blunt-ended, and the tree's profile shows a clear lower trunk topped with long, swooping branches.

True firs are best recognized by their cones: barrel-shaped and smooth to the touch when young, they grow upright from the branches; at maturity the scales disintegrate, leaving a needle-like core that remains on the branch. It is generally believed that these natural 'decorations' inspired the hanging of lights and ornaments on Christmas trees and inspired the German folksong *O Tannenbaum*. The most prevalent of the true firs are the **white fir** *(A. concolor)* and **subalpine fir** *(A. lasiocarpa)*, both growing in the Rocky Mountains, Cascades and Sierra Nevada.

Larches

Larches (*Larix* spp), which unlike other conifers lose their needles in winter, speckle the evergreen forest with shades of gold and orange from October to the first snowfall. At other times, the tree's most defining feature is the way its needles grow in whorled clusters around the branch, with even spaces between each cluster. The **tamarack** *(L. laricina)*, called the eastern larch, is found in the extreme Northeast and grows to 80ft, while the **western larch** *(L. occidentalis)*, whose reddish-brown bark is thicker, grows to 150ft and is found in the northern reaches of the Rocky Mountains and Cascades.

Junipers

Some of the 13 species of juniper (*Juniperus* spp) native to the USA are called 'cedars'. All like dry, rocky soil (but can grow just about anywhere that is not wet), grow low to the ground and have reddish-brown, fibrous bark. The **common juniper** *(J. communis)*, also called the **dwarf juniper**, is found throughout the USA. Its needle-like leaves grow in threes, and its small, round, purplish-blue cones (which resemble blueberries) are usually covered with a white, powdery film. These cones, called juniper berries, are used for flavoring gin (hence the term 'juniper juice').

JOHN ELK III

Juniper trees growing through rocks, Colorado National Monument, Colorado.

Other junipers – including the **eastern redcedar** *(J. virginiana)* which grows throughout the East, and **Rocky Mountain juniper** *(J. scopulorum)* and **Utah juniper** *(J. osteosperma)* found in the Rocky Mountains and Southwest – have similar berry-like cones, but very distinctive foliage that resembles dark-green, rubbery rope (usually 0.1 inch thick, 1 inch long) with small, overlapping scales.

Oaks

The most widespread broadleaf trees in North America, oaks *(Quercus* spp) can be either deciduous or evergreen, depending on locality. Their fruit, the nut-like acorn which wears a 'cap' securing it to the tree, is an important winter staple for many mammals and was ground and prepared as an edible mush by Native Americans. There are 58 species of oak in the USA, divided into two groups: red oaks have tiny bristles at the end of each leaf or each lobe of the leaf (or both), acorns that are bitter and take two years to mature (and thus stay on the tree in winter) and a hairy lining on the inside of the acorn's cup; white oaks have rounded lobes without bristles, sweet acorns that mature in six months and have a smooth interior to their cups.

Most common in the east are the **northern red oak** *(Q. rubra),* **black oak** *(Q. velutina)* and **scarlet oak** *(Q. coccinea),* all growing to 70ft and with deciduous leaves of five or more lobes, squat acorns and dark, furrowed bark. **White oak** *(Q. alba)* and **post oak** *(Q. stellata)* grow along riverbanks and moist valleys. The **blackjack oak** *(Q. marilandica),* called the barren oak, has distinctive, bell-shaped leaves and a leathery texture.

In the western half of the USA, oaks grow mostly in California. An exception is the **gambel oak** *(Q. gambeii),* found in the Southwest and Rocky Mountains. It has deciduous leaves with a smooth top and hairy underside. The **California white oak** *(Q. lobata)* grows to 120ft – the tallest of western oaks – and has long, pointy acorns.

Hickories

Often found with oaks, hickories *(Carya* spp) are native to the East. Their tough wood is used for

JAMES LYON

The distinctive Joshua tree, California.

making tool handles and, when still green, grilling or smoking meats (it imparts a terrific, sweet-smoky flavor that sauces try to replicate). Related to walnuts (*Juglans* spp), which are also found in the East, not all kernels of hickory nuts are edible, but the **pecan** (*J. illinoensis*) is an important food crop in the southern states. Hickories grow to 90ft, have shaggy, fibrous bark and leaves with from five to nine leaflets.

Yuccas

Found only in dry soils of the western hemisphere, yuccas (*Yucca* spp) are perhaps the most whimsical looking trees in the USA. They have long, bayonet leaves that grow from shaggy, irregular branches and light-colored flowers growing around a pointed stem which extends beyond the main body of the tree. The flowers open in the night, pulling back thick, dry petals to reveal smooth, flat ovules. The **Joshua tree** (*Y. brevifolia*), to which a national park is dedicated, grows to 30ft. Filaments along the leaves of the **soap tree** (*Y. elata*) detach and curl, hanging down from the tree like straw ribbons.

WILDFLOWERS

The wide range of climatic conditions in the USA supports more than 1500 species of 'wildflowers', defined loosely as any flowering plant that grows outside cultivation and is neither a tree nor a small shrub.

The part of the country in which you hike will be a determining factor as to what flowers you encounter. The broad, heart-shaped leaves of **Dutchman's-pipe** (*Aristolochia durior*) and **Virginia snakeroot** (*A. serpentaria*), the greenish-white, spiked flowers and deep purple berries of **pokeweed** (*Phytolacca americana*), and clinging vines such as **passionflowers** (*Passiflora* spp) – whose intricate blossoms symbolized the passion of Christ to Spanish explorers – thrive in the rich woods of the East. Specific to the West are **yerba buena** (*Satureja douglasii*) which has pairs of oval (nearly heart-shaped) leaves along a square stem; **sand lilies** (*Leucocrinum montanum*) whose fragrant, white flowers grow low to the ground among grass-like leaves; and **mountain sunflowers** (*Hymenoxys grandiflora*) which grow to 12ft and have yellow flowers with mound-like centers. Despite such examples, however, most flower groups are represented throughout the USA by species which have adapted to their local environment.

The most common alpine flowers are **pearly everlasting** (*Anaphalis margaritacea*), **Mou** (*Erigeron philadelphicus*), **harebell** (*Campanula rotundifolia*), **greater bladderwort** (*Utricularia vulgaris*), **Canada violet** (*Viola canadensis*), **pinesap** (*Monotropa hypopithys*), **Solomon's zigzag** (*Smilacina racemosa*), and at high elevations in every mountain range you'll encounter several kinds of **columbines** (*Aquilegia* spp), **asters** (*Aster* spp), **shooting stars** (*Dodecatheron* spp) and **stonecrops** (*Sedum* spp).

For more information on the flora of each region featured in this book, see the individual hikes chapters or consult region-specific wildflower books (sold at national and state park visitor centers, outdoors stores and bookstores); a good guide for eastern and central USA is *Newcomb's Wildflower Guide.*

Columbines growing among other wildflowers on a grassy hillside in Grand Teton National Park, Wyoming.

Fauna

As the USA continues to develop, reshaping the 'natural' landscape in favor of built environments, wildlife either adapts or becomes threatened. Instead of relying on wild native plants for food and shelter, species must increasingly survive on introduced crops and weeds. This has had drastic effects on some species (see Endangered Species, later) while benefiting others such as pocket gophers, prairie dogs and coyotes. As a rule, the transformation of land is least harmful to species which survive best in border zones, not reliant on the abundance of any one food source.

More than 400 species of mammals and 650 species of birds are at home in the USA. The following are ones you're most likely to see when hiking in areas covered by this book. For more information, see Harper & Row's *Complete Field Guide to North American Wildlife* or the aforementioned Reader's Digest guide.

MAMMALS

There are three species of deer (*Odocoileus* spp) that roam throughout the USA. Most widespread are **white-tailed deer** (*O. virginianus*), named for the white underside of the tail that they flip up at the first sign of danger or excitement. Their coat is light reddish-brown and their throat, underbelly and ear-lining is white.

The **mule deer** *(O. hemionus)*, most common in the West, spends summers at 7000ft to 8000ft and migrates to lower climes for winter. They are recognized by big ears and a round, white tail tipped with black, which they tuck away when running. Considered a close relative of the mule deer, the **black-tailed deer** *(O. columbanis)* is the smallest of North America's deer and is most abundant on the west coast. It has short, broad ears and a bushy tail. The buck (male) of all three species grows antlers which are shed annually in mid-winter.

Related to the Thian stag of Turkestan and the European red deer, the **elk** *(Cervus canadensis)* or wapiti of North America was nearly extinct in the 1860s but has made a valiant comeback, especially in the Rocky Mountains and Pacific Northwest. They grow to 10ft in length, weigh up to 800lb and are around 5ft tall at the shoulder. Antlers, grown by the bull, angle back over the shoulder. The bugling call of the elk starts low and reaches a rather unforgettable cacophonous pitch.

The unmistakable profile of a **moose** *(Alces americana)* shows its long, round nose, broad antlers with finger-like projections, and bell – a growth of skin and hair that hangs down from its throat. These large creatures – they grow to 1400lb and stand 5½ft tall at the shoulder – are remarkably good swimmers, eat mostly water-loving plants and are usually seen near swamps and lakes in northern forests.

Larger than its European and Asian counterparts, the majestic **mountain goat** *(Oreamnos americanus)* lives in the upper reaches of the Cascades and Rocky Mountains. It grows to 300lb and has a long, white coat and short, sharp horns that bow slightly towards its rear.

Seen throughout the dry, rocky regions of the Rocky Mountains and Southwest, **bighorn sheep** *(Ovis canadensis)* are recognized by the large curled horns worn by rams. They have a short, grayish tan coat, a cream-colored rump and black tail.

North America's large cat is known by eight names including 'panther' and 'cougar' but officially only goes by **mountain lion** *(Felis concolor)* or **puma**. Found in arid regions of the West, throughout the Southwest and in limited areas in the East, mountain

JOHN ELK III

The large and agile mountain goat has become a denizen of some Rocky Mountains campsites, thanks to its affection for salty campers' foods.

JOHN HAY

The North American bighorn sheep has staged a successful recovery in places where it was once heavily hunted.

lions grow to 6ft long, have a thick, 2ft-long tail with a black tip, large paws and a short, tan coat. They've been known to travel 25mi in a night hunting deer.

Like an oversized housecat with a bobbed tail, long ear-tufts and large paws, the **lynx** *(Lynx canadensis)* is found throughout the Northeast (especially in the Adirondacks), the Cascades and the Rocky Mountains. Closely related is the **bobcat** *(L. rufus)* whose fur is spotted instead of streaked and whose tail is striped, rather than tipped, with black.

Once found from Alaska to Mexico City, the **black bear** *(Euarctos americanus)* now has a smaller range although it is still found throughout the USA. It actually comes in a variety of shades – light tan, dark brown, reddish brown – so its most recognizable feature is its short, rounded claws. While their traditional diet is of wild plants, the inner bark of conifers, and fish, these bears are great scavengers and known for their dexterity at opening anything containing food. Sadly, black bears have become camping-ground pests at many national parks, including Yosemite, Glacier and Yellowstone.

The **grizzly bear** *(Ursus arctos horribilis)*, related to the brown bear of Europe and Asia, is distinguished by long claws, a heavy brow, a humped back and a big, mane-like chin. Classified as 'threatened', grizzly populations decreased from estimates of more than 50,000 to less than 1000 between 1800 and 1975. They are now found in areas of Montana, Wyoming, Idaho and Washington.

The second-largest rodent in the world (and largest in the USA), the **beaver** *(Castor canadensis)* is found throughout the USA wherever aspen and cottonwood trees are abundant. With four large front teeth they fell the trees and use them to build dams which are watertight and, structurally, very sound. On average, a beaver is the size of a fat housecat. It has a large, flat, oval tail that propels it through water (at around 4mph) and, when slapped on the surface of the water with a great 'thwack!', acts as a signal of danger. Demand for beaver pelts – mostly for hats – was a driving force in westward exploration and expansion in the 19th century.

Star of Native American legends and ranchers' extermination campaigns, the dog-like **coyote** *(Canis latrans)* used to run only in the West but is now found in the East and Northeast as well. The average size of

JOHN HAY

The elusive bobcat will rarely show itself so boldly as this.

SHANNON NACE

An adult grizzly bear with two juveniles fishing at a waterfall; stand well back – a mother with cubs can become very aggressive if threatened.

HUGH D'ANDRADE

The coyote is under pressure across some of its range thanks to competition from re-introduced wolves.

HUGH D'ANDRADE

The pika is best known for its haunting whistle, which echoes around high mountain passes and crags.

a coyote is 20lb to 45lb. It has pointed ears, a pointy nose, and a 12- to 15-inch tail tipped with black.

The graceful little **marten** (Martes americana) is found in coniferous forests from the Adirondacks to the Rocky Mountains. It has a soft layer of fur next to its skin covered by an outer fir that is red to gray, big black eyes, rounded ears and a bushy tail that grows to 10 inches; the average size of a marten is 2ft to 3ft long. It was once killed for its pelts but is now protected and no longer in danger of being threatened.

Related to species in the Himalaya and Urals, the **pika** (Ochotona princeps) lives among rocks at 8000ft to 13,500ft throughout the USA. Usually heard rather than seen, they make a high-pitched chirping sound that echoes off rocks and is difficult to pinpoint to a source. Evidence of pika are the small haystacks they make for winter nourishment. If you do see one, you might find it adorable – its about the size of a small rabbit, has pale gray fur, large dark eyes, round ears and feet that are covered with fur.

Native only to the Americas, the opossum (Didelphis virginia) is the only marsupial in the USA. Believed to have changed little in 70 million years, it has a prehensile (grasping) tail of around 12 inches, a 24- to 34-inch

Common Creatures

Two furry critters that are 'typically American' but foreign to international visitors are raccoons and skunks. Raccoons (Procyon lotor) are nocturnal animals, usually the size of a small dog, that are known for making midnight forays into trash cans and ice chests (or anywhere food is stored). They have long, ringed tails, dexterous hands, small black eyes, a pointed nose and a black mask that befits their love of thievery.

Skunks (Family Mustelidae) are black-and-white, housecat-sized creatures known for the strong-smelling secretion they emit when excited or threatened; it's said that soaking in tomato juice is the best way to erase the smell. The most famous skunk of all time is probably Pepe Le Pew, the dashing love-starved cartoon character who tirelessly courts Flower (a cat who inadvertently ends up resembling a skunk in every episode).

body, a long, pointed snout and tiny eyes. Opossums eat anything and can be terrible pests; they prefer to live in damp woods and swamps.

BIRDS

North America has more than 3300 species of bird, often divided into 'eastern' and 'western' species according to migration and habitation patterns. According to US Department of Fish and Wildlife studies, dry western plains support 0.5 to one bird per acre, eastern fields support one to three birds per acre and deciduous forests have two to 10.5 birds per acre. Its not surprising, then, that birdwatchers find more to look at in the eastern USA than they do in the Cascades and the Sierra Nevada.

Only around 650 species are permanent residents; more than 2650 migratory species are found here but breed in Canada in the summer and fly south (some as far as South America) in winter. Birding is best during these migration periods (especially in spring when the males of most species are in full, or 'breeding', plumage and easier to spot).

No matter where you hike you'll encounter jays – **Stellar's jay** *(Cyanocitta stelleri)* in the West, **blue jay** *(C. cristata)* in central and eastern USA – notable for their bright blue color and sharp, short black bill; **killdeer** *(Charadrius vociferous)*, a plover with two black bars across its upper chest, white collar and forehead, reddish rump and wide white stripe on its wing; and the **American robin** *(Turdus migratorius)*, a member of the thrush family, with its dark gray back and head and round reddish belly.

All birdwatchers should equip themselves with the American Ornithologists Union's *Check-list of North American Birds*, the definitive publication with taxonomic status and geographic ranges of all North American birds; and the Peterson Field Guides *A Field Guide to the Birds*, published by Houghton Mifflin.

Once hunted for their filmy, pearl-colored plumes, the **snowy egret** *(Egretta thula)* and larger **great egret** *(Casmerodius albus)*, also called **common** or **American egret**, live in wetlands and watered pastures throughout the southern half of the USA. Both of these birds are large, white and long-legged; the snowy egret has a black bill and black legs with yellow feet, while the great egret has an orange-yellow bill and black legs and

HUGH D'ANDRADE

Stellar's jay is a commonly seen bird of the western wilderness.

RICHARD CUMMINS

A snowy egret with a meal of shrimp, Tampa, Florida.

The red-tailed hawk, a bold and dramatic predator.

The white-tailed ptarmigan, a flightless member of the grouse family, Glacier National Park, Montana.

The wild turkey, runner up in the contest to become a symbol of America, now Thanksgiving dinner.

feet. The **cattle egret** (Bubulcus ibis), introduced in the 1950s, is smaller (18 to 20 inches) than other egrets and often seen riding on the backs of cattle.

The most common bird of prey in the USA, the **red-tailed hawk** (Buteo jamaicensis) spies small mammals either from the air or from exposed perches and swoops down with alarming speed and accuracy to grasp and kill them with its sharp talons – quite an exciting thing to see. Their 4½ft wingspan and rufous tail make them easy to see from the ground.

Members of the Accipiter genus of hawks are recognized by their long tails and short rounded wings, and known for an undulating rhythm in flight: they flap their wings a few times, then tuck them back and glide, then flap a few more times and so on. The **sharp-shinned hawk** (A. striatus) is the smallest and most widespread accipiter in the USA, found mainly in woodlands and brushy areas; the **Cooper's hawk** (A. cooperii) is found in the same regions but is heavier and has a more pronounced flight pattern; the **goshawk** (A. gentilis) is the largest and lives in the northern forests.

On the whole, grouses (Phasianidae spp) are 16 to 19 inches long (rather football shaped), good runners (they're ground dwellers) and fond of seeds, berries and insects; plumage is mottled tan, white and gray. Their elaborate courtship rituals vary within the species, but all are frenzied and not easy to miss. The **ruffed grouse** (Bonasa umbellus), with distinctive black shoulder patches and a fan-shaped tail edged with white and black, is found throughout the USA, the **spruce grouse** (Dendragapus canadensis) lives in northern forests and the **blue grouse** (D. obscurus) calls the western mountains home.

Ptarmigan (Lagopus spp) are related birds, with feathered legs and toes, found above treeline and in alpine meadows.

Indigenous to North America, the **wild turkey** (Meleagris gallopavo) was almost the USA's national bird (the bald eagle – see Endangered Species, later – prevailed) and is now a representative of Kentucky bourbon and famous as the main dish for Thanksgiving dinner. These are large birds, 3ft to 4ft tall, with a long black-banded tail, bluish head and scaly red piece of skin that hangs loosely from the forehead to the throat. Native to the East but introduced throughout the USA for hunting, turkeys are ground-dwelling birds that roost in the trees of deciduous woodlands and oak forests.

Woodpeckers are noisy birds which cling to the bark of a tree with their feet, brace themselves with their stiff, spiny tails and chisel into the wood using their remarkably strong, pointed bills. Some, like the **pileated woodpecker** *(Dryocopus pileatus)* – on which the cartoon character Woody Woodpecker was based – and **Nuttall's woodpecker** *(Picoides nuttallii)* extract carpenter ants and other wood-burrowing insects for nourishment. Others, such as the **red-headed woodpecker** *(Melanerpes erythrocephalus)* and **acorn woodpecker** *(M. formicivorus)* store nuts and acorns in the holes they drill. The males of most woodpeckers have a black-and-white body and red or yellow head.

In addition to the larger birds, there are hundreds of smaller birds (4 to 6 inches) ranging from 'LBBs' (Little Brown Birds) that are everywhere and difficult to identify due to their bland plumage, to the magnificent **northern cardinal** *(Cardinalis cardinalis)* whose red hood and red-orange bill appear on the uniform of many sports teams (like the St Louis Cardinals).

Nuthatches *(Sitta* spp) are easily identified as the only birds that climb head-first down the trunks of trees, gathering insects and insect eggs. They are normally black on the back of the head and neck, white or red underneath and have a grayish-blue coat.

More than 50 types of warblers stop in the USA, most of which have yellow in their plumage, a thin, straight bill and a tendency towards hyperactivity. The most common warblers include the **American redstart** *(Setophaga ruticilla)*, found in deciduous forests and urban areas, the **yellow warbler** *(Dendroica petechia)* or **common yellowthroat**, and the **yellow-rumped warbler** *(D. coronata)*.

Finches, **sparrows** and **juncos** (Family Fringillidae) are also common, and are characterized by short, round bills (for eating seeds) and are often streaked brown above, pale and slightly streaked below.

HUGH D'ANDRADE

Woodpeckers have extraordinarily strong bills for chiseling into trees and winkling out insects.

Endangered Species

The Environmental Protection Agency (EPA) was created in 1970, and in 1973 Congress passed the Endangered Species Act, meant to 'provide a

HUGH D'ANDRADE

The peregrine falcon has made a spectacular comeback since the ban on DDT insecticides.

means whereby the ecosystems upon which endangered species and threatened species depend may be conserved' and 'provide a program for the conservation of such endangered species'. This piece of legislation has since been instrumental in bringing several species – such as the **peregrine falcon** *(Falco peregrinus)* and **American crocodile** *(Crocodylus actus)* – back from the brink of extinction. Other native species, such as the passenger pigeon, woodland caribou and ivory-billed woodpecker, were not as lucky. They didn't survive the draining of wetlands, building of dams, cutting of forests, laying of roads and building of neighborhoods that have come with the making of modern America.

The **northern spotted owl** *(Strix occidentalis caurina)*, which nests in cavernous 'snags' (dead trees) of old-growth forests (those more than 200 years old

How Extinct is Extinct?

Conservation organizations, scientists and fundraisers use the following categories to classify threatened species. Funding, study and conservation measures are prioritized accordingly. Getting bumped from Endangered to Vulnerable may seem like a good thing for the species, but it may mean funding for its protection gets cut. Do the animals know this when they cooperate and procreate in captivity?

A species is **extinct** when there is no reasonable doubt that the last individual has died. It is **extinct in the wild** when it is known only to survive in cultivation, in captivity or as a naturalised population outside of it's former range. When a species is facing an extremely high risk of extinction in the wild in the immediate future, it is **critically endangered**, if it's risk of extinction is in the near (as opposed to immediate) future it is **endangered**, and if it's risk is in the medium-term future it is **vulnerable**. When a species does not fall into any of these categories, but has been evaluated, it is said to be **lower risk**. Finally, if there is inadequate information to make an assessment of its risk, the species gets 'DD' or **data deficient** status.

and never altered by humans) in the Pacific Northwest has become a symbol of anti-logging sentiment. The National Park Service and US Forest Service have jurisdiction over 90% of the USA's old-growth forests. Traditionally old-growth trees were felled for lumber and snags were dragged away for the same market. Since the mid-1980s, however, serious efforts have been made to limit (if not halt) the extraction of snags to protect the 3000 to 5000 pairs of northern spotted owl thought still to exist in the wild.

Also surrounded by controversy is the **gray wolf** *(Canis lupus)* which once roamed throughout the USA. Nearly extinct by the 1920s – due to habitat degradation and extermination by ranchers – gray wolves were reintroduced to Yellowstone National Park and USFS land in central Idaho in 1994. This caused a major stir with local ranchers who feared for their livestock and horses; thus far, with one shocking exception where a gun-loving fellow in Montana shot (and then hid) one of the strongest males of a pack, the program has been successful.

During WWII, DDT was used to treat lice and other pests brought in from war zones, and after the war it was used on the coasts and in wetlands for mosquito control. The animals and birds which ingest plants and insects from DDT-sprayed areas store the poisonous chemical in their fat tissue, passing it on to their predators. Peregrine falcons, **bald eagles** *(Haliaeetus leucocephalus)* and **whooping cranes** *(Grus americana)* suffered drastically from this poisoning. Bald eagles were the focus of several aggressive restoration campaigns; by 1995 populations were estimated to have risen to between 80,000 and 110,000, so the majestic national bird was 'downlisted' from endangered to vulnerable (see the boxed text 'How Extinct is Extinct?'). Whooping cranes, named for their trumpeting call and famous for their dramatic courtship dance, are still endangered, with an estimated population of 250 to 300 birds, 90 of which are in captivity.

Another bird near extinction is the **California condor** *(Gymnogyps californianus)*, largest of North America's feathered friends with a wing span of 9ft, a 45- to 55-inch body and flight range of up to 15,000ft in elevation. There are 100 condors in captivity and 36 others have been released (in Utah, northern Arizona and California) since 1995.

The magnificent bald eagle is a master at riding thermal updrafts.

MARK NEWMAN

The **American pronghorn** (*Antilocapra americana*) evolved in North America millions of years ago and has never existed anywhere else. As recently as 200 years ago, 40 million of these creatures – which can run at 70 mph and survive without drinking for extended periods – inhabited the semi-arid deserts, grasslands and shrublands of the USA. With the onset of large-scale agricultural practices in the 1920s, their population dropped to around 12,000 where it has remained since.

Perhaps the most tragic tale of near-extinction is that of the **American bison** (*Bison bison*) or **buffalo**, which outnumbered people in North America until less than 200 years ago. In the 1820s there was an estimated 60 million bison roaming the prairies and woodlands of the USA. By the mid-1880s, the population was down to 800 beasts; 99.9% having been killed for their hides, for sport and as part of the military's Indian containment strategy. In 1902 a herd of 41 was placed under government protection in Yellowstone National Park. Currently 2000 or so still survive in Yellowstone and another 28,000 are on private and public reserves throughout the USA.

JOHN ELK III

Cars stop for bison crossing the road through Hayden Valley, Yellowstone National Park, Wyoming.

continued from page 28

In the 1930s, during the Great Depression, President Franklin Delano Roosevelt (FDR) introduced his 'New Deal' which, among other things, provided federal funds to local projects that created temporary jobs. The umbrella Civilian Conservation Corps (CCC) hired people – mostly men – around the country to build roads, dams, bridges and trails. Projects such as the Tennessee Valley Authority and Central Valley Project – both of which dammed hundreds of miles of waterways for hydroelectric power – remain among the most controversial and devastating environmental legacies of that time.

In response to the fervor with which these public works projects were undertaken, Aldo Leopold and Robert Marshall – both forest managers who were sympathetic to the New Deal but uncomfortable with the government's economic-based view of conservation – founded the Wilderness Society (1935) 'to save from invasion...that extremely minor fraction of outdoor America which yet remain free from mechanical sights and sounds and smell.' They constructed ecological ideas that scientifically and philosophically examined the importance of preserving land not for human-centered pursuits (including aesthetic enjoyment) nor for current or future economic wealth, but for the sake of the land itself. Leopold's book *A Sand County Almanac* (1949), in which he developed the idea of a 'land ethic', is still considered a classic.

During WWII the Bureau of Reclamation surveyed a dam site within Dinosaur National Monument, New Mexico, under the pretense of needing more power for reasons of national security. This federal invasion on designated public lands created a backlash that resulted in what came to be called the 'environmental movement'. When Rachel Carson's book *Silent Spring* – which discusses the short-sighted and profit-centered view that has driven people to do irreversible and ultimately self-defeating damage to the earth – hit the shelves in 1962, it popularized ecological thought and forever linked the concepts of wilderness and environmental health.

Two Years in a Tree

For 738 days of her then 25 years on earth, Julia 'Butterfly' Hill lived on two 6ft by 6ft platforms in the canopy of a 200ft tall, 1000-year-old tree. The old-growth redwood she calls Luna, was in danger of being cut down by the Pacific Lumber Company (PL), a major force in the lumber-based economy of Humboldt County and one of the largest old-growth forest land owners in the US.

HUGH D'ANDRADE

During her vigil Hill was visited by celebrities, interviewed by the media and supported by a crew that brought her food, fuel, mail and cell-phone batteries twice per week. Through the course of her two-year sit, she also gained support from environmental organizations across the globe. Besides the tangible goal of saving Luna from the lumber mills, Hill's protest was infused with her hope 'that people can learn to feel their connection to the magnificence of creation.'

Through phone interviews and negotiations, Hill and PL reached an agreement in December 1999. PL committed to preserve the tree and a surrounding 200ft buffer zone in exchange for a $50,000 payment from Hill and her supporters. Hill agreed to never again trespass or tree-sit on PL property, but she gets visiting rights to the tree with 48 hours notice.

A lesson she learned? Not to wash her feet too often, as sap from the tree helped her navigate the branches more easily!

In 1964 the Kennedy administration passed the Wilderness Act, providing for the protection of lands 'where man himself is a visitor who does not remain'. Since then, more than 104 million acres of land have been designated wilderness. The most recent designations were made in 1996 by President Clinton who won environmentalist support by signing the Desert Protection Act and creating the enormous Grand Staircase–Escalante National Monument (see the Southwest chapter).

Conservation Organizations

US conservation organizations have an incredible range of sizes and scopes – from ultra-specialized, locally run campaigns to global concerns. The following are well-founded groups that will be around for awhile.

American Lands (☎ 202-547-9400, fax 547-9213, ☐ www.americanlands.org), 726 7th St SE, Washington, DC 20003. The national clearing house for environmental organizations and a good place to get information about a wide range of topics.

Earth First! (☐ www.efmedia.org), PO Box 324, Redway, CA 95560. Founded in 1979, Earth First! takes a 'direct action' approach which ranges from grassroots organizing and involvement in the legal process to civil disobedience and monkeywrenching.

Earth Island Institute (☎ 415-788-3666, fax 788-7324, ☐ www.earthisland.org), 300 Broadway, Suite 28, San Francisco, CA 94133. Founded in 1982 by veteran environmentalist David Brower, EII provides organizational support in developing projects for the 'conservation, preservation, and restoration of the global environment'. Its Project Network consists of more than 30 projects worldwide.

Environmental Defense Fund In 1967 volunteer conservationists on Long Island formed the EDF to fight the use of DDT (it was finally banned in 1972). These days the EDF raises money to buy lands that are pertinent to regional, national and international environmental issues. Its headquarters are in New York City (☎ 800-684-3322, ☐ www.edf.org) at 257 Park Ave S, New York, NY 10010, but its has regional offices in Washington, DC;

Oakland, California; Boulder, Colorado; Raleigh, North Carolina; Austin, Texas; Boston, Massachusetts; and Los Angeles, California.

National Audubon Society (☎ 212-979-3000, fax 979-3188, ☐ www.audubon.org), 700 Broadway, New York, NY 10003. One of the USA's biggest conservation organizations. It was founded in 1905 to conserve and restore natural ecosystems, focusing on birds and other wildlife. Local chapters throughout the nation hold hikes and clean-up initiatives.

National Wildlife Federation (☎ 703-790-4000, ☐ www.nwf.org), 8925 Leesburg Pike, Vienna, VA 22184. The nation's largest member-supported conservation group and unites individuals, organizations, businesses and government while focusing its efforts on five core issues – endangered habitat, water quality, land stewardship, wetlands and sustainable communities.

Sierra Club (☎ 415-977-5500, fax 977-5799, ☐ www.sierraclub.org), 85 Second St, Second Floor, San Francisco, CA 94105-3441. Since its founding in 1892, with John Muir as its first president and the defeat of a proposed reduction in the boundaries of Yosemite National Park as its first conservation effort, the Sierra Club has grown to a large – some say cumbersome – body of political influence. Local chapters hold hiking, backpacking, biking and ski trips.

The Wilderness Society Founded in 1935, the Wilderness Society focuses on public education, scientific analysis and advocacy. It has its headquarters in Washington, DC (☎ 800-THE-WILD, ☐ www.wilderness.org), 900 Seventeenth St NW, Washington, DC 20006-2506, and regional offices in Anchorage, Alaska; Seattle, Washington; San Francisco, California; Boise, Idaho; Bozeman, Montana; Denver, Colorado; Atlanta, Georgia; and Boston, Massachusetts.

NATIONAL PARKS & RESERVES

The world's first national park, Yellowstone, was created by Congress in 1872 'for the benefit and enjoyment of the people.' Other national parks were created in California, Colorado and Arizona, and in 1916 the National Park Service (NPS) was established within the Department of the Interior to 'promote and regulate their use' and to 'conserve the scenery and the wild life for the enjoyment of future generations.' When all the national monuments and battlefield sites were transferred to the national park system in 1933, the NPS became the all-purpose guardian of the nation's natural and historical treasures.

Although the national parks were once called 'the best idea America ever had,' there are now fears that the parks are being loved to death; as many as 10 million people a year visit some parks, mostly concentrated in the summer months. In the 1970s, national recreation areas were created to help reduce the demand for activities in the most hard-pressed parks. NPS policy is currently to err on the side of preservation rather than public enjoyment and parks are regulated, some quite restrictively, in the interests of conservation.

Because most visitors stick to developed facilities and short trails near main park roads, hikers will often experience solitude once they've walked an hour or two into the backcountry. In the most popular parks (Glacier, Yellowstone, Zion and Yosemite, for example), quota systems regulate the number of people using backcountry trails and campsites; these systems require you to register on or before your day of departure, stick to a day-to-day itinerary (that you plan) and pay a fee. Solo hikers and those who don't have much hiking experience often appreciate the infrastructure (including well-marked trails and the presence of park rangers) that a national park offers. If you can't stand crowds when you're communing with nature, seek out the less popular parks and avoid the summer vacation period.

The NPS budget, allocated by Congress, varies from stringent to miserly and the service finds it difficult to maintain all the buildings, roads and trails for which it is responsible. On the other hand, the standard of NPS interpretive services and publications is extremely high and NPS staff are very dedicated, well informed and helpful (though often a bit stingy in making trail recommendations). The NPS website (🖥 www.nps.gov) has information about, and links to, all the NPS parks and areas.

National Park System

The NPS manages some 367 federal sites in 20 different categories. The best known are the *national parks*, which protect areas of outstanding natural beauty and provide access and facilities for visitors. Some are as small as 40 sq mi; the largest is more than 13,000 sq mi. *National preserves* are created mainly for the protection of a particular natural area and may have few visitor facilities. *Designated wilderness areas* within some national parks do not allow any permanent structures at all. *National monuments* are usually smaller in size and protect a specific natural or historic site. They include both structures like the Statue of Liberty and natural areas like the Grand Staircase in Utah. For the protection, preservation and restoration of historically significant sites, there are also national historical parks, national historic sites, national military parks and national battlefields.

National recreation areas are intended principally for outdoor recreation and enjoyment and often have extensive facilities or concessionaires providing recreational services. In this recreational category are national seashores, national lakeshores and national rivers.

The NPS is also responsible for two *scenic parkways* and administers eight *national scenic trails* (including the Appalachian and Pacific Crest Trails – see the Long-Distance Trails chapter) and nine *national historic trails*. The NPS doesn't control all the land through which the trails pass, but it has a coordinating and advisory role for the various federal, state and private interests.

National Forests

The United States Forest Service (USFS) is under the US Department of Agriculture and administrates the use of forests. Many of the most scenic areas in the Rocky Mountains, Cascades and New England are under USFS jurisdiction. National forests are less protected than parks, being managed under the concept of 'multiple use', which includes timber cutting, watershed management and recreation. Critics have accused the USFS of promoting unsustainable forestry practices at the expense of conservation. As on BLM lands (see next section), hunting is permitted in national forests and hikers should take precautions during hunting season, which varies from state to state (usually October to March).

Current information about national forests can be obtained from ranger stations, listed in the text for each hike under Planning or Information. You can also get information from the USFS website (🖳 www.fs.fed.us/). See Useful Organizations and Accommodations in the Facts for the Hiker chapter for more information.

BLM Areas
The Bureau of Land Management (BLM) manages public use of federal lands, from cattle ranges to backcountry byways (used by 4WD vehicles). There are few restrictions on activity in BLM lands, which means one can often camp, hike, bike, ride horses or do whatever one chooses. A downside to this for those who seek quiet is that this laissez-faire approach also attracts off-road drivers and motorcyclists. Hunting is permitted (with a permit) during the designated hunting season – hikers should be sure to wear bright colors.

Each state has a regional office located in the state capital. Look in the blue section of the local White Pages directory under US Government, Interior Department or call the Federal Information Center (☎ 800-688-9889).

Wilderness Areas
Wilderness areas, which are inaccessible to mechanized travel, are the best places to truly leave the 'civilized' world behind. Since implementation of the Federal Wilderness Act of 1964 (see Conservation earlier in this chapter), roadless areas have been set aside throughout the country in the interest of preserving biological diversity, protecting valuable resources and offering recreational escapes from urban areas.

The NPS, USFS and BLM all manage wilderness areas, the majority of which are on USFS land. While all areas differ slightly in their management, the general philosophy behind them is to 'take only photographs, leave only footprints.' Some areas have restrictions limiting group size, regulating campsites and length of stay, and prohibiting campfires. Many wilderness areas, especially in the desert Southwest, have no developed campsites.

State Parks & Reserves
Each state covered in this book has its own system of state parks, wildlife areas and reserves which are generally smaller and less diverse than those in the federal system. However, they can contain some surprisingly beautiful scenery and often make for good camping options.

POPULATION & PEOPLE
In October 1999 the official estimate of the US population was 273,726,683. Despite this apparent precision, population figures from different sources are often wildly inconsistent. A national census is taken every 10 years, but most states, cities and towns update the census figures from time to time with their own estimates. For literally up-to-the-minute population estimates, check the Census Bureau website (🖳 www.census .gov).

The population is about 83% white, 13% black, 3% Asian and 1% Native American. These figures include the 9% who are of Hispanic origin, but they are not counted separately in the census – many are likely to count themselves as white for census purposes. The proportions vary greatly between states and are changing over time, with a higher-than-average birthrate in the black community and a high proportion of new immigrants coming from Asia and Latin America.

Geographically, the states of the Northeast have about 53 million people; the Great Lakes states, 63 million; the South, 93 million; and the West, 59 million. In the past two decades, population growth has been above average in the West and the South, while the Northeast and Great Lakes states have grown more slowly. Historically there has been a movement away from the countryside, and 75% of people now live in urban areas, defined as cities or towns with more than 2500 inhabitants.

Due mainly to economic inequalities, these populations are not equally represented in the backcountry. In fact, more foreign visitors take overnight hiking trips than do Americans of Hispanic, African or Asian origin. The 'average' American hiker is defined as white, between the ages of 22 and 56 and in the mid-to-upper socio-economic bracket.

SOCIETY & CONDUCT
Traditional Culture

Native American communities are generally based on reservation lands, mostly west of the Mississippi. Areas in which hikers are near reservations are the Pacific Northwest, Rocky Mountains and the Southwest. Many reservations are engaged in commercial activities including farming, tourism and, particularly, casinos and the people have a modern lifestyle while retaining traditional cultures to a greater or lesser extent. Language, customs and religious ceremonies differ from one reservation to the next.

Reservations are governed by federal and tribal law. Each tribe is independent and what is permitted on one reservation may be banned on another (drugs are banned on all). Visitors to reservations are generally welcome, but should behave in an appropriately courteous and respectful manner. Hikers should always get permission from the tribal council (usually located in the largest town on a reservation) before hiking or camping on tribal land (any permits needed for hikes in this book are mentioned in the hike's Permits & Regulations section).

Many tribes ban all forms of recording – photography, videotaping, audiotaping or drawing. Others permit these activities in certain areas only if you pay a fee. Obtain permission before you photograph anyone on a reservation, including children – a tip is usually expected.

The rip-off of Native American arts has become a lucrative business, with imitations from China or Taiwan often passed off as authentic. If you're considering purchasing art, find a legitimate shop or a roadside stand on a reservation and either look for authenticating labels or find out who the artist is.

Dos & Don'ts

The USA is a very well-ordered society and, generally speaking, people stand in line, obey the rules and follow the instructions. In the backcountry talking loudly, discarding litter on the ground, smoking, cutting switchbacks, trampling vegetation (to put up a tent, or otherwise), disregarding permit or fee payments and taking more than your portion of a campsite are practices that are frowned upon.

When passing someone on the trail you should give them advanced notice by asking 'Do you mind if I pass?', and be prepared to make a bit of small talk about the weather or trail conditions; do not pass someone if the trail drops off steeply on one side. When you meet someone coming in the opposite direction, a simple 'How's it going?' or 'Hi' is OK. Technically, people going uphill have the right of way; on a flat trail, whoever has the most room to step aside usually does.

Dress codes are practically non-existent in the backcountry and if you're ever going to witness nudity in the USA it will probably be here. In heavy-use areas such as national parks it's best to keep your clothes on, though men can hike bare-chested and women can hike in shorts and a sports bra without calling attention to themselves (depending on their physique of course!) In towns and national park centers, shirt and shoes are required to enter most stores and all restaurants. Jeans or shorts and T-shirts are accepted just about everywhere, though people dress a little more formally in the East, especially in New England.

LANGUAGE

English is spoken throughout the USA, though it is not designated as the country's official language. Some believe that it should be, especially those concerned about the widespread and increasing use of Spanish. Other minority languages are French (in Louisiana and upstate New York near Quebec), Pennsylvania 'Dutch' (a German dialect), Chinese (mostly Cantonese, in the 'Chinatowns' of several large cities), Yiddish (among Orthodox Jews in New York) and Gullah, an African-American dialect (on sea islands off South Carolina). A few immigrant ethnic communities retain their own languages, but historically these have tended to dissipate within one or two generations. A few Native American communities speak indigenous languages, of which about 200 survive. Some indigenous languages have fewer than a dozen native speakers.

There are regional differences in accent, idiom and use of vocabulary, but American English is relatively uniform when compared to, say, the varieties of English spoken in Britain. Most foreign visitors will be familiar with American English from movies and the mass media, but may have difficulty following the speech of those in the Deep South or the African-American idiom. Equally, many Americans are unfamiliar with foreign accents and may not understand the English of foreign visitors. Apart from speaking clearly and slowly, it may help to mimic an American accent, especially in the use of vowels – say *bathroom* with a short 'a,' rather than 'barth-room.'

In the 18th century Ben Franklin, by trade a printer, sought to rationalize and standardize the disordered spelling of the English language. Although his plans weren't adopted at the time, he did influence Noah Webster, who published the *American Dictionary of the English Language* in 1828. It was Webster who popularized the change in spellings of such words as *theatre* to *theater*, *colour* to *color* and *organise* to *organize*.

But it's not the spelling that makes American English so distinctive – it's the wealth of new words and expressions that it has brought to the language. Several Native American words have come into English including *moccasin*, *moose*, *toboggan* and *kayak*. Many more words have come from European languages via immigrants to America: from German, there are words like *loafer*, *hoodlum* and *kindergarten*; from Dutch, *boss*, *stoop* (a front step) and *nitwit*; from Yiddish, *schmuck*, *schlock* and *schmaltz*; from French, *prairie*, *saloon* and *levee*; and from Italian, *pasta*, *pizza* and other food words. Spanish has contributed *canyon*, *ranch*, *rodeo* and numerous place names in the Southwest and the West.

Nevertheless, the vast majority of Americanisms come from America itself. American inventiveness produces not only new products, but new words to describe them and a new vocabulary to market them. So there's not just *soda pop*, *root beer* and *sarsaparilla* (all American inventions), but the brand names *Coca-Cola*, *Coke* and *Pepsi* are also in the language, along with advertising slogans like 'the Pepsi Generation,' and imaginative new concepts like Coca-Colonization. American business, technology, cars, movies, military forces and especially sports have all contributed words that are so familiar that it's easy to forget they're American. For more on American language, read Lonely Planet's *USA phrasebook* and Bill Bryson's *Made in America*.

Facts for the Hiker

SUGGESTED ITINERARIES

Hikers bound for the USA should make some pre-trip decisions regarding what kind of trip they want. Do you want to see sights and towns between hikes? Do you want to spend time on the road, doing the cross-country *Thelma and Louise* thing? Or do you just want to get to a trailhead and hike, hike, hike? The sheer size of the USA makes it nearly impossible to do it all, so it's smart to start with a game plan – then stay flexible.

Highlights

Each of this book's authors would love to have three months to hike one of the USA's long-distance trails. But most people don't have the large budget (of time and money) for a long-distance journey, and instead develop favorite hikes that can be done in a day or a week. Whether taking a morning or a month, a wealth of experiences and adventures lies within spitting distance of one of the world's most developed societies.

Some of the highlights of our travails and trails include:

- **Hiking** among the granite domes and verdant meadows of the high Sierra Nevada
- **Spotting** moose and bears in the dense woods of remote northern Maine, New England
- **Gazing** at a landscape of sparkling, glaciated peaks from Swiftcurrent Mountain Lookout in Glacier National Park, Rocky Mountains
- **Clambering** over slickrock terraces, through natural arches and past wild rock sculptures in the Grand Staircase–Escalante National Monument, Southwest
- **Tumbling** down a 500ft coastal sand dune in the Oregon Dunes National Recreation Area, Pacific Northwest
- **Standing overshadowed** by one of the Sierra Nevada's monumental giant sequoias, the largest living organisms on earth
- **Lazing** on a bald mountaintop in the Great Smoky Mountains, Southern Appalachia
- **Retracing the steps** of Henry David Thoreau (New England) and John Muir (Sierra Nevada)
- **Snuggling** into your bag in a deserted camp at the toe of a glacier in North Cascades National Park, Pacific Northwest
- **Brushing through** blooming rhododendron in the Roan Mountain wilderness in Southern Appalachia's Blue Ridge Mountains
- **Wandering** the rugged coast of New England with the sea on one side, mountains on the other
- **Summitting** Mt Whitney (14,496ft), the crown of the Sierra Nevada and highest peak in the contiguous USA
- **Exploring** the tooth-like cliffs and domes of Capitol Reef National Park, Southwest
- **Soaking** away your aches in the Ferris Fork hot springs in Yellowstone National Park, Rocky Mountains
- **Slumbering** through your last night under canvas after 'end-to-ending' the Appalachian Trail, part of America's hiking heritage and a dream for every long-distance trekker

The next question to ask yourself is what kind of hikes and scenery you want. Magnificent, old-growth conifer forests? High alpine meadows and lakes? Dense broadleaf forests? Canyons, arches and slickrock? Windswept coastline? Each region in this book has distinct characteristics to be considered. Doing a hike in each of these regions would require at least four weeks (of perfect weather), plus an almost unlimited travel budget and desire to spend as much time getting around as on the trail. If hiking, not touring, is the focus of your trip stick to the hikes in one or two regions.

Geography will also play a part in the planning of your trip: Europeans are much closer to hikes in New England, the Adirondacks and the Appalachian Mountains than to hikes in the western part of the USA; hikers coming from Australia or New Zealand will probably land in Los Angeles or San Francisco, close to hikes in the Pacific Northwest, Sierra Nevada and Southwest.

With only a couple of weeks, you might choose a five-day hike and a shorter hike (or several day-hikes) and spend a few days exploring your point of entry.

With a month, you could hike in several regions by flying between them or sticking to regions that are adjacent to each other. Such a trip might look like this: arrive in San Francisco, spend 10 days in the Sierra Nevada, return to SF, fly to Seattle, spend a week in the Cascades and a week on the Olympic Peninsula (or fly to Denver and spend two weeks in the Rocky Mountains), then fly back to San Francisco (or on to New York). Without flying, you could drive from the Sierra Nevada to the Southwest, north through the Rocky Mountains, then west to the Cascades and back to San Francisco. You could also spend the entire month on one trail, such as the Appalachian, Pacific Crest or Continental Divide. There are many possibilities.

Weather is yet another important factor – hiking in April can be limited by snow while hiking in August can be limited by thunderstorms, depending on where you go. See When to Hike under Planning, later in this chapter, and in individual chapters and/or hike descriptions.

Every itinerary should allow two days for driving to/from the hike and arranging necessary permits, maps and provisions. If you're relying on public transport, your options will be greatly limited and you'll need more time.

PLANNING
When to Hike
In a sweeping generalization, it can be said that May, June, September and October are the best months to hike in the USA. Schools are in session so crowds are light; flies and mosquitoes are either not yet a problem or are past their worst; and temperatures are neither too hot nor too cold. This, of course, has yearly and regional variants.

There's not much hiking in the USA from December to April, when higher trails are covered in snow and lower trails are muddy and wet. Road closures are common during this time and accommodations are limited. National parks usually close their facilities (though the parks themselves remain open) from mid-October to May and ranger stations may be closed or have shortened hours. Exceptions are in the lower regions of the Pacific Northwest (where trails, while often wet and muddy, are rarely too cold and never snowy), parts of the Southwest and Southern Appalachians; the California Coast has year-round hiking, but is not covered in this book (see Lonely Planet's *California & Nevada* book). For more detail, see Climate in the Facts about the USA chapter and the When to Hike sections of individual chapters, regions and hikes.

What Kind of Hike?
Except for rock climbing, spelunking (caving or potholing) and mountaineering routes, hikes in the USA are usually done independently, without guides or special equipment. Longer hikes require more planning and provisions for sleeping, eating, discarding waste and keeping warm and well-hydrated; some also require a permit or registration at the trailhead (a few day-hikes require this too). Most hikes take you through wilderness or forested areas where there are no towns or other re-supply stations, so hikers must leave

the trailhead with all they need. The exception is in New England, where trails cross main roads at regular intervals.

Except for along the Appalachian Trail and in a few places in the Rockies, backcountry huts are uncommon in the USA. Most hikers carry a tent, sleeping bag and sleeping pad (sleeping mat), stove and cooking utensils. Hiring porters, or someone to carry your gear, is virtually unheard of. Special requirements for individual hikes or regions are covered in the Planning section of each.

There are two basic approaches to overnight hikes: radial (where you pack in and set up a base camp and do day hikes from there) and linear (where you move to a different camp each night). The radial model enables you to explore the backcountry with a light day-pack and maximize your time on the trail, since you don't have to strike and set up camp each day. It's a good method for those who have only a few nights, or who have not done much backpacking and/or are uncomfortable wearing a heavy pack; it's also popular with rock climbers, 'summit baggers' and photography enthusiasts.

The linear model (which applies to loop, or circuit, hikes, as well as point-to-point hikes) has the advantage of journeying progressively through an area without backtracking. On long-distance trails this is the only option. If moving each day seems too arduous, plan several rest days throughout the hike.

Most hikes in this book are of the linear kind, but can be made radial by hiking the first (or last) leg and setting up a base camp. This is best done with hikes that have a side trip on the first or last day; if you don't find any in the region you are planning to visit, ask a ranger for suggestions of what to explore from your proposed starting point.

There *are* opportunities to participate in guided trips of various degrees of difficulty and standards of comfort; see Guided Hikes later in this chapter for suggestions.

Maps & Navigation

For information on this book's custom-drawn hiking maps, see Maps in This Book under Hikes in This Book later in this chapter.

Though most of the hikes in this book are along well-marked trails, a good map is essential for identifying landscape features and navigating out of a lost situation. Mark your hiking route on a map with colored pens and it becomes a terrific souvenir.

Small-Scale Maps For getting around the USA, highway maps from the American Automobile Association (AAA) are the most comprehensive and dependable. These range from national, regional and state maps to very detailed maps of cities, counties and even relatively small towns. They are available free to AAA members (see Useful Organizations later in this chapter) and for sale to nonmembers.

Excellent and inexpensive USA road atlases are widely available overseas and may help to plan a driving route. Good ones include the venerable Rand McNally, with annually updated editions ($10), and the *National Geographic Road Atlas* ($15). The DeLorme Mapping series of atlases and gazetteers has detailed topographic and highway maps of individual states at a scale of 1:250,000, with good detail of secondary and rural roads ($20). If you arrive without an atlas, look for one in a local bookstore.

Folded sheet maps published by Rand McNally, Gousha or USA Maps Inc are all good and widely available at gas stations, convenience stores, bookstores, stationary stores and grocery stores for around $3. State tourism offices often give away state maps for free, and will send you one if you contact them in advance.

Large-Scale Maps The United States Geological Survey (USGS), an agency of the federal Department of the Interior, publishes very detailed topographic maps of the entire country at various scales. Maps ($4) at 1:62,500, or approximately 1 inch = 1 mile, are ideal for backcountry hiking and backpacking. Some USGS maps are somewhat dated, but individual cartographers are producing updated versions of old USGS maps at 1:62,500. The USGS standard topographic quadrangles include the '7.5-minute series' at 1:24,000, 1:25,000 or 1:20,000 and

'15-minute series' at 1:25,000. Many of these are also out of print. The United States Forest Service (USFS) produces good topographic maps of national forest areas at a scale of 1:126,720 (2 inches = 1 mile).

To order a map index and price list, phone ☎ 800-435-7627, visit the USGS website at 🖥 www.usgs.gov, or write USGS Distribution Branch, Building 810, Box 25286, Denver Federal Center, Denver, CO 80225. Maps are also available by fronting up to the USGS (☎ 415-329-4390), 345 Middlefield Rd, Menlo Park, California. If you plan to order maps by mail from the government, allow at least six weeks for them to arrive.

Also good is National Geographic's Trails Illustrated series which has well-drawn, easy-to-read topographic maps that usually include information about park regulations and trail distances. These are available for many hiking areas and are sold at park information centers and outdoors stores in paper ($4) and waterproof ($9) versions. For a catalog, contact Trails Illustrated (☎ 303-670-3457, 🖥 www.colorado.com/trails), PO Box 4357 Evergreen, CO 80437. The National Park Service (NPS) gives out good park maps at park entrances, but these should only be used for finding your way around the park and not for hiking. The University of Texas maintains an extensive online library of maps at 🖥 www.lib.utexas.edu/Libs/PCL/Map_collection/National_parks/National_parks.html.

Buying Maps Outdoors stores usually carry both USGS and USFS maps for the surrounding area – you probably won't find maps for a trail in Utah when you're in Tennessee. Most ranger stations and information centers at parks have a good range of topographical maps ($2 to $6). In the absence of a ranger station, try the local stationery store, hardware store or gas station.

For advice on where to buy maps near trailheads, see Maps under Information, or the Nearest Towns section, for each region or hike in this book.

GPS Originally developed by the US Department of Defense, the Global Positioning System (GPS) is a network of more than 20 earth-orbiting satellites that continually beam encoded signals back to earth. Small, computer-driven devices – GPS receivers – can decode these signals to give users an extremely accurate reading of their location – to within 100ft, anywhere on the planet, at any time of day, in almost any weather. The cheapest hand-held GPS receivers now cost less than $100 (although these may not have a built-in averaging system that minimizes signal errors and gives readings of acceptable accuracy.) Other important factors to consider when buying a GPS receiver are its weight and battery life.

It should be understood that a GPS receiver is of little use to hikers unless used with an accurate topographical map – the GPS receiver simply gives your position, which you must then locate on the local map. GPS receivers will only work properly in the open. Directly below high cliffs, near large bodies of water or in dense tree-cover, for example, the signals from a crucial satellite may be blocked (or bounce off the rock or water) and give inaccurate readings. GPS receivers are more vulnerable to breakdowns (including dead batteries) than the humble magnetic compass – a low-tech device that has served navigators faithfully for centuries – so don't rely on them entirely.

What to Bring

For a full list of suggested hiking gear see the Equipment Check List on page 56.

Backpack Most overnight hikes in this book require the use of a dedicated hiking backpack. (Travel packs, a convenient amalgam of traveler's suitcase and hiking pack, are an efficient way to mix airline-hopping and some trail-walking, but are not really suited to multiday hiking in challenging weather.) While styles, constructions and traditions vary from continent to continent, a good hiking backpack should:

• be sturdily constructed from a long-wearing fabric such as canvas or woven synthetic, with high-quality stitching, straps and buckles, a lightweight internal or external frame and resilient and smoothly working zips

Equipment Check List

☐ **Boots** – light to medium for day hikes, sturdy boots for longer hikes with a heavy pack. Most important is that they're well broken in and have a good tread. Waterproof boots are recommended for long hikes.

☐ **Other footwear** – sandals, moccasins or running shoes for around camp, old sneakers for crossing streams. Do not cross streams in sandals (even sport sandals such as Tevas) as your feet will be exposed to debris.

☐ **Socks** – polypropylene and wool stay warm even when wet. Bring at least two pairs. Silk or polypropylene sock liners reduce blisters and wash and dry quickly.

☐ **Underwear** – a sports bra can be worn solo on warm days. Men who swear by cotton boxer shorts should try synthetic or silk ones; cotton takes a long time to dry and is cold when wet.

☐ **Shorts, light shirt** – for everyday wear.

☐ **Long-sleeve shirt** – one undershirt of wool or synthetic and one button-down overshirt for layering and protecting your arms against the sun.

☐ **Long pants** – light cotton, canvas or synthetic pants are good for hiking through brush, and sweatpants (fleece ones, for cold weather) are useful for wearing in camp. Long underwear bottoms with shorts over them are the perfect combo in non-brushy areas.

☐ **Insulating layer** – a polypropylene or fleece pullover with a high zip-neck is recommended. A down vest packs small

and light and keeps your core toasty while your arms stay free.

☐ **Rain gear** – waterproof and breathable is the key, best provided by fabrics such as Gore-Tex. If nothing else is available, use heavy duty trash bags (available at grocery stores) to cover you and your pack.

☐ **Hat, gloves** – a warm hat and one with a brim to protect against sun. About 80% of body heat escapes through the top of the head. Keeping your head and neck warm reduces the chance of hypothermia.

☐ **Bandanna or handkerchief** – good for wiping, washing, drying and keeping hair back.

☐ **Small towel** – one which is indestructible and will dry quickly.

☐ **First-aid kit** – see the Health & Safety chapter for details.

☐ **Stove and fuel** – lightweight and easy to operate. Test the stove, even cook a meal on it, to familiarize yourself with any quirks it may have. Propane and white gas are widely available, and outdoors stores (even in small towns) carry butane cartridges. Long-distance hikers should carry a stove that can burn more than one kind of fuel. Kerosene and methylated spirits (denatured alcohol) are available at most hardware stores, pharmacies and many large supermarkets. Don't forget that it is prohibited to carry fuel – and even matches – on aircraft.

☐ **Pots and pans** – aluminum cooking sets are best, but any sturdy, one-quart

• have an adjustable, well-padded harness which distributes weight evenly
• be large enough to comfortably fit all your hiking gear, eliminating the need to strap bits and pieces to the outside where they can be lost or damaged
• be water-resistant, with a minimum of external nooks and crannies for water to pool and seep in; stitched seams can be treated with a sealant such as beeswax if the weather is likely to be poor

• be equipped with a small number of internal and external pockets to provide easy access to frequently used items such as snacks, maps etc

Single-compartment, top-loading packs are generally the most watertight, though some people prefer the convenience of a dual-compartment pack which allows a sleeping bag or tent to be stowed in a com-

Equipment Check List

pot will do, and a skillet or frying pan is good if you want more than pasta and soup. A pot scrubber is helpful, especially when using cold water and no soup.

☐ **Knife, fork, spoon and mug** – a double-layer plastic mug with a lid is best. Bring an extra cup if you like to eat and drink simultaneously.

☐ **Water purifier** – optional, but really nice to have. Alternatively you can boil water for at least 10 minutes (which takes lots of fuel at high altitude) or use iodine tablets (which you should have regardless, in case the purifier gives out.)

☐ **Matches or lighter** – waterproof matches are a good idea.

☐ **Candle or lantern** – candles are easy to operate but do not stay lit when dropped or wet, and can be hazardous inside a tent. As with a stove, familiarize yourself with a lantern before you hit the trail.

☐ **Flashlight (torch)** – one per person, and bring plenty of extra batteries. Headlamps are good, as they keep your hands free for cooking, putting up a tent and finding toilet paper.

☐ **Sleeping bag** – goose-down bags are warm and lightweight, but virtually worthless when wet; heavier, artificial-fibre bags are the alternative.

☐ **Sleeping pad** – either closed-cell foam or self-inflating. Use a sweater or sleeping-bag sack stuffed with clothes as a pillow.

☐ **Tent** – with a waterproof cover (fly). Make sure you know how to set it up before you reach camp.

☐ **Tarp or ground cover** – to keep the underside of the tent dry. A bright or reflective color can help in emergencies as well.

☐ **Pocket knife** – make sure it's sharp. One with multiple functions, such as a Swiss army knife or Leatherman, is good.

☐ **Whistle** – a vital safety tool that costs $1.

☐ **Water bottles** – two 1 quart (about 1L) bottles per person. Nalgene bottles – of durable, clear plastic – can hold hot liquids.

☐ **Camera and binoculars** – optional, but if you don't bring them you'll wish you had! Don't forget extra film and waterproof film canisters (sealed plastic bags work well).

☐ **Maps and compass** – GPS receiver optional.

☐ **Eyeglasses/contact lenses** – wearers should bring a back-up set.

☐ **Sunglasses and sunscreen** – at least SPF 15.

☐ **Notebook and pen**.

☐ **Sundries** – toilet paper and trowel for digging waste holes; small sealable plastic bags; insect repellent; lip balm; dental floss (burnable and good when there's no water for brushing); deck of cards; books; miniature chess set; swimsuit.

☐ **Emergency high-energy food** – lemonade and hot chocolate powder, energy bars, dried fruit.

---

partment separated from the main space by a zip-flap (and which can be reached by a second external zip-opening). No backpack is utterly waterproof and an internal liner such as a tough garbage bag should be used to ensure at least dry clothes and sleeping bag.

A day-pack or a smaller bum-bag (fanny pack), is perfect for day hikes or side trips radiating from a central base camp, when camera, lunch and wet-weather gear is all that is likely to be required. Backpacks with a detachable day-pack can be well suited to this style of travel, although they often suffer the same design compromises as travel packs.

Tent The choice of a tent largely depends upon the use to which it will be put. An expensive, modern tent may not be appropriate

The Layering Principle

When dressing for the backcountry, keep in mind that it is important to maintain a comfortable body temperature while hiking and yet be warm enough when resting or when in camp at night. The best way to do this is to regulate your temperature by adjusting the amount of clothing you are wearing.

If you only have a couple of bulky items to wear when you're cold, then you don't have the flexibility to keep an ideal temperature while hiking. Several thin layers, on the other hand, mean you can wear as much as is needed for what you are doing, maintaining a comfortable temperature at all times. Layered clothing also traps air, which helps to insulate you from the cold. For example, a thermal undershirt; then a light shirt, wool shirt or pile jacket; and a waterproof jacket to keep the wind out, will be enough to keep you very warm and dry in most situations.

If you find that you are perspiring heavily because you are overdressed, your clothing will get damp; then, when you stop, it will become cold and lose much of its insulation value. The answer is to wear just enough clothing to keep you warm while hiking and have several layers ready in your pack to put on as needed during stops.

Similarly, not wearing sufficient clothing will increase your chances of becoming too cold. If you have only one bulky, warm item to put on, chances are that you'll save it for when it becomes *really* cold and make do with a thin shirt in the meantime. This could cause you to become overcooled, particularly during rest stops along the way. Again, a number of thinner layers are the answer.

Several layers of clothing provide you with the flexibility you need to keep cool or maintain warmth as the weather and terrain dictate.

---

for someone who mostly pitches it in camping grounds or the yards of friendly locals and often seeks out roofed accommodation such as mountain refuges or village hostels. However, a simple, single-skin canvas tent may be a dangerous choice for bivouacking on a high mountain pass in poor weather. Modern tents are usually dome- or tunnel shaped, and have lightweight aluminium poles, sewn-in waterproof floor and detachable fly or outer tent. Such tents, while expensive, are roomy, lightweight, stable in windy conditions and pack into a small space.

Sleeping Bag For serious overnight hiking, a good sleeping bag is essential. The two main types differ largely in the insulating material with which they are filled. Down sleeping bags rely on the extraordinary ability of fine duck or goose feathers to 'loft', or expand, and thus trap a large volume of air within the bag's shell. It is this air, not the fill itself, which is warmed by the body and which insulates you from the cold. Down is extremely light, compresses into a very small volume and has remarkable loft. However, once wet it loses almost all of its insulating ability. A bag with a waterproof, breathable outer shell, while more expensive and a little heavier, can eliminate this drawback.

The alternative is a synthetic-fill bag, in which down is replaced with one of a variety of artificial fibers designed to mimic the lofting ability of the natural product. Early generations of such bags were significantly heavier and bulkier than a down bag of equivalent warmth but this type of bag has the advantage of retaining its loft, and thus warmth, when damp.

Sleeping bags are made either in a tapered ('mummy') shape, which minimises surface area and wasted internal space but to some people is constricting, or are rectangular, which is roomier but not as warm for the weight. A hood and an internal muff, or heat-seal, around the shoulders and along the zip increases warmth, while a dual-ended, full-length zip allows you to fine tune the temperature by selectively opening or closing it at the feet and chest.

Stove Increasingly, with the depletion of wood resources near ever-more-popular campsites and the growing awareness of the fragility of some wild environments, hikers are abandoning the traditional campfire for one of a range of fuel stoves. These fall into three broad categories.

- Multifuel stoves are small, very efficient and run on a variety of petroleum fuels (including automobile and aircraft fuel), making them ideal for use in places where a reliable supply of one type of fuel is hard to find. They tend, however, to be sootier, more prone to blockages due to contaminated fuel and require some care and experience to use and maintain.
- Methylated spirit (ethyl alcohol) burners are slower and less efficient (requiring more fuel to be carried) but are safe, clean and easy to use. They often come as a complete cooking kit, with integrated compact pots, pans and kettles.
- Butane gas stoves are commonly sold in camping shops around the world and rely on disposable cartridges which must be packed into and out of the wilds. While clean and reliable, they can be slow, awkward to pack and are expensive to run over the long term. Cartridges are widely available, which removes the need to negotiate the often confusing variety of names and unreliable supply of liquid fuels.

Buying & Hiring Locally The two largest outdoor-gear retailers in the USA are Recreation Equipment Inc (REI; ☎ 800-426-4840, international 253-891-2500, 🖳 www.REI .com), which was founded in Seattle in 1938; and Eastern Mountain Sports (EMS; ☎ 888-463-6367, 🖳 www.emsonline.com). Both have stores throughout the USA, though REI has more stores in the West (especially California) and EMS has more stores in the Rocky Mountains and the East; call the number listed or access their websites to find the store nearest you. Each store hires tents, backpacks, stoves and lanterns, as well as climbing gear, kayaks and bicycles.

Most major towns in the USA have an REI or EMS, or a discount version such as Big 5 or Sports Authority. In small towns, check the local supermarket and hardware store for things like tent stakes, lanterns, stoves and flashlights. See the Planning and Nearest Towns sections for individual hikes.

Backpacker magazine published an article ('Attention Shoppers', August 1999) that compared gear bought at specialty stores to gear bought at Wal-Mart, America's largest retail chain. They concluded that you can save money on foam sleeping pads, eating utensils, headlamps and flashlights, batteries and pocket knifes at a Wal-Mart style store (other such stores include Target and K-Mart), but should stick to outdoors stores for essentials like tents, sleeping bags and rain gear.

Mail Order Suppliers Many gear-heads swear by the goods they get from catalog shopping. Mail order companies, which are prolific in the US outdoors scene, cut costs by not paying rent, staff and other costs associated with maintaining retail space. As a result they pass tremendous bargains on to their customers. If you have a problem with something you order, you have a year to send it back for an exchange or a full refund. Most companies get your gear to you within 10 days (often sooner) and charge a minimal amount for shipping; international orders are subject to overseas postal rates.

The best of the bunch sell top-quality, name-brand products that range from GPS receivers to mountaineering boots to fleece gloves. Highly recommended are Campmor Inc (☎ 800-230-2151, 🖳 www.campmor .com), PO Box 700-BC97, Saddle River, NJ 07458-0700, and Sierra Trading Post (☎ 800-713-4534, fax 800-378-8946, 🖳 www.sierra tradingpost.com), 5025 Campstool Rd, Dept BP0799, Cheyenne, WY 82007. *Backpacker* magazine's online shopping site at 🖳 www. basecamp.com is also good.

Physical Preparation

How you prepare for a hiking trip is largely a personal preference, but should reflect where you plan on hiking. If you're going to altitude (the Rocky Mountains, Cascades or Sierra Nevada), allow several days for acclimatization at the beginning of the trip, and take it easy on your liver by abstaining from alcohol for a few days and drinking plenty of non-caffinated fluids (water is best).

Hikes that gain or loose 2000ft or more of elevation in one stretch will require strong calf and quadricep muscles: squats, calf raises and running stairs (or, better yet, walking stairs with a full pack on) are good exercises for these. Remember to keep supporting muscles such as the groin, hamstring and IT band, which runs from the gluteus maximus (butt) to the outside of the knee, well-stretched to avoid injury.

The main areas of concern for everyone are feet and shoulders. Walking outdoors 3mi to 5mi, three to four times a week, in the boots you plan to hike in, will wear them in and reduce your chance of blisters and foot fatigue. It will also let you test different socks and lacing systems. Doing this in a hilly area with a half-loaded pack is ideal preparation.

How far in advance you prepare will depend on your age and endurance level. If you're not already accustomed to exercise, start the process gradually: walk a mile with a day-pack and work your way up to 5mi with a half-loaded pack of the kind you plan to wear. In any case, don't wait until a week before your trip to start training. To shortchange yourself will mean a rough week or two of hiking until your body gets in shape or, in a worst-case scenario, lead to injury that will halt your hiking plans altogether.

HIKES IN THIS BOOK
Covering the USA's myriad hiking possibilities could fill volumes of thick, heavy books. Since no-one wants an encyclopedia in their pack, this book, during its planning stages, became a sort of 'best of the USA' hiking guide. There are big chunks of the country that are conspicuously left out, simply because they are not prime hiking destinations. This does not mean that Nebraska, for example, has no hikes at all. But it does mean that if you have a limited time (say, a lifetime) to hike in the USA, you'd probably not want to spend it in the Midwest.

The ratio we've tried to maintain throughout the book is around 70% long hikes (of more than three days) and 30% day hikes. Ideally, every long hike could either be tackled in its entirety or broken easily into stages – but few things are ideal. When it is possible to exit a trail, or turn a side trip into an alternate route out, this is described in the specific hike description. Day trips are usually in an area of remarkable beauty that may not allow overnight camping; they may also be near other trails that you can use to turn the day hike into an overnight (or multiday) trip.

We hope that hikers use this book as an introduction and planning tool, as well as an actual guide for hikes, and that once they become familiar with local circumstances they start planning their own routes to take advantage of the endless possibilities the USA has to offer. The Other Hikes sections at the end of most chapters are used to point you to other great trails in the area that we couldn't cover (due to space limitations) this time around.

Route Descriptions
Most of the hikes are described in stages that take the average hiker one day to complete and end at a campsite or trailhead. When alternative campsites are of interest to stronger or slower hikers, or to hikers who want to do one segment of a longer hike, this is noted under an Alternative Campsites heading. If the hike is an out-and-back one, we've included a description for each day of the return hike even if it's only a sentence or two.

Hikes can usually be done in either direction, but there is often a strong argument for going one way instead of the other and this is explained in the text.

Levels of Difficulty
The hikes in this book are graded easy, easy-medium, medium, medium-hard or hard and the grading appears next to the heading 'Standard' in the summary at the beginning of each hike description. While each author has their own definition of what a 'hard' hike is, we've tried to come to a general consensus. If the definition of difficulty changes slightly from chapter to chapter, it should remain consistent within each chapter. In a region you're visiting for the first time it's not a bad idea to start with a day hike. This will familiarize you with the regional topography and climate, and with the style of the author who has written the chapter. Keep in mind that how much sleep

you've had, how your gastro-intestinal tract is working and similar personal considerations have much to do with the perceived difficulty of any hike.

Most trails in the USA are well defined – route-finding is really only an issue in the Southwest and in mountainous regions above treeline. Thus hard hikes are most often ones with a tough ascent or descent, a long stretch with no camping opportunities, or difficult navigation.

Medium routes can be hiked without undue exertion by people of average fitness who are accustomed to carrying a full pack. Day hikes of this rating have a moderate ascent/descent and, generally, do not take longer than five hours to complete.

An easy route will be relatively flat, will not present navigational difficulties nor require the use of all four limbs at any point and can be comfortably undertaken by a family with children aged 10 and up.

A few hike descriptions, particularly in the Sierra Nevada chapter, refer to sections of trails as being Class 1, Class 2 or Class 3. These grades refer to the Yosemite Decimal System, which classifies terrain by the equipment and techniques required to tackle it. Class 1 is a rocky scramble of the sort frequently encountered on harder hikes. Class 2 is steeper terrain which may require the occasional use of hands but generally not a rope. Class 3 entails frequent use of hands and is essentially simple climbing for which the use of a rope is advisable.

Times & Distances
The approximate time needed to complete a hike is given with each hike description. (This does not include side trips or alternative routes, the details of which are listed separately.) These times are based on actual hiking times and don't allow for rest stops, photography or meandering. Be sure to factor in the extra time taken for these activities so as not to become stranded after dark in a place you'd rather not be. Remember that bad weather and swollen streams will also make hiking times longer.

We've tried to give both distances and times in the text. When given, distances are in miles, yards or feet – see Weights & Measures in this chapter for further definition.

Maps in This Book
The maps in this book are intended to show the general route of individual hikes and to be used in conjunction with the maps recommended in the Planning section of each hike or regional section (also indicated on the map itself).

A wide line of brown stipple shows the entire route covered by the text, and alternative routes are shown with a dashed line of wide, brown stipple. Start and finish points are marked with boxes, and campsites, lookout points and other symbols are also indicated. A wide band of gray stipple shows land boundaries and borders and the coverage of any adjoining or overlapping maps is also shown, along with their page numbers.

The scale and contour interval of each map is different, but is clearly marked beneath the LP north arrow. Make sure to look at this information first when using the map.

A small-scale regional map, with outlined boxes that show the borders of the hike areas mapped in greater detail in the individual hike sections, appears at the beginning of each chapter.

Altitude Measurements
Altitude measurements have been quoted from the maps used during our research. Normally these are USGS topographical maps with a scale of 1:62,500. Bureau of Land Management (BLM) and USFS maps were also used in places.

Place Names & Terminology
The hike descriptions in this book use terms that are familiar to hikers in the USA but may not be common overseas. In regions of the USA where local terminology deviates from that in the book, the local terms are described in the beginning of the chapter or in the comprehensive Glossary at the back of the book.

GUIDED HIKES
There is an increasingly large number of commercial companies that offer organized

hiking vacations in the USA. These vary from ultra-plush 'inn' trips, where you stay and eat in elegant accommodations each night; to base-camp style trips, where you stay in a central lodge and choose a different day hike each day; to guided backpacking trips where everyone helps in cooking and carries their own gear. Mostly, the trips cover a specific geographic area and are conducted during the months that offer the best chance of good weather. Many companies will custom-design a trip for 12 or more people. Contact the companies for information on dates, prices and areas of expertise – most produce a fancy catalog which they'll send, free, to nearly anywhere on the globe.

Alpine Ascents International (☎ 206-378-1927, ☻ aaiclimb@accessone.com, ▯ www.alpine ascents.com) 121 Mercer St, Seattle, WA 98109. Famous for mountaineering and climbing expeditions, but also leads backpacking courses in the Cascades.

American Alpine Institute (☎ 306-671-1505, ▯ www.mtnguide.com) 1515 12th St P-77, Bellingham, WA 98225. A highly reputable guide service that leads rock, ice and mountaineering expeditions.

Backpacking Adventures (☎ 888-734-4453, ▯ www.wildhorizonsexpd.com) PO Box 7627, Jackson, WY 83002. Guided backpacking trips in wilderness areas in Wyoming, Arizona, southern Utah and Montana.

Backroads (☎ 510-527-1555, 800-462-2848, ▯ www.backroads.com) 801 Cedar St, Berkeley, CA 94710-1800. Offers high-end hiking trips throughout the world and is known for its excellent accommodations, food and guides.

Big Wild Adventures (☎ 406-821-3747) 5663 West Fork Rd, Dept B, Darby, MT 59829. Leads small groups on wilderness hikes through Montana, Idaho, New Mexico and Utah.

Country Walkers (☎ 800-464-9255, ▯ www .countrywalkers.com) PO Box 180, Waterbury, VT 05676. Leads small groups of walkers through Maine, Vermont, Arizona, Montana and Canada, staying and eating in small inns.

MountainFIT (☎ 406-585-3506, 800-926-5700, ☻ hike@mountainfit.com, ▯ www.mountain fit.com) PO Box 6188, Bozeman, MT 5977. Integrates mind and body work with deluxe accommodations on trips in Montana, Arizona and Utah.

Wilderness Expeditions (☎ 413-664-6138, ☻ WilderExp@aol.com). Designs custom trips and offers backpacking trips of one to five days throughout Vermont, New York and western Massachusetts.

RESPONSIBLE HIKING

Backcountry areas are fragile environments and cannot support insensitive or careless activity, especially with the increasing numbers of visitors. Conservation organizations, hikers' manuals and the NPS all promote backcountry codes that seek to minimize the impact of hikers on the environment. Make sure you are familiar with these before you set out and always stay on the main trail, even if it means walking through mud or crossing a patch of snow.

Campsites & Fires

To preserve the environment, use old campsites instead of clearing a new one. Make sure you are at least 200ft (70 steps) away from the nearest lake, river or stream. Fires are prohibited in many backcountry areas and in state and national parks during dry seasons. The best advice is to carry a lightweight stove and use it. If you do light a fire, keep it at least 9ft away from flammable material (including grass and wood), watch it at all times and drown it thoroughly with water before going to sleep or leaving the site – you should be able to immerse your hand in the coals.

Water & Toilets

Avoid using soaps and detergents (gravel cleans pots remarkably well!) and wash up at least 200ft from any water source. Bury human waste in a hole dug 6 inches deep (that's deeper than most people realize – familiarize yourself with how deep 6 inches is before you have an emergency) and at least 300ft (105 steps) from water. *Do not* bury your toilet paper: put it in a sealable plastic bag and pack it out.

Garbage

The hikers mantra is 'pack it in – pack it out'; this includes everything from toilet paper to tea bags. It's for this reason that canned goods are frowned upon –an empty tuna-fish tin gets old after day one, let alone for five days. A trash can is provided at nearly every trailhead.

Access

Hikes in this book do not cross private property unless the owners have given clearance for all hikers to pass without prior notification. If there is an exception, it is noted in the hike description. People who own property in scenic areas are often protective of their land. This is especially true where hiking trails cross or border farming communities, such as in Montana and Wyoming. Respect the American ego and let property owners have an unchallenged right to their land.

WOMEN HIKERS

Despite legal equality and enlightened public policies, it's fair to say that sexist attitudes toward women are still widespread. In the outdoors community, however, gender equality is highly valued. There is a general sense that *any* person in pursuit of fresh air and wide-open spaces is as good as any other, and as likely to accomplish the task

---

Women on the Trail

I've been both on the receiving end of, and participated in, the sizing up of women and their backpacks – the weight of their packs, the quality of the gear inside, the height of the climb and length of the hike, how much of the big stuff the male companion is carrying etc. People rarely make overt comments, but I've been on the porch of the ranger station enough times to hear 'Check out the size of her pack,' directed at a female passerby, and have hiked with enough men who can't help but quip 'She must be pretty buff to carry all that,' or 'Looks like he's carrying all the stuff,' after any female hiker we encounter. There are definitely some people who think that a woman shouldn't be in the woods without a guy, but you won't encounter these people on the trail.

Jennifer Snarski

---

at hand (such as thru-hiking the Pacific Crest Trail or bagging a summit). Several of this book's women authors did all of their research alone, without any undue hassle.

That said, women potentially face more challenging situations when hiking alone than men do. If you're unaccustomed to hiking solo, stick to well-trodden trails where you are likely to meet people at campsites, or try to hook-up with a group or companion before hitting the trail; national park visitor centers and ranger stations often have bulletin boards specifically for this purpose. For organized hiking trips to join, see Resources & Organizations later in this section and Guided Hikes earlier in this chapter.

Safety Precautions

Women may be safer on the trail than in bad parts of big cities or backwoods rural areas. Two on-trail issues called to our attention for this section are that women hikers often don't drink enough water for fear of having to find a place to pee along a busy trail (this is to be discouraged), and that stomach upsets (diarrhea or vomiting) can inhibit your body's ability to absorb oral contraceptives – so take necessary precautions.

Between-hike traveling – in cities and rural areas – may present the greater challenges for women traveling alone, so they need to develop an extra awareness of their surroundings. In towns and cities be aware of 'bad,' or unsafe, neighborhoods or districts, particularly after dark. If you must go into these areas it's less risky in a private car or taxi. If you are unsure which areas are considered unsafe, ask at your hotel or telephone the local tourist office or women's center for advice. While there is less crime in rural areas, women may still be harassed.

Hitchhiking is always risky and not recommended, *especially* hitchhiking alone. Don't pick up hitchhikers if driving alone. See also Hitching in the Getting Around chapter.

Rape mostly occurs in cities, but to a lesser degree also in rural areas. Common sense will help you avoid most problems. You're more vulnerable if you've been drinking or using drugs than if you're sober,

Women & Bears

While it's not been proven that bears have an affinity for menstruating women, more than one woman has been attacked by a bear while in the middle of her menstrual cycle. If you have your period while hiking in bear country, be sure to carry plenty of tampons (pads are not recommended as they are more odorous and messy) and plenty of sealable plastic bags in which to dispose of them. If you accidentally bleed on clothing or gear, wash it out immediately when you get to camp. Women who have a heavy menstrual flow may want to try to schedule their trip for before or after their period.

and you're more vulnerable alone than if you're with trusted associates.

If you are assaulted, call the police (☎ 911). In the few rural areas where this number is not active, dial ☎ 0 for the operator. Cities and larger towns have rape crisis centers and women's shelters that provide help; they are listed in the telephone directory, and the police should also be able to refer you.

To deal with potential dangers, many women protect themselves with a whistle, mace, cayenne-pepper spray, some karate training – or a gun (although having a gun may actually *increase* the risk of being seriously hurt.) If you decide to purchase a spray, contact a police station to find out about regulations and training classes. Laws regarding guns and sprays vary from state to state, but federal law prohibits them being carried on planes.

What to Wear

It's usually North American women who get the bad rep for flaunting too much skin abroad. Short shorts and sports bras are de rigueur for many women hikers, but women travelling alone should cover more flesh to preclude implications of promiscuity.

Resources & Organizations

Maiden Voyages (🖳 www.maiden-voyages.com) is an online magazine with a database of hundreds of travel services – including hiking and backpacking companies – owned, run by and/or geared toward women. Other good websites for women travelers are 🖳 www.journeywoman.com, and *Backpacker* magazine's women's page (🖳 www.backpacker.com/womenspage/).

The National Organization for Women (NOW; ☎ 202-331-0066, 🖳 www.now.org/), 1000 16th St NW, suite 700, Washington, DC 20036, is a good resource. NOW can refer you to state and local chapters.

A Journey of One's Own by Thalia Zepatos (1996) contains travel tips, anecdotes and a long list of sources and resources for the independent female traveler. *Adventures in Good Company* (1994), also by Thalia Zepatos, covers a huge range of adventure, outdoor and special interest tours and activities for women in the US and abroad.

For local resources, check in the Yellow Pages phone directory under 'Women's Organizations and Services.' Women's bookstores are very good places to find out about upcoming gatherings, readings and meetings and often have bulletin boards where you can find or place travel and housing notices.

HIKING WITH CHILDREN

There's no need to hang up your boots until the children grow up, and hiking with them in the US is probably easier than anywhere else in the world. Baby food, diapers (nappies), creams and potions, and all the other paraphernalia of traveling with the very young are readily available in supermarkets and pharmacies throughout the US. Though you may not find your favourite brand, all the biggies are here.

Children can be slow to adapt to changes of diet, temperature and altitude, so before undertaking a route of several days it might be wise to first establish a base camp and do a number of day- or half-day hikes to break yourselves in. It's important to choose hikes that have scope for lots of variety – a visitor center at which to spend some time, places for other related activities (beaches are perfect), unusual features such as archeological

Top Left: New England's remarkable deciduous forests burst into a canopy of color in fall.
Top Right: Acadia National Park, Maine, an unusual glacier-carved landscape flanking the Atlantic.
Middle Right: Cape Cod National Seashore, Massachusetts – steeped in history, lashed by the elements.
Bottom: Tranquil waters above a steep cascade in the White Mountains, Vermont.

JON DAVISON

IZZET KERIBAR

KIM GRANT

JON DAVISON

Top Left: Hikers set out from a hut typical of those on the Appalachian Trail, New Hampshire.
Top Right: The Appalachian Trail wends through hundreds of miles of northern deciduous forest, rich with wildflowers and bear-attracting berries, New Hampshire.
Bottom: The distinctive, blue haze of the forested valleys in the Great Smoky Mountains, Tennessee.

LEE FOSTER

LEE FOSTER

JOHN ELK III

sites, or somewhere there is a good chance of seeing wildlife. Touristed regions around large national parks such as Yellowstone and Glacier are well-equipped with (often somewhat odd!) children's entertainment such as go-kart tracks, mini-golf and water slides. Keep in mind that spectacular views and 'interesting' geological formations are usually more of an adult pastime.

Make sure that you carry plenty of food and drinks including the children's favorites. It's important to bring a generous range of warm clothing – children warm up and cool down very quickly (see What to Bring under Planning earlier in this chapter). The distance and duration of the hike you choose should be firmly based on the children's capabilities, rather than your own with a bit taken off.

Lonely Planet's *Travel with Children* (1995) by Maureen Wheeler has lots of practical advice on the subject, along with firsthand travel stories stemming from the experience of a host of Lonely Planet authors and others.

Most nature trails within national parks are very suitable for families with children. Other possibilities are historic trails in New England (where rest stops are readily available) and the relatively flat terrain of Sequoia National Park, Yosemite Valley and parts of Southern Appalachia.

If your children enjoy these hikes, there's a good chance they'll be hikers for the rest of their lives.

USEFUL ORGANIZATIONS
Government Departments

See National Parks & Reserves in the Facts about the USA chapter for more information on government land-management authorities.

National Park Service (☎ 800-365-2267, 🖳 www.nps.gov), NPS Public Inquiry, Department of the Interior, 1849 C St NW, Washington, DC 20013. The NPS will mail maps, park newspapers, park campground and reservations information to domestic and international addresses for free. Its comprehensive website has links to individual parks for specific information.

US Forest Service The US Forest Service is under the Department of Agriculture and manages national forests. Entry to national forests is free, although a new, experimental program charging visitors a $2 to $5 fee to drive on popular roads has been instituted in several areas. National forest campground and reservation information can be obtained by calling ☎ 800-280-2267. Also, visit (🖳 www.fs.fed.us/)

Bureau of Land Management The BLM manages public use of federal lands other than national parks and forests, mostly in the desert Southwest. Regional BLM offices are usually in the state capital – look in the front of the White Pages directory under 'US Government, Department of the Interior', or call the Federal Information Center (☎ 800-688-9889).

Fish & Wildlife Services Each state has one of these, variously called Fish & Game, Fishing & Hunting, Wildlife Resources etc. These issue fishing and hunting licenses and may provide information about viewing local wildlife as an alternative to killing it. Look in the phone book under 'US Government, Department of the Interior', or call the Federal Information Center (☎ 800-688-9889). Licenses are often available at outfitters, tackle shops and post offices.

Hiking Clubs

See also Guided Hikes earlier in this chapter.

If the USA has several hundred hiking clubs, why is it rare to see a pack of people hiking down the trail together? Most clubs are composed of, and cater to, weekend-warrior types who only hike on weekends in areas within three hours drive of an urban center. While there is nothing wrong with such clubs, most outsiders will feel disconnected when hiking with groups of people who all know each other, each other's kids and grandkids etc. On the other hand, hiking in an area with people who know it well can give great insight to local landscape and culture (and will undoubtedly yield the whereabouts of the best nearby beer and pizza).

To find a local hiking club, start at the local outdoors store. It may have members of the club on staff, or bulletins published by the club (usually monthly). Some clubs are listed in the Yellow Pages under 'Clubs – Hiking'. Most clubs allow visitors to participate on most hikes, free of charge. (It's essential to contact the trip leader first.) Colleges and universities often have hiking clubs that open their trips to the public for a small fee; contact the recreation department, often located at the main gymnasium.

American Hiking Society (☎ 301-565-6704, 🖳 www.americanhiker.org), 1422 Fenwick Lane, Silver Spring, MD 20910. Information on volunteer trail-maintenance vacations and regional hiking clubs.

Appalachian Mountain Club (☎ 617-523-0636, 🖳 www.outdoors.org), 5 Joy St, Boston, MA 02108. The AMC sells hiking guides and maps to the White Mountains and other New England backcountry.

Appalachian Trail Conference (☎ 304-535-6331, 🖳 www.nps.gov/aptr), PO Box Harpers Ferry, WV 25425-0807. The ATC administers the Appalachian National Scenic Trail in cooperation with the NPS.

Nature Conservancy (🖳 www.tnc.org) whose mission is to protect the rarest living things for future generations, organizes field tours for its members and can advise on interesting areas for the general public. Find out about the nearest field office from its website or one of it's regional offices:

California: (☎ 415-777-0487) 201 Mission St, 4th floor, San Francisco, CA 94105
Eastern: (☎ 617-542-1908) 201 Devonshire St, 5th floor, Boston, MA 02110
New York: (☎ 518-273-9408) 415 River St, 4th floor, Troy, NY 12180
Southeast: (☎ 919-967-5493) PO Box 2267, Chapel Hill, NC 27515-2267
Western: (☎ 303-444-1060) 2060 Broadway, Suite 230, Boulder, CO 80302

Pacific Crest Trail Association (☎ 800-817-2243, 🖳 www.pcta.org), 5325 Elkhorn Blvd, PMB 256, Sacramento, CA 95842. The PCTA sells maps and guides to the Pacific Crest Trail, which it maintains with paid staff and volunteers.

Sierra Club (☎ 415-977-5500, 🖳 www.sierraclub.org), 85 Second St, 2nd Floor, San Francisco, CA 94105-3441. Founded in 1892 by John Muir, this is the nation's largest outdoors organization. It's regional chapters have a full calendar of hiking and backpacking trips (as well as ski trips, rock-climbing seminars etc) open to the public. Call, visit the website, or look in the White Pages under 'Sierra Club' to locate the nearest chapter. See also Conservation Organizations under Ecology & Environment in the Facts about the USA chapter.

Other Organizations
American Automobile Association (AAA, pronounced triple-A) provides great travel information, distributes free road maps and guidebooks, and sells American Express traveler's checks without commission to its members. The AAA membership card will often get you discounts for accommodations, car rental and admission charges. All major cities and many smaller towns have a AAA office – there's a list at 🖳 www.aaa.com.

AAA also provides emergency roadside service in the event of an accident or breakdown or if you lock your keys in the car. The nationwide, toll-free roadside assistance number is ☎ 800-222-4357 (800-AAA-HELP).

Members of other national and state motoring associations – such as the UK Automobile Association or the NRMA and its counterparts in Australia – can use AAA services if they bring a membership card and a letter of introduction from their home organization.

TOURIST OFFICES
Very few tourist offices have information about hiking, unless there's a half-mile, self-guiding nature trail nearby. Ask for hiking, camping and recreation-related material when requesting information, but be prepared to go elsewhere. Usually, you'll get the best hiking information from local outdoors stores, NPS, USFS and BLM offices.

There is no national tourist office promoting US tourism in other countries, though some states may have an office or agent in a prime market. Information USA has an excellent website (🖳 www.information-usa.com) with links to state and city tourist organizations, consulates, a map page and weather information sites; text is in French and English.

Local Tourist Offices
Tourist promotion and information is done by states, cities and local areas, not by the federal government. Every state has a tourist office, which will send out a swag of promotional materials on request, mostly aimed at domestic tourists and holiday makers.

Listed here are state tourist offices of the states crossed by trails in this book:

California Division of Tourism (☎ 916-323-9882, 800-462-2543, fax 322-3402, 🖳 go-calif.ca.gov) 801 K St, Suite 1600, Sacramento, CA 95814

Colorado Travel & Tourism Authority (☎ 303-296-3384, fax 296-2015, 🖳 www.colorado.com) 1127 Pennsylvania Ave, Denver, CO 80203

Georgia Department of Industry, Trade and Tourism (☎ 404-656-3553, 800-847-4842, fax 651-9063, 🖳 www.georgia.org/itt/tourism/) 285 Peachtree Center Ave NE, Suite 1000, Atlanta, GA 30303

Idaho Division of Tourism Development (☎ 208-334-2470, 800-635-7820, fax 334-2631, 🖳 www.visitid.org) 700 West State St, PO Box 83720, Boise, ID 83720-0093

Maine Office of Tourism (☎ 207-287-5710, 800-533-9595, fax 287-8070, 🖳 www.visitmaine.com) 33 Stone St, 59 State House Station, Augusta, ME 04333-0059

Travel Montana (☎ 406-444-2654, 800-847-4868, fax 444-1800, 🖳 www.visitmt.com) 1424 Ninth Ave, PO Box 200533, Helena, MT 59620-0533

New Hampshire Office of Travel & Tourism (☎ 603-271-2665, 800-386-4664, fax 271-6784, 🖳 www.visitnh.gov) PO Box 1856, Concord, NH 03302-1856

New Mexico Department of Tourism (☎ 505-827-7400, 800-733-6396, fax 827-7402, 🖳 www.newmexico.org) 491 Old Santa Fe Trail, Santa Fe, NM 87501

North Carolina Division of Tourism (☎ 919-733-4171, 800-847-4862, fax 733-8582, 🖳 www.visitnc.com) 301 N Wilmington St, Raleigh, NC 27601-2825

Oregon Tourism Commission (☎ 503-986-0000, 800-547-7842, fax 986-0001, 🖳 www.traveloregon.com) 775 Summer St, NE, Salem, OR 97310

South Carolina Department of Tourism (☎ 803-734-0122, 800-872-3505, fax 734-1409, 🖳 www.sccsi.com/sc/) 1205 Pendleton St, Suite 248, Columbia, SC 29201

Tennessee Department of Tourist Development (☎ 615-741-9001, 800-836-6200, fax 741-7225, 🖳 www.state.tn.us/tourdev/) 320 Sixth Ave N, PO Box 23170, Nashville, TN 37202

Utah Travel Council (☎ 801-538-1030, 800-200-1160, fax 538-1399, 🖳 www.utah.com) Council Hall, Salt Lake City, UT 84114

Vermont Department of Travel & Tourism (☎ 802-828-3230, 800-837-6668, fax 828-3233, 🖳 www.travel-vermont.com) 134 State St, Montpelier, VT 05601-1471

Virginia Tourism Corporation (☎ 800-233-8824, 🖳 www.virginia.org) 901 East Byrd St, Richmond, VA 23219-4048

Washington State Tourism Development Division (☎ 360-664-2560, 800-544-1800, fax 753-4470, 🖳 www.tourism.wa.gov) PO Box 42500, Olympia, WA 98504-2500

West Virginia Division of Tourism & Parks (☎ 304-558-2288, 800-225-5982, fax 558-0108, 🖳 www.state.wv.us/tourism) 2101 Washington St E, Charleston, WV 25305

Wyoming Division of Tourism (☎ 307-777-7777, 800-225-5996, fax 777-6904, 🖳 www.state.wy.us/state/tourism/tourism.html) Frank Norris Jr Travel Center, I-25 & College Dr, Cheyenne, WY 82002-0660

Many cities also have an official Convention & Visitors Bureau (CVB) whose main function is to promote the city and attract the conference trade. Most aren't really set up to assist hikers, but some are really helpful. Generally they keep standard business hours and close on weekends.

In smaller towns, the local chamber of commerce, an organization of local businesses that promotes the town and the commercial interests of its members, will often maintain a list of hotels, motels, restaurants and services. The list will mention only chamber of commerce members and may not include camping options. Most chamber of commerce information centers open on weekdays, some on Saturday and a few on Sunday, especially where tourism is a big local business.

Some state governments maintain 'Welcome Centers,' found on the main highways as you enter a state or approach a city or national park. They are usually open quite long hours and on weekends, especially during holiday times.

VISAS & DOCUMENTS

All visitors should bring their home driver's license and any health- or travel-insurance cards. You'll need a photo identification to show that you are over 21 to buy alcohol. Keep these in a waterproof bag.

It's a good idea to make photocopies of your passport and other essential documents and carry the copies separately from the originals (I keep photocopies of documents, in a waterproof bag, stashed in the frame of my backpack). If you're staying at the same hotel (or with the same friends) before and after a hike, leave valuable documents with them. Also leave a copy at home – it can make it easier to obtain a replacement if you lose the original.

Passports & Visas

All foreign visitors (other than Canadians) must bring their passports. Your passport should be valid for at least six months longer than your intended stay in the USA. Canadians must have proof of citizenship, such as a citizenship card with photo identification, or a passport.

Under the Visa Waiver Program, citizens of Andorra, Argentina, Australia, Austria, Belgium, Brunei, Denmark, Finland, France, Germany, Iceland, Ireland, Italy, Japan, Liechtenstein, Luxembourg, Monaco, the Netherlands, New Zealand, Norway, San Marino, Slovenia, Spain, Sweden, Switzerland and the UK may enter the USA without a US visa for stays of 90 days or less. Under this program, you *must* have a roundtrip or onward ticket that is nonrefundable in the USA, and you may be required to show evidence of financial solvency.

Apart from those entering under the Visa Waiver Program, foreign visitors need to obtain a visa from a US consulate or embassy. In most countries this can be done by mail or through a travel agent. Documents of financial stability, a return or onward ticket and/or guarantees from a US resident are sometimes required, particularly for those from developing countries. The relevant authority is the US Immigration & Nationalization Service (INS), a body not noted for its easygoing attitude. For detailed information about visas, immigration etc, check the US State Department website (⌨ travel.state.gov/visa_services.html).

A visitor's visa is good for one or five years with multiple entries and prohibits the visitor from taking paid employment in the USA. The validity period depends on what country you are from. The length of time you'll be allowed to stay in the USA is determined by the INS at the port of entry.

You can be refused a visa or entry to the USA if you are a drug trafficker, seek to enter the USA to engage in terrorist activities, have ever participated in a genocide or have a 'communicable disease of public health significance' or a criminal record. If you're tempted to conceal something, remember that the INS is strictest of all about false statements – it will often review favorably an applicant who admits to an old criminal charge or a communicable disease, but it is extremely harsh on anyone who has ever attempted to mislead it, even on minor points.

It's a good idea to be able to list an itinerary that will account for the period for which you ask to be admitted and to be able to show you have $300 or $400 for each week of your intended stay. An onward or return ticket helps. These days, a couple of major credit cards will go a long way toward establishing 'sufficient funds.' If you want, need or hope to stay in the USA longer than the date stamped on your passport, go to the local INS office (☎ 800-755-0777, or look in the local White Pages under 'US Government') to apply for an extension *before* the stamped date.

Re-entry While none of the hikes described in this book requires you to cross any national borders, extensions or nearby hikes in the Northern Cascades, Glacier National Park and New England can lead across the USA's northern border into Canada. While these trails are not patrolled specifically for immigration purposes, rangers are required to ask for identification. A hiking permit is usually sufficient; however, it's best to have your passport and immigration card with you (and a photocopy of both stashed in the car or somewhere reasonably secure). If your immigration card has nearly expired, apply for a new card before heading into the backcountry.

Foreigners in Canada who are crossing into the USA through regular border crossings are often hit with a US$6 entry fee (not one hiker I've talked to has been asked to pay this, but it's a good idea to have the $6 just in case).

The Pacific Crest Trail leads to the Mexican border in an area that is heavily guarded against illegal entry. If you're going to cross into Mexico, be sure to have your passport and immigration card with you. The Mexican *Federales* (federal police) are notorious for stopping people who have committed no crime or error. A $20 bill is usually all they want and many people take extra cash south of the border specifically for this reason.

Onward Tickets

A return or onward ticket is compulsory only for the Visa Waiver Program. If you have a visitor's visa, a ticket out of the country may help persuade the INS that you don't intend to stay permanently, but it's not obligatory.

Hiking Permits

The USA does not have a national hiking permit system, and not all hikes require a permit. Hikes on National Forest and BLM land have historically not required permits, though a Fee Demonstration Program, implemented in 1996, now requires hikers to buy a permit (usually a $5 parking pass, purchased at a ranger station) for some areas – see the individual hikes chapters for details.

Most national parks require overnight hikers to carry a *backcountry, wilderness* or *special-use* permit, which can be obtained from national park visitor centers or ranger stations 24 hours in advance and may require you to submit (and follow!) a day-by-day itinerary. The permits are usually free but can cost up to $20 and, in addition, require a per-person, per-night fee to be paid. For the most popular hikes, you often need to make a permit reservation well in advance.

See the Permits & Regulations sections of individual hikes and hikes chapters for more information.

National Park Entry Permits

The cost of entry to a national park ranges from $5 to $20 per vehicle, and from nothing to $10 for pedestrians and cyclists. The fee is collected upon entry to most parks, though a rare few go by the honor system and have you self-register and drop your payment in a box. Cash and traveler's checks are the only accepted payment methods.

If you're going to several national fee areas (including national parks, monuments, historic sites, recreation areas, and national wildlife refuges), it pays to get the $50 Golden Eagle Passport which admits the passholder and any accompanying passengers in a private vehicle. The pass can be purchased on-site, or by mail from the NPS, 1100 Ohio Dr, SW, Room 138, Washington, DC 20242, attention: Golden Eagle Passport, and is valid for one year from the date of purchase.

The Golden Age Passport ($10) gives admission, plus a 50% reduction on camping, parking and other visitor fees to people 62 years or older (with proof of age). The Golden Access Passport, identical to the Golden Age, is a free, lifetime entrance pass for people who are blind or permanently disabled.

Travel Insurance

It is *highly advisable* to take out travel insurance that covers you for medical expenses, hospital treatment and an emergency flight home if necessary. Be sure to read the fine print, as many policies do not cover emergency evacuation or injuries incurred while engaged in 'mountaineering activities' (which can including hiking). If insurance that does cover such activities seems expensive, it's still nowhere near the cost of a medical emergency in the USA. See also Health Insurance in the Health & Safety chapter.

A good option for hikers who travel frequently is an annual policy, offered to the public in the USA starting February 2000. These policies cost around $150 per year and while they do not cover trip cancellation or interruption, they do provide up to $50,000 in medical-evacuation costs and usually have no prohibitive clauses aimed towards adventurous types. Two established providers are Access America (☎ 800-284-8300, 💻 www.accessamerica.com), PO Box 90315, Richmond, VA 23286, and Travelex (☎ 888-407-5404, 💻 www.trav elex-insur-ance.com), 11717 Burt St, Suite 202, Omaha, NE 68154.

Coverage for luggage theft or loss, cancellations, delayed travel arrangements and ticket loss is also advisable, as is coverage against civil liability (sadly, the USA is a very litigious society, and if you accidentally cause someone loss or damage he or she may sue you for millions).

Other Documents

Most visitors can legally drive in America for up to a year with their home driver's license. An International Driving Permit (IDP) is a very useful adjunct – see the Getting Around chapter for details.

If you are a student, bring your school identification to take advantage of the available discounts. Unless you plan to visit quite a few sights or attend movies and performances, an ISIC (International Student Identity Card; US$20) is not necessary. The GO 25 card (US$20), issued to those aged 12 to 25, can help you get a reduced rate on airfares, car rental and other costs. People over the age of about 60 often get discounts. All you need is identification with proof of age.

Most hostels in the USA are members of Hostelling International/American Youth Hostel (HI/AYH), which is affiliated with the International Youth Hostel Federation (IYHF). You can purchase membership ($25 adults, $10 under 17) on the spot when checking in or before you leave home (you'll need an identification).

If you're a member of a national or state motoring association that is affiliated with the American Automobile Association (AAA), bring your membership card and/or a letter of introduction – see Useful Organizations earlier in this chapter.

Copies

All important documents (passport data page and visa page, credit cards, travel insurance policy, air/bus/train tickets, driving licence etc) should be photocopied before you leave home. Leave one copy with someone at home and keep another with you, separate from the originals.

It's also a good idea to store details of your vital travel documents in Lonely Planet's free online Travel Vault in case you lose the photocopies or can't be bothered with them. Your password-protected Travel Vault is accessible online anywhere in the world – create it at 🖳 www.ekno.lonelyplanet.com.

EMBASSIES & CONSULATES
US Embassies & Consulates

Diplomatic representation abroad includes:

Australia
Embassy: (☎ 02-6270 5000) 21 Moonah Place, Yarralumla, ACT 2600
Consulate: (☎ 02-9373 9200) Level 59, MLC Centre, 19–29 Martin Place, Sydney, NSW 2000
Consulate: (☎ 03-9526 5900) 553 St Kilda Rd, Melbourne, Vic 3004
Canada
Embassy: (☎ 613-238-5335) 100 Wellington St, Ottawa, Ontario K1P 5T1
Consulate: (☎ 604-685-1930) 1095 W Pender St, Vancouver, BC V6E 2M6
Consulate: (☎ 514-398-9695) 1155 Rue St-Alexandre, Montreal, Quebec
France
Embassy: (☎ 01 42 96 12 02) 2 Rue St Florentin, 75001 Paris
Germany
Embassy: (☎ 228-33-91) Deichmanns Aue 29, 53179 Bonn
Ireland
Embassy: (☎ 1-687-122) 42 Elgin Rd, Ballsbridge, Dublin
Japan
Embassy: (☎ 3-224-5000) 1-10-5 Akasaka, Minato-ku, Tokyo
Netherlands
Embassy: (☎ 70-310-9209) Lange Voorhout 102, 2514 EJ, The Hague
Consulate: (☎ 20-310-9209) Museumplein 19, 1071 DJ, Amsterdam
New Zealand
Embassy: (☎ 4-722-068) 29 Fitzherbert Terrace, Thorndon, Wellington
UK
Embassy: (☎ 020-7499-9000) 5 Upper Grosvenor St, London W1
Consulate: (☎ 31-556-8315) 3 Regent Terrace, Edinburgh EH7 5BW
Consulate: (☎ 232-328-239) Queens House, Belfast BT1 6EQ

Embassies & Consulates in the USA

Just about every country in the world has an embassy in Washington, DC – call ☎ 202-555-1212 for embassy phone numbers.

Many countries also have consulates in other large cities such as New York, Atlanta, Houston, Seattle, San Francisco and Los Angeles – look under 'Consulates' in the Yellow Pages.

Australia
Embassy: (☎ 202-797-3000) 1601 Massachusetts Ave NW, Washington, DC 20036
Consulate: (☎ 303-297-1200, fax 297-1280) 999 18th St, Suite 1830, Denver, CO 80202
Canada
Embassy: (☎ 202-682-1740) 501 Pennsylvania Ave NW, Washington, DC 20001
Consulate: (☎ 206-443-1777, fax 443-9662) 412 Plaza 600, Seattle, WA 98101-1286
Consulate: (☎ 213-346-2700) 550 South Hope St, 9th floor, Los Angeles, CA 90071
France
Embassy: (☎ 202-944-6000, fax 944-6166) 4101 Reservoir Rd NW, Washington, DC 20007
Consulate: (☎ 212-606-3688, fax 606-3620) 934 Fifth Ave, New York, NY 10021
Consulate: (☎ 415-397-4330, fax 433-8357) 540 Bush St, San Francisco, CA 94108.
Other consulates in Atlanta, Boston, Chicago, Houston, Los Angeles, Miami and New Orleans.
Germany
Embassy: (☎ 202-298-4000, fax 298-4249) 4645 Reservoir Rd, Washington, DC 20007-1998
Ireland
Embassy: (☎ 202-462 3939) 2234 Massachusetts Ave NW, Washington, DC 20008
Consulates in Boston, Chicago, New York and San Francisco.
Japan
Embassy: (☎ 202-238-6700, fax 328-2187) 2520 Massachusetts Ave NW, Washington, DC 20008-2869
Consulate: (☎ 212-371-8222, fax 319-6357) 299 Park Ave, New York, NY 10171
Consulate: (☎ 503-221-1811, fax 224-8936) 2400 First Interstate Tower, 1300 SW 5th Ave, Portland, OR 97201
Consulate: (☎ 415-777-3533, fax 974-3660) 50 Fremont St, Suite 2300, San Francisco, CA 94105
Consulate: (☎ 206-682-9107, fax 624-9097) 601 Union St, Suite 500, Seattle, WA 98101
Other consulates in Atlanta, Boston, Chicago and Detroit.
Netherlands
Embassy: (☎ 202-244-5300, fax 362-3430) 4200 Linnean Ave NW, Washington, DC 20008

New Zealand
Embassy: (☎ 202-328-4800, fax 667-5227) 37 Observatory Circle, Washington, DC 20008
UK
Embassy: (☎ 202-462-1340) 3100 Massachusetts Ave NW, Washington, DC 20008
Consulate: (☎ 312-346-1810, fax 464-0661) Wrigley Building, 400 N Michigan Ave, Chicago, IL 60611
Consulate: (☎ 404-524-5856, fax 524-3153) Suite 2700, 245 Peachtree Center Ave, Atlanta, GA 30303
Consulate: (☎ 617-248-9555, fax 248-9578) Federal Reserve Plaza, 600 Atlantic Ave, Boston, MA 02210
Consulate: (☎ 212-745-0200, fax 754-3062) 845 Third Ave, New York, NY 10022
Consulate: (☎ 415-981-3030, fax 434-2018) 1 Sansome St, Suite 850, San Francisco, CA 94104

CUSTOMS

US Customs allows each person to bring 1 liter (about a quart) of liquor (provided you are 21 years old or older), 100 cigars and 200 cigarettes duty free into the USA. US citizens are allowed to import, duty free, $400 worth of gifts from abroad, while non-US citizens are allowed to bring in $100 worth.

US law permits you to bring in, or take out, as much as $10,000 in US or foreign currency, traveler's checks or letters of credit without formality. There's no maximum limit, but any larger amount of any or all of the above must be declared to customs.

See also Arriving in the USA in the Getting There & Away chapter.

Prohibited Imports

There are heavy penalties for attempting to import illegal drugs. It's also forbidden to import chocolate liqueurs, pornography, lottery tickets and items with fake brand names. Any fruit, vegetables, or other food or plant material must be declared or left in the bins in the arrival area. Most food items are prohibited to prevent the introduction of pests or diseases.

The USA, like 140 other countries, is a signatory to CITES, the Convention on International Trade in Endangered Species. As such, it prohibits the import and export of products made from species that may be endangered in any part of the world, including ivory, tortoise shell, coral, and many fur, skin and feather products. If you want to bring a fur coat, snakeskin belt or bone carving with you, you may have to show a certificate demonstrating that it was not made from an endangered species. The easiest option is simply not to bring anything even remotely suspect. CITES restrictions apply to what you take home, too. Alligator-skin cowboy boots might be a great souvenir, but be ready to convince customs authorities that they're not made from endangered 'gators.

MONEY
Currency
The US dollar is divided into 100 cents (c). Coins come in denominations of 1c (penny), 5c (nickel), 10c (dime), 25c (quarter) and the seldom-seen 50c (half-dollar). Quarters are the coins most commonly used in vending machines, telephones and parking meters, so it's handy to have a stash of them. Notes, usually called bills, come in $1, $2, $5, $10, $20, $50 and $100 denominations – $2 bills are rare, but perfectly legal and considered collectors' items by some.

There is also a $1 coin that the government has tried unsuccessfully to bring into mass circulation; you may get one as change from ticket and stamp machines. Be aware that it looks similar to a quarter.

Exchange Rates
Banks in cities will exchange cash or traveler's checks in major foreign currencies, though banks in outlying areas are not asked to do so very often, and it may take them some time. Thomas Cook and American Express offices, and exchange counters at airports and international borders will also exchange foreign currencies, though you'll probably get a better rate at a bank. Hikers are advised to exchange money at their point of entry. Some national park lodges have currency exchange desks, but the rates are usually terrible. At press time, exchange rates were as follows:

country	unit		US dollars
Australia	A$1	=	US$0.61
Canada	C$1	=	US$0.68
euro	€1	=	US$0.97
France	FF10	=	US$1.47
Germany	DM1	=	US$0.50
Hong Kong	HK$10	=	US$1.29
Japan	Y100	=	US$0.94
Netherlands	NF1	=	US$0.44
New Zealand	NZ$1	=	US$0.50
UK	UK£1	=	US$1.57

Traveler's Checks
American Express and Thomas Cook are widely accepted and have efficient replacement policies. Keep a record of the numbers of checks you purchased and of those you have used, and keep the record separate from the checks themselves. The numbers are necessary for obtaining a refund of lost checks.

Bring traveler's checks in US dollars, in $50 and $100 denominations. Traveler's checks in a foreign currency can only be changed at a bank or exchange counter in a large city. This can be inconvenient, you may not get a good exchange rate, and you may have to pay an exchange fee.

ATMs
ATMs (automated teller machines) are available 24 hours a day at almost every bank, as well as at shopping centers, grocery stores and airports. You can withdraw cash from an ATM using a credit card (Visa, MasterCard etc), which will usually incur a fee. Alternatively, most ATMs are linked with one or more of the main ATM networks (Plus, Cirrus, Exchange, Accel), and you can use them to withdraw funds from an overseas bank account if you have a card affiliated with the appropriate network. This is usually cheaper than a credit card transaction. The exchange rate on ATM transactions is usually as good as you'll get.

Contact your bank or credit card company for information about using its cards at ATMs in the USA. If you will be relying on ATMs, bring more than one card and keep them separate. Don't forget your personal identification number, but don't write it on the card. Contact your bank if you lose your card.

Credit & Debit Cards

Major credit cards are accepted at hotels, restaurants, gas stations, shops and car-rental agencies throughout the USA. It's almost impossible to rent a car or make phone reservations without one. Even if you'll be relying mostly on cash, it's highly recommended that you carry a credit card for emergencies, rentals and reservations. If you're planning to rely primarily upon credit cards, bring more than one and include a Visa or MasterCard in your deck, since other cards aren't as widely accepted.

Places that accept Visa and MasterCard are also likely to accept debit cards. A debit card deducts payment directly from the user's bank account, and users are charged a small fee for the transaction. Check with your bank to confirm that your debit card will be accepted in the USA; you may have to change your PIN (Personal Identification Number) to one with four digits.

Carry copies of your credit card numbers separately from the cards. If you lose your cards or they get stolen, contact the company immediately. Following are toll-free numbers for the main credit card companies:

American Express	☎ 800-528-4800
Diners Club	☎ 800-234-6377
Discover	☎ 800-347-2683
MasterCard	☎ 800-826-2181
Visa	☎ 800-336-8472

International Transfers

You can instruct your bank back home to send you a draft, provided you stay in the city where it will arrive for at least a week. Specify the city, bank and branch to which you want the money directed, or ask your home bank to tell you where a suitable one is and make sure you get the details right. The procedure is easier if you've authorized someone at home to access your account.

Money sent by telegraphic transfer should reach you within a week; by mail, allow at least two weeks. When it arrives it will most likely be converted into local currency – you can take it as cash or buy traveler's checks.

You can also transfer money by American Express, Thomas Cook or Western Union, though the latter has fewer international offices. These services are expensive, but faster.

On the Hike

Most hikers will find that they don't need any money once they are on the trail. Except on trails that pass through or near populated areas, such as the Pacific Crest and Appalachian Trails, there is generally no place to spend money once you've left the trailhead. Before leaving, you may need to buy a permit or parking pass from a visitor center or ranger station, or self-register at a trailhead parking lot; in such situations it is best to have cash, as out-of-state (or country) checks are rarely accepted and traveler's checks are looked askance at. Similarly, in small-town stores or restaurants where credit cards are not accepted, cash is usually the only accepted method of payment.

This doesn't mean that you must carry gobs of cash around. Most stores and restaurants do accept credit cards, and those in towns near heavily touristed areas (such as national parks) are familiar with traveler's checks. Pay for supplies, gas, between-hike food and accommodations with a credit card, and keep cash on hand for permits and entry fees. Knowing how much a permit is going to cost will help you to decide how much cash to carry. It's also advisable to stash $20 (I break it into a $10 bill, $5 bill and five $1 bills) in your pack (or somewhere secure) for unforseen emergencies.

Security

Usually, there's nothing to worry about in the backcountry, but it's a good idea to divide your money and credit cards and stash them in several places. Keep copies of all your documents, and an extra bit of cash, in your car, but keep the originals with you in a waterproof bag; while on the trail you may want to keep them in an inside pocket of your pack, but in public areas (like campgrounds, towns and national park centers) it's best to keep them on your person. Most hotels and hostels provide safekeeping, so you can leave your valuables with them. Using a safety pin or key ring to hold the zipper tags of your pack together can help deter theft. If you're being cautious, put a small combination lock on the zipper.

Costs

The cost of travel in the USA depends a great deal on the degree of comfort you require and the things you want to do. Generally, it's more expensive to travel alone than as a couple, a family or a small group. Spreading the cost of a national park entry fee, backcountry permit and topo map among several people can greatly cut costs. Moving around a lot costs more than staying longer in fewer places. The main expenses are transportation, accommodations, food, sightseeing and entertainment. In addition to permit and park entry fees, which vary from hike to hike, typical expenditures are:

hostel bed	$11 to $17 per person
budget motel room	$30/34 single/double
campground fee	$7 to $14 per site
budget restaurant	$6 per person
glass of wine/beer	$3.50
loaf of bread	$2
brick of cheese	$2.50
instant noodle soup	$1
candy bar	$0.85
map	$9
gasoline	$1.40 per gallon
local phone call	$0.35
major newspaper	$0.50

Tipping

Tipping is expected in restaurants and better hotels and by guides, taxi drivers and baggage carriers. People waiting tables in restaurants are paid minimal wages and rely upon tips for their livelihoods. Tip 15% unless the service is terrible or up to 20% if the service is great. Never tip in fast-food, take-out or buffet-style restaurants where you serve yourself.

Baggage carriers (skycaps in airports and bellhops in hotels) should be tipped $1 for one bag and 50c for each additional bag. In budget hotels, tips are not expected. Guides should be tipped a minimum of $5 per person, per day – more if they go out of their way to explain history, geology and the like, or attend to your personal needs.

Taxes

Public campground fees, entry to public lands (national parks, forests etc) and back-country permits are not taxed – but just about everything else you pay for in the USA is. The tax on restaurant meals and drinks, accommodations and most purchases is added to the advertised cost. Occasionally, the tax is included in the advertised price (eg, gas, drinks in a bar and admission to museums or theaters).

A few states have no sales tax, and in others it varies up to about 8%. In addition, there may be local and city sales taxes (maybe an extra 5%) and sometimes other separate taxes, such as a 'bed tax' (usually 4%) on lodging or a special tax on car rentals. When inquiring about hotel or motel rates, be sure to ask whether taxes are included. Unless otherwise stated, the prices given in this book don't include taxes.

POST & COMMUNICATIONS
Post

The US Postal Service (USPS) is reliable and inexpensive, though Americans often complain about it. It is, by a wide margin, the busiest postal service in the world, handling astronomical numbers of letters and parcels every day.

Postal Rates Rates for 1st-class mail within the USA are 33c for letters up to 1oz (22c for each additional ounce) and 20c for postcards.

International airmail rates (except to Canada and Mexico) are 60c for a half-ounce letter, $1 for a 1oz letter and 40c for each additional half ounce. International postcard rates are 50c. Letters to Canada are 46c for a half-ounce letter, 52c for a 1oz letter and 40c for a postcard. Letters to Mexico are 40c for a half-ounce letter, 46c for a 1oz letter and 35c for a postcard. Aerograms are 50c.

The cost for parcels airmailed anywhere within the USA is $3.20 for 2lbs or less, increasing by $1 per pound up to $6 for 5lbs. For heavier items, rates differ according to the distance mailed – the maximum weight is 70lbs. Books, periodicals and computer disks can be sent by a cheaper 4th-class rate.

For 24-hour postal information, call ☎ 800-275-8777 or check 🖳 www.usps.com. Each gives zip (postal) codes for a given address, the rules about parcel sizes, and the location and phone number of any post office.

Sending Mail If you have the correct postage, you can drop your mail into any blue mailbox. To buy stamps, weigh your mail, or send a package 16oz or heavier, go to a post office. There are branch post offices and post-office centers in many supermarkets and drugstores. National park visitor centers and, occasionally, ranger stations sell stamps and have a mailbox, but do not send packages. For the address of the nearest post office, call ☎ 800-275-8777. Post offices in main towns are usually open 8 am to 5 pm Monday to Friday and 8 am to 2 pm Saturday.

Receiving Mail General delivery mail (ie, poste restante) can be sent to you c/o General Delivery at any post office that has its own zip code. Mail is usually held for 10 days before it's returned to sender; you might request your correspondents to write 'Hold for Arrival' on their letters. You'll need photo identification to collect general delivery mail. In some big cities, general delivery mail is not held at the main post office but at a postal facility away from downtown. Alternatively, have mail sent to the local representative of American Express or Thomas Cook, which provide mail services for their customers. Hotels and national park lodges will often receive mail for people staying with them for several days, as long as you notify them and ask permission in advance.

Telephone

The US phone system comprises numerous regional phone companies (many are Bell subsidiaries), competing long-distance carriers, and lots of smaller mobile-phone and pay-phone companies. Technically, the system is very efficient, but it's geared to the needs of local users and for foreign visitors it's inconvenient and often expensive. Try to bring a telephone card from your home phone company – it may not be the cheapest call option, but it will probably offer better information and service than a US pay-phone company or a phone debit card.

Telephone Numbers If you're calling from abroad, the international country code for the USA is ☎ 1.

All phone numbers within the USA consist of a three-digit area code followed by a seven-digit local number. If you are calling a number within the same area code, just dial the seven-digit number. If you are calling long distance, dial ☎ 1 plus the area code plus the phone number.

The ☎ 800 and ☎ 888 prefixes are for toll-free numbers. These calls are free, though sometimes the toll-free number is not available from the same locality or state, or from outside the state. (The ☎ 900 prefix is for calls for which the caller pays a premium rate – phone sex, horoscopes, jokes etc.)

Directory Assistance For local directory assistance dial ☎ 411. For directory assistance outside your area code, dial ☎ 1 plus the three-digit area code of the place you want to call plus 555-1212 – this is charged as a long-distance call to that area.

To find a number in another country, call the international operator at ☎ 00. International directory assistance can be very expensive from a pay phone.

International Calls To make an international call direct, dial ☎ 011, then the country code (which you can find in the front of most phone directories), followed by the area code and the phone number. The country codes for the following are: Australia (61), France (33), Germany (49), Japan (81), Netherlands (31), New Zealand (64), UK (44). Canadian area codes, similar to those in the USA, are found with American ones in the front of most phone directories.

International rates vary depending on the time of day and the destination. Call the operator for rates. The first minute is always more expensive than those that follow.

Call Charges Most local calls can be made for free from private domestic phones and for a flat fee from a pay phone. Calls made to numbers within the same area code but outside the local calling zone (typically about 15mi) are charged by the minute. Long-distance charges vary depending on the destination and the telephone company you use – call the operator (☎ 0) for rate information. Don't ask the operator to put your call through, however, because operator-assisted calls are much more expensive than direct-dial calls. Generally, nights (11 pm to 8 am), all day Saturday and 8 am to 5 pm Sunday are the cheapest times to call (60% discount). Evenings (5 to 11 pm Sunday to Friday) are mid-priced (35% discount). Day calls (8 am to 5 pm Monday to Friday) are full-priced within the USA.

Phonecards Phonecards are now almost essential for travelers using the US phone system. There are two basic types. A phone credit card allows you to make calls that are billed to your home phone number. Some cards issued by foreign phone companies will work in the USA – inquire before you leave home. When using a phone credit card, be aware of people watching you, especially in public places like airports and bus stations. Thieves can memorize numbers and use them to make calls at your expense. Shield the telephone with your body when punching in your credit card number.

Alternatively, phone debit cards are widely available from vending machines in airports, bus stations and hotel lobbies in big cities. You purchase the card with a specified value, say $5, $10, $20 or $50 for 18, 38, 80 or 220 'units.' To call, you access the company through an 800 number, key in your PIN, and a synthetic voice will tell you how many domestic or international minutes your card is good for. The cost of calls is immediately debited from the value of the card. Rates vary between the debit cards, and the cheapest generally are competitive with rates charged by a US phone company on a domestic phone. If you use a phone debit card from a pay phone or a hotel, many systems will debit two units from your card for the initial connection. If you have several calls to make, use the card's

follow-on option to save the connection fee and the hassle of repeating the PIN.

Lonely Planet's rechargeable eKno Communication Card (see the insert at the back of this book) is aimed specifically at independent travelers and provides budget international calls, a range of messaging services, free email and travel information – for local calls, you're usually better off with a local card. You can join at 🖳 www.ekno.lonely planet.com, or by phone from within the US (48 states) by dialling ☎ 1800-707-0031. Once you have joined, to use eKno from within the continental US dial ☎ 1800-706-1333 (Los Angeles local call: ☎ 927-0100).

Check the eKno website for joining and access numbers from other countries, and updates on super-budget local access numbers and new features.

Hotel Phones Many hotels and motels add a service charge of 50c to $1 for each local call made from a room phone, and they have hefty surcharges for long-distance calls. They even charge you for calling 800 numbers. Ask if they offer free calls before picking up the phone.

Cell (Mobile) Phones For information on the use of cell phones in the backcountry, see Rescue & Evacuation in the Health & Safety chapter.

Fax

Fax machines are easy to find in the USA at shipping companies like Mail Boxes Etc, photocopy services, and hotel business-service centers, but be prepared to pay high prices (more than $1 a page). While generally good for booking accommodations, rental cars and backcountry permits, more and more places prefer to do business online.

Email & Internet

If you want to surf the net or send the occasional email message, most public libraries have a computer with Internet access. Other options are an Internet cafe, a copy center (like Kinko's, which charges about $10 per hour) or a hotel that caters to business travelers. Some hostels even offer Internet access to their guests. The cheapest way to have email access while traveling is to get a free, web-based email account such as Lonely Planet's eKno (🖳 www.ekno.lonelyplanet .com), Hotmail (🖳 www.hotmail.com) or Yahoo! (🖳 www.yahoo.com). This way you can access your mail from cybercafes and other facilities anywhere in the world using any net-connected machine running a standard web browser such as Explorer or Netscape.

INTERNET RESOURCES

Most hiking, backpacking, conservation and government organizations have a web page (listed after the telephone number throughout this book). Some noteworthy sites focused on hiking are:

American Trails Has a 'Trails State by State' page with links to related private and government organizations in each state. 🖳 www.outdoor link.com/amtrails/index.html

Great Outdoor Recreation Pages A bit heavy on mainstream, corporate advertising, but it has interesting articles that are constantly updated to reflect the seasons, and draws a good crowd to its chat rooms.
🖳 www.gorp.com

Life on the Trail Reviews of backpacking gear, recipes and women's issues, and a knowledgeable editorial staff who responds to queries about any of these subjects. 🖳 www.lifeonthe trail.com

Lightweight Backpacking A good place to find equipment information, hiking and packing tips, books and specifics on winter, ultralight and beginning-backpacking skills.
🖳 www.backpacking.net/contents.html

Lonely Planet Information about most places on earth, linked to the Thorn Tree bulletin board and Postcards, where you can catch up on postings from fellow travellers. The website also has travel news and updates to many of Lonely Planet's most popular guidebooks, and the sub-WWWay section links you to the most useful travel resources elsewhere on the web.
🖳 www.lonelyplanet.com

Mountain Zone Updated daily, with news and longer articles about anything to do with mountain sports (mostly mountaineering).
🖳 www.mountainzone.com

Peak to Peak A vast network of links to hiking clubs and organizations, state parks, national parks, national forests and wilderness areas.
🖳 www.peaktopeak.net

Trailplace An interactive site for Appalachian Trail thru-hikers.
🖳 www.trailplace.com

BOOKS
Lonely Planet

For more detailed information about specific regions of the continental USA, look for Lonely Planet's guides to the following destinations:

Alaska	*New York City*
Backpacking in Alaska	*New York, New Jersey & Pennsylvania*
California & Nevada	*Pacific Northwest*
Chicago	*Rocky Mountains*
Deep South	*San Francisco*
Florida	*Seattle*
Los Angeles	*Southwest*
Miami	*Texas*
New England	*Washington, DC & the Capital Region*
New Orleans	

Hiking Guidebooks

The list of regional hiking guides to the USA is grand and ranges from very good to very, very poor (in terms of both organization and accuracy). For this reason it's best to rely on titles from publishers which have established a good reputation in the hiking field. These include Seattle-based The Mountaineers Books, whose titles include *Hiking the Great Northwest* (1998); San Francisco-based Foghorn Press, which publishes the *Complete Guide to California Hiking* (1999); HumanKinetics Publishers, which has a hiking title for each of the 50 states; and Falcon Press, out of Helena, Montana, which publishes regional guides and smaller guides to national parks and wilderness areas.

Individual titles that veteran hikers recommend include *The Complete Walker III: The Joys and Techniques of Hiking & Backpacking* (1984), by Colin Fletcher; *Beyond Backpacking: Ray Jardines Guide to Lightweight Hiking* (1999) by Ray Jardines; Michael Mouland's *Complete Idiot's Guide to Camping & Hiking* (1999); and *How to Shit in the Woods* (1994), Kathleen Meyer's explicit, comical and useful manual on toilet training in the wilderness.

The Appalachian Trail Reader, edited by David Emblidge, is a collection of stories written by and about Appalachian Trail (AT) hikers that gets swapped around many a backcountry hut. For the Pacific Crest Trail, Jeffery P Schaffer's two-volume series, published by The Mountaineers Books, is unsurpassed.

You'll find that some regional guides, such as Rudy Lambrechtse's *Hiking the Escalante*, can achieve nearly biblical status when there is no other published material on an area. When this is the case, buy the book for reference but do not rely on it as a definitive source of guidance (you might ask local hikers who are familiar with the book if it is reliable or has any quirks).

Travel & Exploration
There's a long history of foreigners and Americans traveling around the country and trying to make sense of it. They include Alexis de Tocqueville in 1835–40, with *Democracy in America*; Charles Dickens, who wrote *American Notes* in 1842; Oscar Wilde, who wrote *Impressions of America* (1883); and GK Chesterton, who described his visit in *What I Saw in America* (1923).

Undaunted Courage (1996) by Stephen Ambrose tells the real-life adventure story of the Lewis and Clark expedition, which explored the Northwest in 1804–06. *My First Summer in the Sierra*, and any other book by John Muir, reveals his talent for lighthearted, poetic writing and passion for the outdoors. *In the Spirit of Adventure: A 1914 Smoky Mountains Hiking Journal* (1994) by DR Beeson is a classic for that region.

The Lost Continent (1989) by Bill Bryson is a wonderfully funny, personal and perceptive account of the author's search for the perfect American town. His latest book, *A Walk in the Woods: Rediscovering America on the Appalachian Trail* (1998) is excellent and a 'must' for any AT hikers. *There Are Mountains to Climb* (1996) by Jean Reeds is the inspirational story of her mid-life decision to leave her job and thru-hike the Appalachian Trail. *Blue Highways: A Journey into America* (1991) by William Least Heat-Moon, describes people and places the author encounters in his travels through side roads, rural areas and reservations.

Natural History
Like hiking guidebooks, natural history guides range from ultra-specific to nationwide in scope and are best chosen according to who publishes them. Peterson Field Guides (Houghton-Mifflin) are the definitive birding books in the USA, and also good for just about every outdoors subject – from trees to caterpillars. They also publish Flash Guides which feature at least 100 species on one plastic, foldable sheet. The Audubon Society Field Guides (AA Knopf) have good descriptions and large photos for their wide range of subjects. Golden Field Guides (St Martin's Press) are good for amateur naturalists and are lightweight.

You'll find these guides in local bookstores and large chains, or you can order them directly: Houghton-Mifflin (☎ 800-225-3362, 🖥 www.houghtonmifflin.com), 181 Ballardvale St, Wilmington, MA 01887; Alfred A Knopf (☎ 800-726-0600, 🖥 www.aaknopf.com), 400 Hahn Rd, Westminster, MD 21157. Golden Field Guides are only sold in stores and online (see Buying Books later in this section).

For more specific suggestions see the Flora & Fauna special section earlier in this book.

General
Living & Working in America (1995) by David Hampshire is a thorough and useful guide for anyone planning a long-term visit.

Cadillac Desert: The American West and its Disappearing Water by Marc Reisner is an altogether fascinating environmental history of the West and its quest for water. For the history (or prehistory) of the earliest Americans, see *The American Indians: Their Archaeology and Prehistory* (1976) by D Snow; or *Ancient North America* (1995) by Brian Fagan.

Books by Chicago radio-man Studs Terkel consist almost entirely of interviews in which Americans from every class and culture talk about their lives. His books include *Division Street* (1967), about Chicagoans; *Working* (1972), in which 'people talk about how they feel about what they do'; *American Dreams: Lost and Found* (1999); and *The Great Divide: Second Thoughts on the American Dream* (1988).

Buying Books

The best source for regional guides will be the local bookstore, outdoors store or visitor center in that region's largest town. Bookstores at national park visitor centers are usually managed by the park's natural history association and generally have an excellent selection and fair prices.

US nationwide booksellers such as Barnes & Noble, B Dalton and Crown Books may not have the specific title you're looking for, but they can probably order it for you. See Books under Information in the individual hikes chapters for where to find recommended reading.

If fingering a book before buying it is not important, go online to get the best selection and lowest prices. Amazon (💻 www.amazon .com) is the biggest and probably best source.

MAGAZINES

There's a plethora of outdoors-oriented magazines in the USA including *Outside*, which can be found in airports and supermarkets. It's online version (💻 www.out-sideonline .com) is updated daily and has current news on outdoor gear, destinations and personalities. Specifically for hikers is *Backpacker: The Magazine of Wilderness Travel*, found in some general bookstores, the occasional supermarket and most outdoors stores. It, too, has an excellent website (💻 www.back packer.com) with links to national parks and more.

WEATHER INFORMATION

Most newspapers have local and national weather forecasts (look for 'Weather' on the front page index). In the front section of the White Pages and Yellow Pages phone directories (found at most public phones), listed under 'Weather' in the 'US Government' section, is a local number you can call to get updated weather information for your surrounding area. National park visitor centers and ranger stations get frequent weather updates which they post on bulletin boards in the station, or outside near park entrances.

The government department that handles forecasts, marine warnings and the like is the National Weather Service. Its website, Internet Weather Source (💻 www.weather.noaa .gov/), is detailed and accurate but can be cumbersome if you just want fast facts. Quicker is the University of Michigan's WeatherNet (💻 cirrus.sprl.umich.edu/wxnet), which covers the past 24 hours of weather (including relative humidity, sunrise and sunset times), forecasts and warnings for even the most remote corners of the USA.

Radio hounds can pick up a National Weather Radio receiver for $25 to $100 at electronics stores throughout the USA (Radio Shack is a good one). With the receiver you can access 24-hour weather news, warnings and forecasts on the public band between 162.400 and 162.550 MHz. For a current list of frequencies and transceiver locations, go to 💻 www.nws.noaa/gov/nwr.

PHOTOGRAPHY
Film & Equipment

Stock up on film at your point of entry, as selection is limited and prices are high, high, high in small towns and national park visitor centers. If you do find yourself in the back of beyond and out of film, check the local pharmacy, grocery store (or supermarket if there is one), outdoors store and hardware store, in that order.

Print film is more widely available than slide film, and black-and-white film is rarely sold outside major cities. Advance Photo System (APS) film (such as Kodak's Advantix) is becoming quite popular but is hard to find in smaller towns.

Drugstores are a good place to get your film processed cheaply – around $6 for a roll of 24 exposures. One-hour processing services are more expensive, usually from around $11.

Film can be damaged by excessive heat, so don't leave your camera or film in the top compartment of your backpack or in your car on a hot day. Always bring a spare battery for your camera and tote a good waterproof camera bag or a heavy duty, sealable plastic bag to store camera and film in the wet (a Gore-Tex stuff sack also works well).

Technique

When the sun is high, photographs tend to emphasize shadows and wash out highlights. It's best to take photos during early morning and late afternoon hours, when the light is softer. This is especially true of landscape photography. To photograph elusive wildlife, plant yourself in a meadow or near a water source in the pre-dawn hours, or just after sunset, and be prepared to wait in one spot, camera poised, for an hour or so. A tripod will alleviate cramped neck and finger muscles.

Always protect camera lenses with a haze or ultraviolet (UV) filter. At high altitudes, the UV filter may not adequately prevent washed-out photos; a polarizing filter can correct this problem and dramatically emphasize cloud formations.

Many national parks, eg, Yosemite, offer free photography seminars and/or hikes with a photographer who knows the area and can make suggestions. Look for listings in the national park newspaper, or ask at the visitor center.

Restrictions

There aren't any restrictions on photographing trees or sunrises, so you're not likely to encounter restrictions in the backcountry. When touring around, be aware that most restrictions are for commercial or PR reasons. Many galleries won't let you photograph artwork but will sell photos of it in the museum store. At some attractions, like Disneyland, it's a condition of entry that you won't take photos for commercial purposes. There don't seem to be any restrictions on photographing military hardware or bases – if you're allowed to see it, you're allowed to photograph it.

Photography is commonly prohibited at Native American pueblos, ceremonies and reservations, but sometimes permitted with payment of a fee. Native Americans usually expect to be tipped if you take their photo.

Photographing People

There's usually no problem with medium or long shots, but if you want a close shot, you should always ask – pointing at the camera and smiling will usually get an affirmative nod. Street people and the destitute may refuse or ask for money.

Airport Security

All airline passengers have to pass their luggage through X-ray machines. Technology as it is in the USA doesn't jeopardize lower-speed film, so you shouldn't have to worry about cameras going through the machine. If you have high-speed film (1600 ASA and above), you may want to carry your film spools loose (in a Tupperware or similar clear-plastic container) and ask the X-ray inspector to visually check the film.

TIME

There are four one-hour time zones across the continental USA (Alaska and Hawaii cover two more time zones.) See map on page 81.

When it's noon in New York, Detroit, Atlanta and Miami, it's 11 am in Chicago, Kansas City and Dallas; 10 am in Salt Lake City, Denver and Albuquerque; 9 am in Seattle, San Francisco and Los Angeles; 8 am in Anchorage; and 7 am in Honolulu.

Daylight saving time, when clocks are moved forward one hour, runs from the first Sunday in April to the last Sunday in October in most states. The few exceptions include Arizona and Hawaii.

ELECTRICITY

In the USA voltage is 110V, and plugs have two flat pins, or two flat pins plus a round one. Plugs with three pins don't fit into a two-hole socket, but adaptors are easy to buy at hardware stores and drugstores. Two-pin plugs can easily slip out of the socket, so stretch the prongs apart a little for a tighter fit.

WEIGHTS & MEASURES

Distances are in feet (ft), yards (yd) and miles (mi). Three feet equal 1yd (.914m); 1760yd, or 5280ft, are 1mi (1.61km). Dry

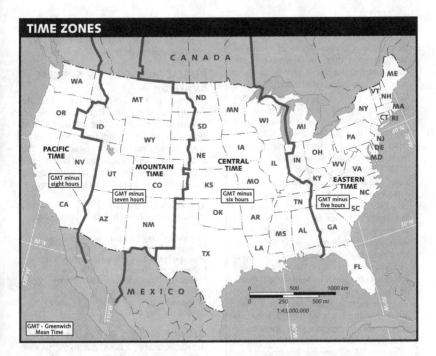

weights are in ounces (oz), pounds (lbs) and tons – 16oz equal 1lb (.45kg); 2000lbs equal 1 ton (907kg), but liquid measures differ from dry measures. One pint equals 16 fluid oz; 2 pints equal 1 quart – a common measure for liquids like milk. Milk is also sold in half gallons (2 quarts) and gallons (4 quarts). US pints and quarts are 20% less than Imperial ones. Gasoline is dispensed by the US gallon, which is also about 20% less than the Imperial gallon. A conversion chart is at the back of this book.

LAUNDRY

There are self-service, coin-operated laundry facilities in most towns of any size and at better campgrounds. Washing a load costs about $1 and drying it another $1. Some laundries have attendants who will wash, dry and fold your clothes for an additional charge. To find a laundry, look under 'Laundries' or 'Laundries – Self-Service' in the Yellow Pages of the telephone

directory. Dry cleaners are also listed under 'Laundries' or 'Cleaners.'

On the trail, never use soap to do laundry. Soak your dirties overnight, scrub them with a rock, rinse them and put them in the direct sunlight. This may not get all of the stink out of well-worn socks, but it will make an improvement. A favorite washing product (for teeth, pots and pans, hair and clothes) is Dr Bronner's, an all-natural liquid available at REI, EMS, other outdoors stores and most health food stores. No soap at all is still a better option, however.

BUSINESS HOURS

Generally businesses open at 9 or 10 am and close at 5 or 6 pm, but there are no hard and fast rules. In large cities, there are a few supermarkets, restaurants and a post office that stay open 24 hours. Some stores are open until 9 pm, especially those in shopping malls, and many open for shorter hours on Sunday (typically noon to 5 pm).

Metrication in the USA

Despite the recommendations of the Metric Study Group in 1971, the USA has not generally adopted the metric system. To do so would require a concerted effort by federal authorities, and this is unlikely with the current cynicism about the role of 'big government.' Metrication is actually raised as a bogeyman by right-wing, Rush Limbaugh-types who regard it as unwarranted government interference and an attempt to foist world government on freedom-loving Americans. The politicians are keeping well clear.

Nevertheless, substantial sections of US society have already adopted the metric system. The largest of these is the military, which had to go metric to be compatible with other NATO forces. Presumably most defense-related industries have to supply the military with goods in metric measures. The whole scientific community has for years been using SI (International System of Units) measurements, which are basically metric. Medicine is metric in the laboratories, but not in the clinics, where patients are weighed in pounds, measured in inches and have their temperatures taken in Fahrenheit. Blood pressure, however, is measured in millimeters of mercury (mmHg).

Most consumer goods are sold in Imperial units, but the metric equivalent is usually marked somewhere on the packaging, either for the convenience of the large immigrant population or to facilitate export sales. One product that is always marketed in metric units is wine – the standard bottle of wine is 750ml.

In most areas, post offices are open 8 am to 4 or 5:30 pm Monday to Friday, and some are also open 8 am to 3 pm on Saturday. Banks are usually open either 9 or 10 am to 5 or 6 pm Monday to Friday. A few banks are open 9 am to 2 or 4 pm on Saturday. Hours are decided by individual branches.

Ranger stations and national park visitor centers are generally open daily 8 or 9 am to 6 or 7 pm from Memorial Day to Labor Day; in the busiest parks they may stay open until 8 pm. After Labor Day they open later, close earlier and may close for an hour in the middle of the day. In winter, many open on weekends only.

PUBLIC HOLIDAYS & SPECIAL EVENTS

National public holidays are celebrated throughout the USA. Banks, schools and government offices (including post offices) are closed and transportation, museums and other services operate on a Sunday schedule. Many stores, however, maintain regular business hours. Holidays falling on a weekend are usually observed the following Monday.

New Year's Day January 1
Martin Luther King Jr Day January – 3rd Monday
Presidents' Day February – 3rd Monday
Memorial Day May – Last Monday
Independence Day ('Fourth of July') July 4
Labor Day September – 1st Monday
Columbus Day October – 2nd Monday
Veterans' Day November 11
Thanksgiving November – 4th Thursday
Christmas Day December 25

Other Holidays & Events

Besides the above holidays, the USA celebrates a number of other events. Some of the most widely observed ones are:

Chinese New Year January – Begins at the end of January or beginning of February and lasts two weeks. The first day is celebrated with parades, firecrackers, fireworks and lots of food.
Valentine's Day February 14 – No one knows why St Valentine is associated with romance in the USA, but this is the day to celebrate.
St Patrick's Day March 17 – The patron saint of Ireland is honored by all those who feel the Irish in their blood as well as by those who want to feel Irish beer in their blood. Everyone wears green (if you don't, you can get pinched).
Easter March-April – Secular rituals of painting eggs, eating chocolate and searching for eggs hidden by the 'Easter bunny.' (Good Friday is not a public holiday.)
Mother's Day May – 2nd Sunday. Children send cards and flowers and call Mom. Restaurants are likely to be busy.
National Trails Day June – 1st Saturday. Events to raise people's trail awareness range from local trail runs to maintenance projects to full-city trail festivals. Contact the American Hiking Society for information.

Father's Day June – 3rd Sunday. Same idea, different parent.

Halloween October 31 – Kids and adults dress in costumes. Children go 'trick-or-treating' for candy. Adults go to parties to act out their alter egos.

Day of the Dead November 2 – Observed in areas with Mexican communities, this is a day for families to honor deceased relatives and make breads and sweets resembling skeletons, skulls and such.

Election Day November – 2nd Tuesday.

Chanukah December – date determined by the Hebrew calendar. An eight-day Jewish holiday (also called Hannukkah or the Feast of Lights) commemorating the victory of the Maccabees over the armies of Syria.

Kwanzaa December 26-31 – This African American celebration is a time to give thanks for the harvest.

New Year's Eve December 31 – People celebrate with few traditions other than dressing up and drinking champagne or watching the festivities on TV. The following day people stay home to nurse their hangovers and watch college football.

ACCOMMODATIONS
Between Hikes

Big cities have every sort of accommodations, from bed and breakfasts (B&Bs) with floral curtains and antique furniture to old motels whose carpet saw platform shoes the first time they were in. Small towns, especially in the West, have a narrow range of accommodations but generally have a few small motels where a double room costs less than $50. Motel and hotel chains are commonly clustered together near freeway exits. AAA (see Useful Organizations earlier in this chapter) publishes an annual guide to accommodations across the USA.

Campgrounds Basic national forest and BLM campsites usually have toilets, fire pits, picnic benches and drinking water (but it's always a good idea to have a few gallons of water with you), and typically cost about $5 to $7 a night. Many are occupied on a first-come, first-served basis. Arrive early, especially on weekends.

State and national park campgrounds, which cost several dollars more, often have hot showers and sometimes RV hookups (powered sites). They may also accept or require reservations. The National Park Reservation System (☎ 800-365-2267, 301-722-1257 outside the USA; 🖥 www.nps.gov) allows you to reserve a park campsite five months prior to your visit, beginning on the 15th of each month for Yosemite and on the 5th for all other national parks. The National Forest Service also has a reservation system (☎ 877-444-7777, 🖥 reserveusa.com) allowing visitors to make camping reservations up to four months in advance. The cost is $8.65 per reservation.

Many private campgrounds look like paved parking lots, but some have grassy, shaded sites for tents. Tent sites start at around $14 for two people, plus $1 to $3 for each extra person. RV sites usually cost around $15 to $20, but $25 or $30 is possible at peak times in popular locations. Facilities include hot showers, coin laundry and often a swimming pool, games area, playground and convenience store. Kampgrounds of America (KOA) is a national network of private campgrounds, with sites usually ranging from $12 to $15, or around $20 with hookups. You can get the annual directory of KOA sites by calling ☎ 406-248-7444 or writing PO Box 30558, Billings, MT 59114-0558.

Hostels Hostels near a national park or outdoors destination are good for meeting other hikers and finding out about the region. The better ones (Bozeman, Montana, and Yosemite Bug come to mind) arrange excursions and offer transportation within the region for a minimal fee. Hostelling International/American Youth Hostels (HI/AYH) are scattered thinly across the country, with the Northeast, Colorado and the west coast having the most facilities. These usually charge $10 to $12 for a dormitory bed ($2 or $3 more for nonmembers), and $25 to $30 for a private room – if they have any. If your sleeping bag looks like its been on the trail for a few weeks, you'll probably have to rent bed linens for around $2.

Independent hostels, often called backpackers hostels, are usually a few dollars cheaper and have a wide range of standards.

Both types of hostel usually have kitchen and laundry facilities, information and advertising boards, a TV room and lounge area. HI/AYH hostels are more likely to have a curfew and prohibit alcohol.

Get information from HI/AYH (☎ 202-783-6161, ✉ hiayhserve@hiayh.org, 🖥 www.hiayh.org), 733 15th St NW, Suite 840, Washington, DC 20005, or use its code-based reservation service at ☎ 800-909-4776 (to use this service you need the access code for the hostel, available from any HI/AYH office or listed in its handbook.)

B&Bs These are for people who want a comfortable, atmospheric alternative to impersonal motel rooms. Typically they are in restored, old houses and are in the $50 to $100 price range, for a room and substantial breakfast for two. B&B owners prefer advance reservations, though some will happily oblige the occasional drop-in. Look for *Bed & Breakfast USA*, the *Complete Guide to American Bed & Breakfasts* or guides concentrating on the areas you fancy.

Hotels & Motels Hotels differ from motels in that they do not surround a car park and usually have some sort of a lobby. Motel and hotel prices vary tremendously from season to season; prices quoted in this book are for the high season, unless otherwise noted. You can often get a cheaper rate for a stay of several days, but you may have to pay it all in advance. Simply asking about 'specials' can often get you a discount.

The cheapest motels are usually small, independent (ie, nonchain) establishments whose prices go as low as $20. Rooms are usually small, and beds may be soft or saggy, but they normally have a private shower, toilet and TV. Some motel rooms have 'kitchenettes' with a small burner, fridge and sink.

Downtown hotels tend to be either very expensive or very seedy, without much in between. Old hotels, often near the train or bus station, sometimes double as transient rooming houses. If you have any doubts about the place, ask to see the room first.

Chain motels usually fall in the mid-range price category and maintain a consistent

level of quality and style (sterile, both) across the country. The cheapest national chain is Motel 6, which charges from $20 for a single in smaller towns, in the $30s in larger towns, plus an extra $6 for each additional person. Motel chains in the next price level (Super 8, Days Inn, Econo Lodge) have firmer beds, cable TV, and free coffee. Stepping up to the $45 to $80 range (Best Western, Holiday Inn, Comfort Inn) you'll find noticeably nicer rooms, on-site or adjacent cafes, restaurants and/or bars, and perhaps an indoor swimming pool, spa or exercise room. At the highest end (Hilton, Hyatt, Radisson, Sheraton) are rooms for $100 or more in places with gourmet restaurants, in-room spas and bathrobes.

Chain motels have central reservation systems and will take reservations days or months ahead. Normally, you have to give a credit-card number to hold the room. If you don't show up and don't call to cancel, you will be charged for the first night's rental.

For reservations, call the following:

Best Western	☎ 800-528-1234
Comfort Inn	☎ 800-228-5150
Days Inn	☎ 800-329-7466
	(800-DAYS-INN)
Econo Lodge	☎ 800-553-2666
	(800-55-ECONO)
Hilton	☎ 800-445-8667
Holiday Inn	☎ 800-465-4329
Hyatt	☎ 800-233-1234
Motel 6	☎ 800-466-8356
	(800-4MOTEL6)
Radisson	☎ 800-333-3333
Sheraton	☎ 800-325-3535
Super 8 Motel	☎ 800-800-8000
Travelodge	☎ 800-578-7878

Lodges Lodges in attractive scenic areas typically affect a rusticated style (lots of logs and stonework) but are usually very comfortable inside. They often have restaurants and excellent services, but can be very expensive. In national parks, the only accommodations other than camping are park lodges. These are usually operated as a concession and are quite comfortable, but overpriced for the quality they offer – around $100 for a double during the high season, when you need to make a reservation months in advance.

On the Hike

Camping Backcountry campsites vary from being a flat piece of earth that you find for yourself (preferably where someone has obviously camped before) to a clearing with logs set up as benches, a high bar from which to hang food and a wooden post giving the number of the site. The type of campsite to expect depends on where you are hiking: a wilderness area has campsites of the first description, national parks mostly have campsites of the second. (Each hike in this book has campground or campsite descriptions highlighted.)

Occasionally there will be more than one party assigned to one camping area. If this is the case, be respectful of your neighbors. Don't pitch your tent right smack next to theirs and don't spread your things out all over camp. Most importantly, don't stay up all night singing if they've gone to bed at 6 pm (and if they stay up all night singing, you have every right to ask them, nicely, to keep it quiet).

For information on trailhead campgrounds and accommodations, see Between Hikes earlier in this section.

Mountain Huts These are most common in New England, the Adirondacks and the Appalachian Mountains. Huts managed by the Appalachian Mountain Club (☎ 603-466-2727) have kitchen facilities, partially heated common rooms and unheated, coed bunkrooms. During the full-service season (June to Labor Day), staff are on hand to cook and serve two hot meals a day. During the shoulder seasons (spring and fall), most of the huts are open for self-service. The cost of hut stays is $64 per person, per night, and reservations and payments must be made in advance. These huts are very popular; if you're planning to go during peak times (summer weekends), reserve well in advance.

Lean-tos (rustic, three-sided shelters) are also scattered throughout New England and the Adirondack and Appalachian mountains. Overnight sites are first-come, first-served

and typically spaced no more than a moderate day's hike apart. Caretakers are sometimes on hand at high-use sites, where moderate fees ($5 to $7 per night) are charged.

FOOD
Local Food

Between hikes, you can entertain your deprived palate with Mexican food for breakfast, Chinese for lunch and Italian for dinner. Even in small rural towns, these three 'ethnic' cooking traditions get good (if not authentic) representation. For a real American meal, head to a 'diner' or 'coffee shop' where breakfast (less than $5) consists of pancakes, hearty omelettes or bacon and eggs (served with fried potatoes and toasted bread); lunch ($4 to $7) is along the lines of a hamburger, BLT (bacon, lettuce and tomato sandwich) or chef salad (with sliced ham, cheese and hard-boiled egg); and dinner ($6 to $11) might be chicken-fried steak (a piece of steak, breaded and pan-fried), spaghetti with meat sauce or fish-and-chips.

Americans love choices, and for every meal you'll have to answer a deluge of questions to complete your order: 'How do you want your eggs?', 'What kind of bread – white, wheat, rye or sourdough?', 'French fries, coleslaw, baked potato, potato salad, cottage cheese or sliced tomatoes with your sandwich?', 'Soup or salad?', 'What kind of salad dressing – Italian, blue cheese, Thousand Island, ranch or honey-mustard?' And these are just the basics.

Not particularly exciting or healthy, fast-food chains are cheap, reliable stand-bys for just about any meal and will usually have clean bathrooms. For hamburgers, the choices include McDonalds, Burger King, Carl's Jr and Wendy's. Jack in the Box (mostly in the Western states) has tacos and burritos as well as burgers, while Dairy Queen is best known for ice cream. Taco Bell serves really cheap and perfectly edible quasi-Mexican food, though often lacks a place to sit indoors. Pizza Hut and Round Table are the most common pizza-parlor chains and require a bit more time and money than other fast-food places. KFC is

Mexican Food

Mexican food deserves a special mention because it's so widespread and because there are interesting regional variations. The farther south you travel, the better and more frequent Mexican restaurants become. Chain restaurants like Taco Bell serve a milder version of Mexican food, which may be better for the faint of stomach.

For the real thing, find a place with red-vinyl booths, Mexican music blaring on the radio and fake flowers hung on the wall. Here you will get authentic enchiladas (chicken, beef or cheese wrapped in corn tortillas and covered with red or green sauce and cheese), tacos (fried corn tortillas filled with beef or chicken, cheese, lettuce and sauce), tamales (cornmeal patties stuffed with chicken or pork and wrapped in corn husks) and *huevos rancheros* (corn tortillas topped with fried eggs and red ranchero sauce), all of which come with chips, salsa, rice and beans. Not for the calorie conscious, most Mexican food contains substantial amounts of cheese and lard.

Tex-Mex food features more beef, beans and wheat-flour tortillas. A burrito is a flour tortilla filled with beans, rice and meat or vegetables. New Mexican food (ie, from New Mexico) can include blue corn tortillas, whole beans (not refried) and chilis served as a vegetable, as in *chilis rellenos* (stuffed chilis). Southwestern food used to be like Tex-Mex – Mexican but with more steak. Nouvelle Southwestern, or Santa Fe-style food, has elements of Mexican, Californian and continental cuisine, which means fresh ingredients, imaginative combinations, tasteful presentation, smaller servings and higher prices.

the most widespread fried-chicken chain. 'Family restaurants' like Sizzler or Denny's often have big servings of good quality but unspectacular food.

Vegetarian Vegetarians will find that most restaurants offer at least one veggie dish. Pasta with tomato sauce, cheese-only pizza and bean burritos are the most mundane, but the variety can be outstanding. If you see something that strikes your fancy but has meat in it, ask if the meat can be left out – most restaurants are very accommodating. At Mexican restaurants, be sure they cook with vegetable oil (instead of lard) before biting into the beans.

On the Hike

The food you take hiking should be nourishing, lightweight and tasty enough to look forward to at the end of the day. Day hikers have more choice in what they can eat, since they only have to carry it until lunchtime. Eat constantly when on the trail – your body needs more fuel than when sitting around at home, and many small meals are easier to digest on the go and at altitude. This does not mean eat to excess. Eat enough to keep your energy up but, as a rule of thumb, don't eat until you're full – just until you're satisfied. A general guideline is to eat 50% carbohydrates, 27% proteins and 23% fats while on the trail.

Pre-measure your rations and employ the strictest willpower to eat only the rations you have allotted for that day. Carrying emergency rations is advisable, although in my experience if these are too appetising they often get chowed before the trip is over. One idea is to carry a can of cat food with you – it will enable you to survive but you'll only eat it in a true emergency!

Outdoors stores supply dehydrated, freeze-dried meals that are pre-measured, pre-spiced, easy to cook and quite expensive. Dependable backpacking food companies are Mountain House, Backpackers Pantry and Alpine Aire (which produces several self-heating packages that require neither water nor a stove). Unless you have no tolerance for advanced food preparation, however, you can easily, and more cheaply, make your own lightweight meals from ingredients bought from a regular supermarket.

For a breakfast pick-up, instant oatmeal which comes in individual, pre-packaged servings or in bulk. Besides cutting down on packaging that you will have to pack out of the backcountry, buying bulk oatmeal lets you add a bunch of goodies to it before you go: try powdered milk, cinnamon, brown sugar, raisins, dried apples and nuts, and put it all together in a sealable plastic bag – then, just add water. Muesli is another option that doesn't require cooking.

Lunch, which is usually more like a bunch of snacks, consist of crackers, bagels, rye bread, peanut butter (no Vegemite here, Aussies!), jerky, trail mix, salami, cheese spread (not very healthy but it keeps forever), pretzels, granola or cereal bars, chocolate and dried fruit.

For dinner items, dried soups are a great base – particularly ramen (noodle soup), instant chili beans and powdered cream soups. Individual cup-like containers of dried soups can be dumped into a big, sealable plastic bag before you go to cut down on packaging (just remember to read or copy down the cooking directions first). Add lunch items (especially jerky and crackers) to soups to thicken them up, and remember to bring a small armada of spices (including powdered garlic), bouillon cubes and a small plastic bottle (with a sturdy top) of olive oil to fortify your stew. Rice is also good as a base, just make sure it's 'instant' or 'quick-cooking.'

Buying Food Large- and medium-sized towns have big supermarkets (Vons, Lucky, Ralph's, Safeway and Alpha Beta are a few) where the choices can be overwhelming. Some are open 24 hours and have a bakery, deli, florist, pharmacy and photo-development all under one roof. Even the smaller markets in smaller towns are likely to have a wide variety of items.

If the supermarket is lacking anything, such as bulk cereal, try a health food store.

Cooking Hikers generally use a stove to cook, so saving fuel is important. This is why pasta and regular-cooking rice are not recommended. Know how much your backpacking mug holds and use it as a measuring cup. When heating water, insulate the

The Counter-Balance Method

When camping in bear country, it is important to put yummy (or smelly) things – particularly food – safely out of reach. (See Safety on the Hike in the Health & Safety chapter for important safety advice on bears.) While ineffective in some popular hiking areas, the 'counter-balance method' is the most widely used technique for suspending your goodies.

Locate an unobstructed branch with a 6-inch diameter at least 20ft above the ground and extending at least 15ft away from the tree trunk. Tie a rock to one end of a rope of at least 50ft and throw it over the branch at least 10ft out from the trunk. Divide your food into two equally weighted portions and put into two sacks. Tie one sack to one end of the rope and hoist it to the branch. Tie the second bag as high on the rope as possible. Secure any excess rope to the second bag, leaving a loop out. Toss or push the second bag up until both bags hang at the same height. Retrieve the food by hooking the loop of rope with a long stick and slowly puling it down.

stove by surrounding it with rocks or an aluminum shield (available at outdoors stores) and keep the lid on the pot until you know the water is boiling (when the pot starts vibrating).

Eliminate dirty dishes by only heating water in your pot and keeping food items to your mug. For items that require lots of cooking this isn't possible, but for instant cereal, soups and noodles it works fine. Again, spices are lightweight and can turn a boring meal into something really tasty.

DRINKS
Alcoholic Drinks
If your identification says you're over 21 and you're not in a dry county, you can enjoy some of the best and cheapest booze in the world. Even in dry counties, some restaurants let you bring your own wine or beer.

Microbreweries, or 'brewpubs', offer beers brewed on the premises and you can get a dozen different types on tap. Supermarkets and big liquor stores can stock a bewildering variety of imported beers and local micro brews. If you're particularly fond of Foster's, Heineken or Moosehead at home, you may be disappointed to find that it has been wimped down for the American market – beer sold in the USA has a lower alcohol content than the beer in most other countries.

California is America's leading wine producer, but there are plenty of other wineries in New York, Pennsylvania, Washington, Oregon, Colorado, New Mexico and elsewhere. A reasonable bottle of Californian red or white can be bought for $6 to $10 at a supermarket or liquor store, but will be much more expensive in restaurants.

All bars have a big range of 'hard liquor': gin, brandy, rum, vodka, whiskey etc, invariably served with lots of ice ('on the rocks') unless you ask for it 'straight up.' If you ask for whiskey, you'll get American whiskey, which is called bourbon if it's made in Kentucky (eg, Jim Beam) or whiskey if it's not (eg, Jack Daniels). If you want Scotch whisky, ask for Scotch. The American taste for cocktails originated during Prohibition, when lots of flavorful mixers were used to disguise the taste of bathtub gin. These days there are thousands of named cocktail recipes, and many bars will have their own special concoction, usually with a fancy or a funny name.

On the Hike

Hydration is crucial. It's recommended that individuals drink 4 to 6L (6 or 7 quarts) per day. (Caffeine and alcohol don't count since they are diuretics, which flush fluids out.) Tea, coffee (available in individual 'tea bags' called 'singles' or as just-add-water instant powder), hot cocoa mix and powdered drink mixes such as Tang, Gatorade or ERG can make iodine-treated water more palpable. If you're relying on a powdered drink for a sugar fix, read the label carefully – many powdered juice-like drinks (such as Crystal Light) contain aspartaime instead of sugar, or are unsweetened.

See the Health & Safety chapter for more.

Health & Safety

The sections that follow aren't intended to alarm, but they are worth a skim before you go. Generally speaking, the USA is a healthy place to visit. There are no prevalent diseases, and the country is very well-served by hospitals and clinics. However, due to the high cost of health care, international visitors should take out comprehensive travel insurance (see Travel Insurance under Visas & Documents in the Facts for the Hiker chapter).

Hospitals and medical centers, walk-in clinics and referral services are easily found in towns and all national parks have a medical clinic. In an emergency call ☎ 911 for an ambulance to take you to the nearest hospital emergency room (ER), but note that both the ambulance and the ER will be incredibly expensive. Many city hospitals have 'urgent care clinics' which are designed to deal with less-than-catastrophic injuries and illnesses and are much cheaper.

Predeparture Planning

HEALTH INSURANCE
Travel health insurance is essential – some hospitals will refuse care without evidence that the patient is covered. If you have a choice between lower or higher medical expenses options, take the higher option for visiting the USA.

You may prefer a policy that pays doctors or hospitals directly, rather than you having to pay first and claim later. If you have to claim later, keep *all* documentation. Some policies ask you to call back (reverse charges) to a help center in your home country for an immediate assessment of your problem.

Check whether the policy covers ambulance fees or an emergency flight home. See also Travel Insurance under Visas & Documents in the Facts for the Hiker chapter.

IMMUNIZATIONS
Immunisations are not required for the USA (though evidence of cholera and yellow fever vaccinations may be necessary for those coming from infected areas) but before any trip it's a good idea to make sure that you are up to date with routine vaccinations such as diphtheria, polio and tetanus. It's particularly important that your tetanus is up to date – the initial course of three injections, usually given in childhood, must be followed by boosters every 10 years.

FIRST AID
It's a good idea at any time to know the appropriate responses to make in the event of a major accident or illness and it's especially important if you are intending to hike for some time in a remote area. Consider learning basic first aid on a recognized course before you go, or including a first-aid manual with your medical kit. Although detailed first-aid instruction is outside the scope of this guidebook, some basic points are listed under Traumatic Injuries later in this chapter. Prevention of accidents and illness is as important – see the boxed text 'Hike Safety – Basic Rules' on page 101 for more advice. You should also be aware of how to summon help should a major accident or illness befall you or someone with you – read the Rescue & Evacuation section later in this chapter.

OTHER PREPARATIONS
Make sure that you're healthy before you start traveling. If you have any known medical problems or are concerned about your health in any way, it's a good idea to have a full check-up before you go. It's far better to have any problems recognized and treated at home than to find out about them halfway up a mountain. It's also sensible to have had a recent dental check-up since toothache on the trail with solace a couple of days away can be a miserable experience (not least because you can't nourish yourself) and dental

Medical Kit Check List

Following is a list of items you should consider including in your medical kit – consult your pharmacist for the names of brands available in your country.

First Aid Supplies
☐ adhesive tape
☐ bandages and safety pins
☐ elasticized support bandage for knees, ankles etc
☐ gauze swabs
☐ nonadhesive dressings
☐ scissors and tweezers
☐ sterile alcohol wipes
☐ sutures and paper stitches
☐ thermometer (note that mercury thermometers are prohibited by airlines)

Medications
☐ Antidiarrhea and antisickness drugs
☐ Antibiotics – consider including these if you're traveling well off the beaten track; see your doctor, as they must be prescribed, and carry the prescription with you
☐ Antifungal cream or powder – for fungal skin infections and thrush
☐ Antihistamines – for allergies, eg, hay fever; to ease the itch from insect bites or stings; and to prevent motion sickness
☐ Antiseptic (such as povidone-iodine) – for cuts and grazes
☐ Calamine lotion, sting-relief spray or aloe vera – to ease irritation from sunburn and insect bites or stings
☐ Cold and flu tablets, throat lozenges and nasal decongestant
☐ Multivitamins – consider for long trips, when dietary vitamin intake may be inadequate
☐ Painkillers, eg, aspirin or acetaminophen (paracetamol) – for pain and fever
☐ Rehydration mixture – to prevent dehydration, eg, due to severe diarrhea; particularly important when traveling with children

Miscellaneous
☐ Insect repellent, sunscreen, lip balm and eye drops
☐ Water purification tablets or iodine

fillings are more likely to come loose at high altitude. If you wear glasses, take a spare pair and your prescription. (You can get new spectacles made up quickly and competently for less than $100, depending on the prescription and frame you choose.)

If you need a particular medicine, take enough with you to last the trip. (Pharmaceuticals are expensive in the USA.) Take part of the packaging showing the generic name, rather than the brand, as this will make getting replacements easier. It's also a good idea to have a legible prescription or letter from your doctor to prove that you legally use the medication.

For more advice on the best way to prepare for your hike, see the Physical Preparation section in the Facts for the Hiker chapter.

HIKING & TRAVEL HEALTH GUIDES
If you are planning to be away or hiking in remote areas for some time, you might consider taking a more detailed health guide.

CDC's Complete Guide to Healthy Travel, Open Road Publishing, 1997. The US Centers for Disease Control & Prevention recommendations for international travel.

Medicine for Mountaineering & Other Wilderness Activities, James A Wilkerson, The Mountaineers, 1999. An excellent reference for the lay person on a remote hike or trek.

Mountaineering Medicine, Fred Darvill, Wilderness Press, 1998. A technical guide specifically for trekkers and mountaineers.

The Outward Bound Wilderness First-Aid Handbook, Jeff Isaac, The Lyons Press, 1998. Comprehensive, well-organised coverage of prevention and first-aid for the wilds.

Travellers' Health, Dr Richard Dawood, Oxford University Press, 1995. Comprehensive, easy to read, authoritative and highly recommended, although it's rather large to lug around.

Where There Is No Doctor, David Werner, Macmillan, 1994. A very detailed guide intended for someone, such as a Peace Corps worker, going to work in an underdeveloped country.

ONLINE RESOURCES
There are also a number of excellent travel health sites on the Internet. From the Lonely

Planet home page there are links at ⌨ www.lonelyplanet.com/health to the World Health Organization and the US Centers for Disease Control & Prevention.

Staying Healthy

HYGIENE

To reduce the chances of contracting an illness, you should wash your hands frequently, particularly before handling or eating food. If you are on an organized hike, make sure that your cooks, and any other people handling your food or utensils, also wash their hands. Antibacterial, no-rinse hand cleanser is available at most pharmacies and many supermarkets in the USA. It's a clear, alcohol-based solution that you pour (just a few drops) on your hands, rub in and go.

NUTRITION

If your food is poor or limited in availability, if you're traveling hard and fast and therefore missing meals, or if you simply lose your appetite, you can soon start to lose weight and place your health at risk. Fast food is generally low in dietary fiber, so try to eat some fresh fruits and vegetables each day if you're becoming a 'junk-food junkie' between hikes. If your diet isn't well balanced or if your food intake is insufficient, you could consider taking vitamin and iron pills. Energy bars, such as Clif, Balance, MetRx, 40-30-30 and PowerBar, usually have more vitamins and minerals than regular candy bars, plus they don't melt (though they can be hard to bite into when temperatures are very low).

FOOD

Most food in the USA is oversterilized, so lack of nutrients is more of a problem than the possibility of infection. What can get overlooked, however, are the bulk-food bins in supermarkets (especially in small markets where the turnover rate is slow). Always look closely in the bin before scooping out nuts, trail mix or cereal.

Raw, unpeeled fruits and vegetables are OK to eat, though many have been treated with pesticides and coated with wax (especially apples) to give them a shiny veneer. Wash them in warm water or with a pesticide-reducing fruit wash (available at most health-food stores) if you're really concerned.

Try to avoid food that has not been freshly cooked or fully reheated. Meat and seafood are generally OK, but not if they've been on a lukewarm buffet for two hours. If a place looks clean and well run and the vendor also looks clean and healthy, then the food is probably safe. An 'A' hanging in the window of a restaurant means that it passed health inspection with no marks against it; a 'B' means that it had a point or two taken off for, for example, less than satisfactory refrigeration or employee food-handling techniques. In general, places that are packed with travelers or locals will be fine, while empty restaurants are questionable. The food in busy restaurants is cooked and eaten quite quickly with little standing around and is probably not reheated.

WATER

Many diseases are carried in water in the form of bacteria, protozoa, viruses, worms, insect eggs etc. Tap water is generally fine to drink throughout the USA, though it may taste bad because it's been treated with chlorine and/or fluoride. To be safe, ask at your hotel or at the ranger station before drinking or filling water bottles from the local tap. Bottled water is available everywhere, in fancy bottles with exotic names. If you just want no-frills, inexpensive water, go to a supermarket and get a gallon (or two-gallon) jug of 'drinking water', which may be Arrowhead, Sparklettes or a local brand.

Water Purification

All river, stream, lake and even spring water needs to be filtered for giardia. Even the most vestigial-looking spring may be contaminated from groundwater that has been affected by cattle feces 20mi away. The simplest way of purifying water is to boil it thoroughly. Vigorous boiling should be satisfactory; however, at high altitude water boils at a lower temperature, so germs are less likely to be killed. Boil it for longer (10 minutes is suggested) in these environments.

The problem with boiling water is that is consumes stove fuel at a rapid rate. Alternatively, you can use a chemical agent to purify water. Chlorine and iodine are usually used for this and are available from outdoors equipment suppliers and pharmacies in powder, tablet or liquid form. Follow the recommended dosages and allow the water to stand for the correct length of time. Chlorine tablets will kill many pathogens, but not some parasites like giardia and amoebic cysts. Iodine is more effective in purifying water though you must follow the directions carefully and remember that too much iodine can be harmful. Some iodine tablets come with neutralizing tablets which make iodine-treated water less harmful and better tasting. Vitamin C crystals (available in most supermarkets and health food stores) work just as well.

Consider purchasing a water filter for a long backcountry trip. There are two main kinds of filter. Total filters take out all parasites, bacteria and viruses and make water safe to drink. They are often expensive, but they can be more cost effective than buying bottled water. Simple filters (which can be a nylon-mesh bag) take out dirt and larger foreign bodies from the water so that chemical solutions work more effectively – if water is particularly dirty chemical solutions may not work at all. It's very important when buying a filter to read the specifications so that you know exactly what it removes from the water and what it doesn't. Assemble your filter and pump a few quarts through it before taking off on the trail. Recommended brands, available at most outdoors stores in the USA, are PUR, Katadyn and MSR.

COMMON AILMENTS
Fatigue

A simple statistic: more injuries of whatever nature happen towards the end of the day than earlier, when you're fresher. Although tiredness can simply be a nuisance on an easy hike, it can be life-threatening on narrow, exposed ridges or in bad weather. You should never set out on a hike that is beyond your capabilities for that day. If you feel below par, have a day off – write in your journal or watch the grass grow. To reduce the risk, don't push yourself too hard – take rests every hour or two and build in a good half-hour lunch break. Towards the end of the day, take down the pace and increase your concentration. You should also eat properly throughout the day to replace the energy used up. Things like nuts, dried fruit and chocolate are all good energy-giving snack foods. Remember to breathe deeply, as oxygen is another important kind of body fuel.

Blisters

Blisters *can* be avoided. Make sure that your hiking boots or shoes are well worn in before your trip. At the very least, wear them on a few short hikes before tackling longer outings. Your boots should fit comfortably with enough room to move your toes; boots that are too big or too small will cause blisters. Similarly for socks – be sure they fit properly, and wear socks specifically made for hikers; even then, check to make sure that there are no seams across the widest part of your foot. Wet and muddy socks can also cause blisters, so even on a day hike pack a spare pair of socks. Silk or capilene sock liners are a worthwhile investment for anyone prone to blisters. Keep your toenails clipped but not too short. If you do feel a blister coming on, treat it sooner rather than later. Apply a simple sticking plaster, or preferably one of the special blister plasters (look for Second Skin or Band-Aid Blister Block in the USA) and follow the maker's instructions.

Knee Pain

Many hikers feel the judder on long, steep descents. When dropping steeply, reduce the strain on the knee joint (you can't eliminate it) by taking shorter steps which leave your legs slightly bent and ensure that your heel hits the ground before the rest of your foot. Some hikers find that tubular bandages help, while others use high-tech, strap-on supports. Hiking poles are very effective in taking some of the weight off the knees.

Medical Problems & Treatment

The following is meant to prepare hikers for possible medical emergencies. It is not a manual for doctors. Don't be alarmed or get psyched-out when reading over the following, just remember that accidents do happen. Most hikers get nothing worse than a bout of constipation, blisters or a scraped elbow.

ENVIRONMENTAL HAZARDS

Hikers are at more risk than most groups from environmental hazards. The risk, however, can be significantly reduced by applying common sense – and reading the following section.

Altitude

Lack of oxygen at high altitudes (over 7500ft) affects most people to some extent. The effect may be mild or severe and occurs because less oxygen reaches the muscles and the brain at high altitude, requiring the heart and lungs to compensate by working harder. Symptoms of Acute Mountain Sickness (AMS) usually develop during the first 24 hours at altitude but may be delayed up to three weeks. Mild symptoms include headache, lethargy, dizziness, difficulty in sleeping and loss of appetite. AMS may become more severe without warning and can be fatal. Severe symptoms include breathlessness, a dry, irritative cough (which may progress to the production of pink, frothy sputum), severe headache, lack of coordination and balance, confusion, irrational behavior, vomiting, drowsiness and unconsciousness. There is no hard-and-fast rule as to what is too high: AMS has been fatal at 6000ft, although 7500ft to 13,000ft is the usual range.

Treat mild symptoms by resting at the same altitude until recovery, usually a day or two. Paracetamol or aspirin can be taken for headaches. If symptoms persist or become worse, however, *immediate descent is necessary*; even 1000ft can help. Drug treatments should never be used to avoid descent or to enable further ascent.

The drugs acetazolamide and dexamethasone are recommended by some doctors for the prevention of AMS; however, their use is controversial. They can reduce the symptoms, but they may also mask warning signs; severe and fatal AMS has occurred in people taking these drugs. In general we do not recommend them for travelers.

To prevent acute mountain sickness:

- Ascend slowly – have frequent rest days, spending two to three nights at each rise of 3000ft. If you reach a high altitude by hiking, acclimatization takes place gradually and you are less likely to be affected than if you fly directly to high altitude.
- It is always wise to sleep at a lower altitude than the greatest height reached during the day if possible. Also, once above 9000ft, care should be taken not to increase the sleeping altitude by more than 1000ft per day.
- Drink extra fluids. The mountain air is dry and cold and moisture is lost as you breathe. Evaporation of sweat may occur unnoticed and result in dehydration.
- Eat light, high-carbohydrate meals for more energy.
- Avoid alcohol as it may increase the risk of dehydration.
- Avoid sedatives.

Sun

Protection against the sun should always be taken seriously. Particularly in the rarefied air and deceptive coolness of the mountains, sunburn occurs rapidly. Slap on the sunscreen and a barrier cream for your nose

---

WARNING

Self-diagnosis and treatment can be risky, so you should always seek medical help. An embassy, consulate or five-star hotel can usually recommend a local doctor or clinic. Although we do give drug dosages in this section, they are for emergency use only. Correct diagnosis is vital.

Note that we have used generic rather than brand names for drugs throughout this section – check with a pharmacist for locally available brands.

Everyday Health

Normal body temperature is up to 98.6°F (37°C); more than 4°F (2°C) higher indicates a high fever. The normal adult pulse rate is 60 to 100 beats per minute (children 80 to 100, babies 100 to 140). As a general rule the pulse increases about 20 beats per minute for each 2°F (1°C) rise in fever.

Respiration (breathing) rate is also an indicator of illness. Count the number of breaths per minute: between 12 and 20 is normal for adults and older children (up to 30 for younger children, 40 for babies). People with a high fever or serious respiratory illness breathe more quickly than normal. More than 40 shallow breaths a minute may indicate pneumonia.

and lips, wear a broad-brimmed hat whenever the sun appears and protect your eyes with good-quality sunglasses with UV lenses, particularly when hiking near water, sand or snow. If, despite these precautions, you get yourself burnt, calamine lotion, aloe vera or other commercial sunburn relief preparations will soothe.

Snowblindness This is a temporary, painful condition resulting from sunburn of the surface of the eye (cornea). It usually occurs when someone walks on snow without sunglasses. Treatment is to relieve the pain – cold cloths on closed eyelids may help. Antibiotic and anesthetic eye drops are not necessary. The condition usually resolves itself within a few days, and there are no long-term consequences.

Heat

Treat heat with respect! Take time to acclimatize to high temperatures, drink sufficient liquids and do not do anything too physically demanding until you are acclimatized. In the hottest season, start your hike early (before sunrise), rest in the shade during the hottest part of the day and then recommence at around 4 pm, hiking until just after dark. Wear light-colored, lightweight long-sleeves and pants to reflect the sun's rays.

Prickly Heat This is an itchy rash caused by excessive perspiration trapped under the skin. It usually strikes people who have just arrived in a hot climate. Keeping cool, bathing often, drying the skin and using a mild talcum or prickly-heat powder or resorting to air-conditioning may help. Fungal infections of the skin also occur more commonly in hot, humid conditions – for more details, see Infectious Diseases later in this section.

Dehydration & Heat Exhaustion Dehydration is a potentially dangerous and generally preventable condition caused by excessive fluid loss. Sweating and inadequate fluid intake are among the commonest causes in hikers, but other important causes are diarrhea, vomiting, and high fever – see Diarrhea under Infectious Diseases for more details about appropriate treatment in these circumstances.

The first symptoms are weakness, thirst and passing small amounts of very concentrated urine. This may progress to drowsiness, dizziness or fainting on standing up and, finally, coma.

It's easy to forget how much fluid you are losing via perspiration while you are trekking, particularly if a strong breeze is drying your skin quickly. You should always maintain a good fluid intake – a minimum of three to four quarts a day is recommended.

Dehydration and salt deficiency can cause heat exhaustion. Salt deficiency is characterized by fatigue, lethargy, headaches, giddiness and muscle cramps. Salt tablets are overkill – just adding extra salt to your food is probably sufficient. Sports drink powders like ERG and Gatorade are also effective.

Heatstroke This is a serious, occasionally fatal, condition that occurs if the body's heat-regulating mechanism breaks down and the body temperature rises to dangerous levels. Long, continuous periods of exposure to high temperatures and insufficient fluids can leave you vulnerable to heatstroke.

The symptoms are feeling unwell, not sweating very much (or at all) and a high body temperature (102° to 106°F or 39° to

41°C). Where sweating has ceased, the skin becomes flushed and red. Severe, throbbing headaches and lack of coordination will also occur, and the sufferer may be confused or aggressive. Eventually the victim will become delirious or convulse. Hospitalization is essential, but in the interim get victims out of the sun, remove their clothing, cover them with a wet sheet or towel and then fan continually. Give fluids if they are conscious.

Cold
Hypothermia Too much cold can be just as dangerous as too much heat. Hypothermia occurs when the body loses heat faster than it can produce it and the core temperature of the body falls.

It is surprisingly easy to progress from very cold to dangerously cold due to a combination of wind, wet clothing, fatigue and hunger, even if the air temperature is above freezing. It is best to dress in layers; silk, wool and some of the new artificial fibres are all good insulating materials. Downfilled clothing is unsurpassable in terms of warmth and ease of packing, but is useless when it gets wet. A hat is important, as a lot of heat is lost through the head. A strong, waterproof outer layer (and an insulating 'space' blanket for emergencies) is essential. Carry basic supplies including food containing simple sugars to generate heat quickly and fluid to drink.

Symptoms of hypothermia are exhaustion, numb skin (particularly toes and fingers), shivering, slurred speech, irrational or violent behavior, lethargy, stumbling, dizzy spells, muscle cramps and violent bursts of energy. Irrationality may take the form of sufferers claiming that they are warm and trying to take off their clothes.

To treat mild hypothermia, first get the person out of the wind and/or rain, remove their clothing if it's wet and replace it with dry, warm clothing. Give them warm liquids – not alcohol – and some high-calorie, easily digestible food. Do not rub victims: instead, allow them slowly to warm themselves. This should be enough to treat the early stages of hypothermia. The early recognition and treatment of mild hypothermia is the only

way to prevent severe hypothermia, which is a critical condition.

Frostbite This refers to the freezing of extremities, including fingers, toes and nose. Signs and symptoms of frostbite include a whitish or waxy cast to the skin, or even crystals on the surface, plus itching, numbness and pain. Warm the affected areas by immersion in warm (not hot) water or with blankets or clothes, only until the skin becomes flushed. Frostbitten parts should not be rubbed. Pain and swelling are inevitable. Blisters should not be broken. Get medical attention right away.

INFECTIOUS DISEASES
Diarrhea
Simple things like a change of water, food or climate can all cause a mild bout of diarrhea, but a few rushed toilet trips without other symptoms are not indicative of a major problem. More serious diarrhea is caused by infectious agents transmitted by fecal contamination of food or water, by using contaminated utensils, or directly from one person's hand to another. Paying particular attention to personal hygiene, drinking purified water and taking care of what you eat (as outlined earlier in this chapter), are important measures to take to avoid getting diarrhea on your hike or travels.

Dehydration is the main danger with any diarrhea, particularly in children or the elderly as dehydration can occur quite quickly. Under all circumstances *fluid replacement* (at least equal to the volume being lost) is the most important thing to remember. Powdered sports drinks, weak black tea with a little sugar, soda water, or soft drinks allowed to go flat and diluted 50% with clean water are all good. With severe diarrhea a rehydrating solution is preferable to replace minerals and salts lost. Commercially available oral rehydration salts (ORS) are very useful; add them to boiled or bottled water. In an emergency, you can make up a solution of six teaspoons of sugar and a half teaspoon of salt to a quart of boiled or bottled water. You need to drink at least the same volume of fluid that you are losing in bowel movements and vomiting. Urine is the best guide to the adequacy of replacement – if you have small amounts of concentrated urine, you need to drink more. Keep drinking small amounts often. Stick to a bland diet as you recover.

Gut-paralyzing drugs such as diphenoxylate or loperamide can be used to bring relief from the symptoms, although they do not actually cure the problem. Only use these drugs if you do not have access to toilets, eg, if you *must* travel. These drugs are not recommended for children under 12 years of age or if you have a high fever or are severely dehydrated.

In certain situations antibiotics may be required: diarrhea with blood or mucus (dysentery), any diarrhea with fever, profuse watery diarrhea, persistent diarrhea not improving after 48 hours and severe diarrhea. These suggest a more serious cause of diarrhea and in these situations gut-paralyzing drugs should be avoided.

In these cases, a stool test may be necessary to diagnose what bug is causing your diarrhea, so you should seek medical help urgently. Where this is not possible the recommended drugs for bacterial diarrhea (the most likely cause of severe diarrhea in travelers) are norfloxacin 400mg twice daily for three days or ciprofloxacin 500mg twice daily for five days. These are not recommended for children or pregnant women. The drug of choice for children would be co-trimoxazole with dosage dependent on weight. A five-day course is given. Ampicillin or amoxycillin may be given in pregnancy, but medical care is necessary.

Two other causes of persistent diarrhea in travelers to be aware of are giardiasis and amoebic dysentery.

Giardiasis is caused by a common parasite, *Giardia lamblia*. Symptoms include stomach cramps, nausea, a bloated stomach, watery and foul-smelling diarrhea and frequent gas. Giardiasis can appear several weeks after you have been exposed to the parasite. The symptoms may disappear for a few days and then return; this can go on for several weeks.

Amoebic dysentery, caused by the protozoan *Entamoeba histolytica*, is characterized by a gradual onset of low-grade diarrhea, often with blood and mucus. Cramping abdominal pain and vomiting are less likely than in other types of diarrhea, and fever may not be present. It will persist until treated and can recur and cause other health problems.

You should seek medical advice if you think you have giardiasis or amoebic dysentery, but where this is not possible Tinidazole or metronidazole are the recommended drugs. Treatment is a 2g single dose of tinidazole or 250mg of metronidazole three times daily for five to 10 days.

Fungal Infections

Sweating liberally, washing less frequently than usual and going longer without a change of clothes, mean that long-distance hikers risk picking up a fungal infection, which, while an unpleasant irritant, presents no danger.

Fungal infections are encouraged by moisture so wear loose, comfortable clothes, wash when you can and dry yourself thoroughly. Try to expose the infected area to air or sunlight as much as possible and apply an antifungal cream or powder such as tolnaftate.

Hepatitis

Hepatitis is a general term for inflammation of the liver. It is a common disease worldwide. There are several viruses that cause hepatitis, and they differ in the way they are transmitted. The symptoms are similar in all forms of the illness and include fever, chills, headache, fatigue, feelings of weakness and aches and pains, followed by loss of appetite, nausea, vomiting, abdominal pain, dark urine, light-colored feces, jaundiced (yellow) skin and yellowing of the whites of the eyes. People who have had hepatitis should avoid alcohol for some time after the illness, as the liver needs time to recover.

Hepatitis A & E are transmitted by contaminated food and drinking water. You should seek medical advice, but there is not much you can do apart from resting, drinking lots of fluids, eating lightly and avoiding fatty foods. Hepatitis E is transmitted in the same way as hepatitis A; it can be particularly serious in pregnant women.

Hepatitis B, C & D. There are almost 300 million chronic carriers of hepatitis B in the world. It is spread through contact with infected blood, blood products or body fluids – for example through sexual contact, unsterilized needles and blood transfusions, or contact with blood via small breaks in the skin. Other risk situations include having a shave, tattoo or body piercing with contaminated equipment. The symptoms of hepatitis B may be more severe than those of type A and the disease can lead to long-term problems such as chronic liver damage, liver cancer or a long-term carrier state. Hepatitis C and D are spread in the same way as hepatitis B and can also lead to long-term complications.

There are vaccines against hepatitis A and B, but currently there are no vaccines against the other types of hepatitis. Following the basic rules about food and water (hepatitis A and E) and avoiding risk situations (hepatitis B, C and D) are important preventative measures.

HIV & AIDS

Infection with the human immunodeficiency virus (HIV) may lead to acquired immune deficiency syndrome (AIDS), which is a fatal disease. Any exposure to blood, blood products or body fluids may put the individual at risk. The disease is often transmitted through sexual contact or dirty needles – vaccinations, acupuncture, tattooing and body piercing can be potentially as dangerous as intravenous drug use. The blood supply in the USA is well screened, so blood transfusions are an unlikely source of infection. The US Center for Disease Control has a helpful AIDS hotline (☎ 800-342-2437). AIDS support groups are listed in the front of phone books.

Rabies

This fatal viral infection is found in many countries. Many animals can be infected (such as dogs, cats, bats and monkeys) and it is their saliva which is infectious. Any bite, scratch or even lick from an animal should be cleaned immediately and thoroughly. Scrub with soap and running water, and then apply alcohol or iodine solution. Medical help should be sought promptly to receive a course of injections, which can prevent the onset of symptoms and death.

Tetanus

This disease is caused by a germ which lives in soil and in the feces of horses and other animals. It enters the body via breaks in the skin. The first symptom may be discomfort in swallowing, or stiffening of the jaw (hence the term 'lockjaw') and neck; this is followed by painful convulsions of the jaw and the whole body. The disease can be fatal. It can be prevented by vaccination, so make sure that you are up to date with this vaccination before you leave.

INSECT-BORNE DISEASES
Lyme Disease

This is a tick-transmitted infection which may be acquired throughout North America, Europe and Asia. The illness usually begins with a spreading rash at the site of the tick bite and is accompanied by fever, headache, extreme fatigue, aching joints and muscles and mild neck stiffness. If untreated, these symptoms usually resolve over several weeks but over subsequent weeks or months disorders of the nervous system, heart and joints may develop. Treatment works best early in the illness. Medical help should be sought.

TRAUMATIC INJURIES
Sprains

Ankle and knee sprains are common injuries in hikers, particularly when walking over rugged terrain. To help prevent ankle sprains in these circumstances you should wear an all-leather boot that has adequate ankle support. If you do suffer a sprain, immobilize the joint with a firm bandage and relieve pain and swelling by keeping the joint elevated for the first 24 hours and, where possible, by using ice (a packet of frozen peas is a good alternative) on the swollen joint. Take simple painkillers to ease the discomfort. If the sprain is mild, you may be able to continue your hike after a couple of days. For more severe sprains, seek medical attention as it may be necessary to have an X-ray to rule out the possibility of a broken bone.

Major Accident

Falling or having something fall on you, resulting in head injuries or fractures, is always possible when hiking, especially if you are crossing steep slopes or unstable terrain. Following is some basic advice on what to do if a major accident does occur; detailed first-aid instruction is outside the scope of this guidebook (but see First Aid under Predeparture Planning earlier in this chapter). If a person suffers a major fall:

• do not move the person unless they are in danger or unable to breathe
• make sure that you and other people with you are not in danger
• assess the injured person's condition
• stabilize any injuries, such as bleeding wounds or broken bones
• seek medical attention – see Rescue & Evacuation under Safety on the Hike later in this chapter.

If the person is unconscious, immediately check whether they are breathing – clear their airway if it is blocked – and check whether they have a pulse (feel the side of the neck rather than the wrist). If they are not breathing but have a pulse, you should start mouth-to-mouth resuscitation immediately. In these circumstances it is best to move the person as little as possible in case their neck or back is broken. Keep the person warm by covering them with a blanket or other dry clothing; insulate them from the ground if possible.

Check for wounds and broken bones – ask the person where they have pain if they are conscious, otherwise gently inspect them all over (including their back and the back of the head), moving them as little as possible. Control any bleeding by applying firm pressure to the wound. Bleeding from the nose or ear may indicate a fractured skull. Don't give the person anything by mouth, especially if they are unconscious.

Indications of a fracture (broken bone) are pain, swelling and discoloration, loss of function or deformity of a limb. You shouldn't try to move a broken bone unless it is obviously displaced, in which case you should attempt to straighten it if possible. To protect from further injury, immobilize a nondisplaced or straightened fracture by splinting it; for fractures of the thigh bone, try to straighten the leg gently, then tie it to the good leg to hold it in place. If you lack proper splinting materials, use tent poles, hiking poles or straight tree branches. Fractures associated with open wounds (compound fractures) require more urgent treatment than simple fractures as there is a risk of infection. Dislocations, where the bone has come out of the joint, are very painful, and should be set as soon as possible.

Broken ribs are painful but usually heal by themselves and do not need splinting. If breathing difficulties occur, or the person coughs up blood, medical attention should be sought urgently, as it may indicate a punctured lung.

Internal injuries are more difficult to detect and cannot usually be treated in the field. Watch for shock, which is a specific medical condition associated with a failure to maintain circulating blood volume. Signs include a rapid pulse and cold, clammy extremities. A person in shock requires urgent medical attention.

Some general points to bear in mind are as follows:

• Note that even large wounds can be sutured (sewn up) several days later, so there is no great hurry to close them unless you know what you are doing.
• Simple fractures take several weeks to heal and don't need fixing straight away, but should be immobilized to protect them from further injury. Compound fractures need much more urgent treatment.
• If you do have to splint a broken bone, remember to check regularly that the splint is not cutting off the circulation to the hand or foot.
• Most cases of brief unconsciousness are not associated with any serious internal injury to the brain, but as a general rule of thumb any person who has been knocked unconscious should be watched for deterioration. If they do deteriorate, seek medical attention straight away.

CUTS & SCRATCHES

Even small cuts and scratches should be washed well and treated with an antiseptic such as povidone-iodine. Dry wounds heal more quickly so where possible avoid bandages and Band-Aids, which can keep wounds wet. Infection in a wound is indicated by the skin margins staying red, painful and swollen for more than three days after the injury is incurred. More serious infection can cause swelling of the whole limb and of the lymph glands. The sufferer may develop a fever, and will need medical attention.

BITES & STINGS

The US doesn't lack biting, stinging things, but it's unlikely that you'll meet anything much worse than bees, wasps and mosquitoes in most situations. In the case of any potentially toxic bite, evacuate immediately and go to the nearest emergency clinic.

Bedbugs

Bedbugs live in various places, but particularly in dirty mattresses and bedding, evidenced by spots of blood on bedclothes or on the wall. Bedbugs leave itchy bites in neat rows. Calamine lotion or a sting-relief spray may help.

Bees & Wasps

These are usually painful rather than dangerous. However, in people who are allergic to them severe breathing difficulties may occur and urgent medical care is required – if this is you be sure to carry a shot of epinephrine, even on day hikes (though remember that it's technically illegal for non-physicians to administer such shots to others).

In most cases calamine lotion or a sting relief spray will ease the discomfort of a sting.

Lice

All lice cause itching and discomfort. They make themselves at home in your hair (head lice), your clothing (body lice) or in your pubic hair (crabs). You catch lice through direct contact with infected people or by sharing combs, clothing and the like. Powder or shampoo treatment will kill the lice and infected clothing should be washed in very hot, soapy water and dried in the sun.

Snakes & Scorpions

There are several varieties of venomous snakes in the US, but they do not cause instantaneous death and antivenins are available. First aid is to place a light, constricting bandage above the bite, keep the wounded part below the level of the heart and move it as little as possible. Administer CPR if breathing stops. Stay calm and get to a medical facility as soon as possible. Bring the dead snake for identification if you can, but don't risk being bitten again. The use of tourniquets and sucking out the poison are now comprehensively discredited.

To minimize your chances of being bitten always wear boots, socks and long trousers when walking through undergrowth where snakes may be present. Don't put your hands into holes and crevices and be careful when collecting firewood.

In the Southwest and other dry regions, both rattlesnakes and scorpions may be an issue. Rattlesnakes usually give warning of their presence and backing away from them (slowly!) usually prevents confrontation. Remember that their bites are seldom fatal and that only one in three adult rattlers actually injects venom when it bites (younger ones are more prone to inject venom, as they haven't learned self discipline!)

Scorpions are not aggressive, but will sting if you sit or step on them. Always

---

Wound Cleaning 101

In every first aid kit should be an unused, sealable plastic bag and a bottle of povidone-iodine solution. If you need to clean a cut that is rather deep and very dirty, fill the plastic bag with clean (ie, filtered or boiled) water, prick a hole in one corner of the bag and squeeze the water out through the hole in a pressurized stream. After the wound is free of dirt and debris, repeat this irrigation technique using a solution of 95% water, 5% povidone-iodine. Never put undiluted povidone-iodine on a wound.

check your shoes before putting them on; shaking out your sleeping bag isn't overly cautious either.

Spiders

Black widow spiders are found throughout the US. Their bites are more toxic than those of rattlesnakes, but they inject a smaller amount of venom. These bites are rarely fatal, but can cause localized and sometimes systemic inflammation – again, stay calm and seek medical help immediately.

Ticks

Ticks are parasitic arachnids that may be present in brush, forest and grasslands, where hikers often get them on their legs or in their boots. Adult ticks suck blood from hosts by burying into the skin and can carry infections such as Rocky Mountain spotted fever or Lyme disease.

Always check your body for ticks after walking through high grass or thickly forested area. If ticks are found unattached they can simply be brushed off. If one has attached itself to you, pulling it off and leaving the head in the skin increases the likelihood of infection. To remove an attached tick, use a pair of tweezers, grab it by the head and gently pull it straight out – do not twist it. (If tweezers are not available, use your fingers, but protect them from contamination with a piece of tissue or paper.) Do not touch the tick with a hot object like a match or a cigarette – this can cause it to regurgitate noxious gut substances or saliva into the wound. And do not rub oil, alcohol or petroleum jelly on it. If you get sick in the next couple of weeks, consult a doctor.

WOMEN'S HEALTH
Gynecological Problems

Antibiotic use, synthetic underwear, sweating and the use of contraceptive pills can lead to fungal vaginal infections, especially when traveling in hot climates. Fungal infections are characterized by a rash, itch and discharge and are usually treated by nystatin, miconazole or clotrimazole pessaries or vaginal cream. If these are not available, a vinegar or lemon-juice douche, or yoghurt

can also help. Maintaining good personal hygiene and wearing loose-fitting clothes and cotton underwear may help to prevent these infections.

Sexually transmitted diseases are another cause of vaginal problems. See the Infectious Diseases section earlier in the chapter for more details. Remember that male sexual partners must also be treated.

Urinary Tract Infection

Cystitis or inflammation of the bladder is a common condition in women. Symptoms include burning when urinating and having to urinate frequently and urgently. Blood can sometimes be passed in the urine. Sexual activity with a new partner or with an old partner who has been away for a while can trigger an infection.

The initial treatment is to drink plenty of fluids, which may resolve the problem. Single dose (nonantibiotic) treatments may be effective in the early stages of mild cystitis. If symptoms persist seek medical attention, because a simple infection can spread to the kidneys, causing a more severe illness.

Pregnancy

Severe stomach upset and the use of antibiotics can decrease the effectiveness of oral contraceptives.

If you are pregnant, see your doctor before you travel.

Safety on the Hike

By taking a few simple precautions, you'll reduce significantly the odds of getting into trouble. See the boxed text 'Hike Safety – Basic Rules' for a list of simple precautions.

For information on the clothes and equipment you should take with you when hiking, consult What to Bring in the Facts for the Hiker chapter. For hazards more specific to each region or hike, see the Warning boxes spread throughout the hikes chapters.

BEARS

Debate about what to do (or *not* to do) in the presence of a bear is ongoing: should you

Hike Safety – Basic Rules

- Allow plenty of time to accomplish a walk before dark, particularly when daylight hours are shorter.

- Don't overestimate your capabilities. If the going gets too tough, turn round.

- If possible, don't walk on your own. Always leave details of your intended itinerary and route, including expected return time, with someone responsible before you set off.

- Before setting off, make sure that you have a relevant map, compass, whistle, flashlight and that you know the weather forecast for the area for the next 24 hours.

walk away slowly, backwards and not make any sudden movements, or should you remain in one spot and raise your hands over your head to appear larger and, perhaps, more daunting? Tactics for dealing with bears vary from region to region, depending on how familiar the bears of that region are with humans: are they likely to get scared because they've never seen humans before? If so, will they run away or charge when scared? Or do they associate humans with candy bars and camp food?

In the USA, where most bears have encountered humans or human activity, people are generally in little danger of being attacked. Still, every year the NPS reports several instances of folks being mauled. How to avoid this?

- Let them know you're coming! Bears are less likely to feel threatened if they have plenty of advanced notice that you are coming (this gives them time to flee, which is what they usually do). Sing, clap your hands or use bear bells (small bells tied to your backpack) when hiking through a densely forested area.
- Heed the warnings about not keeping food or anything scented (including soap, toothpaste and lotion) in your tent. Be extremely diligent about this, dumping out all pockets and packs at the end of each day. Put all smelly things in a bag and hoist it up in a tree (see the boxed text 'The Counter-Balance Method' in the Facts for the Hiker chapter) or, where provided, on a 'bear pole'.

- In regions where hanging is known to be ineffective, use a bear-proof container (available from outdoors suppliers) set 50ft from camp, or take advantage of the metal bear-boxes provided by the park authority.
- Have designated cooking clothes that you put in the 'smelly things' bag, and never let these clothes into your tent.
- Keep an immaculate camp, particularly regarding food scraps and washing up.
- If you do encounter a bear, stay still and slowly raise your arms above your head. If the bear attacks, *do not run*! Drop to the ground in the fetus position and clasp your hands behind your neck to protect your spinal cord. *Do not fight back*! Play dead until the bear leaves.
- Use good sense in tempting situations: don't try to get closer to a bear to get it's photograph! Be particularly careful if you encounter a mother with cubs as she will be extremely protective and more likely to attack if startled.
- Remember that bears hibernate all winter. In the spring they are hungry and active, in the fall they are getting sleepy and slow.

CROSSING RIVERS

You may have to ford a river or stream swollen with snowmelt which is fast flowing enough to be a risk. Before stepping out from the bank, ease one arm out of the shoulder strap of your pack and unclip the belt buckle – should you lose your balance and be swept downstream it will be easier to slip out of your backpack. If linking hands with others, grasp at the wrist; this gives a tighter grip than a handhold. If you're alone, plant a stick or your hiking poles upstream to give you greater stability and help you to lean against the current. Use them to feel the way forward and walk side-on to the direction of flow so that your body presents less of an obstacle to the rushing water.

HUNTING SEASON

If a trailhead parking lot is full of trucks with gun racks, that's a good sign that hunting season has begun (see National Parks & Reserves in the Facts about the USA chapter).

Check with local rangers to find out what areas are currently getting the most use by hunters, and wear bright colors when hiking – you can buy a plastic orange vest, often worn by hunters, at most grocery and hardware stores in popular hunting areas.

LIGHTNING

If a storm brews, avoid exposed areas. Lightning has a penchant for crests, lone trees, small depressions, gullies, caves and cabin entrances, as well as wet ground. If you are caught out in the open, try to curl up as tightly as possible with your feet together and keep a layer of insulation (such as your backpack) between you and the ground. Place metal objects such as metal-frame backpacks and hiking poles away from you.

RESCUE & EVACUATION

If someone in your group is injured or falls ill and can't move, leave somebody with them while another one or more goes for help. If there are only two of you, leave the injured person with as much warm clothing, food and water as it's sensible to spare, plus the whistle and flashlight. Mark the position with something conspicuous – an orange bivvy bag, or perhaps a large stone cross.

If you need to call for help, use these internationally recognized emergency signals. Give six short signals, such as a whistle, a yell or the flash of a light, at 10-second intervals, followed by a minute of rest. Repeat the sequence until you get a response. If the responder knows the signals, this will be three signals at 20-second intervals, followed by a minute's pause and a repetition of the sequence.

Be ready to give information on where an accident occurred, how many people are injured, the injuries sustained and, if a helicopter needs to come in, the terrain and weather conditions at the accident site.

Emergency Transponders, GPS & Cell Phones

As asserted in the Planning section of the Facts for the Hiker chapter, a GPS receiver should not be relied upon in the backcountry. It cannot be emphasised enough how important a topographic map and a compass are to any hiker.

The use of cell (mobile) phones – which are basically 800MHz transceivers relying on a repeater system – in the backcountry is a point of debate in the outdoors community. Many hikers like the security of having a phone with them in case of emergency. Search and rescue team members and most park rangers, however, argue that cell phones are over-used and are thus contributing to a 'boy who cried wolf' scenario that could ultimately be harmful to cell-phone users who really need help. In any case, many remote areas of the USA are 'dead zones' where cell phones do not function. If you do decide to take a cell phone into the backcountry, ask at the local ranger station whether you will be in a useable range. Take extra batteries, plenty of non-technological survival equipment and knowledge, and only call the local authorities if you have broken bones or are in, or witness to, a life-or-death situation.

Emergency satellite beacons are not frequently used by hikers in the US. Backcountry skiers are often equipped with avalanche beacons, but hikers rarely carry such things.

Search & Rescue Organizations

Search and Rescue (S&R) and Mountain Search and Rescue (MSR) organizations throughout the USA are run by the county sheriff's department. The best thing to do in an emergency is to dial ☎ 911, then the operator will alert the relevant parties. If it's not a life-threatening emergency but you need a search and rescue operation, contact the local police or sheriff (listed in the front of the phone book and on most public phones) or, if relevant, the National Park Service.

Helicopter Rescue & Evacuation

If a helicopter arrives on the scene there are a couple of conventions you should be familiar with. Standing face on to the chopper:

- arms up in the shape of a letter 'V' means 'I/We need help'
- arms in a straight diagonal line (like one line of a letter X) means 'All OK'

In order for the helicopter to land, there must be a cleared space of 75ft x 75ft, with a flat landing area of 18ft x 18ft. The helicopter will fly into the wind when landing. In cases of extreme emergency, where no landing area is available, a person or harness might be lowered. Take extreme care to avoid the rotors when approaching a landed helicopter.

Getting There & Away

AIR
Airports

The USA has a number of main 'gateway' airports, and most international flights will arrive at one of them. If you want to fly into a non-gateway city, you'll probably have to land first at one of the gateway airports, where you'll do the immigration and customs thing, then take another flight to your final destination. These are the main international gateway airports:

city	airport	code
Atlanta	Hartsfield	ATL
Boston	Logan	BOS
Chicago	O'Hare	ORD
Dallas–Fort Worth		DFW
Los Angeles		LAX
Miami		MIA
New York	John F Kennedy	JFK
	Newark	EWR
San Francisco		SFO
Seattle	Seattle-Tacoma	SEA
Washington, DC	Dulles	IAD

There are many other so-called international airports, but some have only a few flights from other countries. These include cities with connections to Mexico or Canada and major tourist destinations such as Orlando or Denver that have charter flights and direct connections from their main markets. Even travel to an international gateway sometimes requires a connection in another gateway city. For example, many London–Los Angeles flights involve a transfer connection in Chicago.

Buying Tickets

Numerous airlines fly to the USA, and a variety of one-way, roundtrip and Round-the-World fares are available. It pays to do a bit of research first. Start by perusing travel sections of magazines such as *Time Out* and *TNT* in the UK, or the Saturday editions of newspapers like the *Sydney Morning Herald* and *The Age* in Australia. Ads in these publications offer cheap fares, but they're usually low-season fares on obscure airlines, with conditions attached.

Online travel agencies now list some of the cheapest fares available (see Online Purchasing), but as with bucket-shop advertisements, the best fares sometimes seem to be unavailable or sold out. Try 💻 www.etn.nl or www.travelocity.com to start with. Airlines themselves can supply information on routes and timetables, but unless there's a price war they won't offer the cheapest tickets.

High season for most of the USA is mid-June to mid-September (summer). May and October are often 'shoulder' periods, with the low season November through March, except for the week before and the week after Christmas, which are peak for ski resorts. Airlines often have competitive low-season, student and senior citizens' fares, but they often have complicated conditions and catches. Find out about the fare, the route, the duration of the journey and any restrictions on the ticket.

WARNING

The information in this chapter is particularly subject to change – prices for international travel are volatile, routes are introduced and canceled, schedules change, special deals come and go, and rules and visa requirements are amended. In addition, the travel industry is highly competitive, and there are many lurks and perks.

You should get opinions, quotes and advice from as many airlines and travel agents as possible before you part with your hard-earned cash. Check directly with the airline or a travel agent to make sure that you understand how a fare (and any ticket you may buy) works. The details given in this chapter should be regarded only as pointers and cannot be a substitute for your own careful, up-to-date research.

Airlines

Major international airlines include US-based carriers with domestic and international services as well as foreign airlines that fly to the USA. Calling the following 800 numbers is free within the USA and Canada, but you can dial the numbers from other countries as a regular international call:

Air Canada
☎ 800-776-3000

Air France
☎ 800-237-2747

Air New Zealand
☎ 800-262-1234

Alitalia
☎ 800-223-5730

American Airlines
☎ 800-433-7300

British Airways
☎ 800-247-9297

Canadian Airlines
☎ 800-426-7000

Cathay Pacific
☎ 800-228-4297

Continental Airlines
☎ 800-525-0280

Delta Air Lines
☎ 800-221-1212

Japan Airlines (JAL)
☎ 800-525-3663

Lufthansa
☎ 800-645-3880

Northwest Airlines
☎ 800-447-4747

Qantas Airways
☎ 800-227-4500

Scandinavian Airlines (SAS)
☎ 800-221-2350

South African Airways
☎-800-722-9675

TWA
☎ 800-221-2000

United Airlines
☎ 800-241-6522

US Airways
☎ 800-428-4322

Virgin Atlantic
☎ 800-862-8621

Cheap tickets are available in two distinct categories: official and unofficial. Official tickets have a variety of names including 'APEX', 'excursion', 'promotional' or 'advance-purchase' fares. Unofficial tickets are simply discounted tickets that the airlines release through selected travel agencies (not through airline offices). The cheapest tickets are often nonrefundable and require an extra fee for changing your flight (usually $50). Many insurance policies will cover this loss if you have to change your flight for emergency reasons. Return (roundtrip) tickets usually work out cheaper than two one-way fares – often *much* cheaper.

Use the fares quoted in this book as a guide only. Quoted airfares are not necessarily a recommendation for the carrier.

In some places, especially the UK, the cheapest flights are advertised by obscure bucket shops whose names haven't yet reached the telephone directory. Many such firms are honest and solvent, but some will take your money and disappear. If you feel suspicious about a firm, don't give them all the money at once – leave a deposit of 20% or so and pay the balance on receiving the ticket. If they insist on cash in advance, go elsewhere. And once you have the ticket, call the airline to confirm that you are booked on the flight. You may decide to pay a little more than the rock-bottom fare and opt for the safety of a better-known travel agent. Established firms like STA Travel (🖳 www.sta-travel.com) or Council Travel (🖳 www.counciltravel.com), both of which have offices internationally, or Travel CUTS in Canada (🖳 www.travelcuts.com), offer good prices to most destinations.

Once you have your ticket, make a copy of it, and keep the copy separate from the original ticket. This will help you to get a replacement if your ticket is lost or stolen.

Online Purchasing Most airlines have their own websites with online ticket sales, often discounted for online customers. To buy a ticket via the web, you'll need to use a credit card – this is straightforward and secure, as card details are encrypted. Commercial reservation networks offer airline ticketing as well as information and bookings for hotels, car rental and other services. Networks include:

Atevo Travel
🖳 www.atevo.com
Biztravel.com Inc
🖳 www.biztravel.com
CNN Interactive's Travel Guide
🖳 www.cnn.com/Travel
Excite Travel by City.Net
🖳 www.city.net
Internet Travel Network
🖳 www.itn.net
Microsoft Expedia
🖳 www.expedia.com
Preview Travel
🖳 www.previewtravel.com
Priceline
🖳 www.priceline.com
Travelocity
🖳 www.travelocity.com

There are also online travel agencies that specialize in cheap fares:

1-800-Airfare
🖳 www.1800airfare.com
Cheap Tickets
🖳 www.cheaptickets.com
LowestFare.com
🖳 www.lowestfare.com
Yahoo Travel Last-Minute Special
🖳 travel.yahoo.com/destinations/bargains/

Round-the-World Tickets Round-the-World (RTW) tickets can be a great deal if you want to visit other regions as well as the USA. Often they work out to be no more expensive, or even cheaper, than a simple roundtrip ticket to the USA, so you get the extra stops for nothing. They're of most value for trips that combine the USA with Europe, Asia and Australia or New Zealand. RTW itineraries that include South America or Africa are substantially more expensive.

Official airline RTW tickets are usually put together by a combination of two or three airlines, and they permit you to fly to a specified number of stops on their routes as long as you don't backtrack. Other restrictions are that you must usually book the first sector in advance and cancellation penalties apply. The tickets are valid for a fixed period, usually one year. An alternative type of RTW ticket is one put together by a travel agent using a combination of discounted tickets.

Most airlines restrict the number of sectors that can be flown within the USA and Canada to three or four, and some airlines 'black out' a few heavily traveled routes (like Honolulu to Tokyo). In most cases a 14-day advance purchase is required. After the ticket is purchased, dates can usually be changed without penalty, and tickets can be rewritten to add or delete stops for $50 each.

From Australia, a RTW ticket using United, Lufthansa and Thai, with several stops in the USA, costs about A$2500. A cheap deal with Qantas and Air France flies to Los Angeles, has an open-jaw segment (enabling you to fly into one city and leave from another) across the USA, then includes flights from New York to Europe, Asia and back to Australia, for A$1880.

There are many possibilities with Qantas and various partner airlines, ranging from A$1500 to A$3200.

From New Zealand, a RTW ticket via North America, Europe and Asia with Air New Zealand and others will cost from NZ$2300.

Courier Flights Some firms provide very cheap fares to travelers who will act as couriers, hand-delivering documents or packages. Courier opportunities are not easy to come by, and they are unlikely to be available on other than principal routes. The traveler is usually allowed only one piece of carry-on baggage, with the checked-baggage allowance being taken by the item to be delivered. In London, try Bridges Worldwide (☎ 0189-546-5465), 🖳 www.adventure1.com or www.nowvoyager.com.

Travel Passes & Add-On Fares Some deals for inexpensive air, bus and train travel within the USA can only be purchased overseas in conjunction with an international air ticket. These include Visit USA air passes, Greyhound's International Ameripass and some Amtrak rail passes. Also, you can often get supercheap domestic flights within the USA as an add-on to your international airfare. Think about your travel connections within the USA when you're shopping for your air ticket (see the Getting Around chapter for details).

Baggage
On international flights, the usual baggage allowance is 44lb (20kg), but on flights from the USA, the limit is commonly higher; check with the airline. On most domestic flights, you are limited to two checked bags, or three if you don't have a carry-on bag. There could be a charge if you bring more, or if the size of the bags exceeds the airline's limits. Internal-frame backpacks are usually OK, but many airlines will ask you to sign a waiver that releases them from responsibility should one of the straps get caught and rip your pack open (or something similar). External-frame backpacks are usually frowned upon and sometimes prohibited.

If your baggage is delayed upon arrival (which is rare), some airlines will provide you with a cash advance to purchase necessities. If sporting equipment is misplaced, the airline may pay for rentals. Should the baggage be lost, it is important that you submit a claim. The airline doesn't have to pay the full amount of the claim; instead they can estimate the value of your lost items and reimburse you accordingly. It may take them anywhere from six weeks to three months to process the claim and pay you.

Flight Restrictions

Illegal Items Items that are illegal to take on a plane, either as checked or carry-on baggage, include aerosols of polishes, waxes etc; tear gas and pepper spray; camp stoves with fuel; and divers' tanks that are full. Matches should not be packed in checked baggage.

During check-in, you may be asked questions about whether you packed your own bags, whether anyone else has had access to them since you packed them and whether you have received any parcels to carry. These questions are asked for security reasons.

Traveling with Stoves

You cannot take any fuel (unleaded gasoline, white spirits or any flammable liquid) or gas cartridges on a plane in baggage that you plan to check through or carry on. Temperature and pressure variations can cause containers to leak and result in toxic fumes in the cabin or a highly flammable substance leaking in the luggage containers.

Backpacks are so common these days that most backpackers aren't even asked whether they have fuel in their luggage. But don't take this as a green light to put your own and others' lives in danger! If you have some fuel left in your multifuel stove or a half-used cartridge, burn it off or safely dispose of it before arriving at the airport. Then at the next town purchase more before heading out on the trail. In this situation it doesn't pay to be cheap!

Children Kids less than two years old travel for 10% of the standard fare (or for free on some airlines) as long as they don't occupy a seat. (They don't get a baggage allowance, either.) 'Skycots' should be provided by the airline if requested in advance; these will take a child weighing up to about 22lb. Strollers can often be taken on as hand baggage. Children aged between two and 12 can usually occupy a seat for one-half to two-thirds of the full fare and do not get a baggage allowance. Sometimes there is a child's rate on a discounted fare, sometimes not – it can be cheaper for a child to fly on an adult discounted fare than on a child's fare at two-thirds of the full adult rate. For pricing purposes, the child's age is reckoned at the time of departure on the first leg of the flight.

Arriving in the USA

For visa, passport and additional customs information, see the Facts for the Hiker chapter.

Even if you are continuing immediately to another city, the first airport that you land in is where you must carry out immigration and customs formalities. If your baggage is checked from, say, London to Phoenix, you will still have to take it through customs if you first land in Chicago. Passengers from Asia will go through immigration and customs in Honolulu if their flights stop there on the way to California.

Passengers aboard the airplane are given standard immigration and customs forms to fill out. After the plane lands, you'll first go through immigration. There are two lines: One is for US citizens and residents and the other is for nonresidents. After immigration, you collect your baggage and then pass through customs. If you have nothing to declare, you'll probably clear customs quickly and without a baggage search, but don't count on it. For details on customs allowances and the procedure for foreigners entering the USA, see the Facts for the Hiker chapter.

If your flight is continuing to another city, or you have a connecting flight, it is your responsibility to get your bags to the right place. Normally, there are airline representatives at counters just outside the customs area who will help you. Most airports will have pay phones and car rentals, but other facilities can be pretty minimal. Don't count on a foreign exchange office, tourist information desk or left-baggage service. US airports are run for the benefit of airlines, not travelers, and some are very user-unfriendly.

Departure Taxes

Taxes for US airports are normally included in the cost of tickets bought in the USA or abroad. There's a $7 airport departure tax on all passengers bound for a foreign destination and a $6.50 North American Free Trade Agreement (NAFTA) tax on all passengers entering the USA from a foreign country, both added to the purchase price of your air ticket. See Passports & Visas under Visas & Documents in the Facts for the Hiker chapter for information on entry requirements.

Canada

Travel CUTS has offices in all major cities. The *Toronto Globe & Mail* and *Vancouver Sun* carry travel agencies' ads; the magazine *Great Expeditions*, PO Box 8000-411, Abbotsford, BC V2S 6H1, is also useful. There are daily flights to all the big US cities from Vancouver and Toronto, and many smaller Canadian cities have connections as well.

The best deals for Canadians are flights to the sunny destinations like Florida, California and Hawaii, with prices higher in the winter peak season. Commuter flights to cities like New York and Chicago can be very expensive.

Australia

There are some direct flights from Sydney to Los Angeles and San Francisco and from Melbourne to Los Angeles, with quite a few more going via Auckland. Flights to other US cities will usually involve a stop in Los Angeles, San Francisco or Honolulu, but Los Angeles is the main gateway. Qantas, Air New Zealand and United are the main airlines on the route. Fares from Melbourne, Sydney, Brisbane and sometimes Adelaide and Canberra are 'common rated'. From Hobart and Perth, there's always an add-on fare.

STA Travel and Flight Centre are the main discount travel agencies, with offices everywhere. They usually have rates to the USA within a few dollars of each other and will often match a lower fare offered by the other agency. It's also worth checking the online agency, ⌨ www.travel.com.au. Some sample discount low-season roundtrip fares from Sydney/Melbourne include Los Angeles for A$1500, San Francisco for A$1500 and New York for A$1600. High-season fares will be more like Los Angeles for A$1850 and New York for A$2050. Low season is roughly February, March, October and November. High season is mid-June to mid-July and mid-December to mid-January. The rest of the year is considered shoulder season.

Some of the cheapest fares are with Japan Airlines and involve indirect routes and a night layover in Tokyo. The savings really aren't worth it if your time is limited. The cheapest tickets often have advance-purchase requirements and minimum- and maximum-stay provisions. Full-time students can get an extra discount of A$80 to A$140 on some roundtrip fares to the USA.

New Zealand

Air New Zealand has regular flights from Auckland direct to Los Angeles. Flights from Christchurch and Wellington require a plane change on one of the Pacific Islands or are routed through Auckland. For discount fares, try STA Travel (☎ 09-309-0458), 10 High St, Auckland, or Flight Centre (☎ 09-309-6171), National Bank Tower, 205–225 Queens St, Auckland. Both have offices in other main cities. Some sample low-season roundtrip fares from Auckland include Los Angeles for NZ$1729 and New York for NZ$2049. In high season, a roundtrip flight to New York is about NZ$2600. Low, shoulder and peak seasons are roughly as for Australia.

UK & Ireland

One of the busiest, most competitive air sectors in the world is the UK to the USA, with hundreds of scheduled flights by British Airways, American Airlines, United, Delta, Northwest, Continental, Kuwait, Air India, TWA and discount specialist Virgin Atlantic.

London is arguably the world's headquarters for the no-frills discount travel agencies called bucket shops. These are well advertised and invariably have fares well below the airlines' published standard rates. Check the ads in magazines such as *Time Out*, plus the Sunday papers, *Exchange & Mart* and the free magazines distributed all over London. Most British travel agents are registered with the Association of British Travel Agents (ABTA). If you have paid for your flight to an ABTA-registered agent who then goes out of business, ABTA will guarantee a refund or an alternative. Unregistered bucket shops are riskier but sometimes cheaper.

Two large, well-established and reliable agents for cheap tickets in the UK are STA Travel (☎ 0171-361-6262), 86 Old Brompton Rd, London SW7, and Trailfinders (☎ 0171-937-5400), 215 Kensington High St, London W8. STA has offices in most of the UK's main cities. Trailfinders has offices in Manchester (☎ 0161-839-6969), Glasgow (☎ 0141-353-2224) and Dublin (☎ 01-677-7888).

Other reputable agencies include Flightbookers (☎ 0171-757-2000), 177 Tottenham Court Rd, London W1, and Council Travel (☎ 0171-437-7767), 28A Poland St, London W1. The Globetrotters Club (BCM Roving, London WC1N 3XX) publishes a newsletter called *Globe* that covers obscure destinations and can help you to find traveling companions.

Discounted fares are highly variable, volatile and subject to various conditions and restrictions, but as an indication, see the table below for some sample roundtrip fares from various discount agencies on a variety of carriers (fares include tax).

From UK regional airports, cheap discounted flights may be routed via London, Paris or Amsterdam, and will probably not fly direct to smaller US cities like Las Vegas or Denver.

For these fares, high season is at various times between April and October, and most of the rest of the year is low season. Note that there's also a 'superpeak' season from December 12 to 24, when fares are even higher than in high season.

from	to	low season/ high season (£)
London	Boston	232/355
	Charlotte	260/441
	Chicago	270/413
	Denver	325/521
	Las Vegas	310/521
	Los Angeles	276/516
	Miami	276/468
	New York	184/355
	San Francisco	314/476
Manchester	New York	262/427
	Boston	261/375
	Los Angeles	335/415
Glasgow	New York	262/427
	Boston	261/394
	Los Angeles	335/415
Dublin	New York	348/450
	Boston	261/394
	Los Angeles	419/634

Virgin Atlantic is an airline with consistently low fares, such as 21-day advance-purchase deals from London to New York for £355/566 or Los Angeles for £483/664. Student travel agencies might be able to offer a small discount on these to travelers with proof of student status. There are also occasional special offers, usually in November, January and February, that can be supercheap – to New York for as low as £200!

Continental Europe

There are nonstop flights to many US cities, but many of the discounted fares involve indirect routes and changing planes. The main airlines between Europe and the USA are Air France, Alitalia, British Airways, KLM, Continental, TWA, United, American, Delta, Scandinavian Airlines and Lufthansa. Sometimes an Asian or Middle Eastern carrier will have cheap deals on flights in transit to the USA, if you can actually get a seat. Also try Icelandair connections via London.

The newsletter *Farang*, La Rue 8 á 4261 Braives, Belgium, covers exotic destinations, as does the magazine *Aventure du Bout du Monde*, 116 Rue de Javel, 75015 Paris, France.

Netherlands Amsterdam is one of the best places to get cheap airfares, and its Schiphol airport is excellent. The official student agency, NBBS (☎ 020-624-0989), Rokin 38, is good, but may not have the very lowest prices, so check some of the discount travel agencies along Rokin. Other established agencies include Budget Air (☎ 020-556-3333), Singel 21, and Flyworld/Grand Travel (☎ 020-657-0000), at Schiphol, which does everything by phone and fax. Some of the cheapest advertised fares for low-season roundtrips start around NF920 to New York, NF1345 to Miami and NF1440 to Los Angeles.

Germany For discount fares, try STA Travel (☎ 69 43 01 91), Bergerstrasse 118, 60316 Frankfurt, or Council Travel (☎ 211 36 30 30), Graf Adolf Strasse 64, 40212 Dusseldorf; Council also has an office in Munich (☎ 089 39 50 22) at Adalbert Strasse 32, 80799 Munich. Cheap advertised fares, low-season roundtrip from Frankfurt, start around DM700 to New York, DM900 to Miami and DM1000 to Los Angeles.

France In Paris, Council Travel (☎ 01 44 55 55 44) is at 22 Rue des Pyramides, 1er. Nouvelles Frontières (☎ 08 03 33 33 33) and Havas Voyages (☎ 01 53 29 40 00) both have branches throughout Paris. Some of the cheapest advertised fares, low-season roundtrip from Paris, start around FF2300 to New York, FF3200 to Miami and FF3300 to Los Angeles.

Africa

Only a few cities in West and North Africa have direct flights to the USA – Abidjan (Côte d'Ivoire), Accra (Ghana), Cairo (Egypt), Casablanca (Morocco) and Dakar (Senegal) have about three or four flights per week. South African Airways flies direct from Johannesburg to New York six days a week. All other flights from Africa to the USA go via a European hub, most commonly London.

The USA is becoming a popular destination for young South Africans. The student fares from STA Travel are the cheapest op-

tion, typically with British Airways via London; a 12-month roundtrip ticket costs about R4130 in low season, R5080 in high season. Discounted roundtrip fares for non-students cost from around R5560 in low season, R6400 in high season, with some restrictions. High season is mid-June to mid-September, and December through mid-January. Prices are variable and have been increasing as the rand devalues. STA Travel has offices in Johannesburg (☎ 11-447-5551), at Wits University (☎ 11-716-3045) and Capetown (☎ 21-418-6570). The Flight Center has opened in South Africa with offices in Johannesburg (☎ 11-880-2361), and some other discount travel agencies like Seekers are appearing. Rennies Travel is about the largest and most established travel agency in the country, with several offices in Johannesburg.

Asia

Bangkok, Hong Kong, Kuala Lumpur, Singapore, Seoul and Tokyo all have good connections to the US West Coast on high-quality national airlines. Many flights to the USA go via Honolulu and allow a stopover. Bangkok is the discounted fare capital of the region, though its bucket shops can be unreliable. Hong Kong, Kuala Lumpur and Singapore are also very competitive. STA Travel has branches in Hong Kong, Tokyo, Singapore, Bangkok and Kuala Lumpur.

Central & South America

The main gateway to Central and South America is Miami, but there are also many direct flights from Los Angeles. Check the international flag-carrier airlines of the countries you want to connect to (Aerolineas Argentinas, LANChile, Varig etc) as well as US airlines such as United and American.

Mexico

Regular flights link the major cities of Mexico and the USA. At times, depending on prices and exchange rates, it can be substantially cheaper to fly to a Mexican border town than to the adjacent town on the US side. A flight from Mexico City to Tijuana can cost quite a bit less than a flight to San Diego, just a few miles north on the US side.

LAND

If you're driving into the USA from Canada or Mexico, don't forget the vehicle's registration papers, liability insurance and your home driver's license. Canadian and Mexican driver's licenses are valid, but obtaining an international driver's permit is a good idea. A vehicle rented in the US can usually be driven into Canada and back, but very few car-rental companies will let you take a car into Mexico.

Canada

Bus Greyhound has direct connections between main cities in Canada and the northern United States, but you may have to transfer to a different bus at the border. Note that Greyhound US and Greyhound Canada are two different companies. Greyhound's Ameripass is not valid for travel within Canada, but you can use it to get into Canada; from Boston or New York to Montreal; Detroit to Toronto; or Seattle to Vancouver; and back to the USA by the same routes. See the Getting Around chapter for more on bus passes available through Greyhound.

Train There are regular services from Montreal to New York (four weekly), Toronto to New York via Niagara Falls (daily), Toronto to Chicago (three weekly), and Vancouver to Seattle (three daily). Amtrak rail passes get you to/from Vancouver and Montreal only.

Car If your papers are in order, taking your own car across the US-Canadian border is usually quick and easy, but occasionally the authorities of either country decide to search a car *thoroughly*. Canadian auto insurance is valid in the USA – make sure that your policy is current before you cross the border. On weekends and holidays, and especially during holiday weekends in summer, traffic at the main border crossings can be very heavy and there will be a long wait. Avoid crossing at these times, or try to cross at a smaller, less trafficked border post.

Mexico

Bus There are direct buses between main towns in Mexico and the USA, but northbound buses can take some time to cross the US border – sometimes the whole bus is delayed as the Immigration & Naturalization Service (INS) checks everyone on board.

Train There was a time when you could get on a train in Chicago and get off in Mexico City. No more. Amtrak gets close to the Mexican border at San Diego, California, and El Paso, Texas, but there are no cross-border services. Three Mexican train services travel south from the border towns of Mexicali (across from Calexico, California), Ciudad Juárez (across from El Paso, Texas) and Nuevo Laredo (across from Laredo, Texas). The line from Ciudad Juárez connects at Chihuahua for the Copper Canyon Railway.

Car US auto insurance is not valid in Mexico, so even a short trip into Mexico's border region requires you to buy Mexican car insurance, available for about $6 per day at most border crossings. At some border towns like Tijuana or Ciudad Juárez, there can be very long lines of vehicles waiting to re-enter the USA. For a short visit, it's usually more convenient to leave your car in a lot on the US side and walk or bus across the border. For a longer trip into Mexico beyond the border zone or Baja California, you'll need a Mexican *permiso de importación temporal de vehículos* – see LP's *Mexico* guide for the tedious details.

SEA

In the warmer months only, Cunard's *Queen Elizabeth II* sails from Southampton to New York in about six days – and it's expensive. Most other passenger liners in US ports are cruise ships doing a circuit around the Caribbean. The standard reference for passenger ships is the *OAG Cruise & Ferry Guide*, published by Reed Travel Group (☎ 44-158-2600-111), Church St, Dunstable, Bedfordshire LU5 4HB, UK.

Regular ferries operate from Nova Scotia to Maine in the east, and Vancouver Island to Washington State in the west.

Getting Around

AIR

Flying is the most practical way to get around the USA if your time is limited, especially if you want to spend most of it on the trail. The domestic air system is extensive, with dozens of competing airlines, hundreds of airports and thousands of scheduled flights every day. If you get one of the special deals on internal airfares, flying can be even cheaper than traveling by bus, train or car. Most hikers, once they land, still need to rent a car to get to the various trailheads and thus may benefit from one of the fly-and-drive packages offered by many major airlines.

The best advice if you're thinking of air travel is to consult a good travel agent, which will have all the up-to-the-minute details on fares, routes, discounts and so on, all of which change on a nearly daily basis. Visit several agents if you have time to shop around.

Flights are most frequent, direct and least expensive between main 'hub' airports. These include all the international gateways listed in the Getting There & Away chapter, plus quite a few other cities, especially those which serve as the home base for a big airline. Most cities and towns have a local airport, some bigger and busier than others, but you might have to travel via a hub airport to reach them – this can make flying less convenient and more expensive.

Domestic Airlines

Many US airlines offer both domestic and international services, but some are purely domestic and the small airlines only cover one region or a few states. Domestic airlines include the following:

America West (☎ 800-235-9292)
American Airlines (☎ 800-433-7300)
Continental Airlines (☎ 800-525-0280)
Delta Air Lines (☎ 800-221-1212)
Northwest Airlines (☎ 800-225-2525)
Reno Air (☎ 800-736-6247)
Southwest Airlines (☎ 800-435-9792)

TWA (☎ 800-892-4141)
United Airlines (☎ 800-241-6522)
US Airways (☎ 800-428-4322)

Tickets & Fares

Two of the most reputable discount travel agents in the USA are STA Travel (☎ 800-777-0112, 🖳 www.sta-travel.com) and Council Travel (☎ 800-226-8624, 🖳 www .counciltravel.com). With offices in cities nationwide (call for the nearest location), both companies sell the International Student Identity Card (ISIC) and specialize in low-cost travel for students and those aged under 26. STA and Council often get competitive airfares for nonstudents of all ages as well.

Special fares are sometimes available through other discount travel agents. Check the ads in the Sunday travel sections of the larger newspapers such as the *Los Angeles Times*, *San Francisco Chronicle*, *New York Times* and *Chicago Tribune*. Browsing the Internet for cheap airfares is another option: see Buying Tickets in the Air section of the Getting There & Away chapter for a list of commercial reservation networks and discount travel agencies that offer airline ticketing and other services.

Advance-purchase options often give a series of graduated discounts for purchasing your ticket seven, 14 or 21 days in advance, with the biggest savings on a 21-day advance purchase – while this is the common system, it varies for different airlines and routes. The same flight might cost much less for travel at night, or on a weekend rather than on a weekday. Some airlines offer companion fares that are practically a two-for-the-price-of-one discount from the full coach (economy class) fare. Discount tickets may be subject to a minimum or maximum stay, and often require that you stay over a Saturday night at your destination.

All that said, and depending on availability at the time of booking and purchase, here is a rough indication of the price ranges for some routes with particularly frequent and convenient services of interest to hikers. All prices are for one-way fares:

route	price range ($US)
New York–Chicago–Los Angeles	160 to 240
New York–Las Vegas	185 to 285
Los Angeles–San Francisco	78 to 129
Los Angeles–Las Vegas	65 to 155
Los Angeles–New York	150 to 325
San Francisco–Seattle	95 to 250
San Francisco–Denver	115 to 215
San Francisco–Salt Lake City	70 to 135
San Francisco–Chicago	155 to 370
Seattle–Kalispell–Missoula	120 to 185
Boston–Atlanta	85 to 165

Add-On Fares You can often get supercheap domestic flights in conjunction with an international airfare, and it's worth considering your plans for air travel within the USA while shopping for your international ticket. Add-on fares can include a choice of several destinations within the US, and may permit 'open-jaw' options. For example, you might get a roundtrip fare to New York; spend some time there (and perhaps New England or the Appalachia); use a cheap, add-on fare to fly to Las Vegas; rent a car and hike around the Southwest and Sierra Nevada; then fly from San Francisco back to New York. Cheap add-on fares may be available only to a few cities in the USA, and there will likely be an extra charge (usually US$50) for mid-trip changes to your travel date.

Air Passes

Most US airlines offer some sort of air pass to overseas visitors. They are only sold to non-US or non-Canadian residents in conjunction with an international airfare, and you often have to buy the pass with the same airline as your international ticket. The passes are actually a book of coupons – each coupon equals a flight, good for 60 days from the use of the first coupon. This time restriction may be a drawback for long-distance hikers. Also be aware that if a connection is not a direct flight (ie, if it involves a change of flight number), it will count as two coupons. It's therefore worth getting

your pass with an airline that offers direct flights between the cities you want to visit.

In Australia, US air passes are priced in US dollars, and you pay the Australian dollar equivalent when you book. They must be bought in conjunction with a roundtrip or round-the-world fare, but not necessarily from the same airline. United Airlines has direct flights to many US cities, and its passes cost from US$389/417 for three coupons in the low/high season to US$569/599 for six coupons. It charges quite a bit more if you don't fly United to the USA. Continental Airlines air passes might be a bit cheaper, but Continental doesn't have direct flights to as many cities.

To get the best deal on air passes, you really have to work out your itinerary and schedule and get a travel agent to provide cost estimates for the options. Hikers need to remember that the weather won't always cooperate with your airline schedule, and you must be ready to sacrifice either hiking time or money if you purchase a ticket with many restrictions. Some air passes are quite flexible, requiring only that you book the first flight, after which you can use the remaining coupons to go anywhere you want. Some deals let you leave the flight times open – you reserve your seat at least one day in advance (if seats are available!). Even if you book specific flights when you buy the pass, you can change the dates later without penalty so long as the last flight is scheduled within the 60-day limit. Remember that you need to be in a town, and not in the backcountry, to make such arrangements and will need to schedule your between-hike time carefully if you are to juggle flights effectively.

A Visit USA fare is a point-to-point fare purchased in conjunction with an international airline ticket from outside the USA, Canada and Mexico. It will be cheaper than the equivalent standard US domestic airfare, but probably not as cheap as the best bargain deals available from US travel agents or consolidators.

Getting Bumped

Airlines try to ensure consistently full planes by overbooking, counting on some passengers not showing up. This usually involves 'bumping' passengers off full flights. Getting bumped can be a nuisance because you have to wait around for the next flight, but if you have a day's leeway you can really take advantage of the system.

When you check in at the airline counter, ask if they will need volunteers to be bumped and what the compensation will be. Depending on the desirability of the flight, this can range from a $200 voucher toward your next flight to a fully paid roundtrip ticket. Be sure to confirm a later flight so that you don't get stuck in the airport on stand-by. If you have to spend the night, airlines frequently foot the hotel bill for their 'bumpees'. All in all, it can be a great deal, and many people plan their travel with a day to spare in order to try for a free ticket that will cover their next trip.

Be aware, however, that being just a little late when checking in for your flight could get you bumped with none of these benefits.

BUS

Greyhound (☎ 800-231-2222 for fares and schedules, 800-822-2662 for customer service) is the major long-distance bus company, with routes throughout the USA and to the Canadian cities of Montreal, Toronto and Vancouver. Complete schedule and fare information is also available at 🖳 www.greyhound.com.

Greyhound runs buses several times a day along major highways between large towns, stopping at smaller towns that happen to be along the way. Towns not on major routes are often served by local carriers, and Greyhound will usually have information about them – the name, phone number and, sometimes, fare and schedule information as well. Local phone numbers for Greyhound and other carriers are listed under their respective cities and towns throughout this guide.

Peter Pan Trailways (☎ 800-343-9999), Capitol Trailways (☎ 800-444-2877) and Martz Trailways (☎ 800-432-8069) provide bus services in the northeast of the country, competing with Greyhound. For some less conventional bus services, see Alternative Carriers later in this section.

Most baggage has to be checked-in and should be well labeled. Larger items like skis and bicycles can be transported, but there may be an extra charge; backpacks are OK. Be careful not to leave hand baggage on the bus during rest stops.

The frequency of bus services varies, but even the least popular routes will have one bus per day. Main routes will have buses every hour or so, sometimes around the clock. Buses are reasonably fast and travel mostly on the interstate highways, but bus trips can still be very long because of the great distances – nonexpress buses will stop every 50mi to 100mi to pick up passengers, and long-distance buses stop for meal breaks and driver changes. A cross-country trip from New York to Los Angeles will take about 70 hours.

Generally, buses operated by Greyhound and its main competitors are clean, comfortable and reliable. Buses have air conditioning, onboard lavatories and reclining seats. Smoking is not permitted. The buses stop for meals, usually at fast-food restaurants or cafeteria-style truck stops.

Bus travel is often the cheapest way to cover long distances, and those who rely on bus travel represent a wide cross-section of the population. However, many people in the USA consider buses to be transport for the poor and are put off by the possibility that fellow passengers may be from the lower strata of society. Bus stations *can* be pretty depressing places, often in unsafe areas of big cities. But by the standards of most countries, US bus services are very good, and the unvarnished view of American life is a travel experience you won't get on the airlines.

Tickets & Fares

If purchased 10 days in advance, tickets can be bought over the phone with a major credit card (MasterCard, Visa or Discover) and mailed to you, or you can pick them up at the terminal with proper identification. Greyhound terminals also accept American Express, traveler's checks and cash. Note that you can only reserve a seat by purchasing a ticket. You can buy a ticket as late as 15 minutes before departure, but the busline will only fill the number of seats on the bus – no standing allowed. If possible, buy your ticket in advance to ensure that you get a seat and perhaps a better price.

The cost of bus travel varies tremendously. Sometimes you can get discounted tickets if you purchase them seven or 21 days in advance. Sometimes a roundtrip ticket costs twice the price of a one-way ticket; at other times roundtrips are cheaper than two one-ways. Special promotional fares are sometimes offered (eg, 'Anywhere that Greyhound goes for $99', or 'Anywhere in California for $45'). Other promotions include Greyhound's $59 one-way, unlimited-mileage ticket, which can be a bargain if you're looking for a cheap way to cover a long distance. If you're traveling with a friend, ask about companion fares, where two can travel for the price of one (roundtrip journeys only). As with regular fares, these promotional fares change from season to season – call for current details.

Tickets for children aged two to 11 are half price. Senior citizens are entitled to a 15% discount. A disabled passenger and a companion can travel together for the price of one. Student discounts are occasionally available on specific routes during certain times of the year – call for details.

Here are some examples of Greyhound's long-distance services, one-way fares and travel times:

route	cost ($US)	time (hours)
New York–Chicago	91	16½
New York–Miami	124	27
New York–New Orleans	89	30
New York–Los Angeles	155	64
Los Angeles–New Orleans	103	42
Los Angeles–Seattle	84	28

Bus Passes

Passes can be economical if you want to travel a lot in a short period. The passes are for unlimited travel on consecutive days (for options, see below), not for a number of days spread out over a longer period. Greyhound stamps your pass the first time you use it, and the days start from then. Two short-term passes cost more per day, but may better suit your itinerary.

The pass is valid on dozens of regional bus lines as well as Greyhound and can include side trips to Montreal, Toronto and Vancouver. Passholders can call ☎ 888-454-7277 in the USA for information, but seat reservations must be made in person at a bus station.

Ameripass This pass can be purchased in the USA and costs $179 for seven days of travel, $289 for 15 days, $399 for 30 days, $599 for 60 days. You can buy one by phone or at any Greyhound station.

International Ameripass This pass is available from travel agents in the UK at £85 for five days of bus travel, £110 for seven days, £170 for 15 days, £230 for 30 days, and £340 for 60 days. A £75 four-day pass is good for travel between Monday and Thursday.

In Australia, New Zealand and elsewhere, passes are usually priced in US dollars, and you pay the current equivalent. The pass will cost about US$159 for seven days of travel, US$239 for 15 days, US$319 for 30 days, US$499 for 60 days. The International Ameripass is available in the US to foreign students staying less than one year; buy one by phone from the Greyhound international office in New York City (☎ 212-971-0492, 800-246-8572).

Bus Stations

Some larger towns and cities have a bus station shared by Greyhound and other bus lines, while in others Greyhound and the other companies may have separate stations. The better ones have clean bathrooms, luggage lockers, information boards, pay phones and snack bars. Some bus stations are in unattractive – even dangerous – parts of town, so it's better to avoid arriving at night and to budget for a taxi to and from the station.

In many small towns, Greyhound no longer maintains a bus station but stops at a given location, such as a McDonald's or a post office. To board at these stops, know exactly where and when the bus arrives, be emphatic when you flag it down, and be prepared to pay the driver with exact change.

Alternative Carriers

Green Tortoise The 'alternative' bus line, Green Tortoise (☎ 415-956-7500, 800-867-8647, ☐ www.greentortoise.com), offers 10- to 14-day trips across the USA between San Francisco, New York and Boston, from May to September. The Green Tortoise provides not only transport but an unusual sort of home-on-wheels, with foam-mattress bunks; communal food and cooking; and stops for hiking, swimming, white-water rafting, visits to parks, camping and cookouts. From San Francisco to New York, a Green Tortoise trip will take 10 days at a cost of $279 plus $71 food fund, or 14 days at $349 plus $81 food fund, depending on when you travel.

Green Tortoise also operates a weekly north-south route between Los Angeles and San Francisco, connecting with another twice-weekly route between San Francisco and Seattle; this trip has fewer recreational stops, making it from San Francisco to Seattle in about 24 hours. You can catch either the cross-country or the north-south bus at many points along the way; phone for information or to request a brochure.

Other Green Tortoise adventures include multiday trips from San Francisco to Yosemite National Park ($100 to $150) and to the Grand Canyon ($410); prices include food fund. Call for details.

Trek America Trek America offers activity-oriented bus tours using 12- or 14-seat vans rather than full-size buses. Most nights are spent camping in tents, and everyone helps with the camping chores. Stops are often for two or three nights to permit hiking and more individual sightseeing. The standard Trek America trips are for the 18- to 38-year-old age group, but the 'Footloose' trips are designed for older travelers.

Trips vary from one to four weeks and cost, on average, around $400 a week, including food. For trip descriptions, dates and prices, contact Trek America directly at PO Box 189, Rockaway, New Jersey 07866 (☎ 973-983-1144, 800-221-0596, ☐ www.trekamerica.com); or, in the UK, 4 Waterperry Court, Middleton Rd, Banbury, Oxon, OX16 8QG, England (☎ 0129-525-6777).

Us Bus This new, independent service is aimed at young, budget travelers. From May to October its buses travel on set routes around the main areas of traveler interest on the west coast, the Southwest, the Northeast, in Florida and along the Mississippi River. The buses stop at HI hostels and other budget accommodations, and passholders can get on and off where they want, but should book each sector in advance (toll-free ☎ 877-843-8728).

Buses travel the various routes every two or three days, and all sectors are covered during daylight hours. Most buses are 15-seaters, with air-con, stereo and lots of travel information on board. Sometimes they stop en route for meals and photo opportunities. The emphasis is on flexibility rather than speed – it will take eight days to go from New York to Los Angeles (via New Orleans and Phoenix) with seven overnight stops.

The passes are priced as follows:

days of travel	use within	cost ($US)
5	15 days	199
10	25 days	299
15	40 days	399
30	60 days	639
45	90 days	799

Passes are available from Us Bus sales offices in the UK (☎ 1892-512700, 1892-532060) and the USA (☎ 877-843-8728), or from travel agents. Us Bus passes are widely available in Australia and New Zealand from budget travel agents like STA. For local addresses and agents, contact US Bus via email at ☻ TheUsbus@att.net.

TRAIN

Amtrak (☎ 800-USA-RAIL, ☐ www.amtrak.com) has an extensive rail system throughout the USA, with Amtrak Thruway buses providing convenient connections linking the rail network to some smaller centers and national parks. For information, call or visit the website. The advantages of train travel include comfort, sociability, great scenery and the pleasure of arriving in an elegant station in the heart of a city like New York, Chicago, Boston or Washington. The drawback for hikers is that you'll almost always have to catch a connecting bus or rent a car to get to a trailhead; the exception is in the Rocky Mountains where Amtrak serves small towns near hiking destinations.

Train travel is quicker than bus travel, but the time saved may be offset by less convenient departure and/or arrival times. Traveling by train is usually more expensive than by bus on the same route, but some special deals may make train travel competitive. On a busy, long-distance connection, it's often possible to get an airfare cheaper than a train ticket. In short, trains are rarely the quickest, cheapest or most convenient option, but they can be close on all counts, and people enjoy them for the travel experience.

Tickets & Fares

It can be difficult to get useful information about Amtrak services and prices – try a travel agent who specializes in train travel. Reservations can be made any time from 11 months in advance to the day of departure; since space on most trains is limited, it's a good idea to reserve as far in advance as you can. This also gives you the best chance of getting a discount fare.

Various one-way, roundtrip and touring fares are available, with discounts of 15% for seniors aged 62 and over, 50% for children aged two to 15, and 15% for disabled travelers. Fares vary according to type of seating; you can travel in coach seats or in various types of sleeping compartments. Low-season fares are offered on all tickets from early January to mid-June and from late August to mid-December. Amtrak also offers a variety of all-inclusive holiday tour packages.

The Amtrak website has lots of information about Amtrak services, but it won't give general information about fares – you have to nominate a date and a route and pretend to book a ticket, and it will give a fare for that time and route only; then, the actual fare you pay will probably be different from the amount quoted on the website. Despite the company's monopoly on rail travel, Amtrak's prices are as complex as the ultracompetitive air travel industry. Generally, the earlier you book a ticket, the cheaper the price.

Here are some examples of Amtrak's long-distance services, one-way fares and travel times:

route	cost ($US)	time (hours)
New York–Chicago	99	19
New York–Los Angeles	239	66
Los Angeles–New Orleans	164	43
Los Angeles–Seattle	119	34½
Chicago–Seattle	189	46

International Gateway Fares These discount fares can be purchased overseas in conjunction with an international air ticket for specific one-way trips in the Northeast, including New York–Washington DC ($46; Metroliner express service $56), and New York–Boston ($37).

Train Passes

USA Rail Passes These passes are available from travel agents outside of North America, but foreign-passport holders can purchase them from Amtrak once inside the USA. The pass offers unlimited coach-class travel within a specific region for either 15 or 30 days, with the price depending on region, number of days and season traveled. These are generally best for long journeys:

region	15 days, low/high ($US)	30 days low/high ($US)
National	285/425	375/535
Northeast	175/195	215/230
East	205/250	255/310
West	195/315	260/395
Far west	185/240	240/310
East coast	n/a	225/275
West coast	n/a	225/275

Present your pass at an Amtrak office to buy a ticket for each trip. Reservations should be made as well – as far in advance as possible. You can get on and off as often as you like, but each sector of the journey must be booked. (At some rural stations, trains will only stop if there's a reservation.) Tickets are not for specific seats, but a conductor on board may allocate you a seat. First-class or sleeper accommodations cost extra, and must be reserved separately.

North America Rail Pass A new option offered by Amtrak in conjunction with Canada's VIA Rail, this pass offers unlimited travel on US and Canadian railways for 30 consecutive days for US$450/645 in the low/high season (high season is June 1 to October 15).

CAR

Driving is undoubtedly the most convenient way for hikers to get around. Besides – driving in the USA is a cultural and sensual experience in itself; as you go with the flow on the endless interstates, tune in to the local radio stations and develop a taste for tacky roadside architecture and highway hamburgers.

If your schedule is at all limited, plan to do the long trips by plane or train, and rent a car where you need it. The obvious frustration hikers will encounter is the thought of how much they're spending to let the rental car sit at the trailhead. If you're doing a long hike that's not too far from an urban center, investigate the cost of having a cab or shuttle service take you to/from the trailhead before renting a car.

For young travelers (aged under 25 and especially under 21), car travel is scarcely an option. Car rentals are expensive, or completely unavailable, and if you buy a car, insurance can be prohibitive.

Road Rules

The use of seat belts and child safety seats is required in almost every state.

The speed limit is generally 55 or 65mph on highways, 25mph in cities and towns, and as low as 15mph in school zones (strictly enforced during school hours). It's forbidden to pass a school bus when its lights are flashing. On the interstate highways in designated rural areas, the speed limit is 65, 70 or even 75mph. Always watch for posted speed limits.

Drivers should watch for livestock on highways, especially in the deserts and range country – high-risk areas are signed as Open Range, with the silhouette of a cow or something to that effect. Hitting a steer at 55mph will wreck your car, kill the animal and might kill you as well.

Most states have laws against littering – if you are seen throwing anything from a

Driving by Numbers

Most roads in the USA are identified by numbers – to navigate, you need to know the numbers of the highways to your destination. Don't expect signs saying 'To San Jose' – you need to know the way is via I-880, US 101, Hwy 82 or Hwy 87.

On the main system of interstate highways, even numbers indicate the east-west routes and odd numbers are for north-south routes – I-80 connects New York to San Francisco; I-95 goes from Maine to Miami. I-80 heads north out of San Francisco, but the freeway entrance will be marked I-80 East, because that's where the highway is going. Where an interstate skirts a city, it has an even digit added to the front – I-295 is the bit of I-95 that goes around Washington, DC. Where an interstate goes into or through the middle of a city, an odd number is added to the front – I-395 is the bit of I-95 that goes through central Washington, DC. Where two of the interstate routes merge, the same stretch of highway can have two numbers, like I-70/I-76 between Pittsburgh and Chicago.

The national numbering system was introduced in the 1920s, and old highway names were dropped from use – 'National Old Trails Hwy' became US Route 66. The classic 'US' highways used the system of odds and evens, but the old routes were often buried under new interstates in the 1950s and '60s. Leaving San Francisco, US 50 is the same road as I-80, but it becomes US 50 itself east of Sacramento, and there's an alternate route, ALT 50, going through Reno.

State highways, secondary state highways and country highways all have two- or three-digit numbers. Often three or more highway numbers apply to the same stretch of road. It's all very logical, but it can be confusing.

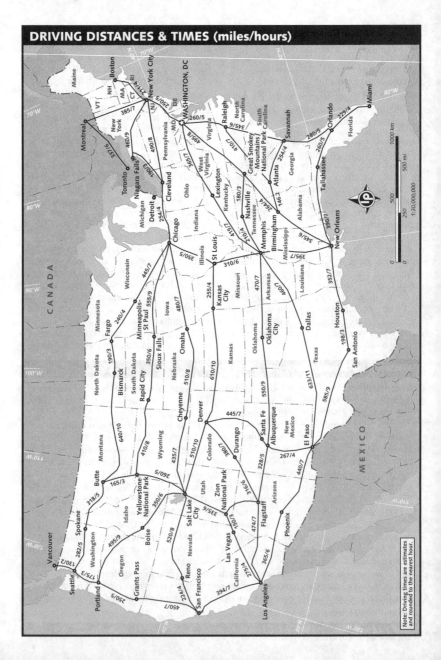

DRIVING DISTANCES & TIMES (miles/hours)

Note: Driving times are estimates and rounded to the nearest hour.

vehicle you can be fined $1000 and be forced to pick up what you discarded.

In winter conditions you may have to carry snow chains and fit them if there is snow on the road. Many cars are fitted with steel-studded snow tires for winter driving.

Penalties are very severe for 'DUI' – driving under the influence of alcohol and/or drugs. Police can give roadside sobriety checks ('touch your nose, walk along this line' etc) to assess whether you've been drinking or using drugs. If you fail, you'll be required to take a breath test, urine test or blood test to determine the level of alcohol or drugs in your body. Refusing to be tested is treated as if you'd taken the test and failed. The maximum legal blood-alcohol concentration is 0.08%. During festive holidays and special events road blocks are sometimes set up to deter drunk drivers.

In some states it is illegal to carry open containers of alcohol in a vehicle, even if they are empty. Containers that are full and sealed may be carried, but if they have ever been opened they must be carried in the trunk.

Rental

Car rental prices vary widely from city to city, company to company, car to car and day to day. Florida and California are generally the cheapest places to rent, and New York and Illinois among the most expensive. As a very rough indication, renting the cheapest, subcompact economy car for one week with unlimited mileage costs around $114 in Florida, $140 in California, $196 in New York and Illinois, and $170 in most other parts of the USA.

If you're arranging a rental before you get to the USA, check all the options with your travel agent. If you get a fly-drive package, local taxes may be an extra charge when you collect the car. Several online travel-reservation networks have up-to-the-minute information on car-rental rates at all the main airports and let you make online reservations (see Buying Tickets in the Air section of the Getting There & Away chapter). Rates are usually lower in main cities with lots of competing companies, but if there's a big conference or sports event in town, rental cars will cost more for a few days before, during and after.

Once you're in a city, shop around. Use toll-free phone numbers to check the big companies but try the local ones, too. Many airports have a courtesy phone and a board with advertisements for local car-rental agencies as well as the big names. You can spend 30 minutes calling a dozen of them toll-free, select the most suitable, and they'll pick you up and take you to their lot. Be sure to ask for the best rate – discounts may be offered for renting on weekends, for three days, by the week or month, or even for renting a car in one place and returning it to another if the company needs to move cars in that direction.

Compare the total cost, including insurance and mileage; one company may charge a little less for the car, but a little more for the insurance. Also estimate the distance you'll be driving; an 'unlimited mileage' plan works out more economically than a 'cost-per-mile' plan if you'll be driving long distances.

Some companies won't rent a car for more than four weeks or so at a stretch or will require you to bring the vehicle in for a mileage check and oil change every four weeks. Arrangements in which car rentals are included as part of a fly-drive package are more likely to permit long-term rentals.

Most rental companies require that you have a major credit card, that you be at least 25 years old and that you have a valid driver's license (your home license will do). Alamo, Thrifty, Budget and Rent-A-Wreck may rent to drivers between the ages of 21 and 24 for an additional charge (usually around $20 per day).

There are several types of insurance to consider. Liability insurance is required by law in most states, but is not always included in rental contracts because many Americans are covered for rental cars under their regular car liability insurance policy. Check this carefully. You need liability coverage, but don't pay extra if sufficient coverage is already included with the rental. Insurance against damage to the car, called Collision Damage Waiver (CDW) or Loss Damage Waiver (LDW), is usually optional

($8 to $12 per day), but will often require you to pay for the first $100 or $500 of any repairs. This cost, called the deductible, may be removed by paying additional premiums. Some credit card companies, like Master-Card Gold or American Express, will cover your CDW if you rent for 15 days or less and charge the full value of the rental to your card. Check with your credit card company before you leave home to determine if this service is offered and the extent of coverage.

A 'one-way' rental – renting a car in one place and returning it somewhere else – can be useful. The extra 'drop-off charge' ranges from nothing to $200. The major nationwide rental-car agencies are as follows:

Alamo (☎ 800-327-9633)
Avis (☎ 800-831-2847)
Budget (☎ 800-527-0700)
Dollar (☎ 800-800-4000)
Enterprise (☎ 800-325-8007)
Hertz (☎ 800-654-3131)
National (☎ 800-328-4567)
Thrifty (☎ 800-367-2277)

Rent-A-Wreck (☎ 800-421-7253) offers older vehicles at lower prices. There are also thousands of smaller local companies that sometimes offer better prices than their national competitors. Check the Yellow Pages under 'Automobiles'.

Driver's License

Visitors can legally drive in the USA for up to 12 months with their home driver's license. An International Driving Permit (IDP) is a very useful adjunct and may have more credibility with US traffic police, especially if your home license doesn't have a photo or is in a foreign language. Your automobile association at home can issue an IDP, valid for one year, for a small fee. You must carry your home license together with the IDP.

Car Sharing

If you're looking for someone to ride along to share the cost of fuel, ask around, put a notice up in local hostels, check the ride boards at universities, or even peruse the newspaper classified ads. Hostels can be especially good places to find riders, not only for long trips but also for sharing the cost of a rental car for local day trips.

Drive-Away Cars

One option for longer trips is a 'drive-away car' from a vehicle transport company that needs drivers to move cars from one place to another.

To be a driver you must be over 21 and be able to present a valid driver's license, personal references and a $200 to $400 cash deposit that is refunded upon safe delivery of the car. Some companies also require a printout of your driving record, a major credit card or three forms of identification. You pay nothing for the use of the car, but you do pay for the fuel you use. The company pays you nothing to drive the car, but they do pay the insurance. Check the car carefully for damage before you start.

You must deliver the car to its destination at a specified time; the time allotted for a trip usually works out at about six hours of driving per day; a maximum mileage is also stipulated, so you have to follow the shortest route. Be clear about the conditions for deposit refund and how you can cash the refund check.

There may or may not be cars available when and to where you want to go, so it helps to be flexible, plan ahead and contact several companies. Availability depends on demand, with the routes most readily available being coast to coast. Some demand is determined by holiday movements – lots of cars need drivers from the Northeast to Florida at the start of winter.

Drive-away car companies are listed in the Yellow Pages telephone directory under 'Automotive Transport & Drive-Away Companies'. They include the following:

AAA Advantage Auto Transport (☎ 800-480-1733)
A-A Auto Transport & Driveaway (☎ 800-466-6935)
A Anthony Driveaway Truckaway (☎ 800-606-2006)
Across America Driveaway (☎ 800-964-7874)
Auto Driveaway Co (☎ 800-346-2277)
Contranz (☎ 800-862-9999)
National Auto Transport (☎ 800-225-9611)

Phone a week or two ahead of when you want to travel.

MOTORCYCLE

Riding a bike in America is an almost mythical experience, with a heritage going back beyond *Easy Rider* and *The Wild One*. The image of the biker on the road descends from that of the cowboy on the range and entails many of the same discomforts as well as the same sense of freedom and the wide-open spaces.

To ride a motorcycle, you need a US state motorcycle license or an International Driving Permit endorsed for motorcycles. A state Department of Motor Vehicles (DMV) can give you the rules relating to motorcycle use. Helmets are required in almost every state.

Motorcycle rental and insurance is expensive, especially if you want to ride a Harley. EagleRider motorcycle rentals (☎ 800-910-1520), with offices in major cities nationwide, charges $135 per day for a 1340cc Harley, including helmet and liability insurance, but collision insurance (CDW) is extra. Buying a bike would be cheaper if you're staying a few months and if you can take a loss to sell it in a hurry.

Bike Tours Amerika (☎ 03-5473 4469 in Australia, 2764-7824 in Germany) offers a choice of escorted group tours on Yamaha XT 600s, including a three-week trip from San Francisco to Vancouver via the Grand Canyon and the Rocky Mountains, from DM3650.

BICYCLE

The country is so big that cycling around it would take a long time, though it's entirely feasible. Bicycles are not permitted on freeways, and you certainly wouldn't want to ride on them anyway. However, even long-distance trips can be done entirely on quiet backroads.

For serious long-distance cycling, you'll need to bring your own bike or buy one in the USA. Some international and domestic airlines will carry bikes as checked baggage without extra charge if they're in a box. Many carriers impose an oversize-baggage charge (for domestic carriers up to $50) for bikes that aren't disassembled first – check before you buy the ticket. Excellent bicycles are available at reasonable prices at specialist bike shops, sporting goods stores and discount warehouse stores. Used bicycles are sold at flea markets and garage sales and advertised in newspapers and on notice boards at hostels and colleges.

Amtrak trains and Greyhound buses will transport bikes within the USA, sometimes with handling charge of about $10. Ask about packaging and boxing requirements and extra charges.

HITCHING

Hitchhiking in the USA is potentially dangerous and definitely not recommended. There have been so many nasty incidents and lurid reports that drivers are very reluctant to pick up hitchhikers anyway. This may be less so in rural parts, but traffic can be sparse, and you might get stranded. Hitchhiking on freeways is prohibited – there's usually a white sign at the on-ramp stating 'no pedestrians beyond this point,' and anyone caught hitching past there can be arrested.

Even hitching to and from a hiking trailhead should be avoided – try to arrange something at a ranger station or with other hikers. If you're flat broke, there are still alternatives to standing by a roadside with your thumb out – look for share rides at hostels, or ask at campgrounds.

LOCAL TRANSPORT

See individual chapters for information on trailhead shuttle services and getting to/from each hike.

New England & Adirondacks

For such a small area of the United States, the New England and Adirondacks region boasts an embarrassment of natural riches. How else but by foot to explore this stunning palette of ghostly white birch and flaming red maple, knife-edged granite and fern-fringed footpath? Here, leafy forest meets icy sea, with a tumble of boulders leading the way.

The New England–Adirondacks hiker is faced with a menu of tempting choices: the challenge of bouldering up the craggy face of an unforgiving peak, the salt-tinged allure of a seaside ramble in the footsteps of Henry David Thoreau, or a jaunt to the spot where the Pilgrims first encountered the Wampanoags.

Moreover, this delightful tapestry is woven together with a well-established, remarkably interconnected trail system. Among the options, this region offers 440mi of the fabled Appalachian Trail (AT), including its oft-kissed northern terminus; some 133mi of the Northville-Placid Trail, connecting the Adirondacks' southern foothills to the range's High Peaks; and America's first long-distance footpath, the 270mi Long Trail, reaching from Massachusetts to Canada along the crest of the Green Mountains. All this in a seven-state area that could easily be tucked into Texas, with room to spare.

You're never really alone here. Besides the usual small mammals and birds, you'll be sharing the territory with moose (Maine has more moose per sq mile than anywhere else, including Alaska), black bears, peregrine falcons, bald eagles, harbor seals and whales. So, as you ramble, take time to look closely for moose tracks, bear sign and, at the highest elevations, rare, tiny alpine wildflowers, seen only here and in the Arctic, hundreds of miles to the north.

CLIMATE

Weatherwise, the most pleasant hiking is from May through October. The East actually has five seasons, the fifth being 'mud season' – from March through April and most

MARK NEWMAN

A classic New England landscape in the northern Green Mountains, Vermont.

- Following moose tracks and bear signs in the remote northern Maine woods
- Traversing New England's highest peaks with extended ridgeline views
- Retracing Thoreau's steps on the windswept beaches of Cape Cod National Seashore
- Exploring the rugged, rocky coastline of Acadia National Park, where the mountains meet the sea

of November – due to rain and snow-melt. Hiking during mud season is tough slogging, not to mention harmful to the environment. Avoid it. Black flies and 'no-see-ums' can be a nuisance from mid-May to mid-June, but some hikers appreciate the light crowds during that time – so what if you have to wear a geeky-looking headnet? Expect the biggest crowds during the high summer months – July and August – and weekends

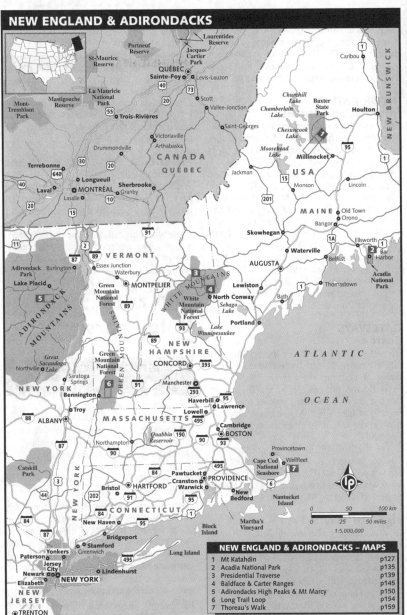

NEW ENGLAND & ADIRONDACKS

NEW ENGLAND & ADIRONDACKS – MAPS

1	Mt Katahdin	p127
2	Acadia National Park	p135
3	Presidential Traverse	p139
4	Baldface & Carter Ranges	p145
5	Adirondacks High Peaks & Mt Marcy	p150
6	Long Trail Loop	p154
7	Thoreau's Walk	p159

Laurentides
Reserve
Portneuf
Reserve
Jacques
Cartier
Park
Caribou
St-Maurice
Reserve
QUÉBEC
Sainte-Foy
Levis-Lauzon
La Mauricie
National
Park
Mastigouche
Reserve
Scott
Churchill
Lake
Baxter
State
Park
Houlton
Mont-
Tremblant
Park
Trois-Rivières
Vallee-Jonction
Chamberlain
Lake
Chesuncook
Lake
Saint-Georges
Millinocket
Victoriaville
Arthabaska
Moosehead
Lake
Drummondville
CANADA
USA
Terrebonne
QUÉBEC
Jackman
Longueuil
Sherbrooke
Jackman
15
Monson
Lincoln
Laval
MONTRÉAL
Granby
Lasalle
MAINE
Old Town
Orono
201
Bangor
Skowhegan
Waterville
Ellsworth
Bar
Harbor
VERMONT
AUGUSTA
1A
Belfast
Adirondack
Park
Burlington
Essex Junction
Waterbury
WHITE MOUNTAINS
Lewiston
Thomastown
Acadia
National
Park
Lake Placid
Green
Mountain
National
Forest
MONTPELIER
North Conway
White
Mountain
National
Forest
Sebago
Lake
Bath
ADIRONDACK
MOUNTAINS
Portland
Lake
Winnipesaukee
Great
Sacandaga
Lake
Northville
Green
Mountain
National
Forest
NEW
HAMPSHIRE
CONCORD
ATLANTIC
Saratoga
Springs
GREEN MOUNTAINS
Manchester
NEW YORK
Bennington
OCEAN
Troy
ALBANY
MASSACHUSETTS
Haverhill
Lawrence
Lowell
Catskill
Park
Northampton
Quabbin
Reservoir
Cambridge
BOSTON
Provincetown
Cape Cod
National
Seashore
Wellfleet
Pawtucket
Cranston
PROVIDENCE
Bristol
HARTFORD
Warwick
New
Bedford
Nantucket
Island
New Haven
CONNECTICUT
New Haven
Bridgeport
Block
Island
Martha's
Vineyard
Paterson
Yonkers
Stamford
Greenwich
Long Island
Jersey
City
Lindenhurst
Newark
NEW YORK
Elizabeth
NEW
JERSEY
TRENTON

0   50   100 km
0   25   50 miles
1:5,000,000

from mid-September to mid-October, when fall paints the hillsides scarlet and gold. Fall is spectacular here; the weather is generally warm by day (50°F to 70°F or so) and cool by night. If you can manage a mid-week trip, you may have the trail to yourself.

INFORMATION
Information Sources
Three clubs are valuable sources of information about the hiking trails featured in this chapter: the Appalachian Mountain Club (AMC; ☎ 603-466-2727, 800-367-3364, 🖳 www.outdoors.org, postal address: PO Box 298, Gorham, NH 03581); the Adirondack Mountain Club (ADK; ☎ 518-668-4447, 800-395-5080, 🖳 www.adk.org, postal address: 814 Goggins Rd, Lake George, NY 12845); and the Green Mountain Club (GMC; ☎ 802-244-7037, 🖳 www.greenmountainclub.org, postal address: PO Box 650, Waterbury Center, VT 05677), Rte 100, RR1, Waterbury Center. These clubs work tirelessly to maintain the trails and to protect the region from development.

GATEWAYS
Boston
Boston is a major hub for the region. The city's airport, Logan International, serves major destinations from around the world. From Boston, one can rent a car at the airport (all the major US rental agencies are represented) or take a bus. Major bus companies link Boston with most cities throughout New England.

For visitor information, contact the Greater Boston convention & visitors bureau (☎ 617-536-4100, 888-SEE-BOSTON, 🖳 www.bostonusa.com), 2 Copley Place, Suite 105, Boston, MA 02116.

Places to Stay & Eat For lodgings in Boston, contact *Hostelling International Boston (☎ 617-536-9455, 888-HOST-222, 🖳 www.bostonhostel.com)*, 12 Hemenway St, Boston, MA 02116, offering dormitory-style rooms, full kitchens and self-service laundry. The hostel is near several colleges, so there are several inexpensive eateries in the vicinity.

Manchester
If you're heading to New Hampshire's White Mountains or Maine, consider using Manchester, New Hampshire's airport. You'll find car rental agencies here and bus services to northern New England cities.

For visitor information, contact the Greater Manchester chamber of commerce (☎ 603-625-6426, 🖳 www.manchesterchamber.org), 889 Elm St, Manchester, NH 03101-2000.

Places to Stay Manchester has a handful of economical lodgings; try the *Rice Hamilton (☎ 603-627-7281, 123 Pleasant St)* or *Hill-Brook Motel (☎ 603-472-3788)* at 250 Rte 101, Bedford (3mi south of Manchester). Both offer basic but clean digs, some with kitchenettes for about $40 to $55 a night. At the airport, try the *Highlander Inn (☎ 603-625-6426, 2 Highlander Way)* with free airport shuttle; rooms start at $99.

100 Mile Wilderness

Appalachian Trail to Mt Katahdin

Duration	6 days
Distance	46mi (74km)
Standard	medium-hard to hard
Start	Lake Nahmakanta
Finish	Katahdin Stream campground
Nearest Town	Millinocket
Public Transport	no

Summary This hike traverses Maine's northern lake country and deep woods, culminating with a rigorous climb up Maine's highest peak. It features pristine, remote mountain lakes, postcard-pretty streams, waterfalls and cascades, and lofty summit views.

This magnificent hike offers a sustained backwoods experience through Maine's northern lakes region. You'll hike the famed

Appalachian Trail through dense woods, skirting pristine mountain lakes and streams, culminating with an arduous climb up Mt Katahdin.

The southern portion of this hike is relatively easy, travelling on level, well-marked paths through lush, lakeside forests, with short climbs up Nesuntabunt Mountain and Rainbow Ledges. Along the way you'll hear loons and beavers and are likely to see moose on the banks of pretty Nahmakanta and Rainbow Lakes. You might even see the black, furry tail-end of a bear as it scrambles into the woods.

The hike ends in Baxter State Park, where you'll need advance reservations. The climb up Mt Katahdin is one of the toughest in the east, offering the finest views.

HISTORY

During the 19th century the woods in this region were filled with loggers and the rivers and streams were the main highways for moving timber. Dams were built, ledges dynamited and roads carved to make way for logs en route to Maine's mills. Remnants of the old logging days remain (look for stanchions in the rocks near Nesowadnehunk Stream and at the dynamited ledges along Rainbow Stream) and sounds of trucks can still be heard on the private logging roads criss-crossing the backwoods.

Today, much of the area is under special-use or multiple-use management. The Katahdin Iron Works/Jo-Mary Forest is a privately-owned, commercial forest of about 175,000 acres between Millinocket, Greenville and Brownville. The North Maine Woods Company (☎ 207-435-6213, postal address: PO Box 425, Ashland, ME 04732) manages recreation in the forest including campsites, road use and fees. The National Park Service (NPS) and the Bureau of Land Management (BLM) own much of the land surrounding Nahmakanta Lake.

Mt Katahdin lies within Baxter State Park, some 204,733 acres donated to the state by former Governor Percival Baxter. The park has 46 mountain peaks, 18 of which exceed 3500ft. As a condition of his gift, Baxter declared that the land 'shall forever be left in the natural wild state...' The state goes to great lengths to hold up its end of the bargain, controlling the recreational impact on the park by enforcing strict regulations and limiting the number of visitors (see Planning).

NATURAL HISTORY

Katahdin, the Abenaki's name for 'greatest mountain', holds a special place in the hearts of New Englanders. At 5267ft elevation, it is not the region's tallest summit (Mt Washington holds that honor at 6288ft), but it is arguably its most dramatic. It's a cloud-shrouded giant of massive cliffs, steep ridges, craggy peaks and glacial cirques, rising abruptly from the dense northern-Maine forest. Three giant basins with towering granite walls surround Katahdin's six peaks: Baxter (the highest peak on the west side); South, Chimney and Pamola Peaks to the east; and Hamlin and Howe Peaks to the north. Circling the basins and connecting Baxter and Pamola Peaks is the famous Knife Edge, a narrow, jagged ridge of fractured granite, with slopes falling some 1500ft on each side.

Katahdin's broad, above-treeline plateaus (formed thousands of years ago when a glacier planed off the mountain top) support a variety of alpine tundra, carpeting barren areas in diapensia, sedge, snowbank and alpine heath communities. The smallest plants found here are among the oldest perennials in Maine.

Native American legend says that Katahdin is guarded by Pamola, god of wind and storms. She's believed to be a giant storm-bird, threatening those who get near the mountain with unpredictable, harsh weather.

PLANNING

This hike requires work, logistically and physically, and should not be underestimated or taken on at the spur of the moment. The hike includes 18mi (from the start on Nahmakanta Lake to Abol Bridge) of the '100 Mile Wilderness', a stretch extending from Monson, Maine, to the Abol Bridge said to be the most wild and remote on the Appalachian Trail. There are a few logging roads, but you'll not find services or supplies along this route.

What to Bring
Bring food and supplies for at least six days. Weather is unpredictable so be prepared with rain gear, warm clothes and cold-weather sleeping bag. Insect repellent is a must. Consider packing a black-fly headnet; these pesky buggers can ruin a trip if you're not prepared. You can pick one up at most outdoor gear shops for less than $12. Bring rope, preferably with a pulley system, for hanging food packs away from black bears. (See the boxed text 'The Counter-Balance Method' in the Facts for the Hiker chapter.)

Maps
The 1:62,500 *Appalachian Trail in Maine (Map 1)* covers this hike in its entirety. The accompanying book, published by the Maine Appalachian Trail Club (postal address: PO Box 282, Augusta, ME 04332) features seven maps of the Appalachian Trail through Maine.

The compass declination in Maine is about 18 degrees west.

Permits & Regulations
Advance reservations are required for all campsites within Baxter State Park. Camping is permitted only in authorized campgrounds and campsites. Reserve sites well in advance; some fill up in January for the summer season. Call or write Baxter State Park (☎ 207-723-5140), 64 Balsam Dr, Millinocket, ME 04462, for information and reservation forms. Then mail in the fee and a completed reservation form; no phone reservations are taken; no refunds. Shelters, lean-tos and tent sites are $6 per person per night.

Everyone must register when entering the park (register at the Daicey Pond campground). Use of plastic sheeting is prohibited at some sites and use of soap or the disposal of food scraps is prohibited in any water.

Fires are permitted at designated sites only. During extended dry periods no fires or open-air burning is allowed. Lean-tos and shelters outside Baxter State Park are first-come, first-served.

NEAREST TOWN
Millinocket
Millinocket is a hub of activity with a host of fast food restaurants and services. Contact the Katahdin Area chamber of commerce (☎ 207-723-4444, fax 723-4459, ℮ kacc@kai.net) at 1029 Central St for visitor information.

Places to Stay & Eat *Katahdin Area B&B* (☎ 207-723-5220, 94–96 Oxford St) has five rooms with private baths for $45 to $60. *Big Moose Inn* (☎ 207-723-8391) has 11 rooms with shared baths for $32 to $36 per person. The more deluxe *Best Western Heritage* (☎ 207-723-9777, 935 Central St) has a hot tub – a welcome amenity at the end of the trail. Double rooms are $89 per night.

The *Appalachian Trail Cafe* (☎ 207-723-6720) off Main St caters to hikers with daily specials, hot and cold sandwich platters, homemade breads and salads.

Getting There & Away From Boston, follow I-95 north to exit 56. Follow Hwy 11/157 west into Millinocket. From Manchester, follow Hwy 101 east to I-95, then proceed north as above.

GETTING TO/FROM THE HIKE
Getting to the trailhead on Nahmakanta Lake is a long haul, much of it on gravel logging roads. Plan on at least two hours – more if the roads are in poor condition. Take Jo-Mary Rd, off Hwy 11, about 15mi south of Millinocket. This is a private road and you'll be required to pay a $7 per person fee at the checkpoint gate to enter. The gate is open 6 am to 10 pm. For more information and road conditions contact the North Maine Woods Company or call the gatehouse (☎ 207-723-8944). From the gate it's a slow-going 24mi to the trailhead at Nahmakanta Lake.

Katahdin Stream campground, where this hike ends, is accessed through the Togue Pond Gate at Baxter State Park's south entrance. It's about 24mi from Millinocket.

The best plan is to arrange a shuttle service with the Katahdin Taxi Company (☎ 207-723-2000). The cost is about $45 from Millinocket to the trailhead at the south end of Nahmakanta Lake and $35 from Katahdin Stream campground back to Millinocket. You can leave your car in the taxi company's parking lot (free of charge) while you're hiking.

THE HIKE
Day 1: Nahmakanta Lake to Wadleigh Stream Lean-To
2–3 hours, 2.6mi (4.2km)
This is a short day, considering that it will take two to three hours to reach the trailhead.

The trail skirts **Nahmakanta Lake** – a pristine, 4mi-long glacial lake considered by many hikers to be one of the prettiest along the entire Appalachian Trail. Towering aspen, hemlock, northern white cedars and birch trees line its rocky beaches.

The trail leaves the gravel logging road, heading northwest across Nahmakanta Stream bridge. At 0.3mi a side trail leads to the shoreline of Nahmakanta Lake for a good peek at the lake. The main trail skirts the lake's southwest shore, passing over smooth granite slabs, before rising steeply away from the water and into a forest of towering aspen, cedar, hemlocks and birch. For the next two or so miles the trail travels up and down gently from the lakeshore to the woods. At 1½mi the trail descends and the shoreline to a small gravel beach, a nice place to dip your toes. The trail then rises sharply to about 200ft above the lake and open rock ledges with good views of the lake, before descending steeply. At 2.2mi, a 50ft side trail leads to a pretty sand beach.

You'll cross the **Wadleigh Stream** before reaching the **lean-to** at 2.6mi. The lean-to sits at the edge of Wadleigh Stream and there are several tent sites in the nearby woods, surrounding the lean-to. After setting up camp, consider a short walk back to Nahmakanta Lake, where you can listen to the loons, spot moose along the shoreline and watch bats dart back and forth gobbling up insects.

Day 2: Wadleigh Stream to Rainbow Stream Lean-To
5–6½ hours, 8.1mi (13km)
Fill your water bottles before leaving camp in preparation for your climb up Nesuntabunt

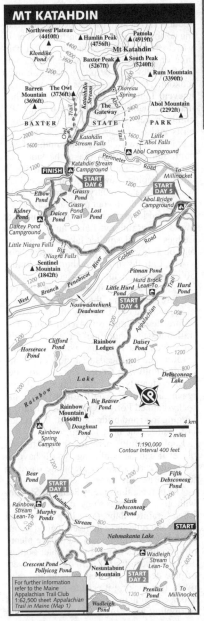

Mountain – you won't find reliable water for about 4mi. The trail leaves the lean-to, heading north through a thick conifer forest on its way to Nesuntabunt Mountain. For a half-mile or so the trail climbs gently, gaining 250ft in elevation before reaching an open lookout. The trail continues to ascend on an uneven footpath, descends briefly, then makes a final, steep climb. The 0.6mi, 650ft climb snakes back and forth through rock cliffs and over a series of stone steps. At 1.9mi you'll reach the 1540ft **summit of Nesuntabunt Mountain**. Take the side trail leading 250ft to an open ledge, where you'll have sweeping views of Maine's northern woods and lake country. Nahmakanta Lake lies to the south; to your north and east you'll get a good look at where you're going, with views of Rainbow Lake and Rainbow Ledges, several smaller lakes and streams and, on a clear day, the peaks of Mt Katahdin.

The trail down Nesuntabunt is a kinder 500ft descent, with rocky ledge lookouts along the way, until it descends gently into the forest. At 3.1mi, the trail crosses a logging road and climbs easily through woods before descending to **Crescent Pond**. The trail hugs the shoreline for about a half-mile, then heads into the woods. At 4.4mi, a 150ft side trail leads to a view of the upcoming **Pollywog Gorge**. The trail now descends steadily into the gorge until you reach the bottom. You'll follow along the rocky-banked Pollywog Stream, reaching a logging road and bridge at 5.7mi. This is the last road for the next 17½mi.

Look carefully here for the white trail blaze; it can be confusing. You'll have to cross the road and find the white blaze on the opposite side.

The trail parallels pretty **Rainbow Stream**, with clear waters rushing down over polished granite slabs. You'll pass several shoots and falls and a number of good swimming holes along the way, and have plenty of opportunities to refill your water bottles. The well-worn trail is softened with layers of pine needles. It's well marked and relatively flat, making it easy to relax and meander, enjoying the smell of cedar and sound of rippling water. At 8.1mi, you'll meet up with the stream again and the *Rainbow Stream lean-to* comes into sight.

The lean-to sits on the banks of Rainbow Stream, with plenty of swimming holes nearby. The shelter has room for about six people, a fire pit and privy. There are also several surrounding tent sites.

Alternative Campsites
Rainbow Spring If you'd like to continue (see Day 3), you'll find a small *campground* just off the shores of Rainbow Lake, another 3.8mi down the trail. There's a privy and a spring for water. Sites are set in the woods but a short trail leads to the lake's shoreline, the perfect place for a day's end swim.

Day 3: Rainbow Stream to Hurd Lean-To
6–8 hours, 11½mi (18.5km)
This is a long day, hiking beside one of the East's prettiest lakes, up Rainbow Ledges and through dense forest. A worthwhile side trip up Rainbow Mountain for lofty views adds another 2.2mi. If you prefer, you can shorten your day by pitching a tent along the way. You'll find a number of choice shoreline spots near the southeast end of Rainbow Lake. This will cut off about 4½mi, adding it to Day 4's shorter stage.

The trail leaves the shelter, crossing **Rainbow Stream** on slippery logs that can be especially tough in high water. In a few minutes you'll see the Rainbow Lake Deadwaters. It's an easy, level walk through white pine and cedar forest, with water views, for about the next 1½mi. If you arrive at the Deadwaters early in the morning, and quietly, you may see moose feeding on the aquatic plants in the shallow shoreline waters.

At 1.8mi, the trail heads away from the Deadwaters, climbing gently toward Rainbow Lake. Listen for owls that are plentiful in these woods and for the slap of beavers' tails on the lake. The trail flanks the **Rainbow Lake** shoreline for about a half-mile before descending slightly into the forest and through a small meadow, before reaching the side trail to the *Rainbow Spring campsite* at 3.8mi. Even if you don't stay for the night, stop to walk down the short trail leading to the lake. You'll find a cold spring for filling your water bottles and a fine spot to plunge in the water. Rainbow Lake is perfect for swimming, with tepid water, a hard, sandy bottom and clear, clean water. Spending an evening near Rainbow Lake has the added benefit of a nightly serenade, courtesy of the large number of loons that live on the lake. Unfortunately, you're also likely to hear the frequent whirr of float planes as they leave and return to a nearby fishing camp.

At 5½mi, you'll see a sign marking the side trail to the summit of **Rainbow Mountain**. The 2.2mi roundtrip is a moderate hike, well worth the time and effort. The mountaintop features an open ledge covered in soft lichen, moss and blueberries, with sweeping views of the surrounding forest, lakes and mountains.

Back on the trail, you'll travel in a forest of mosses, ferns and conifers, with tree-filtered glimpses of the lake's shimmering waters. The footing becomes gnarly with roots and large rocks, but it maintains an even grade. There are several clearings to the lake, if you need water or refreshing. You'll find a few cleared spots for overnight camping as you near the south end of the lake, a good option if you're tenting.

At 7.3mi, a side trail leads 0.1mi to Little Beaver Pond and an additional 0.4mi to Big Beaver Pond. Both spots are secluded and quiet, but too murky for swimming and a very popular hang-out for hordes of pesky no-see-ums and mosquitos. We'd skip it.

The trail now leads to **Rainbow Ledges**, a moderate 550ft climb to open slabs of granite. A fire here in 1923 razed the mountaintop forest, leaving today's unobstructed views. Reindeer lichen and lush mosses carpet the ledges. In summer the area is filled with wild blueberries, making this a great spot for a rest and a snack.

The trail crosses the ledges before descending into a deep forest. You'll travel up and down at a moderate grade before reaching the *Hurd Brook lean-to* at 11½mi. The three-sided, tin-roofed shelter fits about six people, has a privy, and a nearby spring for water. It sits in a deeply-shaded forest and

can be quite dark and dreary. Of redeeming value is the comradeship of fellow hikers; some who may be thru-hikers on the Appalachian Trail, willing to share their experiences. Check out the shelter's guest book for interesting reading. This is one of the last stops for northbound AT thru-hikers close to the end of their multimonth journey. The book is filled with messages and goodbyes to hikers met along the way and personal reflections of life on the trail.

You have the option of continuing on another 2.8mi to **Abol Bridge** – see Day 4.

Day 4: Hurd Lean-To to Abol Bridge

2–3 hours, 3½mi (5.6km)

This is the shortest day of the hike, but with plenty of options for side trips and excursions. It will also give you time to recuperate from the previous day and to prepare for the next two. You'll be leaving the 100 Mile Wilderness section of the hike at Abol Bridge, your last stop before entering Baxter State Park.

The trail leaves the shelter, entering a dense, fragrant pine forest. A thick blanket of pine needles carpets the trail and giant tree boughs form a canopy overhead. Giant glacial boulders, covered in velvety mosses and lichen, dot the forest. The hike to Abol Bridge is a gentle up-and-down meander, made a bit tougher at times by the boulders strewn across the trail. At 3mi, you'll reach the trailhead sign marking the northern entrance to the 100 Mile Wilderness, and warning hikers of the area's remoteness and the need to carry adequate food and supplies. In a few steps you'll reach civilization, coming out on Golden Rd and Abol Bridge.

Cross the bridge and you'll see the sign for the *Abol Bridge campground (postal address: PO Box 536, Millinocket, ME 04462)*. This is the only private campground on the AT and is a very welcome site for most hikers. The store stocks real food, like fresh donuts, fruit, brewed coffee, sandwiches and snacks, and a limited amount of supplies. Tent sites are $7.50 per person, each furnished with a picnic table and fire pit. There are coin-operated showers, flush toilets and potable water. We'd suggest visiting the store and showers, but saving the camping fees by turning left out of the store, crossing the street and walking a few yards to a *free camping area*. The wooded sites overlook the river, with picnic table, fire pits and a privy.

You can spend the rest of your day on the banks of Maine's famed **Penobscot River**. The waters of the 'Penob' roar over worn boulders, slipping in and out of the shadows of Mt Katahdin. Centuries ago, the famous fishing guide Joe Polis and Henry David Thoreau journeyed the river, and Penobscot Indians hunted the surrounding woods and fished the waters. Today, it remains a favorite with anglers fishing for wild salmon, whitewater rafters who ride the fast-moving waters and contemplative visitors who watch moose at dusk, or eagles overhead. If you're feeling restless, load a day-pack and head for one of several trails in the area.

Day 5: Abol Bridge to Katahdin Stream Campground
5–6½ hours, 9.9mi (16km)
Roaring rivers, bubbling streams, tumbling falls and pristine mountain ponds highlight the day's hike into Baxter State Park.

Walk down the road, heading west; just after crossing the Katahdin Stream, the trail leaves the road and heads into the woods. At 1.9mi, a footbridge crosses the tiny Foss and Knowlton Brook. From here, you'll follow the shore of the **Penobscot River**, in and out of view of the water. It's a flat, easy meander for about the next 2mi. At 4.1mi, you'll reach Pine Point, the junction of the West Branch of the Penobscot River with Nesowadnehunk Stream. The trail curves to the right to follow the stream, but take a peek up the Penobscot River for a pretty view of falls. You might also see whitewater rafters on the river.

Nesowadnehunk Stream is postcard-pretty, with clear waters rippling over rocks into pools and eddies. You'll follow the stream for more than 3mi, hiking easily along its banks. There are plenty of places to swim and picnic along the way. At 4½mi, rock hop across the stream, and again on the upper

branch at 5½mi, before climbing gently to a rocky ledge on your way to a series of waterfalls. At 6.3mi, a 150ft side trail leads to a scenic overlook of **Big Niagra Falls** and, in another hundred or so yards, you'll have a peek at **Little Niagra Falls**. Both are beauties.

It's a level, short hike of 1.1mi to the *Daicey Pond campground*. This pretty, and very popular, Baxter State Park site offers 11 wilderness cabins (equipped with beds, a stove for heat and gas lights), lean-tos and tent sites. The setting, on the banks of a secluded mountain pond in the shadows of Katahdin, is hard to beat. Staying here, with advance reservations (see Permits & Regulations under Planning), is an option; but it means that you'll have an additional 2.3mi to tag on to your very tough and long trip up to Katahdin's peak the next day. In any case, plan to spend a little time at Daicey – there's great swimming, picnic tables and canoes to rent. There's also a small library housed in a log cabin and a pleasant porch, complete with comfy rocking chairs. You'll need to register with the ranger before continuing on.

Back on the white-blazed trail, you'll skirt **Daicey Pond**, **Elbow Pond** and **Tracy Pond** before reaching the Perimeter Rd at 9.1mi. The trail turns right along Perimeter Rd until 9.8mi, when you reach *Katahdin Stream campground*, 0.1mi off the road. Katahdin Stream campground has 12 lean-tos and 11 tent sites, a picnic area and a ranger station. Water is available from the stream.

This is the time to check out the weather forecast for the following day, load up on carbohydrates and water, and get a good night's sleep. Mt Katahdin is up next.

Alternative Route: Daicey Pond to Katahdin Stream Campground via Grassy Pond Trail
1–2 hours, 2mi (3.2km)
The Grassy Pond Trail is a shorter route to the Katahdin Stream campground from Daicey Pond, cutting off about a half-mile. The disadvantage is that you'll miss seeing Elbow and Tracey Ponds (though you'll get a bird's eye view of both ponds when you hike up Katahdin).

The trail is a pleasant, level walk through woods and on boardwalks. Pick up the trail at the Daicey Pond campground.

Day 6: Katahdin Stream Campground to Mt Katahdin Return
10–13 hours, 10.4mi (16.7km), 4167ft (1250m) ascent/descent

Be prepared for a long, strenuous day of climbing. Though not technical, this hike requires a good deal of bouldering. You'll gain more than 4000ft in 5.2mi, and much of your day will be spent above treeline. The reward of lofty, ridgeline views of Maine's wild northern country is worth every grunt and groan and bump and bruise you're likely to get along the way.

The AT follows the Hunt Trail to Katahdin's peak. It's the oldest route up the mountain, blazed in 1900 by Irving Hunt, the owner of a local sporting camp. The trailhead and hiker sign-up register is at the Katahdin Stream campground. The first couple of miles are a bit of a teaser. The trail moves at a moderate, sometimes level, grade along a stream and through a mixed hardwood forest of tall birch, maples and white

> **WARNING**
>
> Start your ascent of Mt Katahdin early so that you're down below treeline before dusk. All hikers are required to sign in before attempting the climb. The trail is often closed due to wind, rain, snow or, more rarely, heat. If weather conditions are not optimal, the rangers will not let you go up. Stay alert and be prepared to turn back if the weather takes a turn for the worse – which it often does. Consider yourself lucky if you get to climb Katahdin with clear skies and calm winds, on the day you planned – Pamola, the storm-god, is on your side.

pine. Who said this was tough? At 1mi, the Owl Trail leaves to the left. Now, your work begins as the AT begins to rise steeply, reaching **O-Joy Brook** at 1.7mi. You'll keep climbing at a steep incline for another mile to the **'Cave'**, a den formed by two gigantic boulders. In less than a half-mile you'll reach treeline, a land of wind-twisted krummholz and rough terrain, clogged with giant, pink-colored boulders. The trail becomes tougher,

Struggling Upward

Wild, rugged, and remote Mt Katahdin holds a special place in the hearts of hikers. It's the northern terminus of the Appalachian Trail, and it's not uncommon to hear compelling stories from hikers on the trail to its peak, or to witness emotional outbursts from thru-hikers who've made it to the summit, completing a 2100mi plus odyssey.

On a recent hike to Katahdin Peak, we met an unlikely couple: well-dressed seniors from Georgia, enjoying orange juice and donuts on the trail. We engaged in the usual trail banter. They told us they'd spent the night at a local B&B 'as close as we could get to the trail', rose before dawn, and we're committed to 'making it to the top'.

Yeah, right, we thought. We wished them good luck and headed on, convinced that they probably wouldn't make it up the relentlessly steep trail and exposed, skyrocketing boulder fields that lie ahead.

We passed them again on our way back down, looking a lot more bedraggled but still moving upward. 'I'd like to tell you why we're here', the woman said to us. 'Today is our son's birthday. He would have been 32 years old.'

Their son was an AT thru-hiker, she explained. He had died a year previously by his own hand. 'Every night, we read something from the journal he kept while hiking the AT,' she revealed. 'Today, we've come to spread his ashes on the top of Mt Katahdin. It's what he wanted.'

We don't know whether they made it to the top and have never connected with this couple again, but we think of them every time we climb a mountain.

Diane Bair & Pamela Wright

following an exposed, boulder-strewn ridgeline marked by white paint slashes and cairns and climbing steeply over fractured rocks. The route (at this point it's more a way up than a trail) will undoubtedly give you pause. ('It goes *where*?')You'll find a few iron rungs to help you up the steepest boulders. Be careful to follow the trail marks; many people have been seriously injured after getting off the trail.

At 3.6mi, the trail passes **'The Gateway'**, a pass between two granite slabs, and continues east to Thoreau Spring, at 4.2mi. To the left is the Baxter Peak Cutoff, your best alternative route down the mountain if the weather turns bad. From the spring, the trail climbs moderately across the open, exposed tablelands for 1mi to **Baxter Peak**.

The peak is 13ft shy of 1mi high, hence the 13ft cairn marking the spot. You'll have eye-popping views from the summit of Maine's remote, wild north country, dozens of shimmering lakes and Katahdin's slides and ridges.

Descend carefully by the same route.

Side Trip: Owl Trail
4–5 hours, 6.4mi (10.3km)
This up-and-back hike is a good alternative for those not wanting to make the arduous climb up Katahdin. At 3736ft, the Owl Mountain domed summit boasts splendid panoramic views of northern Maine and Mt Katahdin.

Follow the AT/Hunt Trail from the Katahdin Stream campground. At 1mi, pick up the Owl Trail, cross a tributary of Katahdin Stream and begin to climb on a well-marked route. You'll reach the summit 2.2mi after leaving the AT. Note that this trail is sometimes closed in the summer due to nesting hawks.

Acadia National Park

Acadia National Park, surrounded by the cold, pounding Atlantic waters, is blessed with scenic riches. Rugged, granite cliffs and glacier-carved mountains jut from the sea and deep lakes and glistening ponds dot the inland valleys, forest and marshlands.

This popular park occupies 41,000 acres on Mt Desert Island along Maine's northern rocky coastline and draws more visitors per acre than any other national park in the United States. The island, attached to the mainland by a bridge, is also the home of sleepy fishing villages, harbor towns and bustling Bar Harbor, the hub of activity, services and lodging.

Hikers have plenty of choices: more than 120mi of trails, ranging from flat beach hikes to more strenuous cliff climbs. In addition, there are 55mi of motorless carriage roads weaving through the park, offering hikers and bikers a look at the less-visited interior landscape. The carriage road system, including 16 stone bridges, was a gift of John D Rockefeller Jr and remains one of the finest examples of hand-cut stone roads left in America.

The two hikes featured here are representative of what Acadia has to offer, with rewarding vistas of mountains, valleys, harbors and open ocean.

HISTORY
The Abenaki Indian tribe occupied the island when Samuel de Champlain landed in 1604. He named it 'L'isle de Mont Desert' for its rocky, desert-like peaks. For many years, hearty fishermen and lumbermen who harvested logs for shipbuilding lived on the rugged island.

The island's beauty would not go unnoticed for long; by the mid-19th century it had become a summer playground for America's rich and famous. The Fords, Carnegies, Rockefellers and Vanderbilts built elegant summer cottages on the island. In 1919, President Woodrow Wilson sought to preserve and protect the area, establishing the Lafayette National Park, the first national park east of the Mississippi. Ten years later it was renamed Acadia.

In 1947, a devastating fire swept the island, changing its appearance forever. The fire destroyed many of the elegant homes and summer mansions, razing 17,000 acres of forest land, including 10,000 acres in Acadia.

Today, a young, rejuvenated forest has grown back and Acadia National Park remains a top tourist destination, drawing visitors from around the world.

NATURAL HISTORY

The geological sculpting of Acadia National Park began tens of thousands of years ago when glaciers carved through an east–west granite ridge. As a result, most of Acadia's mountains have steep east–west sides, with more gently sloping north–south ridges. When the glaciers receded they left whaleback-shaped mountain ridges, deep lakes and ponds, and Somes Sound, the only fjord on the eastern seaboard.

The forest is young and largely deciduous, a result of the massive 1947 fire. There are 273 species of birds that frequent the park including osprey, endangered peregrine falcons, and puffins that nest on the nearby isolated islands. More than 50 bald eagles nest in the area. A variety of whales – including humpback, fin-back, minke and right whales – as well as porpoises and seals are found in the surrounding waters.

PLANNING

Even in the summer months it can be quite wet, windy and raw. No matter when you go, be sure to bring a raincoat or slicker. The salty sea air and dense fog seep into your pores quickly. Heavy fog can also make trail visibility difficult, especially on treeless ridges marked by cairns. Note that the Precipice Trail is often closed in July and August due to peregrine falcon nesting. For an alternative way up Champlain Mountain take the Beachcroft Path from the west or the Beehive and Bowl Trails to the south.

For information, contact the NPS (☎ 207-288-3338, 🖳 www.nps.gov/acad, postal address: PO Box 177, Bar Harbor, ME 04609). The park's visitor center is at the Hulls Cove Entrance off Rte 3, at the start of Park Loop Rd; it's open 8 am to 4:30 pm mid-April to October (until 6 pm in July and August).

Consider adding other activities to your agenda. Sea kayaking, biking, nature tours

and boat excursions are popular here and there are several outfitters and equipment rental shops in Bar Harbor.

Maps

Free hiking maps for many of the park's trails are available at the visitor center (☎ 207-288-5262) at Hulls Cove on Rte 3.

Friends of Acadia's *Hiking Trail & Carriage Road Map* at about 1:40,000 covers trails on Mt Desert Island and within Acadia National Park.

A Walk in the Park by Tom St Germain features history, descriptions and maps of all Acadia's hiking trails. It's available for about $12 at many of the outdoor or gift shops in Bar Harbor.

Permits & Regulations

There's a $10 per automobile fee to enter Acadia National Park, valid for seven consecutive days. Bikers and hikers into the park are not charged. Backcountry camping is not allowed in the park; you must camp at established campsites. Fires are permitted only in designated rings or fireplaces in campgrounds and picnic areas.

NEAREST TOWNS & FACILITIES
Bar Harbor

This busy resort town, just outside Acadia National Park, is chock-full of restaurants, ice-cream shops, gift stores, B&Bs, motels, hotels and full-scale vacation properties. Guided tours, bike and kayak rentals, whale watches, nature cruises and boat trips leave from here. For information, contact the Bar Harbor chamber of commerce (☎ 207-288-5103, 800-288-5103, postal address: PO Box 158, Bar Harbor, ME 04609).

Places to Eat Try breakfast or lunch at *Two Cats* (☎ 207-288-8595) on Cottage St. Treat yourself to a lobster feast at *Bar Harbor Lobster Bakes* (☎ 207-288-5031) on Rte 3 in Hulls Cove. Pick up groceries at *Don's Shop & Save* on Cottage St.

Getting There & Away From Boston, follow I-95 north into Maine. Take Hwy 395 to Rte 1A. Follow this south to Ellsworth, then take Rte 3 to Acadia National Park and Bar Harbor.

Vermont Transit Lines Day (☎ 207-772-6587) offers a bus service between Boston and Bar Harbor, mid-June through Labor Day. Free bus services are available to and from Bar Harbor and major park sites.

Campgrounds

The park runs two campgrounds. ***Blackwoods campground*** (☎ 800-365-2267), off Rte 3 5mi south of Bar Harbor, has 300 sites and is open year-round. You must reserve in advance. Sites cost $18 a night; free from December through mid-April. ***Seawall campground*** (☎ 207-288-3338), on Rte 102A 5mi south of Southwest Harbor, is open late May through late September. Its 200 sites are first-come, first-served and fill fast, so arrive early in the day to secure one. Sites are $18 a night. Both campgrounds have restrooms (no showers), picnic areas and fire rings.

Champlain Mountain

Duration	2½–4 hours
Distance	1.6mi (2.6km)
Standard	medium-hard
Start/Finish	Park Loop Rd
Nearest Town	Bar Harbor
Public Transport	no

Summary This short, tough hike is the steepest in the park and arguably one of its most dramatic. A series of ladders helps you ascend sheer cliffs to the top of Champlain Mountain for rewarding views extending out to the open waters of the Atlantic Ocean.

GETTING TO/FROM THE HIKE

From Bar Harbor, take West St to Rte 3 and follow it to Park Loop Rd. The Precipice Trailhead will be on your right, just before Sand Beach and Thunder Hole. The trailhead is before the toll gate, so you won't have to pay the park entrance fee to hike this trail.

THE HIKE

Champlain Mountain is the easternmost summit on the island, rising sharply to 1058ft. This footpath is one of the park's most popular, offering great views and the unique experience of a ladder trail.

The Precipice Trail leaves from the well-marked parking area off Park Loop Rd. You'll hop boulder to boulder through a large talus slope, ascending moderately. After 0.4mi you'll reach a junction with the East Face Trail, which leads to the Bear Brook Trail. The Bear Brook Trail offers a more gradual approach to the peak and is often preferred for the descent because it avoids backing down ladders and maneuvering the steepest sections of the Precipice Trail (see the Alternative Route at the end of this hike description).

The Precipice heads to the left, climbing steeply, with stomach-dropping views of plunging cliffs below. If you're afraid of heights it's probably time to turn back. Braver souls can look out beyond the drop-off cliffs at a view of the rocky coastline. You'll head northwest, negotiating the steepest stretches with the help of well-placed iron rungs and railings. Here, the trail requires more mental gumption than physical stamina as it rockets skyward with the aid of well-placed, straight-up ladders.

The trail levels off for the last 500ft, traversing open ledges to the peak, where you'll have a stunning view of island mountains, Frenchman Bay, Great Head, Sand Beach and open ocean. Follow the same trail back down.

Alternative Route: Bear Brook Trail

2 hours, 2mi (3.2km)

The trail begins off Park Loop Rd, just east of the Bear Brook picnic area, heading south toward the summit of Champlain Mountain. The trail ascends gently through sun-dappled forest, climbing the mountain's broad north face. At half a mile, the Champlain East Face Trail heads to the left. This trail intersects with the Precipice Trail, 0.4mi from the Precipice Trail parking area off Park Loop Rd.

Bear Brook Trail continues straight, emerging from the trees for great views of Frenchman Bay. Continue another half-mile to the summit.

Cadillac Mountain

Duration	4–5 hours
Distance	7mi (11.3km)
Standard	medium
Start	Blackwoods campground
Finish	Sieur de Monts
Nearest Town	Bar Harbor
Public Transport	yes

Summary This is one of the longer hikes on Mt Desert Island, climbing to the summit of Cadillac Mountain (1530ft), the tallest peak on the Atlantic coast north of Brazil. You'll have some of the best views from the top – of island mountains, harbors and the Atlantic Ocean. The downside is that at the summit you'll be greeted by crowds of people who made it up via the Cadillac Mountain Auto Rd. You'll descend in the valley between two mountains, through a deep-sided gorge.

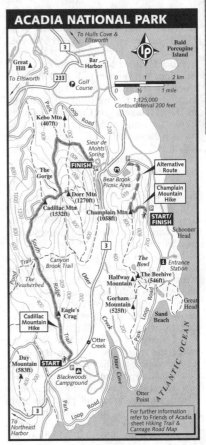

GETTING TO/FROM THE HIKE

From Bar Harbor, take West St to Rte 3. Follow Rte 3 to Park Loop Rd. The Blackwoods campground is off Park Loop Rd, near Otter Cove. The Cadillac South Ridge Trail begins at the campground. From the end of the hike at Sieur de Monts Spring, take Park Loop Rd to Rte 233, then follow Rte 3 to Bar Harbor. Park buses (free) make stops at both Blackwoods campground and Sieur de Monts.

THE HIKE

The first section of the hike, from Blackwoods campground to Cadillac Peak, takes 2½ to three hours and covers 3½mi. Pick up the trailhead at the Blackwoods campground. You'll head north, up the south side of Cadillac Peak. The chances are high that you won't be alone on this part of the hike – this is a popular trail with plenty of foot traffic. The trail heads into the woods, passing over roots and stones along the way. At 1mi, the trail reaches the Eagle's Crag junction, a 0.2mi loop, with plenty of views to the coast and Otter Creek. The trail emerges above treeline, rising moderately over open ledges. In another mile or so you will arrive at

'The Featherbed', a small pond. Canyon Brook Trail, to the right, and Pond Trail, to the left, converge at this point. The South Ridge Trail continues straight over a short, steep stretch and then across more moderate, open expanse. The trail comes close to the Cadillac Mountain Auto Rd; alas, you'll hear the traffic on this road before the final steep, but short, climb to the top. You'll likely be greeted at the summit by crowds of people who've made it up via the road. So what? Relax and enjoy the lofty, unobstructed views from the bare, ledgy summit. Some romantic souls head out in pre-dawn hours, getting to Cadillac's summit to be among the first in the US to see the sun rise. Too early for you? Sunsets are mighty nice, too.

From Cadillac Mountain to Park Loop Rd is one to 1½ hours (1.8mi). Follow the Dorr Mountain Notch Trail from Cadillac's summit. The trail links the summits of Dorr Mountain and Cadillac Mountain. Look for signs and paint splotches on rocks indicating the trail leading into the notch.

From the summit, just past the auto road, the trail turns left and crosses a small brook. You'll head northeast, descending gently. At half a mile, you'll reach the junction with the Gorge Path and Murray Young Trails. The Dorr Mountain Notch Trail continues straight to Dorr Mountain summit (see Side Trip).

Take a left onto Gorge Path, heading north. The trail heads into a **deep gorge**, with granite walls towering 30ft to 40ft above. Even in the heat of the summer this narrow gorge remains cool and wet. A pretty, bubbling stream snakes through the bottom of the gorge. Watch for slippery rocks along the trail. As you leave the gorge the trail follows Kebo Brook. In 1.3mi, you'll reach the Park Loop Rd. Note: Take a right onto the Hemlock Trail, just before Park Loop Rd, for the Sieur de Monts parking area and park bus stop. Cross the stream and follow Hemlock Trail to Hemlock Rd, leading to the parking area in front of Sieur de Monts Spring and Abbe Museum.

Side Trip: Dorr Mountain Summit
30 minutes–1 hour, 0.8mi (1.3km)

Peak baggers and those who never tire of bare summit views will enjoy this short side trip. Heading down from Cadillac Mountain's summit, you'll reach the junctions of Dorr Mountain Notch, Gorge Path and Murray Young Trail. Continue straight on the Dorr Mountain Notch Trail. The trail climbs quickly and steeply, and in 0.4mi reaches the open, ledgy summit. You'll have good views of Cadillac and Champlain Mountains, and open ocean.

White Mountains

Presidential Traverse

Duration	4 days
Distance	25.8mi (41.5km)
Standard	hard
Start	Crawford Notch
Finish	Pinkham Notch
Nearest Town	Jackson
Public Transport	yes

Summary One of New England's finest and most challenging hikes, this traverse in the White Mountains of New Hampshire takes in seven mountain summits, including Mt Washington, the highest peak in the region.

At the top of the list for New England hikers is a climb up mighty Mt Washington. This four-day excursion combines a series of interlocking trails, taking you up the west side of Mt Washington and looping around its east side through a rare, alpine garden before plunging into the lush Great Gulf Wilderness. From here, you'll clamber back up to the ridgeline traversing the Northern Presidential Range.

Much of this trip is spent above treeline on wind-slapped ledges, along the bare, rocky bone of the northern peaks. The effort is immense: leg-quivering climbs, knee-pounding descents and exposure to ornery – and often severe – weather. But the rewards are worth it: top-of-the-world, show-stopping vistas of wild terrain, plunging cliffs, cascades and waterfalls and spill-away views into several states.

There's a well-developed system of connecting trails in the Presidential Range, offering unlimited opportunities to ramble. This trip can easily be shortened or lengthened as you like.

NATURAL HISTORY

Mt Washington, at 6288ft, is the highest mountain in the Northeast, with steep sides, deep ravines and a jutting cone-shaped summit. The Northern Presidentials, with peaks rising above 5000ft, march northwest from Mt Washington, surrounding the Great Gulf. This U-shaped valley, with steep-sided headwalls rising to 1600ft, was formed by vanishing glaciers before the last ice age. It is the largest glacial cirque in the White Mountains. (See the boxed text 'Glaciers & Glacial Landforms' on page 214).

Rare alpine vegetation grows above tree-line on the mountain summits. Some plants, like the endangered dwarf cinquefoil, are found only on the tops of New Hampshire's Presidential and Franconia Mountains.

WARNING

Mt Washington is said to have the worst weather in the world; 231 mph winds whipped the summit on April 12, 1934, the highest velocity ever recorded. Even on the best days Mt Washington can be cold and windy, with average summer summit temperatures hovering in the low 50s°F. Frequent snow storms (sometimes in mid-summer) and bone-chilling rain spank the summit, raising the risks of becoming lost and suffering hypothermia. There have been several serious injuries and more than 100 fatalities on the mountain. Do not let the short distance of this climb lull you into a false sense of security. Be prepared for a rigorous mountain hike and study maps for alternative routes down should the weather change suddenly.

PLANNING

The AMC operates three backcountry huts along this route – Mizpah Hut, Lakes of the Clouds Hut and Madison Hut. Reservations and payment must be made in advance to stay overnight in the huts. This is especially true for the Lakes of the Clouds Hut, the closest shelter to the summit of Mt Washington and the AMC's most popular. Cost for hut stays is $64 per person per night including dinner and breakfast.

When to Hike

Summer is the safest and most popular time for this hike. Severe weather can occur above treeline during spring and fall. It's said

that Mt Washington makes its own weather; it may look nice when you start out, but be prepared for that to change for the worse as you climb. During mid- to late June, the alpine gardens along this route are in bloom.

What to Bring

Carry warm, winter clothing including mittens, hat and windbreaker. Rain gear is a must.

Maps

The AMC's *White Mountain Guide* covers all the trails in the White Mountain National Forest. *Presidential Range (Map 1)* covers the trails in the Presidential and Northern Presidential Ranges at 1:47,500. Compass declination is 17 degrees west.

Permits & Regulations

Permits are not needed to hike in the White Mountain National Forest but you will need a permit for trailhead parking. Permits cost $5 for seven days or $20 for the year and can be picked up at several nearby outdoor shops, ranger stations, the Crawford Notch hostel and the AMC headquarters in Pinkham Notch.

There is no overnight camping on top of Mt Washington. No camping is permitted above treeline except at designated backcountry huts (see earlier in this section for hut fees). Camping is not permitted within 200ft of trails or a quarter-mile of shelters. Campfires are permitted only in firepits at shelters.

NEAREST TOWNS & FACILITIES
Jackson

This postcard-pretty town is a favorite New England vacation destination. Two-thirds of Jackson lies within the White Mountain National Forest so there's plenty of outdoor recreation and scenery. The town is quintessential New England, with a historic covered bridge, white-steepled church and a plethora of *country inns* and *B&Bs*. Bustling North Conway (see Nearest Town & Facilities for the Baldface & Carter Ranges hike) is only a few minutes drive south. For information, contact the Jackson

150 Years of 'Improvements'

There are purists who grouse about the development on top of Mt Washington. But this is nothing new. The first building was constructed at the summit in 1852, followed by a resort hotel in 1853. Several other buildings followed. From 1870 to 1886, there was a weather observatory; in 1932 the observatory was reactivated and continues in operation today.

A carriage road from the Glen House on Route 16 to the summit was opened in 1856. This 8mi road, now called the Mt Washington Auto Rd, is a top tourist attraction. Visitors are charged a fee to drive the road or to join a guided, 45 minute bus trip to the summit. Throughout New England, you're likely to see cars sporting 'This Car Climbed Mt Washington' bumper stickers.

The Mt Washington Cog Railway, ascending the west ridge, was completed in 1869. The historic, steam-powered train hits inclines that reach 35% grade, making it the second steepest railway track in the world. Visitors can purchase tickets for the three hour roundtrip.

Today, you'll find several buildings at the summit, including a cafeteria, souvenir shop, post office, weather obervatory and small museum in the Sherman Adams summit building; the historic Tip Top House, a former hotel; and radio transmitter facilities.

chamber of commerce (☎ 603-383-9356, 800-866-3334, postal address: PO Box 304, Jackson, NH 03846). The chamber also covers the nearby villages of Bartlett and Glen.

For good-tasting, hefty portion grub try the *Wildcat Inn & Tavern (☎ 603-383-4245, 800-228-4245)* on Rte 16A, Jackson Village.

Getting There & Away From Boston, take I-95 north to Rte 16/Spaulding Turnpike (New Hampshire exit 4). Stay on Rte 16 through North Conway to Jackson. Concord Trailways (☎ 800-639-3317) runs bus services from Boston's South Station to North Conway ($25.50 one way) and from

the airport at Manchester, New Hampshire, to North Conway ($16.85 one way).

Campgrounds
Crawford Notch State Park (☎ 603-374-2272), off Rte 302, is tucked in a scenic mountain pass and has 30 rustic tent sites at its *Dry River campground (☎ 603-271-3628),* within walking distance of the Crawford Path trailhead where you begin this hike. The *AMC Crawford Youth Hostel (☎ 603-466-2727)* off Rte 302 (adjacent to Crawford Notch State Park) has two coed bunkhouses, showers and kitchen facilities for $18 per night. *AMC Pinkham Notch headquarters (☎ 603-466-2727)* has coed bunks and private rooms. Bunks are $30; rooms start at $65 for a double. Packages including lodging, breakfast and dinner start at $49.

GETTING TO/FROM THE HIKE
From Jackson, take Rte 16 south to the Rte 302 intersection. Turn right on Rte 302 toward Crawford Notch. Take a right onto Mt Clinton Rd, just past Crawford Notch State Park. The trailhead parking lot is off this road, a short distance from Rte 302.

The hike ends at the Pinkham Notch visitor center on Rte 16, 8mi north of Jackson. The AMC runs a hikers' shuttle service between Pinkham Notch and Crawford Notch from June to mid-October.

THE HIKE
Day 1: Crawford Notch to Lakes of the Clouds
5–6 hours, 7mi (11.3km), 3130ft (939m) ascent

The historic Crawford Path Trail takes you from lush forest, punctuated with brooks, streams and falls to rugged, above-treeline terrain. You'll gain more than 3000ft in elevation, ending at Lakes of the Clouds (5050ft), the highest lake in New England.

Much of the day will be spent above treeline, with magnificent views but with full exposure to fickle weather. Be prepared to turn back quickly if the weather turns bad.

Follow the Crawford Path Cutoff from the parking lot for 0.4mi to a bridge over Gibbs Brook and the junction with Crawford Cliff

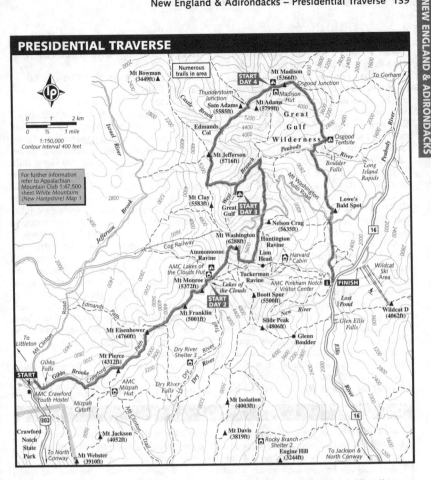

PRESIDENTIAL TRAVERSE

0   1   2 km
0   ½   1 mile
1:150,000
Contour Interval 400 feet

For further information refer to Appalachian Mountain Club 1:47,500 sheet *White Mountains (New Hampshire) Map 1*

spur trail. The spur is a steep side trip leading to a small cascade and ledge overlooking Crawford Notch, and adds 0.8mi to the hike. You'll have a pretty view of the notch, but you may want to save your legs.

Continue on the Crawford Path Cutoff over the bridge and take an immediate left onto Crawford Path, leading northeast. This wide, well-marked trail blazed in 1819 is the oldest continuously maintained footpath in the country. It's also one of the most popular routes up Mt Washington.

Almost immediately you'll pass a spur trail on your left leading to lovely **Gibbs Falls**

and at 1.9mi the Mizpah cutoff trail enters on the right, leading to the *AMC Mizpah Hut*. The Crawford Path marches up the shoulder of Mt Pierce with your first hint of what's to come: a peek at the southern Presidentials and the Dry River Wilderness. The views only get better from here.

At 3.1mi the Webster Cliff Trail leads right to **Mt Pierce** summit (4312ft). Peak baggers shouldn't miss this short, moderate climb, with open views to Mt Washington.

Continue northeast on Crawford Path following cairns on your way to Mt Eisenhower. Here, you'll reap big rewards: expansive,

360-degree views along a moderate climb. In about a half-mile the trail begins to climb more steeply, scaling rocky ledges to the Mt Eisenhower Loop junction at 4.3mi. Trees on the exposed terrain are squashed and stunted, and begin to disappear. If the weather has held, consider the short 300ft scramble to **Eisenhower summit**. At 4761ft, the exposed mountaintop offers great views and the trail loops to rejoin Crawford Path, adding only 0.2mi to your hike.

Back on Crawford Path, you'll begin a breathless half-mile ascent up Mt Franklin. At 6mi, a loop trail on the right leads to 5004ft **Mt Franklin summit**. Go for it – you'll have jaw-dropping vistas into the plunging Oakes Gulf.

At 6.2mi, a loop trail on the left leads to the 5372ft **Mt Monroe summit**. The trail requires a little climbing (about 350ft or so) but gives more open views and is about the same distance as staying on the Crawford Path. The loop trail traverses a lovely and rare alpine garden and, if you've planned it right, you'll reach Mt Monroe summit at dusk, when you can witness a fading sun streaking the horizon with swatches of pink and purple on its way to the other side of the world.

It's an easy descent by either trail to the *Lakes of the Clouds Hut* at 7mi. The high mountain hut sits at the foot of two alpine lakes, overlooking the Ammonoosuc Ravine.

Day 2: Lakes of the Clouds to Great Gulf
6½–7 hours, 5.8mi (9.3km)

If the weather gods are on your side, you'll climb Mt Washington today – a rough and tumble scramble over jagged rocks and granite slabs – and descend its southeast slope before dropping into the protected Great Gulf.

From the hut, the Crawford Path climbs between the two alpine lakes and then passes the junction with Crossover and Camel Trails. It continues past an alpine garden before beginning its relentlessly steep scramble up the cone-shaped **Mt Washington summit**. Be forewarned: it looks a lot easier and closer than it really is. By the time you reach the top your legs will be quivering and you will have earned the immense satisfaction of having made it. Alas, summit-struck hikers are joined by the tour-bus folks who've driven the auto road or taken the railway. Welcome back to civilization. Treat yourself to some cafeteria goodies and then take in the magnificent view.

There are plenty of ways down the mountain (you can even hop aboard the Cog Railway) but this trip takes you a short distance

Doing Tucks

The crocuses were up. The robins were back. The sidewalk vendors were hawking bouquets of tulips and daffodils. And we were shouldering pounds of ski gear, ascending slippery ridges of granite with slopes angled at a precipitous 55 degrees. Below us lay the vast and open bowl of Tuckerman's Ravine.

Every spring, when avalanche danger subsides and the sun crests the edge of the bowl and softens the ice, this wild and challenging region in northern New Hampshire opens to daredevil skiers. The backcountry powderhound paradise can draw more than 2000 skiers on a spring day – not counting the spectators.

'Doing Tucks' is not for the faint of heart. The infamous ravine, an enormous glacial cirque on the southeast side of Mt Washington, has sudden fall-line shifts, plunging drops and over-the-head powder.

The hike up to the headwall is a tortuous climb. You can stay at the Hermit Ranger Station, two-thirds of the way up. It's a first-come, first-served lean-to, more often than not covered in snow. You'll wake to a crystalline splendor, an incredible expanse of white-capped mountains, black jagged rocks, shimmering ice and forests. You'll also be one of the first to tackle the bowl.

Pick a line; hang your ski tips over the edge, take a deep breath – and plunge.

Diane Bair & Pamela Wright

into spectacular Tuckerman's Ravine, across the Mt Washington Alpine Garden, and into the Great Gulf.

From the summit, follow the cairns south to Tuckerman Ravine Trail, descending steeply over giant boulders and jagged rocks. At 0.6mi, the Alpine Garden Trail enters on the left. You'll find relief for your legs on this lovely, level traverse, heading north, with open views: Mt Washington rises to your left; to the south is spectacular Lion Head, the towering ridge overhanging the north wall of Tuckerman's Ravine; to the east is the dizzying headwall of Huntington's Ravine. At your feet is a pretty **alpine garden**, a carpet of mosses, lichen, diapensia, alzalea, Lapland rosebay, and more. The garden is at its blooming best in mid- to late June.

The Alpine Garden Trail crosses the Huntington Ravine Trail at 1.2mi, the Nelson Crag Trail at 1.4mi, and reaches the Mt Washington Auto Rd at 1.8mi. Cross the road and pick up the Wamsutta Trail, which runs 1.7mi from the Auto Rd to the Great Gulf Trail. It's a very steep, rough descent through woods and down a ledgy ridgeline. You'll find several good **tent sites** overlooking the West Branch of the Peabody River, along the Great Gulf Trail near its junction with the Wamsutta Trail.

Day 3: Great Gulf to Mt Madison
4–5 hours, 5.9mi (9.5km)
The day begins in the valley of a large glacial cirque, dotted with wild rivers, shimmering cascades and tumbling waterfalls and surrounded by mountain headwalls. You'll climb steep slopes to the Northern Presidential ridgeline for open, expansive views of mountaintops, towering walls and the luxuriant Great Gulf Wilderness on your way to the Madison Hut.

Follow the Great Gulf Trail southwest (left off the Wansutta Trail), flanking the West Branch of the Peabody River. The trail passes several pretty cascades and crosses the river, before reaching its junction with the Sphinx Trail at 1.1mi. Turn right onto the Sphinx Trail, heading west. The short, 1.1mi **Sphinx Trail**, running in the col between Mts Clay and Jefferson, is arguably

one of the prettiest in the White Mountains. The climb is steep, sometimes slippery, and requires a bit of stamina and willpower but the visual rewards are plentiful. You'll pass several cascades, tumbling down in a hurry from the steep-sided slopes, and crisscross a number of small brooks on your climb through the col. The trail pokes out into the open in about a half-mile, with views of falling waters and drop-off cliffs. Continue the precipitous climb to the ridgeline where you'll intersect the Gulfside Trail.

Turn right onto the Gulfside Trail, heading north, traversing the ridgeline in the open and exposed terrain – though it's well marked with cairns and paint splotches. You'll cross a relatively easy grassy meadow before the Mt Jefferson Loop Trail enters on the left 0.6mi from the Sphinx Trail junction. By all means, head to the summit. It's about a 300ft climb but won't add much to the distance, as it parallels the Gulfside Trail. The views from the top of **Mt Jefferson**, at 5716ft, are breathtaking, covering the Northern Presidential Range, Mt Washington and Great Gulf Wilderness.

The Gulfside Trail dips down, where you'll clamber over rugged rocks, with dizzying views into Jefferson Ravine. The trail reaches Edmands Col, marked with a plaque commemorating the blazer of most of the Northern Presidentials' peak trails, at 1½mi.

From Edmands Col, you'll climb moderately along the ridgeline separating Jefferson Ravine and Castle Ravine along the Gulfside Trail. The rugged terrain has an otherworldly feel to it, with jagged, bare rocks and giant, lichen-covered boulders – a great expanse, fully exposed to the elements.

At 2.8mi, you'll reach a towering cairn marking **Thunderstorm Junction**, where several trails intersect. From here, you'll begin a gradual descent, with views straight ahead to Mt Madison. The *Madison Hut* is 0.9mi from Thunderstorm Junction.

Day 4: Mt Madison to Pinkham Notch
5½–6½ hours, 7.1mi (11.4km)
Today you'll climb to the summit of Mt Madison before heading back down into the

An Extreme Hike in the Presidentials

(Best Undertaken Thus – as an Armchair Adventure)

So you've hiked virtually every mountain in New England. Now what? You do something totally crazy – try to conquer 13 mountain summits in one day. This idea originated with Appalachian Mountain Club hut crew members, who would tackle all the summits to keep themselves occupied when things got slow. They called it the Death March.

The idea: to take on 13 peaks – including the biggie, Mt Washington – at once, squeezing the effort into 16 hours of daylight. Tempted to try it? Alas, we can't recommend this one to most visiting hikers. Those who undertake it need to be completely familiar with the area and terrain, in addition to being in top physical form and extremely well prepared. As with any strenuous mountain hike, trekkers need to know all the routes off every summit to reach help or get out quickly if something goes wrong.

Here's how one intrepid hiking duo did it.

After three months of planning, the pair decided to trek from Gorham Notch to Crawford Notch, a distance of 28.6mi, between sunrise and sunset. To give themselves an edge, they chose one of the longest days of the year (late June, here) and a forecast of great weather. The trip shaped up something like this:

- 5 am, left Dolly Copp campground in Gorham. Conquered Mt Madison (5363ft)
- 8 am-ish, arrived at AMC's Madison Hut.
- Hiked up Mts John Quincy Adams, John Adams (5798ft) and Sam Adams.
- Reached summit of Mt Jefferson (5717ft). The pace? Trotting, jogging, even running up the peaks, stopping to rest only at summits.
- 1 to 2 pm, conquered Mt Washington (6288ft), the highest point in New Hampshire. Took a longish break, ate lunch, changed clothes, then:
- Lakes of the Clouds and summits of Mts Monroe (5385ft), Franklin (5028ft) and Eisenhower (4775ft), pausing to savor each summit.
- Early evening, fatigue sets in. Duo continues in drone mode, climbing Mts Jackson (4012ft) and Webster (3876ft) by 8 pm.
- 8 pm, uh-oh… Gazing at the pink-tinged sky, they realized it was now a race with the sun. Would they make it to Crawford Notch before nightfall?
- Seriously tired, they misjudge the distance from the notch, thinking they were a mile closer to their goal than they were. The woods are getting dark. Fortunately, the trail is good, because the hikers' boots were dragging the ground.
- 9 pm, stumbled out of the forest at Saco Lake, totally exhausted, but sporting the biggest grins of their lives.

Diane Bair & Pamela Wright

Great Gulf Wilderness and Pinkham Notch. It's a steady descent (once over the Madison summit) with plenty of scenic spots and water along the way. There are also a few overnight camping options if you can't bear to leave the mountains and woods.

From the hut, follow the Osgood Trail to the summit of **Mt Madison**. It's a huff and puff climb up the steep ridge, with views to your right of Madison Gulf. In a half-mile you'll reach the 5366ft summit. (Can you

stand more views?) The Watson Path enters to your left, but continue straight from the summit, passing the Howker Ridge Trail on your left and descending a promontory. The trail reaches Osgood Junction at 1mi and then begins a steep descent, dropping below treeline and reaching the Osgood Cutoff trail at 3mi. You can call it quits for the day, if you like, setting up your tent on one of the platforms at the *Osgood campsite*, located at this junction. If you continue, you'll have an even more secluded and picturesque site at the Bluff, about a half-mile away.

Turn right onto the Osgood Cutoff, heading west to the Great Gulf Trail. A pretty *campsite* is located at this junction, sitting on a bluff overlooking the Northern Presidentials and Great Gulf. Turn left onto the Great Gulf Trail and follow it to the Madison Gulf Trail, just a few steps (0.1mi) away. Turn left again, heading southeast on Madison Gulf Trail. This trail makes an up and down route through the Great Gulf Wilderness. It requires several stream crossings that may be difficult in high water.

You'll climb the banks of the West Branch of the Peabody River, and then ascend more gently into the river valley. The trail continues in moderate dips and rises, crossing several brooks before reaching the Mt Washington Auto Rd at 2.1mi. Pick up the Old Jackson Rd, located directly across the road. This well-marked trail will take you 1.9mi, on an even descent, past a small waterfall and across several brooks to Pinkham Notch visitor center and the AMC headquarters, where showers, food and shuttle buses await.

Baldface & Carter Ranges

Duration	3 days
Distance	20.2mi (32.5km)
Standard	medium-hard
Start/Finish	NH 113, just south of North Chatham
Nearest Town	North Chatham
Public Transport	yes

Summary Meandering rivers, emerald green pools and 4mi of open ledges yielding remarkable views of New Hampshire's and Maine's peaks and valleys make this traverse of the Baldface and Carter Ranges one of the finest hiking loops in the Northeast.

Rising more than 3500ft from the valley of the Wild River, Baldface is often overshadowed by some of the more popular ridges to its west. So while the crowds head to mighty Mt Washington, the Presidentials and the Franconia mountain ranges, Baldface stays

relatively untrammeled once you get beyond the day-hiker zone.

Eight trails connect to form this three-day, 20.2mi trek that loops back to the trailhead. The hike combines ascents of North and South Baldface, a drop into the wide, lush Wild River Valley and a climb to the bare-topped Carter Dome and Mt Hight summits. You'll pass Emerald Pool and No-Ketchum Pond, cross several rivers and streams including the scenic Wild River and see some of the finest mountaintop views in the region.

This is not a hike to be taken lightly. The Baldface Circle Trail, where this adventure begins, lies in the valley at 520ft. Steep ledges ascend to the 3591ft summit of North Baldface. You'll top out at 4832ft at Carter Dome. There's a total elevation gain of more than 8000ft, with some exposed ridgeline hiking. Stretching the hike to four days would lower daily mileage and make it more leisurely, but it's certainly doable in three.

This is a land of many options. Baldface is located in the 775,000 acre White Mountain National Forest, which boasts a large network of connecting trails. You can enlarge your loop to continue for days or weeks, and end up back at your car without retracing a step.

NATURAL HISTORY

The Carter-Moriah Range features eight peaks with elevations over 4000ft. The rocky peaks of the Baldface Range rise from a low valley, with South Baldface at 3570ft and North Baldface at 3610ft. The Wild River slices through the valley between the two ranges.

A spread of fires in the early 20th century left many of the summits bare, resulting in sweeping, open views from the peaks of Carter Dome (4832ft), Mt Hight (4675ft) and North and South Baldface.

PLANNING

The AMC (see Information Sources under Information at the beginning of this chapter) and the White Mountain National Forest headquarters (☎ 603-447-5449), Saco ranger station, 33 Kancamagus Hwy, Conway, are excellent sources of information about hiking in the region.

When to Hike

Day hikers tend to crowd the first mile of the Baldface Circle Trail on hot summer days, seeking the cool waters of Emerald Pool. Carter Dome and the Wild River also draw some traffic during the summer season.

What to Bring

Bring extra water. There may be long stretches, especially along the ledges and ridges, where water is unavailable.

If you have room, consider bringing a packable fly rod or other fishing gear – the Wild River offers good trout fishing.

Maps

The bible for this region is the AMC's *White Mountain Guide*, including six maps and covering more than 500 trails. The AMC's *Carter Range–Evans Notch (Map 5)* at 1:95,000 covers this hike. Another good resource is *DeLorme's Trail Map to the White Mountain National Forest* at 1:100,000.

Permits & Regulations

Permits are not needed to hike and backpack in the White Mountain National Forest but are required to park at trailheads. Parking permits cost $5 for seven days ($20 annual pass) and can be picked up at ranger stations, the AMC Pinkham Notch headquarters and many outdoor stores in the area.

No camping is permitted above treeline (where trees are less than 8ft tall). The point where the restricted area begins is marked on most trails with small signs. No camping is permitted within a quarter-mile of most facilities such as shelters and surrounding tent sites, except at the facility itself. Camping is not permitted within 200ft of trails. Campfires are permitted only in fire pits at shelters.

NEAREST TOWN & FACILITIES
North Conway

North Conway has a motherlode of lodging and dining options. For information, contact the North Conway chamber of commerce (☎ 800-367-3364) or Mt Washington Valley chamber of commerce (☎ 603-356-3171, 800-367-3364, ▢ www.mountwashington

valley.org). For outdoor gear and supplies, head to Eastern Mountain Sports on Main St.

Places to Stay & Eat For classic New England flavor, check in to the 18-room *Cranmore Inn* (☎ 603-356-5502, 800-526-5502, 80 Kearsage St). A double room, with breakfast, is $64 per night.

The *Eastern Slope camping area* (☎ 603-447-5092) off Rte 16 in Conway is a big, family-oriented (mini-golf, anyone?) place with 140 tent/trailer sites. Beachfront campsites on the Saco River go for $26 per night; wooded sites are $20.

For pizza, *Elvio's* (☎ 603-356-3307) reigns. Dig into pub grub at *Horsefeathers* (☎ 603-356-6862), offering mammoth burgers as well as trendier fare and locally-brewed pints. Both are on Main St.

Getting There & Away From Boston, take I-95 north to NH 16. Follow Rte 16 north to North Conway. From Manchester, take I-93 north to NH 112 (the scenic Kancamagus Hwy). Follow Rte 112 east to Rte 16, turn left and follow it north to North Conway.

Concord Trailways (☎ 800-639-3317) runs bus services from Boston's South Station to North Conway ($25.50 one way) and from Manchester airport to North Conway ($16.85 one way).

GETTING TO/FROM THE HIKE

From North Conway, follow Rte 16 south to Rte 113, turn left and follow it north. The trailhead parking lot is off NH 113 about 0.2mi north of the AMC Cold River Camp driveway in North Chatham. This is a loop hike, so you'll end up back at your car at the end of the trip.

Rowell's Rolling Wheels (☎ 603-447-2105) runs a private shuttle service in this area.

THE HIKE
Day 1: Baldface to Perkins Notch Shelter

6–7½ hours, 8.6mi (13.9km), 2470ft (741m) ascent

Strap on your sturdiest boots, get plenty of rest and throw in some extra Power Bars for

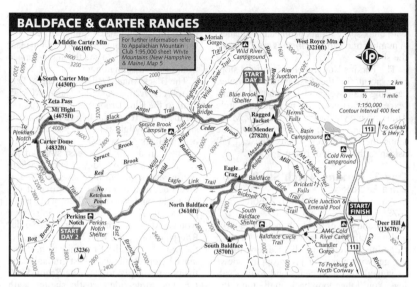

BALDFACE & CARTER RANGES

the first day of this trek. You'll gain almost 2500ft in elevation and hike more than 8mi before reaching the Perkins Notch shelter on the banks of the Wild River.

Follow the Baldface Circle Trail to Circle Junction (0.7mi). Watch for a well-worn path leading north; this will take you 0.1mi to pretty **Emerald Pool**. The deep, icy-cold pond, the color of cat's eyes, is fringed with cool granite slabs. The spot is popular with summer day hikers and picnickers.

Take a right back onto the Baldface Circle Trail, skirt the Charles Brook and ascend through second-growth hardwood forest. At 1.4mi the Bicknell Ridge Trail enters on the left. The Bicknell Ridge Trail offers an alternative route to the summit, rising through the forest to open ledges. Elevation gain and distance are about the same on both the Baldface Circle and Bicknell Ridge.

The Baldface Circle Trail climbs gradually northwest to the ridgeline. (At 2.1mi, a side path leads left across the brook above Eagle Cascade, again connecting with the Bicknell Ridge Trail.) On the Baldface Circle Trail, you'll enter an old logging road, cross a small brook, then begin to climb steeply over open, rough ledges. You'll

have excellent views to the ridgetop, where the trail connects with the Eagle Link and Meader Ridge Trails.

Take the Eagle Link Trail, which runs 2.4mi from Baldface Circle Trail to the Wild River Trail. Eagle Link Trail descends the steep north slope of North Baldface mountain, before heading west at moderate grade. The trail meanders through a birch forest, crosses a large brook and gradually descends into the valley of the **Wild River**. The trail crosses two channels of the Wild River (this can be difficult during high water) before connecting with the Wild River Trail on the west bank of the river. If the river crossing looks dicey, stay along the river bank and pick up the trail at a later point.

The Wild River Trail follows the river, crisscrossing it several times during the 1.7mi hike to Perkins Notch shelter. It's an easy hike, with plenty of scenic overlooks of the river as it tumbles over polished boulders. The trail skirts the south side of **No-Ketchum Pond** (a good place to see moose feeding during the early morning and evening hours), before climbing slowly to Perkins Notch. The *shelter* is on the south side of Wild River (you'll see a sign pointing the way), where you'll find a covered platform with bunk space for six people, and latrines. A number of cleared *campsites* are also near the shelter.

The Perkins Notch shelter is a good stopping point for the first night. However, camping is allowed anywhere along the trails (except above treeline on the Baldface Circle Trail), giving you plenty of flexibility. Many hikers prefer to stake out their own campsite along the Wild River, where they can fall asleep to the sound of rushing waters.

Day 2: Perkins Notch Shelter to Blue Brook
6–7 hours, 11.7mi (18.6km), 2260ft (678m) ascent

The second day of this loop includes a huff-and-puff climb to Carter Dome and a short ridgeline traverse on the Carter-Moriah Range, with plenty of jaw-dropping views of jagged mountain peaks and rolling valleys. You'll then loop back on the long, flat Black Angel Trail, before a short ascent to the Spruce Brook Shelter. In all, you'll cover 11.7mi, gaining and losing more than 4000ft. Pack plenty of water before you take off; you won't find much along the way until you reach Cedar Brook near day's end.

Follow the Wild River Trail 0.8mi as it makes a gradual climb west to Perkins Notch. At Perkins Notch, take the Rainbow Trail, leading to Carter Dome. The Rainbow Trail starts out slow and easy. Don't be fooled. In a half hour or so, you'll begin a steep hike up the southeast slope of Carter Dome. The trail climbs steadily through the woods, with little relief until you reach the south knob of Carter Mountain, at 1½mi. Here, the trail runs in the open with great views as it climbs more moderately to the **Carter Dome summit**, where it hooks up with the Carter-Moriah Trail. Turn right onto this. The Carter-Moriah Trail follows the crest of the Carter Range and is part of the Appalachian Trail. Follow the Carter-Moriah Trail 0.4mi to the Black Angel Trail. At this junction, you'll see a side path leading north to **Mt Hight**. The extra 0.8mi (roundtrip) climb is well worth the effort. Mt Hight was swept by a fire in 1903 leaving its

summit bare but offering sweeping views of the White Mountain National Forest, the Carter Range and the Presidentials. On clear days you'll be able to see the snow-capped peak of Mt Washington to your west.

The Black Angel Trail, the last leg of Day 2, travels 7.2mi from the Carter-Moriah Trail to the Blue Brook Shelter, your home for the night. If you tire before reaching the shelter, or daylight runs out, you can camp off the Black Angel Trail.

The trail descends the east slope of Mt Hight across steep, ledgy sections, where footing is rough, but the views are fine. It levels out as it enters a small grove of virgin timber and crosses a tributary of Spruce Brook at 2.6mi, before entering open woods. At 4.8mi, the trail reaches **Spider Bridge**, crossing the Wild River. From here, the trail skirts Cedar Brook for a short distance before climbing, at first gradually and then more steeply, to the *Blue Brook Shelter*. The three-sided, rustic shelter, with wooden platform and roof, sits in a clearing near the Blue Brook.

Day 3: Blue Brook to Baldface
6½–7½hours, 10mi (16.1km), 1840ft (552m) ascent

Fill extra water bottles before heading out this morning. Much of your day will be spent above treeline, traversing the Baldface Mountain Range, where water is often unavailable.

Follow the Black Angel Trail as it climbs to Rim Junction, where it intersects with the Basin Rim Trail. Take Basin Rim Trail south along the ridgeline to Mt Meader. Almost immediately, at 0.1mi, you'll pass a great view overlooking the Basin. Next up is your first hump of many for the day, as the trail climbs steeply over ledges, leading to Mt Meader. The Mt Meader Trail forks left, heading back to Hwy 113 – a good bail-out route if the weather turns bad. Otherwise, follow the Meader Ridge Trail along the ridgeline to link up with the Baldface Circle Trail. The up-and-down trail has several scenic outlooks along the way. The north branch of the Baldface Circle Trail enters on your left (this is where you hiked in). You'll pass Bicknell Ridge Trail, also on your left, as you begin to climb to the summit of **North Baldface**. The trail ascends steep, wide ledges to the 3610ft summit, and backs downs the other side with an equally steep pitch. From here, the trail runs in the open to South Baldface, with non-stop, unobstructed views in all directions. For a short distance (0.2mi), you'll hike through a protected, small grove of mature conifers before ascending the broad **South Baldface** ridge and reaching its bare summit. (Snack alert! Grab a handful of tiny, wild blueberries growing here and on the south side.) The trail descends very steeply over open rock slabs before reaching the *South Baldface Shelter* and Last Chance Spring. You're now only 1.7mi from Circle Junction and a short jaunt more to inviting Emerald Pool. Take the plunge into its clear, cold waters – what better way to wash away three days of trail dust?

Adirondack State Park

The Adirondacks, or 'dacks' as it's known to the locals, covers six million acres, an area larger than the Grand Canyon, Yellowstone and Yosemite combined. The figures are impressive: 2000 mountain peaks, 100 greater than 3000ft, 46 greater than 4000ft; more than 2400 lakes and ponds; and 1200mi of rivers, fed by 3000mi of brooks and streams. Outdoor recreation abounds in this popular New York park, with plenty of facilities nearby and easy access. Hikers will find a large network of trails, some 2000mi weaving through deep forests, gentle hills and up and down the highest summits.

The hikes featured here are in the High Peaks region, located in the northeastern section of the park The region includes all the Adirondack peaks with elevations over 4000ft. It is well traveled and in some places quite crowded, but it offers some of the most varied terrain and loftiest views in the park.

HISTORY

In 1609, Samuel de Champlain and Henry Hudson separately explored the Adirondacks. During the next several decades it was the stomping grounds only of the Iroquois and Algonquin. The Iroquois called the Algonquins 'Adirondack', which means 'bark eater', because when the waterways froze in the winter the Algonquins would survive off the buds and barks of the trees.

It was not until the late 19th century that the area became popular for recreation, vacationing and recuperating. Dr Edward Livingston Trudeau set up a treatment center for tuberculosis and the Adirondacks soon drew patients from around the world. At the same time, the region began to attract wealthy vacationers. Grand sports lodges and hotels were constructed, giving birth to the rustic Adirondack-style architecture. Many of the grand camps still exist as private homes and elegant hotels and lodges.

Conservation and preservation went hand-in-hand with tourism. In 1885, the New York State government created the Adirondack Forest Preserve, declaring that the forest lands must remain wild. It was the first preserved wilderness in the country. In 1892, the state created the Adirondack State Park, consisting of the preserved land and private lands surrounding its boundary. Today, the forest preserve occupies 2.5 million acres of the park.

NATURAL HISTORY

The Adirondacks, the only mountains in the eastern United States that are not part of the Appalachians, are about 10 million years old. They're part of the vast, ancient Canadian Shield and the exposed bedrock on the summits is among the oldest in the world.

The Adirondacks is composed of several vegetation zones. The northern regions are mostly conifer forests. Further south the forest becomes deciduous, with stands of birch, beech and maple. The highest peaks host alpine communities, with mosses and lichen.

There are more than 70 species of tree, 218 species of bird, and 55 mammals, mostly beavers, raccoons, porcupines, deer and black bears.

PLANNING

If you can, plan a midweek trip from May through October. The Adirondack Mountain Club (ADK; ☎ 518-668-4447, postal address: 814 Goggins Rd, Lake George, NY 12845-4117) is the best source of information for hiking in the park.

Maps

The 1:62,500 *Trails of the Adirondack High Peaks Region* by the ADK covers both hikes featured here.

Permits & Regulations

Lean-tos are first-come, first-served. Tents must be erected more than 150ft from a trail, lake or stream or at designated sites. No tents can be erected in or beside a lean-to. No camping is permitted above 4000ft, except in winter months.

NEAREST TOWN
Lake Placid

This resort and lakeside village at the doorstep of the Adirondacks hosted the 1932 and 1980 winter Olympics. Today, it's a mecca for outdoor enthusiasts and vacationers who come to see the Olympic sites and watch current US national teams train. Stop by the visitor center (☎ 800-447-5224, 🖳 www.lakeplacid.com) on Main St next to the Olympic Center. There are a number of outdoor equipment, clothing and supply shops in town including Eastern Mountain Sports, Outdoor Gear Exchange and Mountain Run, all on Main St.

Places to Stay & Eat The ADK operates the *Adirondack Loj at Heart Lake (☎ 518-523-3441, postal address: PO Box 867, Lake Placid, NY 12946)*, about 9mi south of Lake Placid (take Adirondack Rd off Rte 73). This is the most convenient place to stay as both hikes described in this section start here. Cabins, lean-tos and campsites are available. There are showers, a dining room, a small nature museum, camping supplies and ranger-led programs. It will take walk-ins, but it's better to reserve your site in advance, especially on a summer or fall weekend. In Lake Placid, the *Whispering*

Pines campground (☎ 518-523-9322), on Rte 73, has wooded tent sites starting at $12 a night. The *Mt Van Hoevenberg Bed & Breakfast (☎ 518-523-9572)*, also on Rte 73, is an Adirondack-style country lodge with pretty views and a wood-fired sauna. Rooms are $65 to $78.

Begin the day with pancakes the size of your head at *Goldberries (☎ 518-523-1799)* at 137 Main St. Locals load up on carbs at *Mr Mike's (☎ 518-523-9770)* at 332 Main St. For groceries, try Grand Union on Saranac Ave.

Getting There & Away From Boston, take the I-90 (Massachusetts Turnpike) to Albany. Pick up I-787 north to Cohoes. Connect with Rte 7 west to I-87 and follow this north to exit 30. Take Rte 9 north for 2mi to Rte 73. Continue on Rte 73 for 28mi to Lake Placid. Drive time is about five hours.

From Burlington, Vermont, take the car ferry across Lake Champlain (☎ 802-864-9804, 🖳 www.ferries.com). Car and driver costs $23 roundtrip. Trips run May 19 to mid-October. The ferry lands in Port Kent, New York; crossing time is one hour. From Port Kent, follow Rte 9N southwest to Jay, then pick up Rte 86 to Lake Placid.

Adirondack Trailways (☎ 800-225-6815) runs a bus service from Albany and New York City to Lake Placid. Amtrak has a rail service ($100 roundtrip) from New York City to Westport, and Champs Express (☎ 518-523-4431; 40 minutes, $15) runs a bus service from Westport to Lake Placid – book when you make your train reservations.

GETTING TO/FROM THE HIKES

From Lake Placid, follow Rte 73 south about 4mi to Adirondack Rd. There's a sign directing you to Adirondack Loj and 'High Peaks' area. Turn right here and follow this road to the park entrance booth, about 4½mi. The parking lot is on your left, just past the booth. Both the Adirondacks High Peaks and Mt Marcy hikes begin here. Parking is $7 a day. Arrive early; when the parking lot fills, you'll be turned away – this is how numbers are controlled within the park.

Adirondacks High Peaks

Duration	3 days
Distance	21.9mi (35.3km)
Standard	medium
Start/Finish	Heart Lake
Nearest Town	Lake Placid
Public Transport	no

Summary This three-day loop in the High Peaks region of the Adirondacks includes mountain lakes and falls, a steep-sided gorge, and a spectacular mountain pass. Interlocking trails offer unlimited opportunities to increase or shorten this hike.

THE HIKE
Day 1: Heart Lake to Wallface Ponds
3½–5 hours, 6.9mi (11.1km)

You'll leave the busy Heart Lake area, climbing gently to Rocky Falls and then on to Wallface Ponds. There are two lean-tos along the way should you decide to stop earlier, but if solitude is what you crave, keep going – the side trail to Wallface Ponds leads to a cluster of pretty mountain ponds and seclusion.

Pick up the Indian Pass Trail near the Adirondack Loj entrance booth. The trail, No 75 and marked with red disks, follows an old road flanking Heart Lake. You'll find the trail register about a half-mile down the trail. Shortly after, the Old Nye Ski Trail enters on the right and the Indian Pass Trail continues straight ahead, a gentle up-and-down meander through the forest. At 2.1mi, you'll cross a brook and in a few steps reach the junction of the side-trail leading to **Rocky Falls**. Indian Pass Trail continues straight, but turn right for a look at the falls and a chance to cool your 'dawgs' in the lower falls swimming hole. There's also a *lean-to* just above Rocky Falls. If you like to fall asleep to the sound of falling waters, this may be a good overnight spot (though you'll have to make up the miles another day). The 0.3mi side trail loops around the falls to rejoin Indian Pass Trail.

It's a pleasant, though sometimes wet, hike from here through marshy areas and across streams. You'll reach *Scott Clearing*

lean-to at 3.8mi If you like, plop your sleeping bag in the lean-to, claiming home for the night, and go explore. You can visit nearby Wallface Ponds, a 5.6mi roundtrip, and return to the lean-to to sleep.

Those who prefer tent camping in a more remote site should continue. The Wallface Ponds Trail junction and Scott's Dam is 0.3mi from the Scott Clearing lean-to. Turn right at the dam onto Wallface Ponds Trail, No 76, heading west. The trail follows an old logging road, climbing at a steady, moderate pace for about a mile before dropping toward Scott Pond. At 1½mi, you'll get a good view of a pond straight ahead. The trail passes an old dam and briefly follows the river before heading away. Look for clearings along the pond's shoreline for *possible campsites*.

In about a mile, you'll enter an open meadow area, with great views of the picturesque valley, a small mountain pond and the MacIntyre mountain range. Continue for another half-mile, hopping your way on logs and across bridges through soggy woods to pretty **Wallface Ponds**. Pick a clearing overlooking the ponds, with views of MacNaughton Mountain, and settle in for a quiet night. Chances are it'll only be you, the moon and the stars sharing this site.

Day 2: Wallface Ponds to Lake Colden
4½–6 hours, 9.2mi (14.8km)

Try to get an early start today, as you'll encounter some steep, rough climbs up to Indian Pass and lots of up and down on your way to Lake Colden.

From peaceful Wallface Ponds, retrace your steps 2.8mi back to Indian Pass Trail. Follow Indian Pass Trail 0.8mi to the junction with trail No 72, entering from the left. You'll come back here later. Now, stay straight on Indian Pass Trail as it climbs steeply into the pass. It's a huff and puff, with rocky, uneven footing. At 4.2mi, you'll reach an altitude marker and get your first glimpse of the tall, **sheer-sided cliffs**. Continue another half-mile for the best view from Summit Rock. The 1000ft cliffs are some of the highest in the East, and views of the rocky, boulder-strewn gorge are jaw-dropping.

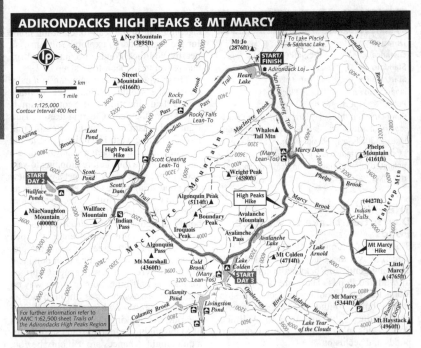

ADIRONDACKS HIGH PEAKS & MT MARCY

When you've seen enough, retrace your steps 1.1mi to the junction with trail No 72. Turn right onto this trail, heading east. For the next two or so miles you'll climb up and down, passing waterfalls and crossing several brooks along the way. The trail then climbs very steeply up **Algonquin Pass**, between Iroquois Peak and Mt Marshall, before leveling at an open, grassy area at 7.6mi. From here, you'll descend quickly, slabbing across the granite slopes of Iroquois Peak at a knee-throbbing pace.

The trail crosses the south branch of **Cold Brook** and continues to climb down along the brook's steep banks. You'll cross Cold Brook or its tributaries three more times on your way to the northwest shore of **Lake Colden**. Lake Colden, at 2764ft, is surrounded by forests, in the shadows of Mt Colden, Avalanche Mountain, Iroquois Peak and Mt Marshall. It's a popular destination and campsite. There are four *lean-tos* in the area, two on the Opalescent River,

and two on the south shore of Lake Colden. If these are full, as they often are during peak times, you can usually find *tent sites* along the Opalescent River; several *lean-tos* are also located further south, near Calamity and Livingston Ponds. (Follow trail No 121 at the south end of Lake Colden near the Opalescent River outlet.)

Day 3: Lake Colden to Adirondack Loj

3–4 hours, 5.8mi (9.3km)

You'll be trekking a shorter distance today, leaving plenty of time to linger at Lake Colden in the morning and to take your time through Avalanche Pass. The trip through the pass is considered one of the best short trips in the Adirondacks. It's also very popular, so expect company, including teen and school groups.

Leaving Lake Colden, follow trail No 69 northeast from the Indian Pass Trail junction. Immediately, you'll pass yellow trail

No 71, heading left to Algonquin Peak. Continue straight, walking about a half-mile before reaching the Avalanche Pass Trail, No 68. Turn left onto this trail, heading south toward Avalanche Lake and Marcy Dam. The trail climbs gently for 0.3mi to **Avalanche Lake**, then skirts the west bank. At 0.4mi, you'll cross a bridge and have a good view of Mt Colden. From here, you'll begin your descent through **Avalanche Pass**, where impressive, towering cliffs rise steeply from the lake. The trail snakes its way around and up and over large boulders and rocky ledges. A series of bridges and ladders makes the going a bit easier, but butt-crawling and sliding down a few of the larger boulders is sometimes necessary. There are spectacular views of the Mts Colden and Avalanche slopes.

At 0.8mi, you'll reach the northern edge of **Avalanche Lake**, a great place to shed boots (and clothes, if you like) for a refreshing dip in the lake. There's a small, pebbly beach strewn with driftwood and rocks.

The trail climbs gently into sparse forest and then begins the moderate but steady descent (sometimes on log stairs) to Marcy Dam. Marcy Dam, with its pretty overlooks, is usually crawling with campers and day hikers. There are five *lean-tos*, nicely tucked into woodsy sites, and several possible tent sites.

Follow the Van Hoevenberg Trail, an easy 2.3mi descent through sun-dappled woods, back to Heart Lake.

Mt Marcy

Duration	7½–9 hours
Distance	14.8mi (23.8km)
Standard	hard
Start/Finish	Heart Lake
Nearest Town	Lake Placid
Public Transport	no

Summary This up-and-back hike follows one of the oldest routes up Mt Marcy, New York's highest peak. At 5344ft, you'll have sweeping views from its bare-topped summit.

THE HIKE

This up-and-back hike follows one of the oldest and shortest routes up the mountain.

Expect crowds; on summer and fall weekends the parking lot often fills by 8 am.

This is a long, strenuous hike with 3166ft of ascent, but you can tackle it in two days by staying overnight at Marcy Dam.

Begin on the Van Hoevenberg Trail at the Adirondack Loj parking area. The trail crosses the Algonquin Brook and begins to veer away, climbing gently through mixed forest. At 1mi, the Algonquin Peak Trail, No 64, enters. Turn left (southeast). For the next mile or so, the trail is a breeze, with gentle up-and-down dips on wide, level, and well-traveled ground. You're likely to meet joggers, families and day hikers along the way.

At Marcy Dam, with five *lean-tos* and several *tent sites*, stop to take a gander at the view: Phelps Mountain to the east, Algonquin to the west, and Colden to the north. From the dam, the Van Hoevenberg Trail climbs to the bank of **Phelps Brook** and follows the brook at an easy grade. At 3.2mi, trail No 62 enters on the left, leading to Phelps Mountain. Bear right and you'll begin to climb more steeply for a mile or so, before leveling off in an open, wet area.

At 4.4mi, you'll cross Marcy Brook, and have a good look at **Indian Falls**, framed by the MacIntyre mountain range. You'll hike at a moderate grade for another mile or so, then climb steeply for a short distance (0.2mi) before reaching the **ridgetop** at 5.4mi. This is what you've worked for: open ridgeline views of forest and mountain peaks, with good views of Marcy summit ahead.

At 6.2mi, the Hopkins Trail, No 2, from Keene Valley, enters from the left. At 7mi, you'll begin bouldering your way up Marcy's rocky slope. Cairns and yellow paint splotches mark the route over boulders. Take care to stay on the trail – it's easy to get lost, especially in cloudy weather. Fragile alpine vegetation grows in the rock crevices, and can be easily damaged. You'll reach the smaller east summit first; keep going. It's only a short distance to **Mt Marcy's true summit** at 7.4mi. The bare-topped summit pokes out of the valley at 5344ft, offering a splendid 360-degree view.

Retrace your steps to Marcy Dam and Heart Lake.

Green Mountains

Long Trail Loop

Duration	2 days
Distance	21.8mi (35.1km)
Standard	medium
Start/Finish	Woodford
Nearest Town	Bennington
Public Transport	no

Summary This two-day hike offers the chance to traverse a southerly section of Vermont's Long Trail, running north to south in the Green Mountain National Forest. It features an overnight in a log lean-to and a trip to a fire tower, where panoramic views await. Combining a day of trekking a section of the Long Trail/Appalachian Trail with a day on a remote side trail, this hike offers a rare opportunity to do a loop tour on the Long Trail.

Hikers on the Long Trail (LT) feel like they're part of history. The LT is said to be the oldest long-distance hiking trail in the US, and served as the inspiration for the Appalachian Trail. These two famous trails share some 100mi of terrain in the southern third of Vermont. This hike offers a rare opportunity to make a loop hike off the south–north running Long Trail. Day 1 takes you along terrain shared with the AT, while Day 2 features a little-used footpath up and down Bald Mountain.

HISTORY
Constructed in 1910 by the Green Mountain Club (GMC) 'to make the mountains of Vermont play a larger role in the lives of the people', the Long Trail follows the main ridgeline of the Green Mountains. The trail extends for 270mi from the Massachusetts line through Vermont to the border of Canada.

Each year, according to the GMC, about 80–100 'end-to-enders' complete the whole hike (typically in three to 3½ weeks). The total number of confirmed end-to-enders is about 2350 at this writing. The Long Trail

is alluring to the hiking 'purist' who likes the idea that it's a relatively primitive footpath. The trail's long history, not to mention that Vermont mystique, adds to its appeal.

Managed and maintained by the GMC, the system features 175mi of side trails and 62 rustic cabins and lean-tos. It is steep in places, boggy in others, and always rugged and natural. The Long Trail meanders through the Green Mountain National Forest, wilderness areas, state park land, and some private property, skirting several ponds and climbing to the summits of numerous peaks.

NATURAL HISTORY
Three hundred and fifty million years ago, the Green Mountains were part of an inland sea, transformed by heat and pressure into a mountain range. During the ice age, glaciers sculpted the sharp peaks and steep slopes of the range. The average elevation of the Green Mountain ridgeline is 2000ft, although five peaks exceed 4000ft. Hikers along this Long Trail Loop will find evidence of Vermont's stony spine of granite and marble, especially on the West Ridge side trail.

The lower slopes of the Green Mountains are forested by a mixture of hardwoods including beech and sugar maple. Between 2400ft and 3000ft, a transitional forest features yellow and white birch and red spruce, while balsam fir dominates at higher elevations.

PLANNING
The heaviest crowds turn out on fall weekends to admire the flame-colored foliage. Contact the GMC (☎ 802-244-7037, 🖥 www.greenmountainclub.org, postal address: Box 650, Waterbury Center, VT 05677), Rte 100, RR 1, for more information.

Maps
The GMC is the best source for maps. It is currently updating its Long Trail End-to-End maps. Its widely available *Long Trail Guide* sells for $14.95 and covers the entire trail. Maps 1 and 2 detail this hike.

Permits & Regulations

Camp at least 200ft from any trail, stream or pond. No camping in the vicinity of Hell Hollow Brook.

NEAREST TOWN
Bennington

This town, 5.2mi east of the trailhead, is the home of Bennington College; an arts-flavored town – Vermont's first, chartered in 1749 – it is welcoming to hikers. Much of the action happens on Main St (VT 9). Visit the Bennington Area chamber of commerce (☎ 802-447-3311, 🖳 www.bennington.com) on Veteran's Memorial Dr for visitor information. For hiking and camping supplies, try CB Sports (☎ 802-447-7651) at 190 North St.

Places to Stay & Eat If your first order of business is a hot meal, try *Madison Brewing Co (☎ 802-44-BREWS, 428 Main St)* for hefty, inexpensive burgers, sandwiches and tasty options for vegetarians. A classic choice is *Blue Benn Diner (☎ 802-442-5140)*, a 1948 dining car on Rte 7. For do-it-yourselfers, the nearest grocery stores are Salem's Super Market at 831 Main St and Grand Union at 300 Depot St.

For hot showers and cheap sleeps, try the *Midtown Motel (☎ 802-447-0189, 107 Main St)*, where rooms run from $38 to $58 per night.

Getting There & Away From Boston take Rte 2 west to Hwy 91 and head north toward Brattleboro, Vermont. At the Brattleboro exit, take Rte 9 west through Woodford (and the trailhead) to Bennington.

Amtrak has a daily rail service from Washington DC and New York City to Brattleboro. Vermont Transit (☎ 800-451-3292, 800-231-2222, 🖳 www.greyhound.com) has a daily bus service between Boston and Bennington.

GETTING TO/FROM THE HIKE

Look for the sign marking the trailhead of the LT/AT and parking lot on Rte 9, 1mi west of the village of Woodford and 5.2mi east of Bennington. Alternatively, a taxi from Brattleboro (20mi east) to the trailhead would take one hour and cost about $50. Try Federal Taxi (☎ 802-254-5411).

The trail ends approximately 2mi from the trailhead. To get back to your car, you'll hike 0.8mi south on a dirt road, Harbor St, to Rte 9, then turn left on Rte 9 and hike 1.2mi back to the LT/AT parking lot. If you're hiking with a companion, you have another option: leave one hiker and the backpacks at the picnic table located beside the Town of Woodford municipal building/meeting house at the junction of Rte 9 and Harbor St. The other hiker, minus gear, then heads left on Rte 9 for the 1.2mi hike to the parking lot at the trailhead to pick up the car.

THE HIKE
Day 1: Rte 9 to Goddard Shelter

6–7 hours, 10.1mi (16.3km), 2640ft (792m) ascent

Welcome to the Green Mountain National Forest. A bulletin board and a latrine mark the entrance to the white-blazed LT/AT, heading north. Entering the forest, you'll cross City Stream using a footbridge. Follow the stream for a short distance, then bear right. There's no getting used to this one gradually; you'll now begin a steep climb. Rocky switchbacks lead you up the ridgeline. At 0.6mi, you'll reach your first landmark, **Split Rock**, a halved boulder. Pass through the rock, then begin a moderate ascent. At 1.1mi, you'll cross an old road. As you continue along the woodsy trail, you'll reach a spur trail at 1.7mi, which leads 200ft to the *Melville Nauheim Shelter*. This frame shelter offers bunk space for eight. Surrounding the shelter are a few campsites. A latrine is located a few yards away. If you got a late start on the hike, consider spending the night at this shelter and getting an early start the next morning.

Back on the trail, you'll head north, crossing a power line cut at Maple Hill (2mi). Take a minute or two to view the Bennington Valley and Mt Anthony, to the west, and Mt Snow and Haystack Mountain, looking east. If you're hiking in midsummer, look

LONG TRAIL LOOP

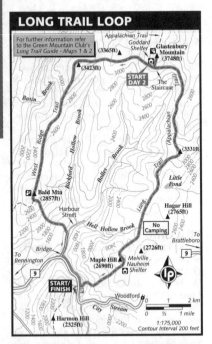

For further information refer to the Green Mountain Club's Long Trail Guide - Maps 1 & 2

Appalachian Trail
Goddard Shelter (3365ft)
Glastenbury Mountain (3748ft)

(3423ft)

START DAY 2
The Staircase

Appalachian Trail

(3331ft)

Basin

Hell Hollow Brook

Little Pond

Hagar Hill (2765ft)

No Camping

To Brattleboro

West Ridge Trail

Bickford Brook

Bolles Brook

Long Trail

Bald Mtn (2857ft)

Harbour Street

(2726ft)

9

To Bennington

Bridge

Maple Hill (2690ft)

Melville Nauheim Shelter

START/ FINISH

9

Woodford City Stream

0   1   2 km
0   ½   1 mile
1:175,000
Contour Interval 200 feet

Harmon Hill (2325ft)

Day 1. The next landmark is Glastenbury lookout at 7.4mi, offering views of Glastenbury and the connecting ridge to Bald Mountain, the highlight of Day 2.

Now comes the toughest stretch of this two-day hike: a series of steep, thigh-testing stairstep boulders, **'the staircase'**, that climb toward *Goddard Shelter*. Just when you've had enough of this, the trail levels off, you cross a stream, and the shelter pops into view at 9.8mi.

This popular shelter, a log lean-to, has bunks that sleep 10–12 people. Its best feature: lofty views of distant mountains and hills, shrouded in misty blue. Refresh your water supply at the nearby spring, then fire up the stove for dinner. Plan your evening so that you can take in the sunset at **Glastenbury Mountain's summit**, a densely-wooded 0.3mi hike.

Climb the 50-plus steps up the old fire tower. Built in 1927, the old tower was abandoned in the 1940s but renovated by the United States Forest Service (USFS) as an observation deck for hikers. From the top, enjoy a 360-degree view of the wilderness. This spot is the most remote point on the Long Trail; the nearest road is 10.2mi away. Look south to the Berkshire Hills of Massachusetts; to the north are Mt Equinox and Stratton Mountain; Haystack Mountain and Mt Snow rise to the east; and the Taconic Mountains loom to the west. As the sky turns to scarlet, you'll feel the wind begin to pick up and the temperature drop quite noticeably.

Day 2: Goddard Shelter to Rte 9
7–8 hours, 11.7mi (18.8km), 1000ft (300m) ascent
Awaken to vistas of faraway peaks, then, if you're not a 'bag worm' (local hiker slang for folks who stay nestled in their sleeping bags for as long as possible), hike back to the summit tower to catch the sunrise. After breakfast, load up your pack and head for the blue-blazed trail, designated as West Ridge Trail/Bald Mountain, just to the left of the shelter. This is a little-used side trail. The other backpackers you've encountered here will likely continue north or south on

for wild raspberries growing along trail-sides. From this point, amble along easygoing terrain to **Hell Hollow Brook** at 3.1mi. Refill your water bottles here, and treat your feet to a cool plunge in the ripply water. The water looks rusty, but it's drinkable if treated. The brook is part of the Bennington water supply. (Camping is not permitted here.)

Cross the bridge over the brook and continue your ascent of the ridge, hiking across a swamp toward a lookout at 4.3mi. Stretching before you, on your right, are views of Haystack Mountain; from this vantage point you'll realize how much elevation you've gained (2500ft plus) thus far. This small clearing is a good place for lunch or a snack break.

From here, the trail continues a gradual, steady climb over two hills. You'll begin a long, uphill stretch, with little reward save the knowledge that you're getting closer to Glastenbury Mountain, your destination for

the Long Trail so you'll leave them behind now. After the sociability of a day of the LT/AT, where the presence of other souls is a given, Day 2's hike is a marked contrast: quiet and contemplative, this route provides a real sense of being alone in the deep wilderness.

Soon, you'll enter a dense forest where the only other footprints you're likely to see in the damp earth are moose tracks. In most places, the trail is fairly overgrown and a mere boot-width wide. The lead hiker may well break through dewy nets of cobweb, gauzily strung between tree boughs. This trail follows the western ridge of the mountain and takes in a minor peak before it reaches the summit of Bald Mountain.

Look closely for blazes (not always easy to find) and follow the trail toward a beaver pond. With the pond on your left, hike over the marsh on wooden planks, then enter the woods again.

Pass through a tangle of thorny bushes to a fern-lined stretch of trail that leads to an old logging road at 2½mi. Turn right on the road, then head left, into the forest. Here, you'll begin a short, narrow, rocky climb leading to a 3423ft **minor summit**. From this point, the trail becomes a gentle, lushly-ferned footpath as it follows the hillside.

The hike continues like this for some time. You'll feel far off the beaten path as you tramp over some fallen trees and encounter dense brush. The route will feel more like bushwacking than backpacking at some points.

You'll pass a small stand of hemlocks, then return to a more open forest. The trail bears to the right again and begins a more obvious descent. You'll follow the ridgeline for a long distance, but it'll be hard to tell what's on either side of you since a mixed hardwood forest envelopes you on both sides. Eventually you'll begin a gradual ascent, following switchbacks as the forest changes to evergreen.

A series of steep, rocky switchbacks will lead you to the flat **Bald Mountain summit** at 7.7mi. A pile of chalky boulders marks the spot. Enjoy the views and try to locate the route you just hiked from Glastenbury

Mountain (hint: look for the fire tower). This is a sweet spot for a rest.

Following the blue blazes, tramp about 0.1mi to the junction of Bald Mountain Trail. Head left (westward), following blue blazes all the way, and begin your descent. It's a rocky trip down, with little relief for the knees on the downhill, over several large, white marble boulders. Some are loosely stacked; watch your footing.

At 0.2mi into the descent a spur trail marked with a light-blue blaze leads to Bear Wallow, a spring (0.2mi in). Via switchbacks, you'll continue to pound your way down the mountain, leaving behind the pines for deciduous forest.

As you make your way down, you'll begin to hear the distant hum of traffic on Rte 9 – music to your ears, if you've had enough of this downhill grind. Close as it sounds, you still have a couple of miles of hiking ahead of you.

Follow the blazes through the woods and over an old stream bed. As the traffic sounds get louder you'll pass a road on your left with a 'no trespassing' sign – civilization! A short distance ahead, on the right, you'll see a cabin and an outbuilding. Bear to the left, following the blazes, until you reach a driveway (9.7mi). Follow it, downhill, to the Bald Mountain/West Ridge Trail sign (barely readable at our last visit) and head right on a dirt road.

Running alongside a river, the road, Harbor St, leads south. You'll pass a few houses, then cross a bridge, meeting Rte 9 – none too soon, since this dusty road is a tiresome jaunt – at 10½mi. To your right you'll see the Woodford Municipal Building/Meeting House (c1733), a white structure topped with a weathervane. Beside it is a small parking lot with a picnic table, a good place to stop and rest for a minute. Behind you, the river gurgles along, beckoning you to follow the footpath to the water's edge and dip your toes in the cold water.

Hard as it will be to leave this spot, leave it you must. At least one of your party must turn left on Rte 9 and hike back to pick up the car in the LT/AT parking lot at 11.7mi.

Cape Cod National Seashore

Thoreau's Walk

Duration	6 hours
Distance	6mi (9.7km) or 8.5mi (13.7km)
Standard	easy
Start	Eastham
Finish	Wellfleet
Public Transport	yes

Summary Retrace the footsteps of Henry David Thoreau on Cape Cod National Seashore. This day hike revisits the first day of Thoreau's three-day trek, along the outer beach on the cape's eastern shore.

Retrace the footsteps of Henry David Thoreau on Cape Cod National Seashore in Massachusetts. Thoreau hiked the entire 25mi peninsula in three days; this day hike features the first day of Thoreau's trek. You'll wander a string of pristine beaches along the windswept Atlantic side of the cape, on the peninsula's eastern shore. Enjoy a stunning landscape of salt marsh and sand dune, lapped by a froth of pounding surf. Plan a good six hours to hike the 6mi from Coast Guard Beach to LeCount Hollow. Even though it's fairly flat terrain, don't underestimate the effort it takes to trudge through ankle-deep sand. You'll be rewarded with tantalizing views every step of the way, enhanced by the scent of the sea and the rhythmic roar of the surf.

HISTORY
Thoreau called it a 'wild rank place' in his travel classic, *Cape Cod*, a land where one encounters 'naked nature, nibbling at the cliffy shore'. The wildness of the Outer Cape, or eastern shore, of Cape Cod so enticed Thoreau that he set out on a stormy day in mid-October of 1849 to walk it – all 25mi of it. Thoreau took three days to complete the trek, sleeping in the cottages of an oysterman and a lighthouse keeper, fishing and foraging for food.

Hikers who retrace Thoreau's footsteps today will find that remarkably little has changed in the intervening century-and-a-half. The Cape Cod National Seashore was established in 1961 to protect the cape's outer 'arm'. Because the seashore is under federal jurisdiction, it hasn't been developed, although a few old houses still stand. The seashore includes six ocean beaches, a white-cedar swamp, a beech forest, several hiking trails and two visitor centers.

'Everything told of the sea', Thoreau wrote of the cape. Indeed, the sea is the dominant force here, where 'nor'easter' storms lash the Atlantic coast and shipwrecks once washed ashore quite regularly. There have been an estimated 3000 shipwrecks off Cape Cod, although it's a rare occurrence these days.

Cape Cod's first known residents were the Wampanoag Indians, who lived peacefully here. On November 9, 1620, the *Mayflower* landed at the tip of the cape, off Provincetown. In December, 19 men set off in an open boat, headed down the coastline. They camped on the beach near the present site of Eastham. The next morning, they were surprised by the Wampanoags, at the site of what is still known as First Encounter Beach.

NATURAL HISTORY
Cape Cod was formed during the last ice age, when a glacier covered what is now the cape and the islands of Martha's Vineyard and Nantucket. When the ice melted the ocean level rose 400ft. Miles of land were underwater; only the highest parts rose above it. The glacier left behind a moraine ridge of clay, sand, rocks and gravel in a pile which forms the land that is now Cape Cod. As the ice retreated it left behind giant blocks of ice which, when they melted, left behind hollows in the ground that have since become cranberry bogs, freshwater ponds and, when connected by channels to the sea, salt ponds.

Cape Cod National Seashore is an ever-changing landscape. Wind and waves sculpt the coastline. Pounding waves and relentless currents erode the sea cliffs, reducing

Cape Cod Pirates

Wild-eyed pirates off the tranquil coast of Cape Cod? Believe it. About a quarter-mile from the town of Wellfleet, the ocean's floor is littered with the booty of the treasure-laden *Whydah* (WIH-dah), the first pirate ship ever discovered in North America

The *Whydah* was a 100ft, three-masted ship, launched in London in 1715. Involved in the slave trade between West Africa, the Caribbean – where slaves were traded for gold and silver, among other bounty – and England, the *Whydah* was attacked by two pirate ships near the Bahamas in February of 1717. Pirate Samuel 'Black Sam' Bellamy claimed the *Whydah* as his flagship.

The bad boys headed up the east coast, robbing vessels along the way. Just two months later, Bellamy sailed the *Whydah* into the jaws of a raging nor'easter storm. Accounts of the event describe wind gusts topping 70 miles per hour and 30ft seas. Within sight of the beach, the ship rammed into a sandbar and was crushed by powerful waves. Her cannon fell from its mounts, sending a hail of cannonballs onto the decks. Finally, the *Whydah* split apart in the middle, leaving more than 100 corpses among the ship's timbers.

Of the *Whydah* 's crew of nearly 150, two men survived the ordeal, telling tales of mind-boggling stores of gold and silver – 180 bags in all, they reported – hidden in chests between decks. Local folk wasted no time in plundering the wreck, even cutting gem-studded rings off the fingers of the dead.

A local cartographer kept journals and noted the location of the shipwreck on a map. This material has led professional treasure-hunter Barry Clifford on a 15-year search for the lost loot. To date, Clifford and his expedition team have recovered more than 100,000 artifacts, including the ship's bell. Although preservationists have cried foul, Massachusetts' high court ruled that it's 'finders, keepers' for Clifford and the *Whydah* wreck. For now, Clifford and his crew keep diving at the site, consumed by the thought of those 180 bags of treasure. Take a look at some of the spoils at the Whydah Museum on MacMillan Wharf in Provincetown (☎ 508-487-8899).

the beach by nearly 3ft each year. Winds and tides build and demolish sand dunes, which then migrate inland, sometimes burying ponds and marshes in the process. Violent storms attack the cape in fall and winter, sometimes flattening entire dune systems. Beach grass has been planted on bare dunes to help the sand resist erosion; still, the seashore is a work in progress.

This region is an important destination for migratory birds. About 368 species have been sighted within the seashore. Fall is the time when the greatest variety and number of birds can be found. A recovery plan for a threatened species, the piping plover, is ongoing; in spring and summer, hikers may encounter closed areas and posted nesting sites.

Surf casting for saltwater fish is a popular pursuit here. Fishing seasons run from May through October for striped bass, bluefish, mackerel, cod, flounder and fluke. (A state license is not required.)

From spring through fall, whales are sometimes seen off the coast. Race Point Beach, near Provincetown, is a good vantage point. Stellwagen Bank, 7mi northeast of Provincetown, is a rich feeding ground for whales.

PLANNING
When to Hike

Cape Cod National Seashore is open year-round from 6 am to sunset. No matter in which season you visit, this undulating stretch of crystalline sand offers stunning beauty. This hike is best in fall, when the crowds have gone and you'll share the beach with, perhaps, a surf fisherman or two and a solitary hiker. Plus, it's more authentic that way; Thoreau began his beach walk on October 11, 1849. Cape Cod's weather is generally delightful in fall. Except during storm conditions, the beach is accessible during high tide, but you'll enjoy a wide expanse and firmer footing during ebb tide. Call the national seashore's Salt Pond visitor center (☎ 508-255-6860) for weather advisories and tide information.

What to Bring
Thoreau traveled with nothing more than a knapsack; there's no reason to bring more. Water, food, sunblock, insect repellent, maybe a swimsuit in case you get the urge to swim. There are restrooms at some access points along the beach, open through mid-October.

Maps
National Geographic's Trails Illustrated map *Cape Cod National Seashore (No 250)* at 1:38,000 is available at Salt Pond visitor center bookshop (☎ 508-255-6560) on Rte 6 at Eastham and also by mail, for $9. The declination of Cape Cod is 16 degrees east.

Permits & Regulations
Open fires are not allowed except by permit, obtainable at visitor centers. Keep off sand dunes – they are extremely sensitive to erosion – and protected nesting sites. Camping and overnight use of the national seashore is not permitted. Plan your hike so you'll be off the beach by sundown.

NEAREST TOWNS
Eastham
The gateway to Cape Cod National Seashore, Eastham was settled by the Pilgrims in 1644. With a year-round population of about 5000, Eastham has a smattering of shops along Rte 6, with a few more in North Eastham, at the corner of Rte 6 and Brackett Rd. The town's landmark is an old windmill off Rte 6, across from town hall. Visit Salt Pond visitor center, on Rte 6, for maps and information.

Places to Stay Eastham has *Hostelling International, Mid-Cape* (☎ 508-255-2785, 800-909-4776 for reservations in-season, 617-779-0900 off-season, 75 Goody Hallet Dr)*, open mid-May to mid-September (reservations essential for July and August). A bed in one of the eight cabins is $14/17 for members/non-members. For a list of motels

and B&Bs in Eastham, contact the Eastham chamber of commerce (☎ 508-240-7211, postal address: Box 1329, Eastham, MA 02642).

Getting There & Away From Boston, follow I-93 south to the Sagamore Bridge over Cape Cod Canal, then follow Cape Cod's Rte 6 east to Eastham. Plymouth & Brockton (P&B) Bus (☎ 508-778-9767) operates a service from Boston to Eastham.

Wellfleet
This day hike ends near Wellfleet, a town with the feel of an old fishing village. Whether you choose to end the hike at LeCount Hollow (6mi) or Newcomb Beach (8½mi), you'll have easy access to the town of Wellfleet, home to 3000 year-round residents. Wellfleet is famous for oysters, but its rich shellfish beds also produce tasty bay scallops, quahogs, mussels, blue crabs and sea clams. Wellfleet has several art galleries and a bell clock that strikes at ship's time – two bells at one, five, and nine o'clock; four bells at two, six, and ten o'clock, and so on. Wellfleet also has one of the few remaining drive-in theaters in New England. This former whaling village, where pirate ships have sunk, is fun to explore. Plan to spend the night here after hiking, if you can.

Places to Stay & Eat *Maurice's campground* (☎ 508-349-2029), on Rte 6 just north of the Eastham town line, has tent sites/cabins for $20/60. *Paine's campground* (☎ 508-349-3007, 800-479-3017), on Old Colony Rd off Rte 6, is open mid-May to mid-October and has 150 sites for $18 to $24.

Mainstay Motor Inn (☎ 800-346-2350) in South Wellfleet is convenient to LeCount Hollow. Room rates are $44 to $46. Wellfleet is loaded with good seafood restaurants. Try *Bayside Lobster Hutt* (☎ 508-349-6333) on Commercial St and *The Lighthouse Cafe* (☎ 508-349-3681) on Main St.

GETTING TO/FROM THE HIKE
If you begin this hike at Eastham's Coast Guard Beach, there's parking available at

the national seashore's Little Creek Staging Area on Doane Rd, a half-mile from the start. A fee is charged from late June through Labor Day. At other times of the year, call the visitor center first to make sure the gate is open. Also, you'll need permission to keep your car here after midnight.

If you choose to hike the entire 25mi of Cape Cod National Seashore, you'll wind up at land's end in Provincetown. To get back to Eastham from Provincetown, take the P&B bus (several daily, $5) from MacMillan Wharf.

THE HIKE

Begin the hike at Coast Guard Beach, 1.8mi east of the Salt Pond visitor center. Before beginning your south-to-north hike, take a quick stroll down the fingerlike spit of land that stretches about 2mi to the south. This strip of beach separates the tidal flat of Nauset Marsh from the ocean. Looking across the marsh, you'll see Fort Hill where, in 1927, naturalist Henry Beston spent the year alone in a small cottage. He recounted his experiences in the book *The Outermost House*. The cottage was destroyed in a powerful nor'easter storm in 1978.

Heading north, with the ocean on your right, you'll pass an abandoned coast guard station, marking Coast Guard Beach. This structure, painted bright white with green shutters, is now used year-round as an education center

From here, the beach stretches lazily ahead of you, luxuriously wide, its crystalline grains twinkling in the sun. About a mile up the beach you'll reach **Nauset Light Beach**, where a quick jog to the parking lot will bring Nauset Light, a working red-and-white lighthouse, into view. If you want to see more, and don't mind adding a half-mile to your hike, head left (inland) on Cable Rd about a quarter-mile to see a trio of lighthouses called **Three Sisters Lighthouses**, moved from other locales due to beach erosion.

As you continue hiking, you'll notice ripply sea cliffs rising abruptly from the shore. Here and there tufts of beach grass sprout from the sand; in summer, tumbles of wild roses bring spots of fuchsia to the tawny

THOREAU'S WALK

bluffs. On the sea side, foamy waves lap the beach, depositing an assortment of treasures: skate egg-cases (called 'mermaid's purses' by children), bits of seashell and bits of seaweed entangled in fish net.

Two more miles of hiking will get you to Marconi Beach, where there's a parking lot, restrooms with outdoor showers (open all summer through mid-October) and a sand-dusted stairway that leads to the beach. A bit farther north, perhaps a mile up the beach, is **Marconi Station**, where the first trans-Atlantic cable was transmitted. Here, the dunes rise sharply, sometimes as high as 100ft. At

6mi, you'll reach **LeCount Hollow Beach**, in South Wellfleet. This is where Thoreau stopped for lunch (sea clams he caught himself) on his walk. If you're stopping here, note that LeCount Hollow Rd, off the parking lot, connects with Rte 6, the cape's main drag. Arrange for pickup at the parking lot or walk the two or so miles into Wellfleet.

If you want to keep going, a la Thoreau, head up the beach for 2½mi. You'll pass through White Crest Beach and Cahoon Hollow Beach, with parking lots marking each, leading to Newcomb Hollow Beach, where Thoreau called it quits on his first day. You probably won't luck into an oysterman to take you in for the night, as he did, so you'll need a ride into Wellfleet. From the beach parking lot, take Gross Hill Rd into Wellfleet, a distance of about 2mi.

Other Hikes

100 MILE WILDERNESS
Gulf Hagas Trail
This deep, slate canyon sliced by the fast-moving Pleasant River features drop-off cliffs, towering rocks and tumbling falls. It's on the National Natural Scenic Register and is considered one of Maine's, if not the East's, most spectacular natural sights. The Gulf Hagas Trail is reached by a road leading west off Hwy 11 about 25mi south of Millinocket through Katahdin Iron Works/Jo-Mary Forest. Go through the Katahdin Iron Works checkpoint gate to the parking area at the West Branch of the Pleasant River ford.

The 8.2mi (13.2km) trail can be steep and slippery; plan on four to six hours. The trail traverses the canyon rim, with open ledges overlooking a series of falls, cascades and pools, passing several unique rock formations and stomach-dropping views into the gorge.

Remote Appalachian Trail
It'll take 10 days to travel the 100mi (161km) of the 'most remote section' of the AT from Monson to Abol Bridge. This is a demanding hike, with lots of elevation gain and loss and no services or supplies available along the way. Reach the trail off Hwy 15, about 3½mi north of Monson, Maine. Lean-tos are about a day's hike from one another. The trail climbs and traverses the Barren Chairback Range, Gulf Hagas Mountain and White Cap Mountain,

passing dozens of ponds, lakes, rivers and streams along the way. The best source of information and maps is the Maine Appalachian Trail Club's *Appalachian Guide Trail to Maine; Maps 1–3* cover the hike.

WHITE MOUNTAINS
Franconia Notch
This spectacular, steep-sided notch lies between the Franconia Range and the Kinsman Range in the central region of New Hampshire's White Mountains. Surrounded by high peaks and the lush Pemigewasset Wilderness, the region offers unlimited opportunities for great hiking. Start at the scenic Franconia Notch State Park. You'll have a choice of trails nearby; try the Falling Waters Trail – a misty, 3.2mi (5.2km) climb to the Franconia Ridge Trail. You'll pass a series of impressive waterfalls before reaching the high peaks' ridgeline. From here you can climb mountains, drop into forests or ramble along rivers and streams. A well established network of trails leads you in all directions including a hook-up with the Appalachian Trail. The AMC's *White Mountain Guide* covers the area. *Franconia-Pemigewasset (Map 2)* details trails in the Franconia Range at 1:95,000.

ADIRONDACK STATE PARK
The Northville-Placid Trail
If you want a good sample of what the Adirondacks has to offer, consider this 133mi backpack trek connecting the southern foothills with the High Peaks region. This north–south trail was originally laid out by the Appalachian Mountain Club in 1922–23. The trail winds through low, rolling terrain and picturesque valleys; travels through remote, seldom-visited country; crosses ridgelines and climbs over mountains – with plenty of lakes, streams, waterfalls and lofty views along the way. You'll pick up the trail near Northville, at the southern boundary of Adirondack State Park and snake northward to Lake Placid. It takes about 18–20 days to hike its length, but you can easily do it in sections. The best resource is the Adirondack Mountain Club's *Guide to Adirondack Trails: Northville-Placid Trail*.

GREEN MOUNTAINS
Camel's Hump Loop
If you're looking for a good, strenuous day hike in Vermont, Camel's Hump is a worthy choice. Rewarding but, alas, discovered – to the tune of 10,000 to 15,000 hikers annually. Tied with Mt Ellen for third-highest mountain

in Vermont at 4083ft, Camel's Hump is the only undeveloped high peak in the state.

Access the trail from Couching Lion Farm, about 11mi from exit 10 off I-89 in Waterbury. Make a 7.4mi (11.9km) loop hike by following the blue-blazed Monroe Trail to Dean Trail (also blue-blazed), then turn right to connect with the white-blazed Long Trail. Head north on the Long Trail (quite steep in places) to the exposed western face of Camel's Hump. Take in spectacular views, including Owl's Head in Canada, New Hampshire's White Mountains and the Presidential Range, and New York's Adirondacks and the Champlain Valley. A steep and rocky descent will then take you from the Long Trail to the Monroe Trail, until you arrive at the junction of the Monroe and Dean Trails, completing the loop. Plan at least six hours for this hike. Vertical rise is 2645ft. Trail maps (USGS 1:62,500 sheets *Waterbury* and *Huntington*) are available from the Green Mountain Club.

CAPE COD NATIONAL SEASHORE
Great Island Trail

The Cape Cod National Seashore offers 11 self-guided hiking trails. The longest, and most difficult, is Great Island Trail, a 6mi, sandy ramble to Jeremy Point overlook. To extend the hike to an 8mi (12.9km) roundtrip, choose the Tavern Site route, where a colonial-era tavern once stood. Careful, though – it's devilishly easy to get lost on the many side trails and you will find portions of the hike are submerged at high tide. West of Wellfleet, the trail meanders around sand dunes and skirts salt marsh, edging along tidal flats as it reaches Jeremy Point. At the highest points along the trail, peer through openings in the pitch-pine forest for splendid ocean views. Make sure that you wear sturdy shoes; the trail is mostly soft sand, with a few log steps. Allow about six hours to hike it – you certainly won't want to rush through this one. Maps are available at the Great Island parking lots off Chequesett Rd or at the Salt Pond visitor center.

Southern Appalachia

The Appalachian Mountains, stretching from Georgia to Maine, form the spine of the eastern United States. They divide the waters between the Gulf of Mexico and the Atlantic Ocean, and provide some of the last wild areas in the East. Southern Appalachia runs from northern Georgia to the Virginias. The highest peak east of the Mississippi River, Mt Mitchell in North Carolina, reaches only 6684ft. However, these are not easy mountains. An intricate geography of narrow gorges, tree-choked hollows and lonely balds make this a region of diverse life, difficult travel and cultural isolation.

There is much here that humans have enjoyed; abundant wildlife and water provided the Native Americans with hunting grounds and holy places. When Europeans arrived, Native Americans were forced out by ambitious settlers who cleared much of the land for farming and built small communities where stern religious beliefs and hard work kept them alive. As the rest of the east coast developed, the need for resources eventually affected Appalachia and timber and coal were extracted from old forests and mineral-laden hills. Southern Appalachia especially was devastated by the coal and timber industries, which provided work for many years but left no lasting infrastructure. This legacy still haunts many a small town along the old, curvy roads of Tennessee, North Carolina, Virginia, West Virginia and Kentucky.

NATURAL HISTORY

Even if material wealth hasn't come to these communities, the beauty of the mountains has reasserted itself. Very little of the old-growth forests remain, but incredibly diverse second-growth forests are well established and thriving in the lush and humid climate of the south. The biological diversity of the southern Appalachian Mountains is astonishing. There are 160 different species of trees blanketing the hillsides. These in turn provide shade for the dense understory where spring

HIGHLIGHTS

JOHN ELK III

The historic Cable Mill, Cades Cove, Great Smoky Mountains, Tennessee.

- Watching peregrine falcons near the top of Mt Leconte in the Great Smoky Mountains
- Walking over the great balds of Roan Mountain during the blooming season of pink rhododendrons
- Experiencing the Appalachian Trail near Mt Rogers including views, wild ponies, and a taste of AT camaraderie.
- Scrambling over the granite boulders and nature-hewn stairs on the way to the summit of Old Rag in Shenandoah National Park

wildflowers grow profusely, summer blooms of orange azalea, pink rhododendron and white mountain laurel illuminate the trails with their blossoms, and autumn leaves achieve a range of color from yellow to red to purple to brown that is one of the most beautiful shows nature can orchestrate.

Small creatures which like the moist atmosphere wear bright colors to advertise

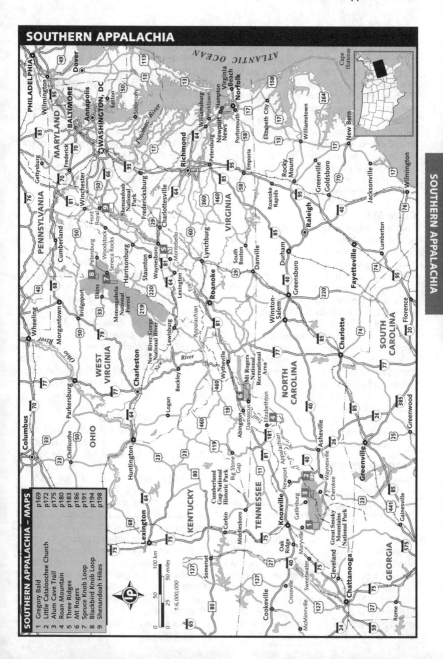

SOUTHERN APPALACHIA

SOUTHERN APPALACHIA – MAPS
1 Gregory Bald p169
2 Little Cataloochee Church ... p172
3 Alum Cave Trail p175
4 Roan Mountain p180
5 Three Ridges p183
6 Mt Rogers p186
7 Spruce Knob Loop p191
8 Blackbird Knob Loop p194
9 Shenandoah Hikes p198

0   25   50 miles
0   50   100 km
1:6,000,000

they won't make good eating – like scarlet salamanders, bright green snakes, and scarlet tanagers. Large animals occasionally cross the trails or pass nearby on their way to a water source – red deer, foxes, bobcats or black bears. Water is abundant and creeks and rivers flow unimpeded (except for an occasional beaver dam) from these mountain streams. Even in dry years, steam rises from the land, creating the misty atmosphere which gives the distinctive blue haze to long views and is the reason for the naming of the 'Blue Ridge' and 'Smoky' Mountains, both part of Southern Appalachia.

CLIMATE

Southern Appalachia boasts a long hiking season, from April to October. It is most accessible in spring and fall when temperatures are generally in the 70°sF. However, there can be dips to freezing temperatures at night and the occasional snow storm in the mountains during these shoulder seasons, so check the forecasts before packing that overnight backpack.

In summer, daily high temperatures average 85°F and it is still a wonderful time to escape to the mountains. It's usually cooler there than in the lowlands, and much of Appalachian hiking is in the shade of the very leafy forests. Creeks and waterfalls are frequent and the summer flowers are a delight. Thunderstorms are common in late summer afternoons, complete with lightning – beware of ridgetop hikes in stormy weather.

INFORMATION
Maps

For a general overview of Southern Appalachia, the American Automobile Association (AAA) provides several useful maps including *Southeastern States and Provinces* which shows all the states within Southern Appalachia (Georgia, Tennessee, North Carolina, Kentucky, West Virginia and Virginia.)

For hiking trails and topographical information, there are several choices. As well as the National Park Service (NPS) and United States Forest Service (USFS), Trails Illustrated produces excellent maps that are only available for trails in Shenandoah and Smoky Mountains National Parks. United States Geological Society (USGS) maps are available for every region in this chapter, but they are often unwieldy since you might need three different maps for one single hike. (See Planning in the Facts for the Hiker chapter for pre-ordering details.)

For all maps pertaining to the Appalachian Trail (see also the Long-Distance Trails chapter), the best source is the Appalachian Trail Conference (ATC; ☎ 304-535-6331, 888-AT-STORE, fax 304-535-2667, ☐ www.atconf .org, postal address: 799 Washington St, Harpers Ferry, WV 25425-0807).

Books

There are innumerable books about the hiking in Southern Appalachia. Each visitor center in the national parks and national forests offers wonderful selections of books covering every aspect of their respective regions. Highlights along the Appalachian Trail (AT) can be found in two books: *The Best of the AT Day Hikes* and *The Best of the AT Overnight Hikes* by F & V Logue ($14.95). For a historical overview of Appalachia, read *Night Comes to the Cumberlands*, a classic book (still in print), written in 1964 by H Caudill recalling the environmental and cultural devastation Appalachia has suffered from mining interests.

GETTING AROUND

As with most of the US, there aren't many public transportation options for the hiker. At best, the Greyhound Bus Co or Amtrak can deliver you to the nearest large town or city, and from there you must rely on taxis or shuttle services. A grass-roots movement started for AT hikers needing rides, and now shuttle services dot the landscape in and around the AT. Look for little notes posted on grocery store bulletin boards, at visitor centers, or at hiking outfitters. (Several are listed in this chapter under Getting To/From the Hike for the individual hikes, or under Getting Around for the regions.) A current list of all AT shuttle services can be obtained from the ATC.

The easiest way to get around is to have a vehicle of one's own. Rental cars are readily available in the larger towns of Appalachia; check the websites of the better known rental car agencies (see the Getting Around chapter for a list).

Some care should be taken when leaving a vehicle at a trailhead. Make sure that all valuable items are stowed in the trunk or completely out of sight (better yet, take them along or leave them at home). Don't leave a note on the windshield as to when you are coming back or when you left. If possible, leave the car in a parking area where there are other cars and lots of activity.

Hitchhiking is common practice in and around more popular trailheads and in hiking towns. Common sense and safety practices should apply to all hitchhiking forays (see Hitching in the Getting Around chapter).

Great Smoky Mountains

The Cherokee people first occupied this densely forested land leaving little sign of their presence. The history of the mountains changed dramatically when, in 1820, a treaty took the land from the Cherokee and divided it between the states of North Carolina and Tennessee. Land speculators bought large tracts in hope of making a profit by selling it to settlers, who struggled to clear the dense forests for farming and grazing. Much of the land was logged in the 19th century, leaving about 20% virgin forest.

By 1920, all of what is now national park was held in private hands. There was a growing desire, however, to save the beauty and pristine quality of the Smokies from further development, so a group of people began the arduous process of getting funds together to purchase the land and give it National Park status. It was an effort which swept the southeast, from grade-school coin collecting to a generous grant from John D Rockefeller. Through this process 6600 separate land purchases were made and the Great Smoky Mountains National Park was declared in 1934. One of the stipulations of

the original charter was that there would never be a fee charged for entering the park, and this remains the case today. Perhaps that is why nearly 10 million visitors come through the Smokies every year, the most visited park in the entire system. (The Grand Canyon is second, with 4 million visitors annually.)

A large percentage of visitors never get out of their cars, or limit their time outside to the Clingmans Dome half-mile. A serious hiker can spend the better part of a day by themselves. Hiking trails are numerous with more than 850mi of well-marked paths criss-crossing the mountains on which one can experience the incredible biodiversity of the Smokies. There are 1500 species of flowering plant, and more species of trees than in all of northern Europe. Wildlife is flourishing in the park, with deer, fox, bear and many species of birds to be seen. The Smokies have been declared a World Biosphere Preserve because of this incredible abundance and diversity.

INFORMATION

There are three visitor centers in the park: two in Tennessee – at Sugarland (near Gatlinburg) and Cades Cove (near Townsend) – and at Oconaluftee (near Cherokee, North Carolina). Besides offering useful and informative displays and other ranger services, all three are able to give out backcountry information and will check on the availability of backcountry permits for certain campsites. Sugarland and Oconaluftee are staffed with backcountry rangers who will give advice on where to hike, where bears have last been seen and what the crowds are likely to be.

Maps

The most complete topographic map of the entire park is published by Trails Illustrated at 1:62,500 ($9.95) and is available at all park visitor centers. USGS maps (see Maps & Navigation in the Facts for the Hiker chapter) of a larger scale (1:24,000) sell for $4.95, but you may need several to cover all the areas you may want to hike (see Planning for each hike).

Books

Each visitor center also has a book store featuring many excellent guidebooks to the various hikes in the park. The favorite is *Hiking Trails of the Smokies* published by the Great Smoky Mountains Natural History Association, for sale only in the park for $16.95. It is a very complete tome with elevation profiles and historical tidbits on every trail in the park.

Permits & Regulations

Although it's free, the permit system is quite strict and you must fill out a permit before spending the night anywhere in the backcountry. For most sites you can self-register at any ranger station, campground or visitor center. However, some campsites require a reservation from the backcountry reservation office (☎ 423-436-1231), open every day from 8 am to 6 pm. The park sells a map showing which sites are 'rationed' (requiring a reservation) and which are first-come, first-served. During the high season, permits for rationed sites must be obtained several days, or even weeks, in advance. For 'non-rationed' campsites, you can self-register the day you arrive in the park. If you haven't reserved one of the rationed campsites ahead of time, there's always the chance that there are still spaces available so check with the rangers in the wilderness office.

NEAREST TOWNS & FACILITIES
Gatlinburg

The traditional gateway city to the Great Smokies, Gatlinburg has grown in the last few years from an old-fashioned corn-ball resort town into a ticky-tacky carnival still under construction, competing with the depressingly commercial Pigeon Forge – one of the finest examples of late-20th-century urban sprawl – to the north of Gatlinburg. Now many visitors come to the region to go to the malls and shows of Pigeon Forge and the park is just an afterthought. If you can, try to arrive through Townsend or Cherokee instead.

For AT hikers who want a hot shower or a new pair of boots, try the Happy Hiker (☎ 423-436-5632), a backpacking/hiking store

located behind the Burning Bush restaurant at the last signal before the park entrance. It has unlimited advice for hikers and suggestions for hikes in the park.

Places to Stay & Eat If you must find accommodation in Gatlinburg, *Grand Prix Motel* (☎ 423-436-4561) is on Ski Mountain Rd. In town, dining might include a visit to *The Brewery*, a local favorite with in-house brewed beer, burgers and wood-fired calzones. It's off the main drag (Hwy 441) behind Calhoun's. Good Italian fare can be found at *The Best Italian Restaurant* in Elk's Plaza on the main road.

Among several commercial campgrounds, only two allow tents. These are both located on Hwy 321E, which is the road that heads east and north out of Gatlinburg. *Trout Creek* (☎ 423-436-5905) has shady, flat sites with river access, pool, laundry and showers. Sites are $14 for a tent and $20 to $22 for a Recreational Vehicle (RV). *Le Conte Vista* (☎ 423-436-5437) has smaller tent sites on a hillside for $20 to $25. A good restaurant out that way is the *Black Bear*, which is family owned and serves dinner, or the *Mountain Lodge* which only serves breakfast and lunch but is an old favorite.

Getting There & Away Gatlinburg lies along Tennessee Hwy 441, which leads through the middle of the park to North Carolina. From Knoxville, off I-40, take Hwy 441 south through Sevierville, then past the awful Pigeon Forge sprawl to reach Gatlinburg.

Cherokee

Cherokee is the main town on the Cherokee Indian Reservation of North Carolina. This is the eastern branch of the tribe which managed to hide out in the Smokies despite the best efforts of the North Carolina government in the early 19th century to run them off. The majority of the Cherokee tribe was moved off their lands in the Appalachian Mountains and forcibly marched to Oklahoma where the Cherokee Nation has a much larger reservation and population. The town makes the most of its Cherokee heritage, featuring a Museum of the Cherokee Indian, a long-running summer outdoor performance called 'Unto These Hills', and many an Indian craft shop. There are plenty of hotels, motels, campgrounds, restaurants, and one giant casino, as well as the Reservation Grocery Store (closed on Sundays). For more information, stop at the Cherokee information center on Business 441 South, the main street of town.

Places to Stay & Eat *Ocona Valley Motel* (☎ 828-497-4618) on Acquoni Rd has riverside rooms, a pool and is close to the park entrance. Doubles start at $48. *Cool Waters Motel* (☎ 828-497-3855) is farther out of town, along Hwy 41 toward Maggie Valley. Rooms are $45 to $65, with a pool and riverside location.

KOA Cherokee campground (☎ 828-497-9711, 800-825-8352, @ gsmkoa@aol.com) is on Big Cove Rd. This very Euro-style campground has tent sites ($19 to $31, depending on season and location) and cabins ($36 to $63, plus $10 for an extra room). Food at the *Poolside Cafe*, features all-you-can-eat dinners ($7 or $10).

In addition to the standard collection of fast-food joints, there are a small number of 'Ma and Pa' style restaurants in Cherokee. *Granny's Kitchen*, across the street from Cool Waters Motel, serves a classic southern buffet ($7.99). (The restaurants in Cherokee don't offer wine or beer since this is a dry reservation.) A non-buffet option is the *Hungry Bear*, on the road to Atlanta. This has a salad bar ($6), steak, chicken and fish, as well as burgers.

Getting There & Away To reach Cherokee, take I-40 west from Asheville, then Hwy 19 through Maggie Valley to Cherokee.

Townsend

Townsend is on the 'peaceful side of the Smokies' and will hopefully stay that way, what with kitchy Gatlinburg only 40mi away. Everything you need is here: a grocery store, two camping outfitters, a helpful visitor center (☎ 423-448-6134, 800-525-6834), and food and lodging.

Places to Stay & Eat There are some expensive log cabins and B&Bs here in the $90 to $100 range per night (ask at the visitor center for a listing). A bit more reasonable is the *Riverstone Lodge* (☎ 423-448-6677, 800-854-7358) with rooms for $49 to $59. *Headrick's RiverBreeze Motel* (☎ 423-448-2389, 800 879-0047) has rooms for $55 to $65. Both establishments have a pool. Several campgrounds are located along the main highway running through town. The last campground before the park is the *Little Mountain Village campground* (☎ 423-448-2241, 800-261-6370) with tent sites for $18 to $21, a pool, *restaurant*, store and playground. It also has log cabins for $40 to $45 per night. The hippest place to eat in town is *Deadbeat Pete's* (☎ 423-448-0900) often featuring live bluegrass music.

Getting There & Away Take Hwy 129 south off I-40 in Knoxville. In Maryville, take Hwy 321 which will lead to Townsend.

In the Park

The best camping in the area is in the park itself, where there are 10 campgrounds which between them have a total of about 1000 sites. The three large campgrounds that can be reserved from May 15 to October 31 are *Cades Cove* (closest to Townsend), *Elkmont* (closest to Gatlinburg) and *Smokemont* (closest to Cherokee). Cades Cove has the most visitors of any campground in the park, and for good reason. It's close to many good hiking trails and is the starting point for the Cades Cove driving loop, which is a big attraction. To reserve a campsite in these campgrounds, call ☎ 800-365-2267 (toll free). From abroad, call ☎ 301-722-1257 or check the NPS website (🖳 www.nps.gov). The best of the smaller and less visited campgrounds are *Balsam Mountain* and *Cosby*, both on the eastern side of the park. *Cataloochee campground* is in an isolated part of the park; this campground has 27 sites, all first-come, first-served. Try to get there early in the day, and avoid weekends. For the latest update on campsite availability, check at the nearest ranger station after 1 pm.

SOUTHERN APPALACHIA

GETTING AROUND

Call A Walk in the Woods (☎ 423-436-8283) to speak to Erik or Vesna who run this small guiding and shuttle company out of Gatlinburg.

Gregory Bald

Duration	5–6 hours
Distance	11mi (17.7km)
Standard	medium
Start/Finish	End of Forge Creek Rd, Cades Cove
Nearest Towns	Townsend, Gatlinburg
Public Transport	no

Summary Follow a creek through old-growth forest, then a rhododendron- and azalea-covered ridge to a heathy bald with stunning views and spectacular flowers in season. A good chance of seeing bears.

The hike to Gregory Bald is one of those experiences that is different each time you follow this path. In early spring the trail is flanked with wildflowers, and in June mountain laurel and the Catawba rhododendron's magenta blossoms line the trail. By July, orange and fuchsia azaleas are bursting into bloom. After a hefty climb of 3000ft (900m) in 5.4mi, the hiker is rewarded with not only a nearly 360-degree view, but a flower-cloaked (in season) bald and a chance at meeting one of the Smokies' black bears over an August crop of mountain blueberry. Fall is also spectacular since the autumn leaves of all the deciduous trees are featured and the views begin to open up along the ridge as the trees lose their leaf cover. For many, this is the quintessential Smokies hike that can be done year after year.

WARNING

As for many hikes in the Smokies, there is always a chance of meeting black bears on the trail. See the Health & Safety chapter for important information about bears.

PLANNING
When to Hike

This is a wonderful hike in any season, although different seasons have their distinctions. For the most spectacular scenery (rhododendron and azalea) on the bald, go in late June. For wildflowers along the forest floor on the ridge, try to hike in May or early June. The heat of summer is not oppressive since the majority of the hike is in the shade. Fall colors hit their peak in the last two weeks of October. However, after the leaves have fallen the views open up considerably.

What to Bring

This hike offers a good opportunity to bring along binoculars as there is a great view from the top of the bald and many birds along the trail. Rain gear is always a good idea to have along as well as two quarts of water since the steep grade of the climb will cause the most seasoned hiker to lose quite a bit of liquid in sweat alone. There is no access to water after the first 2mi, although just below the bald there is a spring (all water in the Smokies should be treated before drinking either with tablets or a filter).

Maps

For this well-marked, easy-to-follow route, the trail map provided by the park is fine. However, if more detail is desired, use the Trails Illustrated *Great Smoky Mountains National Park* topographic map (see Maps at the beginning of this section).

GETTING TO/FROM THE HIKE

Take the Cades Cove Loop Rd from Townsend and at the turnoff for the visitor center and Cable Mill area, go straight onto Forge Creek Rd for 2.3mi until it ends in a small parking area. Forge Creek Rd runs through an area once called Chestnut Flats, which was a notorious haunt of moonshiners (makers of illegal home-made corn whiskey). Many a shootout took place in these parts over whose moonshine was whose. Its nefarious activity continued well into the 20th century – right up until people began to sell out to make room for the national park.

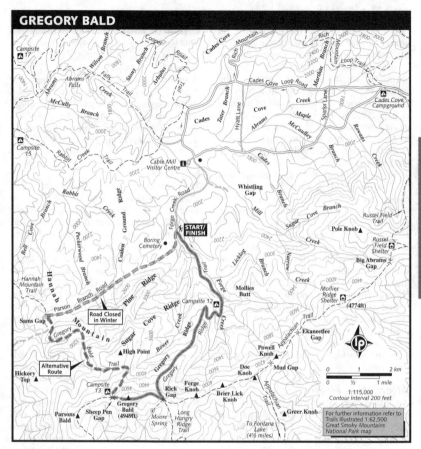

GREGORY BALD

THE HIKE

The Gregory Ridge Trail begins with a short uphill over a ridge that eventually levels out as it follows Forge Creek. This is a second-growth hemlock forest, and in spring wild-flowers carpet the forest floor. The trail crosses the creek several times over foot-bridges. The little gray junco may flit out from its nesting site (in June) on the ground near the trail as you walk by. After the second crossing of Forge Creek, a section of old-growth tulip trees appears. After the third crossing of Forge Creek there will soon appear primitive (unrationed) *campsite No 12*.

This is the last chance to fill up on water (although this is from the creek, and needs to be treated).

From here, the climbing begins in earnest. The ascent is of a moderate grade and will continue for the next 3mi, gaining about 2400ft. After about a mile of oak forest the ridge itself is reached. Mountain laurel are plentiful along this stretch, with white clusters of cup-shaped flowers that bloom in June. At about 4.6mi there is a final, flat stretch with views out to the east. With luck Spence Field and Thunderhead Mountain above it are visible. At

4.9mi is **Rich Gap** and the junction with the Gregory Bald Trail. Moore Spring is straight ahead from this point on an unmarked, single-track trail, about a third of a mile further on. The side trip to the spring is worthwhile not only for the water, which wells up beneath a boulder, but also to view the former site of a popular Appalachian Trail shelter when the AT passed this way. The shelter burned down in the 1970s and was not replaced, and since the fire the AT has been re-routed to pass Fontana Lake.

To the right from Rich Gap intersection is **Gregory Bald**, a further 0.6mi. The rocky and steepish climb is mercifully short and soon the bald opens out in all its splendour. If the timing is right (late June), the flame azaleas are competing for the many bees that buzz around their lovely white, pink, yellow and red blossoms. It's a unique genetic challenge for the azaleas; even the British Museum of Natural History in London has felt compelled to investigate by collecting a number of specimens to take home. In August the blueberries are the attraction for bees, bears and humans.

From the bald, the hike returns along the same path.

Alternative Finish

An alternative to returning the way you came is to continue over the bald on Gregory Bald Trail, passing *campsite No 13* (a rationed campsite), and descending 4mi to the intersection with Parson Branch Rd. Turn right onto this forest-service road and walk 4.4mi to the intersection with Forge Creek Rd. The car will be just to the right. This would make a total hike of 14.4mi (plus 0.6mi if the Moore Spring side trip is added). Another interesting side trip is just before the intersection with Forge Creek Rd, where there's a small jeep trail on the left. Follow this trail 150ft to the Boring cemetery where the Baptist preacher William Boring, his wife and three daughters are all buried. All of the women died in a typhoid epidemic in the late 19th century.

Little Cataloochee Church

Duration	5–6 hours
Distance	10.4mi (16.7km)
Standard	medium
Start/Finish	Cataloochee Valley, Pretty Hollow Gap Trail
Nearest Towns	Cherokee, Maggie Valley
Public Transport	no

Summary A forest hike to historic structures in a less visited area of the park.

HISTORY

The Cataloochee Valley was the last area of the Smokies to be settled after the Cherokee were driven out. Rough topography made it one of the more difficult to reach, but it was eventually tamed and by 1910 boasted a population of 1251 people. The 'Big' Cataloochee, where the campground and ranger office are now located, was settled first. The original families came in 1814 and the valley was pretty well occupied by 1850. When the children of those families needed land, they began settling the Little Cataloochee valley, the two valleys being separated by Noland Mountain. These folks had their work cut out for them clearing the dense forests of old-growth timber for growing corn and apples and creating grazing land for their cattle. The old Palmer House in the Big Cataloochee has an excellent exhibit, as well as a video production with interviews of some of the old-timers. It's located down the gravel road which forks off to the left if you leave the campground heading back on the pavement toward Maggie Valley. (This fork also leads to Hwy 284).

What was once a settled agricultural community has now returned to a dense though different forest. When the efforts to make this region a national park began, the people of Cataloochee were not pleased. Some families had been there several generations, but they eventually agreed to sell their land and move elsewhere. The park service at the time was anxious for the land to become wilderness once again, so they demolished or removed many of the buildings However, one of the early park rangers felt that the human element of Cataloochee was also important to the history of the land; thus, a few places were saved and restoration of various buildings has continued ever since. The most recent restoration is Dan Cook's log cabin, along the Little Cataloochee Trail. Little Cataloochee Church is just beyond Dan Cook's place, and is in pristine condition, lovingly whitewashed and watertight. The families who still live nearby keep it in its present state and the fresh (and plastic) flowers in the graveyard are a sign that someone comes here often.

NATURAL HISTORY

The hike to Little Cataloochee is lonely and beautiful. There are many birds, wildflowers, trees, and a good chance to see wildlife. The forest is mostly of tulip trees (yellow-orange blossoms in May and early June), maple, American beech, yellow birch and silverbell. Catawba rhododendron are prevalent, blooming pink flowers in June.

PLANNING
When to Hike

Spring and fall are probably the best times, for spring wildflowers or for the autumn turning of the leaves. However, at any time of the year this is a shaded, cool forest hike with many streams.

If it has been raining the hike will be very muddy. Even in good weather, there is a lot of water coming off the mountain and several easy stream crossings are required. Horses are allowed on the trail, which sometimes makes the muddy sections that much worse.

What to Bring

This is the steamier side of Smoky Mountains National Park; in summer there are nearly daily afternoon thundershowers. Bring rain gear and plenty of drinking water – while the hike is in the shade for nearly its entire length, it's usually so humid that a person will sweat out a lot of moisture. Any water available along the trail, even at the Ola Spring, needs to be filtered or treated before drinking.

Maps & Books

The small, brown *Smoky Mountain Hikes* book is a great resource, and the Trails Illustrated Smoky Mountains map is also useful. The two differ slightly on their mileages and *Smoky Mountain Hikes* has the benefit of an elevation profile for each hike. It also comes with a map showing all the hikes and how they connect – necessary if one is considering doing an overnight loop. The trails are clearly sign-posted at every junction.

GETTING TO/FROM THE HIKE

From Cherokee, take Hwy 19E toward Maggie Valley and I-40. Follow the signs for I-40 but turn left on Cove Creek Rd, just before crossing the bridge over the river (I-40 itself is visible ahead). If you're on I-40, take exit 20, cross the bridge over the river and take an immediate right onto Cove Creek Rd.

Proceed on this curvy residential road for a few miles before it turns to dirt and goes dizzily up and then down. Watch at the curves for large RVs brave (or ignorant) enough to drive this narrow stretch.

It's only a 10mi drive on Cove Creek Rd, but it takes a while. Once in the park a paved section begins and Cataloochee campground soon appears on the left. Beyond the campground another mile or so is the trailhead for Pretty Hollow Gap and Palmer Creek Trails. (Don't take the bridge over Palmer Creek or you've gone too far – however, there are a few interesting buildings up that road, including the Beech Grove Schoolhouse, the Caldwell house and the Woody House.)

THE HIKE

Beginning at the trailhead for the Pretty Hollow Gap Trail, the path follows Palmer Creek and soon passes the horse camp where there's generally a lot of activity. There's plenty of signs of horses on the trail, but they won't interfere with an enjoyable hike since their pace is faster than that of a hiker. After 1.1mi, make the first of several crossings of the Davidson Branch (a tributary into Palmer Creek), walking along a wide (former) road that used to be lined with fields to the left, now overgrown with forest. This is a rocky path with many seeps that can make it rather wet and slippery.

At 1.8mi, a right switchback diverges to follow a fork of the Davidson Branch, shaded

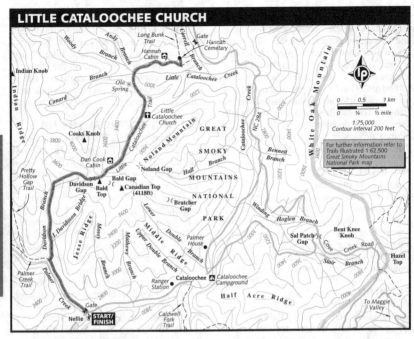

LITTLE CATALOOCHEE CHURCH

by second-growth forest which replaced the formerly cleared agricultural land. At 2.2mi you might notice on the left some hand-hewn chestnut logs and a stone wall which are the remains of an old farm. Although the trail has been steadily gaining altitude, a steep climb begins soon after this point, reaching **Davidson Gap** at 2½mi. The gap and the creek are named for William Davidson, an old Cataloochee cattle man. There are hitching posts as well as an easily missed, single-track trail which leads up to Bald Top and Bald Gap.

After the Davidson Gap, the trail descends at a moderate pitch into the Little Cataloochee Valley. This is all second-growth forest, and one must try to imagine what it was like 100 years ago: all of the land was cleared up to the gap, corn fields were in the valley bottom and apple orchards lined the hillsides. Just as it seems that nature has vanquished all signs of human habitation, the restored cabin of Dan Cook comes into view at 3.1mi. It was the

finest log cabin of the 'little Catalooch' and it was lovingly restored by the park service in 1999, using logs left from the original structure (disassembled in 1975 and put into storage). Dan Cook had originally built the cabin in 1856 and lived there for more than 50 years with his wife, Harriet. His grave is in the Baptist church graveyard.

The **Little Cataloochee Church** is reached at 3.9mi. It was built by the people of the community in 1889, and held services once a month when a travelling preacher came around. The graveyard is filled with familiar Cataloochee names as well as earlier graves marked only with a stone. Passing the church, the trail winds down to the lowest point of the hike, a rock covered spring on the left. This is where the community of Ola began – the 100-acre spread of Will Messer, who married Dan Cook's daughter, Rachel. They did well in the apple business and in 1905 moved to this end of the valley. In 1910 he built a fine, large house with 11 rooms, hot water and acetylene lighting. The post office was registered under the name 'Ola' after the Messer's daughter, Viola. The site of the old Messer home can be found by looking about 75ft beyond the spring on the right where two tall, pyramid-shaped ornamental shrubs are overgrown.

At 4.3mi, the Little Cataloochee creek is crossed. The trail immediately begins to go up, and at 4.6mi there is a trail on the left leading 220ft to the Hannah cabin. This structure dates from 1864, and was restored in 1976. Newspaper still clings to the interior walls where it was tacked to keep out cold drafts. The trail descends again to the junction with the Long Bunk Trail at 5mi. Follow it for 0.2mi to the Hannah cemetery – a worthwhile side trip. This is the turn-around point of the out-and-back version of this hike.

Alternative Finish

If you are lucky enough to have someone who will shuttle your car, you can continue to the terminus of Little Cataloochee Trail (don't take Long Bunk Trail, but continue straight on Little Cataloochee Trail) that ends at the dirt road of Hwy 284 where your car could be waiting for you. Or, you could walk the rarely travelled Hwy 284 back to Little Cataloochee, passing Palmer House and arriving at the campground – a long day.

Alum Cave Trail

Duration	6–8 hours
Distance	12.7mi (20.5km)
Standard	medium-hard
Start	Newfound Gap Rd
Finish	Newfound Gap parking area
Nearest Towns	Gatlinburg, Cherokee
Public Transport	no

Summary A long climb (3000ft ascent) through old-growth forest, past Arch Rock and Alum Bluff Cave, leads to the top of 6593ft Mt Leconte, the second-highest peak in the park. Return on the Boulevard and Appalachian Trails.

NATURAL HISTORY

The Alum Cave Trail passes through some of the most spectacular scenery in the park.

The Peregrine Falcon

Two types of falcon are seen in the Appalachian Mountains: the small American kestrel (males are reddish brown with gray wings, and females are larger with red-brown wings and a finely striped tail) and the peregrine falcon, which is larger and beautiful to watch. This distinctive raptor, with its dark head and white neck and cheeks, has only recently made a startling comeback from the abyss of pesticide-induced annihilation. There were none left in the East until re-introduction programs (and tighter pesticide laws) began to bear fruit in only the last few years. Listen for their shrill cry and watch as they swoop on their prey (usually small birds) knocking them out of the sky. The underside of their wings is striped with black and white, which you'll notice as they circle in the thermal currents above.

Much of the trail is in the Anakeesta Formation, a slaty rock left over from the oceanic mud the Smokies were before they were pushed upward as the continent collided with Africa many millennia ago. The rock has a weak structure – when it was being deformed in the uplifting action, its layers shifted, creating weakness and the crumbling, jagged layers visible to the hiker. These vulnerable layers make the Anakeesta more susceptible to freeze-thaw erosion; this trail has many examples of this natural tendency for landslides and interesting rock formations, especially at Arch Rock and Alum Cave.

After 5000ft elevation is reached, the spruce-fir forest will be in evidence, although the 'fir' part of that combination has been devastated by the woolly adelgid bug. Most of these trees at the high elevations are old growth. At the beginning of the trail are many old-growth hardwood trees (eastern hemlock, beech, birch and buckeye). In the final approach to Mt Leconte, a massif of four peaks, keep an eye out for the peregrine falcons which usually nest here in summer.

The Lodge on Mt Leconte

At the turn of the century there was nothing at Newfound Gap but a warden's cabin and empty hills of old-growth forest. Early explorers often began their journeys from here, until the 1920s when Newfound Gap Rd was built. This attracted adventurers such as the Gatlinburg hotelier, Jack Huff, who in 1925 built a wilderness lodge on the top of Mt Leconte. Offering very spartan accommodation, and no electricity or running water, it became a haven for those early hikers. Today, Mt Leconte Lodge is the only privately owned accommodation in the park, although it is just as spartan as ever. However, making a reservation is nearly impossible. Call (☎ 423-429-5704) 9 am to 5 pm Monday to Friday. Sometimes there are cancellations, so call before you hike just to check. It's $75 per person, including dinner and breakfast. The food is said to be quite good – it's brought in on the backs of llamas which come up Trillium Gap Trail three times a week. Day hikers can fill up with water at the lodge, buy candy bars, and sit in the rocking chairs on the big front porch.

PLANNING
When to Hike

This popular trail can be very crowded on weekends. Fortunately, the majority go only as far as Alum Bluffs Cave, just 2.2mi from the trailhead. If you start early you will probably have a nearly empty trail ahead. Bring plenty of water (although you can refill at Mt Leconte Lodge without using a filter).

Maps & Books

The Trails Illustrated *Great Smoky Mountaind National Park* map is fine for this well-marked trail. *Hiking Trails of the Smokies* is an excellent resource book for all the trails in the park, and comes with the park trail map and elevation charts.

GETTING TO/FROM THE HIKE
To the Start

From Sugarland visitor center, travel 8.6mi on Newfound Gap Rd to a parking area on your left. The trailhead is here. This is 21mi from Oconaluftee visitor center.

From the Finish

The trail ends in the large parking area at Newfound Gap (13.2mi from Sugarland visitor center on Newfound Gap Rd and about 16mi from Oconaluftee.) It is 5.4mi between the trailhead and the end of the trail, so you will need to shuttle your car to one end, and either hitch back at the end of the day or arrange a morning shuttle to leave your car at Newfound Gap.

Those without a car could try A Walk in the Woods – see Getting Around earlier in this section. In North Carolina, call Charlie Watts (☎ 828-479-2504).

THE HIKE

The first 1½mi of the hike to Arch Rock is through old-growth hemlock forest along Alum Cave Creek. If there are large hemlocks in a forest, it indicates that the area was probably never logged. Unfortunately, the hemlock is threatened by an epidemic of woolly adelgid bug that has already attacked the Fraser fir trees of the Smokies. This new hemlock-attacking adelgid cousin has already arrived in Shenandoah National Park farther to the north and is making its way south. The deciduous yellow birch trees are prevalent here too, and the young trees can be distinguished by their peeling yellowish bark which becomes flakier as the trees grow older.

At the third footbridge, you'll reach **Arch Rock** – actually more of a tunnel. The rock inside the 'arch' is not smooth, but jagged and rough, indicating that this was not formed by the creek waters but by the freeze-thaw erosion that is so effective in the Anakeesta rock. You'll see the remnants of many landslides along this trail, a common occurrence on this mountain of unstable slate.

After the next footbridge and a stretch through rhododendron bushes, the trail opens up to the remains of a big slide which in 1993 took a 20ft layer of debris into this gorge, uncovering the mountainside down to bedrock. Now the debris is in the process of re-adjusting to its new environment,

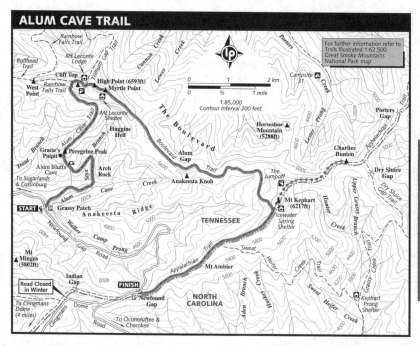

ALUM CAVE TRAIL

growing fern, hardwood, and rhododendron. After nearly 2mi (about an hour) the trail leaves the old forest and climbs Peregrine Peak, named for its falcon population which disappeared for many years and has only recently reappeared. Keep a lookout for falcons, especially from Inspiration Point, an inviting rocky face surrounded by rhododendron, sand myrtle and mountain laurel bushes. It has wonderful views of Little Duck Hawk Ridge across the valley. (There are also some aggressive chipmunks here who live on hiker handouts – please don't give them any!) From here, the trail begins to climb steeply and arrives at **Alum Bluffs Cave** after 2.2mi, about 1¼ hours from the trailhead.

If you smell a gunpowder odor it is the naturally occurring sulfides and saltpeter found in the bluffs. During the Civil War, a Confederate colonel attempted to mine them out. But the access here is so difficult that not much was ever taken. From here,

the trail will be much less populated, since most hikers go only as far as the bluffs.

From the bluffs, the trail climbs and then wraps around to the other side of the ridge. At the turning-point there is a small trail off to the left that leads a few yards to **Gracies Pulpit**, a small rock promontory named for Gracie McNichol who climbed this trail many times, including once on her 92nd birthday. This point offers a good view of the four peaks that comprise the Mt Leconte massif: West Point, Cliff Top, High Point and Myrtle Point. From here the trail descends for about 0.3mi; the climb up to Mt Leconte then begins in earnest. Alternating between red spruce forest and grassy, landslide-cleared stretches, the trail eventually emerges just below Cliff Top at the Rainbow Falls Trail (about 3½ hours and 4.9mi from the trailhead). Turn right here toward the lodge and the Boulevard Trail. For the view from **Cliff Top**, take the side trail that begins just before reaching the lodge. It climbs over

What's happening to the trees?

The Smokies get their name from the haze rising from the humid plant life below. The haze, however, has become thicker in the last few decades. A guidebook from 1955 described the view from Clingmans Dome (the highest point in the Smokies) as stretching for 85mi. Today, on a clear day you can see perhaps 25mi. Numerous studies by the NPS have declared that this is mostly due to coal-burning electric plants in nearby states. The moist, thick air traps these 'acid' fumes, making the upper elevations of the Appalachians more polluted than the streets of some east coast cities.

The trees living at the higher elevations have been suffering. Already weak from the bad air, a bug accidentally imported into the US 30 years ago (the balsam woolly adelgid) has systematically killed most of the Fraser fir trees of the Appalachian Mountains. This devastation of the fir forests is most evident above 6000ft. A close relative of that bug is now poised to kill the hemlocks, already having wreaked havoc in Shenandoah National Park and now heading south to the Smokies. The only strategy the NPS has come up with is to try to influence local governments to reduce coal-burning emissions.

a further 0.2mi to the viewpoint from which you can see **Clingmans Dome** (the highest peak in the park, and the second highest in the East at 6643ft) and sometimes downtown Knoxville. The trees above 6000ft are mostly Fraser firs, or what's left of them after the devastation of the little adelgid bug. At the stairs leading down to *Mt Leconte Lodge*, continue straight to shortly begin the Boulevard Trail, leading uphill to the right.

At the lodge you can get drinking water from a pump, take a rest in one of the rocking chairs on the porch, and purchase a candy bar or a Mt Leconte T-shirt if a staff member is around. The lodge staff stay all summer, and go back to civilization only rarely. But if they go, they go fast – the unofficial record for hiking Alum Cave Trail is held by a former staff member, Greg Ernsberger, who descended the trail in 28 minutes, and climbed back up in 1 hour 12 minutes.

The Boulevard Trail begins just after passing the lodge, and is a beautifully scenic meander that never dips below 5500ft. Plenty of wildflowers linger along its length well into the summer since it stays cooler up here than at lower elevations. Just after leaving the lodge the trail passes the *Mt Leconte shelter*, a rationed site.

After 15 minutes (about 0.3mi) is **High Point** at 6593ft, the highest point on Mt Leconte. It's marked by a pile of stones on the left, which are an attempt by Mt Leconte

enthusiasts to build the peak up to a higher elevation than Clingmans Dome. They've got some stone-lugging ahead of them. Just after is a short side trail leading 0.2mi to Myrtle Point. The next section of trail is along the steep northeastern side of Mt Leconte. The trail itself is not steep, but gradually descends across many old landslides and open forests. After a gradual descent of 1000ft over 2½mi (about 1½ hours) **Alum Gap** is reached.

Now the trail is more forested. About two hours from the lodge the trail hits the lowest point along the Boulevard Trail (at 5500ft); the last mile gains 500ft before intersecting the AT at 10.3mi. Turn right here for the last 2.7mi of mostly descending trail to the parking area at Newfound Gap. This section of the AT used to be quite protected by a large and healthy Fraser fir forest which in the last decades has been reduced to great stands of matchstick trees offering little shade. However, the views are more spectacular than ever, and the additional sunlight is encouraging a whole new set of plants to grow. Blackberries are all along this trail bearing fruit in August. (Bears also love the sweet berries, so keep an eye open.) The trail ends at Newfound Gap, a welcome sight even if it is teeming with motorized tourism.

Only 0.2mi to the left of the intersection of the Boulevard and Appalachian Trails is (rationed) *Icewater Spring shelter* which boasts an ice-cold spring and a composting toilet. About a mile beyond the shelter is Charlies Bunion, an unusually denuded rock outcrop that is named for its resemblance to an early Smoky explorer's foot. The section of the AT that leads from Charlies Bunion to Newfound Gap is one of the oldest trails in the park, built in 1931 with pick and shovel.

Blue Ridge Mountains

The Blue Ridge Mountains are the easternmost rampart of the Appalachian Mountains and stretch from northern Georgia to central Pennsylvania. The Blue Ridge Parkway (BRP) is a 469mi road along the crest of the Blue Ridge. The road was approved in 1935 by President Roosevelt as a link between the Shenandoah National Park and the Great Smoky Mountains. The road meanders through the Blue Ridge with stunning views every few hundred yards. However, it is surprisingly devoid of the human element so intrinsic to these hills – no one lives along it and there are no commercial enterprises. The BRP itself is administered by the NPS which maintains the road and operates several visitor centers, some campgrounds, and more than 100 trails that emanate from the ridge. It is organized by mile marker, starting from Shenandoah.

The Blue Ridge has an amazing human history because of its isolation up until the 1930s, when the first roads opened up the region to communication and newcomers. All that's left up here of that legacy – bluegrass music, artisan wood-working, moonshine production, and a particular dialect of the English language – is recreated in some of the visitor centers, but it's still living down in the valleys on either side of the Blue Ridge. The 're-created' communities (the Johnson Farm at Mile 85.9, Basin Cove at Mile 243.7, and the Black Ridge at Mile 169, among others) make for good day-hikes but the inhabitants are long gone, their descendants having moved downhill. Most of the trails along the Blue Ridge are only a mile or two in length, except for the AT which often parallels the road for long stretches.

Roan Mountain

Duration	7 hours
Distance	13.3mi (21.4km)
Standard	medium
Start	Carvers Gap
Finish	Near Elk Park on Hwy 19E
Nearest Towns	Roan Mountain, Elk Park
Public Transport	no

Summary A stunningly beautiful hike over three bald mountaintops offering open views, expanses of rhododendron gardens, and an optional overnight stay.

It's such a treat to hike in the Blue Ridge without the ever-present forest canopy. This hike takes great advantage of the open balds of Roan Mountain's wilderness. Hiking on the AT for the entire length, there are several good climbs and great views from Round Bald, Little Hump and Big Hump Mountains. An optional 1½mi side trail goes to the top of Grassy Ridge, the only natural 360-degree view above 6000ft close to the AT.

It's possible to make this an overnight hike by staying in one of the shelters or camping along the way. (The Overmountain Shelter is highly recommended.)

NATURAL HISTORY

The balds of Roan Mountain display vast stretches of rhododendron bushes which in the second half of June will attain their full pink splendor. Most people will only go as far as the Rhododendron Gardens Trail, on the west side of the road at Carvers Gap, featuring a very easy 1mi path that meanders through the big bushes. This extensive garden was actually created after the spruce-fir forest was logged in the early part of the century and most of the rhododendrons were dug up for sale to exotic plant nurseries. But the roots of the rhododendron went deeper than the shovels could go and they have had an amazing recovery, taking over whole hillsides.

The Balds of Roan Mountain

The balds of Roan Mountain are an example of a mysterious phenomenon found in the Appalachians. 'Balds' are open mountain tops or meadows that occur well below treeline and have been treeless as long as people have been writing about them. Theories abound as to how they were originally cleared: were fires set by Native Americans wanting open hunting ground or space for religious ceremonies? Or did wild herds of elk and bison clear the space by their grazing? In any case, the balds were here when Europeans arrived and they provided good grazing lands for domestic stock animals, so were kept open. Only in the last few decades, with encroaching development and fewer grazing animals, has the forest begun to reclaim these open spaces. The USFS has tried several methods to keep the balds bald, including controlled burns and roaming herds of goats. It's not yet clear if nature needs help or if the forest service should let nature take its course. Time will tell.

PLANNING
When to Hike

The second half of June is the classic time to walk the trail. This is when the vibrant pink of the catawba rhododendron bushes are in full, spectacular bloom. However, it is a beautiful hike during the entire hiking season; because of the open expanses there are always colorful views of spring wildflowers, summer blueberries, or autumn leaves.

What to Bring

This area receives lots of rain, so even if it starts out hot and sunny bring rain gear. The higher balds are quite exposed and can be windblown so rain gear can double as wind protection. Less time in the forest means more sun, so bring a hat. Plan on two quarts of water per person, although there are creeks along the way (with water that should be filtered or treated). Good boots, preferably waterproof, are helpful since many sections of the trail are stone-stepping, steep, and often wet and muddy.

Maps

Use the ATC map *Moreland Gap Shelter to Sams Gap, US 23 – Cherokee and Pisgah National Forests (Map 2)*, although it is very difficult to find on sale anywhere near Carvers Gap. However, the trail is well-marked with the AT white blazes, so there is little opportunity to get lost.

Information Sources

There is a ranger station at Roan Mountain Gardens, on the west side of the road at Carvers Gap. There is another ranger station down in Roan Mountain State Park, near the campground.

NEAREST TOWNS & FACILITIES
Roan Mountain

This town has some small grocery stores, a laundromat, a bank with an ATM, medical services and a pharmacy.

Places to Stay & Eat *Roan Mountain State Park* (☎ 423-772-4178, 800-250-8620) is a full-service campground with primitive sites for $9.50 and sites with electricity and water for $14.50. There are hot showers and a swimming pool. The campground is 3mi from the town itself, where there are some very authentic southern eating establishments. The *Roan Mountain Motel* is officially closed, but owner Ken Hodges (☎ 423-772-4404) will rent rooms to hikers. Try *Dairyland Bob's* for his great burgers and huge, flaky biscuits for breakfast.

Getting There & Away From Knoxville, head north on I-81 about 100mi then turn right onto I-181 south to Johnson City. Turn onto Hwy 321 and take it east to Elizabethton, then join Hwy 19E towards North Carolina for about 20mi to Roan Mountain. For the campground and trailhead, turn right on Hwy 143 just west of Roan Mountain, go 3mi to Roan Mountain State Park (the trailhead is five more miles on Hwy 143).

From the BRP, follow the directions for Carvers Gap (see Getting To/From the Hike), then continue a further 8mi to Roan Mountain.

Elk Park

Places to Stay & Eat The *Times Square Motel* (☎ *828-733-9271*) has doubles for $35 and a *restaurant*. However, the nearby *King of the Road Restaurant* serves giant steaks with all the extras for about $15. The closest big food stores are to be found in Newland, just east of Elk Park a further 7mi along the road to the BRP.

Getting There & Away Elk Park is just east of the town of Roan Mountain on Hwy 19E. It is 12mi west of the BRP at the Pineola exit, off the BRP just north of Linville Falls area, at about Mile 312.

Hampton

Places to Stay & Eat The *Kincora Hiking Hostel* (☎ *423-725-4409*) is an AT thru-hiker hangout, with great owners, Bob and Pat Peoples, who run their very simple but clean operation asking for a donation of only $4 per night. Showers, kitchen facilities, laundry and private rooms are available. Bob will also shuttle hikers to Carvers Gap (see Getting To/From the Hike).

Getting There & Away Hampton is 6mi south of Elizabethton; from here, turn onto Dennis Cove Rd, go over a big hill and the Kincora mailbox is on your right. It's a further 0.2mi to the AT junction. From the junction, it's one to two days of hiking (about 20mi) to Hwy 19E, so about two to three days to Carvers Gap.

GETTING TO/FROM THE HIKE
To the Start

Carvers Gap is on the border of Tennessee and North Carolina. From the BRP, go through Spruce Pine from Gillespie Gap (Mile 331) onto Hwy 226. Continue until you reach a right turn onto Hwy 261 toward Bakersville and Roan Mountain. Carvers Gap is about 26mi from the BRP. From Roan Mountain State Park campground (near Roan Mountain) take Hwy 143 right out of the campground and drive for about 5mi up to Carvers Gap. The trail begins at the white blazes on the east side of the road.

From the Finish

The trail emerges onto Hwy 19E, just 2½mi west of Elk Park and 3.4mi east of Roan Mountain. This is a busy highway, although there is a wide shoulder. You can walk uphill (east) 0.6mi to the pay phone outside Vick's Market to call for a shuttle back to your car.

Shuttle Services

For a shuttle, try Cloudland Wrecker Service (☎ 423-772-4301) in Roan Mountain. It should be arranged ahead of time to bring your car to their shop in the morning, and then shuttle to Carvers Gap, and upon finishing call from Vick's Market to be picked up. The charge is $25.

Bob Peoples, the owner of Kincora Hiking Hostel (see Places to Stay & Eat for Hampton), will shuttle hikers from his place at Dennis Cove Rd outside Hampton to Carvers Gap, and then pick them up at Hwy 19E for $25 total per van load. Or you can leave your car at Kincora, shuttle to Carvers Gap, and spend two to three days hiking the AT back to Kincora. The charge is $20 for this shuttle.

THE HIKE

Beginning at 5520ft at Carvers Gap, take the white-blazed trail on the east side of the road. It climbs steeply on a well-worn path, reinforced with railroad ties to prevent erosion. The trail will quickly become less-travelled as the car-hikers retreat back to the car park at Carvers Gap. After 15 minutes you'll come to the top of Round Bald (5820ft) followed by Jane Bald, reached about 45 minutes into the hike. There are stunning views all along this section. After this second bald, the trail will shortly hit an intersection where the AT veers off to the left to skirt **Grassy Ridge Bald**. If you want a great view from the only natural 6000ft plus viewpoint near the AT, go straight for about 0.3mi. From the top of Grassy Ridge, another trail leads off to the left and down to meet up with the AT again.

Continuing on the AT at the left-hand intersection before Grassy Ridge, enter the hardwood forest on the northwest flank of Grassy Ridge. This is a shady and moist section of the trail with fern and berry bushes

SOUTHERN APPALACHIA

SOUTHERN APPALACHIA

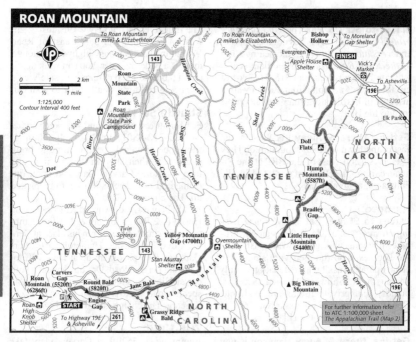

ROAN MOUNTAIN

To Roan Mountain (1 mile) & Elizabethton · To Roan Mountain (2 miles) & Elizabethton · Bishop Hollow · To Moreland Gap Shelter · Evergreen · Apple House Shelter · FINISH · Vick's Market · 143 · Hampton Creek · Shell Creek · To Asheville · 19E · Elk Park · Roan Mountain State Park · Roan Mountain State Park Campground · Doe River · Heaton Creek · Sugar Hollow Creek · Doll Flats · NORTH CAROLINA · TENNESSEE · Hump Mountain (5587ft) · Bradley Gap · Twin Springs · Yellow Mountain Gap (4700ft) · Overmountain Shelter · Little Hump Mountain (5440ft) · 143 · Stan Murray Shelter · Yellow Mountain · Big Yellow Mountain · Horse Creek · 19E · TENNESSEE · Carvers Gap · Round Bald (5820ft) · Jane Bald · Roan Mountain (5520ft) · Roan Mountain (6286ft) · Roan High Knob Shelter · START · Engine Gap · Grassy Ridge Bald · 261 · NORTH CAROLINA · To Highway 19E & Asheville · For further information refer to ATC 1:100,000 sheet The Appalachian Trail (Map 2)

0   1   2 km
0   ½   1 mile
1:125,000
Contour Interval 400 feet

below, and tall rhododendron and hardwood canopy above. With only a short break from the forest cover, the trail will mostly descend for the next 45 minutes until reaching Roan Highlands Shelter (renamed **Stan Murray Shelter**). There is a creek nearby for water, although it must be treated. You've come about 3mi from Carvers Gap.

The next 1.7mi are through forest of maple, buckeye and yellow birch. It's generally downhill, reaching the lowest elevation of the hike so far (4700ft) at Yellow Mountain Gap. There is an intersection here with Overmountain Victory Trail, the path of the Overmountain Men, a brigade of southerners who passed this way en route to the Revolutionary War battle of Kings Mountain. The **Overmountain Shelter** (highly recommended for overnighters) is 0.2mi to the right on this blue-blazed trail in an old red barn.

Continue straight on the AT, the next section of which is mostly uphill, in and out of the forest and along the edge of a bald which

is becoming overgrown. After 45 minutes there will be a big view of the climb to Little Hump Mountain. A further 20 minutes brings you near the top of Little Hump Bald, where a group of rocks marked with AT blazes invites the weary hiker to rest. Just beyond is the top of Little Hump (5440ft) and ahead can be seen the last big climb of the hike, to the top of Hump Mountain (5587ft). There's a descent of 500ft to Bradley Gap before the climb begins to Hump Mountain and about 40 minutes from the top of Little Hump, the **Hump Mountain summit** is reached.

The wind here can be fierce but the views are stunning. There are some rocks on the other side where one could enjoy a well-deserved rest, especially considering that most of the hiking from here is in the forest. A plaque here commemorates Stan Murray, an active advocate for the Southern Highlands Conservancy who managed to have this region permanently protected from any kind of development or mineral extraction.

Heading downhill from Hump Mountain the trail is still on the open, grassy bald when the AT veers left (a double track continues straight) and soon passes through a wooden gate. A few minutes later the trail enters the forest. It's a hardwood forest which in fall is spectacular. Many little creeks and rivulets cross the trail. If it has been raining at all recently, keep your eyes open for the hard-to-miss red salamanders which come out when it's wet. They are brilliantly hued and don't move very fast so it's easy to get a close look.

In less than an hour from Hump Mountain you'll come to a clearing on the hillside with a fence below. These are farmlands of the town of Elk Park. Very soon after this view you will enter a cleared area with trees overhead. The AT makes a sharp left in this clearing – watch for the AT blazes! The trail is densely forested from here to Apple House Shelter and descends, sometimes steeply, on stairs and switchbacks. It's very well maintained – sometimes brutally so, with errant roots chopped out of the hiker's way. Some of this is an AT re-route, a decision made by the local AT club, in this case the Tennessee Eastman Hiking Club in Kingsport.

At the 12.9mi mark, about two hours after Hump Mountain, *Apple House Shelter* is reached. It's only 10 minutes on flat trail to the intersection with Hwy 19E.

Three Ridges

Duration	3 days
Distance	22.3mi (35.9km)
Standard	medium-hard
Start	Crabtree Falls Trailhead
Finish	Tye River AT Bridge
Nearest Towns	Montebello, Waynesboro
Public Transport	no

Summary A forest hike past the longest falls east of the Mississippi, on the Appalachian Trail over Priest Mountain, then crossing the Tye River to climb Three Ridges, returning along a mountain stream.

The Three Ridges is one of the dreaded uphills of this portion of the AT, but you'll warm up on this hike of 6700ft ascent/ descent by climbing past Crabtree Falls (the longest waterfall east of the Mississippi) to the Priest. After climbing the Three Ridges, the return is on Mau-Har Trail which follows Campbell Creek with its 40ft waterfall and an enticing swimming hole.

This entire hike is within George Washington National Forest so camping is allowed anywhere, although there are some shelters for those who are travelling tent-free. Be sure to follow the rules of low-impact camping since this is a popular area. The forest is dominated by oak, blackberry bushes and the usual selection of hardwoods. Wildlife is abundant – red deer, hawks, snakes, flying squirrel, a selection of birds and the occasional bear can all be seen during this hike.

Use the USFS 1:62,500 sheet *Appalachian Trail (Map 5)*.

NEAREST TOWNS & FACILITIES
Montebello
Places to Stay & Eat The *Montebello Camping and Fishing Resort (☎ 540-377-2650)* is run by the Montebello store, which is surprisingly well-supplied with wheels of Wisconsin cheese and homemade jam, besides the usual small grocery store stock. The campground has showers and a coin-operated laundry with shady tent and RV sites and a few cabins. Prices are $12 for a tent, $17 to $19 for an RV, and cabins are $45 to $95 for four people. There is a post office and gas station at the store.

Crabtree Falls campground (☎ 540-377-2066) is about half a mile east of the Crabtree Falls trailhead with riverside sites for $17, showers, laundry and a small store. The owners can arrange shuttles. Free camping is allowed along the Tye River, but only near the AT crossing.

Getting There & Away Montebello is 2mi east of the BRP at Mile 27.2, along Hwy 56.

Waynesboro
Waynesboro is an all-American town whose downtown is struggling while malls fill the perimeter, with plenty of fast food and chain motels. What it lacks in charm it makes up for in helpfulness to hikers. Most

AT thru-hikers manage to make a stop here to re-supply and have a night in a hotel.

Places to Stay & Eat The only motel downtown is the *Comfort Inn (☎ 540-942-1171)* where doubles are a whopping $60. A bit further from downtown is the *Colony House Motel (☎ 540-942-4156)* with doubles ($43) and a pool. Free camping is available near the local *YMCA*, down Wayne Ave next to the river. Other campgrounds nearby are the *Shenandoah KOA (☎ 540-248-2746)* in Verona, and the *Waynesboro N 340 campground (☎ 540-943-3888)* both out of town.

There are several *fast food* choices at the west end of Main St, a few *Chinese restaurants* downtown, and the usual selection of *coffee shops* and *Mom and Pop cafes*. There's a hardware store for white gas, a shoe repairman, a laundromat, a big grocery store, and a hiking outfitter (in Rockfish Gap).

Getting There & Away Waynesboro is the largest town south of Shenandoah National Park just off I-64, 21mi west of Charlottesville and a few miles east of Rockfish Gap (Mile 0 of the BRP). The Greyhound bus will deliver you to the east end of Main St, from which point you must get a taxi or shuttle service to the trailhead.

GETTING AROUND
Operating from Vesuvius, Ed and Mary Anne Williams (☎ 540-377-6049) run a 'donations accepted' shuttle service and will consider picking up and dropping off as far as Waynesboro. Call them at least a day ahead of time and leave a message as they sometimes 'screen' their calls. Other shuttles may be arranged with the owners at Crabtree Falls campground. The taxi service in Waynesboro is Al's Radio Cabs (☎ 540-949-8245). For other shuttle services, contact or go to the very helpful chamber of commerce (☎ 540-949-7740) at 301 W Main St.

GETTING TO/FROM THE HIKE
To the Start
On Hwy 563, a half-mile east of Montebello store, is the Crabtree Falls Trailhead parking area with a phone and drinking water.

From the Finish
From Hwy 56, with the Tye River AT bridge just behind you, go west 1.1mi to the little (closed) store where there is a working pay phone. You can call one of the shuttle services from there (see Getting Around), or have your car delivered to the parking area at the Tye River bridge the morning of your return.

THE HIKE
Day 1: Crabtree Falls to Tye River Bridge
5–6 hours, 9.2mi (14.8km), 2500ft (750m) ascent, 3000ft (900m) descent
Though the 'experts' disagree on the exact height of Crabtree Falls, they are without a doubt one of the loveliest and loftiest east of the Mississippi. To begin the hike, start from the Crabtree Falls Trail parking lot and cross the impressively massive, laminated bridge. There is a hand pump just across the bridge that provides drinking water – when it is working. Best to come prepared. The trail winds gently through hemlocks and mossy logs to the first of several overlooks built of native stone and timber before climbing about 1000ft over the next mile and a half. Steep stone steps and switchbacks keep ascending through the forest, leaving and rejoining the falls at various points. Though it is tempting to wander out on the slippery rocks for a better look, heed the signs to stay on the trail. At 1.7mi the trail reaches the top of the upper falls. There is a sitting area on the far side of the creek that provides a welcome place to rest, as well as views of the valley below and Fork Mountain to the north. Recross the creek and turn left, following the now almost level trail through hemlocks and mountain laurel. After 0.3mi veer right onto an old road and continue 0.8mi to a parking area. There are outhouses here for the needy.

Turn left onto the dirt road (VA 826) and walk uphill for about half a mile. The AT intersects this road at the top of a grassy saddle. Turn left and follow the friendly white blazes of the AT. After another 600ft of climbing over 0.8mi there is a blue-blazed path to the right leading to the *Priest Trail Shelter* and spring. About 0.3mi later along the AT is a

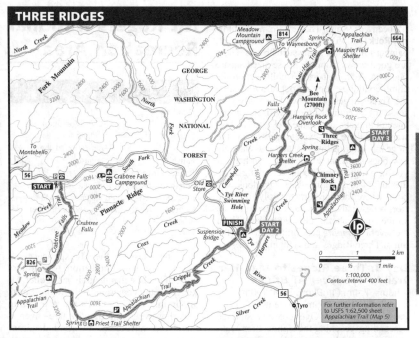

THREE RIDGES

short side trail to a rock outcrop, with views of the Three Ridges and a preview of the descent that lies ahead. In about a quarter-mile you will pass over the wooded summit of the Priest (4060ft) and begin the steep descent into the Tye River valley beneath the familiar canopy of mixed hardwood forest.

The next four or so miles are all downhill. After crossing Cripple Creek, the trail leaves the tight switchbacks behind and takes a more direct route to the valley floor, arriving at paved Hwy 56. You are 9.2mi from where you began and have climbed 2500ft and descended 3000ft. *Camping* is allowed all along this stretch of the AT since it is within George Washington National Forest. A store (now closed) with a still-working pay phone is 1.1mi to the left (west). An excellent Tye River swimming hole is just across the street from this store. To the right (east) 1.4mi is another *store* that sells Ben & Jerry's ice cream (very popular with AT thru-hikers) but has no phone.

Day 2: Tye River Bridge to the top of Three Ridges
5 hours, 5.7mi (9.2km), 3300ft (990m) ascent, 300ft (90m) descent

The AT continues over the Tye River on a recently rebuilt suspension bridge. The trail ascends via several switchbacks through a poplar grove, reaching a ridge line after a half-mile. Now the forest is dominated by oak and will remain so over the entire Three Ridges. From here there is sometimes a view of the three famous ridges to the right, but only if the leaves have fallen. The next section is a steep climb on an old road to a gap 1.8mi from the bridge. This is where the Mau-Har Trail goes off to the left. (You'll emerge here on your way back.)

Stay on the white-blazed AT, veering to the right, and descend just a bit over the next 20 minutes (0.8mi) to a signpost indicating that *Harpers Creek Shelter* is straight ahead (about 0.2mi), while the AT continues to the right. The shelter is a good one, with a clean privy and a trickling stream for water (unless it's been a dry year.) The next 2.2mi to **Chimney Rock** (3200ft) are the steepest of the hike, gaining 1500ft over many switchbacks. There are good views from the house-sized square boulders. After a short downhill section the climb continues, topping out at 3900ft atop the Three Ridges (no view). Hopefully your sense of accomplishment will be strong enough to make up for the lack of visual reward, and there are several *campsites* on the ridge top, offering lovely shade and relatively few bugs since there's no water up here. If you've got the energy, consider hiking a further 0.7mi to Hanging Rock Overlook at a point where the trail turns sharply right and steeply descends. You're facing due west here so the sunset should be spectacular. (There are several *camping* possibilities between the top of Three Ridges and Hanging Rock.)

Day 3: Three Ridges to Mau-Har Trail to Tye River AT Bridge
4 hours, 7.4mi (11.9km), 300ft (90m) ascent, 3350ft (1005m) descent

Pass Hanging Rock Overlook and continue descending, reaching the signpost for Mau-Har Trail and Maupin Fields Shelter 2.6mi and 1½ hours from Three Ridges high point. Turn left here for *Maupin Fields Shelter* after 0.3mi. Continue on the level blue-blazed Mau-Har Trail for a few minutes before a steep descent begins. About 1½mi (45 minutes) from the shelter is the 40ft waterfall of Campbell Creek, marked with a yellow blazed sign 'Waterfall'. This can be a popular spot for AT hikers, but mostly in the afternoon. There's a lovely little swimming hole at the top of the falls (and at the bottom, too, although it is more difficult to access). Be prudent climbing on these rocks since help is far off and the rocks are slippery. The trail is easy from here, going up and down over small streams as it makes its way to the junction with the AT. This narrow, stream-carved valley is a haven for wildlife, so keep your eyes open.

Three miles from Maupin Fields Shelter is the intersection with the AT, passed on Day 2. Turn right onto the AT and re-trace your steps down to the AT bridge over the Tye River.

Mt Rogers National Recreation Area

Mt Rogers

Duration	4 days
Distance	40.7mi (65.5km)
Standard	medium
Start	Fox Creek Trailhead
Finish	Damascus
Public Transport	no

Summary A delightful hike over the vast, rhododendron-covered hillsides of Mt Rogers Recreation Area, with craggy pinnacles and wild ponies.

For a little taste of the AT experience, Mt Rogers National Recreation Area offers some of the best that the trail has to offer. Mt Rogers is the centerpiece, the highest peak in Virginia at 5729ft. It's not a towering peak, however, but a friendly, tree-covered, round top surrounded by rhododendron-filled meadows, grassy balds 'maintained' by the local herd of wild ponies, and rocky ridges with stupendous views of the Blue Ridge Mountains. The last leg of the journey follows the crest of Straight Mountain before descending to the Virginia Creeper Trail, a former railroad bed, into the hiker haven of Damascus.

PLANNING
When to Hike
This is a beautiful trail at all times of the hiking season. For the rhododendron blooming season, hike this trail in the second half of June. Try to avoid the Wilburn Ridge section (Day 2) on weekends, as this is a very popular day-hike area.

What to Bring
There are no re-supply possibilities along this four-day stretch, so you must bring enough food for the entire hike. Water sources are plentiful but all water must be treated. Bring rain/wind gear – much of the

first two days is exposed to the weather. While it's not a particularly technical climb, there are a few steep descents so comfortable boots with good support are recommended.

Maps

The brown USFS *Mt Rogers High Country and Wilderness* map (1:24,000) is excellent, but only covers Days 1 & 2. Optionally, the ATC's *Mt Rogers National Recreation Area (Map 1)* at 1:64,500 covers the entire four days, but is on a smaller scale and a bit harder to read. Both are available in Damascus.

Permits & Regulations

There are no permits necessary to camp overnight in Mt Rogers National Recreation Area. However, there is no camping allowed in Grayson Highlands State Park (except in designated campgrounds or the Wise Shelter), along Wilburn Ridge, or within 1000ft of Mt Rogers.

NEAREST TOWN
Damascus

Tucked in the far southwest corner of Virginia, Damascus is named for the Syrian city because the city fathers of the 19th century assumed they were going to build a great steel industry here. (In ancient times, Damascus, Syria, was an important center of mining and iron production.) Fortunately, the surrounding hills only produced a low grade ore, so the vision was never fulfilled. But the little town survived on its timber industry and, more recently still, a new boom from tourists seeking recreation has put Damascus on the map. The Mt Rogers area attracts every kind of outdoor-pleasure seeker and the AT passes right through town. So does the Trans-Continental bike trail, as well as the 33mi Virginia Creeper trail, a popular day-trip for cyclists from near and far.

The town also hosts the Trail Days festival, which was begun in 1987 on the 50th anniversary of the creation of the AT and has continued every year since. Hundreds of hikers converge on the town for music, a parade, slide shows and talks from past AT thru-hikers. It's a grand reunion that takes place in May on the weekend after Mother's Day.

Two hiking outfitters are on the main street a few doors apart. Mount Rogers Outfitters (☎ 540-475-5416) is a top-notch backpacking store whose owner, Dave, was an AT thru-hiker in 1990. (He rents out backpacking gear.) Adventure Damascus (☎ 540-475-6362, ✉ AdvDam@naxs.com) is a mountain-bike outfitter, but has maps and helpful advice on surrounding trails. Ask for Tom, the resident mountain-bike tour guide.

Places to Stay & Eat The cheapest place to stay is the *free camping* downtown next to Laurel Creek. Because of Trail Days the town of Damascus is very accommodating to its hiking population and has even built a bathroom with shower next to the grassy camp. It isn't always sparkling clean, and there isn't any hot water, but what can you expect for free? Alternatively, for $2 you can spend the night in *The Place*, a dilapidated but welcoming old house behind the Methodist church where AT thru-hikers can be found recovering from their first several months on the trail. Kitchen, showers and hostel accommodations are available. Everyone who stays is asked to pitch in to clean some portion of the place before leaving.

There are no motels in Damascus, but the largely retired population has joined the tourism trade by opening up B&Bs by the drove. One of the most friendly, and purported to have the best breakfast in town, is the *Lazy Fox Inn (☎ 540-475-5833)* on Imboden St, just a few blocks east of the free camping area on Laurel Creek. Rooms are $45 to $55 for two. Other B&Bs in town are the *Maples (☎ 540-475-3943; $40 to $70)*, the *Apple Tree (☎ 540-475-3280; $45 to $55)* and, just west of downtown, the slightly fancier *Mountain Laurel Inn* ($69 to $89).

Grindstone campground is 3mi before the trailhead on Hwy 603; sites are $14 and there are shower facilities.

If you want to eat with the locals, go to *Dot's Inn* on the east side of town, while *Quincey's Pizza* is popular with ATers and locals alike. *Dairy King* has wonderful, soft ice-cream cones, and *Cowboy's Deli* is popular for carbo-loading breakfasts of the grits 'n' gravy variety. A newcomer to town, and

SOUTHERN APPALACHIA

MT ROGERS

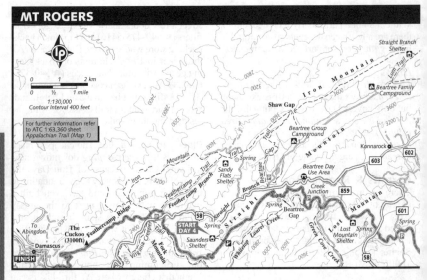

0   1   2 km
0   ½   1 mile
1:130,000
Contour Interval 400 feet
For further information refer
to ATC 1:63,360 sheet
Appalachian Trail (Map 1)

Straight Branch
Shelter

Beartree Family
Campground

Shaw Gap

Beartree Group
Campground

Konnarock

Sandy
Flats
Shelter

Beartree Day
Use Area

Creek
Junction

Spring

Beartree
Gap

START
DAY 4

Saunders
Shelter

Lost
Mountain
Shelter

To
Abingdon

The
Cuckoo
(3100ft)

Damascus

FINISH

an indication of the changing times, is *Javaleena's*, a coffee bar with excellent espresso drinks, bagels, pies, pastries, and free Internet access. There is one large grocery store in town, across the street from Javaleena's.

Getting There & Away Damascus is 12mi east on Hwy 58 from Abingdon – a large town with big food stores and a Greyhound bus station – 120mi south on I-81 from Roanoke. From Tennessee, Damascus is just a few miles north of the Tennessee border on Hwy 91, which is reached by taking Hwy 421 north into the northeastern corner of Tennessee from Boone, North Carolina.

GETTING AROUND
Dave at Mount Rogers Outfitters in Damascus provides shuttles to Fox Creek Trailhead ($30). Adventure Damascus also provides shuttles ($22 for two people).

GETTING TO/FROM THE HIKE
To reach the Fox Creek Trailhead, take Hwy 58 east out of Damascus. After 8mi or so, where Hwy 58 turns abruptly south, continue straight on Hwy 603. Stay on Hwy

603 for the next 13mi to Fox Creek Trailhead, on the right (south) side of the road. There is a horse camp across the street.

THE HIKE
Day 1: Fox Creek Trailhead to Wise Shelter
5 hours, 7.7mi (12.4km), 1800ft (540m) ascent, 900ft (270m) descent
This is a fine day of hiking on the AT, with just enough trees, distant vistas, open meadows, gurgling streams and a mixture of climbing and cruising to please just about anyone. From Fox Creek Trailhead (3460ft), follow the white blazes of the AT to enter a hardwood forest with a familiar mix of rhododendrons, birch, maple and oak. Winding gracefully, the trail slowly gains in elevation, passing through airy stands of maple before crossing the Old Orchard Horse Trail. (Throughout this hike you will be entering and leaving various recreation areas, wilderness areas, a state park and private property. Not all transitions will be noted. If in doubt follow the never-failing white blazes.) After 45 minutes of gentle hiking, you arrive at the *Old Orchard Shelter* in a fine setting overlooking a verdant meadow with good *tent*

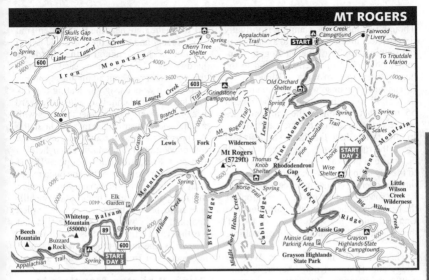

MT ROGERS

sites and a spring. It is fun to check out the register book to get insider tips on the local hiking, shelters and local cuisine.

Continue on the AT up towards Pine Mountain. The trail maintains the same grade but gets considerably rockier in spots, with ferns, moss and downed trees adding a fairyland feel to the forest. Forty minutes later you intersect the Pine Mountain trail at an elevation of 5000ft. Continue straight on the AT. This is the high point of this portion of the hike. Fine views are just ahead. When you reach the Scales corral and parking area, go around the corral to the right, through a gate, and continue around left to the east side of the corral where you'll begin to see more white blazes. Climb the bald **Stone Mountain**, enjoying the exceptionally open views which in fall are ablaze with yellows, reds and golds of the changing foliage on the surrounding hills and valleys.

Thirty minutes from the Scales is Little Wilson Creek Wilderness. Ten minutes later watch for a small spring flowing from the rocky roots of a tree by the side of the trail. The trail continues descending, passing through small meadows of mountain laurel before meeting the Scales Trail. Turn

downhill and 50ft later turn right to continue on the AT. Minutes later, cross Wilson Creek. This is not only a good source of treatable drinking water, but a chance to take a quick dip as well. This is within a quarter-mile of the very popular *Wise Shelter*. Begin checking out possible *camping spots* in case the shelter is overcrowded. Many good spots exist near the two creeks before you enter the Grayson Highlands State Park. There is no camping allowed near the shelter. This newer shelter, still missing from many maps, is about 8mi from the trailhead and is finely made from well-joined timbers in a typical three-sided style.

Day 2: Wise Shelter to near Whitetop Mountain

5–6 hours, 11.7mi (18.8km), 1850ft (555m) ascent, 1100ft (330m) descent
Continue on the AT up the Quebec Branch of Wilson Creek. The trail continues to climb at a constant but gentle rate over various rhododendron-studded balds with views in all directions. After 30 minutes the trail arrives at **Massie Gap** (the parking area is visible down to the left). Shortly thereafter, the AT leaves Grayson Highlands State

Park and re-enters the national forest. Though this means the camping is virtually unrestricted, hikers are asked to avoid camping within a 1000ft of the Mt Rogers Summit, within 250ft of Deep Gap, and in the heavily used areas of Wilburn Ridge.

The next mile or so will take you up more than 500ft to the high point of the hike at 5526ft. This section of the trail provides ample views to reward the increased effort. In mid- to late June the rhododendrons that cover the rock outcrops along the way will be a blaze of pinks and purples. After skirting to the east of one rocky knob the trail passes directly over a second, an excellent spot to have a snack and take in the view. Drop off the back side of the rocks into **Rhododendron Gap** and follow the white blazes of the AT through the jumbled intersection of multiple trails.

This stretch of the AT, between Wilburn Ridge and Thomas Knob Shelter, is quite gentle and wooded with many good *campsites* (although they are somewhat trodden). The views, however, are very peaceful and the early morning sun is a treat. From Rhododendron Gap it takes about 30 minutes to reach *Thomas Knob Shelter*. Keep an eye open for some of the wild horses that call these highlands home. The shelter is protected from the elements by a large outcrop of rock to the south. It has a spring (protected from horses) down the hill on the far side of the outcrop. There is a permanent toilet between the shelter and the tent *camping area*, indicating the great popularity of this spot.

Just past the shelter is the Mt Rogers spur trail. This is about a mile roundtrip and climbs 330ft. Other than the added elevation, the partial views from the top cannot compare to the past couple of miles. Continue along the AT through sweet-smelling Fraser firs and the rocky downhill section to Deep Gap. Make sure you take a sharp right-hand turn uphill when you reach the wooden stile at the beckoning green meadow. After a relaxing cruise along Elk Garden Ridge, the AT leaves Lewis Fork Wilderness and drops to the Elk Garden parking area along paved road VA 600.

From Elk Garden parking area, find the AT off to the right near the Elk Garden Trail (for horses) and enter the forest. This is a section of lush undergrowth and dense hardwoods. The trail climbs easily through this cool canopy. About 50 minutes from Elk Garden is a wooden sign indicating that Elk Garden is 2½mi behind you. Just afterward is a good *camping spot* under the trees with a water source nearby. Ten minutes later, the AT crosses the gravel road that goes to the top of **Whitetop Mountain**. From here to Buzzard Rock the trail is open. If the weather permits, *camp* out in the open rather than in the forest – however, you'll notice that many of the stunted trees out on the hillside have broken branches or are gnarled and bent by the wind, an obvious sign that weather can be fierce on this open hillside. Don't miss the sunset though, which should be spectacular from this west-facing slope.

Day 3: Whitetop Mountain to Saunders Shelter
6 hours, 12mi (19.3km), 800ft (240m) ascent, 3300ft (990m) descent
From the Whitetop road crossing, it's about 25 minutes of easy hiking through blueberry, azalea and old fruit trees to the top of **Buzzard Rock** (5100ft). Plan to spend some time here since this is the last high point of the hike, and the view is exceptional. To the north is visible the ridge of the Iron Mountains and to the south are the endless Blue Ridge Mountains. From Buzzard Rock, a steep descent begins which will quickly enter the forest where it stays for most of the day. A further 40 minutes from Buzzard Rock is a good *campsite* behind a large boulder with a trickling creek not far away. Before this point the trail has been descending steeply with no real camping options.

One hour from Buzzard Rock (the descent has slackened considerably) you'll cross USFS Rd No 601 where there's a small brick house and a parking area for hikers. This is at 3600ft, and the maple, oak and tulip-tree forests you are walking through reflect the change from the flora above 5000ft. A further 30 minutes from the USFS road, is the intersection with Hwy 58, the main road back to Damascus. Across the road the AT plunges into a tall forest and the first rhododendron bushes of the day appear, sometimes in thick tunnels. These are the July-flowering white rhododendron.

Twenty minutes from Hwy 58 is *Lost Mountain Shelter*. This is a newer shelter with a pit toilet and a sometimes sluggish water source about 400ft along a separate trail. A sign tells you that Saunders Shelter is a further 6mi. Another 20 minutes from Lost Mountain Shelter cross USFS Rd No 859. The creek you've been following becomes steadily larger, beckoning the sticky hiker to come for a dip. However, access is quite difficult through tangled underbrush. Fifteen minutes from USFS Rd No 859 there is an abrupt left turn uphill to the Virginia Creeper Trail, although stream access is easier if you go straight a little ways. Once at the Virginia Creeper Trail, turn right to cross the bridge.

The Virginia Creeper is the name of the lumber transporting train that used to travel this route until 1977 when the last steam engine slowly chugged its way up this path. The Rails-to-Trails people (a national organization that converts old railroad beds into hiking trails) got wind of it, and the tracks were removed to become a very popular bike and hike trail. The AT follows the Virginia Creeper for only 20 minutes before the AT blazes appear on your right. (An option here is to follow the Virginia Creeper Trail into Damascus, a slightly downhill grade for 9mi. *Camping* is allowed along the trail, except in the sections that are on private property.)

The AT begins to climb away from the Virginia Creeper, soon crossing Whitetop Laurel Creek. About 2mi from that first creek crossing, steadily gaining altitude, the trail arrives at the Beartree Gap Trail intersection, a magenta-blazed trail heading north 0.3mi to intersect Hwy 58, and then 0.2mi to the Beartree Day Use Area parking with a big swimming lake nearby. From the Beartree Gap Trail intersection, the AT follows the crest of Straight Mountain until reaching the right-hand turnoff for *Saunders Shelter*, a short distance from the trail at a place with a great view.

Day 4: Saunders Shelter to Damascus

5–6 hours, 9.4mi (15.1km), 1000ft (300m) ascent, 2200ft (660m) descent

From Saunders Shelter, go back to the AT and turn right. A series of steep, downhill switchbacks and scrambles lie ahead. The trail eventually will run parallel to the Virginia Creeper Trail and then after 4mi, crosses Hwy 58 to pass through the Feathercamp parking area. From here the trail gently climbs the southern ridge of Iron Mountain to **The Cuckoo** (3100ft) and then descends more steeply (1000ft over 2mi) back to Hwy 58. Once at the highway, the AT crosses the road and continues east into Damascus. The Virginia Creeper Trail is on this side of the road too, so you can choose to follow this into town (arriving at the caboose park) or take the AT, which follows the sometimes busy Hwy 58 into town. The Creeper passes by the city pool, open in the hot months of summer.

Allegheny Mountains

The Monongahela National Forest lies squarely within the Allegheny Mountains, part of the myriad of mountain chains located in West Virginia, known as the 'mountain state'. It could also be called the 'tree state' as it is 70 percent forest covered, although only 10 percent of that forest is government owned. Citizen's groups have lobbied to protect these great forests from timber and coal industries, and they have had varying degrees of success. In 1984, the USFS proposed a 50-year plan to increase the amount of timber, coal and road-building in national forests by 70%. When the Monongahela National Forest attempted to implement this plan, locals rallied and managed to have the plan rejected, claiming that the forest should retain its natural character and remoteness. A new, more restrictive, plan was adopted in 1986, with the result that the Monongahela is still a wild place with many possibilities for the adventurous hiker. There aren't many organized camp-grounds, and most access roads are unpaved. However, camping is allowed anywhere in the national forest, with only a few restricted areas.

Spruce Knob Loop

Duration	2 days
Distance	14.2mi (22.9km)
Standard	medium-hard
Start/Finish	Spruce Knob
Nearest Town	Seneca Rocks
Public Transport	no

Summary Starting at West Virginia's highest point, this hike has long views of the Alleghenys, spruce forest, waterfalls and swimming holes.

There is nowhere to go but down on this two-day hike starting at the top of West Virginia's highest peak, Spruce Knob (4861ft), in the heart of the Monongahela National Forest. If clear skies are in your favor, a quick warm up hike around the interpretive Whispering Spruce Trail to the observation tower is highly recommended.

The entire 13½mi Spruce Knob Loop hike can be done in a day or can be short-ened 2mi by staying on the Huckleberry Trail all the way down to Seneca Creek.

PLANNING
When to Hike
The Monongahela enjoys the same climate as the rest of Appalachia, with rhododen-dron and mountain laurel blooms in the early summer, blueberries in late summer and beautiful colors in the autumn.

What to Bring
This is a rocky trail up on the plateau so good boots are helpful. Water is available near the recommended campsite, although it must be treated or filtered. Good rain gear is essential.

Maps & Books
There is no 'one' map available for this trail. You need three USGS 1:24,000 maps to cover the entire route (*Spruce Knob*, *Whit-mer* and *Onego*) or you can use the free but

not very detailed photocopied map given out by the forest service. The Monongahela Na-tional Forest map sounds good but is not a topo and doesn't show any trails.

The guidebook *West Virginia Hiking Trails* by Allen de Hart ($17) is very complete with trail maps, although it's a bit hard to piece the trails together. A more specific book is the *Monongahela National Forest Hiking Guide* by Sunquist & de Hart, published by the West Virginia Highland Conservancy.

All of these choices are available at the Seneca Rocks Discovery Center.

NEAREST TOWN
Seneca Rocks
This town is named for the impressive rock wall on the far side of the river. Climbers from near and far come to this place to ex-perience some of the best climbing routes on the east coast. The Seneca Rocks Discovery Center is the only visitor center in the north-ern section of the Monongahela and looks out at Seneca Rocks. Besides helpful rangers, clean bathrooms, a limited selection of maps and books and a worthwhile video, the center is a bit disappointing compared to its grand (and brand new) building. For those interested in climbing, the Seneca Rocks Climbing School (☎ 304-567-2600, 800-548-0108) is behind Harper's General Store.

Places to Stay & Eat *Yokum's Motel* (☎ *304-567-2351, 800-772-8342*) has a pool, restaurant, store, laundry, campground ($5 per person for tent sites), motel rooms ($40 for two) and log cabins ($75 to $95 for four). Another motel near the turn-off for Spruce Knob is the *4-U Motel* (☎ *304-567-2111*) with rooms for $40 to $55. A beauti-ful new national forest campground called *Seneca Shadows* (☎ *304-567-2415*) has hot showers and shady sites for $11 to $13. Try *Harper's General Store and Front Porch Restaurant* for a meal; it seems to be the preferred spot of the climbing crowd.

Camping 3mi from the trailhead can be found at *Spruce Knob Lake campground*. There are no showers or hot water, and the large lake is only for fishing (no swimming). See Getting To/From the Hike for directions.

Getting There & Away From Harrisonburg, travel 45mi west on Hwy 33 to Franklin, continue 14mi west on Hwy 33 to Judy Gap, then turn right (north) onto Hwy 28 for 11mi to Seneca Rocks. From Front Royal (at the north end of Shenandoah National Park) travel west on I-66 for 7mi, take I-81 south for 4mi, then take Hwy 55 west toward Petersburg. You'll be on Hwy 55 for 43mi to Petersburg, and then it's 21 more miles to Seneca Rocks. Both of these state highways are curvy mountain roads, so don't plan on making the drive in a hurry.

GETTING TO/FROM THE HIKE

Follow Hwy 28 south 20mi from Seneca Rocks (2.8mi south of Cherry Grove) to Sawmill Run Rd. Go right onto this small, unmarked road which soon turns to dirt. After 8.6 uphill miles, take the right fork to Spruce Knob. In another mile is another intersection; go straight to Spruce Knob where there's a big parking lot, picnic tables and an observation tower. (To the left at the last intersection is Spruce Knob Lake campground.)

THE HIKE
Day 1: Spruce Knob to Judy Springs
5½ hours, 9½mi (15.3km), 1760ft (528m) descent

From the Spruce Knob parking area find the Huckleberry Trail on the northern edge and enter the tight, dark world of dense spruce forest. The almost imperceptibly falling path is easy to follow but a bit difficult to navigate due to scattered rocks mixed with tufts of grass. After a half hour there are fine vistas to the west from a heath meadow, and in another half-mile there are the remains of a small-plane crash on the left of the trail. Continue left at the 'Huckleberry Trail No 533' sign and the 'Seneca Creek 2.9' sign.

Fifteen minutes later, after entering a stand of maple, turn right onto the Lumberjack Trail as it intersects the Huckleberry Trail. (If it is a particularly wet time of year, you may consider forgoing this section and stay on the Huckleberry Trail to reach Seneca Creek after about a mile, shortening

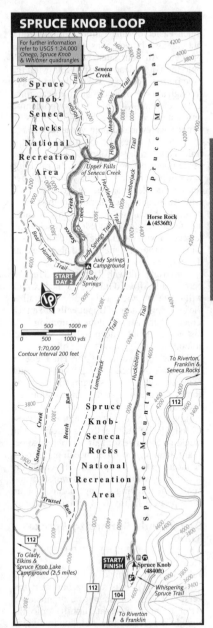

SOUTHERN APPALACHIA

the route by 2mi.) The walking becomes much easier on this former railroad grade but can be a bit soggy as it crosses a series of seeps. An hour later, veer left downhill onto the High Meadows Trail following the blue blazes. For the next 2mi the trail drops through a series of woods and the occasional grassy clearing with thistle, daisy, goldenrod and asters, providing fantastic views of **Seneca Valley** and distant verdant ridges to the west. At times the exact course of the trail is a bit tricky to follow as it crosses old fence lines and intersects with the rambling paths of grazing cows. Keep your eyes open for the blue blazes on trees or meadow posts, while maintaining a generally southwesterly descent. When you come to an old cattle salt-feeder, continue to the left to reach an intersection with the Huckleberry Trail (this is where the short-cut mentioned above rejoins the main route).

Turn right (downhill) onto the Huckleberry Trail. After 20 minutes, Seneca Creek will come into view and parallel the trail to the crashing waters of **Upper Falls** of **Seneca Creek**. There is a fabulous swimming hole just below the falls, deep and cool with fine, smooth rocks on which to dry off.

At the intersection of the Huckleberry and Seneca Creek Trails, turn left onto Seneca Creek Trail, upstream, and rock-hop across the creek. Use extreme caution, especially at high water. You can either begin looking for a place to *camp* at the many established sites along this section of the creek, or continue for half an hour or so beneath a canopy of birch, beech and rhododendron up to **Judy Springs**. The canyon is wider here with many good *campsites* and boasts the flowing spring, named for an early pioneer family who settled the area.

Day 2: Judy Springs to Spruce Knob

4 hours, 4.7mi (7.6km), 1760ft (528m) ascent

Take the Judy Springs Trail on the east side of the creek. This is a steep but short traverse through an open grassy meadow. After 0.7mi turn right (uphill) onto the Huckleberry Trail. In a few hundred yards

the trail crosses the Lumberjack Trail. Stay on the Huckleberry Trail as it winds its way back to the Spruce Knob parking area, 4mi away, over familiar ground. You'll be happy to reach smooth pavement after navigating the uneven rocks of the final 3mi.

Blackbird Knob Loop

Duration	5–6 hours
Distance	9mi (14.5km)
Standard	easy-medium
Start/Finish	Red Creek campground
Nearest Towns	Petersburg, Seneca Rocks
Public Transport	no

Summary Splendid Allegheny Mountains hiking, solitude, and a well-timed swim in a large pool at the bottom of Red Creek cascade. Wildflowers, mountain laurel, red deer, hawks and other wildlife are abundant.

Dolly Sods Wilderness is one of four wilderness areas within Monongahela National Recreation Area, and is a unique part of the Allegheny plateau. Ranging in elevation from 2600ft to over 4000ft, this windswept and rocky plateau resembles parts of Northern Canada in its plant life and climate. Forests of red spruce, yellow birch, heath-covered meadows of blueberry, mountain laurel, azalea, rhododendron, and cranberry bogs are dispersed over the upper elevations, while classic Appalachian hardwood forests cover the lower reaches. This hike stays on the highest part of the plateau, dipping only briefly to enjoy a swim in Red Creek, in order to experience the most beautiful section of the Sods. Rambling through the open meadows of knee-high blueberry, with azalea and mountain laurel adding color (in early summer), and long stretches with views in all directions, this hike is very different from the usual Appalachian hike.

HISTORY

The wonderfully open, heath-covered slopes of the Dolly Sods weren't exactly created through acts of nature. In the early 19th century, this plateau was covered in a thick red spruce forest with trees of up to

Top Left: Sunset over the Cataloochee Valley, Great Smoky Mountains National Park, Tennessee.
Top Right: Southern Appalachia is dotted with reminders of past industry, such as this water mill.
Middle Left: A Smoky Mountains church and graveyard, testament to the struggles of the pioneers.
Bottom: The Cades Cove Valley, Tennessee, is surrounded by the Great Smoky Mountains.

JOHN ELK III

PETER PTSCHELINZEW

JOHN ELK III

JOHN ELK III

Highlights of Yellowstone National Park, Wyoming. Clockwise from Top: The garish Grand Prismatic Springs of Midway Basin; a hiker contemplates the country around Mt Washburn; the Yellowstone River meanders peacefully through the Hayden Valley; the Grand Canyon of the Yellowstone River is 1300ft deep in places.

12ft in diameter. A logging operation soon cleared the land completely, leaving a thick layer of rich humus made from centuries of dropped spruce needles. This peaty layer quickly dried without its protective shade and then became tinder for the first spark. Perhaps it was lightning or an errant logger's campfire that started the blaze, but when it was over there was nothing left but rock. The humus layer had burnt away and the only thing that could grow was the scrubby heath that is still here today. For many years it was grazed by herds belonging to the Dahle family, German immigrants whose name was Americanized to 'Dolly'. 'Sods' refers to the name for grassy grazing lands. In the 1930s the Civilian Conservation Corps (CCC) planted some trees and attempted to restore some of the original vegetation, but their efforts could not bring back the lost layer of rich nutrients that used to feed the large trees. Still, much of the forest has recovered over time and it presents an interesting study in how a heavily logged region can recover.

PLANNING
When to Hike
This particular wilderness area is quite popular, although on a beautiful Sunday in June you can meet only a few other hikers the entire day. If possible, however, try to avoid weekends, especially if planning on camping at Red Creek campground which has only 12 sites. Most people who plan to spend the night do a backpacking trip and stay in the wilderness somewhere.

What to Bring
Since this hike is over an often rocky surface with some bogs, there is a good possibility that the trails will be muddy with slick rocks. A good pair of waterproof boots with ankle support are recommended. Weather is changeable; this is the west side of the Allegheny Front, the eastern divide (water falling on this side of the mountains flows west, eventually to the Gulf of Mexico). The western side receives substantially more rain than the east, so be prepared for a change in the weather even if the day starts out clear.

Maps
Use two USGS 1:24,000 maps, available at the Seneca Rocks Discovery Center, on this trail: *Blackwater Falls* and *Blackbird Knob*.

NEAREST TOWN
Petersburg
Just 9mi north from the southern end of Jordan Run Rd on Hwy 55, Petersburg is a bigger town than Seneca Rocks (11mi south on Hwy 55; see Spruce Knob Loop hike) with a large supermarket and many motels and other conveniences.

Places to Stay & Eat Try *Fort Hill Motel* (☎ 304-257-4717), where rooms start at $38, with a pool. Several 'Ma and Pa' restaurants are in town, and the steaks at *Poor Joe's* are recommended. *Smoke Hole Caverns* (☎ 304-257-4442 or 800-828-8478) is just half a mile north on Hwy 55 from Jordan Run Rd, where a *motel* offers rooms for $45 to $55, or $100 for a log cabin with kitchen. There is a small *restaurant* too.

Getting There & Away See Getting There & Away for Seneca Rocks in the Spruce Knob hike.

GETTING TO/FROM THE HIKE
To the Start
From Seneca Rocks, head north on Hwy 28/55 toward Smoke Hole Caverns and Petersburg. After 12mi, turn left onto Jordan Run Rd (just before Smoke Hole Caverns) where there's a big, brown sign for Dolly Sods. After 1mi, veer left onto USFS Rd No 19, and continue a further 6mi (on dirt). At the junction with USFS Rd No 75, turn right toward Red Creek campground, reached after 4.9mi.

If coming from Petersburg, travel 9mi on Hwy 28/55 south to Smoke Hole Caverns, then turn right on Jordan Run Rd. Follow above instructions from there.

From the Finish
After the hike, keep going on USFS Rd No 75 toward Bear Rocks, which is a further 2.6mi up the dirt road. You can park here and take the little path up to the rocks which offer

SOUTHERN APPALACHIA

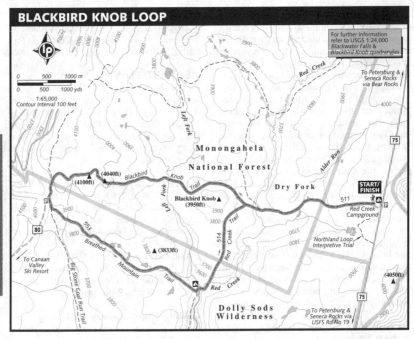

BLACKBIRD KNOB LOOP

For further information refer to USGS 1:24,000 Blackwater Falls & Blackbird Knob quadrangles

0   500   1000 m
0   500   1000 yds
1:65,000
Contour Interval 100 feet

Monongahela

National Forest

To Petersburg & Seneca Rocks via Bear Rocks

Red Creek

Blackbird Knob Trail

(4040ft) Blackbird Knob
(4100ft)

Blackbird Knob ▲
(3950ft)

Dry Fork

Alder Run

START/FINISH
511
Red Creek Campground

Northland Loop Interpretive Trail

Breathed Mountain Trail

▲ (3833ft)

Red Creek Trail

Red Creek

Dolly Sods Wilderness

To Canaan Valley Ski Resort

Big Stone Coal Run Trail

(4050ft) ▲

To Petersburg & Seneca Rocks via USFS Rd No 19

a wonderful view of the valley below and the mountains all around. Continue downhill from here on USFS Rd No 75 (you don't need to go back the way you came). About 4mi along this road you'll hit pavement and 0.7mi later a T-intersection with Jordan Run Rd. Turn right, and travel to the intersection with Hwy 28/55 near Smoke Hole Caverns (which are a half-mile to your left). Turn right onto Hwy 28/55 to reach Seneca Rocks (11mi), or left toward Petersburg (9mi).

THE HIKE

From Red Creek campground parking area, at about 4000ft elevation, follow the trail that begins just east of the campground, on a stretch of boardwalk. It's clear that this area is sometimes completely water-logged. Pass through a couple of groves of white pine and red spruce before reaching the first heath meadow, 10 minutes from the trailhead. The trail is marked with cairns here and there, but is in generally good shape and

the route is clear. After 30 minutes, mostly descending, cross the small stream of Alder Run, a tributary to Red Creek. The heath stretches are full of blueberry, so if you're here in mid- to late summer there should be plenty of them for eating along the trail. Twenty minutes from the Alder Run is a crossing of an upper branch of Red Creek. This is a nice spot for a rest, especially in June when the banks of the river are lined with mountain laurel in bloom. Ten minutes beyond the creek crossing is a signpost for Blackbird Knob Trail. Continue straight on Blackbird Knob Trail. To the left is Red Creek Trail (there's no sign) which is the trail you'll be returning on later in the hike.

This is the prettiest stretch of the hike, and is actually outside the wilderness boundary of Dolly Sods. Perhaps that's why it's not as traveled, since this section of the trail is not on the USFS map. Open balds of blueberry, azalea and mountain laurel go for long stretches amid stands of beech and other hardwoods, with good views of the surrounding Allegheny plateau and peaks. The trail skirts **Blackbird Knob** itself (off to your left) and 15 minutes from the signpost it crosses the left branch of Red Creek where there is a decent *campsite*. The trail continues on the other side uphill.

Ten minutes from the creek campsite, after climbing steeply through a hardwood forest, is a tricky left turn in the middle of an open bald covered in mountain laurels, although it is marked with a cairn. The path is quite overgrown with grass here, but is still discernible. After passing over the top of another bald, the trail doubles in width and climbs to yet another grassy bald with excellent views of the surrounding mountains. At 4120ft this is the highest point of the hike. The trail curves to the left off the top of this bald and in 15 minutes arrives at the intersection with Breathed Mountain and Big Stone Coal Run Trails. Take a hard left to begin Breathed Mountain Trail. Now you are back in the official wilderness area. This 2mi stretch alternates between fir forest, marshy bog and open heath. Rhododendrons appear for the first time on this hike. The trail is fairly straightforward, except for one place where a path goes off to the left toward a large marshy area. Be sure to stay right here – many cairns make the choice obvious.

One hour from the beginning of Breathed Mountain Trail you'll begin to descend quite steeply to the Red Creek Trail, reached in about 10 minutes. Turn left onto the trail, with the rather large creek down below. A great swimming hole is just below this point, and a good access trail is only another 200yd or so. It's marked by a 4ft stump and descends abruptly to the creek. Once beside the creek, go downstream until you come to the base of the long, gradual cascade. There is a large pool that is deep enough for a refreshing swim. There are a couple of *campsites* along the creek. (Please use existing sites and fire rings. Burn only downed or dead wood.)

Continuing upstream on Red Creek Trail, cross the creek (after passing some more good *campsites*) and begin to climb out of the Red Creek gorge. Stay left of the campsite and on the opposite side of the creek,

following cairns uphill. In 15 minutes you'll come to the top of the steep part (gaining about 300ft), arriving at a grassy meadow with a metal post declaring this the boundary of the wilderness area. There are lovely views from this open meadow; to the right are the hills you're heading back toward. The intersection with Blackbird Knob Trail is 25 minutes from Red Creek crossing. Turn right and retrace the path you took earlier in the hike for the next 2.2mi to return to Red Creek campground.

Shenandoah National Park

This stretch of the Blue Ridge Mountains was nominated to become a park in 1926. It took ten years for the people who had lived here to relocate, and in 1936 President Roosevelt dedicated the park, naming it Shenandoah. It was considered a novel experiment to take an over-logged and grazed area and allow it to return to its natural state. In 1939, the 105mi Skyline Dr was completed, running down the spine of the Blue Ridge and then continuing as the Blue Ridge Parkway all the way to the Smoky Mountains. Skyline Dr allows great access to most of the trails in Shenandoah, although some trails must be accessed from outside the park. There are commercial ventures along Skyline Dr, but the park feels somehow old-fashioned, with most buildings dating from the 1930s when the CCC provided the labor to build the many rest stops, visitor centers, campgrounds, and two grand lodges. Meanwhile, the 'experiment' worked, and the former croplands and pasture once again have become wild forest, complete with a healthy population of black bears, deer, bobcats, turkeys and 200 species of birds.

INFORMATION
Maps
The Potomac Appalachian Trail Club (PATC) produces three excellent maps at 1:62,500 that cover the entire park, since the

AT parallels Skyline Dr for its entire length. These are available for $5 each at all visitor centers or from the PATC (☎ 703-242-0693). Trails Illustrated publishes one map for the entire park ($10) but the scale is 1:100,000.

Information Sources

Dickey Ridge visitor center (Mile 4.6 on Skyline Dr) is the northern-most source for information in the park including maps and books and the opportunity to obtain back-country permits. Byrd visitor center (Mile 51) and Loft Mountain information center (Mile 79) provide the same services.

Permits

You must have a permit (free) to camp in the backcountry. These can be obtained at all entrance stations, visitor centers, or at park headquarters on Hwy 211, between Thornton Gap and Luray. In 1999 it was possible to camp almost anywhere within the park; however, regulations were in the process of being changed so check with park officials.

NEAREST TOWNS
In the Park

There are four campgrounds in the park: *Mathews Arm* (Mile 22.2), *Big Meadows* (Mile 51.3), *Lewis Mountain* (Mile 57½) and *Loft Mountain* (Mile 79½). These are primitive campgrounds, without showers, electricity or water hookups, although there are bathrooms with cold water. There are coin-operated showers and laundry facilities near Big Meadows, Lewis Mountain and Loft Mountain. Campgrounds charge $11 to $14 and can be reserved by way of the NPS reservation service (see Accommodations in the Facts for the Hiker chapter). Campgrounds are open from spring to the end of October.

There are two lodges within the park: *Skyland Lodge* (Mile 41) and *Big Meadows Lodge* (Mile 51.2). Both are rustic lodges with cabins and hotel rooms, *restaurants*, shops etc. Prices start at $50 to $65 for two. *Lewis Mountain* has cabins with beds, baths, lights and heat. For reservations, call ☎ 800-999-4714 or 540-743-5108 or visit the website at 🖳 www.visitshenandoah.com. There are six backcountry rustic *cabins* available

for rent from the PATC – the keys are sent to you upon reservation.

Luray

Luray is a large town with an excellent supermarket and many lodging options. *Hillside Motel* on the east side of town has rooms for $45, and a pool. The *Brookside Restaurant* is recommended for classic American fare.

Sperryville

Sperryville is a lovely little town, but it is quite limited on accommodations. In order to get on the trail early, the only reasonable choice is to *camp* in the woods with your car parked in the upper lot so you can leave your camping gear behind when you take the hike. Otherwise, there are expensive *B&Bs* in Sperryville, or the various lodging options in the park itself (see Nearest Town & Facilities early in this section), which is only about 18mi from the trailhead.

Food can be purchased at the Mountain Market in Sperryville, a big natural-food store with a wonderful deli, bulk foods, organic fruits and veggies. There's a good restaurant next door too, the *Blue Moon* with live music on weekends, closed on Tuesday and Wednesday. A good deli/cafe called *Appetite Adjustment* is on the main street in downtown Sperryville (open for breakfast and lunch only).

Cedar Run–Whiteoak Canyon Loop

Duration	5–6 hours
Distance	10.4mi (16.7km)
Standard	medium
Start/Finish	Hawksbill Gap parking area
Nearest Town	Luray
Public Transport	no
Summary	A forest hike past two cascading streams with many pools and waterfalls.

Cedar Run is a creek that flows down the side of Haywood Mountain and this hike follows it for 2000ft of that elevation loss.

The trail passes many pools and cascades, populated by colorful salamanders which love the moist atmosphere of this tumbling stream. Near the bottom of the gorge, the trail heads to Whiteoak Canyon where Whiteoak Run falls several thousand feet. This route goes upstream so you'll encounter the six named waterfalls from the bottom up. Many pools beckon, and several of the falls are more than 50ft high. It's a narrow, cool gorge with rock faces oozing moss and water from Blue Ridge springs, so even in dry years it's wet and the waterfalls are flowing. After the final waterfall, the trail loops up through old-growth hemlock groves, and finally returns to Hawksbill Gap on the AT.

PLANNING
When to Hike
This is one of the most popular hikes within the park, so plan on leaving early in the day and avoiding the weekends.
What to Bring
Even though you are near a stream for most of the hike, bring at least two quarts of water to drink.

Maps
The best map for this hike is the PATC *Appalachian Trail (Map 10)* sold for $5 at all visitor centers.

GETTING TO/FROM THE HIKE
The hike begins and ends at Hawksbill Gap, on Skyline Dr north of Big Meadows between Mile 45 and Mile 46.

THE HIKE
From the parking area at Hawksbill Gap, cross Skyline Dr to the east side where the Cedar Run Trailhead is indicated. Descend into the forest on a blue-blazed trail. In a few hundred yards, another, yellow-blazed, horse trail enters from the right and then goes off to the left a short while later. Stay on the blue-blazed trail. After 10 minutes (half a mile) the trail meets Cedar Run, which it follows for the next hour or more. In summer this narrow and not well-used path is flanked by stinging nettles, so you must stay on the trail. The creek remains difficult to access until 25 minutes into the hike, where a big boulder affords a good resting place with a pool at the base of a cascade that spreads a wide sheet of water across the rock face. The next section of trail mostly descends, occasionally crossing the creek. About 1 hour 10 minutes from the trailhead (2½mi), the trail crosses the creek to pass a metal post with a 'Leave no trace' message. Turn right after the crossing, continuing on the blue-blazed trail. After 10 minutes (at 2.8mi) veer left at the Y-intersection onto Whiteoak–Cedar Run Link Trail. (To the right is the continuation of Cedar Run Trail which goes to Berry Hollow parking area on VA 600.) Cedar Run Link is a pleasant meander through a hardwood forest with a few struggling hemlock on a smooth dirt path. Birdsong replaces the sound of the tumbling creek waters.

After 10 minutes you'll arrive at **Whiteoak Run** (and a good swimming hole) which you'll cross a minute later to a cement trail marker. You have come 3.6mi. Turn left here to begin climbing upstream. This is a more popular trail than Cedar Run, although because of its difficulty there are relatively few hikers this far downstream. The forest here has some very large, old white oak and hemlock, and a few large red cedars. It's lush and verdant along this narrow gorge, and the moisture seeps from the rock walls at all times of the year.

About 15 minutes from the trail marker, after some switchbacks, cross the largest of the many tributary streams that flow into Whiteoak Run. This one has its own waterfall. In a few minutes you will reach the first of the six waterfalls in this gorge (several are unidentifiable because you're either not able to get near them without a steep scramble, or they are so close together that it's difficult to tell where one starts and another begins), just after a sign saying 'Avoid poison ivy, stay on the trail'. Unfortunately, just after passing the pool at the base of the falls there's a fork in the trail with a well-used but illegitimate trail going up steeply to the left. Take the right path which ascends much more reasonably on a switchback. Twenty minutes later, after a steep climb over some rock faces, there appears a clearing where the trail levels out and a very inviting rock face offers a place to rest, with a big view of the east side of the park.

Another 15 minutes of climbing follow, and the trail comes to a pool at the base of the second falls, about 60ft high. If you haven't had a swim yet, this is the place to do it. The First Falls, coming up, invariably have other visitors since most people only go that far. Ten minutes from the Second Falls, begin to climb a set of rock-and-cement steps, and a further 10 minutes of climbing will bring you to the base of the first and longest waterfall, about 90ft high.

Veer left off the trail to see the falls themselves and access the pool at their base. The top of First Falls is reached after a further seven minutes on the trail. There's an intersection with a horse trail, an old wagon road built by George Pollock in the 1890s. He built Skyland Lodge and brought wealthy city folks out here to the clear air of the high mountains, then toted them around in wagons to see the sights and fed them elaborate meals as they observed nature. Turn left at this intersection, and you'll see the top of First Falls. Veer right before reaching the creek to stay on the blue-blazed trail and cross the walking bridge. At the far end of the bridge is a trail marker. Turn right to continue upstream on the Whiteoak Canyon Trail and enter a stretch of old-growth hemlock, the healthiest bunch in the park.

About 30 minutes from the bridge is the intersection with Limberlost Trail. Turn left onto this very manicured trail; it was recently the recipient of a grant to make it wheelchair-accessible. For 0.3mi enjoy the gentle uphill climb on a wide, pebble-covered path with comfy wooden benches every few hundred yards. Turn left onto Crescent Rock Trail which is marked by a cement trail marker. Within 15 minutes Skyline Dr is reached at its Mile 45. Go across the street, veering to the right to enter the driveway of Crescent Rock Overlook. Follow the driveway; just before the car park, turn right onto Bettys Rock Trail, but only for a few seconds before turning left downhill to reach the AT after 150yd. Once

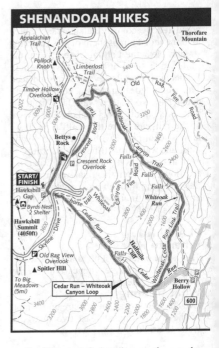

on the AT turn left, heading south on a descending path. At the next intersection, about 10 minutes later, turn left toward Hawksbill Gap parking area.

Old Rag Loop

Duration	4–6 hours
Distance	7.7mi (12.4km)
Standard	medium-hard
Start/Finish	Old Rag Trailhead, Hwy 600
Nearest Town	Sperryville
Public Transport	no

Summary A climb to the summit of 3620ft Old Rag, scrambling over granite boulders and crawling under rock formations to the 360-degree view.

Old Rag – a solitary peak, separate from the main crest of the Blue Ridge – is one of the best hikes in the park and has unique views.

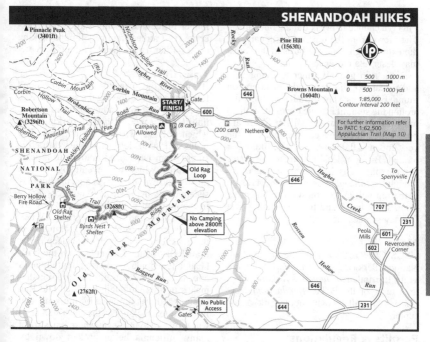

After a climb through the forest (total ascent/descent for the hike is 2300ft), the trail arrives at a section of granite boulders that must be scrambled over to get to the bald granite summit. The scrambling is not particularly technical, but it's still quite challenging. Once on top – if it's a clear day and the scout troop hasn't yet caught up to you – this is an incredible chance to see in all directions from a completely unfettered viewpoint. The descent is easy in comparison to the climb as there are no more boulders to navigate. There are two shelters on the way down, although they are not supposed to be used for sleeping unless there's a surprise storm. This isn't prime camping territory – the lower part of the trail is mostly on a hillside with dense undergrowth including poison ivy and stinging nettles, and the upper part of the hike would be very difficult while carrying a big backpack. Really the only camping is at the beginning of the trail near the creek in the hemlock forest where there

is much less undergrowth. In this way, a person could camp and leave their camping gear in the car while making this into a day loop – entirely feasible since it's only a 7.7mi trek.

PLANNING
When to Hike

This is a beautiful hike at all times of the year, although in the winter there is often snow on the trail. The strategy for the best possible experience, however, is to avoid the crowds which pack this trail on weekends and holidays. During the week, and especially early in the morning, this can be a completely solitary experience. Try to get on the trail by 7 am on a Monday in spring or late June (for the flowers), or even earlier in October when the park experiences a last surge of interest thanks to the changing leaves. If it is raining or foggy, choose another hike since this one has so much rock to climb over and the views should be enjoyed on a clear day.

What to Bring

This is a chance to break out the binoculars. The views from the top are worth carrying the extra weight, and the birds in the forest may deserve a closer look, too.

Bring rain gear. Weather is changeable and a clear morning may end with afternoon thundershowers. The middle of the hike around the summit is quite exposed, with no trees from which to seek shelter. There are no water sources except the creek at the very end, and the water has to be filtered or treated. Bring at least two quarts of water per person – this is a strenuous hike, although the mileage is short. The experience at the top will make you want to linger, so bring some lunch and plan on making it a full day's endeavor.

Maps

USGS *Old Rag Mountain*, the Shenandoah National Park *Old Rag Trail Map* (free), the Trails Illustrated *Shenandoah National Park* topo map, or the PATC *Appalachian Trail (Map 10)* are all available at the park visitor centers.

Permits & Regulations

Carry the green national park entrance fee receipt (it's good for a week from when you first entered). If you haven't previously entered the park, you must pay $5, or $10 for a family. Fees can be paid at either parking area and it is an honor system. If a ranger comes along asking for your receipt he can fine you if you can't produce one.

Backcountry permits (free) are required for camping and can also be filled out at the lower parking area. On Fridays and weekends in the summer, a ranger is in attendance at the trailhead or down in the parking area.

GETTING TO/FROM THE HIKE

From the park's Thornton Gap Entrance (Mile 31½) head east to Sperryville. Take a right onto Hwy 522 heading south and within a mile turn right onto Hwy 231. Stay on this road until you turn right onto VA 707. It's a short distance before turning right onto VA 600, and continue 2mi to a large parking area in a field on your left. This is

not park service land, but there is a small ranger office that is only staffed on weekends. The trailhead and very limited parking are a further 0.8mi ahead. Parking is free.

THE HIKE

If you're in the lower parking area, head out left on the road following the sign 'Old Rag 0.8 mile'. After the last house, the road goes uphill to a second, smaller parking area which only has space for eight cars. The trailhead is to the left with some interpretive signs. From here, head uphill into a hemlock forest which will eventually become mostly hardwoods. This is a gentle but persistent climb in the shade of tall trees. Early in the morning is the best time of day for birdwatching and animal sighting. When the path isn't too rocky, keep looking up in the trees for bears, which often sleep in the branches. About 45 minutes from the trailhead, a few boulders offering limited views appear next to the trail. The granite that makes up this mountain is called Old Rag Granite and was formed a billion years ago from molten rock under the earth's crust. It was thrust up to this level where it has spent many millennia being broken down by wind, water, and hot and cold temperatures to create the great, rounded boulders and cracks you're climbing through today.

After a little more than an hour, the rock scrambling begins. There are a few more views to the ridge that you'll be scrambling on and to the rocky top of Old Rag itself.

This next section is only 0.6mi long but it will take you longer than any simple hike in the woods. After 1½ hours from the trailhead you'll negotiate a **natural stairway** between two giant boulders. After two hours, arrive at the top of the first of two flat, moonscape mountaintops. From here are excellent views; up to the left can be seen the top of Old Rag. Twenty minutes later is the **summit** itself, marked on the trail with a cement trail marker. Scramble up the rocks past the trail to get to the precipitous viewpoint which offers many comfortable resting places to contemplate a 360-degree panoramic view, one of only four in the park. Due west is Hawksbill, and to the right below Bettys

Rock are the multiple falls of Whiteoak Canyon. A bit more to the right is Stonyman, and Marys Rock is due north. Down below is Weakley Hollow which is where the return path travels. Back over toward the crest of the Blue Ridge you can make out the large, green expanse of Big Meadows. To the southeast are the farmlands of Piedmont.

After filling your senses with the view from atop this rocky crag, continue on the blue-blazed trail down into the forest. This descent seems extremely tame after the boulder-dashing of the ascent. After 15 minutes you will arrive at a trail marker and **Byrds Nest Shelter**. This is a stone, open-sided structure with a huge stone fireplace. It is for day use only, except in the case of extreme weather. A further half hour of descent on the Saddle Trail will bring you to **Old Rag Shelter**, on a little knoll in a clearing of green grass and ferns. From here, the Saddle Trail doubles in width, evidence of its former use as a logging road. After 10 minutes the Post Office intersection is reached. There is an interpretive sign explaining that this was once the hub of a small mountain community where several roads met As well as a post office, there was a schoolhouse and church, and many fewer trees than there are today. From here, go right on Berry Hollow Fire Rd, and then quickly right again onto Weakley Hollow Fire Rd. A few trails diverge from this road, but stick to Weakley Hollow Fire Rd for the next 2½mi until reaching the upper parking area of Old Rag.

Other Hikes

GREAT SMOKY MOUNTAINS
Joyce Kilmer Memorial Forest–Slickrock Wilderness
Southwest of Great Smoky Mountains National Park, north on Hwy 29 from Robbinsville, is Nantahala National Forest. One of the best places to experience a virgin hardwood forest in the East, this uncrowded wilderness area features trails and camping in the area. Use the topo map from the Cheoah district ranger office on Massey Branch Rd, 2mi northwest of Robbinsville.

BLUE RIDGE MOUNTAINS
Mt Mitchell
At 6684ft, this is the highest peak east of the Mississippi River. The summit is close to the road but there is a 6mi trail from Black Mountain campground to the top of Mt Mitchell. Get to Black Mountain campground by taking USFS Rd No 472 off the BRP just north of Mile 352.

Craggy Gardens
This area offers many trails, but the 1.2mi roundtrip to Craggy Pinnacle gives the most spectacular views. These open heath balds are rare on the BRP and Craggy Gardens is almost entirely bald.

Peaks of Otter
Here are many choices for hikers, but the most famous hike is the 3mi climb to the top of Sharp Top (one of three Otter Peaks) giving commanding views of the surrounding countryside.

ALLEGHENY MOUNTAINS
Cranberry Wilderness Area
This haven of biodiversity is located in the southwestern section of the Monongahela, east of Richwood, West Virginia. The Cranberry Mountain visitor center (at the intersection of Hwy 55 and Hwy 150) can provide information. Hiking in this area is highly recommended due to the abundance of birds and other wildlife, as well as the exceedingly diverse flora along the trail. Try the Cranberry Glades Botanical Area Loop for a start and consider the more challenging 17.7mi Tea Creek–Gauley Mountain–Right Fork Connector–Tea Creek Mountain Trail loop from the Tea Creek campground, 13mi north of the nature center. Maps are available at the visitor center.

Rocky Mountains

Dividing the continent into the great Pacific and Atlantic (including the Arctic) watershed basins, the Rocky Mountains earn their title of the 'backbone of North America.' The Rockies – an area of roughly 250,000 sq miles – are a broad and geologically complex range that extends south from the Canadian border through Montana, Wyoming and Colorado as far as northern New Mexico, with major lateral extensions reaching deep into Idaho and Utah. Around a third of the protected lands – national parks, national forests and wilderness areas – in the lower 48 states lie within the greater Rocky Mountains area, and the Rockies boast four of America's great parks, Glacier, Yellowstone, Grand Teton and Rocky Mountain. A vast system of hiking trails gives access to even the most remote roadless areas. The great Continental Divide Trail traverses the entire length of the US Rockies for a distance of some 3000mi.

HISTORY

Various Native American peoples inhabited the Rocky Mountains before the arrival of Europeans. The Shoshone and the Absaroka (Crow) of western Wyoming and the Ute people of western Colorado and Utah were less resistant to the first European explorers and traders who ventured onto their lands, but the warlike Blackfeet of Montana were feared by their neighbors and bitterly fought the foreign advance. From the 16th century the Spanish began pushing north into the Rocky Mountain region from Mexico, introducing horses to Native American tribes. In the northern Rockies, French explorers and fur traders did not begin to arrive from eastern Canada until the early 18th century.

In the Louisiana Purchase of 1803, France (presumptuously) sold present-day Montana along with most of Wyoming and western Colorado to the USA. To survey this vast acquisition, President Thomas Jefferson despatched the famous Lewis and Clark expedition of 1804–06 (see the boxed text in the Facts about the USA chapter), which

HIGHLIGHTS

JOHN ELK III

Bison grazing at Jackson Hole, Grand Teton National Park, Wyoming.

- Looking out over rows of superb glaciated peaks from Swiftcurrent Mountain Lookout in Glacier National Park
- Hiking along the base of the majestic Chinese Wall escarpment in Bob Marshall Wilderness
- Bathing in the unspoiled Ferris Fork hot springs along the Bechler River in Yellowstone National Park
- The staggering view of Cirque of the Towers from Jackass Pass in the Wind River Range
- Watching herds of bighorn sheep grazing on the alpine tundra of Bighorn Flats in Rocky Mountain National Park

journeyed across the Rocky Mountains to the Pacific. Other important expeditions through the Rocky Mountains were led by Zebulon Pike in 1806–07 and Major Stephen Long in 1819. From the early 1820s the first white

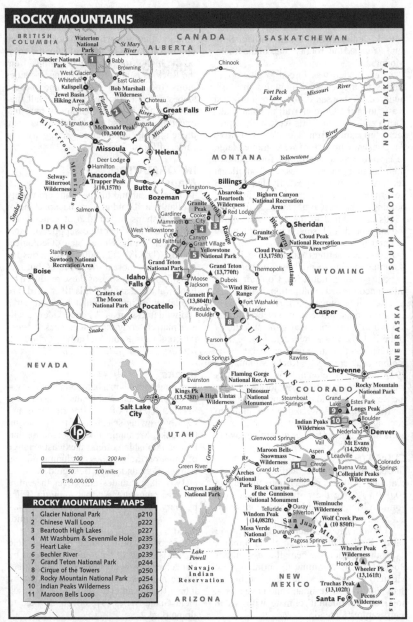

ROCKY MOUNTAINS

BRITISH COLUMBIA

CANADA

ALBERTA SASKATCHEWAN

Waterton National Park

St Mary River

Glacier National Park Babb

West Glacier Browning

Whitefish East Glacier

Kalispell

Jewel Basin Hiking Area

Polson

St Ignatius

McDonald Peak (10,300ft)

Bob Marshall Wilderness

Choteau

Great Falls

Augusta

Chinook

Fort Peck Lake

Missouri River

Missouri River

Missoula

Deer Lodge

Hamilton

Helena

MONTANA

Yellowstone River

Anaconda

Trapper Peak (10,157ft)

Butte

Bozeman

Billings

Livingston

Selway-Bitterroot Wilderness

Salmon

IDAHO

Granite Peak

Gardiner

Mammoth

Cooke City

Red Lodge

Absaroka-Beartooth Wilderness

Bighorn Canyon National Recreation Area

Cody

Sheridan

Cloud Peak National Recreation Area

West Yellowstone

Old Faithful

Canyon

Grant Village

Yellowstone National Park

Granite Pass

Big Horn Mountains

Cloud Peak (13,175ft)

Grand Teton National Park

Grand Teton (13,770ft)

Thermopolis

WYOMING

Stanley

Sawtooth National Recreation Area

Moose

Jackson

Dubois

Wind River Range

Boise

Craters of The Moon National Park

Idaho Falls

Gannett Pk (13,804ft)

Fort Washakie

Lander

Pocatello

Pinedale

Boulder

Snake River

Farson

Casper

Rock Springs

Rawlins

NEVADA

Evanston

Flaming Gorge National Rec. Area

Cheyenne

COLORADO

Kings Pk (13,528ft)

High Uintas Wilderness

Dinosaur National Monument

Steamboat Springs

Rocky Mountain National Park

Grand Lake

Estes Park

Longs Peak

Salt Lake City

Kamas

Green River

UTAH

Glenwood Springs

Vail

Indian Peaks Wilderness

Nederland

Boulder

Denver

Green River

Maroon Bells-Snowmass Wilderness

Aspen

Leadville

Mt Evans (14,265ft)

Colorado River

Grand Jct

Crested Butte

Buena Vista

Collegiate Peaks Wilderness

Colorado Springs

Canyon Lands National Park

Gunnison

Black Canyon of the Gunnison National Monument

Arches National Park

Telluride

Ouray

Silverton

Weminuche Wilderness

Sangre de Cristo Mountains

Windom Peak (14,082ft)

San Juan Mtns

Wolf Creek Pass (10 850ft)

Mesa Verde National Park

Durango

Pagosa Springs

Lake Powell

Wheeler Peak Wilderness

Navajo Indian Reservation

Hondo

Wheeler Pk (13,161ft)

NEW MEXICO

Truchas Peak (13,102ft)

Pecos Wilderness

ARIZONA

Santa Fe

0 100 200 km
0 50 100 miles
1:10,000,000

ROCKY MOUNTAINS – MAPS

1	Glacier National Park	p210
2	Chinese Wall Loop	p222
3	Beartooth High Lakes	p227
4	Mt Washburn & Sevenmile Hole	p235
5	Heart Lake	p237
6	Bechler River	p239
7	Grand Teton National Park	p244
8	Cirque of the Towers	p250
9	Rocky Mountain National Park	p254
10	Indian Peaks Wilderness	p263
11	Maroon Bells Loop	p267

ROCKY MOUNTAINS

trappers – legendary 'mountain men', with evocative names like Jim Bridger, Tom Fitzpatrick, Jedediah Smith and William Sublette – roamed the frontier lands of the Rocky Mountains.

After Mexico was forced to give up all claims to the Rocky Mountains in 1848, hundreds of thousands of settlers journeyed west along the Oregon Trail to Utah, California and Oregon. Forts were built to protect emigrants from attack by Native Americans, who in turn were granted large reservations as compensation for the loss of their hunting grounds. Pressure from illegal settlers, however, repeatedly led the US government to reduce or relocate tribal land holdings. The arrival of railroads from the 1860s contributed to the extermination of the huge herds of bison on which the many Indian tribes were dependent.

Permanent settlers came to the Rocky Mountain region to establish lumber, mining and grazing industries. Concern at the often uncontrolled exploitation of the Rockies' natural resources gave rise to an early conservationist movement. The creation of the world's first national park at Yellowstone in 1872 was a precedent for the later establishment of other national parks in the region: Glacier in 1910, Rocky Mountain in 1915 and Grand Teton in 1950. Tourism has gradually grown to be the major industry in the Rockies, and today outdoor recreation – anything from rafting, skiing and hiking to hunting, fishing and mountain biking – supports many former timber or mining towns.

CLIMATE

Closer proximity to the Pacific and lower elevations – with few peaks rising much above 10,000ft – give the northern Rockies (of northern Montana and Idaho) a more moist but relatively moderate climate.

Although their much higher altitude partly compensates for their closer proximity to the equator, the central and southern Rockies (from Wyoming to northern New Mexico) – where a valley may be higher than 9000ft – lie far inland and have a pronounced 'continental' climate with wider temperature fluctuations.

The Rocky Mountains form a massive barrier to the moist westerly winds – most notably the powerful chinook – which dump 200 inches or more of rain and snow on the higher ranges annually. Water from the Rockies is vital for the farms and cities along the parched western and eastern slopes. Even in summer, snow can fall anywhere in the Rockies, but much more frequent are thunderstorms which bring cold, drenching rain or hail and lightning, a major cause of forest fires.

INFORMATION
Maps

Topographical and hiking maps are widely available, and sold at local backpacking or outdoor shops (often also at general and hardware stores or office suppliers). Most hikers rely on the United States Geological Society (USGS) 1:24,000 'quad' series for longer and/or more difficult routes, but special hiking maps, such as those produced by Earthwalk Press and Trails Illustrated, are available for most popular national parks and wilderness areas. A good, widely available map covering the greater Rocky Mountain region is Rand McNally's *Central & Western United States* ($2.95).

Books

Regional book shops, outdoor suppliers, national park offices and United States Forest Service (USFS) offices stock a large and rapidly growing selection of titles relevant to Rocky Mountain hikers. In particular, Falcon Publishing offers an extensive range of titles on the Rockies, including hiking, fishing, flora and fauna field guides.

Two hiking guides that cover the entire Rockies range are: *Rocky Mountain Walks* by Gary Ferguson ($15.95), and *Adventuring in the Rockies* by Jeremy Schmidt ($16).

One of the best general botanical field guides is *Plants of the Rocky Mountains* by Linda Kershaw et al ($19.95), while *A Field Guide to Rocky Mountain Wildflowers* by John J Craighead et al, part of the Peterson Field Guide Series ($18.00), is devoted to alpine flora.

ROCKY MOUNTAINS

WARNINGS

Particularly in the central and southern Rockies, high elevations bring a significant risk of altitude sickness to people who are not properly acclimatized (see Environmental Hazards in the Health & Safety chapter).

Fire danger in the Rockies varies from year to year, but is often extreme in late July and August. Now recognized as a regulator of forest ecosystems, fires started naturally are often allowed to burn if they do not endanger life or property. Local USFS offices can advise hikers about fires burning out of control. Fire warnings are usually posted at wilderness access points.

Summer in the Rockies brings out mosquitoes, deer flies and other blood-sucking insects in often plague proportions. Many a hike has been ruined by unpreparedness, so carry plenty of insect repellent. Some hikers also use head nets. Ticks carry Rocky Mountain spotted fever and other diseases, and it is advisable to check your body after walking through forest.

In summer major electrical storms are common in the Rockies, and typically occur in mid-afternoon. On mountain tops and ridges the exposure to lightning strike is extreme, and hikers should watch the weather and plan to be off-summit by early afternoon. Heavy rain storms also bring the danger of hypothermia.

Giardia, campylobacter and other microorganisms that cause intestinal disorders with severe diarrhea are present in waterways throughout the Rockies. Drinking water taken from lakes and streams should always be treated by boiling, filtering or chemical sterilization.

Wildlife can be very unpredictable and should never be approached. This is particularly important should you encounter a grizzly bear or mountain lion (see Safety on the Hike in the Health & Safety chapter), but deaths also occur when bison, moose and elk charge people who venture too close. Never feed animals or allow them near your food.

Birds of the Rocky Mountains by Chris C Fisher ($19.95) and *Mammals of the Central Rockies* by Jan L Wassink ($14) are two books which cover regional fauna and may enrich your experience on the trail.

Information Sources

National Park Service (NPS) and United States Forest Service (USFS) regional offices can give up-to-date information on anything from local weather, trail conditions, snow cover, forest fires, river levels and even local bear or mountain-lion sightings (see Nearest Towns for each region or hike for convenient offices).

Permits

With certain exceptions, such as Colorado's Indian Peaks Wilderness, hikers do not require a backcountry permit to camp in (USFS administered) national forests and wilderness areas, though in some USFS picnic or recreation areas a fee applies for day use and/or trailhead parking. Hikers who enter Native American lands, including the Mission Mountains Tribal Wilderness in Montana and the Wind River Roadless Area in Wyoming, need to buy a 'fishing' or use permit from the local tribal authority.

In each of the Rockies' four national parks – Glacier, Yellowstone, Grand Teton and Rocky Mountain – you must have a backcountry permit to camp in backcountry areas. Rules vary, but all parks issue only a set number of permits per day for each backcountry campsite. In most cases, no more than half of the campsites can be reserved, with the remainder available the day before on a first-come, first-served basis. The backcountry permit lists the dates for which each campsite has been reserved – once issued, the itinerary cannot be changed without approval. Permits are regularly checked by patroling park rangers, and hikers caught camping out without a valid permit are likely to be fined.

Anglers should note that fishing licenses – issued by state, national park or Native

American tribal authorities – are required on all waterways. Rules and fees vary considerably, so consult the appropriate land management authority.

GATEWAYS

Kalispell

Kalispell lies at the junction of US Hwys 2 and 93 in northwestern Montana. This small, otherwise unexciting center of the Flathead Valley serves as a gateway to Glacier National Park, Jewel Basin Hiking Area and the Mission Mountains, as well as the somewhat more distant Bob Marshall country.

Amtrak's daily *Empire Builder* train stops at Whitefish, 13mi north of Kalispell. Intermountain Transport (☎ 406-755-4011) runs a daily bus between Whitefish and Missoula via Kalispell.

Several airlines have flights between Missoula, Salt Lake City, Spokane, Seattle and the local Glacier Park International Airport (☎ 406-527-5994).

Missoula

This small university city in western Montana is well positioned as a gateway to the Mission Mountains, Bitterroot Mountains and Glacier National Park.

The Greyhound depot (☎ 406-549-2339) at 1660 W Broadway has regional buses to Whitefish (via Kalispell), Billings (via Butte) and Bozeman (via Anaconda and Butte), as well as interstate services to San Francisco, Seattle and Mineapolis. Buses CART (☎ 1800 258 4937) runs a shuttle bus three times weekly in either direction between Missoula and Hamilton ($7 or $11 to/from Missoula airport) with direct connections between Hamilton and Salmon. Missoula airport (☎ 406-728-4381) has flights to/from Kalispell, Seattle, Salt Lake City and Minneapolis.

Great Falls

At the geographical heart of Montana, Great Falls straddles the Missouri River where I-5 meets Montana Hwy 87. Great Falls boasts the enormous Giant Springs, which gushes out to form the 201ft-long Roe River – the shortest river in the world.

Great Falls International Airport (☎ 406-727-3404) has flights to Helena, Missoula and Salt Lake City. From the Great Falls bus terminal (☎ 406-454-1982), near the airport baggage claim, there are busses at least daily to Helena, Butte, Lewistown and Billings.

Bozeman

Bozeman is situated on Montana's I-90 north of Yellowstone National Park, surrounded by the Absaroka, Beartooth, Bridger, Crazy and Gallatin Mountains.

Regional and interstate bus connections including to West Yellowstone leave from the Greyhound depot (☎ 406-587-3110) at 625 N 7th St. Several airlines fly into the local Gallatin airport (☎ 406-388-6632) to/from Salt Lake City, Washington and Alaska.

Idaho Falls

This drab agricultural and mining center in southeastern Idaho is within a day's drive of the Sawtooth National Recreation Area and the Craters of the Moon, Yellowstone and Grand Teton National Parks.

From the Greyhound depot (☎ 208-522-0912) at 850 Denver St there are buses to/from Bozeman and Salt Lake City, CART (☎ 208-522-2278) buses to Salmon (with connections to Missoula), Rexburg and Jackson (see Grand Teton National Park), and SLASH (☎ 800-359-6826) shuttles between Salt Lake City and Idaho Falls.

Salt Lake City

Salt Lake City, nestled at the foot at the Wasatch Mountains, is Utah's largest city and convenient to the High Uintas and Wind River Range.

Greyhound (☎ 801-355-9579), 160 W Sth Temple, provides at-least-daily bus services to much of the rest of the US including Las Vegas, Los Angeles, Denver, San Francisco, Seattle and Portland. Amtrak trains (☎ 801-531-0188) serve Chicago via Denver.

Salt Lake City's international airport is served by a number of major carriers.

Denver

Sprawling across the rolling prairies on the eastern foot of northern Colorado's Front

Range, Denver is a pleasant city with a broad range of attractions.

Amtrak's *California Zephyr* runs daily between Chicago and San Francisco via Denver's Union Station. From the downtown Denver bus terminal (☎ 303-293-6555) at 19th and Arapahoe Sts, there are frequent (connecting) services to/from all major US cities.

Denver's international airport (☎ 303-342-2000 or 800-247-2336) is the Rockies' main point of entry for air travelers. Some 20 airlines fly into DIA, of which United Airlines has by far the largest number of flights – see the Getting There & Away chapter.

Boulder

Boulder sits right under the slab-rock mountainsides of Front Range just northwest of Denver. This pleasant, laid-back university city is the gateway to Rocky Mountain National Park and Indian Peaks Wilderness.

RTD (☎ 303-299-6000) buses run at least hourly between Boulder and downtown Denver.

Santa Fe

Santa Fe lies at the southern end of the Sangre de Cristo Mountains of northern New Mexico.

TNM&O-Greyhound (☎ 505-471-0008) runs regularly to Albuquerque and Taos. United Express (☎ 800-241-6522, 800-822-2746) flies to/from Denver, and Aspen Mountain (☎ 800-877-3932) flies to/from Dallas.

Glacier National Park

The 1583-sq-mile Glacier National Park of northern Montana extends south along the Continental Divide from the Canadian border. Glacier adjoins Canada's much smaller Waterton Lakes National Park, and together the two form an International Peace Park. Largely because animal populations on both sides of the border can readily communicate, the greater Glacier area is regarded by many ecologists as the most important biosphere reserve in the lower 48 states. Its outstanding wilderness scenery and wildlife attract hoards of tourists during the short summer season, though most visitors leave their cars only briefly (if at all) on their way across the Going-to-the-Sun Rd between West Glacier and St Mary.

HISTORY

At the time of the first European contact, the Blackfeet people occupied most of northern Montana. After a series of land-grabs and dishonored treaties throughout the latter 19th century, the Blackfeet finally sold the area now comprising the park to the US government in 1896. The construction of the Great Northern Railway in the 1890s led to rapid settlement and often rapacious exploitation of the region's resources, especially timber.

In 1895 Waterton Lakes National Park was established just across the border in Canada. Having long recognized the area's uniqueness, Dr George Bird Grinnell finally convinced the US government to create Glacier National Park, which came into being in 1910. In the early 1910s the Great Northern Railway built a series of hotels and mountain chalets in the park, but the completion of the Going-to-the-Sun Rd over Logan Pass in 1927 and the rising popularity of motorized transport brought the end of Glacier's short era of 'railroad tourism'.

NATURAL HISTORY

The moderating influence of the moist Pacific winds is particularly pronounced on the slopes west of the Continental Divide. For this reason many tree species found in the greater Glacier region do not grow much farther south in the Rockies, most notably western red cedar, mountain hemlock, western hemlock and western yew as well as grand fir and white spruce. Tree species more readily associated with upper montane and subalpine forests of the Rocky Mountains include Engelmann spruce and subalpine fir.

These rich forests support diverse birdlife. The varied thrush is typically present in the moist, lower forests of western red cedar and hemlock on the western side of the park. Steller's jay can be found in Engelmann spruce, while the gray-crowned rosy finch favors the subalpine shrub willow thickets. The well camouflaged spruce grouse is found in the coniferous montane and subalpine forests. The white-tailed ptarmigan lives mostly in the tundra, largely feeding on wildflowers and the buds of alpine shrub willows.

In early summer Glacier's alpine wildflowers bloom with almost unparalleled splendor. The park's diverse alpine flora species include hardy creamy-white globeflowers, yellow blanket flowers, deep blue mountain bog gentians and purple pasqueflowers, which pop out of the ground as the winter snows melt. Yellow glacier lilies carpet the highest alpine meadows, and their tubers are dug out and eaten by grizzly bears. Coarse, blade-like beargrass produces fragrant white flowers on a long stalk that are eaten by elk and bighorn sheep (but seldom by bears).

Viewing wildlife is one of the great pleasures of Glacier. Moose browse on saplings, shrubs and other plants of the waterlogged valleys, at times even diving to feed on the aquatic vegetation in lakes. Herds of bighorn sheep graze the alpine tundra in summer. Mountain goats are another of Glacier's often-sighted larger mammals (partly because salt-addicted mountain goats frequent many backcountry campsites). These remarkably agile animals pick their way through the steepest slopes in search of alpine grasses, shrubs or lichen.

The greater Glacier area is an important breeding ground for grizzly bears. Local grizzlies are largely vegetarian, but sometimes take old or sick mammals and are quickly attracted by animal carcasses. Grizzlies are by nature solitary animals, but will congregate anywhere food is abundant, such as alpine berry fields. In late autumn grizzlies dig out hollows, typically under tree roots just below treeline, where they hibernate until the winter snows are gone. Researchers keep track of Glacier's grizzlies by nailing short lengths of barbed wire to tree trunks, which the bears rub against to mark their territory.

Other wildlife includes whitetail deer, mule deer and Rocky Mountain elk (or wapiti). Several feline species, mountain lion (or cougar), lynx and the bobcat inhabit the park but are rarely seen.

PLANNING
Maps
Most hikers use Trails Illustrated's 1:142,747 *Glacier/Waterton National Park* ($9.95), which covers the whole of Glacier and includes a 1:83,930 inset map of the Many Glacier area. The USGS 1:100,000 *Glacier National Park* ($5) covers the entire park at a larger scale, but is rather unwieldy.

Permits & Regulations
Park entry fees (valid seven days) are: $10 for private vehicles and motorcycles, $5 for individuals on foot or bicycle.

Backcountry permits are required for all overnight trips within the park. These cost $4 per person per night from June through September (otherwise free of charge). Up to 50% of backcountry sites are available for advanced reservation after 15 April for an additional fee of $20. Details and forms are available in the park's free annual *Backcountry Guide*. There are backcountry offices at Apgar, Many Glacier, St Mary (visitor center), Two Medicine, Polebridge and Waterton Lakes (visitor center). For backcountry information call park headquarters (☎ 406-888-7800), or write to Backcountry Reservations, Glacier National Park, PO Box 395, West Glacier, MT 59936.

NEAREST TOWNS
Many Glacier
Many Glacier is 12mi from Babb off US Hwy 89 in the park's northeastern sector. With at least half a dozen or so excellent routes in the surrounding mountains, this scattered, summer-only village is probably the best base for hiking in Glacier.

The basic NPS *Many Glacier campground* (☎ 406-888-7800 for availability) has sites for $12. First opened in 1914, the large *Many Glacier Hotel* (☎ 406-732-4411 or 602-207-6000), on the north shore of Swiftcurrent Lake, has medium-range accommodations. About 1.2mi on at the end of the road is the **Swiftcurrent Motor Inn** (☎ 406-732-5531), which serves as an annexe for Many Glacier Hotel. The motor inn also has a restaurant and a general store, which sells tokens for the nearby shower and laundry but – apart from maps – few backpacking supplies.

St Mary

St Mary lies at the junction of Hwy 89 and the Going-to-the-Sun Rd. The visitor center at the park entrance has natural history exhibits and issues backcountry permits. There is an expensive supermarket. The **KOA campground** (☎ 406-732-4122) and **Divide Creek campground** offer sites with facilities.

East Glacier

At the junction of Hwy 49 and US 2, East Glacier gives access to the southeast side of the park. The **East Glacier Motel** (☎ 406-226-5593) has budget rooms. Amtrak's *Empire Builder* train, which runs the 2200mi between Chicago and Seattle/Portland daily in each direction, stops (around 9 am eastbound, around 7 pm westbound) at the local Glacier Park Station.

Apgar

Apgar is just inside the park boundary at the scenic southern shore of Lake McDonald, 2mi from West Glacier. There is a small visitor center and a separate backcountry office (for permits). There is a general store, camping at the basic NPS **Apgar campground** and rooms at **Apgar Village Inn** (☎ 406-888-5632).

West Glacier

Just outside the park on US 2 at the west turnoff to the Going-to-the-Sun Rd, West Glacier is the park's main entry point. The park headquarters in West Glacier is on the road towards Apgar. The nearest camping with all facilities is at **Glacier campground** (☎ 406-387-5689), on the southern side of US Hwy 2, 1mi west of the park entrance. The **Vista Hotel** (☎ 406-888-5311), 2mi west of the park entrance, has rooms for $46/55.

Amtrak's *Empire Builder* train stops (around 8.30 am eastbound, around 7.30 pm westbound) at the local Belton Station.

GETTING AROUND

In summer the Hiker Shuttle (☎ 406-888-9187) runs between Many Glacier and Apgar via St Mary. For private shuttles call Many Glacier Hotel (see Many Glacier under Nearest Towns).

Swiftcurrent Mountain Lookout

Duration	7½–10 hours
Distance	15.8mi (25.4km)
Standard	medium-hard
Start/Finish	Many Glacier (Swiftcurrent Motor Inn)
Public Transport	yes

Summary One of the most panoramic lookouts anywhere in the Rockies, Swiftcurrent Mountain Lookout makes a long, tiring yet unceasingly scenic roundtrip day hike from Many Glacier.

This spectacular route transits the upper valley of Swiftcurrent Creek (a summer feeding ground of local grizzly bears – so be 'bear aware' at all times) – a long roundtrip day hike from Many Glacier with an elevation gain of almost 3500ft (1050m). Some hikers stay at Granite Park chalet or campground, a short way west of Swiftcurrent Pass. It is also the first (or last) day of the Highline Trail/Ptarmigan Tunnel Loop (see next hike).

When to Hike

It is unlikely that the upper sections of the trail will be in condition much before the end of June or after September. Afternoon thunderstorms are a danger in summer, so try to get an early start. The trails around Many Glacier are heavily used during the summer months, even on weekdays.

Maps

Two USGS 1:24,000 quads cover the hike: *Many Glacier* and *Ahern Pass*. In this book, see the Glacier National Park map on page 210–211.

ROCKY MOUNTAINS

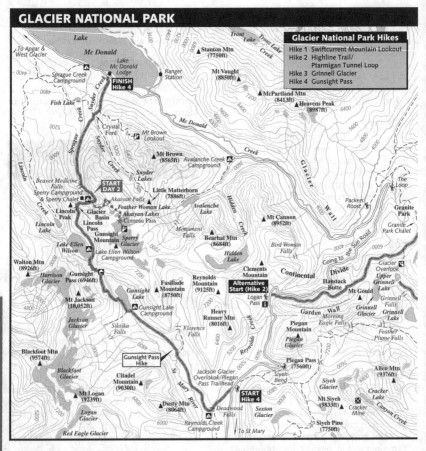

GLACIER NATIONAL PARK

Glacier National Park Hikes
Hike 1 Swiftcurrent Mountain Lookout
Hike 2 Highline Trail/
Ptarmigan Tunnel Loop
Hike 3 Grinnell Glacier
Hike 4 Gunsight Pass

GETTING TO/FROM THE HIKE

The trailhead is at Many Glacier, 120yd past the Swiftcurrent Motor Inn on the northwestern side of the large parking area.

THE HIKE

Follow the Swiftcurrent Pass Trail left at the junction a few paces on and cross the footbridge over Wilbur Creek. This low lodgepole forest sprinkled with aspen is regrowth following the 1936 fire that burnt out much of the upper Swiftcurrent Valley.

After passing largely hidden Fishcap Lake, the trail rises gently through beargrass meadows to Redrock Lake and heads up beside Redrock Falls, where the inlet cascades in several stages over the red mudstone. Pass through wildflower fields and brush willow past an unnamed lake to cross a side stream (the outlet of Windmaker Lake) on a small suspension bridge. The view to the north is dominated by Mt Wilbur, Iceberg Peak and the North Swiftcurrent Glacier. The trail continues past the greenish Bullhead Lake, then follows the small inlet almost to the base of the sheer headwalls at the head of the valley, two to three hours from the trailhead.

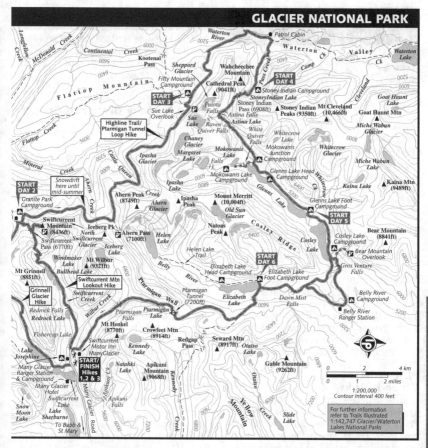

The climb now begins in earnest as the trail – in places cut into the precipitous rock – winds its way up past meltwater cascades coming off the nearby Swiftcurrent Glacier. Now high above the valley, you get a spectacular overview of the landscape you have just passed through. Cut on up over mountain meadows to reach **Swiftcurrent Pass** (6770ft), 1½ to two hours after you began climbing. This broad, low saddle scattered with yellow glacier lilies is bordered by stands of battered firs, and gives the first views of Heavens Peak and other summits in the southern Livingston Range.

The signposted 1.4mi trail to the lookout turns off north just west of the pass and climbs in repeated switchbacks along the steep shingle ridge to arrive at the summit shelter on **Swiftcurrent Mountain** (8436ft) after 45 minutes to one hour. The sublime panorama includes several dozen of Glacier's classic stratified peaks; the sight of the north wall of Mt Grinnell rising up from Swiftcurrent Glacier is especially impressive. Far below in the Swiftcurrent Valley you can easily make out the Many Glacier Hotel. Exercise caution, however, as the summit drops away abruptly into cliffs on its northern side.

Highline Trail/Ptarmigan Tunnel Loop

Duration	5–7 days
Distance	58mi (93.4km)
Standard	medium-hard
Start	Many Glacier (Swiftcurrent Motor Inn) or Logan Pass
Finish	Many Glacier (Swiftcurrent Motor Inn)
Public Transport	yes

Summary Also called the 'North Circle', this spectacular route around the northern Lewis Range probably offers the most varied scenery of any longer hike in the park.

This route combines several popular trails – Highline, Stoney Indian Pass and Ptarmigan Tunnel – to give up to a week of marvellous hiking. Some of the route sections also make excellent shorter hikes. Although there are a number of long, undulating sections, this route involves several strenuous ascents. Remember that the entire hike is in prime grizzly territory – make plenty of noise on the trail and rigorously observe the rules for handling food in bear country.

PLANNING
When to Hike
Due to heavy winter snow, the Highline Trail (particularly a tricky section near Ahern Pass), Stoney Indian Pass and the western approach to Ptarmigan Tunnel may remain closed well into July. From June through September thunderstorms with heavy lightning often occur in the early afternoon.

Maps
The following USGS 1:24,000 quads cover the hike: *Many Glacier*, *Ahern Pass*, *Mount Geduhn*, *Porcupine Ridge* and *Gable Mountain*. In this book, see the Glacier National Park map on pages 210–11.

GETTING TO/FROM THE HIKE
The hike begins and ends at the end of the road just past the Swiftcurrent Motor Inn in the town of Many Glacier (see Nearest

Towns). Alternatively, hikers can begin at Logan Pass on the Going-to-the-Sun Rd and take the Highline Trail to Granite Park (Day 1B). The Hiker Shuttle (see Getting Around earlier in this section) stops at the large car park at Logan Pass.

THE HIKE
Day 1A: Many Glacier to Granite Park
4–5½ hours, 7½mi (12.1km), 2223ft (677m) ascent

Follow the route directions for Swiftcurrent Mountain Lookout (see previous hike) as far as Swiftcurrent Pass. The trail continues 0.9mi down through low firs to intersect with the Highline Trail just above the historic **Granite Park Chalet** (*$60 per person;* ☎ *406-387-5555 for reservations*). This stone-built hut (and annexe) is open 1 July to 12 September, and offers basic accommodation for 34 hikers. The chalet stands on a tiny plateau giving superb views towards Heavens Peak and Logan Pass.

Another trail drops for several minutes down to **Granite Park campground**, with four clustered sites. The campground lies along a transit corridor for grizzlies, so be particularly attentive to hanging food.

Day 1B: Logan Pass to Granite Park
3–4 hours, 7.6mi (12.2km), 830ft (253m) ascent

The alternative first day, via the Highline Trail, begins from the car park atop Logan Pass. Head north around sheer cliffs above the Going-to-the-Sun Rd, whose groaning traffic noise blends strangely with the rushing of Logan Creek. Across the valley, Bird Woman Falls dives down from hanging glaciers on Clements Mountain and Mt Cannon. Leaving the road behind, the trail traverses seepage streamlets emerging from the craggy Garden Wall ridge to cross a broad saddle between Haystack Butte and Mt Gould, 1½ to two hours from Logans Pass.

Sidle over high terraces that fall away left into the deep glacial trough draining southwest into Lake McDonald. Mountain goats, ground squirrels, marmots and pikas frequent these rocky meadows of coarse alpine grasses and hardy wildflowers. The trail gradually descends along the upper treeline to pass the Garden Wall Trail turnoff. This 0.8mi side trail (30 to 45 minutes roundtrip) makes a steady diagonal climb up scree slopes to **Glacier Overlook**, a scenic gap in the Garden Wall that offers excellent views of Grinnell and Salamander Glaciers. The Highline Trail skirts briefly around the mountainside to arrive at *Granite Park Chalet* (see Day 1A), 1½ to two hours from the saddle near Haystack Butte.

Day 2: Granite Park to Fifty Mountain
4¼–5½ hours, 11.8mi (19km), 1908ft (581m) ascent
From the chalet, the Highline Trail cuts five minutes north to a small crest, where it is joined by a trail that leads up from the campground. Proceed north, traversing up and down alpine meadows and dipping occasionally into low stands of whitebark pine and subalpine fir at the upper forest fringe. There are almost uninterrupted views to the glaciated peaks of the Livingstone Range to the west. After mounting a minor spur the trail momentarily turns right along a cliff face. A steep snowdrift here often blocks the way until midsummer, and may require an ice-axe (and perhaps crampons) to cross safely.

The trail sidles on into a shallow cirque and crosses Ahern Creek, 1½ to two hours from Granite Park. Here it meets the 0.3mi turnoff to **Ahern Pass** (7100ft), an easy 45-minute (roundtrip) side trip. Ahern Pass falls away dramatically on its eastern side (where it may be dangerously corniced). For clearer views walk briefly right onto coarse talus slopes looking out on Ahern Glacier. Waterfalls gush from this spectacular icefall, which drops occasional ice chunks into the tarns above Helen Lake.

The Highline Trail skirts the mostly open mountainsides into the grassy amphitheater of **Cattle Queen Creek**, where early season snow along the stream may be tricky to cross. Head on steadily upward over sparse meadows opposite the ridge of Flattop

Mountain to reach a high crest. Here, a short side trail cuts up right to **Sue Lake Overlook**, an abrupt shelf commanding an impressive view of this wild lake in a deep glacial trough 500ft below. Mountain goats are often spotted among the meadows on the far side of Sue Lake.

Cut down left over stabilized scree slopes into rich wildflower meadows to reach *Fifty Mountain campground*, 2¾ to 3½ hours from Ahern Creek. There are six sites here right at treeline, though a number of the firs were killed in the 1988 fire. Grizzly bears frequent Fifty Mountain in summer – evidenced by the dug-over ground where they grub for glacier-lily tubers.

Day 3: Fifty Mountain to Stoney Indian Lake
3¼–4¾ hours, 7mi (11.3km), 1787ft (544m) ascent
Follow the trail northwest from the campground up through glorious wildflower tundra strewn with boulders to reach a crest at the foot of **Cathedral Peak**. Here, by the ruins of an old stone shelter, you get the best and last views back along the Lewis Range and across to the peaks of the adjacent Livingston Range. The trail drops into subalpine fir mixed with beargrass, then begins a long sidling descent over scrubby avalanche slopes overlooking the wild upper Waterton Valley to meet the Waterton River. The trail leads on through rich spruce forest along the river, passing a NPS patrol cabin at Pass Creek just before it comes to the signposted Stoney Indian Trail turnoff, two to 2½ hours from Fifty Mountain.

Turn right here and start a steady but moderate eastward climb through shrubby slopes which give way to dwarf birch and willow thickets. The trail flanks Pass Creek past a cascade to arrive at **Stoney Indian Lake** after 1¼ to 1¾ hours. This beautiful emerald lake lies in a classic cirque underneath Wahcheechee Mountain. The frost-burnt tips of the low firs around the lake show the effects of the harsh winds and winter avalanches. *Stoney Indian campground* has three sites just across the small lake outlet.

Glaciers & Glacial Landforms

Many of the world's finest walks are through landscapes which have been – or are being – substantially shaped by glaciers. As a glacier flows downhill under its weight of ice and snow it creates a distinctive collection of landforms, many of which are preserved once the ice has retreated (as it is doing in most of the world's ranges today) or vanished.

The most obvious is the *U-shaped valley* (1), gouged out by the glacier as it moves downhill, often with one or more bowl-shaped *cirques* (2) at its head. Cirques are found along high mountain ridges or at mountain passes or *cols* (3). Where an alpine glacier – which flows off the upper slopes and ridges of a mountain range – has joined a deeper, more substantial valley glacier, a dramatic *hanging valley* (4) is often the result. Hanging valleys and cirques commonly shelter hidden alpine lakes or *tarns* (5), such as those featured in so many of the hikes in this book. The thin ridge which separates adjacent glacial valleys is known as an *arête* (6).

As a glacier grinds its way forward it usually leaves long, *lateral moraine* (7) ridges along its course – mounds of debris either deposited along the flanks of the glacier or left by sub-ice streams within its heart (the latter, strictly, an *esker*). At the end – or *snout* – of a glacier is the *terminal moraine* (8), the point where the giant conveyor belt of ice drops its load of rocks and grit. Both high up in the hanging valleys and in the surrounding valleys and plains, *moraine lakes* (9) may form behind a dam of glacial rubble.

The plains which surround a glaciated range may feature a confusing variety of moraine ridges, mounds and outwash fans – material left by rivers flowing from the glaciers. Perched here and there may be an *erratic* (10), a rock carried far from its origin by the moving ice and left stranded when it melted.

View of area before glacier's retreat

Day 4: Stoney Indian Lake to Glenns Lake Foot

3–4¼ hours, 8½mi (13.7km), 598ft (182m) ascent

Skirt the eastern shore to the lake head, then switchback your way up to reach **Stoney Indian Pass** (6908ft) after 30 to 45 minutes. The pass directly overlooks Stoney Indian Lake and presents inspiring new views into the head of the pristine Mokowanis valley. The local salt-addicted marmots pounce on *anything* left unattended.

Cut down southeast into the alpine basin filled with white globeflowers and Indian hellebore. The trail leads around a large shallow tarn and over its outlet to cross another side stream that descends from Sue Lake in the leaping cascades of **Raven Quiver Falls**. Ahead, lakes snake along the bottom of the U-shaped valley like a wide, meandering river. Continue past the twin **Paiota Falls** and (farther back) **Atsina Falls** gushing over an escarpment shelf, before winding down to cross the young Mokowanis River just above where it enters Atsina Lake.

Head through shrub willow and dwarf birch fringing the lake's northern side before dropping steeply past a series of waterfalls into the forest to reach *Mokowanis Junction campground* (five sites). The trail proceeds quickly past the Mokowanis Lake Trail turnoff (see Side Trip) to *Glenns Lake Head campground* (three sites with fireplaces). It then rises and dips through old spruce forest some way from the lake's northern shore to arrive at *Glenns Lake Foot campground*, 2½ to 3½ hours from the pass. There are four pretty lakeside sites here.

Side Trip: Mokowanis Lake

1–1½ hours, 2mi (3.2km)

The detour to this beautiful lake in a tiny side valley surrounded by craggy spires is short and very easy. The trail quickly crosses footbridges over the Mokowanis River and the outlet of Mokowanis Lake, where the White Quiver Falls rush over a natural rock spillway into Glenns Lake. It then gently rises on up to the two lovely (but mosquito infested) sites at *Mokowanis Lake campground* on the lake's northeastern shore. An overgrown trail goes on to a churning waterfall descending from the outlet of Margaret Lake and fed by the eternal snows of the valley head.

Day 5: Glenns Lake Foot to Elizabeth Lake Foot

2¼–3 hours, 5.8mi (9.3km)

The trail heads northeast across the swift-flowing Whitecrow Creek then along the shore of Cosley Lake to *Cosley Lake campground* (four sites). Cosely Lake is a nesting area for bald eagles, and public access to parts of the shore is restricted. Continue toward the lone rump of Chief Mountain and take the right-hand Ptarmigan Trail turnoff leading directly to a ford at the lake outlet. After this serious wade, the trail turns southeast through lush forest with sporadic stands of white spruce. The trail meets the Belly River just before the turnoff to the Belly River ranger station, then climbs up past **Dawn Mist Falls**, which spray fine droplets into the air as they crash 45ft.

If the ford seems risky, take the (one hour longer) left-hand detour leading past the Bear Mountain Trail (see Side Trip) and the thundering **Gros Ventre Falls** to cross the Belly River on a suspension bridge. The historic Belly River ranger station is on the uphill side of the fenced paddock here; *Gable Creek campground* (four sites) lies below it.

Continue south above the east bank of the river, recrossing on another suspension bridge to intersect with the trail below Dawn Mist Falls. The trail leads up along the west bank of the river through berry fields and firs to reach the scenic *Elizabeth Lake Foot campground*. The six sites here along the lake's pebbly north shore look out to the towering crags of Ptarmigan Wall. The mournful call of loons and other waterbirds often resonates across these tranquil waters.

Side Trip: Bear Mountain Overlook

2–2½ hours, 3.4mi (5.5km), 1130ft (345m) ascent

The trail up to this scenic overlook turns off near a perennial golden eagle's nest, five minutes on (left) from the Ptarmigan Trail junction. It climbs through Douglas fir and stands of hardy whitebark pines on steep scree slopes to a high ridgetop. From here there are fine views both up and down the Mokowanis valley.

Alternative Campsites

Elizabeth Lake Head campground (with four sites) is at the southwest corner of the lake. Alternatively, try the *Helen Lake campground* (two sites) at the east end of Helen Lake.

Day 6: Elizabeth Lake Foot to Many Glacier

3¾–4¾ hours, 9.6mi (15.5km), 2515ft (767m) ascent

Recross the lake outlet on a suspension bridge and begin climbing through fir-spruce forest to high above Elizabeth Lake. Next, the trail sidles on up past the Redgap Pass Trail turnoff and out onto steep slopes of fir and whitebark pine, many of which show the signs of avalanche damage. There are excellent views down to Helen Lake in the upper Belly River valley as well as across to the majestic, glaciated forms of Natoas Peak, Mt Merritt and Upasha Peak. The trail now skirts left into a scree-filled cirque to reach the base of Ptarmigan Wall. At this point there is a stone-walled path cut into the cliff face; this leads up under the surrounding craggy spires to **Ptarmigan Tunnel** (7200ft). This damp, 120ft-long shaft was blasted through the ridge in 1931. You are now two to 2½ hours from Elizabeth Lake.

The tunnel takes you into the Swiftcurrent drainage basin. Next, descend steep, eroding slopes to Ptarmigan Lake, then drop more gently through forest of fir and spruce to the Iceberg Lake Trail turnoff (see Other Hikes at the end of this chapter). The trail continues past Ptarmigan Falls, then traverses open berry fields above the broadening valley – these are prime grizzly bear feeding grounds, so beware – to a fork. Here, either cut down (right) back to the *Swiftcurrent Motor Inn*, 1¾ to 2¼ hours from the tunnel, or go ahead (left) for 25 minutes to *Many Glacier Hotel*.

Grinnell Glacier

Duration	4–5½ hours
Distance	10.4mi (16.8km)
Standard	easy-medium
Start/Finish	Swiftcurrent picnic area or Many Glacier Hotel
Nearest Town	Many Glacier
Public Transport	yes

Summary The hike up to the Grinnell Glacier, the largest in the park, takes you right up into Glacier's most awesome alpine scenery with a minimum of time and effort. Bighorn sheep and other wildlife can usually be observed on the alpine slopes at the valley head.

This highly scenic roundtrip day hike has enough steep gradient to be challenging without becoming too strenuous, although the elevation gain is almost 1600ft (490m). Taking shuttle boats across the Swiftcurrent and Josephine Lakes cuts 1½mi each way off the hike. Backcountry camping is not possible on this route.

PLANNING
When to Hike

Large snowdrifts normally block the upper Grinnell Glacier Trail at least until early July. The trail remains closed until the manual clearing work is completed. The trail may become dangerously icy after mid-September. This hike is extremely popular, and the trail becomes rather crowded on fine summer days.

Maps

Use the 1:83,930 inset map on Trail Illustrated's general *Glacier/Waterton National Park*, or the USGS 1:24,000 *Many Glacier* quad.

GETTING TO/FROM THE HIKE

The trailhead is at Swiftcurrent picnic area, roughly 300yd east of the Many Glacier campground. There is a large car park here. An alternative starting-point is Many Glacier Hotel, from where the electric boats run across Swiftcurrent Lake to connect with boats on Lake Josephine.

THE HIKE

The first part of the hike follows the Swiftcurrent Nature Trail through fir-spruce forest quickly across the Swiftcurrent Creek footbridge, then around Swiftcurrent Lake to the upper Swiftcurrent boat dock at its southern shore. (A minor route alternative is to leave from the trailhead car park above Many Glacier Hotel and hike around the eastern side of Swiftcurrent Lake, before skirting right across the Grinnell Creek (inlet) bridge past the upper boat dock.)

A short, paved path lined by corn lilies and thimbleberry bushes brings you to another dock on a serene little pebble beach at the north end of the turquoise **Lake Josephine**. The trail heads around the lake's west side over wildflower meadows of yellow columbines, Indian paintbrush and cinquefoil bushes alternating with slopes of birch scrub and low firs battered by the avalanches that crash into the valley during winter. Sidle steadily up (past a minor turnoff that diagonals down back to the lake shore) to a junction above the southwestern shore of Lake Josephine, 40 to 50 minutes from the trailhead. Note how the lake deepens dramatically beyond the narrow shelf of sediment swept in by the inlet.

Turn right along the Grinnell Glacier Trail (the left turnoff drops to the upper Josephine boat dock just across the inlet footbridge) and begin a winding ascent high above Grinnell Lake. These steep slopes look south toward Piegan Pass and give the first views of the spectacular cirque ahead. The trail traverses the almost sheer mountainside through a splashing waterfall and persistent patches of snow to reach a picnic area with a pit toilet just below treeline. A final climb leads to the moraine-dam wall of **Upper Grinnell Lake**. You are now 1½ to 2¼ hours from the trail turnoff. This dramatic lookout lies below the narrow ice-shelf of The Salamander and the spectacular, fractured Grinnell Glacier; until quite recently these two features were joined together.

Retrace your steps to the trailhead.

Gunsight Pass

Duration	1–2 days
Distance	20mi (32.2km)
Standard	medium-hard
Start	Jackson Glacier Overlook/ Piegan Pass Trail
Finish	Lake McDonald village
Nearest Towns	Apgar/West Glacier, St Mary
Public Transport	yes

Summary The hike over the 6946ft Gunsight Pass in the southern Lewis Range is arguably Glacier's most scenic pass route, with an extensive assortment of snow fields and glaciers and the particularly lovely Lake Ellen Wilson.

This classic east-to-west crossing of the Continental Divide is a shuttle hike involving a gradual but long ascent totaling around 3700ft (1130m) (easiest going east to west). The Gunsight Pass area is real mountain-goat country, and hikers are virtually assured of seeing the animals. The popularity of this hike is lessened by its length, which makes it a rather challenging day hike.

PLANNING
When to Hike

Gunsight Pass normally melts out by mid-July, but before then the trail can be dangerously icy, especially on the northern approach to Gunsight Pass. Watch the sky for approaching electrical storms, a common hazard in summer.

Maps

Three USGS 1:24,000 quads cover the route: *Logan Pass*, *Mount Jackson* and *Lake McDonald East*.

GETTING TO/FROM THE HIKE

The hike starts at the Jackson Glacier Overlook (Piegan Pass Trailhead), roughly 4mi east of Logan Pass on the Going-to-the-Sun Rd, and ends at Lake McDonald Lodge, on the Going-to-the-Sun Rd, 6.8mi from West Glacier. The Hiker Shuttle (see Getting Around earlier in this section) stops at both trailheads.

ROCKY MOUNTAINS

THE HIKE
Day 1: Jackson Glacier Overlook to Sperry Chalet
6–9 hours, 13.4mi (21.6km), 3283ft (1000m) ascent

The Piegan Pass Trail cuts down southeast through fir-spruce forest to meet Reynolds Creek, following it downstream past Deadwood Falls to reach a trail junction after 25 to 30 minutes. Here, take the (right) Gunsight Pass Trail leading directly over a sturdy footbridge past **Reynolds Creek campground** (two sites with fireplaces). Head southwest along the northern side of the St Mary River, which flows through waterlogged meadows and small beaver ponds past the 0.6mi (right) turnoff to Florence Falls, a cascade that drops in several stages.

Continue upvalley below the sheer walls of Citadel Mountain and Fusillade Mountain through avalanche clearings of thimbleberry shrubs and pearly everlastings. There are fine views across to the half-dozen glaciers clinging to the high ridge between Blackfoot Mountain and Mt Jackson as you pass **Gunsight Lake campground** (seven sites) a short way before reaching Gunsight Lake, 1¾ to 2½ hours from Reynolds Creek.

Cross the lake outlet (St Mary River) on a suspension bridge to pass a rough turnoff that leads left (south) to the base of **Jackson Glacier**, then begin the ascent in numerous switchbacks through chest-high cow parsnip and alder shrubs. The reassuringly broad and well constructed trail makes a winding upward traverse via cliff ledges high above the lake, and opposite interesting folded ripples in the multicolored rock strata on Gunsight Mountain, to arrive at **Gunsight Pass** (6946ft) after two to three hours. A basic, emergency stone shelter (day-use only) stands on this narrow, high saddle.

Drop in steep switchbacks almost to the north shore of **Lake Ellen Wilson** (5929ft), a spectacular alpine lake lying in a deep trough ringed by sheer, glaciated rock walls. The trail continues around the lake's western shore over grouseberry meadows, passing above **Lake Ellen Wilson campground** (four sites). Skirt diagonally up the slope to a high shelf of glacier-scratched slabs overlooking

Lincoln Lake. The trail turns gradually west to cross the highest point of the hike, **Lincoln Pass** (7050ft), just north of Lincoln Peak, then winds its way down past **Sperry campground**, 1½ to 2½ hours from Gunsight Pass. There are four scenic sites here on a bench overlooking Lake McDonald far below. Mountain goats regularly visit the camp, so always use the pit toilet. (Water taken from the stagnant pond here should be treated.)

The trail leads after five to 10 minutes to the historic **Sperry Chalet** (open 1 July to mid-September), several stone buildings dating from 1913. After closing for some years (due to waste-disposal problems), the chalet reopened in 1998. Rooms cost $150/240 for one/two persons. The chalet is run by Belton Chalets Inc (☎ 406-387-5654, PO Box 188 West Glacier, MT 59936).

Day 2: Sperry Chalet to Lake McDonald Lodge
2¼–3 hours, 6.4mi (10.3km)

Drop quickly past the Sperry Glacier Trail (see Side Trip) across the small Sprague Creek. The trail leads down into fir-spruce forest scattered with columbines past Beaver Medicine Falls, continuing 2½mi downvalley mostly well above the creek to cross Snyder Creek on a footbridge at the so-called Crystal Ford. Pass in quick succession turnoffs (left) to Fish Lake, (right) to Snyder Lakes, where there is a scenic backcountry **campground**, then (right) to Mt Brown Lookout. The trail descends through mossy montane forest rich in cedar, hemlock, grand fir, larch and yew to reach the Going-to-the-Sun Rd just above the upmarket **Lake McDonald Lodge**.

Side Trip: Sperry Glacier Overlook
3½–5½ hours, 7½mi (12.1km), 1615ft (492m) ascent

From the turnoff below Sperry Chalet, follow the Sperry Glacier Trail up into the heavily glaciated upper valley of Sprague Creek. The often steep trail ascends past Akaiyan Falls, Feather Woman Lake and Akaiyan Lake, before climbing a stairway blasted into the cliff face to reach Comeau Pass overlooking **Sperry Glacier**. Cairns lead on to melt-water tarns at the edge of the glacier, from where a mountaineers' route continues north along the range to **Hidden Lake**, itself accessible via a highly popular trail from Logan Pass.

Bob Marshall Wilderness

Named in honor of Robert Marshall, one of America's greatest advocates of wilderness protection, the 1,009,356-acre Bob Marshall Wilderness of northwestern Montana straddles the Continental Divide, taking in the headwaters of the Flathead River to its west and the Sun River to its east. Two smaller wilderness areas adjoin the 'Bob': the Great Bear Wilderness bordering on Glacier National Park to the north, and the Scapegoat Wilderness in the south. Together they form the largest contiguous tract of officially gazetted wilderness in the lower 48 states.

NATURAL HISTORY
The Bob is dissected by massive, tilted limestone escarpments running north to south, of which the finest example is the Chinese Wall. Mountain goats and bighorn sheep find shelter in these inaccessible precipices. Grizzly bears in the Bob communicate with populations in the adjoining Glacier National Park, though the local black bears, which tend to be large and brownish in color, are often mistaken for grizzlies. Other important wildlife species are wolverines, deer, elk, moose and mountain lions. The Bob Marshall country is an important habitat for the grayish-blue and chestnut harlequin duck, which winters on the Pacific coast but breeds along the fast-flowing streams, where it feeds on insect larvae.

Permits & Regulations
Permits are not required for overnight hikes in Bob Marshall Wilderness. Anglers will need a Montana fishing license. Camping is not allowed within 100ft of waterways or 200ft of trails. The popular, high-level trail along the base of the Chinese Wall featured

here leads through a sensitive alpine environment and is closed to camping. Hikers should plan to camp on the sections before and after the Chinese Wall.

NEAREST TOWNS & FACILITIES
Augusta
This pleasant if unexiting little town south of Choteau at the junction of US Hwy 287 and Montana Hwy 21 is the eastern gateway to Bob Marshall Wilderness. The USFS office (☎ 406-562-3247), 405 Manix St, Box 365, Augusta, MT 59410, is open daily in summer and sells maps (check here about possible fire warnings). There is also a chamber of commerce (☎ 406-562-3493).

Augusta is 26mi south of Choteau and 53mi west (via Vaughn and Simms) of Great Falls. Driving from Helena, follow I-15 north 2mi past Wolf Creek, then turn off north along Hwy 287.

Campgrounds
There are two basic USFS campgrounds at Benchmark: *South Fork Sun* ($6, 15 sites), at the trailhead, and *Benchmark* ($5, 18 sites), 1mi farther back. The USFS *Wood Lake campground* ($5, 10 sites), 6.2mi before the trailhead, is also very attractive. These campgrounds fill quickly on weekends in July and August.

Chinese Wall Loop

Duration	5–7 days
Distance	60mi (96.6km)
Standard	medium
Start/Finish	Benchmark
Nearest Town	Augusta
Public Transport	no

Summary This hike circumnavigates Bob's most striking geological formation, the Chinese Wall, a 1000ft-high tilted limestone escarpment extending some 22mi along the Continental Divide.

This long hike crosses the Continental Divide at the north and south ends of the Chinese Wall, and its highlight is the exhilarating, high-level trail along the base of the wall itself. With the exception of the

ROCKY MOUNTAINS

long ascent to White River Pass, gradients are fairly unchallenging, but the trail is often badly chewed up due to (excessive) horse traffic. Grizzlies roam the Bob backcountry, so stay alert.

PLANNING
When to Hike
Hiking in the Bob can be rather hot in July and August. In summer hikers will also encounter numerous (often large) horseback-riding parties. Trails can be appallingly boggy in June.

Maps
The large-format 1:100,000 USFS map *Bob Marshall, Great Bear and Scapegoat Wilderness Complex* covers the entire area; note that contours are shown in metric measurements. Six USGS 1:24,000 quads also cover the hike: *Benchmark* (optional), *Pretty Prairie*, *Prairie Reef*, *Slategoat Mountain*, *Amphitheatre Mountain* and *Haystack Mountain*.

GETTING TO/FROM THE HIKE
The hike begins and ends at Benchmark, 31mi from Augusta (see Nearest Towns). Take the road to the Nilan Reservoir then continue west.

THE HIKE
Day 1: Benchmark to Indian Point Meadows
3½–4½ hours, 10.3mi (16.5km)
Follow the initially broad Sun River Trail from the *South Fork Sun campground* quickly across a sturdy pack bridge over the South Fork Sun River (a summer nesting site for harlequin ducks) to intersect with a trail diverging left. Proceed right (downstream) well above the river through mixed forest of mostly lodgepole pine, Douglas fir and Engelmann spruce dotted with purple lupines, yellow groundsels and low huckleberry brush. The often muddy trail crosses the wilderness boundary (register trip details here) and passes the Bighead Creek Trail turnoff before it swings west through dry clearings to cross the West Fork Sun River on another pack bridge.

Pick up the West Fork Sun River Trail at the junction on the river's north bank and continue left (west) across Wapiti Creek. The crags of Nineteen Ridge emerge up to your left as you head over moist, riverside meadows of yellow cinquefoils and pink wild roses alternating with drier slopes of sagebrush and Rocky Mountain juniper. The trail passes pleasant *campsites* among the trees on the left as the rusty ridges of Red Butte (8590ft) come into view ahead. A gentle climb through thickets of regenerating lodgepoles brings you to the Prairie Reef Fire Lookout Trail (see Side Trip), three to four hours from Benchmark. Here, a well-worn path also leads down left to attractive *campsites* on the sunny river flats of the West Fork.

The trail continues on a further 20 to 30 minutes through forest and grassy river flats to the Camp Creek Pass Trail turnoff at In-dian Point Meadows. There are good *campsites* here for hiking parties but stock are not allowed in the meadows.

Side Trip: Prairie Reef Fire Lookout
3½–4½ hours, 4.8mi (7.7km),
3482ft (1061m) ascent
The day hike up to the USFS fire lookout atop the limestone summit known as Prairie Reef – the highest point in Bob Marshall Wilderness accessible by trail – is strenuous but highly rewarding. Carry plenty of water, as none is normally available en route.

Climb steeply to wildflower terraces overlooking the West Fork valley, then sidle northwest over rocky meadows and through fir-spruce forest. The views open out steadily as you get higher, and after crossing the (usually dry) bed of White Bear Creek the trail comes into a minor saddle. A steep ascent brings you out of the stunted limber pines, from where a final, gentler climb across rocky tundra slopes sprinkled with mountain buttercups and globeflowers leads to the **Prairie Reef fire lookout** (8858ft), two to three hours from the turnoff. The superb panorama takes in the highest summits of the Bob Marshall country and associated ranges, and the view of the white outline of the adjacent Chinese

Wall is particularly impressive. The lookout is staffed (in summer only) by a friendly USFS warden who enjoys the intermittent visits of day hikers.

Day 2: Indian Point Meadows to Chinese Wall

3½–4½ hours, 8.1mi (13km), 975ft (298m) ascent

Make your way over a small stream, where the USFS Indian Point guard station can be seen just up to the right, to meet the intersecting White River Pass Trail. There are more good *campsites* here. Proceed right (north) and follow the often boggy trail through riverside forest scattered with blue gentians. The trail crosses Black Bear Creek and No Name Gulch before fording the West Fork, 1¾ to 2¼ hours from Indian Point Meadows. In summer this is a quite shallow wade, but a makeshift log bridge can be found 10yd upstream. There are a few damp *campsites* on the eastern bank.

Continue 1mi along the west bank of the river before recrossing and following Burnt Creek, its headwater tributary. The trail gradually steepens as it crosses the creek and turns west, making a second crossing before it climbs through limber pine and subalpine fir onto beautiful, flowery meadows under the spectacular towering face of the **Chinese Wall**. There are scenic *campsites* scattered among the trees here, just before the (signposted) start of the no-camping zone.

Alternative Campsites

Good campsites can also be found along much of the upper West Fork and Burnt Creek.

Day 3: Chinese Wall to Brushy Park (Upper White River)

4¾–6¼ hours, 12mi (19km), 908ft (276m) ascent

Head gently up through the trees to a saddle on a ridge buttressing Cliff Mountain. This point offers marvellous views along the escarpment in both directions, and you also get a different perspective on Prairie Reef across the valley. The trail drops down through fir and whitebark pine to cross the

The spectacular limestone escarpment known as the Chinese Wall, Bob Marshall Wilderness, Rocky Mountains, Montana.

ROCKY MOUNTAINS

CLEM LINDENMAYER

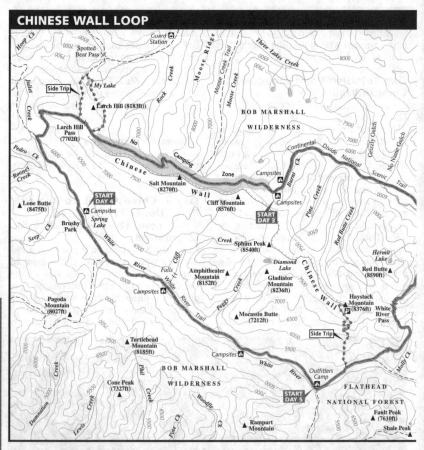

CHINESE WALL LOOP

outlet of a long, shallow tarn, then continues over lovely alpine meadows under the towering precipices. Seepage springs emerge from the rubbly cliff base, where colonies of whistling marmots shelter. Higher up are picturesque isolated clumps of stunted trees clinging to narrow terraces between the bluffs. After one to 1½ hours you meet the intersecting Moose Creek Trail.

Head north over a ridge crest coming off Salt Mountain, before dipping into the upper valley head of Rock Creek. The trail sidles up steeper slopes above the creek's northern tributaries, from where there are good views west toward the Sawtooth Range. After rising over two more low grassy crests, the trail makes a steeper ascent through spruce forest to intersect with the Spotted Bear Pass Trail (see Side Trip). Head left here and climb on briefly to reach **Larch Hill Pass** (7702ft), 1¾ to 2¼ hours from the Moose Creek Trail junction. The pass, which marks the northern extent of the Chinese Wall, gives a first view northwest to the snow-capped Silvertip Mountain and (a few paces down) southwest to Pagoda Mountain.

CHINESE WALL LOOP

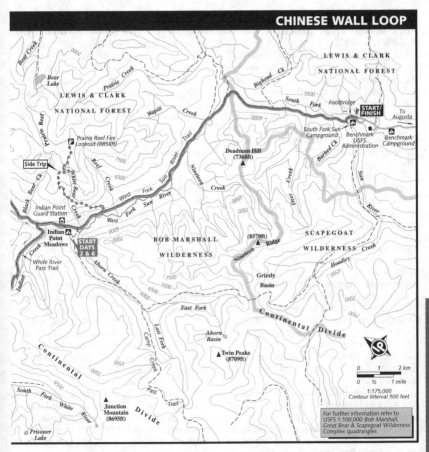

For further information refer to
USFS 1:100,000 *Bob Marshall,
Great Bear & Scapegoat Wilderness
Complex* quadrangles

1:175,000
Contour Interval 500 feet

Cut down northwest onto open, fire-cleared ridge tops past a second trail turnoff to Spotted Bear Pass, then wind your way down into the lodgepole forest to join the White River Trail on the banks of Juliet Creek. Turn left and proceed south through narrow clearings beside the (usually dry) gravelly creek bed into an extended strip of forest burnt in the mid-1990s. Up to your right, idyllic alpine lawns on Lone Butte contrast with the starkness of the charred trees. The trail fords the **White River** by a small grassy pasture, where there are good *campsites* at the edge of the spruce forest,

then crosses channels of the river as it passes through the string of meadows known as **Brushy Park**, two to 2½ hours from the pass. Hummingbirds flutter around the many good *campsites* here.

Side Trip to My Lake
1½–2 hours, 5mi (8km)
The attractive My Lake is reached from the trail junction below Larch Hill Pass. Take the Spotted Bear Pass Trail up around the eastern side of Larch Hill to a minor saddle, then descend northeast. My Lake is closed to camping due to past overuse.

Day 4: Brushy Park to South Fork White River Junction

3½–4¾ hours, 10½mi (17km)

Head downvalley through intact fir-spruce forest. The tracks of bears and other animals that frequent this more isolated part of the valley show up on the often muddy trail, which descends only slightly as it passes the Pagoda Mountain Trail turnoff and skirts a shallow, marshy lake. The trail fords the cold, knee-deep river at some *campsites* on its stony western bank, 1¼ to 1½ hours from Brushy Park.

Continue down along the white-pebbled, meandering river through flowery herbfields in the lodgepole forest, which would make ideal *campsites*. Note as you go how the direction of tilt on the eastern side of the valley – part of the so-called White River Syncline – is opposite to that of the surrounding ranges. The rock strata lean downward into the valley, so there is no escarpment. The trail skirts the reedy Oasis Pond to cross Peggy Creek, then climbs past swirling pools to reach a scenic overlook high above the river, 1½ to two hours from the ford. Here, the thundering **Needle Falls** flow beneath a natural rock bridge before plummeting 100ft into a pool in the ravine far below. There is also a good view south along the valley toward Fault Peak.

Descend gradually through Douglas fir and Rocky Mountain juniper. After meeting the river again the trail follows the west bank – one of the best fishing spots in Montana – to reach an intersection at the much smaller **South Fork White River**, 50 minutes to 1¼ hours on. The large horse-outfitters' encampment here between the two forks is occupied throughout the summer. There are also *campsites* along on the forested flats of the White River.

Day 5: South Fork White River Junction to Indian Point Meadows

4–5¼ hours, 9.3 mi (14.5km), 2180ft (664m) ascent

Turn left along the White River Pass Trail and climb steadily east into the wild South Fork valley past the Haystack Mountain Trail turnoff (see Side Trip). The trail continues high above the steep-sided gulch through lodgepole and Douglas fir past another turnoff, where the (largely disused) South Fork White River Trail goes off right. Ascend on left in steep switchbacks, before sidling up southeast into the tiny valley head of Molly Creek. There are scenic *campsites* among fir-spruce forest on the south bank.

The trail rises gently along the creek's north bank, then begins a steep winding climb northeast over fire-denuded slopes that lead up to a saddle. Take a last look southwest to the Flathead Alps before cutting right around the slope into the rocky gully that is **White River Pass** (7626ft), 2¼ to three hours from the trail junction at White River. The pass offers a sudden view of tilted limestone crags ahead and a final glimpse of Silvertip Mountain to the northwest.

The trail drops left into the upper valley of Indian Creek. Here, semi-sheltered *campsites* can be found among the regenerating subalpine firs and whitebark pines, where boisterous Clark's nutcrackers, a black and white jay, can sometimes be seen (or heard). A side trail detours a half-mile north up to the small saddle overlooking the wild upper valley of Red Butte Creek.

Cross the tiny Indian Creek and follow its north bank down through heath and wildflower meadows past a waterfall splashing down over the trail from the red mudstone slopes. As the valley broadens, the trail dips into lodgepole forest and passes several more streamside *campsites* to ford the West Fork Sun River in a knee-high wade, 1¾ to 2¼ hours from White River Pass. Climb the embankment to rejoin the West Fork Sun River Trail a half-mile north of Indian Point guard station (see Day 2).

Side Trip: Haystack Mountain

3–4 hours, 6½mi (10.5km), 3631ft (1106m) ascent

The 8376ft Haystack Mountain is the best lookout point for the Chinese Wall. From the South Fork turnoff, the trail climbs steeply northwest in numerous switchbacks

Rocky Mountains splendor. Top Left: Spectacular craggy peaks of Bitterroot Wilderness, Montana.
Top Right: Subalpine spiraea produce flat-topped clusters of deep-pink flowers, Glacier National Park, Montana. **Middle Right:** Scarlet paintbrush, Wyoming's floral emblem, Glacier National Park.
Bottom: Teton Range, Grand Teton National Park, Wyoming – one of the Rockies' most striking ranges.

CLEM LINDENMAYER

CLEMLINDENMAYER

CLEMLINDENMAYER

JOHN ELK III

Top Left: Open, grassy valleys fringed by stands of lodgepole pine, Yellowstone National Park.
Top Right: Swiftcurrent Lake and Mt Grinnell, Glacier National Park. **Middle:** Cooling off at Swiftcurrent Pass, Glacier National Park. **Bottom Left:** A stand of trembling aspen in Collegiate Peaks Wilderness, Colorado. **Bottom Right:** Sunlight (left) and Windom Peaks, Weminuche Wilderness, Montana.

out of the lodgepoles and up the open western slopes of Haystack Mountain, before cutting southeast to gain the summit. From here the views stretching along the mighty escarpment are quite breathtaking.

Day 6: Indian Point Meadows to Benchmark
3½–4½ hours, 10.3mi (16.5km)
This final stage is Day 1 in reverse.

Absaroka-Beartooth Wilderness

The 1475-sq-mi (943,377-acre) Absaroka-Beartooth Wilderness stretches along Montana's southern border with Wyoming – a small section on its eastern side lies inside Wyoming – in the Gallatin, Custer and Shoshone National Forests. The wilderness area takes in two distinct mountain ranges, the Absarokas and the Beartooth Plateau (the 'Beartooths'). The Absarokas are characterized by steep, forested valleys and craggy peaks, while the Beartooths are essentially high plateaus dotted with more than a thousand lakes and tarns. The Absaroka-Beartooth offers a solitude and serenity less easily found in other wilderness areas of the Rockies.

NATURAL HISTORY
The Beartooths are composed of ancient uplifted granite some 3 billion years old. Most of the wilderness is rock and ice or high plateau above 10,000ft – an 'arctic' type of environment where the vegetation and wildlife depend on a comparatively short growing season. Low forests of Engelmann spruce scattered with subalpine fir cover the less elevated valleys, with limber pine in more exposed places higher up. Grizzly and black bears are not common in the wilderness, but hikers have a better chance of seeing bighorn sheep, mountain goats or elk. The Beartooths are a paradise for anglers, with brook, cutthroat, golden, lake and rainbow trout abounding in the countless streams and rivers and almost 1000 lakes.

Permits & Regulations
Permits are not required to hike in the Absaroka-Beartooth Wilderness. In order to protect the fragile alpine vegetation, however, hikers should not light campfires above treeline (and preferably not at all). Note that the southern area of the wilderness is part of a grizzly bear management zone, and – although bears rarely venture into the higher country – encounters with grizzlies occasionally occur.

Maps
The contoured USFS map *Absaroka-Beartooth Wilderness* ($9.75) at 1:63,360 covers the whole wilderness and is adequate for most hikes.

NEAREST TOWNS & FACILITIES
Red Lodge
This quaint mining town is at the northern end of the scenic Beartooth Hwy (Hwy 212) in southern Montana. The chamber of commerce (☎ 406-446-1718) is at 601 N Broadway Ave. Silver Peak Mountain Shoppe on N Broadway Ave sells backpacking gear and some maps, but USGS quads are available only at Red Lodge Office Supply, 12 N Broadway Ave. The USFS office (☎ 406-446-2103), 3mi south of town on Hwy 212, is open daily in summer. *Perry's campground* (☎ 406-446-2722), 2mi south of town on Hwy 212, has sites with facilities for $10.

Cooke City
This small, isolated town lies on Hwy 212 near the northeastern entrance to Yellowstone National Park. The general store sells topographical maps. The *Yellowstone Yurt Hostel* (☎ 800-364-6242) has dormitory accommodations ($12) and the *High Country Motel* (☎ 406-838-2272) offers rooms from $38.

Along Beartooth Hwy
The basic USFS *Island Lake campground* has campsites for $9. The *Top of the World Motel* (☎ 307-899-2482), 1mi east of the Island Lake turnoff on the Beartooth Hwy, offers rooms for $30 but has only RV sites.

Beartooth High Lakes

Duration	4 days
Distance	35½mi (57km)
Standard	easy-medium
Start/Finish	Island Lake
Nearest Towns	Red Lodge, Cooke City
Public Transport	no

Summary This hike leads from the gentle lake landscape of the southern Beartooth Plateau into the interesting and extraordinarily varied raw terrain around the intensely glaciated peaks on the Continental Divide. An adventurous route for hikers who are well acclimatized.

This is a loop hike through a glaciated, high-alpine landscape dotted with lakes. Waymarkings and signposts are unreliable, numerous unofficial trails exist and off-trail (side) trips are easy. Hikers should be acclimatized to the high altitude. The first section of the route to Becker Lake (perhaps even as far as Albino Lake) makes an excellent, easy roundtrip day hike with gentle gradients ideal for children.

PLANNING
When to Hike
The Beartooths hiking season is very short. Snow is likely to be encountered in many places above treeline at least until the end of July, and starts to accumulate again after mid-September. Remember that localized afternoon thunderstorms with hail are common in the Beartooths during summer.

Maps
Recommended are two 1:67,000 waterproof hiking maps published by Rocky Mountain Surveys: *Wyoming Beartooths* and *Alpine–Mount Maurice* (or, if the latter is unavailable, *Alpine/Cooke City*) – $7.50 each. Four USGS 1:24,000 quads also cover the hiking route: *Beartooth Butte*, *Silver Run Peak*, *Castle Mountain* and *Muddy Creek*.

GETTING TO/FROM THE HIKE
The trailhead is at Island Lake, 38mi from Red Lodge (or is 3.7mi west of Beartooth Pass) along the scenic Beartooth Hwy (US

212). There is trailhead parking on the east side of the boat ramp for around 50 vehicles (the $3 day-use fee for Island Lake Recreational Center does not apply to hikers).

The Red Lodge Shuttle (☎ 406-446-2257, 888-446-2191) runs a service from Red Lodge to Billings and Cody, Wyoming, and taxis hikers to trailheads.

THE HIKE
Day 1: Island Lake to Becker Lake
1½–2 hours, 3.6mi (5.8km)
Follow the Beartooth High Lakes Trail over fields of purple fleabane and yellow asters at the western shores of Island Lake and Night Lake. The trail continues northwest across a minor watershed and on past reedy tarns and **Flake Lake**, where an inlet stream splashes down over polished pink slabs. There are enticing views toward the interesting, flat-topped ranges ahead as you rise gently over grassy meadows to an unsignposted trail junction by some boggy ponds, one to 1¼ hours from the trailhead.

Take the right-hand turnoff (not shown on USFS maps as it is not an official trail) and head north between Jeff Lake and Mutt Lake, crossing the short outlet/inlet on stepping stones. The trail skirts marshy grassland on Jeff Lake's northern shore, before climbing on over a slight crest to reach **Becker Lake**, 30 to 40 minutes from the turnoff. Walking pads lead off left down to a tiny peninsula with *campsites* on grassy lawns. Boulders left by ancient glaciers ('erratic boulders') lie stranded among smooth granite slabs around the shore and sheer cliffs drop 150ft directly into the lake's western side.

Alternative Campsites
Camping is possible along most of Day 1, including the forested terraces just across the inlet to Jeff Lake.

Day 2: Becker Lake to Wright Lake (Junction Trail 619)
3½–4½ hours, 7½mi (12km), 1777ft (541m) ascent
Head around the eastern side of Becker Lake past several more *campsites* in the low

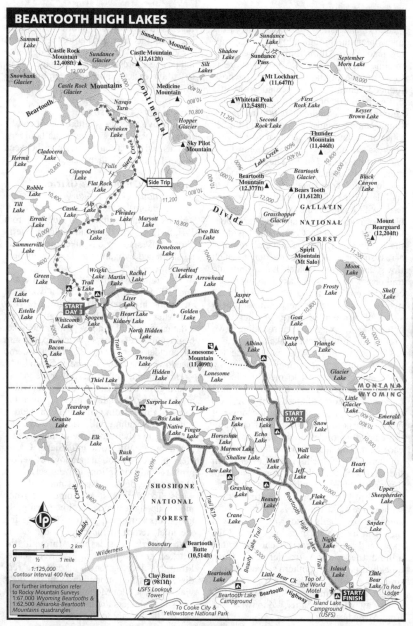

BEARTOOTH HIGH LAKES

ROCKY MOUNTAINS

forest. The trail cuts north across tundra meadows and follows the east bank of the inlet stream up through a lovely grassy valley leading to Albino Lake, at the upper treeline. Rising from its western shore is Lonesome Mountain (11,409ft), whose rounded summit can be scaled with little difficulty via its broad southern ridge (one hour roundtrip). Sheltered *campsites* can be found among stands of spruce and limber pines at the lake's southeastern corner.

Cross the outlet just below Albino Lake and skirt its western shore. The trail ascends more steeply to an almost bare, rocky saddle overlooking **Jasper Lake**, a deep trough in a stark landscape of glacier-polished slabs littered with boulders and other moraine rubble. Beartooth Mountain and the Bears Tooth jut up from behind the Continental Divide to the northeast. Drop for several minutes across stepping stones over the outlet, which flows directly into Golden Lake, until the trail peters out at Jasper Lake's northwestern corner. From here a vague route darts west over a rocky ridge to reach the southern shore of **Arrowhead Lake**, another deep alpine lake in raw, glacial surroundings, two to 2½ hours from Becker Lake.

Cut down left (southwest) beside the trickling outlet then through a dry, rocky gully that curves west to meet the lovely **Cloverleaf Lakes**. A faint trail leads around the southern shores of these deep-blue lakes over bouldery talus and moist meadows of marsh marigolds. Follow the left bank of the cascading outlet down past small escarpments, then around the waterlogged southern side of **Rachel Lake**. Lower down the stream flows subterraneously beneath dry rock rubble, allowing an easy crossing just before you descend to **Martin Lake**, a picturesque sight with its island hillock. In summer, bluebells and yellow arnicas bloom in the watery meadows around the inlet, and good *campsites* can be found around the lake. A trodden trail leads quickly around the southern shores of Martin Lake and the smaller, almost adjoining Wright Lake to intersect with Trail 619 a short way below the outlet, 1½ to two hours from Arrowhead Lake.

A (30 minute) alternative from Martin Lake is to take a rough shortcut trail leading around its northern shore, then up west through a small grassy gap before descending beside a forested streamlet to meet Trail 619 at the eastern shore of Green Lake (see Side Trip).

Alternative Campsites
Even above treeline, sheltered sites can be found in many places among the boulders, such as at the pleasant alpine lawns between Jasper Lake and Golden Lake.

Side Trip: Castle Rock Glacier
5½–7½ hours, 15mi (24km),
1770ft (539m) ascent
This excellent medium-hard side trip from Wright Lake into the headwaters of Sierra Creek makes a long day hike; the days can be shortened by camping almost anywhere along the way.

The trail crosses the Wright Lake outlet and climbs northwest above a waterfall streaming into Spogen Lake down to your left. After rising to the tranquil Trail Lake, on a flattened ridge high above Whitcomb Lake, begin a gradually steeper descent past a tarn on boulder-strewn slopes to reach a damp meadow on the eastern shore of Green Lake.

Head around to the start of some grassy clearings on Green Lake's north side, where an (unsignposted) trail cuts up over the forested ridge; from here you get a fleeting glimpse of Summerville Lake, before descending to where the lake outlet splashes down the granite rock into Sierra Creek. Head upstream through meadows of yellow arnicas and dandelion-like agoseris past Queer Lake below glacier-smoothed rock walls. To avoid a small gorge, the route moves up right through a tiny, open gully and steers left to Alp Lake. After crossing the inlet, return to the creek and head up past waterfalls splashing through the cracked granite to reach **Flat Rock Lake**. From this deep, greenish lake among reddish, scree-filled mountains you get clear views of Sky Pilot Mountain up to the right and small glaciers around Castle Mountain (12,612ft) directly to the north.

Head past the whale-shaped island on the lake's eastern side, then cut across flowery meadows and follow the rubble-choked gully of the inlet stream to Forsaken Lake (shown on USFS maps as Varve Lake). This stark lake lies just below the upper vegetation line and is surrounded by craggy ranges. Trace the forsaken eastern shore, then ascend steeply beside its (main) inlet to make an icy ford just below where the gushing stream leaves the turgid, turquoise Navajo Tarn. After skirting around the tarn's irregular shore, a short, steep climb over raw moraines, fine glacial mud and lingering snowdrifts brings you up to **Castle Rock Glacier**, which slides smoothly down into a large meltwater pool from below Castle Rock Mountain (12,408ft) on the Continental Divide.

Return to Wright Lake by the same route.

Day 3: Wright Lake to Island Lake

5¼–6½ hours, 9½mi (15.3km), 420ft (128m) ascent

From halfway around Wright Lake, the trail climbs southeast past Kidney Lake onto an undulating granite plateau, granting excellent full views north to the glaciers and flat-topped summits of the Beartooth Mountains. The trail picks its way past tarns in this interesting glaciated landscape high above Heidi and Granite Lakes. The fin-like summits around Pilot Peak (11,699ft) fall abruptly into the Yellowstone Valley to the southwest, beginning an arc of other jagged ranges that stretch along the southern horizon.

The often badly eroded trail winds down through fir-spruce forest carpeted with shin-high grouseberry shrubs. Continue high above Thiel Lake before dropping to cross several inlet channels flowing into Mule Lake at an attractive grassy meadow. The trail heads up past sporadic tarns to **Surprise Lake**, ascending high above Box Lake and past the slimy-green Native Lake to reach a broad, boulder-strewn saddle at the northern foot of the impressively craggy rock ridge marking the wilderness exit point, 2½ to three hours from Wright Lake. A signposted turnoff leads southwest to Clay

Butte (where a staffed USFS lookout tower is open to the public).

Walk south down open hillsides of pink asters to a turnoff (signposted 'Island Lake') below the castle-like formations (Trail 619 continues ahead to Beartooth Lake.) The turnoff trail leads northeast through bouldery woods to intersect with the Beartooth High Lakes Trail above the beautiful **Horseshoe** and **Finger Lakes**; scenic *campsites* exist on the moraine bar separating the lakes. (There is also a rough shortcut to Horseshoe Lake going east across the largely open, glaciated terrain from the saddle.) Sidle down over grassy slopes of shrub willows and yellow arnicas above Marmot Lake and Shallow Lake.

The trail crosses the stream where it enters Claw Lake, then leaves this charming valley as it rises and dips over low forested ridges and stream gullies to reach Beauty Lake. Cross the twin inlets on stepping stones to a turnoff, where the Beauty Lake Trail departs southward to Beartooth Lake on the Beartooth Hwy, then make a short, steep ascent east to arrive back at the junction with the Becker Lake turnoff, 1¾ to 2¼ hours from the saddle above Native Lake. Retrace your steps from Day 1 to reach Island Lake in a further 50 minutes to 1¼ hours.

Alternative Campsites

Camping is possible almost anywhere along Day 3, but good campsites can also be found on the eastern side of Surprise Lake, near the trail high above Box Lake, on the southwestern shore of Claw Lake, and around the Beauty Lake outlet or along the Beauty Lake Trail.

Yellowstone National Park

NATURAL HISTORY

Some 80% of the Yellowstone is forested. Lodgepole pine is easily the most widespread tree species, largely due to the high silica content of the common (volcanic) rhyolite rock, which breaks down into infertile soils unfavorable to other species. Lodge-pole has also benefited from periodic forest fires, which kill off more sensitive species. Subalpine fir and Engelmann spruce forest covers the higher ranges, especially in the park's moister southwestern quarter, where Colorado blue spruce is also present.

Around 60% of Yellowstone's forest was destroyed or damaged in the catastrophic fires of 1988, which left behind vast areas of charred trees. Although fire is a natural process in Rocky Mountain ecosystems, the shocking severity of the 1988 fires was due to the park's (now defunct) policy of fighting all fires regardless of their cause and extent. This allowed a dangerous overabundance of combustible material to build up in Yellow-stone's forests. The forest's gradual regener-ation – still scarcely evident in some areas – is being studied by biologists.

Having been protected from human hunters for well over 100 years, Yellow-stone's wildlife is less wary of people than elsewhere in the Rockies. Yellowstone has the Rockies' largest numbers of bison and elk, and herds of these muscular animals graze in the grassy valleys. Bull elk gather on lower ridges in the rutting season, when their bugling calls resonate through the mountains as they challenge far-off rivals. In winter bison and elk often leave the park in search of food, and many are killed by ranchers fearing they will infect their cattle with brucellosis, a bovine disease carried by the animals. Moose frequent bogs and shal-low lakes; each year the solitary males grow massive antlers (weighing 100lb or more) purely to impress the moose cows during mating season (fall).

Wolves were reintroduced in the mid-1990s (having previously been eradicated by the NPS). Although biologists believed this would reestablish natural controls on the high numbers of elk, which had created an imbalance in the Yellowstone ecosystem, there has (still) been no significant impact on Yellowstone's elk population. Coyote num-bers have declined, however, as wolves force them back into a more typical scavenging role. At times wolves take sheep and cattle from neighboring ranches and – although livestock producers are compensated for such losses – many locals continue to oppose the spread of wolves.

Yellowstone's large number of mammals ensures plenty of carrion for scavenging black-billed magpies, easily identified by their shiny greenish-black backs and strik-ingly long black tails. The 'common or gar-den' American robin – actually an adaptable thrush species, found throughout the Rock-ies – often overwinters around the park's hot springs.

Yellowstone's lakes and streams contain five species of trout, plus mountain white-fish and grayling. Biologists are concerned about the recent (illegal) introduction of the lake trout into Yellowstone Lake, one of the last sanctuaries for the native Yellowstone cutthroat trout. Competition and predation from this aggressive species has already caused an alarming decline in the numbers of cutthroat trout, which in turn provide food in spring for threatened grizzly bears and bald eagles as well as many other predators.

PLANNING
Maps
Trails Illustrated's *Yellowstone National Park*, scaled at 1:168,500, covers the whole park in a single sheet, but is less than ideal for hiking. See the Maps sections for the in-dividual hikes.

Permits & Regulations
Park entry fees (valid seven days) are $20 for private vehicles, $15 for motorcycles (one person only) and $10 for individuals on foot or bicycle.

Backcountry permits are required for all overnight trips in Yellowstone. Backcountry

WARNING

Bathing in natural hot pools not only carries the risk of scalding burns, but is not permitted in the park except for at the following three sites: Boiling River (between Gardiner and Mammoth), Madison Hot Pot (near Madison) and Ferris Fork (on the Bechler River).

Grizzly & Black Bears

Perhaps the ultimate symbol of American wilderness, grizzly bears were once widespread throughout western North America. Within the lower 48 states, grizzlies are now largely confined to the northern Rocky Mountains between Glacier and Yellowstone National Parks. Black bears are more adaptable than grizzlies, and remain fairly common throughout much of the USA. Grizzlies can be distinguished from black bears by their prominent shoulder hump, long claws, and broad, dish-shaped face. Color is not a reliable indicator – black bears can have pale brown coats, and grizzlies can be quite dark.

Grizzly bears are by nature shy of humans, but may become aggressive if suddenly encountered at close range. Female grizzlies with cubs are likely to charge anyone who gets too close. Always stay alert and make plenty of noise on the trail and never hike after dusk. (Many hikers carry pepper sprays – containing the severe irritant oleoresin capsicum – as a defense, although their effectiveness has been questioned.) Bears have an acute sense of smell and can best catch your scent when you are upwind of them.

Bears very often 'bluff charge' an intruder – veering away at the last instant – but if an attack does ensue, do not resist. Lie down and pull your knees against your chest, and (if not wearing a large backpack) pull in your head and shield your neck with your hands. Remain as quiet and motionless as possible (even if clawed or bitten). In most cases bears will eventually leave the scene once assured that you present no danger.

Bears are obsessed with food, and rarely 'unlearn' knowledge acquired in finding it. In the past, bears were regularly fed (often as a spectacle for tourists) and allowed to pick over garbage dumps. Conditioned to associate humans with food, large numbers of these so-called 'habituated' bears harassed picnickers or aggressively raided camps. Some grizzlies even began to prey on people – in a few chilling cases, sleeping campers were dragged from their tents. Such behavior, quite atypical for wild grizzly bears, is the ultimate consequence of habituation.

Nowadays, even mildly troublesome bears are destroyed. For their own welfare, bears must be prevented from eating any kind of human food. See the Facts for the Hiker and Health & Safety chapters for more important advice about bears; the boxed text 'The Counter-balance Method' on page 87 describes the essential practice of hanging food.

permits are free, unless you book more than 48 hours in advance (when a fee of $15 is payable). There are backcountry offices at: Bridge Bay, Canyon, Grant Village, Lake Village, Mammoth, Old Faithful and South Entrance. Reservations are accepted by mail to Backcountry Office, PO Box 168, Yellowstone National Park, WY 82190. For more information call the Central Backcountry Office at ☎ 307-344-2161.

Anglers (over 16 years of age) need only a park fishing permit ($10/$20 for 10 days/season), available at backcountry offices and Hamilton general stores. State fishing licenses are not required or valid. Note that many waterways, including the Bechler River, are catch-and-release only (mandatory for cutthroat trout).

NEAREST TOWNS
Gardiner

Gardiner straddles the Yellowstone River on Hwy 89 (to Livingston) at the northwestern boundary of Yellowstone National Park. The chamber of commerce (☎ 406-848-7971) is on Park St. The local USFS office (☎ 406-848-7375) is south of the river. The *Rocky Mountain campground* (☎ 406-848-7251) has campsites with facilities from $18.50. The *Yellowstone River Motel* (☎ 406-848-7303) has rooms from $50.

West Yellowstone

This small, tourism-based town in Montana serves as the western gateway to the park.

continued on page 234

YELLOWSTONE – THE WORLD'S FIRST NATIONAL PARK

The 3472-sq-mile Yellowstone National Park in the northwest corner of Wyoming is the world's oldest national park and the largest in the lower 48 states. This vast, intensely active volcanic plateau has an incredible range and concentration of fascinating volcanic phenomena, from geysers and fumaroles to hot springs, thermal pools and boiling mud-pots. Millions of visitors are attracted to this volcanic wonderland each year, though only a tiny percentage ever hike into the Yellowstone backcountry.

Although the Yellowstone basin was traversed by Shoshone and Absaroka (Crow), who sometimes hunted its bighorn sheep and fished the local rivers, only small numbers of Native Americans lived permanently in the area. The Lewis and Clark expedition of 1804–06 (see boxed text on page 20) bypassed Yellowstone without an inkling of its remarkable geology, but soon afterwards John Colter, a trapper who had accompanied the explorers, ventured into this strange country. His accounts of finding bubbling mud-pools, steaming brooks and jets of boiling water were ridiculed back in St Louis, but returning frontiersmen continued to tell these fantastic stories.

JOHN ELK III

In 1871 Dr Ferdinand Hayden, director of the US Geological Survey, resolved to lead an expedition into the Yellowstone area. His party included photographer William Jackson and landscape painter Thomas Moran. Their photographs and paintings provided crucial evidence of Yellowstone's outstanding features, which – together with Hayden's exhaustive report – convinced Congress to establish Yellowstone as the world's first national park the following year.

The non-treaty Nez Perce, fleeing the US Army in a desperate attempt to reach Canada, crossed Yellowstone in the summer of 1877, briefly seizing several tourists. As poaching and other illegal activities began to get out of hand, the US Army assumed administration of the park in 1886, a role it held until the formation of the NPS in 1916. In 1972 Yellowstone became a UN-designated World Heritage Site.

Hot Spot

Yellowstone's intense volcanic activity is caused by a massive bubble of molten magma close to the earth's crust – known as a 'hot spot' – which is floating gradually northeast. The Yellowstone hot spot is extraordinary, as it sits below thicker continental crust rather than relatively thin oceanic crust (such as Hawaii).

The present landscape of the park was created some 600,000 years ago by a massive volcanic explosion. The force blew out the immense Yellowstone Caldera, which takes in a 1316-sq-mile area between Mt Washburn and Mt Sheridan. Geologists believe that the gradual upward bulging of the Yellowstone Caldera indicates that another major eruption will occur some time in the future.

Facing page: Tourists watch the Old Faithful geyser, Yellowstone National Park, Wyoming.

Right: The Castle geyser in the Upper Geyser Basin, Yellowstone National Park, Wyoming.

JOHN ELK III

continued from 231

Eagle's Store and Tackle (☎ 406-646-9300) on W Yellowstone Ave sells backpacking supplies. The *Madison Hotel (☎ 406-646-7745, 139 W Yellowstone Ave)*, has rooms from $80 and hostel beds for $15. Greyhound buses stop at the Western Union office at 126 Electric St (next door to the Sleepy Hollow Motel).

Mammoth

Mammoth, at the northwest corner of the Yellowstone, is the park headquarters. The village lies at the foot of the fascinating Mammoth Hot Springs, where calcium-rich thermal waters have formed an extensive system of limestone terraces. The visitor center (☎ 307-344-2263), in a section of the old Fort Yellowstone, has exhibits on the establishment and early history of the park. *Mammoth Hot Springs & Cabins* and *Mammoth campground* (85 sites, $12) are open all year.

Old Faithful

This large complex is focused on the famous Old Faithful geyser, which pleases the crowds by erupting (more or less) regularly every 80 minutes. The visitor center (☎ 307-344-7353) has a film on the park's geothermal features (a new center is under construction).

The *Old Faithful Hotel*, a grandiose log construction, has rooms for $56 and cabins from $42. (There is no campground.)

Grant Village

Grant Village is on the West Thumb (bay) of Yellowstone Lake at the junction of the Lower Loop Rd and the South Entrance Rd. The visitor center (☎ 307-242-2650) deals with effects of forest fires on Yellowstone's ecology. The separate backcountry office is beside the gas station. There are *motel* rooms from $79 and *cabins* from $47. The *campground* (425 sites, $15) is by the lake shore.

Canyon

Canyon is at the southern end of the Grand Canyon of the Yellowstone River at the eastern junction of the Upper and Lower Loop roads. Its visitor center (☎ 307-242-2550) includes a backcountry office and has exhibits devoted to the ecology of bison. *Canyon campground* has 271 sites ($15) and cabins are available.

GETTING AROUND

Yellowstone has no real hiker shuttle service, but hikers can board tour buses around the Grand Loop Rd. Fares to/from Mammoth are: Roosevelt Lodge (18mi) $5.50; North Gate (5mi) $1.65. For current timetables call the park concessionaire, Amfac (☎ 307-344-7311).

Mt Washburn & Sevenmile Hole

Duration	1 or 2 days
Distance	16.6mi (26.7km)
Standard	easy–medium
Start	Dunraven Pass
Finish	Canyon
Nearest Town	Gardiner
Public Transport	no

Summary This long day or overnight shuttle hike climbs 1400ft (425m) from Dunraven Pass to the summit of Mt Washburn, continuing along the rim of the spectacular Grand Canyon of the Yellowstone (with a side trip to Sevenmile Hole) to Canyon village.

The 10,243ft Mt Washburn is all that remains of a volcano that exploded some 600,000 years ago, forming the vast Yellowstone Caldera. A popular short hike (3.2mi roundtrip) goes to the fire lookout tower on Mt Washburn's summit, which overlooks the caldera basin to its south. An excellent continuation drops down to Sevenmile Hole on the impressive Grand Canyon of the Yellowstone, an area of hot springs, high waterfalls and superb eroded cliffs.

PLANNING
When to Hike

Bear in mind that there are lots of grizzlies in the Mt Washburn area in late summer and early autumn. Also be wary of lightning associated with afternoon thunderstorms.

Maps

Trails Illustrated's 1:83,333 *Tower/Canyon NE Yellowstone* covers the hike. Two USGS 1:24,000 quads also cover the route: *Mount Washburn* and *Canyon Village*.

GETTING TO/FROM THE HIKE

The hike starts from Dunraven Pass, on the Grand Loop Rd 4.8mi north of Canyon; there is trailhead parking only for around 20 vehicles. An alternative is the somewhat steeper route (mostly along a road) from the Chittenden parking area.

THE HIKE

The wide trail (a rough, long, disused road) makes a comfortable but steady sidling ascent through forest of subalpine fir to a minor gap. Continue up northeast in broad switchbacks, then follow a spectacular, narrow rock-ridge scattered with a few stunted whitebark pines to meet the gravel road from the Chittenden parking area at the Mt Washburn Spur Trail turnoff. The road curves around a few minutes up left to reach the **fire lookout tower** on Mt Washburn (10,243ft). From the public observation room (which has a free telescope) there are majestic views across the Yellowstone basin south to the Tetons and north to the Beartooths.

The Mt Washburn Spur Trail drops southeast along an undulating ridge of alpine wildflower meadows. After dipping through a saddle to another little gap at treeline, cut down right and make a winding descent through tiny clearings to reach ***campsite 4E1***, 1¼ to 1½ hours from Mt Washburn. Keep your wits about you, as you are now in a prime grizzly bear habitat.

The trail continues southwest through areas of boggy grassland grazed by deer and elk to **Washburn Hot Springs**, a small field of boiling mud pools and fumaroles. It may be dangerous to leave the trail here. Proceed past more minor thermal springs to reach the Sevenmile Hole Trail turnoff (see Side Trip), 1¼ to 1½ hours on from 4E1 campsite.

The now broader trail leads on along the northern rim of the almost 1300ft deep **Grand Canyon of the Yellowstone** through lodgepole forest carpeted with fragrant, low

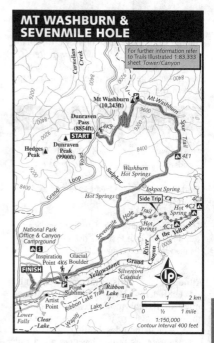

MT WASHBURN & SEVENMILE HOLE

grouseberry shrub. The views become increasingly spectacular as you continue past the long thin **Silvercord Cascade**, falling through its own precipitous little chasm, and amazing yellow, white and red columns in the canyon's eroding sides to reach the Glacial Boulder Trailhead near **Inspiration Point** (1.3mi from Canyon), 1¼ to 1½ hours from the Sevenmile Hole Trail turnoff.

Side Trip: Sevenmile Hole

3½–4½ hours, 5.2mi (8.3km),
1382ft (421m) descent/ascent
Remember that unattended food must be out of reach of bears – do not just dump your pack here.

The trail quickly begins dropping in switchbacks through old Douglas firs, passing a 10ft-high geyser cone in the forest before coming out onto another area of hot springs. Continue down among these bubbling pools and small geysers past ***campsite 4C1*** (on right), crossing a tiny thermal stream to pass *campsite 4C2* right beside the **Yellowstone River**. Large springs emerge from the reddish chalky cliffs on the river's east side. To reach *campsite 4C3* cross the small Sulphur Creek, then walk along the edge of the river past a tiny hot pool in the rock bed.

Heart Lake

Duration	2 or 3 days
Distance	16mi (26km)
Standard	easy (medium to Mt Sheridan)
Start/Finish	Heart Lake Trailhead
Nearest Town	Grant Village
Public Transport	no
Summary	An interesting and uncomplicated out-and-back hike to a lake rich in wildlife and flanked by a geothermal field.

Although large parts of the area were hit by the 1988 fires, Heart Lake has retained much of its charm. Stretching around its northwestern shore is an extensive thermal field, which includes boiling pools and a large geyser. Its tranquil waters are a rich habitat for waterbirds, and plentiful stocks of cutthroat and lake trout make Heart Lake a popular fishing spot. The 10,308ft Mt Sheridan, the highest point in the small Red Mountains range, rises up directly from the lake's western shore and makes a wonderful panoramic point. Although very fit parties sometimes hike to Heart Lake and climb Mt Sheridan in a long roundtrip day hike, it makes more sense to camp a night (or two) at Heart Lake.

WARNINGS

- The Heart Lake area is prime grizzly bear country, so stay alert.
- There is no water until near Heart Lake.

PLANNING
When to Hike
Due to the high bear activity in the area, the trail to Heart Lake does not open until July 1.

Hikers may encounter heavy snow on the way up to Mt Sheridan until mid-July or later.

Maps
Yellowstone Lake published by Trails Illustrated at a scale of approximately 1:83,333 adequately covers the hike. Two 1:24,000 USGS quads also cover the route: *Mount Sheridan* and *Heart Lake*. American Adventures Association's approximately 1:100,000 *South Yellowstone Park* is an acceptable alternative.

GETTING TO/FROM THE HIKE
The hike begins at the Heart Lake Trailhead (8N1), 5.3mi south of Grant Village on the South Entrance Rd. There is trailhead parking for around 25 cars.

THE HIKE
Day 1: Heart Lake Trailhead to Heart Lake
3½–4½ hours, 8mi (12.9km), 342ft (104m) ascent
Follow the wide trail southwest through lodgepole forest severely affected by the 1988 fires and the voracious mountain bark beetle. The trail rises very slightly over a minor watershed to the first group of smoking fumaroles at the northern foot of the bald-topped Factory Hill (9607ft), 1½ to two hours from the trailhead. From here you get your first view of the lake, still 2mi away.

Wind your way down into the intensely active **Heart Lake Geyser Basin** past numerous spurting hot springs and boiling pools, most of which are a short way off to the right. The trail crosses and recrosses the tepid Witch Creek to reach Heart Lake ranger station, just back from the northern shore of **Heart Lake**. In summer this log hut is usually occupied by a park ranger. From here Trail Creek Trail departs left (east) around the lake's northeastern side.

The Heart Lake Trail continues right, first following the gray sand beach to cross the inlet then tracing the lake's western shore to reach *campsite 8H6*. This is the first of five sites along the unburnt strip of firs and spruces fringing the shore. A path leads a few paces off right to another small

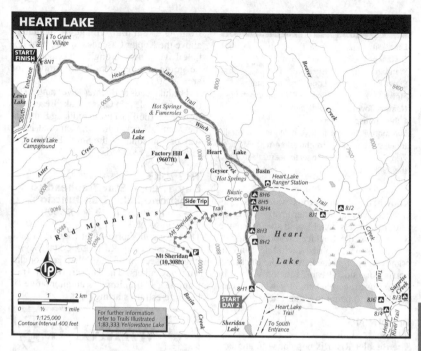

HEART LAKE

but fascinating thermal area. Here, the **Rustic Geyser** shoots up at irregular intervals, while other hot springs bubble up into large calcified bathtubs. Tread carefully in these fragile and dangerous places.

The trail leads directly past ***campsite 8H5*** to meet the Mt Sheridan Trail turnoff (see Side Trip) continuing 20 minutes south past ***campsites 8H4, 8H3*** and ***8H2***. There are good views out across the placid waters east to Overlook Mountain and southeast to the flat-topped Mt Hancock. In the evenings, courting pairs of grebes can be seen diving and calling to each other in mellow, lilting voices.

Side Trip: Mt Sheridan
4–5½ hours, 7mi (11.2km),
2858ft (871m) ascent/descent
The Mt Sheridan Trail cuts up briefly over open meadows before beginning a spiralling ascent along a steep spur largely covered by whitebark pine that leads up into a saddle

among wind-battered firs. Continue left (southeast) up the narrowing tundra ridge over old snowdrifts to reach the 10,308ft summit of **Mt Sheridan**. The fire lookout (staffed in summer, otherwise locked) enjoys a complete panorama encompassing the Pitchstone Plateau to the west, Shoshone Lake to the northwest, Yellowstone Lake to the northeast and the jagged outlines of the Tetons to the south.

Day 2: Heart Lake to Heart Lake Trailhead
3½–4½ hours, 8mi (12.9km),
342ft (104m) descent
Retrace your Day 1 steps to the trailhead.

Alternative Campsites
There are half a dozen other campsites around Heart Lake: ***BJ1*** and ***BJ2*** on its eastern side; ***8J6*** and ***8J4*** on the southeastern shore; ***8J3*** nearby along Surprise Creek; and ***8H1*** at the lake's southwestern corner.

ROCKY MOUNTAINS

Bechler River

Duration	4 days
Distance	28mi (48km)
Standard	medium
Start	Lone Star Trailhead
Finish	Bechler River ranger station
Nearest Town	Old Faithful
Public Transport	no

Summary This is a long but largely downhill (downstream) hike to southwestern Yellowstone's wild Cascade Corner, the sector least affected by the 1988 fires.

Known for its numerous waterfalls, this area receives rather higher levels of precipitation than elsewhere, and the extensive wetlands of the Bechler Meadows support numerous water birds, including sandhill cranes and great blue herons. The Bechler's Ferris Fork side stream is the only place in the Yellowstone backcountry where hikers can (legally) bathe in natural hot springs.

PLANNING
When to Hike
The Bechler River is popular with anglers, and backcountry campsites can be difficult to get, even outside the busy months of July and August. The mosquitoes can be appalling along the Bechler until the end of July. The route also requires a serious ford – which may be impassable in early summer or after heavy rain – so enquire about river levels before departing.

Maps
Recommended is the approximately 1:83,333 Trails Illustrated map *Old Faithful* ($9.95). Five USGS 1:24,000 quads also cover the route: *Old Faithful*, *Shoshone Geyser Basin*, *Trischman Knob*, *Cave Falls* and *Bechler Falls*. The approximately 1:100,000 *South Yellowstone Park* ($3.95) published by American Adventures Association is an acceptable alternative.

GETTING TO/FROM THE HIKE
The hike begins at the Lone Star Trailhead, which is around 2mi (25 to 30 minutes'

hike) southeast along the Grand Loop Rd from Old Faithful village immediately above the Kepler Cascades, where the Firehole River flows through a spectacular little gorge. There is trailhead parking for around 30 cars.

The hike ends at Bechler River ranger station, accessible (via Grassy Lake Reservoir) from the turnoff just north of Flagg Ranch in the John D Rockefeller Jr Memorial Parkway or 2mi south of the South Entrance. A car shuttle is required.

THE HIKE
Day 1: Lone Star Trailhead to Shoshone Lake Trail Junction
2¼–2¾ hours, 5.8mi (9.3km), 900ft (275m) ascent

The easy and short (4.6mi roundtrip) hike from Grand Loop Rd to Lone Star Geyser (the first section of Day 1) is very popular with day hikers. The Howard Eaton Trail from near Old Faithful is an alternative (if less interesting) starting point.

WARNING

MANY VISITORS HAVE BEEN GORED BY BUFFALO

BUFFALO CAN WEIGH 2000 POUNDS AND CAN SPRINT AT 30 MPH, THREE TIMES FASTER THAN YOU CAN RUN

THESE ANIMALS MAY APPEAR TAME BUT ARE WILD, UNPREDICTABLE, AND DANGEROUS

DO NOT APPROACH BUFFALO

In other words, use a telephoto lens when taking snaps of buffalo.

Take the old road (closed to public vehicles since 1972) past a tiny weir diverting water to the Old Faithful village. The road crosses the Firehole River bridge, following the stream up past the Spring Creek Trail turnoff (and a route diverging right) to end at **Lone Star Geyser** after 40 to 50 minutes. This isolated geyser erupts for 10 to 15 minutes at intervals of around three hours, sending a jet of boiling water up to 40ft into the air. A foot trail continues 0.3mi to intersect with the Howard Eaton Trail.

Turn left and proceed southwest past *campsite OA1*, recrossing the river on a footbridge around a small thermal field of scalding hot pools and hissing steam vents. The trail passes *campsites OA2* and *OA3*, then climbs away south over the broad rolling ridge top to cross **Grants Pass**, which lies on the Continental Divide at around 8010ft. Head down through superb stands of tall, old-growth Engelmann spruce and whitebark pine to reach the Shoshone Lake Trail turnoff, 1½ to two hours from Lone Star Geyser. *Campsite 8G1* is a short way down by the meadows around Shoshone Creek.

From here a worthwhile (3mi roundtrip) side trip can be made to the **Shoshone Geyser Basin** at the western end of Shoshone Lake.

Day 2: Shoshone Lake Trail Junction to Three River Junction
3½–4½ hours, 9.2mi (14.8km), 620ft (189m) ascent

Take the right-hand Bechler River Trail and cut briefly through meadows before again making a steady (but rarely steep) climb into montane forest interspersed with small moors. The undulating trail crosses the (approximately 8500ft) watershed of the Continental Divide before descending past *campsites 9D4* and *9D3* (no fires allowed). Cross a shallow, marshy basin at the northern foot of the prominent Douglas Knob and continue gently down past *campsite 9D2* to cross the small Gregg Fork.

The trail follows the stream past the 20ft-high, lightly tumbling **Twister Falls** (a short way over to the right), then drops along a

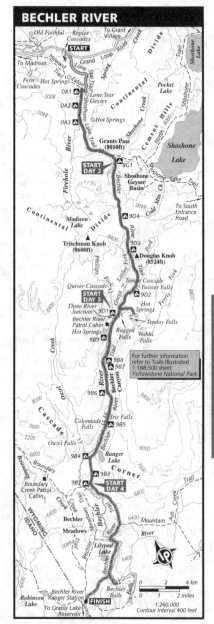

fir-covered ridge to a left turnoff (not shown on most maps) under the northwestern rim of Pitchstone Plateau.

Don't miss the short side trip from here to some interesting bubbling thermal pools and spurting geysers along the Ferris Fork. A vigorous hot spring gushes out of the stream bed itself in one of the park's few permitted **bathing sites** – but beware of scalding as the boiling water mixes erratically with the stream. A rough route goes on upstream to Tendoy Falls and beyond.

The trail leads on to *campsite 9D1* and past **Ragged Falls**, crossing the Ferris Fork on a footbridge before arriving at Three River Junction. Here the two previously mentioned forks merge with the Phillips Fork to form the **Bechler River**. The river has plentiful rainbow trout and attracts backcountry fly fishers.

Day 3: Three River Junction to Bechler Meadows Trail Junction
3–4 hours, 7.7mi (12.4km)
Make your way over lovely river flats of the wild upper valley past a string of steaming, algae-rich pools opposite Bechler River patrol cabin to *campsite 9B9* (no fires), near a pretty waterfall. The trail continues downstream into the steep-sided **Bechler Canyon** past *campsite 9B8* to ford the river below an area of recently burnt forest. Follow the often muddy trail across numerous cold springs and reford the river – a slightly more serious wade – just upstream of *campsite 9B6*. The trail leads through old fir-spruce forest past gliding cataracts with picturesque islets to reach the spectacular **Iris Falls**, a 40ft-high curtain of water spraying thick mist into the air, 1¾ to 2¼ hours from Three River Junction.

Descend quickly past the damp *campsite 9B5* to a short turnoff leading down to a scenic overlook right in front of **Colonnade Falls**, where the Bechler drops another 85ft in two stages. The trail continues close to the river through fir-spruce forest alternating with boulder fields and meadows fringed by birch or native cherry scrub to *campsite 9B4*. It then breaks away southwest past *campsite 9B3* at the edge of a broad clearing to pass the Bechler Meadows Trail turnoff. This is a slightly shorter (5mi) but less interesting route to Bechler River ranger station; it leads directly past *campsite 9B2* to ford the Bechler River, then continues southwest across the boggy Bechler Meadows.

Day 4: Bechler Meadows Trail Junction to Bechler River Ranger Station
3–4 hours, 7mi (11.3km)
Proceed left along the open grassy plains of the meandering river. The trail leads on southeast through forest patches to pass the Mountain Ash Creek Trail turnoff after one to 1¼ hours. Turn off right here and head 1mi south to make a last (normally knee-high) ford of the Bechler River. The trail follows the river's right bank for 2mi to another trail junction, from where a rewarding side trip (30 to 40 minutes roundtrip) leads on downstream to **Bechler Falls**, the largest and most impressive of the Bechler's many waterfalls. The trail cuts right (roughly west) to arrive at the remote Bechler River ranger station in Yellowstone's southwestern corner.

Grand Teton National Park

Grand Teton National Park lies south of Yellowstone National Park in northwestern Wyoming. On its western boundary the park merges with Jedediah Smith Wilderness (within Targhee National Forest). The park stretches some 40mi along the spectacular but compact 15mi wide Teton Range (known simply as 'the Tetons').

Unlike any other range in the Rockies, the Tetons rise with stunning abruptness in a row of 'witch hat' peaks that tower 1½mi above the saltbush plains to the east. Gradual westward tilting has created numerous rock escarpments separating high 'belvedere' terraces that serve as marvellously scenic walkways. The Teton Range boasts a dozen peaks over 12,000ft and a similar number of high hanging glaciers. The Tetons' tallest – and Wyoming's second-tallest – peak is the 13,770ft Grand Teton itself.

The vast majority of hikers visit the especially picturesque and easily accessible southern Tetons, having a severe impact on the most heavily used or fragile areas. Backcountry visitors should keep to designated trails and established campsites.

HISTORY

The Blackfeet, Shoshone and Gros Ventre Native American tribes all frequented Jackson Hole – the broad Snake River valley at the eastern foot of the range – over the summer season, but moved to lower elevations to avoid the harsh winter. Ranchers began settling in the area from the late 19th century. The Carrington expedition of 1879 proposed that the Teton Range be incorporated into Yellowstone National Park, but it took until 1929 for the area to gain such protection as a separate Grand Teton National Park. This original park excluded Jackson Hole, but much of the land in the valley was secretly purchased by the billionaire John D Rockefeller Jr, who donated it to the US government in 1950 to form the present boundaries of Grand Teton National Park.

NATURAL HISTORY

Although they are composed of some of the most ancient (Precambrian) rocks in North America, the Tetons are the Rockies' youngest mountain range. Their classic pointed forms are due to the relatively recent uplifting of the range – a process that began only 9 million years ago – and the even more recent ice-age glaciations that sharpened their summits.

As well as elk (see the boxed text), mountain goats, bighorn sheep, mule deer, moose and black bears are common in these mountains. Grizzly bears are found in the northern half of the park (beyond Mt Moran).

The Tetons' beautiful montane and subalpine forests preserve the largest whitebark pines found anywhere in North America. These slow-growing conifers have reached heights exceeding 80ft and diameters of 6ft at the base. Other typical forest species are Douglas fir, Engelmann spruce and subalpine fir with stands of aspen, cottonwood

An Excess of Elk

The National Elk Refuge just north of Jackson borders the park, and the Jackson Hole area has the densest population of elk (or wapiti) in the Rocky Mountains. In summer a large number migrate out of the valley to graze in the Teton high country. As there are few predators to control elk numbers – mountain lions and bears only occasionally take elk, and wolves were eradicated in the 1930s – the elk population has gradually risen above sustainable levels. This has forced the NPS to introduce seasonal elk hunting, a move unparalleled in US national parks.

and lodgepole pine on better-drained lower slopes.

Wildflowers of the moist forests include the delicate, yellowish-white, three-petaled western trillium, white corn-lilies, starflowered false Solomon's seal, and fairybells – whose twin red 'pom-pom' berries are eaten by grouse and rodents. Yellow arnicas and pink and white phlox are found in forest clearings and subalpine meadows. Scarlet paintbrush, the floral emblem of Wyoming, is abundant in the moraine soils of the Tetons' canyon valleys.

Gray jays dart around the spruce forests, audaciously pecking for leftovers around campsites, while the dark-eyed junco hops through the underbrush. Here you may also hear the distinctive calls of ruby-crowned kinglets – otherwise recognizable by the male's red crest, raised when wooing the female – and the white-crowned sparrow. Water birds, including American coots, sandhill cranes and double-crested cormorants are common on the park's lakes, especially the shallows of the large Jackson Lake.

PLANNING
Maps

Two waterproof maps covering the whole park are the Earthwalk Press 1:72,500 *Recreation Map Grand Teton National Park* ($7.95), with a 1:48,000 inset of its popular southern sector, and Trails Illustrated's

ROCKY MOUNTAINS

1:78,000 *Grand Teton National Park* ($8.95), with a 1:24,000 inset of the Grand Teton climbing area.

Permits & Regulations

Park entry fees (valid seven days) are $20 for private vehicles, $15 for motorcycles and $5 for individuals on foot or bicycle.

Backcountry permits are required for all overnight trips in Grand Teton. Currently, backcountry permits are free unless you book in advance ($15 fee). There are backcountry offices at Colter Bay, Jenny Lake and Moose. Reservations are accepted by mail (postal address: Grand Teton National Park, Draw 170, Moose, WY 83012) or fax (307-739-3438) from 1 January to 15 May.

In southern Grand Teton, backcountry camping is restricted to various Camping Zones. Hikers (with backcountry permits) are free to choose their own tent sites, but in the most heavily used zones all sites are designated (indicated by marker posts). Fires are prohibited and campsites must be at least 200ft from lakes and streams.

NEAREST TOWNS
Colter Bay

Colter Bay is on the east side of Jackson Lake on US 89/287. The backcountry office is at the visitor center (☎ 307-739-3595). *Colter Bay Village* (☎ 307-543-2828) has a range of accommodations, from tent village ($26) to four-person cabins (from $87). A laundry and hot showers are available.

Jenny Lake

The village of Jenny Lake is 7mi north of the park entrance at the lake's southeast shore. The backcountry office is open in summer only. *Jenny Lake campground* is on the lake's southeast shore. The upmarket *Jenny Lake Lodge* (☎ 307-733-4647) is on its northeast side.

Moose

Moose, roughly 10mi north of Jackson at the Teton Park Rd turnoff, is the park headquarters. The backcountry office (☎ 307-739-3309) is at the visitor center, north of the shopping center.

Jackson

The southern gateway to Grand Teton National Park, Jackson is at the junction of Hwy 22 (to Teton Pass) and US 89/US 26/US 191. The National Museum of Wildlife Art, 3mi north of town, has works by important US outdoor and landscape painters, including Bierstadt and Rungiers. The USFS and Grand Teton National Park have a joint counter at the Jackson Hole and Greater Yellowstone visitor center (☎ 307-733-3317) at 532 N Cache Dr (but backcountry permits are not issued here). Teton Mountaineering (☎ 307-733-3595) at 170 N Cache Dr, has a good range of climbing and backpacking gear.

The *El Rancho Motel* (☎ *307-733-3668, 215 N Cache Dr)* has budget rooms and runs *The Bunkhouse* in the basement, with hostel-style accommodations.

Jackson Hole Express (☎ 307-733-1719, 800-652-9510) runs shuttles to Salt Lake City ($45) via Idaho Falls ($20), which both have Greyhound connections.

Teton Village

This modern ski resort lies at the foot of Rendezvous Mountain, 6mi west of Jackson on Hwy 22. The Jackson Hole Aerial Tram (☎ 307-739-2753) runs up 4139ft vertical to Rendezvous Mountain, providing easy access to the high trails of southern Grand Teton National Park. The aerial tram operates daily from 9 am to 5 pm between late May and late September (to 7 pm between late June and early September). Uphill fares are $15/13/6 for adults/seniors/children, but – hikers note! – the downhill trip is free.

Hostel X (☎ *307-733-3415)* has basic rooms for around $40.

GETTING AROUND

Local START (☎ 307-733-4521) buses run regularly between Teton Village and Jackson. Alltrans (☎ 307-733-1112) can do hiker shuttles.

Teton Boating Company (☎ 307-733-2703) runs frequent boats from the southern shore of Jenny Lake to the dock near Hidden Falls on its western shore; the one-way fare is $2/3.25 children/adults.

Paintbrush Divide Loop

Duration	2–3 days
Distance	17.8mi (27km)
Standard	medium
Start/Finish	South String Lake Trailhead
Nearest Towns	Moose, Jackson
Public Transport	no

Summary The high (10,645ft) shelf known as Paintbrush Divide stands between the deep Paintbrush and Cascade Canyons. This superb natural lookout gives outstanding vistas of the surrounding peaks, particularly Mt Moran.

This circuit route crosses a scenic high pass giving marvellous views of the park's classic summits. The hike over Paintbrush Divide can be linked with the Teton Crest Trail to give a marvellous five days' hiking.

PLANNING
When to Hike
Paintbrush Divide usually remains snowbound well into July. Between late June and early September thunderstorms often bring heavy rain, and the danger of lightning strike is acute on high-level routes such as this.

Maps
Two USGS 1:24,000 quads cover the route: *Jenny Lake* and *Mount Moran*.

GETTING TO/FROM THE HIKE
The hike begins at South String Lake Trailhead, near Jenny Lake Lodge. A minor variant is to finish at the trailhead at South Jenny Lake Junction. There are large car parks at both trailheads.

THE HIKE
Day 1: South String Lake Trailhead to Holly Lake
3–4½ hours, 6.2mi (10km), 2540ft (774m) ascent
Cross the outlet on a footbridge where it leaves String Lake (6870ft) by the trailhead car park. Bear right at the intersection a few minutes on and follow the String Lake Trail quickly around the lake's western shore. The trail rises steadily north over avalanche slopes of snapped-off firs – from where

String Lake's unusually narrow, elongated form becomes apparent – to reach a junction, 35 to 45 minutes from the trailhead.

Turn left along the Paintbrush Canyon Trail and climb on gently through fir-spruce forest (with a generous scattering of Douglas fir and occasional white fir). The trail swings west into the deep, enclosed valley of **Paintbrush Canyon** under the towering walls of Rockchuck Peak to meet Paintbrush Canyon Creek. Continue on up into the *Lower Paintbrush Camping Zone* (eight campsites), crossing the creek just before you pass the two uppermost sites. As you get higher, fine views open out downvalley to Leigh Lake and Spalding Bay in Jackson Lake.

The trail ascends through rocky avalanche chutes colonized by wild raspberry shrubs and small meadows sprinkled with columbines and Indian paintbrush, the flamboyant red wildflowers that lend their name to the canyon. After passing the *Outlier campsite* (a reservation-only site not marked on most maps) the trail forks. The left trail climbs an old lateral moraine covered by whitebark pines past a scree-filled tarn, while the more scenic right trail leads up to **Holly Lake** (9410ft), a beautiful alpine lake directly below Mt Woodring (11,590ft). There are a number of designated *campsites* at the lake's southeast corner.

Day 2: Holly Lake to Cascade Creek Forks Junction
3–3½ hours, 4.2mi (6.8km), 1235ft (376m) ascent
From Holly Lake make a steep 300ft climb to join the left trail from the end of Day 1. The trail leads through the *Upper Paintbrush Camping Zone* into the treeless tundra of the upper basin to reach a high, flat shoulder. Traverse quickly (as this slope is prone to rockfall) over persistent snowdrifts above some icy tarns, then make a short, winding ascent through the coarse rubble to arrive at **Paintbrush Divide** (10,645ft), one to 1½ hours from Holly Lake. The views from this pass include the amazing slab walls on Mt Moran to the north, and the rock needles of the Jaw, Mt St John, and the Rock of the Ages poking up along the southern rim of Paintbrush Canyon.

ROCKY MOUNTAINS

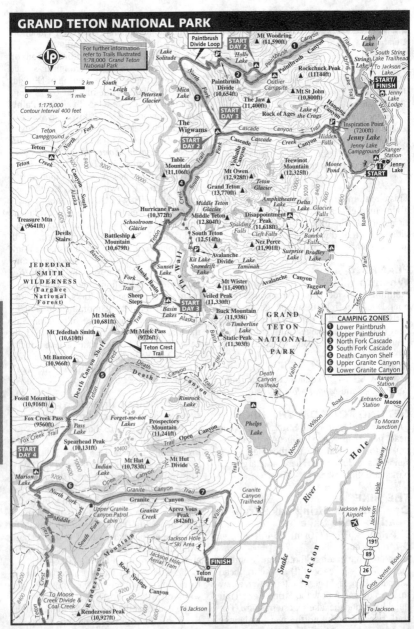

GRAND TETON NATIONAL PARK

ROCKY MOUNTAINS

The trail descends west in broad switchbacks to reach **Lake Solitude** (9035ft), an enchanting tarn in a snowy cirque surrounded by grassy lawns, after 50 minutes to 1¼ hours. Head down through the U-shaped glacial valley toward the north faces of Mt Owen (12,928ft) and (later) Grand Teton (13,770ft), the two highest peaks in the park.

Cross Cascade Creek to enter the *North Fork Cascade Camping Zone*, with 10 campsites scattered among moraine boulders and old firs. The trail crosses and recrosses the creek, descending through the forest to an intersection a short way above the confluence of Cascade Creek's North and South Forks, 50 minutes to 1¼ hours from Solitude Lake. Here, the Teton Crest Trail (see the next hike) turns south up the South Fork.

Day 3: Cascade Creek Forks Junction to South String Lake Trailhead

2¾–3½ hours, 7.4mi (11.9km)
Most of this section is covered – in reverse (uphill) direction – by Day 1 of the Teton Crest Trail hike. From the boat dock on Jenny Lake, head north across the stream coming from Hanging Canyon and proceed around the lake's northwestern shore through the fir-spruce forest to arrive back at the South String Lake Trailhead after 40 to 50 minutes.

Teton Crest Trail

Duration	4 days
Distance	31.4mi (55km)
Standard	medium-hard
Start	Jenny Lake
Finish	Teton Village
Nearest Towns	Jenny Lake, Teton Village, Moose, Jackson
Public Transport	no

Summary One of the most spectacular hikes in the Rockies, the Teton Crest Trail leads over several passes and along broad, high terraces with sheer dropoffs.

This is an exhilarating, high-level route (often above 9000ft) through the wild heart of Grand Teton, offering some quite superb

vistas. As its name suggests, this trail follows a high-level scenic route, dipping in and out of the neighboring Jedediah Smith Wilderness. Numerous side routes lead up the canyons or passes on either side of the trail, allowing easy access and exits. Various additions are possible, including the Paintbrush Divide route (see previous hike), the Valley Trail (north from the Granite Canyon Trail junction to Jenny Lake), or the continuation of the Teton Crest Trail to Hwy 22.

PLANNING
Maps
The following 1:24,000 USGS quads cover the route: *Jenny Lake*, *Mount Bannon* and *Grand Teton*.

GETTING TO/FROM THE HIKE
The hike starts at Jenny Lake (and can be shortened slightly by taking the boat – see Getting Around), and finishes at Teton Village. Shuttle hikers can park vehicles at Jenny Lake and at the Granite Canyon Trailhead (on the Moose-Wilson Rd, 2mi northeast of Teton Village). From Teton Village there are regular buses back to Jackson. Hitchhiking is officially against park regulations, but not uncommon.

THE HIKE
Day 1: Jenny Lake to Cascade Creek Forks Junction
3¼–4¼ hours, 7mi (11.3km), 1057ft (322m) ascent
The trail heads around the western shore of Jenny Lake, then follows Cascade Creek up past small ravines to a footbridge. A short side trail from here leads upstream to the concealed cascades of **Hidden Falls**. (Hikers coming from the boat dock should follow signs southeast up to the falls.) Ascend in spectacular switchbacks through a precipice to **Inspiration Point** (7200ft), an overlook giving fine views across Jenny Lake to the Gros Ventre mountains, to meet the Cascade Canyon Trail, 1¼ to 1¾ hours from Jenny Lake village.

Continue left (east) up into the lower canyon, where the summit of Grand Teton can be seen pushing up behind Mt Owen and

ROCKY MOUNTAINS

Teewinot Mountain. The trail rises gently through meadows alternating with pockets of spruce and lodgepole forest past stream ponds, where you have an excellent chance of spotting moose, to reach the Cascade Creek Forks Junction, two to 2½ hours from the junction above Inspiration Point. *Camping* is in either the North Fork Camping Zone (see Day 2 of the Paintbrush Divide Loop hike) or the South Fork Camping Zone (see Day 2 of this hike).

Day 2: Cascade Creek Junction to Alaska Basin
3–4 hours, 6½mi (10.5km), 2472ft (753m) ascent

Head up the forested western bank of the South Fork, where American dippers can sometimes be seen ducking in and out of the cascading water. The trail soon enters the *South Fork Cascade Camping Zone*, switch-backing only briefly as it makes a mainly gentle climb over almost level stages below abrupt spurs coming off the Tetons and Table Mountain. A junction in the upper valley is reached after 1½ to two hours. The left trail is a worthwhile side-trip (1.6mi) south to **Avalanche Divide** (approximately 10,600ft), a scenic lookout above Snowdrift Lake at the edge of the escarpment known as the Wall.

Follow the (right) Teton Crest Trail (directly past the zone's two uppermost camp-sites) over slopes of purple asters and stunted shrub willows. The trail makes an increasingly steep zigzagging ascent past the now much diminished Schoolroom Glacier – a murky tarn has formed within the circular moraine walls in the wake of the glacier's recession – to arrive at **Hurricane Pass** (10,372ft) after 30 to 45 minutes. The pass offers unsurpassed views of Grand, Middle and South Teton as well as west across interesting stratified ranges.

Head briefly south along the top of the range, then cut down right past limestone sinkholes into Jedediah Smith Wilderness. The trail gently descends a broad ridge past the striking, mesa-like outcrop of Battleship Mountain (10,679ft) before switchbacking down over alpine meadows of blue lupines to **Sunset Lake** (9608ft).

Continue south past several turnoffs – two that lead up left over Buck Mountain Pass (a shortcut route to Moose or Teton Village via Phelps Lake) and a right trail that goes 7.7mi down the canyon to the USFS Teton camp-ground. The Teton Crest Trail skirts around into the scenic Alaska Basin (at roughly 9500ft), where the scattering of shallow tarns known as the **Basin Lakes** look out across the tiers of massive escarpments that fall directly into Teton Canyon.

Alternative Campsites
Sheltered campsites can be found in the low trees above Sunset Lake and around the tarns of Alaska Basin. This area is extremely pop-ular with campers (partly because it is outside the national park and backcountry permits are not required). Remember that you must camp at least 300ft from lakes and 50ft from streams. Campfires are not allowed.

Day 3: Alaska Basin to Marion Lake
3¼–4¾ hours, 8.2mi (13.2km)

Continue around west to cross the small South Fork Teton Creek on stepping stones. After switchbacking steeply up the Sheep Steps, make a smoother climb over open, rolling slopes past another turnoff down to Teton campground (via the Devils Stairs) to reach the wide grassy saddle of Mt Meek Pass (9726ft) after one to 1½ hours.

The trail dips slightly to reenter the na-tional park at the start of **Death Canyon Shelf**. This remarkable terrace stretches nearly 3mi between two great precipices, offering breathtaking 'belvedere' views of Prospectors Mountain and adjacent peaks across the 1500ft-deep canyon. For most of the way the trail transits the (unrestricted) *Death Canyon Shelf Camping Zone*, rising and dipping through clusters of whitebark pine and subalpine fir alternating with meadows of cow parsnip. A final easy climb past the left (east) Death Canyon Trail and the right (west) Fox Creek Trail turnoffs brings you up to **Fox Creek Pass** (9560ft), 1¼ to 1¾ hours from Mt Meek Pass.

Continue southwest across open, undulat-ing slopes west of Spearhead Peak. To the north, just left of the elongated pyramid of Fossil Mountain, steep ravines have cut through the forested mountainside to create a series of narrow, green bands. The Teton Crest Trail cuts up gradually left to follow a broad, flowery ridge into a vague saddle (at roughly 9600ft), then drops south to arrive at **Marion Lake**, one to 1½ hours from Fox Creek Pass. This lovely emerald lake lies just below treeline under the stratified east face of Housetop Mountain; there are a number of designated *campsites* across the outlet.

Day 4: Marion Lake to Teton Village via Granite Canyon
4–5¼ hours, 9.7mi (15.6km)

Head southwest over a low ridge, then sidle down across trickling streams of the upper North Fork Granite Creek to a trail junction.

Turn left along the Granite Canyon Trail and start the gentle descent through the *Upper Granite Canyon Camping Zone*. There is excellent, unrestricted camping (with backcountry permit) among the fir-spruce forest and wildflower meadows of this charming alpine valley. The trail leads past turnoffs (left) to Mt Hunt Divide and (right) to Rendezvous Mountain near the Upper Granite Canyon patrol cabin, 1¼ to 1½ hours from Marion Lake.

Proceed down into the (unrestricted) *Lower Granite Canyon Camping Zone* through old Douglas firs below the high granite cliffs. The slope's steepness makes it hard to find good campsites until near the end of the canyon, where elk, moose, mule deer and black bears frequent meadows fringed by thickets of mountain ash and Rocky Mountain maple. The trail intersects with the broad Valley Trail, 1¾ to 2¼ hours from the patrol cabin.

Follow the Valley Trail south directly across Granite Creek past the Granite Canyon Trailhead turnoff (which goes 1½mi southeast to recross Granite Creek before cutting east over sagebush plains to the trailhead car park). The trail rises over slopes of aspen overlooking the wide, flat plain of Jackson Hole. Go right at a fork on the national park boundary and continue to a gravel road, following this down left under

ski lifts to arrive at Teton Village, one to 1½ hours from the Granite Canyon Trail turnoff.

Alternative Finishes
From North Fork Granite Creek trail junction on Day 4, the Teton Crest Trail continues 13½mi south across Moose Creek Divide and Phillips Pass to the southern trailhead at Coal Creek, 2mi west of Teton Pass.

The trail to the upper station of the Jackson Hole Aerial Tram on Rendezvous Mountain turns left (east) off the Teton Crest Trail after 1.4mi (see Teton Village under Nearest Towns).

Wind River Range

Extending some 100mi northwest–southeast along the Continental Divide through central western Wyoming, the spectacular Wind River Range offers some of the best hiking anywhere in the Rockies. Virtually the entire range is protected wilderness, divided into four large, contiguous tracts comprising some 900,000 acres. Bridger Wilderness takes in most of the Winds' western side, while the Fitzpatrick and Popo Agie wilderness areas and the Wind River Roadless Area (part of the Wind River Indian Reservation managed by the Shoshone and Arapaho Tribes) take in its eastern slopes.

NATURAL HISTORY
Past ice ages have left a stunningly glaciated landscape of hundreds of jagged peaks, ice-ground cirques, and lakes. 'The Winds' have several dozen '13-thousanders' (peaks cresting 13,000ft) including Wyoming's highest summit, Gannett Peak (13,804ft). The higher northern half of the Wind River Range also boasts seven of the 10 largest glaciers in the lower 48 states. This remarkable topography makes the Winds one of the Rockies' best regions for mountaineering and alpine rock climbing.

Forests of lodgepole pine, sometimes mixed with ponderosa pine, cover the Winds' lower slopes, giving way to fir-spruce forest in moister and/or higher areas. Whitebark pine is fairly common up to treeline. Wildlife in the Winds, especially elk and mule deer, is subject to hunting and hence wary of humans. Pronghorn antelope are common on the sagebrush plains fringing the range, and moose are often spotted in the waterlogged valley floors or around lakes. Bighorn sheep, which were almost wiped out in the Winds by overhunting and the introduction of livestock, are now so abundant that they are used to restock other wilderness areas. There are plans to reestablish grizzly bears in the Winds.

PLANNING
Permits & Regulations
No permit is needed for trips in the (USFS administered) national forest areas of the Winds.

Camping is not permitted within 100ft of streams or 200ft of trails and lakes (within a quarter-mile of certain heavily visited lakes); fires are prohibited above treeline.

Fishing Permits

Hikers will require a tribal fishing permit if they enter the Wind River Roadless Area (not covered by this guidebook). Seven-day tribal fishing permits are available for $25/35 for a child/adult from regional fishing and backpacking stores, or from the Shoshone and Arapaho fish and game office (☎ 307-332-7207), Fort Washakie. Anglers must have a Wyoming fishing license to fish in national forests.

NEAREST TOWN
Pinedale
The friendly beef and timber town of Pinedale lies at the western foot of the Wind River Range on US 191, 77mi southeast of Jackson. The Rendezvous, an annual reenactment of the early trappers' meetings, is held in the second weekend of July. The Museum of the Mountain Man, off the Fremont Lake Rd, deals with the early fir trade in western Wyoming and offers special historical lectures and presentations during Rendezvous.

The local USFS office (☎ 307-367-4326) at 210 West Pine St, and the BLM Pinedale Resource Area office (☎ 307-367-4358),

432 E Mill St, have information on the Wind River Range. The Great Outdoor Shop (☎ 307-367-2440) at 332 W Pine St sells gear and maps, and rents out ice-climbing equipment and packing llamas.

Pinedale campground (☎ 307-367-4555) has grassy but unshaded tent sites for $11; showers for non-guests cost $4. *Riviera Lodge (☎ 307-367-2424, 442 W Marilyn St)* has rooms from $48.

Cirque of the Towers

Duration	3 days
Distance	20.4mi (32.8km)
Standard	medium (Texas Pass medium-hard)
Start/Finish	Big Sandy campground
Nearest Town	Pinedale
Public Transport	no

Summary An out-and-back hike (with a loop option via Texas Pass) to a spectacular, sheer-sided amphitheater ringed by a dozen or more sheer-sided granite 'towers' at the head of the North Fork Popo Agie River.

The Cirque of the Towers, one of the Rockies' most spectacular cirques, is a favorite hiking destination. This hike involves a long, steady ascent of around 2000ft (600m) to Jackass Pass. Many hikers (especially families) make a base camp at Big Sandy Lake and explore the cirque and other nearby features on day hikes.

PLANNING
When to Hike
Jackass Pass normally melts out by mid-July, but the slightly higher Texas Pass (optional) takes somewhat longer. Lightning associated with summer electrical storms is a major hazard, especially anywhere above treeline. Note that mosquitos can be extremely bothersome in summer.

What to Bring
Early in the season hikers tackling the Texas Pass route may need an ice-axe and crampons (available for hire at Pinedale Outdoor Shop; see Nearest Town).

As this is a heavily impacted area, hikers should carry a fuel stove and refrain from lighting campfires.

Maps

Two USGS 1:24,000 quads cover the hike: *Temple Peak* and *Lizard Head Peak*; if you do the optional Texas Pass loop you will also need *Mount Boneville* and *Big Sandy Opening*. The waterproof 1:48,000 hiking map *Southern Wind River Range* published by Earthwatch Press ($7.95) covers the entire area. The contoured 1:126,720 *Teton-Bridger National Forest* ($4.50, waterproof edition $6.50) takes in almost all of the Wind River Range; it is useful as an overview map, but is insufficiently detailed for accurate navigation.

NEAREST FACILITIES

The free USFS **Big Sandy campground** at the trailhead has 10 primitive sites; treat water collected from the river.

Big Sandy Lodge (☎ *307-382-6513*) at Mud Lake (take the turnoff 1mi south of the Big Sandy campground) offers cabins from $45 and may be able to arrange transport for guests.

GETTING TO/FROM THE HIKE

Turn off Hwy 353 at Boulder, 12mi south of Pinedale, and take the left turn just after the pavement ends (17mi from the highway). Proceed across the Big Sandy River to take another turnoff (26mi from the highway) and continue past Dutch Joe guard station to Big Sandy campground. There is trailhead parking for perhaps several dozen cars, but space is scarce on summer weekends. Sublette Stage (☎ 307-367-6633) does shuttles to local trailheads, including private vehicle transfers.

THE HIKE
Day 1: Big Sandy Campground to Lonesome Lake

4¾–6 hours, 10.2mi (16.4km), 2332ft (711m) ascent

This is most direct route to the cirque. From the campground parking area, follow the Big Sandy Trail along the banks of Big Sandy River, bearing right at its junctions with the

Mud Lake Trail and the V Lake Trail. The trail rises incrementally through lodgepole pines and narrow meadows of pink asters and lupines above the alternately meandering and tumbling river. Climb gently away to the left into spruce forest past the V Lake Trail turnoff, continuing upvalley through stands of whitebark pine to reach the southern shore of **Big Sandy Lake**, two to 2½ hours from the trailhead.

Sheltered *campsites* can be found among boulders in the forest along the lake's southern shore, as well as on its eastern side on terraced meadows looking out over a picturesque island toward the massive slabs of Haystack Mountain's western face. Marauding black bears were a major problem at both camping areas until steel food storage containers were put in place – use them.

Make your way around to a junction on the lake's northern shore. The right-hand turnoff leads to Little Sandy Lake and Clear Lake, then to Temple Pass – a scenic, medium-difficulty, 5–6½ hour, 12mi side trip with 1880ft of ascent/descent which leads past several lakes in the glacial trough between Haystack Mountain and East Temple Peak.

Bear left and climb north onto meadows beside North Creek. As you ascend, clear views open out southeast toward Temple Pass, with the slanting 'beret' form of East Temple Peak, the tooth-like Lost Temple Spire, and Steeple Peak on the northern side of the pass. After fording the creek the trail enters a less gentle glacial landscape, where hardy conifers cling to the polished rock or shelter among raw boulders, before sidling down to cross a minor inlet to **North Lake** on moist lawns at the lake head. There are a few pleasant *campsites* around the shore here.

Climb steeply past some gnarled, old whitebark pines onto rubbly slopes. The trail follows sporadic cairns over open slab shelves and up low bluffs to reach an (unofficial) junction high above the emerald-green Arrowhead Lake, which lies in a deep trough below the sheer walls of Warbonnet Peak. Cut right – the left turnoff leads across the ridge to Hidden Lake – up the eroding slope to reach **Jackass Pass**, also known as **Big Sandy Pass** (10,812ft), 1¾ to 2¼ hours

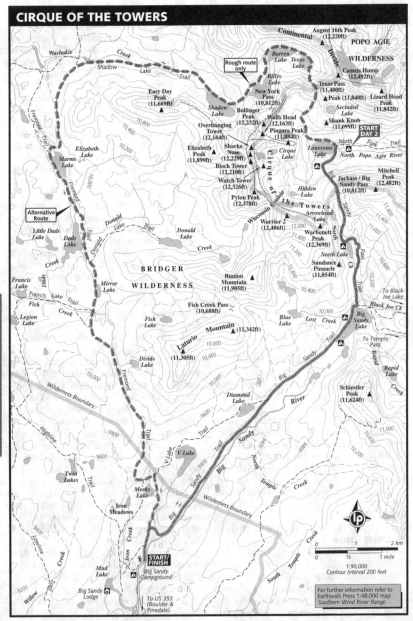

CIRQUE OF THE TOWERS

August 16th Peak (12,220ft)
POPO AGIE WILDERNESS
Continental
Washakie Creek
Shadow Lake
Easy Day Peak (11,669ft)
Barren Lake
Texas Lake
Rough route only
Billys Lake
Camels Hump (12,492ft)
Texas Pass (11,400ft)
New York Pass (10,812ft)
Peak (11,840ft)
Lizard Head Peak (11,842ft)
Secluded Lake
Shadow Lake
Bollinger Peak (12,232ft)
Wolfs Head (12,163ft)
Skunk Knob (11,099ft)
START DAY 2
Overhanging Tower (12,164ft)
Pingora Peak (11,884ft)
Cirque Lake
Lonesome Lake
North Popo Agie River
North Fork Trail
Elizabeth Peak (11,899ft)
Sharks Nose (12,229ft)
Block Tower (12,210ft)
Watch Tower (12,326ft)
Hidden Lake
Jackass / Big Sandy Pass (10,812ft)
Mitchell Peak (12,482ft)
Pylon Peak (12,378ft)
Wisconsin Couloir
Arrowhead Lake
Warrior 2 (12,406ft)
Warbonnet Peak (12,369ft)
Fremont Trail
Marms Lake
Elizabeth Lake
Alternative Route
Little Dads Lake
Dads Lake
Donald Lake
Donald Creek
Donald Lake Trail
Sundance Pinnacle (11,054ft)
North Fork Trail
North Popo Agie Pass
Francis Lake
Dads Creek
Mirror Lake
BRIDGER WILDERNESS
Bunion Mountain (11,905ft)
To Black Joe Lake
Black Joe Ck
Francis Lake Trail
Fish Creek
Legion Lake
Fish Lake
Fish Creek Pass (10,688ft)
Laturio Mountain (11,342ft)
Blue Lake
Lost Creek
Big Sandy Lake
To Temple Pass
Divide Lake
Laturio Mountain (11,305ft)
Schiestler Peak (11,624ft)
Rapid Lake
Rapid
Fremont Trail
Wilderness Boundary
Highline Trail
Diamond Lake
Big Sandy River
V Lake
V Lake
Big Sandy Trail
North Temple Creek
Twin Lakes
Meeks Lake
Iron Meadows
Wilderness Boundary
Big Sandy Creek
Lowline Trail
Iron Creek
START/FINISH
Big Sandy Campground
Mud Lake
Big Sandy Lodge
To US 353 (Boulder & Pinedale)
South Temple Creek
Willow Creek

0   1   2 km
0   ½   1 mile
1:90,000
Contour Interval 200 feet

For further information refer to Earthwalk Press 1:48,000 map Southern Wind River Range

from Big Sandy Lake. The pass, where you cross into Popo Agie Wilderness, offers an excellent overview of the spectacular **Cirque of the Towers**. The broad amphitheater is ringed by more than a dozen jagged 'towers' of gray granite running around to Lizard Head Peak (11,842ft) at its northeastern rim.

Descend (with a brief glimpse of Hidden Lake to the left) into meadows scattered with shrub willows and stands of subalpine firs to arrive at **Lonesome Lake** after 30 to 40 minutes. This beautiful tarn lies in the forested glacial bowl below the striking horn-shaped **Pingora Peak** (11,884ft). Moose are sometimes spotted around the shore or swimming in the lake. Camping is not permitted within a quarter-mile of Lonesome Lake due to the high number of visitors, but suitable (legal) *campsites* can be found on the slopes well up from its southern shore or beside meadows 10 minutes downstream along the small North Popo Agie River (the lake outlet).

Day 2: Lonesome Lake to Big Sandy Campground
4–5 hours, 10.2mi (16.4km), 2332ft (711m) descent
Return to the trailhead by hiking Day 1 in reverse.

Alternative Finish: Texas Pass Loop
7–10 hours, 16mi (25.5km), 1230ft (375m) ascent
This medium-hard alternative loops back to Big Sandy campground. The (unofficial) route climbs up along the northwestern inlet of Lonesome Lake to **Texas Pass** (11,400ft), then descends to Texas Lake and follows the Washakie Creek drainage down past several lakes to meet the Fremont Trail. The trail leads south past **Marms, Dads** and **Mirror Lakes** back to Big Sandy campground.

Rocky Mountain National Park

The 415-sq-mile Rocky Mountain National Park lies northwest of Denver in northern Colorado. Packed into an area hardly a tenth the size of Yellowstone, 'Rocky' is a superb alpine landscape of granite summits, high tundra plateaus, tiny relict glaciers and more than 150 lakes accessible by dozens of scenic trails.

HISTORY
The Rocky area was originally inhabited by groupings of the Ute tribe. Immediately prior to the arrival of Europeans, however, Ute territory was increasingly encroached upon by Arapaho and Cheyenne tribes displaced from the eastern plains by advancing pioneers. In 1819, while leading an expedition on the South Platte River, Major Stephen Long sighted the prominent 14-thousander that today bears his name.

In 1859, Joel Estes tried unsuccessfully to settle the open 'park' meadows along the Big Thompson River. A dozen years later the English earl Lord Dunraven established a private hunting estate here, depicted in 1877 by the great landscape artist Albert Bierstadt in the work *Estes Park*. The inventor FO Stanley purchased Dunraven's estate and in 1909 opened the luxurious Stanley Hotel, establishing Estes Park as a vacation destination for wealthy tourists. Alarmed by the unrestrained development and expansion of the pastoral and logging industries, the conservationist Enos Mills campaigned for the preservation of the area, and in 1915 Congress finally passed the act creating Rocky Mountain National Park. The Fall Ridge Rd over the Continental Divide was completed in 1920, but was largely replaced by the more scenic, high-level Trail Ridge Rd opened in 1932.

NATURAL HISTORY
Lodgepole and ponderosa pine forest predominates in the lower drier edges of the park. As altitude increases, Douglas fir mingles with subalpine fir, Engelmann spruce and aspen. These montane and subalpine forests are often carpeted by fragrant heath-like grouseberry (known locally as whortleberry) shrubs. Colorado blue spruce, readily recognized by its striking bluish-green foliage, grows along mountain streams. Wildflowers such as the radiant red Indian

paintbrush, purple monkshood and blue and white Colorado columbines are found in the subalpine forest clearings, while in moist areas pink moss campion, primroses, and white marsh marigolds are common. Glacier lilies, mountain gentians and alpine sunflowers bloom on the alpine tundra which makes up more than a fourth of the park's area.

In summer red squirrels and chipmunks busily work the lodgepole and fir-spruce forests, harvesting nuts and seeds (or picking over crumbs left by picnickers). Yellow-bellied marmots and pika shelter in coarse talus slopes, feeding on grasses or lichen in the alpine tundra. Nuttall's cottontail rabbits and snowshoe hares shelter in the alpine shrub willow. These herbivores are kept under control by various small predators including the marten, the red fox and bobcat. Rocky's black bears are small and shy, but can occasionally be spotted in meadows munching berries or digging grubs out of rotted trunks in the forest. Mule deer browse in the forests while elk graze in the meadows around dawn and dusk.

Rocky's range of mountain environments allows a diverse birdlife. The red crossbill – note the male's orange-red (especially breast) plumage – constantly moves around the ponderosa and lodgepole forests in search of pine nuts. The radiant-green broad-tailed hummingbirds feed on flowers in the lower montane forests, though they breed in the alpine zone. Greenish-yellow Wilson's warblers and mountain chickadees flit about the alpine krummholz.

The streams in Rocky Mountain National Park have been restocked with the threatened Colorado River cutthroat trout, a subspecies originally distributed throughout the headwaters of the Colorado River.

PLANNING
Maps
Trails Illustrated's 1:59,000 *Rocky Mountain National Park Recreation Map* ($8.95) covers the entire park. The USGS 1:50,000 *Rocky Mountain National Park* ($7) also covers the whole park, but routes are not always shown clearly and it is less widely available.

Permits & Regulations
The park entry fee (valid seven days) for private vehicles is $10, while individuals entering on foot, bicycle, motorcycle or taxi pay $5. Annual passes (individual or private vehicle) cost $20.

Backcountry permits are required for all overnight trips in Rocky. These cost $15 from May through October (otherwise free of charge), regardless of the number in the hiking party and the length of hike (maximum six nights). There are backcountry offices at Estes Park (near the NPS visitor center), Grand Lake (West Unit office) and the Kawuneeche visitor center. Backcountry permits can be reserved after March by writing to the Backcountry Office, Rocky Mountain National Park, Estes Park, CO 80517, or by telephone from March to May 20 (otherwise only one day prior to pick-up) – call ☎ 970-586-1242. Fires are not permitted at most backcountry campsites.

Anglers need park fishing licences. Certain streams are catch-and-release only.

NEAREST TOWNS
Estes Park
The main gateway to Rocky Mountain National Park, the sprawling town of Estes Park lies at the eastern foot of the Front Range just outside the park boundary. The USFS visitor center (☎ 970-586-2317), 161 Second St, is open daily in summer. Outdoor World (☎ 970-586-2114), 156 Elkhorn Ave, has a good range of backcountry gear.

Glacier Basin campground (call the NPS reservation center ☎ 800-365-2267) and *Estes Park campground (☎ 970-586-4188)*, at the East Portal on Tunnel Rd, have tent sites. The huge *YMCA of the Rockies (☎ 970-586-3341)* on Tunnel Rd has rooms from $37. The *H-Bar-G Ranch Hostel (☎ 970-586-3688)* has beds for $10.

The Hostel Hauler (☎ 970-586-3688) runs a shuttle between the Boulder and Estes Park hostels ($15/20 one-way/roundtrip).

Grand Lake
This attractive if very touristy town lies on the north shore of Grand Lake. The chamber of commerce (☎ 970-627-3402) is at the

junction of Hwy 34 and W Portal Rd. Never Summer Mountain Products (☎ 970-627-3642) has hiking gear and maps. *Elk Creek campground (☎ 970-627-8502)* has sites with facilities from $15. The homey *Shadow Cliff Mountain Lodge (☎ 970-627-9220)* has dorm beds from $10 and rooms for $30/35 single/double. Home James (☎ 970-726-5060) runs a shuttle from Denver (also DIA airport) via Granby to Grand Lake ($56).

GETTING AROUND
The Ram's Run (☎ 970-627-8400) operates a scenic backpacker shuttle from Grand Lake to Bear Lake via Trail Ridge and Estes Park.

Odessa Lake

Duration	1–2 days
Distance	10.8mi (17.3km)
Standard	easy-medium
Start/Finish	Bear Lake Trailhead
Nearest Town	Estes Park
Public Transport	yes

Summary This relatively undemanding but rewarding hike leads past half a dozen or so of the park's loveliest lakes.

This longer day (or, better, overnight) hike crosses two minor watersheds (with one moderately steep climb) as it circles Mt Wuh past lovely subalpine lakes. Although much of the route is in the forest, there are plenty of spectacular views.

PLANNING
When to Hike
The relatively low elevation of this hike means it can usually be undertaken from early June at least until early October.

Maps
One USGS 1:24,000 quad covers the route: *McHenrys Peak*.

GETTING TO/FROM THE HIKE
The hike begins at the extremely popular Bear Lake Trailhead, at the terminus of the Bear Lake Rd. The car park here fills quickly in busy periods. In midsummer a frequent, free shuttle service runs back and forth to/from the larger Glacier Basin Shuttle parking area, where the hike ends, so it is best to leave your car there.

THE HIKE
Day 1: Bear Lake Trailhead to Fern Lake
2–2½ hours, 6mi (9.6km), 1150ft (350m) ascent

A broad path from the trailhead car park leads almost immediately to **Bear Lake** (9475ft). With a backdrop that includes Longs Peak and Pagoda Mountain, this lovely tarn is possibly the most visited place in the park. The short circuit of the lake is worth hiking if you have time.

Take the Flattop Mountain Trail turnoff on the lake's northeast side, climbing away through bouldery terrain colonized by hardy aspen and conifers past a turnoff to Bierstadt Lake. There are some good views south into the valley of Glacier Gorge before you reach another trail turnoff among fine stands of aspen.

Follow this trail (right) as it swings northwest up into the Mill Creek catchment through winter avalanche chutes and old limber pines among jumbled boulder moraines. You pass the *Sourdough campsites* and Two Rivers Lake just before crossing a minor watershed, where the gushing **Grace Falls** come into view. Here an unsignposted foot track goes off left to Lake Helene, a broad, shallow tarn lying on a small shelf below Flattop Mountain, which makes a rewarding 10-minute side trip.

Return to the main trail (avoiding a hazardous, old side trail that drops directly from Lake Helene into the basin). The trail sidles down above the spectacular **Odessa Gorge** through course talus slides to meet Fern Creek. Here, a short side trail leads off left, crossing the stream on a neat footbridge to reach *campsites* near the northern shore of **Odessa Lake** (10,020ft). This sapphire lake fills a small but deep glacial trough overlooked by the striking craggy peaks of Notchtop Mountain and the Little Matterhorn. The main trail continues down, quickly curving east past *campsites* by the

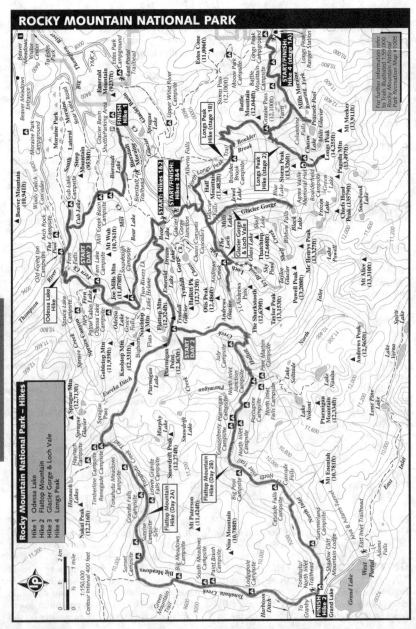

ROCKY MOUNTAIN NATIONAL PARK

ROCKY MOUNTAINS

tranquil **Fern Lake**, where, just across the outlet, you come to a NPS patrol cabin.

A side trip to Spruce Lake leaves from just below the cabin (1.6mi, one hour roundtrip). The unimproved trail climbs west over a ridge (with some minor boulder-hopping) to this picturesque tarn. There are *campsites* on Spruce Lake's northeast shore.

Day 2: Fern Lake to Glacier Basin Shuttle Parking Area

3–4 hours, 6.4mi (10.3km), 1250ft (381m) ascent

Drop more steeply through fir-spruce forest carpeted with grouseberry shrubs past the pleasant if unspectacular Fern Falls. The path descends between the deep gullies of Spruce Creek and Fern Creek, recrossing the latter and passing the *Old Forest Inn camp-sites* to reach The Pool, where the two streams meet the Big Thompson River. Don't cross the river here, but take the right-hand trail and sidle up high above the valley opposite sheer granite cliffs to a route junction. Here, it's worth making the short detour off to the reedy, lily-covered Cub Lake (8620ft); there are *campsites* near the outlet.

As you continue ascending there are some good views back northwest across the wild valley of Spruce Creek to Stones Peak, identifiable by the snowdrift near its summit. You pass through lodgepole and occasional bristlecone pines (regenerating after the fires of 1972) before dropping down into **Mill Creek Basin**.

Head through this pretty little meadow bordered by stands of aspen past a trail departing left to Hollowell Park (a shorter, 1.7mi alternative exit-route that comes out on the Bear Lake Rd closer to the YMCA complex) and the *Mill Creek Basin camp-site*. Continue across the wooden bridge over **Mill Creek** past a second left turnoff to reach the *Upper Mill Creek campsite*.

Climb gently for a half-mile then go left (east) at the first turnoff, which quickly leads onto the foot track ringing **Bierstadt Lake**. Short trails run off through the forest to the lake shore itself, from where you get great views of Longs Peak and other mountains along the Continental Divide.

Two nice alternative routes can be taken from here: the 1.4mi trail leading gently southwest back up to Bear Lake; or the 1.2mi trail down the Bierstadt Trailhead to the Bierstadt Moraine on the Bear Lake Rd.

Otherwise, continue down east through more lodgepole pine forest, where young mule deer browse on herbs and edible fungi, to reach Glacier Basin Shuttle parking area. *Glacier Basin campground* is a five-minute hike across Bear Lake Rd (a 1.3mi trail to the *YMCA* leaves from near campsite No 21).

Flattop Mountain

Duration	2–3 days
Distance	16½mi (25.5km)
Standard	medium-hard
Start	Bear Lake Trailhead
Finish	Grand Lake
Nearest Towns	Estes Park, Grand Lake
Public Transport	yes

Summary The hike up to Flattop Mountain and the extensive undulating plateau known as Bighorn Flats is unquestionably one of the most scenic in the park.

This is a marvellous, high-level crossing of the Continental Divide. Stage 1 to Flattop Mountain (and back) makes a popular roundtrip day hike by itself. For overnight hikers, two route alternatives to Grand Lake are described: Stage 1 – less than a day's hike – followed by either Stage 2A or 2B (with campsites along the way). Those wanting an even longer hike can make a loop by returning to Bear Lake via the stage they shunned on the way out.

The area is a vital summer pasture for bighorn sheep and elk, and sizeable herds of the animals graze these high tundra plains throughout the summer months.

PLANNING
When to Hike

Except for possible smaller drifts on the upper slopes, the trail is normally snow-free from late June to mid-September. Note that electrical storms are a major hazard in Rocky Mountain National Park throughout the summer. Hikers have been killed by lightning strikes on the high, exposed plateau of Flattop Mountain.

Maps
Two USGS 1:24,000 quads cover the route: *McHenrys Peak* and *Grand Lake*.

GETTING TO/FROM THE HIKE
The hike begins at Bear Lake Trailhead (see the Odessa Lake hike) and ends at Grand Lake. There are two car parks with space for 30 vehicles across the Tonahutu Creek bridge just past the Tonahutu Creek Trailhead (Stage 2A); if full, park along the West Portal Rd. The North Inlet Trailhead (Stage 2B) is at the smaller, lower car park.

THE HIKE
Stage 1: Bear Lake Trailhead to Flattop Mountain
2½–3¼ hours, 4½mi (7.2km), 2824ft (860m) ascent
Follow the directions for Day 1 of the Odessa Lake hike as far as the Odessa Lake turnoff. The trail curls up to reach an overlook high above the elongated Dream Lake, 50 minutes to 1¼ hours from the trailhead.

The path zigzags up the broad ridge through steadily thinning alpine scrub of prostrate limber pine and dwarf birch to reach another, more spectacular overlook. From here Emerald Lake is visible directly below in the 1300ft-deep, talus-filled Tyndall Gorge, while there are fine views northeast down the valley to Bierstadt and Sprague Lakes.

Climb into rocky alpine tundra. Pikas scurry about with mouthfuls of lichen and yellow-bellied marmots sound a shrill alarm as you approach. Over to your left is **Tyndall Glacier**, now a tiny remnant of its former self, and behind it Hallet Peak, whose rounded summit makes a straightforward and worthwhile one-hour side trip. The gradient eases as you come onto **Flattop Mountain** (12,324ft), a grassy plateau dotted with yellow avens and other alpine wildflowers, to reach a signposted trail junction 1½ to two hours from the Dream Lake overlook. Day hikers turn around here.

Both overnight hike alternatives described below cross relatively long sections of open and exposed alpine terrain. Here summer storms can bring freezing conditions and/or a considerable danger of lightning strikes, so keep a close watch on weather and be prepared to retreat quickly if conditions look threatening.

Stage 2A: Flattop Mountain to Grand Lake via Tonahutu Creek Trail
4¾–6 hours, 12mi (19.3km)
Head northwest above tarns at the head of Fern Creek past Ptarmigan Point. From here a short deviation left off the trail gives a spectacular view of (otherwise unseen) **Ptarmigan Lake**, set in a glacial cirque. As these names suggest, the white-tailed ptarmigan, a flightless alpine grouse, inhabits these treeless highlands and (although well camouflaged by its speckled plumage) can sometimes be spotted here. The main path rises on past Knobtop Mountain and Eureka Ditch, a small canal dug in 1902 to divert water west, before making a long, gentle descent through the lovely rolling tundra of **Bighorn Flats**.

Sidle down around into the fir-spruce forest of the charming Tonahutu Creek, where half a dozen cascading streamlets merge in a steep-sided alpine valley. The path crosses a larger side stream near *Timberline campsite* (groups only) shortly before reaching a right turnoff, 1¾ to 2¼ hours from Flattop Mountain. This 1.2mi trail mostly follows a forested lateral moraine ridge up past *Renegade* and *Haynach campsites* to the Haynach Lakes, in an imposing setting below Nakai Peak.

Cross a side stream (the Haynach Lakes outlet) and proceed down the narrow, enclosed valley through moist forest draped with lichen past *Tonahutu Meadows campsite* to Granite Falls, a series of small cascades that fall a total of about 60ft. Two campsites are nearby: *Granite Falls* just above the falls, and *Lower Granite Falls* on attractive river flats below them.

The path continues past *Sunrise* and *Sunset campsites* along the northern bank of the Tonahutu Creek, whose Arapaho name alludes to the open grassy flats known as **Big Meadows** through which the stream now increasingly meanders. After passing the Onahu Creek Trail turnoff and the ruins of two cabins built by settler Sam Stone in the early 1900s, the route intersects with the Green Mountain Trail, 1½ to two hours from the Haynach Lakes turnoff.

The 1.8mi Green Mountain Trail is a shorter exit route to Trail Ridge Rd. It leads west over a minor watershed then follows a brook down to reach the trailhead car park after 40 to 50 minutes.

The Tonahutu Creek Trail continues downvalley through lodgepole pine forest fringing the soggy meadows. The easy, if rather monotonous, trail passes the **Big Meadows** (group or stock only), **South Meadows**, **Paint Brush** and **Lodgepole campsites** to meet a trail leading off right after 1½ to two hours.

This half-mile route leads along the small Harbison Ditch to arrive at the Kawuneeche visitor center after 15 to 20 minutes. Another right-hand branch a short way on goes to **Grand Lake Lodge**.

The main trail continues along the creek to terminate by the water-treatment plant at Tonahutu Creek Trailhead after a final 15 to 20 minutes. From here it's a five-minute hike down the dirt road past **Shadow Cliff Mountain Lodge** and across the West Portal Rd to Grand Lake.

Stage 2B: Flattop Mountain to Grand Lake via North Inlet Trail
4¾–6 hours, 11mi (17.7km)
From the Flattop Mountain trail junction, follow cairns south across the plateau of alpine tundra. Andrews Peak stands in front of you and there are great views northwest to the summits of the Never Summer Mountains. Skirt above a deep basin on your right, then drop down through heath of dwarf birch and shrub willow cropped by browsing ungulates. The well-formed trail zigzags down through wildflower slopes into the first trees to cross Hallett Creek after one to 1¼ hours.

A quick side trip into the beautiful upper valley – recommended even if you haven't reserved one of the idyllic **July campsites** (individual and group) here – leads up past

old, stout-trunked firs to near the base of a waterfall splashing down from the Bighorn Flats.

Back on the main trail, head gently down past a swathe of avalanche-cleared forest littered with uprooted trees and snapped-off trunks. A steeper descent in broad switchbacks brings you past the **North Inlet Junction campsites** to a left-hand turnoff (at North Inlet Junction) after 40 to 50 minutes. From here a 3½mi side trail leads across the North Inlet stream and winds its way up through the forest past the **North Inlet Falls** and **Pine Marten campsites** to Lake Nokoni, rising on more gently to **Lake Nanita**. This picturesque tarn nestled at timberline below the craggy outlines of Ptarmigan Mountain and Andrews Peak is probably Rocky's loveliest lake.

The main trail continues downvalley under sheer cliffs past **Porcupine campsite** to cross Ptarmigan Creek. This restocked stream is a refuge for the threatened Colorado River cutthroat trout and presently a no-fishing zone, though it will eventually be opened to anglers on a catch-and-release basis. The muddy trail quickly passes the **Ptarmigan**, **Grouseberry** and (on the creek's south side) **North Inlet campsites**, skirting the waterlogged meadows to reach **Big Pool**, a small churning pond popular with fly fishers with an attractive **campsite**. Drop steadily beside the gushing torrent to Cascade Falls, 1½ to two hours from the Lake Nanita turnoff. Here, North Inlet dives 50ft in several stages; take care as the moistened rocks are dangerously slippery. The **Cascade Falls campsite** is just above the falls.

The path is cut into the cliff-side in places and leads into the lower valley, a glaciated landscape with ice-polished bedrock and the occasional erratic boulder. The fir-spruce woods are plentiful in wild fungi and gradually give way to lodgepole pine forest as you meet a dirt road (closed to unauthorised traffic) near a holiday cottage. Follow the road quickly across the riverside flats of Summerland Park, where there are pleasant **campsites**. The road leads on past the rustic log fence of a private ranch until it comes out at the lower car park at North Inlet Trailhead, 1½ to two hours from Cascade Falls.

From here it's a five-minute hike down to the West Portal Rd just above Grand Lake.

Glacier Gorge & Loch Vale

Duration	1–2 days
Distance	10.2mi (16.4km)
Standard	easy-medium
Start/Finish	Glacier Gorge Junction
Nearest Town	Estes Park
Public Transport	yes

Summary This roundtrip day hike – backcountry camping is possible but limited – leads up into the enclosed valley of Glacier Gorge. A longer side trip into the adjacent Loch Vale is also covered.

The alpine valleys of Glacier Gorge and Loch Vale have an almost magical beauty. Easily accessible (though not overly crowded) trails lead up to jewel-like lakes and tarns in these wild valley heads, where small remnant glaciers cling to the peaks of the Continental Divide.

PLANNING
When to Hike
The trail normally melts out by mid-June and remains passible into October. Winter hikers sometimes make the climb to Mills Lake and The Loch on snowshoes.

Maps
One USGS 1:24,000 quad covers the route: *McHenrys Peak*.

GETTING TO/FROM THE HIKE
The hike begins and ends at Glacier Gorge Junction, a sharp bend on the Bear Lake Rd. The small car park here fills very quickly, so it is best to park at Glacier Basin Shuttle parking area and take the shuttle bus to the trailhead.

THE HIKE
At the trail junction immediately above the car park, head left (east) across Chaos Creek. The trail leads first into mixed aspen

and fir-spruce forest growing on ancient, bouldery moraines, then climbs on beside Glacier Brook to the impressive **Alberta Falls**, where the creek spills over the pink granite bedrock. Continue up slopes still regenerating from a fire in 1900 past the (left) North Longs Peak Trail turnoff to reach a three-way fork, 40 to 50 minutes (or 1.9mi) from the trailhead.

Take the left trail (the right and middle branches go to Lake Haiyaha and Loch Vale – for the latter, see Side Trip), which crosses Icy Brook and Glacier Brook before ascending past Glacier Falls to reach Mills Lake after 30 to 40 minutes. Arriving hikers are wonder-struck by the sudden views up **Glacier Gorge**, dominated by massive scree-strewn slabs below the rump of Longs Peak and the sheer valley headwalls under Pagoda Mountain and Chiefs Head Peak.

Continue around Mills Lake, whose smoothed-rock shore is fringed by erratic blocks and weathered limber pines. The trail leads upvalley past boggy **Jewel Lake** and the *Glacier Gorge campsites*, beginning a steady climb beside Glacier Brook past Ribbon Falls to reach **Black Lake** after 1¼ to 1½ hours. This tarn lies in a spectacular cirque under the east face of McHenrys Peak.

Return to the trailhead by the same route.

Side Trip: Sky Pond
3–4 hours, 4.8mi (7.7km),
1112ft (339m) ascent/descent
The middle trail (from the three-way fork) rises above Icy Brook in a few minor switchbacks to reach The Loch at the start of the enchanting **Loch Vale**. The trail proceeds around the lake's north side and through the valley to *Andrews Creek campsite*. From here a steepening side trail goes up 1mi west along the Andrews Creek drainage to a tarn fed by the meltwater from **Andrews Glacier** (one hour roundtrip). The main trail crosses moist meadows before making a moderate ascent past Timberline Falls to **Glass Lake**. More often called Lake of Glass, in still conditions this tarn in the raw bedrock gives a classic mirror reflection of the surrounding

peaks. The trail rises on smoothly to arrive at Sky Pond (approximately 10,900ft), nestling under the abrupt east wall of Taylor Peak (13,153ft).

To return, retrace your steps to the three-way junction.

Longs Peak

Duration	1–3 days
Distance	13.6mi (21.9km)
Standard	hard
Start/Finish	Longs Peak ranger station or Glacier Gorge Junction
Nearest Town	Estes Park
Public Transport	yes (Glacier Gorge Junction options)

Summary This long, strenuous hike with an ascent of almost 5000ft (1500m) climbs to Granite Pass, then follows a well-trodden but rough route to the broad summit.

The distinctive 'box' shape of Longs Peak (14,255ft) is Rocky's great landmark, and rises almost 1000ft higher than any other summit in the park. Longs Peak is also the most climbed 14-thousander in the Rockies, and can be reached in a very long day hike from either the (eastern) Longs Peak Trailhead – described here as Stage 1A – or the (western) Glacier Gorge Junction – Stage 1B.

Hikers making the ascent in a day usually make a pre-dawn start (using a headlamp), and should carry plenty of water and carefully watch the weather. The route is not suited to sufferers of vertigo. Camping is possible, but backcountry sites are often heavily booked.

PLANNING
When to Hike
The upper route may be snowed over or dangerously icy before July or after late September, when ice-axe and crampons are often required for a safe ascent. In summer the danger of lightning strike on the exposed ridgetops of Longs Peak is usually extreme by early afternoon, so it is essential

to move quickly and watch the weather. Plan to be off the summit by midday.

Maps
Two USGS 1:24,000 quads cover the route: *McHenrys Peak* and *Longs Peak*.

GETTING TO/FROM THE HIKE
Most hikers set out from Longs Peak ranger station, 1mi from the turnoff on Hwy 7 (Peak to Peak Scenic Byway), 9mi south of Estes Park. In midsummer the large trailhead car park often fills up well before dawn.

The NPS *Longs Peak campground (☎ 800-365-2267 for reservations)* near the trailhead makes an excellent base camp.

Alternatively, hikers can set out from and/or finish at the Glacier Gorge Junction (Stage 1B) below Bear Lake (see the Glacier Gorge & Loch Vale hike).

THE HIKE
Stage 1A: Longs Peak Ranger Station to Granite Pass
2–3 hours, 3.8mi (6.1km), 2700ft (823m) ascent
Take the trail from the ranger station (9400ft) and begin a gentle ascent through mostly fir and spruce forest past the Storm Pass turnoff to meet Alpine Brook. Climb on past *Goblins Forest campsite*, in a stand of thick-trunked limber pines.

The trail winds up past the idyllic *Battle Mountain campsite*, crossing the stream before it rises above treeline onto open wildflower slopes. There are some good views of Longs Peak up to your left, while behind you the Twin Sisters Peaks (11,413ft) rise beyond the Tahosa Valley. The winding trail now skirts up the side of Mills Moraine to eventually reach a ridgetop trail junction, 1½ to two hours from the trailhead.

From here a side trip to **Chasm Lake** can be made in 45 minutes roundtrip. The narrow path dips slightly past **Columbine Falls**, where Roaring Fork Creek cascades 100ft to Peacock Pool, then continues across the stream to a patrol cabin at the end of a lovely meadow. Follow cairns on up a rough moraine ridge for a **stunning vista** of this highland tarn nestled right at the granite foot of Longs Peak's east face.

The main trail sidles above shallow pools in a soggy basin down to your right to arrive at **Granite Pass** (approximately 12,100ft), 30 to 45 minutes from the Chasm Lake junction. The pass offers no good views of Longs Peak, but note the interesting cairn-like outcrop to your right.

Stage 1B: Glacier Gorge Trailhead to Granite Pass
3–4 hours, 7mi (11.2km), 2850ft (868m) ascent

From the trail junction above Alberta Falls (see the Glacier Gorge & Loch Vale hike) bear left and cross Glacier Creek just above an impressive water slide. The trail rises gently over regenerating slopes high above the valley to cross Boulder Brook, where there are *campsites*, 1½ to two hours from the trailhead.

Sidle up around the mountainside, then climb in several switchbacks through the last stunted limber pines, from where there are the first clear, close-up views of Longs Peak. A final, long, sweeping rise through the alpine tundra brings you to **Granite Pass**, after a further 1½ to two hours.

Stage 2: Granite Pass to Longs Peak Summit
3¾–5¼ hours, 3mi (4.8km), 2125ft (647m) ascent

Head up west in steep switchbacks, then climb more smoothly and cross the now tiny Boulder Brook to reach Boulder Field, a jumble of glaciated granite blocks under the abrupt north wall of Longs Peak. The nine sheltered *Boulderfield campsites* here are at around 12,800ft – by far the highest in the park.

The trail climbs on past the Agnes Vaille Memorial Hut, a stone emergency shelter dedicated to two mountaineers who died in 1925 during the first winter ascent of Longs Peak, to reach the **Keyhole** after 1¾ to 2¼ hours. This gap in the ridge at around 13,000ft gives you a first spectacular view down into Glacier Gorge, a valley head

ringed by McHenrys Peak, Chiefs Head and Pagoda Mountain.

From here on the way becomes much more serious. Be wary of rockfall – watch for falling debris from climbers above you and avoid dislodging rocks yourself. Be alert to approaching bad weather and be prepared to turn back; thunderstorms bring an extreme danger of lightning strikes.

Follow red-and-yellow paint markings on rocks southeast slightly downhill into the (often snow-filled) gully of the **Trough**. The route continues up the so-called **Narrows**, a sheer-edged shelf with some exhilaratingly tight and exposed sections. Give way to descending hikers you may encounter on this narrow trail. A final, steeper ascent over the polished-granite slabs known as the **Homestretch** leads onto the broad open top of **Longs Peak** (14,255ft), two to three hours from the Keyhole.

The summit area is bigger than a football field and – fortunately – easily accommodates the scores of climbers up here on an average summer day. Sign the register book and explore the panoramic views taking in much of the northern Colorado Rockies. Begin your descent before midday.

Indian Peaks Wilderness

The 73,391-acre Indian Peaks Wilderness lies 25mi west of Boulder in the Colorado Front Range. Its western half lies in Roosevelt National Forest, while the eastern side takes in Arapaho National Forest. On its northern boundary the Indian Peaks Wilderness merges with Rocky Mountain National Park (whose early advocates pushed unsuccessfully for its inclusion). Most of its highest summits bear the names of Native American tribes.

Indian Peaks Wilderness is an interesting landscape of wild, forested valleys and large expanses of alpine tundra, mountain cirques with tiny relict glaciers, and more than 50 lakes and tarns. It is also subject to extremely heavy recreational use due to its closeness to the sprawl of the Boulder-Denver metropolitan area.

PLANNING
Permits & Regulations
Between 1 June and 15 September a backcountry permit is required for overnight trips in Indian Peaks Wilderness. The USFS offices in Boulder, Estes Park and Granby, as well as Ace Hardware in Nederland (see Nearest Town) issue backcountry permits ($5 per group) for 17 of Indian Peaks' 18 travel zones. Only a limited number of permits is available for each zone per day. You do not need a backcountry permit for hikes that do not involve an overnight camp.

Camping is not permitted at all in the Four Lakes Travel Zone (the eastern approach to Pawnee Pass), and permitted only in designated campsites (with backcountry permit) in the Diamond Lake, Crater Lake, Caribou Lake and Jasper Lake Travel Zones. Outside these areas campers (with backcountry permits) are free to choose their own sites. Camp fires are not allowed anywhere on the east side of the Continental Divide, nor around most lakes on its west side. Tents and fires must be at least 100ft away from lakes, streams and trails.

NEAREST TOWN
Nederland
Nederland stands at the junction of Hwy 119 and Hwy 72 (Peak to Peak Scenic Byway) on the eastern foot of Indian Peaks Wilderness. The town is 17mi west of Boulder (follow Boulder Canyon Dr). Ace Hardware (☎ 303-258-3132, open daily) at the Village shopping mall, sells maps and guidebooks and issues state fishing licenses and backcountry permits for Indian Peaks Wilderness. The Nederland visitor center (☎ 303-258-3936) is diagonally opposite the Village shopping mall. The Bucking Brown Trout Co on First St has hiking and fishing gear and supplies.

Nederland International Hostel (☎ 303-258-7788, 8 W Boulder St) has dorm beds for $15 and rooms for $25/30 single/double. RTD buses run up to a dozen times a day between Nederland and Boulder.

Pawnee Pass

Duration	1–2 days
Distance	15mi (24km)
Standard	medium
Start	Brainard Lake (Longs Lake Trailhead)
Finish	Monarch Lake
Nearest Town	Nederland
Public Transport	no

Summary This west–east crossing of the Continental Divide is one of the most beautiful and popular hikes in the wilderness. The 12,541ft Pawnee Pass gives excellent views of the principal summits in the Indian Peaks and is often visited as a roundtrip day hike from Brainard Lake.

This hike from Long Lake makes a stiff ascent over Pawnee Pass before following the Cascade-Buchanan drainage down to Monarch Lake. The route involves an ascent of 2500ft (760m), and can be combined with the Arapaho Pass hike to make a wonderful (semi-) loop tour.

In 1882 Pawnee Pass was surveyed as a possible railroad route (which was ultimately built over Rollins Pass), but a trail was constructed over the pass in the 1930s by the Civilian Conservation Corps (CCC). Although fit hikers manage to complete the route in a single day, it's best to get a backcountry permit and take at least two days.

PLANNING
When to Hike
Pawnee Pass usually melts out by the beginning of July, but the route is often already out of condition by early October. From late June to mid-September thunderstorms bring heavy rain and extreme danger of lightning strike.

Maps
The 1:40,680 Trails Illustrated map *Indian Peaks/Gold Hill* ($9.95) is recommended for the hike. Two USGS 1:24,000 quads also cover the route: *Ward* and *Monarch Lake.*

GETTING TO/FROM THE HIKE
The hike begins at the Long Lake Trailhead in the Brainard Lake Recreation Area. To get

there follow Hwy 72 (Peak to Peak Scenic Byway) 8mi north from Nederland (see Nearest Town) to Ward, then drive 5mi west to Brainard Lake. The large trailhead car park is a half-mile on, west of the lake. There is an entry fee of $5 per vehicle, but free parking exists at the recreation area entrance, 2½mi before Brainard Lake.

Basic sites at the USFS **Pawnee campground** (☎ *1877-444-6777, 1800-280-2267 for reservations)* at Brainard Lake cost $12. Backcountry permits are not available for the Four Lakes Travel Zone east of Pawnee Pass – the ban on camping in this sensitive area is strictly enforced.

The hike ends at the western shore of Monarch Lake. From Granby take Hwy 34 to the Arapaho National Recreation Area, then drive 10mi east on the unpaved USFS Rd 125 via the southern side of Granby Lake to the large car park at Monarch Lake Trailhead.

THE HIKE
Day 1: Long Lake Trailhead to Pawnee Lake
3¼–4½ hours, 6.6mi (10.6km), 2540ft (774m) ascent

The Pawnee Pass Trail heads through fir-spruce forest (past a left trail from Brainard Lake) to Long Lake, continuing around its north side before climbing over a crest to reach **Lake Isabelle** (10,855ft). This lake lies slightly below treeline in a horseshoe of craggy peaks. From here, a popular side trip (two hours roundtrip) leads off left along the lake's northern shore, then follows the drainage of the inlet (South St Vrain Creek) to a tarn under Shoshoni Peak, Isabelle Glacier and Navajo Peak.

On the main trail, climb away right beside a splashing stream, then follow a revegetated moraine ridge out of the trees. Steep switchbacks cut into the rock lead to a rocky shelf high above the lake. Ascend tundra slopes, that look east to the smoggy sprawling suburbs of Boulder and Denver, to reach the broad, blustery ridge of **Pawnee Pass** (12,541ft), 2¼ to three hours from the trailhead.

Drop west (where Granby Lake comes briefly into view) to begin a long, spiralling descent through rough, bouldery rubble underneath mushroom-like outcrops on the western flank of Pawnee Peak. The trail leads out onto meadows before cutting down to the north end of Pawnee Lake, a lovely, subalpine lake nestling in a cirque one to 1½ hours from the pass. Nice **campsites** (undesignated, fires prohibited) can be found across the outlet among tall spruces.

Day 2: Pawnee Lake to Monarch Lake Trailhead
3–4 hours, 8.4mi (13.5km)

Head downvalley opposite glistening glaciers under the jagged summit of Mt George past the turnoff to Crater Lake. (This is another spectacular lake, ringed with abrupt rock ridges, that makes a worthwhile side trip taking 1½ hours there and back; eight backcountry permits are available per day for the designated **campsites** in the surrounding Crater Lake Travel Zone.) The main trail descends along Cascade Creek past the tumbling, 40ft-high Cascade Falls, crossing and recrossing the stream as it passes occasional beaver dams and **campsites** in the lodgepole forest.

Proceed down to Buchanan Creek just before you pass the Buchanan Pass Trail turnoff (on the right). The trail leads on across Hell Canyon Creek to intersect with the Southside Trail (this is a 0.6mi cutoff that crosses the creek, then goes southwest through lodgepole forest to Arapaho Creek – see the Arapaho Pass hike). The trail continues on to the eastern end of **Monarch Lake** (8351ft), skirting its northern shore to arrive at Monarch Lake Trailhead.

Alternative Campsites
There is undesignated camping along the Cascade Creek Travel Zone (for which there are 16 backcountry permits available per day), which extends down the whole valley from Pawnee Lake almost to Monarch Lake. The **Arapaho Bay campground**, at the (north) eastern end of Lake Granby, is 1½mi from the Monarch Lake Trailhead.

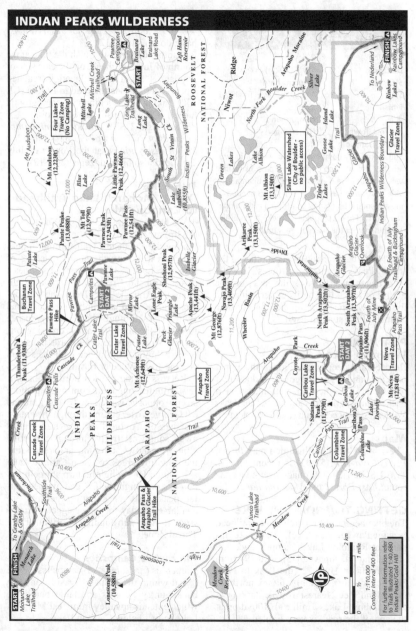

INDIAN PEAKS WILDERNESS

Arapaho Pass & Arapaho Glacier Trail

Duration	2 days
Distance	19mi (30km)
Standard	medium-hard
Start	Monarch Lake Trailhead
Finish	Rainbow Lakes campground
Nearest Towns	Nederland
Public Transport	no

Summary This combined route involving two lengthy ascents approaches the pass from the wild Arapaho Creek, west of the Continental Divide, and continues across open ridges overlooking the interesting string of artificial lakes along the North Fork of Boulder Creek. It is easily combined with the Pawnee Pass route.

The 11,906ft Arapaho Pass is another of the Indian Peaks' scenic pass routes. In 1904 work began on a road over the pass from the Fourth of July Mine on its eastern side, but the road was never completed farther than Arapaho Pass summit itself.

PLANNING
When to Hike
Before July deep snow blocks the upper pass area and higher ridges, as it does after mid-October. Remember, you must have a backcountry permit to camp in Indian Peaks Wilderness between 1 June and 15 September.

Maps
The 1:40,680 Trails Illustrated map *Indian Peaks/Gold Hill* ($9.95) is recommended. Two USGS 1:24,000 quads also cover the route: *East Portal* and *Monarch Lake*.

GETTING TO/FROM THE HIKE
The hike begins at Monarch Lake Trailhead (see the Pawnee Pass hike). The hike terminates at Rainbow Lakes campground, 6mi west along the unpaved USFS Rd 298 from the turnoff on Hwy 72 (the Peak to Peak Scenic Byway), roughly 6½mi north of Nederland (see Nearest Town). Parking at the Rainbow Lakes Trailhead, 100yd on at the end of the road, is very limited.

Rainbow Lakes campground (☎ 1877-444-6777, 800-280-2267 for reservations) has a dozen sites ($12).

Another option is to finish the hike at the Fourth of July Trailhead, on the east side of Arapaho Pass. This trailhead is reached from Nederland via the road to Eldora (CR 130), taking the Buckingham campground turnoff (CR 111) just west of Eldora.

The basic USFS **Buckingham campground** *(☎ 877-444-6777, 800-280-2267 for all reservations)* at the Fourth of July Trailhead also has a dozen sites ($12).

THE HIKE
Day 1: Monarch Lake Trailhead to Caribou Lake
4½–6 hours, 9.3mi (15km), 2799ft (853m) ascent

Follow the Southside Trail through lodgepole forest around the southern shore of Monarch Lake (8351ft). Proceed southeast across Arapaho Creek, then turn off right along the Arapaho Pass Trail. The trail begins a long, gradual climb with occasional switchbacks through the bouldery spruce forest of the narrow valley, crossing numerous streamlets before it fords the small creek below its confluence with the stream coming from Wheeler Basin.

Recross to the creek's northern bank a few minutes on, then continue up more steeply opposite white craggy ridges around Mt George. After cutting through the grassy marshes of Coyote Park, the trail climbs away southwest (right) through attractive alpine meadows, crossing and recrossing the now tiny creek to reach **Caribou Lake** (11,150ft). This delightful tarn at treeline is perched on a high shelf ringed by spectacular peaks. Six backcountry permits are available per day for the designated **campsites** in the surrounding Caribou Lake Travel Zone.

Alternative Campsites
Numerous (undesignated) campsites can be found within the Arapaho Travel Zone (10 backcountry permits available per day), which extends upvalley from near Monarch Lake to just below Caribou Lake.

Day 2: Caribou Lake to Rainbow Lakes Campground

4½–6 hours, 9.6mi (15.5km), 1795ft (547m) ascent

The trail heads southeast across the meadow to make a 750ft ascent in numerous steep switchbacks onto the tundra ridge top, then follows this briefly right to reach the scenic **Arapaho Pass** (11,906ft) after 45 minutes to one hour. For better views of Mt Neva (12,814ft) and Lake Dorothy, follow the Caribou Pass Trail off right (west) a short way.

The main trail traverses gently down slopes above the North Fork of Middle Boulder Creek to pass shafts and tailings – even an old steam engine – of the long abandoned **Fourth of July Mine** to reach the Arapaho Glacier Trail turnoff after 25 to 30 minutes. (From here you can simply continue 1.8mi on the Arapaho Pass Trail down to the Fourth of July Trailhead – see Getting to/from the Hike.)

Turn left and begin a sustained eastward ascent in sidles and switchbacks high above the valley to reach **Arapaho Glacier Overlook** after one to 1½ hours. This gap in the ridge south of South Arapaho Peak gives an awesome (if incomplete) view of the Arapaho Glacier – the most southerly glacier in North America – whose snout is fringed by moraine masses damming a tiny melt-water tarn.

Head east over rolling tundra giving wonderful views south toward Rollins Pass and southeast to Nederland, before cutting through a minor saddle (approximately 12,085ft) to the north side of the ridge. These slopes overlook the picturesque chain of small reservoirs in the upper North Fork Boulder Creek which supply water to the City of Boulder. (Public access to this watershed is prohibited – trespassers risk a $100 fine.) The trail sidles down toward the dozen or so lowland ponds called the Rainbow Lakes, ducking into the first stunted limber pines to make a long descent beside a wire fence (marking the watershed boundary) to arrive at the USFS *Rainbow Lakes campground*, 2½ to three hours from Arapaho Glacier Overlook.

Alternative Campsites
This section passes through the Neva Travel Zone (upper valley of North Fork of Middle Boulder Creek; nine backcountry permits) and the Glacier Travel Zone (along the Arapaho Glacier Trail; seven permits), both of which have undesignated camping.

Maroon Bells–Snowmass Wilderness

The 180,962-acre Maroon Bells–Snowmass Wilderness lies within the White River and Gunnison National Forests directly south of Aspen in central Colorado. Forming the spine of the wilderness, the mighty Elk Mountains include half a dozen 14-thousanders, among them the famous Maroon Bells. Here, the massive ice-age glaciations have produced some classic glacial lakes and tarns. The ranges are fringed by extensive alpine meadows and highland forests of Engelmann spruce, subalpine fir and the rarer white fir, with sporadic stands of graceful aspen.

PLANNING
Permits & Regulations

Permits are not necessary to hike in the Maroon Bells–Snowmass Wilderness, but anglers must have a state fishing license. Designated campsites have been established at some of the most popular camping areas (including Crater Lake and Geneva Lake on the Maroon Bells Loop featured here); always use these where they exist. Camps are not allowed within 100ft of trails, streams and lakes (in certain cases within a quarter-mile of lakes); fires must be at least a half-mile below treeline.

NEAREST TOWN & FACILITIES
Aspen

Aspen is 41mi southeast of Glenwood Springs on Hwy 82. A former mining town, Aspen has become one of the Rockies' premier ski resorts as well as a second home for the rich and famous. The USFS office

(☎ 970-925-3445) at 806 W Hallam St has free brochures on local hikes. Ute Mountaineers (☎ 970-925-2849) at 308 S Mill St sells gear, books and hiking maps.

The historic *Little Red Ski Haus (☎ 970-925-3333)* has dorm accommodations for $23. There are six basic *USFS campgrounds (sites $10 to $12; ☎ 877-444-6777 for reservations)* nearby along Maroon Creek and Roaring Fork River. The closest camping with facilities is at *Aspen Basalt campground*, on Hwy 82 about 20mi north of Aspen.

Aspen is one of the Rockies' few hiking centers accessible by public transportation. The regional RFTA buses run regularly between Aspen and Glenwood Springs ($6), which is on the Greyhound bus and Amtrak rail networks. Several airlines operate regular daily flights between Denver and Aspen.

GETTING AROUND

For trailhead shuttles call High Mountain Taxi (☎ 925-8294, 800-925-8294) or Alpine Express (☎ 800-822-4844). Town Taxi (☎ 970-349-5543) runs hiker shuttles to/from Crested Butte; Aspen Aviation (☎ 970-925-2522, 800-289-1369) does the same by air.

Maroon Bells Loop

Duration	4 days
Distance	29mi (47km)
Standard	medium
Start/Finish	Maroon-Snowmass Trailhead (Maroon Lake)
Nearest Town	Aspen
Public Transport	yes

Summary This very high-level route is largely above 11,000ft and crosses four passes exceeding 12,000ft. Also known as the 'Four Passes Loop', this classic hike completely circumnavigates the Maroon Bells, giving constantly changing views of these remarkable peaks.

The majestic twins, Maroon Peak (14,156ft) and North Maroon Peak (14,014ft), are composed of reddish-brown sedimentary rock and have a stratified appearance more typical of the northern Rockies.

Despite a few steep sections, the ascents on this hike are generally mild; however, hikers should be acclimatized to the high altitude. Hiking in a clockwise direction is slightly easier and more scenic.

PLANNING
When to Hike

Lingering winter snow may keep this route closed well into July and after September. In early summer some of the streams are serious fords. Throughout the summer, powerful electrical storms are common in the early afternoon. Hikers seeking solitude should avoid the Maroon Bells area on summer weekends.

Maps

Trails Illustrated's waterproof 1:40,680 *Maroon Bells Redstone Marbles* ($9.95) map covers the hike; otherwise use two USGS 1:24,000 quads: *Maroon Bells* and *Snowmass Mountain*.

GETTING TO/FROM THE HIKE

The loop begins and ends at the Maroon-Snowmass Trailhead near Maroon Lake, at the end of the Maroon Creek Rd. To use the trailhead parking lot (below the large picnic/parking area) you must pick up a pass at the USFS entrance gate. Due to the popularity of the Maroon Lake area, private traffic is restricted in summer. From 19 June to 6 September (plus weekends through September) the road is closed to private traffic above the T Lazy 7 Ranch between 8.30 am and 5 pm. During road closures the RFTA (☎ 925-8484) runs half-hourly shuttle buses between Aspen and Maroon Lake (children/adults $3/5 roundtrip). The last bus leaves Maroon Lake at 5 pm.

THE HIKE
Day 1: Maroon-Snowmass Trailhead (Maroon Lake) to Upper West Maroon Creek

2¼–3 hours, 4.6mi (7.4km), 1270ft (387m) ascent

The Maroon-Snowmass Trailhead is at the upper end of a new picnic area and car park below the red crags of Sievers Mountain. A mudslide in 1989 forced the permanent

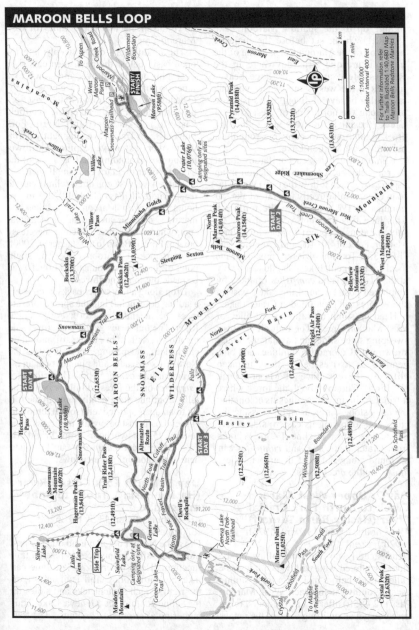

MAROON BELLS LOOP

closure of the campground here. Walk for a minute up to the shallow **Maroon Lake** (9580ft), which, set before the majestic backdrop of the Maroon Bells, is one of the most picturesque tarns anywhere in the Rockies. Head around past large beaver mounds to the west shore, where you can take either of several diverging trails; these lead along the north side of West Maroon Creek (the inlet), or cross and follow the creek's south side to converge roughly a half-mile past Maroon Lake.

Climb through mixed coniferous forest over a rocky crest to a trail junction in an aspen grove, then follow the (left) West Maroon Creek Trail directly to **Crater Lake**, 50 minutes to 1¼ hours from the trailhead. This lake fills a trough (drained only by subterraneous seepage) right below North Maroon Peak (14,014ft) and Pyramid Peak (14,018ft). To minimize the impact on the local environment, hikers should camp only at the 11 designated *campsites* (marked by numbered posts) around the lake's eastern shore. Fires are prohibited at Crater Lake.

Head up south into the upper valley of West Maroon Creek. The trail climbs over sweeping scree slides and avalanche slopes strewn with Colorado columbines and blue gentians as it rises below sheer terraced cliffs on the east face of Maroon Peak (14,156ft). Cut up through the forest where it fringes wild raspberry thickets colonizing the talus slopes on your right, crossing the creek and following its eastern side before you recross it near treeline, 1¼ to 1¾ hours from Crater Lake. Pleasant *campsites* can be found along much of the upper valley, mostly on the creek's eastern side.

Day 2: Upper West Maroon Creek to North Fork Crystal River (Hasley Basin Turnoff)
4½–6 hours, 8½mi (13.7km), 1975ft (602m) ascent

Head steadily up over the rolling tundra slopes scattered with willow heath into the valley head, before making a long, sidling ascent southwest to reach **West Maroon Pass** (12,495ft) after 1¼ to 1¾ hours. From here you get an uplifting view of the ranges to the west, as well as a final look back down the spectacular upper valley of West Maroon Creek.

The muddy trail drops steeply into the open basin below the pass, then cuts right over glorious wildflower meadows to a junction marked only by a cairned pole. (The left turnoff goes down to the East Fork of West Maroon Trailhead on the Schofield Pass Rd.) Take the (right) North Fork Fravert Basin Trail, traversing gently northwest over extensive alpine-wildflower meadows surrounding the East Fork of the Crystal River to a tarn on a small shelf.

Make a very steep, direct climb east to reach **Frigid Air Pass** (12,410ft), 1½ to two hours from West Maroon Pass. Pikas and marmots scamper around this spectacular spot, which looks directly across the grassy bowl of Fravert Basin to the staggered, 2000ft western face of Maroon Peak. The slight point of Snowmass Mountain (14,092ft) can be made out to the northwest.

Drop along a few switchbacks, then begin a sidling descent left into the spruce forest to meet the meandering North Fork Crystal River. The trail leads gently past streamside meadows visited by flocks of mountain chickadees, steepening increasingly as the North Fork cascades and plunges over an escarpment into beaver ponds. Here, look for *campsites* on the forested hillock below the falls. Continue more gently through the forest to an unsignposted left (south) turnoff to Hasley Basin, just before the trail crosses the stream, 1½ to two hours from Frigid Air Pass. Many good *campsites* can be found here at the edge of the meadows.

Day 3: North Fork Crystal River (Hasley Basin Turnoff) to Snowmass Lake
4½–6 hours, 8.4mi (13.5km), 2526ft (670m) ascent

Cross the North Fork and head quickly past more *campsites* in the trees to reach a trail junction. (Here, hikers with less time can take the North Fork Cutoff Trail turnoff, on the right, which switchbacks and sidles up the slope to join the Geneva Lake Trail higher up after one to 1½ hours.) The trail continues downvalley through meadows fringed by raspberry shrubs and stands of aspen, crossing a small torrent (which may be tricky to cross in early summer) to intersect with the Geneva Lake Trail. (The left branch leads 0.3mi down to the Geneva Lake North Fork Trailhead.)

Turn right and climb steeply in tight switchbacks up slopes that look out southwest toward tiny remnant glaciers on Treasury Mountain. The trail levels out shortly before you reach **Geneva Lake** (10,936ft), a pleasant, greenish tarn tucked into a hanging terrace high above the North Fork valley 1¾ to 2¼ hours from the Hasley Basin turnoff. There are several designated *campsites* above the steep western shore (no fires – camping otherwise not permitted within a quarter-mile of the lake).

Skirt around to a stand of firs and spruce, where a route departs (left) to Siberia Lake (see Side Trip). The trail cuts around Geneva Lake's north side and up southeast to a little saddle, where Maroon Peak reappears, before sidling gently upward high above the North Fork to meet the incoming cutoff trail. Climb on over grassy hillocks past a reedy pond, then make a final traversing ascent to arrive at **Trail Rider Pass** (12,418ft), 1¾ to 2½ hours from Geneva Lake. Marked by a thin band of powdery limestone separating the gray and red rock strata, this dip in the ridge offers an excellent overview of the Snowmass basin ahead.

Drop in several broad switchbacks before beginning a high, sidling descent to reach the northwestern end of **Snowmass Lake** (10,980ft), 50 minutes to 1¼ hours from the pass. There are ideal *campsites* near the lake outlet. At the lake head vast scree fields sweep down from a mighty trio of semidetached summits: Snowmass Peak (south), Hagerman Peak (middle) and Snowmass Mountain.

Side Trip: Siberia Lake
2½–3½ hours, 3mi (4.8km), 916ft (279m) ascent/descent
The mostly prominent trail (not shown on maps) leads north along the slopes high above the western side of the Geneva Lake

inlet. After passing the shallow Little Gem Lake follow the tiny valley stream to **Siberia Lake** (11,852ft), a raw tarn at the upper vegetation line. A rougher route continues over the rocky pass at the head of the valley into the drainage of Avalanche Creek.

Day 4: Snowmass Lake to Maroon-Snowmass Trailhead (Maroon Lake)
3–4½ hours, 7.6mi (12.2km), 1482ft (451m) ascent
Follow the muddy Maroon-Snowmass Trail through the forest gradually southeast to pass some *campsites* beside the marshy meadows just before you cross Snowmass Creek. There are good views south to the west faces of the Sleeping Sexton (ridge) and the Maroon Bells. The trail soon passes a right turnoff (going to *campsites* on the creek's east side), winding up past several more *campsites* at treeline before it heads up across wildflower meadows and old moraines dotted with shrub willow. A long, sweeping switchback over the alpine tundra brings you gently up to **Buckskin Pass** (12,462ft), two to three hours from Snowmass Lake. The pass gives uplifting views in both directions, including the mighty Pyramid Peak ahead.

Descend in steep curves past the Willow Lake Trail turnoff, continuing (right) down over alpine meadows into the forest. The trail winds down through **Minnehaha Gulch**, crossing the stream to pass *campsites* under the east walls of the Sleeping Sexton. Sidle down through groves of aspen to arrive back at the West Maroon Trail junction near Crater Lake, one to 1½ hours from the pass. The hike back down to the trailhead at Maroon Lake (see Day 1) takes 45 minutes to one hour.

Other Hikes

JEWEL BASIN HIKING AREA
Situated in the Swan Range between Kalispell and Glacier National Park, the 15,349-acre Jewel Basin Hiking Area is one of Montana's

ROCKY MOUNTAINS

most heavily visited outdoor recreation areas. The basin's 'jewels' are its two-dozen-odd, scattered glacial lakes. Various route combinations are possible, including a medium-standard, 8½mi loop linking the Twin Lakes, Blackfoot Lake, the Jewel Lakes and Black Lake. Due to the area's great popularity, backcountry camping is in designated sites only.

Jewel Basin Hiking Area is most easily accessible via the Echo Lake Rd turnoff on Hwy 83, roughly 20mi southeast of Kalispell. Two USGS 1:24,000 quads cover most of the basin: *Jewel Basin* and *Crater Lake*.

MISSION MOUNTAINS

When viewed from the rolling farmland along northern Montana's Hwy 93 on their western fringe, the high crags and deep lateral valleys of the Mission Mountains are a striking sight. The Mission Mountains' east side comprises Flathead National Forest, while the Mission Mountains Tribal Wilderness, owned by the Federated Salish and Kootenai Tribes, takes in their western side. To enter the Tribal Wilderness hikers need a permit ($7/11 for three days/one year) and campers also need a camp stamp ($10 for one year), available from the Tribal Office on Hwy 93 in Pablo; regional Montana Fish & Wildlife offices; or local outdoor stores.

On the range's west side, a rewarding, long (10.4mi) day- or overnight hike climbs 3371ft over Mollman Pass (6893ft) to **Mollman Lakes**, just outside the tribal wilderness. From here an excellent 19mi, four-day loop leads via Elk Lake and Summit Lake (the trail between these lakes is not shown on maps) to Lake McDonald. The Mollman Trailhead is 6mi east off Hwy 93 via a turnoff 3mi south of Ronan; a track along the Pablo Feeder Canal leads back to Mollman Trailhead. McDonald Lake is 5mi off Hwy 93 via a turnoff 6½mi north of St Ignatius, where the once-daily Missoula-Whitefish bus stops. For the loop use the 1:50,000 *Mission Mountains and Mission Mountains Tribal Wilderness map*, or two USGS 1:24,000 quads: *Fort Connah* and *Mount Harding*.

The **Cold Lakes**, on the eastern side of the Mission mountains in the Flathead National Forest (no permit required), are popular with local anglers. The easy and short (3mi roundtrip) day hike leads to the attractive lower Cold Lake, from where a rougher trail can be followed to the upper lake (camping prohibited within a quarter-mile of lakes). Trailhead access is via the Cold Creek turnoff, 23mi south of Swan Lake on Montana Hwy 83, then turn right after 2½mi. Apart from the 1:50,000

USFS map referred to above, two USGS 1:24,000 quads cover the route: *Piper-Crow Pass* and *Peck Lake*.

SELWAY-BITTERROOT WILDERNESS

The most pristine tracts of wilderness in the Bitterroot Range, which stretches roughly 200mi along Montana's western border with Idaho, are within the 1.3-million-acre Selway-Bitterroot Wilderness.

The Bitterroots are typified by deep valleys reaching far into the range, such as **Blodgett Canyon** near Hamilton, which is fronted by superb, towering granite bluffs. The lower canyon can be explored on easy day hikes from the trailhead near the free USFS *Blodgett campground*, or in a longer (20mi roundtrip) hike to High Lake. Two USGS 1:24,000 quads cover the lower Blodgett Canyon: *Hamilton North* and *Printz Ridge*; a third, *Blodgett Mountain*, covers the upper canyon.

The only peak in Selway-Bitterroot Wilderness above 10,000ft, **Trapper Peak** (10,157ft), makes one of the area's most rewarding day hikes. The (12mi roundtrip) hike up to this spectacular, horn-like summit is often heavy going, however, involving a strenuous ascent of 3807ft. The generally steep route follows a long, broad spur northwest to the bare, rocky summit, which affords a sweeping panorama over rows of craggy ridges. Trapper Peak Trailhead is accessible via a turnoff from Route 473 (West Fork Rd), 11½mi south of its junction with Hwy 93; turn left at the fork 1mi on and follow the rough USFS Rd 5630-A for 4mi. Use two USGS 1:24,000 quads *Boulder Peak* and *Trapper Peak*; a third, *Piquet Creek*, is optional.

CLOUD PEAK WILDERNESS

The 295-sq-mile Cloud Peak Wilderness is within Big Horn National Forest, west of Sheridan in central-northern Wyoming. The best entry point to the wilderness is from West Ten Sleep Lake, accessible via USFS Rd 27 from the turnoff 18mi north of the small town of Ten Sleep on Hwy 16. The USFS *West Ten Sleep Lake campground* is here.

A very satisfying and reasonably easy long day- (12½mi) or overnight hike climbs along Middle Ten Sleep Creek via Mirror Lake to the **Lost Twin Lakes**, which are rimmed by 1000ft precipices. Another popular (12mi roundtrip) overnight hike follows the West Ten Sleep Creek north to past Lake Helen and Lake Marion to **Mistymoon Lake**. This stark alpine tarn makes an ideal base for the long (11mi roundtrip) day hike to the panoramic 13,175ft summit of **Cloud Peak**; the route leads north across the cascading Paint Rock Creek, then up northeast along a steep ridge requiring some rock-hopping.

Two USGS 1:24,00 quads *Lake Angeline* and *Lake Helen* are required for these hikes (plus *Cloud Peak* for the latter).

SAWTOOTH WILDERNESS

The 340-sq-mile Sawtooth Wilderness lies within the larger Sawtooth National Recreation Area of central-southern Idaho. This is classic alpine country with jagged peaks, lakes and tarns, tranquil streams and waterfalls.

The town of Stanley is at the junction of Hwy 75 and Hwy 21 (the Ponderosa Scenic Route) on the eastern foot of the Sawtooth Range. The USFS Red Fish Lake visitor center (☎ 208-774-3376) is 5½mi south of Stanley. Note that vehicles parked at trailheads must show a recreation pass ($2/5/15 one day/three days/year). The Earthwatch Press 1:48,000 *Sawtooth Wilderness Map* covers the entire area.

A wonderful (8mi roundtrip) long day- or overnight hike of easy-medium difficulty leaves from the USFS **Iron Creek campground**, accessible via Iron Creek Rd off Hwy 21 from just west of Stanley. The route climbs 1720ft past Alpine Lake (best *camping*) to the photogenic **Sawtooth Lake**, which fills a deep basin below Mt Regan. One USGS 1:24,000 quad, *Stanley Lake*, covers the hike.

A popular three-day (18mi) loop of medium difficulty leads from Pettit Lake over **Snowyside Pass** (9390ft) past Alice Lake, the Twin Lakes, Toxaway Lake and Farley Lake. The trailhead turnoff is on Hwy 75, roughly 20mi south of Stanley (45mi north of Ketchum). One USGS 1:24,000 quad, *Snowyside Peak*, covers this route.

HIGH UINTA WILDERNESS

Utah's 460,000-acre High Uintas Wilderness lies within the much larger Wasatch National Forest along the northern border with Wyoming. Unlike other mountain ranges in the lower 48 states, the Uintas run east–west. Despite their relatively unspectacular profile, the High Uintas contain Utah's highest summit, Kings Peak (13,528ft). The best access is from the 'two passes area', between Bald Mountain Pass and Hayden Pass on Hwy 150 (the Mirror Lake Scenic Byway) linking Kamas with Evanston in Wyoming. Vehicles parked at trailheads, picnic areas and USFS campgrounds along the Scenic Byway must display a recre-

ation pass ($3/6/25 for a day/week/year). The USFS Kamas ranger station (☎ 801-783-4338) is at 50 E Center St, Kamas, UT 84036.

An easy (10½mi roundtrip) day hike follows the Highline Trail from near the **Butterfly campground**, then turns off north to the pleasant **Naturalist Basin**. A (roughly 20mi) loop of two or three days can be made via **Four Lakes Basin** and **Pinto Lake**.

Use the USGS 1:24,000 quad *Hayden Peak* or the Trails Illustrated 1:75,000 *High Uintas Wilderness* map, which covers the entire area.

COLLEGIATE PEAKS WILDERNESS

Running northwest–southeast through the center of Colorado, the 167,994-acre Collegiate Peaks Wilderness has the Rockies' most clustered concentration of 14,000ft summits – eight in total – most of which bear the names of eminent universities. The range also marks the highest point on the Continental Divide.

Mt Belford (14,197ft) makes a strenuous and long (9mi) day hike from historic Vicksburg, 7.8mi along Clear Creek Canyon Rd (USFS Rd 390/120) from the turnoff on Hwy 24 just south of Granite. The most direct route (4557ft total ascent) follows the Missouri Gulch Trail, with a short loop via Elkhead Pass to Belford's panoramic summit (plus an optional 2½mi side trip to the adjacent 14,153ft Mt Oxford) and down its long, steep northwest ridge. A longer (18mi total) alternative semi-loop from the Colorado Trailhead (on Clear Creek Canyon Rd, 3½mi from the highway) leads south to Pine Creek, then upvalley via the wild Missouri Basin to Elkhead Pass. Use the Trails Illustrated 1:40,680 *Buena Vista Collegiate Peaks*, or two USGS 1:24,000 quads: *Mount Harvard* and *Winfield*.

The summit of **Mt Yale** (14,196ft), another scenic 14-thousander, can be reached in a long (14mi roundtrip) day hike from the Denny Creek Trailhead (*not* Denny Gulch, just east), 12mi from Buena Vista on the Cottonwood Pass Rd. The route makes a winding ascent (of around 4300ft) via Yale's southwest slopes. Use the Trails Illustrated map or the USGS 1:24,000 quad *Mount Yale*.

WEMINUCHE WILDERNESS

The 492,418-acre Weminuche (**wem**-a-nooch) Wilderness lies in the middle of the San Juan Mountains in southwestern Colorado. The historic town of Silverton is at the junction of Hwys 550 and 110 (Alpine Loop) at the northwestern side of the wilderness. The narrow-gauge Silverton & Durango Railroad provides

CLEM LINDENMAYER

The Continentail Divide Trail passes through the high peaks of the Weminuche Wilderness in southwestern Colorado.

access to several trailheads along Weminuche's western edge. Silverton visitor center (☎ 970-387-5654) serves as the local USFS information office. The Trails Illustrated 1:60,667 *Weminuche Wilderness* map covers the entire area.

A very popular, 16mi roundtrip hike of medium difficulty goes from the railroad drop-off point at Needleton to **Chicago Basin** in the upper valley of Needle Creek. Chicago Basin (no campfires) is fronted by the 14-thousanders Mt Eolus, Windom Peak and Sunlight Peak, all of which are non-technical climbs. The hike can be extended to an excellent four-day (41mi) loop via Columbine Pass and Hunchback Pass to Elk Park. The Drake Mountain Maps 1:60,000 *Mountains between Silverton and Durango* covers the whole route. Otherwise, use USGS 1:24,000 quads: *Mountain View Crest* and *Columbine Pass* (plus *Storm King Peak* and *Snowdon Peak* for the loop extension).

One of the wildest sections of the 3000mi **Continental Divide Trail** runs 85mi northwest–southeast through Weminuche Wilderness. This 10-day hike starts at Stony Pass – accessible via USFS Rd 737 from the turnoff at Howardsville on the Alpine Loop, 4½mi north of Silverton – to Wolf Creek Pass on Hwy 160, 22½mi northeast of Pagoda Springs. While one of the most spectacular in the Rockies, it is a

serious undertaking. The rugged, high-level route averages 12,000ft altitude (at times water is scarce) and requires good fitness, attention to impending bad weather (especially electrical storms) and a lengthy car shuttle. The Trails Illustrated map referred to above covers the route. Otherwise, use the following USGS 1:24,000 quads: *Howardsville, Storm King Peak, Rio Grande Pyramid, Weminuche Pass, Granite Lake, Little Squaw Creek, Cimorrona Peak, Palomino Mountain, South River Peak, Mount Hope, Wolf Creek Pass.*

SANGRE DE CRISTO MOUNTAINS

The Sangre de Cristo Mountains of northern New Mexico are usually considered to be the Rockies' most southerly range. This surprisingly high, 100mi-long range boasts a number of 13-thousanders and several interesting wilderness areas.

The small (20,000 acre) Wheeler Peak Wilderness is northeast of the town of Taos within Carson National Forest. Its main attraction is the state's highest summit, **Wheeler Peak** (13,161ft), usually climbed from the Taos Ski Area (16mi from Taos via the turnoff on Hwy 150 just north of town) in a lengthy day- or overnight hike. A long (14½mi roundtrip) but less steep route climbs northeast to Bull of the Woods Pasture, then heads up south through ancient bristlecone pines and on via La Cal

Basin (*campsites*) to the top of Wheeler. A shorter (10½mi roundtrip) route leads south via the Lake Fork to Williams Lake, a pretty tarn at Wheeler's west foot (camp away from shore, no fires), then makes a strenuous direct ascent to the summit. Both routes entail a climb of 3720ft, and loop together nicely. Use the 1:63,360 USFS map *Latir Peak & Wheeler Peak Wildernesses*, or the USGS 1:24,000 quad *Wheeler Peak*. For more information contact the USFS office (☎ 505-758-6200) in Taos.

Directly northeast of the historic city of Santa Fe is the much larger (223,667 acres) and wilder Pecos Wilderness. A popular, long-day (12mi roundtrip) or overnight hike of medium standard goes to **Lake Katherine**. This idyllic tarn can be reached from the Santa Fe Ski Basin (south of the lake at about 8900ft), or via a slightly shorter (10mi roundtrip) route from Cowles (east of Katherine Lake at about 8200ft); side trips or loops can be made via Stewart Lake or Spirit Lake. Camping is not permitted at either of the three lakes, but there are good sites en route. Use either the (approximately 1:60,000) USFS map *Pecos Wilderness*, which covers the entire area; the Drake Mountain Maps 1:50,000 *Mountains of Santa Fe*; or two USGS 1:24,000 quads: *Aspen Basin* and *Cowles*.

Two other long-day or overnight hikes of medium standard can be undertaken from the USFS Trampas campground, in the northern part of Pecos Wilderness, accessible via USFS Rd 207 – take the southeast turnoff 1.1mi north of the tiny town of Las Trampas on Hwy 76. An excellent route (13mi roundtrip) leads up the avalanche-prone Trampas Canyon to the **Trampas Lakes**, twin tarns in an impressive high-walled cirque; a short side trail just below Trampas Lakes goes to Hidden Lake. A somewhat steeper but shorter (8½mi roundtrip) route from the campground leads up to the **San Leonardo Lakes**. Use the *Pecos Wilderness* map or two USGS 1:24,000 quads: *El Valle* and *Truchas Peak*.

GLACIER NATIONAL PARK
Boulder Pass
Boulder Pass lies in Glacier's isolated northwest corner. Almost certainly the most spectacular hike in the park (four days), on most summer days the majestic, glaciated beauty of Boulder Pass attracts a full quota of backcountry hiking parties. The trailhead is reached from Apgar (see Nearest Towns under Glacier National Park) by driving north via the park's Camas Creek Entrance, continuing along the North Fork Rd to Polebridge, then following the (very rough) Glacier Route 7 to the basic Kinta Lake campground ($10 per site).

The route skirts the north side of Kinta and Upper Kinta Lakes, climbing steeply over Boulder Pass before descending (across icy snowdrifts, difficult to cross without ice-axe and crampons well into July) via the superb Hole-in-the-Wall cirque to Brown Pass. From here there are two main alternative routes: continue east to Goat Haunt on Waterton Lake (from where there are regular launches to Waterton township at the lake's northern end in Canada), or drop southwest to the trailhead at the southern end of Bowman Lake.

Three USGS 1:24,000 quads cover the main route: *Kinta Lake*, *Kinta Peak* and *Mount Carter*; for the Waterton Lake route add *Porcupine Ridge*; for Bowman Lake add *Quartz Ridge*.

Iceberg Lake
Enclosed by 3000ft-high, vertical headwalls on three sides, Iceberg Lake is one of the most impressive glacial lakes anywhere in the Rockies. The lake makes an easy day hike (9mi roundtrip, 1200ft ascent) from Many Glacier (see Nearest Towns under Glacier National Park), or a short side trip from the turnoff on the Ptarmigan Trail (see Highline Trail/Ptarmigan Tunnel Loop hike).

Cracker Lake
Cracker Lake, a lovely tarn nestled against the valley headwall below the towering Mt Siyeh, makes a relatively unstrenuous but long (12mi roundtrip) day hike from Many Glacier Hotel. The trail climbs some 1100ft as it follows the Canyon Creek drainage to the scenic (if rather unsheltered) backcountry campground on the lake's southeastern side below the long-disused Cracker Mine.

Three USGS 1:24,000 quads cover the route: *Many Glacier*, *Lake Sherburne* and *Logan Pass*.

Triple Divide Pass
This 7397ft pass lies on the eastern side of Triple Divide Peak, the meeting point of North America's vast Atlantic, Pacific and Arctic drainage basins. From Cutbank ranger station, 17mi north of East Glacier (see Nearest Towns under Glacier National Park), Triple Divide Pass makes an easy-medium (14½mi roundtrip) hike with a gradual (2400ft vertical) climb. A worthwhile two- to three-day extension is to continue north along Hudson Bay Creek and Red Eagle Creek to St Mary (see Nearest Towns), camping at Atlantic Creek

ROCKY MOUNTAINS

CLEM LINDENMAYER

The spectacular alpine panorama from Swiftcurrent Mountain includes Swiftcurrent Glacier and Ahern Mountain (the prominent peak behind), Glacier National Park, Rocky Mountains, Montana.

ROCKY MOUNTAINS

campground and/or at Red Eagle Lake. Two USGS 1:24,000 quads cover the route: *Cut Bank Pass* and *Mount Stimson*.

Dawson Pass

Dawson Pass is directly west of Two Medicine at the southeastern corner of the park, 13mi from East Glacier. The 7598ft-high pass gives wonderful vistas of Mt Phillips and adjacent peaks in the southern Lewis Range. Take the North Shore Trail from the trailhead just north of Two Medicine campground, or a boat from the east end of Two Medicine Lake, to the lake's western side, then continue northwest past No Name Lake to Dawson Pass (11½mi roundtrip). A more adventurous loop alternative – just feasible as a rather long (19mi) day hike, but best overnight – follows the exhilarating, high-level trail north along the western flank of Flinsch Peak and Mt Morgan to the no-less-scenic Pitamakan Pass. Return to Two Medicine by dropping to Oldman Lake and following Dry Fork valley. There are backcountry campgrounds at No Name and Oldman Lakes.

Three USGS 1:24,000 quads cover the hike: *Squaw Mountain* (optional), *Mount Rockwell* and *Cut Bank Pass*.

Nyack–Coal Creek Loop

The Nyack–Coal Creek Camping Zone on Glacier's wild southwestern side is the only

place in the park where camping is permitted – with a backcountry permit – outside a designated campground. Due to its remoteness, the area is best suited to longer trips by more experienced parties. Hikers must negotiate rougher trails and several serious fords.

The 38mi Nyack–Coal Creek Loop begins and ends near Nyack, roughly 11mi southeast from West Glacier (see Nearest Towns under Glacier National Park) on Hwy 2, and takes a minimum of three days. The route follows Nyack Creek gently up to the low Surprise Pass, then descends gradually along the valley of Coal Creek. Most parties make the short detour to the interesting double-cirque of Martha's Basin.

Five USGS 1:24,000 quads cover the route: *Nyack*, *Stanton Lake*, *Mount St Nicholas*, *Mount Stimson* and *Mount Jackson*.

BOB MARSHALL WILDERNESS
Sunburst Lake

This impressive alpine lake sits in a cirque at the foot of the glacier-studded Swan Peak in the Bob's most northwesterly corner. Sunburst Lake makes a long-day (15mi roundtrip) or overnight hike of medium difficulty. The lake offers excellent fishing. The Sunburst Lake Trailhead is accessible via the town of Hungry Horse, on Hwy 2 roughly 20mi northwest of

Kalispell; drive south around Hungry Horse Reservoir to the junction near the USFS Spotted Bear campground, then follow the Bunker Creek Rd (2826).

The USFS 1:100,000 *Bob Marshall, Great Bear and Scapegoat Wilderness Complex* map is adequate, but the following USGS 1:24,000 quads also cover the route: *Meadow Creek, String Creek* and *Sunburst Lake.*

ABSAROKA-BEARTOOTH WILDERNESS
Granite Peak

Montana's highest summit, Granite Peak (12,799ft), is an irresistible goal for many Beartooth backpackers. Most hikers set out from the West Rosebud Trailhead, reached via the (west) turnoff on Hwy 78, roughly 30mi north of Red Lodge (or 3mi south of Absarokee); at the fork 1mi west of Fishtail proceed left (south) to the Mystic Lake hydroelectricity station. This is a steep and strenuous (24mi roundtrip) hike with a total ascent of almost 6200ft.

The route climbs to a saddle (10,140ft) southwest of Prairieview Mountain, then continues south around the northern slope of Froze-to-Death Mountain to a windy plateau on the west side of Tempest Mountain (exposed camping at roughly 11,600ft). The ascent of Granite Peak – although not technically difficult – requires ice-axe and crampons, but the summit of Tempest Mountain is more easily reached and offers comparably marvellous views.

Use two 1:67,000 sheets by Rocky Mountain Surveys, *Alpine–Mount Maurice* and *Cooke City–Cutoff Mountain*, or two USGS 1:24,000 quads: *Granite Peak* and *Alpine*. The USFS has a free brochure on Granite Peak.

Lake Plateau

This delightful plateau in the western Beartooths contains two dozen lakes. The easy (24mi roundtrip) hike departs from Box Canyon guard station, roughly 50mi south from Big Timber on the Boulder River Rd, and gradually climbs 12mi to the Rainbow Lakes. From here a side trip can be made to Lake Pinchot. Lake Plateau offers excellent camping and (rainbow trout) fishing.

Two waterproof 1:67,000 maps by Rocky Mountain Surveys cover the route: *Mount Douglas–Mount Wood* and *Cooke City–Cutoff Mountain*. You can also use three USGS 1:24,000 quads: *Mount Douglas, Tumble Mountain* and *Haystack Peak.*

YELLOWSTONE NATIONAL PARK
Black Canyon of the Yellowstone

Despite its lack of thermal activity, the Black Canyon is one of Yellowstone National Park's classic hikes. This 22mi route from Tower Junction to Gardiner (see Nearest Towns under Yellowstone National Park) leads downstream through a wild gorge, where the Yellowstone River alternately surges into rapids, plunges over waterfalls or just drifts gently along. The hike is of medium standard, but the final section of trail (near Gardiner) crosses steep eroding slopes that become dangerously slippery after rain. It takes several days to hike the Black Canyon, which has 15 backcountry campsites.

Two Trails Illustrated maps (approximately 1:83,333) cover the hike: *Tower/Canyon* and *Mammoth Hot Springs.*

Electric Peak

One of the higher summits in the park, Electric Peak (10,992ft) overlooks the town of Gardiner. The summit is reached via a 3mi side trail off the Sportsman Lake Trail, 4.8mi north from the Glen Creek Trailhead (itself roughly 4mi south of Mammoth on the Grand Loop Rd – or hike directly from Mammoth via Snow Pass). The almost 3000ft of ascent along the rocky southern spur is strenuous and requires some minor scrambling. There are no really dangerous dropoffs except for the summit itself, which offers fine panoramic views of Yellowstone's northwestern corner. Although Electric Peak is sometimes climbed as a long day hike, it is better to book campsite 1G3 or 1G4.

Trails Illustrated's 1:83,333 *Mammoth Hot Springs* map covers the route. Otherwise, use three USGS 1:24,000 quadrangles: *Mammoth, Quadrant Mountain* and *Electric Peak.*

Mary Mountain Trail

The 21mi Mary Mountain Trail runs southwest to northeast across Yellowstone's wild Central Plateau, passing several thermal fields. The area is frequented by large herds of bison as well as elk and deer, and is an important habitat for grizzly bears and (recently reintroduced) wolves. As camping is not permitted anywhere along the route, the full Mary Mountain Trail makes a very long day hike, requiring an early start and a late finish – carry a light pack to quicken your progress. Many hikers explore the valleys on shorter day hikes from either trailhead.

The western trailhead is just south of Nez Perce Creek on the Grand Loop Rd, 6mi south of Madison or 9½mi north of Old Faithful (see

Nearest Towns under Yellowstone National Park). The eastern trailhead is on the Grand Loop Rd just north of Alum Creek, 4½mi south of Canyon.

Use two Trails Illustrated 1:83,333 maps, *Old Faithful* and *Yellowstone Lake*; or several USGS 1:24,000 quads: *Lower Geyser Basin*, *Mary Lake* and *Crystal Falls*.

GRAND TETON NATIONAL PARK
Northern Grand Teton National Park

The inaccessible area north of Mt Moran and west of Jackson Lake receives far fewer visitors than the southern half of Grand Teton National Park. More experience and preparation is required for hikes in this wild (though topographically somewhat less rugged) area, which is also a prime grizzly-bear habitat. Trail maintenance is minimal and hazardous fords must be undertaken where there are no bridges. The easiest access is by (hired) canoe or chartered boat.

The marina at Signal Mountain Lodge (☎ 307-543-2831, ext 250) hires out canoes and does boat shuttles to trailheads around Jackson Lake. From Wilcox Point ($150 roundtrip for up to nine people) there are some good multi-day routes including a loop via Moose Basin Divide and a hike west over Jackass Pass into the adjoining Jedediah Smith Wilderness.

Hermitage Point Trail

This easy (roughly 9mi) loop leads south from Colter Bay (see Nearest Towns under Grand Teton National Park) past Heron Pond and/or Swan Lake to the narrow tip of Hermitage Point peninsula in Jackson Lake. The low-level trails are largely in the lodgepole forest but allow some quite awesome views of the Tetons. It can get hot in midsummer, so take plenty to drink.

Teton Glacier Overlook

This day hike (10.2mi roundtrip) leaves from the Lupine Meadows parking area, about 1mi south of Jenny Lake (see Nearest Towns under Grand Teton National Park). The trail makes a strenuous and winding 3000ft ascent past the Garnet Canyon turnoff (a key access route for mountaineers) to Surprise Lake. A gentler climb leads past Amphitheater Lake to Teton Glacier Overlook, one of the most spectacular spots easily accessible to hikers anywhere in the Tetons.

Use the 1:48,000 inset map on the Earthwalk Press *Grand Teton National Park*.

WIND RIVER RANGE
Titcomb Basin

Titcomb Basin, an intensely glaciated alpine valley enclosed by superb craggy ranges, is probably the most visited area in the Winds. The basin is accessible from Elkhard Park in a roundtrip hike of several days. Many parties base themselves at the lovely Island Lake, at the foot of Titcomb Basin, and explore the area on day hikes from there. Fremont Peak (13,745ft), the Winds' second-highest summit (and Wyoming's third-highest), rises on the west side of the basin and can be climbed via its southern ridge from the nearby Indian Basin. A spectacular loop (only for hikers with ice-climbing gear and basic mountaineering experience) can be made from near the basin head by climbing west over Knapsack Col (12,240ft) to connect with the Highline Trail at Peak Lake.

To reach the trailhead, take the turnoff from near the USFS office in Pinedale (signposted 'Museum of the Mountain Man' – see Nearest Town under Wind River Range) and follow the pavement to Elkhard Park. There is trailhead parking for around 100 cars above the basic USFS Trails End campground ($5 per site).

The Earthwatch Press 1:48,000 *Northern Wind River Range* map ($7.95) covers the entire route. Two USGS 1:24,000 quads, *Bridger Lakes* and *Gannet Peak*, cover the Titcomb area; while two others, *Fremont Peak North* and *Fremont Peak South*, take in the area immediately to its east.

ROCKY MOUNTAIN NATIONAL PARK
Lawn Lake

The medium-difficulty hike to Lawn Lake (12.4mi roundtrip) is both attractive and educational. On 15 July 1982, the dam wall, built across the lake outlet in 1902 to provide water to farms around Estes Park, burst. This released a catastrophic flood that killed several campers downstream and covered central Estes Park in a thick layer of mud. The trail begins at Horseshoe Park near the Old Fall River Rd turnoff, and follows the deeply scoured gully of Roaring Creek (the lake outlet) up to Lawn Lake, whose original grassy shore has now returned. A second day can be spent hiking up to the Saddle, from where Fairchild Mountain is easily climbed via its north ridge. The best camping is at Lawn Lake itself, although there are also several campsites along Roaring Creek.

Ouzel & Bluebird Lakes

This easy-medium, day- or overnight hike (9.2mi roundtrip) in the park's less-visited southern end involves a climb of around 1500ft. From the trailhead just east of Wild Basin ranger station, the route traverses above the valley of North St Vrain Creek to Ouzel Falls. It follows Ouzel Creek up to the lovely Ouzel Lake, where there are backcountry campsites. A short (2.4mi roundtrip) continuation leads to Bluebird Lake.

MAROON BELLS–SNOWMASS WILDERNESS
Conundrum Hot Springs

This is a highly popular, two-day (19mi roundtrip) hike from the Conundrum Trailhead, reached via a turnoff 5mi south of Aspen (see Nearest Towns under Maroon Bells–Snowmass Wilderness) on the Castle Creek Rd. The route follows the deep valley of Condundrum Creek to Conundrum Hot Springs under the 14-thousanders Cathedral Peak and Conundrum Peak. A recommended alternative to backtracking is to continue south over the 12,900ft Triangle Pass (with minor side trips to Copper Pass and Copper Lake) to the Gothic Trailhead, 6.8mi from Crested Butte.

Use the Trails Illustrated 1:40,680 *Maroon Bells Redstone Marble (No 128)* map, or three USGS 1:24,000 quads: *Highland Peak*, *Maroon Bells* and *Gothic*.

Southwest

The Southwest in an enthralling yet unusual hiking destination, where buttes, mesas and solitary junipers dominate the landscape and little water-reliant flora and fauna exists. As one early explorer wrote, 'the lover of nature whose perceptions have been trained in the Alps...New England...Scotland or Colorado would enter this region with a shock...the colors would be the ones he had learned to shun as tawdry and bizarre...the shades and forms in which he had taken delight would be the ones which are conspicuously absent'. Yet the vast expanses of natural space that characterize the USA's deserts are hardly found in other developed nations, and can be mesmerizing to body and soul.

The obvious challenges that hikers face are the lack of water, the power of the natural elements, and the great distances between trails. For this reason, Canyonlands and Arches National Parks are conspicuously absent from this chapter. Both are excellent destinations, but Arches is small enough to be explored without aid of a hiking guide and Canyonlands, where trails mostly require a day and a 4WD vehicle just to access, is large enough to require its own book.

Most routes described here follow the bed of a river, creek or canyon. Wading through water for 80% of a five-day hike (Paria Canyon, for example) is not unheard of or even uncommon.

NATURAL HISTORY

The area covered in this chapter rests atop the 130,000-sq-mile Colorado Plateau which was uplifted between 10 and 15 million years ago. During its uplift, it broke the earth on and around it into smaller plateaus which exposed thick sequences of sedimentary rock and lifted them thousands of feet above sea level.

Water on the plateau drained off as the Colorado River and its tributaries, and this remains the primary land-shaping force of the region. Because each rock layer erodes at a rate dependent on its structure (the more

HIGHLIGHTS

NEIL WILSON

The winding switchbacks of Bright Angel Trail, Grand Canyon, Arizona.

- Descending into the Grand Canyon, through 2 billion years of rock, to the mighty Colorado River
- Sitting atop the Navajo Knobs (Capitol Reef National Park) and looking down the length and height of the Waterpocket Fold
- Feeling very small next to the towering sandstone walls of Paria Canyon, and contemplating the pictographs decorating them
- Exploring the less-traveled reaches of Zion National Park

dense a rock layer is, the better it withstands the forces of water, wind and freeze-thaw cycles), the landscape does not have a uniform shape but is carved into amphitheaters, promontories, buttes, cliffs and mesas.

Look at *Canyon Country Geology* (1996) by FA Barnes for a better idea of how the Southwest attained its current shape.

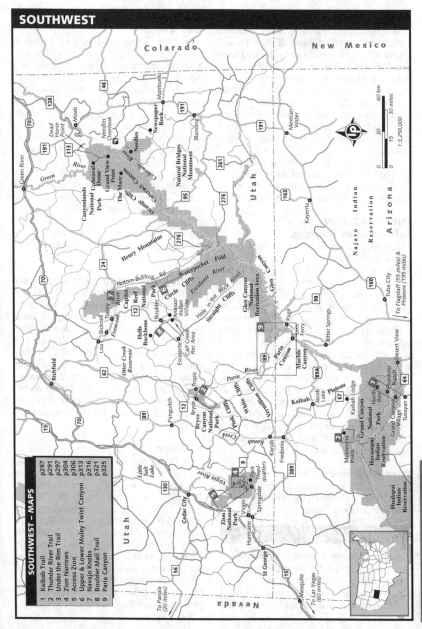

Colorado

New Mexico

Utah

Arizona

Navajo Indian Reservation

To Flagstaff (55 miles) & Phoenix (195 miles)

Moab

Dead Horse Point

Needles Overlook

Newspaper Rock

Monticello

Blanding

Mexican Water

Green River

Canyonlands National Park

Grand View Point

Upheaval Dome

The Maze

Green River

Colorado River

Cataract Canyon

Needles

Orange Cliffs

Natural Bridges National Monument

Kayenta

Henry Mountains

Waterpocket Fold

Escalante River

Hole in the Rock Road

Glen Canyon National Recreation Area

Glen Canyon

Tuba City

Capitol Reef National Park

Notom-Bullfrog Rd

Straight Cliffs

Page

Bitter Springs

Torrey

Fremont River

Boulder

Circle Cliffs

Anasazi Indian Village

Bicknell

Loa

Hells Backbone

Calf Creek Rec Area

Escalante

Lees Ferry

Richfield

Otter Creek Reservoir

Paria Canyon

Marble Canyon

Desert View

Bryce

Tropic

Panguitch

Bryce Canyon National Park

Paria River

White Cliffs

Vermilion Cliffs

Kaibab

Jacob Lake

Kaibab Plateau

Kaibab Lodge

Grand Canyon National Park

North Rim

Phantom Ranch

Grand Canyon Village

Tusayan

Pink Cliffs

Tropic Creek

Kanab Creek

Kanab

Fredonia

Monument Point

Havasupai Indian Reservation

Little Salt Lake

Cedar City

Virgin River

Zion National Park

Park Head-quarters

Springdale

Hurricane

Virgin

Hualapai Indian Reservation

St George

Mesquite

To Panaca (20 miles)

To Las Vegas (60 miles)

Nevada

Utah

0   30   60 km
0 15 30 miles
1:3,250,000

SOUTHWEST – MAPS

1 Kaibab Trail   p287
2 Thunder River Trail   p291
3 Under the Rim Trail   p297
4 Zion Narrows   p304
5 Across Zion   p306
6 Upper & Lower Muley Twist Canyon   p313
7 Navajo Knobs   p316
8 Boulder Mail Trail   p321
9 Paria Canyon   p325

SOUTHWEST

CLIMATE

The climate of the Southwest depends largely on elevation: much of the region is above 6000ft and is subject to freezing temperatures from November to March. Late July and August are generally the wettest months, with downpours during regular afternoon thunderstorms. In other regions these storms may merely soak you, but here they increase a hundred-fold the risk of flash floods and make many canyon hikes impossible.

That said, the area is exceptionally dry for the rest of the year: moisture is sucked from clouds by either the Rocky Mountains to the east or the Sierra Nevada to the west.

INFORMATION
Information Sources

Much hiking in the Southwest is done in national parks, mostly because they provide access to an otherwise inaccessible landscape. The free information the National Park Service (NPS) provides is usually quite good, and supplemental books and guides are available from most parks' natural history associations. They will send all information to you in advance free of charge, though it may take up to three weeks to arrive after you've requested it.

The *Plateau Journal*, a quarterly magazine published jointly by the Museum of Northern Arizona in Flagstaff and the Grand Canyon Association, discusses a wide range of contemporary issues in a historical context and has wonderful photo-journalistic articles.

Permits & Regulations

See the individual regional sections and hikes for information on the permits required to undertake these hikes.

WARNINGS

Read carefully the information on dehydration, heat and hypothermia in the Health & Safety chapter. In the Southwest the natural elements are unfiltered, and can make life uncomfortable for the unprepared or unaware.

GATEWAYS
Las Vegas

The glitz, glitter and gaming found on Nevada's Las Vegas Strip is about as contrary to the natural desert landscape as is possible. Some hikers love to finish a long trek by indulging themselves in all-you-can-eat buffets and air-conditioned rooms; others find the concentration of human-made 'stuff' a depressing way to re-enter civilization. In any case, Las Vegas does provide a good airport and plenty of places to stay and eat.

Contact the Las Vegas Convention & Visitors Authority (☎ 702-386-077, 800-332-5333), 3150 Paradise Rd, or the Las Vegas chamber of commerce (☎ 702-735-1616), 3720 Howard Hughes Parkway, for information. Two helpful websites are 🖳 www.lasvegas.com, and 🖳 www.lasvegas24 hours.com.

Getting There & Away McCarran international airport (☎ 702-261-5211) is 3mi from the Strip and is serviced by most major airlines, including Air Canada, American Airlines, Delta, Continental, United Airlines, TWA, US Airways and Japan Airlines.

Citizens Area Transit (☎ 702-228-7433) runs a regular bus service from the airport to the Strip and there are numerous door-to-door shuttles that make the trip for around $10. Car rental companies at the airport include Budget, Avis, Dollar, National and Hertz.

St George

This Utah town of 45,000 is of little interest except for its direct shuttle to/from Las Vegas and its proximity to Zion National Park. The St George Shuttle (☎ 435-628-8320, 800-933-8320) provides regular buses ($20) between Las Vegas' McCarran international airport and the Fairfield Inn, off I-15 (exit 6) in St George. Car rental companies in town include Enterprise Rent-A-Car (☎ 435-634-1556), Budget (☎ 435-673-6825), Dollar (☎ 435-628-6549) and National (☎ 435-673-5098); all provide free pick-up/drop-off service from the Fairfield Inn or elsewhere.

SOUTHWEST

For lodging information, contact the St George Area chamber of commerce (☎ 435-628-1658, fax 673-1587; 🖳 ci.st-george.ut .us), 97 East St George Blvd, St George, UT 84770.

Flagstaff

The third-largest city in Arizona is home to the University of Northern Arizona, a good dose of sprawl and a historic downtown that is good for a half-day's exploration. Of more importance is its location at the base of the San Francisco Peaks, just 120mi from the South Rim of the Grand Canyon.

Many visitors actually stay in Flagstaff when Grand Canyon National Park lodges and campgrounds are full. For local lodging and campground information, contact the City of Flagstaff Convention and Visitors Bureau (☎ 520-779-7611, 800-892-8687, fax 556-1305), 323 West Aspen Ave, Flagstaff, Arizona 86001-5399. The 🖳 www.flagstaff .az.us website is useful, as is 🖳 www.flag guide.com.

Flagstaff has all major car rental companies and is a main stop on east–west Amtrak trains. For information about transportation between Flagstaff and the Grand Canyon, see Getting There & Away in the Grand Canyon section.

Grand Canyon

'The Grand Canyon of the Colorado is a great innovation in modern ideas of scenery, and in our conceptions of the grandeur, beauty and power of nature... It is perhaps unfortunate that the stupendous pathway of the Colorado River was ever called a canyon', wrote Clarence Dutton in the mid-19th century. His sentiment rings true today, for no other 'canyon' comes close to matching the size or awe-inspiring configuration of the Grand Canyon.

Hikers will find it a harsh environment: all trails are steep and offer little shade or water. That said, hiking to the bottom of the Grand Canyon and back is certainly one of the most rewarding experiences hikers can have in the Southwest.

HISTORY

Before split-twig figurines set the earliest date of human occupation in the canyon at about 2000 BC, Anasazi were thought to be the canyon's earliest inhabitants. From about AD 500 to 1500, the Anasazi lived within the canyon, joined by the Cohonina on the South Rim in about 700. After a prolonged drought, both tribes left the area around 1500. In 1250, the Cerbat migrated to the South Rim from the lower deserts. Their descendants, the Hualapai and Havasupai, still live in the area on tribal land that borders the canyon's south rim east of US 180.

García López de Cárdenas, sent by Coronado (see the Chronology of US History in the Facts about the USA chapter) to look for the legendary Seven Cities of Gold, is considered the first European to have seen the canyon. He tried for three days to descend to the river before turning back. Lieutenant Joseph Ives had similar trouble with the canyon when he surveyed the region in 1857, following the Treaty of Guadalupe Hidalgo. He made the now famous and ironic prediction that 'Ours...will doubtless be the last party of whites to visit this profitless locality. It seems intended by nature that the Colorado River, along the greater portion of its lonely and majestic way, shall be forever unvisited and undisturbed'. How could he imagine that 140 years later the canyon would receive more than five million visitors in one year?

Probably the most famous account of the canyon's exploration is that of Major John Wesley Powell, a one-armed Civil War veteran who led four wooden boats down the 'big cañon' of the Colorado into the 'great unknown' in 1869 (see the boxed text on page 300).

By the end of the 19th century, prospectors had discovered sizeable deposits of copper, lead, zinc and asbestos in the canyon. John Hance, a pioneer from Texas, came to the canyon in 1880 and was among the first to hike from rim to river and back. He guided the earliest tourists, including President Theodore Roosevelt, through the area and established trails that are still in use.

The most tumultuous period in the park's history came in 1965 – 46 years after

President Woodrow Wilson declared the Grand Canyon a national park – when the federal government proposed the construction of two dams that would flood the canyon (as Glen Canyon Dam has done to create Lake Powell). The Sierra Club put up a strong enough fight that the proposal was eventually abandoned. David Brower, the club's president, asked the astute analogous question, 'Should we also flood the Sistine Chapel so tourists can get nearer the ceiling?'.

NATURAL HISTORY

With rocks dating back two billion years (about half of the earth's history) and climatic zones typical of Mexico and Canada within one vertical mile of each other, the Grand Canyon is certainly one of the planet's most exciting natural places.

Geology

Whether hiking from the newest rock layers to the oldest (from the canyon's rim toward the river), or the other way around, the patterned layering is evident. Let's start at the top. The yellow-gray rock that forms the Grand Canyon's rim is *Kaibab Limestone,* deposited 250 million years ago. The sea that covered the land at this time was rich with marine life, so the Kaibab holds many coral and primitive shark fossils. Below the Kaibab, but hardly distinguishable from it, is *Toroweap Limestone.*

Beneath the Toroweap formation is a large layer of slate-like *Coconino Sandstone,* deposited when sand dunes blew across the area during the Permian era, about 270 million years ago. Unlike the horizontal patterns of the limestone layers above it, the buff-colored Coconino is patterned with undulating lines which geologists refer to as 'cross-bedding'.

At the bottom of the Coconino formation the rock becomes slick and very red and the buttes which are visible from the canyon's rim tower up on all sides. This rock is shale, which is mud turned to stone and is divided into the *Hermit Shale* and, below it and older, the *Supai Shale,* almost identical in appearance. Directly below the Supai is the most conspicuous rock in the Grand Canyon, the *Redwall Limestone* that forms a 550ft band around the canyon and is responsible for most of its cliffs. The red color comes from iron oxide leaching down from above – beneath the surface it's a yellowish blue-grey. Fossils in this layer show that marine animals of this time – 340–600 million years ago – were similar to modern day corals, clams and oysters.

At the base of the Redwall the *Tonto Plateau* juts out like a shelf, creating a false image of being at the canyon bottom and obstructing the view of the Colorado River (1500ft below) from the rim (3200ft above). Though the plateau acts as a platform for the Redwall, it is 200 million years older than the red cliffs above it.

Descending from the plateau takes you into the Inner Gorge, through eight layers of Cambrian rock laid more than 600 million years ago. Finally, at the bottom of the canyon's Inner Gorge, is some of the world's oldest exposed rock – Archean rock, commonly called the *Vishnu Schist.* The roots of an ancient mountain range, this black, shiny, metamorphic rock was formed more than 1.5 billion years ago. Veins of rose quartz lace the schist, left from the time when molten material permeated the base of the ancient mountains.

Flora & Fauna

In its vertical mile from top to bottom, the Grand Canyon contains four of North America's seven types of temperate zone. And because travelling 1000 vertical feet is equivalent to travelling 100 north-south miles, going from the top of the canyon to the bottom is like going from British Columbia, Canada, to Sonora, Mexico.

Ironically, the animals you'll probably see most – burros – are not canyon natives, but were introduced by miners in the 1850s. Though popular with tourists who'd rather ride than hike from rim to river, the burros may soon be relocated because they trample the slow-growing desert vegetation and compete for food with native animals.

Atop the South Rim, where only 16 inches of rain falls annually, trees cannot

The Carving Colorado River

The Colorado's role in forming the Grand Canyon is something of a mystery. Though the river is obviously responsible for eroding layers of earth to create a path for itself, the question as to why and how the river made this path is debated. A plateau that averages 7000ft above sea level, and which slopes off to lower ground in all directions, surrounds the canyon (rain that falls at the rim of the canyon does not drain into the canyon, but flows downhill away from it). So why did the Colorado not, as most rivers naturally do, flow around this bump in the landscape?

A hundred years ago, the common notion was that the Grand Canyon resulted from a great upheaval in the earth's crust caused when the molten ball of the earth cooled and dried. Another theory was that the Colorado was an underground river whose roof collapsed, leaving the chasm behind. That would have been quite a splash!

Modern geologists are generally divided into two camps. The 'stream piracy' theory holds that the Colorado once flowed through Marble Canyon (upriver from the Grand Canyon), then through the bed of the Little Colorado, into a big lake. At this time a smaller stream that flowed through the present-day Grand Canyon eroded its way over to the Little Colorado and intercepted the main flow of the Colorado. The sudden change in water direction caused rapid erosion and immense pressure which enabled the river to cut the earth to such extreme depths.

The other well-regarded postulation suggests that the earth around the Colorado has lifted while the river has maintained – due to the uplifting of the Rocky Mountains, which flow into the Colorado, and the end of several ice ages – a strong enough flow not to be tilted out of its bed. While the river certainly cut through the Kaibab Limestone that rims the Grand Canyon, according to this theory the rims weren't always at 7000ft above sea level. When exactly the Colorado River began its downward journey is less of an issue – it's generally agreed that the erosion responsible for the Grand Canyon we see today started one million to seven million years ago (which geologists assure is a very small discrepancy in the grand scheme of things).

grow to their normal heights for lack of water. Here are small versions of pinyon pine and Utah juniper, and a few ponderosa pines; fernbush and cliffrose grow from cliffs and cracks, flowering in late summer. Other flowers you'll find in abundance are thistle, which blooms from May to September or sometimes to October, and pentstemon, which blooms in June and/or July. Porcupine, squirrels, chipmunks and skunks are plentiful, as are chickadees, swallows and scrub- and Stellar's jays.

Ten miles away but 1000ft higher, the North Rim receives an average 28 inches of rain and 140 inches of snow per year. This moisture supports thick forests of spruce, fir, aspen and yellow- and ponderosa pine, and meadows that bloom with goldenrod, phlox, asters and mountain dandelion in May and June. The soil in the meadows is deeper than that of the Coconino Plateau, of which the South Rim is a part, and houses burrowing critters like weasels, gophers and woodrats. Mule deer, coyote and the Kaibab squirrel – distinguished by a bushy white tail and tufted ears – also call the North Rim home. Birds here include the great horned owl, red-tailed hawk and an occasional wild turkey.

The bottom of the canyon is a totally different world. Akin to Mexico's Sonoran Desert, the Inner Gorge gets less than 10 inches of annual rainfall. Willows and cottonwoods grow along the creeks, but otherwise there is very little leafy vegetation. The living things that do well here are cacti – prickly pear and barrel – yucca, ocotillo, mesquite, creosote bush and agave. Desert birds like the black-throated sparrow, and nocturnal creatures such as deermice, spotted skunk and bats, also survive by avoiding the brutal heat of day. Larger animals that depend on the creeks for survival include mule deer and bighorn sheep.

PLANNING
When to Hike

The average maximum temperature in June is 81°F at the South Rim, 73°F at the North Rim and 101°F at the canyon bottom. Winter temperatures on both rims drop below freezing and roads can be impassable due to snow and ice. Even the Inner Gorge stays well below 60°F from December to February.

If you're planning on spending time at low elevations, come mid-April to May or October to mid-November. If you don't plan on going far below the rim, June and September are ideal. Most precipitation falls as snow from December to March, and in August during heavy thunderstorms.

What to Bring

Hikers always need to plan ahead here: wear light layers beneath warm outer gear when heading into the canyon and be ready to don warm layers as you climb out.

Maps & Books

The 1:73,530 National Geographic Trails Illustrated *Grand Canyon National Park (No 207)* is the best overall map; it's sufficient for the corridor trails described here and good for identifying land formations.

The best selection of books is at the Grand Canyon Association store (☎ 520-638-2481, 🖳 www.grandcanyon.org) on the South Rim in the Kolb Studio at the top of the Bright Angel Trail. The *Official Guide to Hiking the Grand Canyon* (1997) by Scott Thybony has detailed descriptions and trail profiles. John Harvey Butchart's classic *Grand Canyon Treks – 12,000 Miles Through the Grand Canyon* recounts the adventures of, arguably, the canyon's most famous long-time resident and is a fun historical read.

Permits & Regulations

The entrance fee here is $20 per vehicle, $10 per cyclist or pedestrian, valid for seven days. Overnight hikes into the canyon require a backcountry permit ($20) plus a $4 per person, per night backcountry fee.

Reservations are accepted in person or by mail or fax beginning the first day of the month, four months prior to the planned trip (ie, you can make a reservation for a trip in September as of May 1st). Obtain a backcountry permit request form at 🖳 www .thecanyon/nps or ☎ 520-638-7888, fax 638-2125.

Submit requests by fax to the above number, or send them to Grand Canyon National Park, Backcountry Reservations Office, PO Box 129, Grand Canyon, AZ 86023. Permits must be picked up in person at the Backcountry Reservations Office on the South Rim or the North Rim ranger station by 9 am on the day your hike begins. If you're willing to be flexible about where and when you hike you can show up in person at the Backcountry Reservations Office (open 7 am to noon and 1 to 5 pm) and get on a waiting list by submitting a request in writing for a permit for the next day. To get an idea of how long the waiting list is, call the Backcountry Office (☎ 520-638-7875) the day before.

GETTING THERE & AWAY

Park headquarters at the South Rim (see Nearest Towns) are 80mi north of Flagstaff, Arizona, via US 180. Nava-Hopi Bus Lines (☎ 520-774-5003), 114 West Rte 66, operates buses between Flagstaff and the South Rim ($12.50 one-way, plus $6 for the park entrance fee). There is a morning bus daily from October to mid-May, with an afternoon bus added from mid-May to September. The morning bus meets the Amtrak train from Los Angeles to Flagstaff ($52 to $94 one-way) all year.

South Rim Travel (☎ 520-638-2748) is a private shuttle service that will pick you up anywhere in Flagstaff and take you to the South Rim for $30 per person (minimum two people).

There are limited air services from Las Vegas to the small Grand Canyon airport south of the South Rim Entrance.

NEAREST TOWNS
South Rim

Often likened to Disneyland because of its crowds and plethora of concessions, this is the Canyon's year-round tourism hub.

Coin-operated showers ($1 for five minutes) and a laundrette are located at Camper

Services (near Mather campground), open 7 am to 7:45 pm daily (6 am to 11 pm Memorial Day to Labor Day). Babbitt's General Store (☎ 520-638-2262), near the visitor center and Yavapai Lodge, has fair prices and a good selection of camping and backpacking gear (including stoves, water filters and footwear), books, maps and groceries; it's open daily 7 am to 8 pm. Rent walking sticks and crampons here.

Places to Stay & Eat At the heart of South Rim activity and within walking distance of all services is the enormous *Mather campground* (☎ 800-365-2267). Sites are $12 (no hook-ups available) and reservations are recommended. The NPS *Desert View campground*, near the east entrance 25mi from Grand Canyon Village, has first-come, first-served sites ($10); closed mid-September to May. In the Kaibab National Forest, off Hwy 64 5mi south of the south entrance, is *TenX campground* (☎ 520-638-2443), closed September to May.

Amfac (☎ 303-29-PARKS, fax 297-3175, 🖳 www.amfac.com) operates all lodging on the South Rim. Least expensive is *Bright Angel Lodge & Cabins* with rooms for $60 and cabins (up to four people, no kitchen) for $70 to $100; *Maswik Lodge*, near the Backcountry Permit Office, has double cabins for $60 ($9 each additional person up to six people), older rooms for $75 and new rooms for $115; the *Yavapai Lodge*, near the visitor center, has $84 rooms; rooms at the *Katchina-Thunderbird Lodge*, near the top of the Bright Angel Trail, are new and

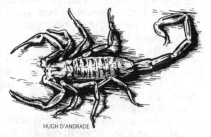

HUGH D'ANDRADE

Southwest hikers may need to shake the scorpions from their boots each morning.

cost $109 to $119; the *El Tovar* is a wonderfully historic park lodge with rooms for $114 to $180. If you arrive without a reservation (a bad idea), go to the Bright Angel Lodge which handles bookings within a four-day period.

If park lodges are full, there are a few budget hotels in Tusayan, 3mi south of the South Entrance on Hwy 64.

The rustic *pub* at the El Tovar serves excellent bar food (salads, quesadillas, soup) for less than $10; dinner reservations are required in the adjacent *dining room* where meals are $14 to $28. The Maswick *cafeteria* has a large selection and is open daily 7 am to 10 pm.

North Rim

Only open from May 15 to October 15, services at the North Rim are concentrated in and around the Grand Canyon Lodge which was built by the Union Pacific railroad company in 1937. A large deck and 'great room', both with spectacular views, are popular for reading, playing cards and enjoying a beer or coffee. The Camper Store (open daily 8 am to 8 pm) has firewood, limited groceries and camping gear, and there are coin-operated showers and a laundry (open daily 7 am to 9:30 pm).

Places to Stay & Eat The *North Rim campground* (☎ 800-365 2267) has $15 sites, half of which are reservable. As at the South Rim, *Grand Canyon Lodge* concessions are handled by Amfac: motel rooms cost $75 and cabins that sleep up to four people are $95 to $140. The *dining room* has breakfast and lunch for less than $10, dinner (reservation only, same-day is OK) is around $15. Next to the lodge is a *snack bar* (open until 9 pm) with pizza and sandwiches for around $7, and a *saloon* (open until 10 pm).

On Hwy 67, 18mi north of the North Entrance, the *Kaibab Lodge* (☎ 520-638-2389 *May 15 to October 15, 526-0924 in winter*) has a restaurant, store, gas station and cabins for $60 to $95. Further north by 17mi, the *Jacob Lake Inn* (☎ 520-643-7232) serves the best burgers around and rents cozy motel rooms for $65 to $80.

Kaibab Trail

Duration	3 days
Distance	20.6mi (33.2km)
Standard	hard
Start	South Rim
Finish	North Rim
Public Transport	yes

Summary This maintained route meets the highly popular Bright Angel Trail at the bottom of the Grand Canyon (near Phantom Ranch) and continues up the North Rim to complete the only maintained cross-canyon traverse.

The Kaibab Trail is the only corridor trail that crosses the Grand Canyon. It requires strong legs and lungs and good judgment regarding the elements. The South Kaibab Trail is recommended for the descent because it offers no water and little shade; climbing up it in warm weather is foolish. From the bottom you can return to the South Rim via the well-traveled and ultra-maintained Bright Angel Trail, or continue to the North Rim on the North Kaibab Trail to complete a cross-canyon hike.

PLANNING

The cross-canyon hike can only be done from May 15 to October 15 when services at the North Rim are open.

GETTING TO/FROM THE HIKE

From mid-March to mid-October there is a free hikers' shuttle to the South Kaibab Trailhead from the Bright Angel Lodge, the Backcountry Office and Yavapai Lodge. No private vehicles are allowed access to the South Kaibab Trailhead at this time. Trans Canyon Shuttle (☎ 520-638-2820) runs a rim-to-rim shuttle from mid-May to mid-September, weather permitting, for $60 one-way. The shuttle takes five hours and leaves the North Rim at 7 am, the South Rim at 1:30 pm. There are parking lots at the Bright Angel and North Kaibab trailheads.

THE HIKE

This classic rim-to-river hike descends along the South Kaibab Trail, the only trail in the Grand Canyon that follows ridge crests the entire way into the Canyon. The ascent to the South Rim on the Bright Angel Trail can be completed in a day, though many prefer to spend a night half-way at Indian Garden campground. The same is true for the ascent via the North Kaibab Trail, though an overnight stop at Cottonwood campground is strongly recommended due to the length and steepness of that trail. In either case, the hike is most enjoyable if spread over at least two nights; three is even better, allowing a rest or exploration day at the bottom of the Canyon.

Day 1: South Kaibab Trailhead to Bright Angel Campground

5–6½ hours, 6.4mi (10.3km), 4725ft (1418m) descent

The South Kaibab Trail begins its descent along a set of switchbacks that look like a staircase for Paul Bunyan. If freezing temperatures have left ice on the trail (check with any ranger station), you may need crampons to avoid slipping; the small ones ($6.50) sold at Babbitt's General Store are sufficient.

Views from here span the spectrum of colors from the bluish-green rim to the purplish-red platform of the Tonto Plateau stretching out below. After 25 minutes or so a sandstone promontory at the elbow of a switchback gives a wide view of the Tonto Plateau and the dramatic canyon cut by Cremation Creek.

At the end of the switchbacks the trail meets Cedar Ridge, which it follows toward **O'Neill Butte**, named for Buck O'Neill whose cabin (near the Bright Angel Trail on the South Rim) is one of the park's oldest structures. Before reaching the butte you'll come to a wide spot in the ridge where a viewpoint and toilet (on the east side of the trail) make a good rest stop.

Around 15 minutes of hiking brings you to the east side of O'Neill Butte. After another 25 minutes the trail descends steeply from Cedar Ridge via scree-covered switchbacks on to the Tonto Plateau. A 15-minute traverse across the relatively flat skirt of the Tonto Plateau brings you to its edge and the junction with the Tonto Trail; a restroom and emergency telephone are 50ft east.

From the junction, the South Kaibab Trail swings down into the Inner Gorge. After the first 150ft, the first of a series of switchbacks cuts into the Tapeats Sandstone at the brink of the Tonto Plateau, exposing fossils. Another 300ft beyond this point black, craggy spires of Vishnu Schist and the Colorado River come into view.

Within two hours you'll reach a junction with the River Trail, which skirts the south side of the Colorado, and, shortly after, the Black Bridge, a suspension bridge built in 1928. Cross the bridge and turn west (left) to pass an ancient Anasazi dwelling. Within 30 minutes you'll reach Bright Angel Creek and the *Bright Angel campground*.

Alternative Campsites
Phantom Ranch Built in 1922, this picturesque cluster of buildings is a popular destination with people who descend the canyon on mules and with hikers who don't want to carry sleeping and cooking gear. Private cabins with four to 10 bunks cost $66 per person; a bunk in a 10-bed, single-sex dormitory is $23 per person. Bedding, soap, shampoo and towels are provided. Reservations (☎ 520-638-2631) must be made far in advance, and you must check in at the Transportation Desk in the Bright Angel Lodge by 4 pm on the day prior to the hike.

Reservations for breakfast and dinner must be made at the same time as room reservations (guests have the option of cooking if they bring their own food and stove); people camping at Bright Angel campground can also eat here, with advanced reservations.

After dinner each night, from 8 to 10 pm, the dining room (called the Canteen during these hours) is open to all for beer, wine, hot drinks and snacks ($2 to $5). There are board games, books, magazines and plenty of lively conversation.

Day 2A: Bright Angel Campground to Cottonwood Campground
2–3½ hours, 7.3mi (11.8km), 2350ft (705m) ascent
Past Phantom Ranch the North Kaibab Trail begins a gentle, steady climb along Bright

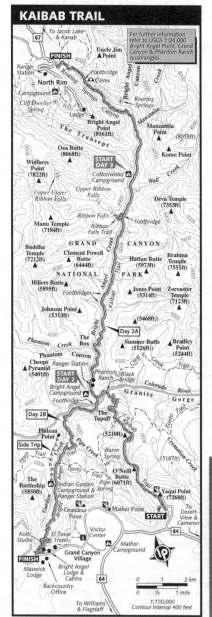

SOUTHWEST

Angel Creek through the **Box**, a mile-long section of narrows where the canyon walls are laced with vertical seams of red gneiss. At the end of the Box, Phantom Creek cuts through the canyon's western wall and Sumner Butte towers above the east side of the trail. Several bridges aid the trail's snake-like path along the next half-mile of Bright Angel Creek to where a wide amphitheater dripping with white silicate makes an impressive sight.

From here, the trail corridor widens. Soon the points and buttes of the North Rim come into view. The next 2½mi of trail roll gently through this low-desert terrain, with occasional seeps where tadpoles reside and fresh mint grows in abundance; the water from these is high in mineral content and hard on water filters.

A sign for Ribbon Falls (see the Side Trip at the end of this day's hike description) indicates the need to stay on the east side of Bright Angel Creek during periods of maximum run-off, though footrails on the west side of the creek may lead you to believe otherwise. Just past the sign you'll crest a knob and see a bridge below; continue straight to reach **Cottonwood campground**, another 1½mi up Bright Angel Creek. Surrounded by a healthy stand of cottonwoods, the campground has drinking water (May 15 to October 15), pit toilets, a ranger station, emergency medical facility and phone.

Side Trip: Ribbon Falls
2 hours, 1mi (1.6km)
The lush oasis created by Ribbon Falls is certainly worth a visit for anyone hiking the North Kaibab Trail and makes a good day-hike destination from Bright Angel campground or Phantom Ranch.

Cross the bridge on the north side of the Ribbon Falls sign and turn south (left) to reach Ribbon Creek. Here the trail turns west into a narrow sandstone canyon and climbs quickly up the creek bed to where the falls come in to view. Follow the signed route up the south side of the canyon to a grotto behind the **Ribbon Falls** – a fairyland of green heather, moss and rust-stained rock.

Return the way you came, taking care on the potentially slippery descent through the

creek bed. Turn left (north) when you reach Bright Angel Creek and right (east) to cross the bridge and re-join the North Kaibab Trail. From here, Cottonwood campground is north (left, if your back is to the falls) and Bright Angel campground is south (right).

Day 2B: Bright Angel Trail to South Rim
6½–9 hours, 9.3mi (15km), 4460ft (1338m) ascent
This is the most heavily used trail in the Grand Canyon, though most traffic is concentrated on the upper half, between Indian Garden campground and the South Rim. Mule teams ferrying people and supplies between the South Rim and Phantom Ranch are encountered the entire way. The route follows a natural fault line that extends from river to rim, so the pitch is less steep than that of the South Kaibab Trail.

From Bright Angel campground, turn toward the Colorado River and cross the footbridge to the west side of Bright Angel Creek. Pass the ranger station and posted maps and cross the Colorado on the pedestrian-only **suspension bridge** (a good photo spot) to join the River Trail. Turn west (right) and follow the River Trail for 1½mi as it undulates above the south bank of the Colorado River, offering good views of river activity and of 7123ft Zoroaster Temple which looms above on the river's opposite side.

There's a small, wooden shelter, emergency telephone and a place to gather water (which needs to be treated) where Pipe Creek flows into the Colorado River. Here the trail turns south and begins to climb steadily along Pipe Creek. After 20 minutes you'll see a waterfall on the west side of the creek, after which you'll start a steep zigzag up, away from Pipe Creek and toward the Redwall cliff. At the top of the switchbacks, the trail levels out and the remains of the **Bright Angel Mine**, active from the late 1880s to 1908, are visible on your left. Shortly afterward you'll encounter Indian Garden Creek which has cut caves and ledges into Tapeats Sandstone and Bright Angel Shale found here.

The climb continues along Indian Garden Creek for nearly a mile before the Tonto

Trail joins from the east. Another half-mile brings you to Indian Garden (3760ft), where there is drinking water, a ranger station, toilets, benches and plenty of shade; this is a good lunch stop for those continuing to the South Rim today. To reach the *Indian Garden campground* and trail to Plateau Point (see the Side Trip at the end of this day), follow the signs to cross to the west side of Indian Garden Creek.

After Indian Garden, the trail continues its steady ascent along the creek bed for 1¼mi to where switchbacks begin cutting across the massive faces of Muav and then Redwall limestone. This is generally where you'll start seeing hikers at regular intervals, if not in a constant stream.

The remaining 3½mi comprise a steep, zigzagging climb – through the nearly vertical Redwall, more sloping Supai Group, cross-bedded Coconino Sandstone, Toroweap Formation and the sandy limestone and shale of the Kaibab Formation – to the Bright Angel Trailhead at the South Rim. There are two rest houses en route (3mi and 1½mi below the rim); the last half-mile of trail is paved.

Side Trip: Plateau Point

1½–3 hours, 3mi (4.8km)

This out-and-back trail (which, from the South Rim, looks like it drops straight off into the Inner Gorge) begins at Indian Garden campground and traverses the Tonto Plateau to end at the nose of northeast-facing **Plateau Point** (3727ft). If you're overnighting at Indian Garden campground, plan on watching the sunrise or sunset from here. The sweeping views extend from the Inner Gorge and Colorado River to Zoroaster Temple with its outstretched arms of Sumner Butte, Bradley and Demaray Points. The canyon directly opposite Plateau Point is that of Bright Angel Creek.

Day 3: Cottonwood Campground to North Rim

5½–8 hours, 6.9mi (11.1km), 3491ft (1047m) ascent

The rest of the North Kaibab is a straightforward haul, first along Bright Angel Creek

and then up the south side of the tremendously steep Roaring Springs Canyon. From Cottonwood campground, turn north to continue along Bright Angel Creek in a similar setting as the hike from Bright Angel campground.

After 1½mi, the trail skirts the foot of west-facing Manzanita Point and **Manzanita Creek** makes an impressive entrance from the east. From here, three-quarters of a mile of this gentle climbing remain until, at a well-signed Y-junction, an unmaintained path continues north to join the Ken Patrick Trail while the North Kaibab Trail turns west to cross Bright Angel Creek, enter Roaring Springs Canyon and begin its arduous upward journey home.

Thunder River Trail

Duration	4 days
Distance	25.4mi (51km)
Standard	hard
Start/Finish	Bill Hall Trailhead
Nearest Towns	Jacobs Lake, Kanab
Public Transport	no
Summary	This unmaintained route to the Colorado River passes the wonderful oases of Thunder River and Tapeats Creek.

The highlight of this hike, which begins west of Grand Canyon Lodge on the canyon's North Rim, is the lush riparian environment of Thunder River. From where it pours out of the Thunder Spring member of Redwall Limestone in a powerful cascade to its end at Tapeats Creek, the river is barely a half-mile long, but supports a wonderful oasis of cottonwoods, striking cacti and monkeyflowers.

WARNING

Lack of water can be a real problem on the Thunder River Trail, especially on the hike out. Most people stash water (a plastic gallon jug taped at the top works well) under the rock overhangs on the Esplanade, near the rim of Surprise Valley, on the way in.

SOUTHWEST

NEAREST FACILITIES

There are many undesignated campsites at the trailhead and in the Kaibab National Forest, off the approach road, but no gas and no water so be sure to take all you need before departing. It's advisable to spend the night before your hike at the trailhead to gain a few hours of hiking time in the morning.

GETTING TO/FROM THE HIKE

The approach to this trail is the longest in the Grand Canyon. The dirt roads through the Kaibab National Forest are usually good, passable with a regular 2WD car, and very scenic. Be careful of deer on the road in the evening and early morning.

To reach the trail, turn west from Hwy 67 onto USFS Rd No 22; this is 26½mi from Jacob Lake, 1mi south of the Kaibab Lodge and 4mi north of the North Rim Entrance. Follow this road for the next 17.6mi, bearing right where a direction sign faces away from you on the road which enters from the left. Turn left on USFS Rd No 425, marked 'Thunder River Trail 13', and follow it for 7½mi. Do not turn right on USFS Rd No 232, marked 'Thunder River 5', but instead follow the sign to 'Crazy Jug Point 4/Monument Point 5'. Continue for 1.7mi to where the unmaintained USFS Rd No 425 branches left near an old cabin. Bear right on the good gravel of USFS Rd No 292 then bear right again toward Crazy Jug Point. At the next four-way junction, continue straight to stay on USFS Rd No 292A which leads after 1½mi to the large, grassy parking area at the Bill Hall Trail trailhead.

THE HIKE

This is a fairly remote and rugged route which descends from Monument Point (on the North Rim) via the Bill Hall Trail to the Esplanade where it meets the Thunder River Trail and continues down to the Colorado River. Starting at Indian Hollow campground adds 2½mi to the hike and is not recommended. There are several established campsites along Tapeats Creek, which flows from Thunder River to the Colorado, but no water or emergency facilities. Even park rangers consider this a difficult hike.

Many hikers make the mistake of thinking that when they arrive at Upper Tapeats campsite the hard part is over. In fact, the 2½mi between Upper Tapeats and Lower Tapeats campsites is steep and rocky and the trail is difficult to find. This is why it's recommended to spend two nights at Upper Tapeats campsite and hike to the river as a day trip: not only do you have the advantage of hiking this part of the trail without a large pack, you also avoid having to hike it just before ascending the switchbacks along Thunder River. The climb out of the canyon from either campsite is best broken up with a night on the Esplanade, though it is possible to hike from Upper Tapeats to the rim in a day.

An alternative route, not detailed here, goes west to Deer Creek where it descends to the Colorado then skirts the river to approach Lower Tapeats; this makes a loop of the last half of the trip.

Day 1: Bill Hall Trailhead to Upper Tapeats Campsite

6–8 hours, 10.4mi (16.7km), 4730ft (1419m) descent

Go through the gate in the old fence at the west end of the trailhead parking lot and, avoiding the road that bears right, descend toward the 'Closed to All Vehicles' sign. Almost immediately the trail splits: the route on the right is the main trail, while the other leads briefly to a viewpoint (nice views of Tapeats Amphitheater from here) and plaque commemorating Bill Hall who died during construction of this trail.

The next mile takes you through a pinyon and juniper forest, burned in a fire started by lightning in 1996, to the top of **Monument Point** at 7206ft. Views from here are unique, as you can see northwest to the Kanab Plateau (on clear days you may see all the way to the Vermillion Cliffs), into the Tapeats Amphitheater immediately south and down the main body of the Grand Canyon stretching west. The elongated mesa in the foreground is 6603ft Bridgers Knoll, a good landform by which to mark your progress; it's actually attached to the cliffs on which you are standing, as will become evident upon reaching the Esplanade, 3mi below.

THUNDER RIVER TRAIL

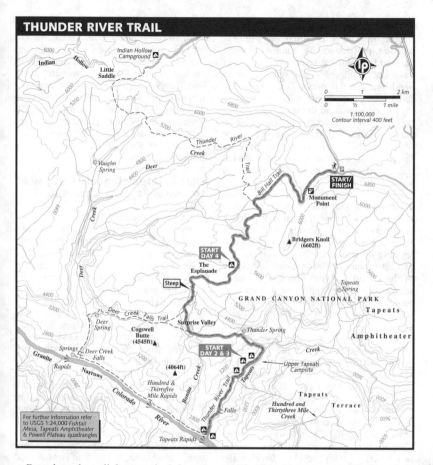

For further information refer to USGS 1:24,000 *Fishtail Mesa, Tapeats Amphitheater & Powell Plateau* quadrangles

From here the trail drops to the left over an exceedingly steep and rocky bit of Kaibab Limestone that may require as much arm work (for support and lowering yourself) as leg work. The stepping then mellows to a very steep switchback descent followed by a half-mile, undulating traverse beneath southwest-facing Monument Point. To the west it appears as though you're seeing all the way through the Grand Canyon, but in fact even on the clearest days only 8mi – between Deer and Kanab Creeks – are visible, after which the canyon again turns south.

After the trail bends west, it begins a steep descent from 6400ft to the Esplanade at 5440ft. A concave pour-off of knobby limestone may require you to lower your pack with a rope on the descent. A wide ledge and overhang at the bottom of this make a shady rest stop. Now begins a steep quarter-mile of switchbacks, after which the trail straightens out and proceeds directly downhill before mellowing out and entering a draw on the left (east). Another quarter-mile brings you to the well-cairned (no signs) junction with the Thunder River Trail (which starts at Indian Hollow campground to the northwest).

SOUTHWEST

Turn left (east) here to begin a lovely 3mi ramble (marked with cairns) along the **Esplanade**, past red knobs, humps, balanced hats and mushroom-like formations that have been sculpted in the red Esplanade Sandstone by tributaries to Deer Creek. The route hugs the inside of the Esplanade's terrace to curve around the southwest end of Bridgers Knoll. At length the trail passes a makeshift rock wall beneath an impressive overhang. This is a good area to cache water for your return, as there are many shaded holes nearby and the wall is an obvious and unique landmark.

Past the wall the trail bends west to enter a narrow draw, lined with yucca and scrub live oak, which ends at a flat spot perched at the edge of the Esplanade and the rim of Surprise Valley. The first records of this valley describe it as an oddity since it runs east to west (perpendicular to almost all others in the Grand Canyon) and has no water source running through it. Geologists now contend that is was formed when two cliff blocks dropped 1500ft – a landslide of proportions that geologists say has happened only rarely in the Canyon's history.

Thanks to that slide the next section of trail, down the Redwall cliff, is manageable. It's a steep descent, but the rock (Redwall Limestone) is more stable than the limestone of the Bill Hall Trail above. At the bottom of the switchbacks the trail straightens out to continue south above a draw, then swings east toward Tapeats Canyon. In the next mile you'll encounter two junctions with the Deer Creek Falls Trail: both are marked with cairns – turn left at both. At the second junction, the trail turns west then climbs briefly north toward two hills on the valley's southeast edge. Soon, Thunder River becomes audible.

There is a broad saddle just before the next descent; this is another good place to cache water. The next set of switchbacks, though longer and steeper than the other two, tends to feel less arduous due to the constant rumble of Thunder River and the refreshing sight of cottonwoods and monkeyflowers.

Half-way down, on the left, is a short trail to the bottom of the falls. It's easy to collect water here, but it still needs to be purified. The main trail continues its descent, flanked by large swaths of desert prickly pear and impressive barrel cacti, before cutting down close to Thunder River then swinging south into Tapeats Canyon. Here is the upper extent of ***Upper Tapeats campsite*** which lines Tapeats Creek for about a quarter-mile. It's a picturesque spot surrounded by reeds and cottonwoods and scrunched between towering walls of Shinumo Quartzite formed a billion years ago.

Day 2: Upper Tapeats Campsite to Lower Tapeats Campsite Return

2½–5 hours, 4.6mi (7.4km)

From Upper Tapeats campsite, the trail skirts the west side of Tapeats Creek then climbs west (right) past a green-and-burgundy-colored shale pour-off to reach the edge of a precipitous and unstable overhang – not-at-all friendly to those with a fear of heights. Below, the canyon narrows as the creek drops rapidly over red shale cliffs and smooth Bass Limestone ledges. The trail continues along the creek's west side, undulating from creekside to around 80ft above the water.

At length the trail climbs higher than usual above the creek to skirt the base of a large, red outcrop and the confluence of Tapeats Creek and the **Colorado River** comes into view. The trail splits here, with the most attractive route appearing to be slightly uphill, straight ahead – *do not* continue straight here, as you'll end up high and dry at the edge of Bonita Creek. Instead, bear left and descend the rockfall via lightly trodden and sometimes cairned switchbacks which end at the sandy beach below.

The beach is a popular pull-out for river rafts and can be quite busy in peak season; Tapeats Rapids are immediately downstream from where Tapeats Creek flows in to the Colorado. Both sides of Tapeats Creek are considered *Lower Tapeats campsite*. There are good campsites on the sand and against the cliffs on the west side of the creek, but for shade you'll need to cross the creek and camp on its east side. If you want to continue hiking, there is a trace of a trail that continues west, downstream, along the Colorado River toward Granite Narrows (1mi downstream) and Deer Creek (1mi further).

For the four-day version of this hike, return to Upper Tapeats campsite the same day.

Day 3: Upper Tapeats Campsite to the Esplanade

6½–9 hours, 7mi (11.3km), 2039ft (612m) ascent

Never begin the return hike after 5 am or before 4 pm. It's recommended only to start with as much water as you need for the first quarter-mile (a quart should be plenty), then fill up and filter at the base of Thunder Spring, reached by a short trail on the right half-way up the switchbacks. There's a false summit just above this turn-off.

Gather any water you have cached on the saddle at the top of the switchbacks, and head west over the undulating terrain of **Surprise Valley**. The break in the Redwall cliff that caused this valley is evident from this vantage point. After 1mi, you'll cross a draw and reach the two Deer Creek Falls Trail turn-offs (marked with cairns) a quarter-mile apart; bear right at both. From here the trail begins to climb toward the base of the Redwall cliff. If you have a good cache of water at the top of the Redwall, you may want to drink or dump any excess (not all of it, in case of emergency) at the base of the Redwall switchbacks.

Upon reaching the Esplanade, the trail climbs through a draw and swings left then right before reaching the makeshift rock wall mentioned on Day 1; retrieve your water cache. There are good *campsites* along the trail from here to the Bill Hall Trail junction.

Day 4: The Esplanade to Bill Hall Trailhead

3–5 hours, 3.4mi (5.5km), 1800ft (540m) ascent

Hiking from the rim of the Esplanade to the Bill Hall Trailhead takes about three hours, moving swiftly without stopping. After following the cairns northwest over the slickrock and through the sandy patches of the Esplanade to the Bill Hall Trail junction,

turn northeast (right) and mount the long, straight approach to the base of Monument Point. Climb the 49 switchbacks, taking care over the limestone pour-off you may have shimmied down. As the trail veers east at the top of the switchbacks, remember to look behind you for parting views; the beautiful expanse of Tapeats Amphitheater lies ahead. Climb up through the white, crumbly Toroweap and Kaibab formations and follow the trail back through the charred forest to the Bill Hall Trailhead.

Bryce Canyon National Park

Bryce Canyon National Park encompasses 14 amphitheaters, of which Bryce Canyon is biggest, carved into the eastern rim of the Paunsaugut Plateau. The relatively small park is most famous for its hoodoos – vertical limestone formations likened to the 'ruins of prisons, castles and churches', and 'monks and cardinals with their robes, attendants, cathedral and congregation'. These hoodoos, carved into the bright pinkish-orange cliffs of the Claron Formation, are easily seen on a day hike (or from drive-up viewing points), so few people (less than 1% of visitors) venture into the backcountry. Even when crowds are intense, normally June through August, there is breathing room when you step away from the heavily trodden

Paiute Legend of Bryce's Hoodoos

According to Paiute legend, the hoodoos in what is now Bryce Canyon National Park were created when Coyote turned the Legend People into stone. These Legend People could make themselves look like small animals and thus played tricks on Coyote and his friends. One night, when all the Legend People were gathered together to celebrate the full moon and were in their animal guises, Coyote turned them all to stone.

trails. The Under the Rim Trail, featured here, skirts the base of cliffs and amphitheaters through pine and aspen forests for most of the length of the park.

HISTORY

The Paiutes lived in the canyon from 1200 to 1500. Major John Wesley Powell (see the boxed text on page 300) and Clarence Dutton climbed the Pink Cliffs in 1872 en route to the Grand Canyon. Three years later, when Ebenezer and Mary Bryce, Mormons of Scottish origin, homesteaded the main canyon of what is now the national park, it became known as 'Bryce's Canyon'. Despite their lasting influence, they stayed only five years. Bryce is often quoted as describing 'his' canyon as 'one hell of a place to lose a cow'.

Inspired by journalist JW Humphrey, who visited the area in 1915, Ruben C Syrett moved to Bryce Canyon and built the Tourist Rest Lodge & Cabins in 1917. Utah Parks Company, a subsidiary of Union Pacific Railroad, bought the lodge from Syrett that same year and built Bryce Lodge. Syrett retreated to his original homestead to build Ruby's Inn, which still stands at the junction of Hwy 12 and Bryce Canyon's main road.

The canyon was designated a national park in 1928. In 1931 its size was doubled – to what it is now – and its name made official.

NATURAL HISTORY

Bryce's unique landscape is due to several factors: the presence of uplifted Claron Formation rock whose layers contain iron and manganese; vertical stress fractures – called joints – which formed when the land was uplifted; and an average of 200 freeze-thaw cycles per year.

Bryce's high elevation means it erodes more than neighboring parks of similar geologic structure. Water seeps into fractures in the rocks, freezes and expands, thus breaking apart the rock from within, on both small and large scales. The resulting fins, pinnacles, ridges and hoodoos are thus susceptible to further erosion by spring snowmelt and summer rains. The fanciful colors are a result of oxidation which turns iron deposits in the rocks various shades of red and brown, and manganese deposits hues of blue, green and gray.

CLIMATE

Bryce is a good place to escape the summer heat, due to its average elevation of 7800ft. On average, Bryce gets 235 days per year of below-freezing temperatures, and only seven days above 90°F.

June and September are usually the best months, with little rain, days about 75°F and nights close to freezing. July and August days are usually about 85°F, with nights about 55°F, but there are frequent thunderstorms. Snow usually comes in October or November and can last as late as April, making hiking in spring unpredictable. Most facilities stay open year-round for cross-country skiers.

INFORMATION
Maps & Books

The 1:37,270 National Geographic Trails Illustrated map *Bryce Canyon National Park (No 219)* covers the entire park on one side and has a backcountry-campground and hiking-trail map on the other; it's available at the Bryce Canyon visitor center for $9.25.

The visitor center also has a good selection of books published by the Bryce Canyon Natural History Association (☎ 888-362-2642); *Shadows of Time – the Geology of Bryce Canyon National Park* is user-friendly and easy to read.

Permits & Regulations

Entrance to the park, good for seven days, costs $10 per private vehicle, $5 for cyclists and pedestrians. The backcountry here is a designated primitive area and managed as such: no open fires are allowed and camping is permitted only at designated sites. Backcountry permits (free) are required for all overnight hikes; they're available on a first-come, first-served basis at the Bryce Canyon visitor center from 8 am until two hours before sunset.

GETTING THERE & AWAY

Hwy 12 runs through the north of Bryce Canyon National Park, connecting to US 89

19mi west. Panguitch, Utah, is 25mi west, Tropic is 11mi east via Hwy 12, and the east entrance to Zion National Park is 78mi southwest via US 89.

NEAREST TOWNS & FACILITIES
Bryce Canyon Area
Services in the national park are limited: apart from the visitor center (☎ 435-834-5322; @ brca_reception_area@nps.gov, ☐ www .nps.gov/brca), there is only Bryce Canyon Lodge (see Places to Stay & Eat), and the general store at North campground which has decent prices but a limited selection of camping supplies and groceries. Showers and a laundrette (open 8 am to 7 pm, until 8 pm in summer) are adjacent to the general store.

In the small settlement of Bryce, half a mile north of the park entrance on Hwy 63, are several gas stations and automotive shops. Ruby's Inn (see Places to Stay & Eat, below) has a large general store with a good selection of groceries and camping supplies (including footwear, stove cartridges and freeze-dried foods); it's open daily 7 am to 10 pm.

Places to Stay & Eat Within the park, *North* and *Sunset campgrounds* have $10 sites (first-come, first-served), water and flush toilets; loop A of North campground is open year-round.

The *Bryce Canyon Lodge* (☎ 435-834-5361), built of local stone and wood in 1924, is managed by Amfac (☎ 303-298-2757) and open April to November. It has a post office, large hearth and a cozy *dining room* with excellent food ($3 to $10, dinner up to $18; vegetarian options) and a casual atmosphere.

Ruby's Inn (☎ 435-834-5301 April to October, 834-5341 November to March, fax 834-5481, ☐ www.rubysinn.com), on the west side of Hwy 63 half a mile north of the park entrance, is still run by the Syrett family who helped establish Bryce Canyon National Park (see History). There are 396 rooms ($85 to $125), a pool and spa, cross-country ski rentals, a general store, gas station, coffee shop and the *Cowboy's Buffet and Steakroom* with an enormous buffet ($6 breakfast, $7 lunch, $14 dinner) and a la carte menu ($6

to $12). The adjacent *Ruby's RV Park & Campground* has $12 tent sites, $22 recreational vehicle (RV) sites, a laundrette, hot showers, pool and spa.

On Hwy 12, less than a mile west of Ruby's Inn, are the *Pink Cliffs Bryce Village Inn* (☎ 435-834-5351, 800-892-7923, fax 834-5256), which charges $45 for a double room or cabin, and the *Bryce Canyon Pines Motel* (☎ 435-834-5441, 800-892-7923, fax 834-5330) with rooms beginning at $50. Each has a swimming pool and restaurant.

Panguitch
Seat of Garfield County and the largest town in the Bryce area, Panguitch (pronounced Pang-wich) is at the junction of US 89 and Hwy 143, 24mi northwest of Bryce Canyon. Most services, including gas stations, a laundrette and several grocery stores, are on Main St (US 89 north of the junction) and Center St (east of the junction).

Places to Stay & Eat Small, inexpensive motels line the highway at the east and north ends of town. Ones to try are the *Adobe Sands Motel* (☎ 435-676-8874, 800-497-9261, fax 676-8874, 390 N Main St); the *Color Country Motel* (☎ 435-676-2386, 800-225-6518, fax 676-8484, 526 N Main St), which has a pool; the *Hiett Lamplighter Inn* (☎ 435-676-8362, 800-322-6966, 581 N Main St); and the *Purple Sage Motel* (☎ 435-676-2659, 800-676-8533, fax 676-8533, 104 E Center St). All of these charge around $30/35 for a single/double from October to April, $45/50 from May to September.

Cowboy's Smokehouse Bar-B-Q (☎ 435-676-8030, 95 N Main St), is a popular place for chicken and ribs and all the fixin's. *Grandma Tina's Spaghetti House* (☎ 435-676-2377, 523 N Main St), makes its pasta sauces from scratch and has several vegetarian selections; both cost $6 to $11. For breakfast, try the *Country Corner Cafe* (☎ 435-676-8851, 80 N Main St).

Tropic
This one-street town 11mi east of Bryce Canyon via Hwy 12 is as good a place to stay as any. Doug's Place (☎ 435-679-8600),

141 N Main St, and Bryce Pioneer Village (☎ 435-679-8546), 80 S Main St, both have groceries, limited camping supplies and a laundrette.

Places to Stay & Eat The *Bryce Canyon Inn (☎ 435-679-8502, 21 N Main St)* has comfortable rooms for $28 October to April, $45 May to September; it also runs the adjacent *Pizza Place (☎ 435-679-8888)* which locals seem to like.

The *Bryce Valley Inn (☎ 435-679-8811, 800-442 1890, fax 679-8846, 200 N Main St)* is probably the nicest lodging in town. Rooms are $54 to $80 and there are nightly barbecue dinners in summer.

Only open April to October, *Bryce Pioneer Village (☎ 435-679-8546, 800-222-0381, 80 S Main St)* has cabins and motel rooms for $40 to $60, a large breakfast buffet ($6) and campsites for $15.

Under the Rim Trail

Duration	3 days
Distance	23mi (37km)
Standard	easy-medium
Start	Bryce Point
Finish	Rainbow Point
Nearest Towns	Bryce
Public Transport	no

Summary Linked segments – each accessible from the main park road by connecting trails – comprise this one-way trail that skirts the base of Bryce Canyon's remarkable Pink Cliffs.

This one-way hike can be done in two days, though three is recommended for those not used to the altitude here. In either direction you have a hefty ascent over the last 3mi. The advantage of hiking north to south (as described here) is that you'll have the sun at your back in the afternoon and Rainbow Point as the grand finale.

There are three connecting trails, each near a backcountry campsite, from Under the Rim Trail to the main park road – any section can be done as a day hike. The following itinerary breaks the hike into three such sections. You could also hike down to

one of the campsites, set up a base camp and do day hikes in either or both directions. At the hike's southern end, the 8.8mi Riggs Springs Loop Trail would be a good addition if you want a few more days out.

PLANNING
When to Hike
Most of the trail is covered with snow from late October to March or April; even in May, the water sources along the trail may be frozen. June and September are ideal months, while in July and August you'll have to deal with thunderstorms and mosquitoes.

Maps
The Trails Illustrated map (see Maps & Books under Information earlier in this section) is sufficient for this hike.

WARNINGS
- Remember that most of this hike is above 7000ft. Take time to acclimatize and drink plenty of fluids.
- The areas along the rim of Bryce Canyon are losing five percent of their naturally occurring vegetation per year due to foot traffic. Watch your steps – you'll be fined $100 for damaging natural resources.

GETTING TO/FROM THE HIKE
This is a one-way hike, beginning from the north end of the Bryce Point parking lot off the Bryce Canyon Rd 5mi south of Hwy 12, so you'll need to leave a car at one or both ends. Hitchhiking is not allowed in the park, and there is no hiker shuttle. That said, hikers have been known to drive to Rainbow Point (the hike's terminus) and catch a ride back to Bryce Point without difficulty.

THE HIKE
Day 1: Bryce Point to Swamp Canyon Connecting Trail
5–6 hours, 11.6mi (18.7km)
Beginning this hike at Bryce Canyon Lodge or Inspiration Point and hiking to Bryce Point via the Rim Trail will add 2¼mi or 1¼mi, respectively.

Follow the 'Under Rim Trail to Peekaboo Loop/Hat Shop' signs. The trail descends steeply almost due east, affording expansive views of the main Bryce amphitheater, Paria River valley and Escalante Point which is the southern tip of the Aquarius Plateau. The flat expanse below (south of) Escalante Point is the next tread of the Grand Staircase; it goes· south to the White Cliffs.

After this first, brief descent, the trail swings high and south through sparse manzanita and pine growing atop nutrient-poor Clarion Mud. After a half-mile the trail starts to descend in earnest, winding down to a ridge where the color of the earth changes from gray to light orange and rust. Over the next a half-mile of switchbacks, the top layer of the Clarion Formation is slowly eroding into the shape of hoodoos. Rainbow Point, looking like a lump atop a distant amphitheater, becomes visible above the unnamed ridge in the foreground.

As the trail stretches along a south-facing promontory, a grand panorama of the Pink Cliffs is visible to the north (behind you). On the right (west) the Right Fork of Yellow Creek forms a steep-sided drainage. Just below the trail, the gray 'hats' of the **Hat Shop** are precariously displayed atop softer rock that is eroding beneath them. The Hat Shop will not go out of business: as the trail winds down to the west off the ridge, you'll tread across the hard cap-rock that will provide hats in the future.

At the bottom of this descent, 2.9mi from the Bryce Point, is the ***Right Fork Yellow Creek campsite***, a good spot in a clearing bounded by a stream that runs most of the year.

From the campsite, follow the left (east) bank of the creek for half a mile through a stand of oak trees, then cross the creek and bear south around the base of an unnamed plateau. Here the landscape is a semi-desert, with little shade and plenty of pungent sage growing in the sandy soil. As the trail turns west, the ***Yellow Creek Group campsite*** is on the left.

A quarter-mile beyond the campsite, you'll encounter the main body of Yellow Creek. The trail follows the creek's west

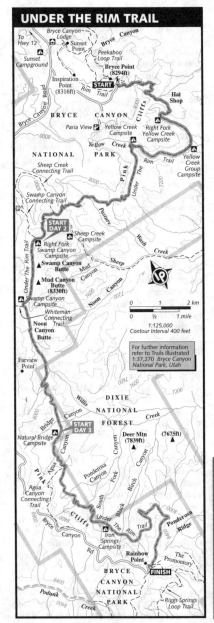

UNDER THE RIM TRAIL

SOUTHWEST

bank and gently ascends toward the Pink Cliffs at the head of the creek, atop which – 1000ft above – sits Paria View. Soon the trail corridor narrows between Yellow Creek and a buff-colored chunk of rock. Within a quarter-mile you'll have to cross Yellow Creek; look for cairns to guide your way to the trail on the opposite bank.

Another quarter-mile of hiking brings you to the *Yellow Creek campsite*; next to the creek with plenty of shade and only a smattering of ponderosas between the campsite and Pink Cliffs, this is as scenic as any campsite in the park.

From the campsite, the trail turns southwest to climb a short but steep hill, revealing a section of salmon-hued cliffs. Upon cresting the hill, Rainbow Point is visible directly south. Now the trail undulates in a steady, gentle rhythm for about 2mi, crossing the slope of a point that separates two of Bryce's amphitheaters. After 1½mi, the trail wraps into the next amphitheater south and descends steeply to the bottom of Pasture Wash. The trail may be hard to follow here, especially during wet periods: follow cairns to the south edge of the wash and look for a sharp uphill turn (southwest) where the trail becomes clearly visible as it zig-zags up and out of the wash. The reward at the top of this climb is the view of (north to south) Swamp Canyon, Mud Canyon and Noon Canyon Buttes.

Just around the corner you'll come face to face with an **unnamed spire** the gothic proportions of which make it one of the most impressive rocks along this trail. From here, the descent takes you into the valley carved by Sheep Creek. Soon you'll meet the Sheep Creek Connecting Trail which leads north, then west, then south, 2mi to the Swamp Canyon Connecting Trail trailhead on the main park road. From this same junction, a well-signed trail goes south, half a mile, to the *Sheep Creek campsite*, whose beauty is second only to the Yellow Creek site; there is water here most of the year.

From the Sheep Creek Connecting Trail junction, the trail climbs 150ft as it crosses from the Sheep Creek amphitheater to the Swamp Canyon amphitheater, where Sheep

Creek Butte stands front and center. The trail descends gently to reach the bottom of Swamp Canyon, where a stand of large quaking aspen trees give a taste of what's to come further south. On the left (southeast) side of the trail, in a clearing among large ponderosa pines, is the *Right Fork Swamp Canyon campsite*; water is usually available in upper Swamp Canyon, 100yd north of the campsite.

The Swamp Canyon Connecting Trail, which climbs north for 1mi to the Swamp Canyon Connecting Trail trailhead on the main park road, is 300ft past the campsite.

Day 2: Swamp Canyon Connecting Trail to Agua Canyon Connecting Trail
5½–7 hours, 10.6mi (17.1km)
From the Swamp Canyon Connecting Trail junction, the trail climbs steadily south through a passage flanked by the Pink Cliffs and the west faces of Swamp Canyon and Mud Canyon Buttes. After 1¼mi, the passage pinches together and the trail turns west to climb a series of switchbacks which afford an excellent profile view of Noon Canyon Butte; its coat of pine and manzanita, dwarfed by the depth of cliff beneath, gets shorter toward the higher point of the butte due to the higher elevation and exposure it receives, and because the butte's tilt causes the topsoil to erode downward away from the highest part.

Around 300ft beyond the top of the switchbacks, at 8200ft, is *Swamp Canyon campsite*. There is not much flat ground here and the site is quite close to both the Under the Rim Trail and the Whiteman Connecting Trail (which joins from the west), but its altitude makes it a nice, cool spot in summer. The best place to find water is a quarter-mile from the campsite, up the Whiteman Connecting Trail. This trail climbs 0.9mi to the main park road where there's a picnic area and trailhead.

The trail next makes a flat, half-mile traverse through aspen and pine before descending to the base of the west-facing Fairview Cliffs. Here, the trail meets Willis Creek which it follows for 1mi until the creek turns southeast. It's often difficult to distinguish the trail from the numerous small creeks that run into Willis Creek here; continue bearing south and west.

A sign indicates the boundaries of the Dixie National Forest, which you'll traverse for a quarter-mile to where the trail curves sharply east to ascend the eroded mudstone slope on the southwest side of Willis Creek. As you ascend, there are large chunks of conglomerate rock that resemble asphalt; locally this rock is called 'Boat Mesa' rock, because it forms the durable cap of Boat Mesa in the north part of the Bryce Canyon National Park.

At the top of this ascent the trail becomes very sandy as it snakes around the east edge of a promontory to gain a **view of the full Pink Cliffs skyline** – from Natural Bridge in the north, to Ponderosa Ridge. Pineapple cacti, prickly pear and yucca are abundant here.

The trail descends again to where thick brush and old ponderosa pines stand along the banks of a southern tributary to Willis Creek. Half a mile of hiking (you may need to cross the creek several times if water is running high), brings you to *Natural Bridge campsite*. There's plenty of shade here and usually ample water, but the site can be hot and bug-infested in summer.

Half a mile past the campsite the trail traverses a splendid meadow of (mostly) sage whose backdrop is the amphitheater of cliffs at the head of Agua Canyon. Traversing Agua Canyon can be difficult: topo maps show the trail turning slightly west and cutting directly across the canyon but, due to numerous floods, you now need to hike upcanyon for three-quarters of a mile before bearing south to ascend the canyon's south ridge. The switchbacks that make the climb are heavily shadowed and usually under snow until late spring. (At the top of the ridge the Agua Canyon Connecting Trail climbs 1.6mi to the main park road at the Ponderosa View parking lot.)

Day 3: Agua Canyon Connecting Trail to Rainbow Point
4–5 hours, 7.9mi (12.7km)
From the junction of the Agua Canyon Connecting Trail and Under the Rim Trail is a

sweeping view of scalloped canyons carved in the southern section of Bryce Canyon's Pink Cliffs, with Rainbow Point as the southern climax. From here the trail cuts a transverse line as it descends, angling west to the base of the Pink Cliffs. The proximity of the trail to the Pink Cliffs here makes it a good point from which to walk up and see their castle-like formations at close range.

The trail wraps around the south end of a pink promontory and descends into Ponderosa Canyon. Crossing the canyon in a half-mile, the trail then zig-zags up the ridge that separates Ponderosa from South Fork Canyon. Again the trail descends, this time for a quarter-mile to the bottom of South Fork Canyon. After crossing the head of this canyon, *Iron Springs campsite* is on the right; the east-facing ridge that the site occupies leaves little room to spread out. Iron Spring – upcanyon (southwest) 600ft from the campsite – is a year-round water source.

The trail continues its undulating rhythm between ridge tops and canyon bottoms for the next mile as it dips south and east to cross both arms of Black Birch Canyon; cairns mark the way, which can disappear under debris in this area. After mounting and descending the lower slopes of a promontory that juts northwest toward Black Birch Canyon, you'll enter the southernmost amphitheater of Bryce Canyon's Pink Cliffs.

The trail traces the outline of the hammer-shaped ridge below Rainbow Point, bearing north, then east, then south, then west again, climbing steadily all the way. Here are **unsurpassed views** of Escalante Mountain to the east and the lowlands that rise to the White Cliffs in the south. The final 1½mi of trail takes you along the back (south) side of the amphitheater. Climbing to the edge to peer into the amphitheater is not advised, but almost irresistible; use caution, as the edges are unstable and constantly eroding.

Half a mile before reaching Rainbow Point you'll be hiking between and above hoodoos, surrounded by some of the most expansive vistas in the park. The Rigg Springs Loop trail intersects the Under the Rim Trail 100ft below and 100yd east of the parking lot at Rainbow Point.

SOUTHWEST

Zion National Park

Perhaps because its spectacular red canyon is so accessible, Zion is often declared the favorite park of people touring the Southwest.

HISTORY

The Anasazi and Fremont Indians occupied the area from 500 to 1200, the Anasazi farming the southern part of Zion Canyon while the Fremonts inhabited the north. The Paiutes came in the mid-19th century but, believing that Zion Canyon was inhabited by evil spirits who dwelled in the reaches that never feel the sun, they didn't venture much past Oak Creek.

Isaac Behunin came, with other Mormon missionaries, to settle the nearby town of Springdale in 1862. Behunin reportedly entered the canyon and at once felt at home. He built a one-room log cabin in the canyon and called it Zion, which in Mormon theology means 'Heavenly City of God'. Major John Wesley Powell surveyed the canyon 10 years later and gave it another name, Mukuntuweap, which has a variety of meanings but is generally translated as 'big canyon'.

Powell's name stuck, and when Stephen P Mather convinced Congress to designate the area as a national treasure in 1909, it was named Mukuntuweap National Monument. Ten years later, President Woodrow Wilson put his pen to the legislation that changed its name and gave it an 'upgrade' to Zion National Park. During the 1930s, when the Civilian Conservation Corps (CCC) was hard at work on various projects in the park, the Kolob Canyons area was added, bringing the park to its current size of 229 sq miles.

NATURAL HISTORY

During the uplift of the Colorado Plateau, Zion was carved from the smaller Markagunt Plateau by the North Fork of the Virgin River. The Moenkopi and Chinle Formations are both exposed in parts of the park, but Zion's most remarkable landmarks are formed of Wingate, Kayenta and Navajo Sandstones (nearly indistinguishable from one another).

John Wesley Powell

A self-taught biologist and Civil War veteran with only one arm, John Wesley Powell made the first recorded descent of the Grand Canyon by boat. On expeditions in 1869 and 1871, Powell and his men (and they were all men) traveled from the Green River in Wyoming to its junction with the Colorado (in what is now Canyonlands National Park). They then continued down the Colorado into 'the Great Unknown', as the Colorado River past Marble Canyon was called. Their findings filled in the largest gap remaining on the map of the United States, ushering in a new period in Grand Canyon history.

The expedition spent 26 days in the canyon, much of the time strapped into wooden boats that were used to navigate the river. On one expedition, two men decided that venturing any further downriver was a virtual suicide mission. They attempted to walk out of the canyon, but were never seen again.

The NPS nearly exterminated the park's mule deer in the 1930s by removing cougars, the mule deer's natural predator, and allowing the deer population to grow to a point where it could no longer be supported by the environment. After the resulting mass starvation, the deer population regained its natural balance and the cougar was reintroduced.

CLIMATE

Zion has around 110 days per year (over half of which are in July and August) when the temperature is above 90°F, and 75 days when the temperature drops below freezing. Most precipitation occurs from December to May, though July and August experience frequent thunderstorms which make hiking perilous due to flash floods.

INFORMATION
When to Hike

The best months to visit are late May to June, and September to October; autumn colors usually peak in mid-October.

Maps & Books

The Zion Natural History Association (☎ 435-772-3264, 800-635-3959) sells a wealth of books and maps at the Zion Canyon visitor center. The 1:37,700 Zion Natural History Association map *Zion National Park Utah*, available in paper ($3.95) and waterproof ($9.50) editions, is the best map for hiking and backpacking; the backcountry desk at the Zion Canyon visitor center will post a copy of this map marked with campsites, current water sources and trail closures.

Zion, the Trails by Rob Lineback is well-regarded and has a handy format. *Exploring the Backcountry of Zion National Park, Off-Trail Routes* by Thomas Brereton & James Dunaway is for advanced backpackers who want to get off the trails.

Permits & Regulations

The entrance fee to Zion is $10 per vehicle, $5 per pedestrian or cyclist (good for one week). Backcountry permits ($5 per person, per night) are required for all overnight trips. Camping is restricted, in most areas, to designated campsites, assigned when the backcountry permit is issued. Obtain a permit in person at the Zion Canyon or Kolob Canyons visitor centers no more than three days before the start of the trip. Special regulations apply to the Zion Narrows hike (see Permits for that hike).

NEAREST TOWNS
Zion Canyon Area

The services within Zion Canyon form the hub of Zion National Park. While you can't buy supplies here, the Zion Canyon visitor center (☎ 435-772-0170, 💻 www.nps.gov/zion), 1mi north of the park's South Entrance, is the site of the backcountry information desk (closed from noon to 1 pm) and the best place to get information about the park; open 8 am to 7 pm daily.

The other visitor center – at Kolob Canyon – is off I-15 at exit 40, 47mi northeast of Zion Canyon.

Places to Stay & Eat *Watchman* and *South campgrounds* at the park's South Entrance have water, flush toilets and sites for $10; Watchman is by reservation-only (☎ 800-365-2267, 8 am to 8 pm) and South is first-come, first-served.

Zion Lodge (☎ 435-772-3213), 3mi north of the South Entrance on Zion Canyon Scenic Dr, is a rustic old national park lodge open year-round. It has motel rooms ($85 to $100 for up to five people), cabins that sleep four ($95) and suites ($116 to $260). The *dining room* serves excellent meals (breakfast and lunch less than $10, dinner $10 to $16); dinner reservations (☎ 435-772-3213) are advised.

Springdale

Thanks to the wealth and creativity of out-of-town investors, this little town which borders Zion's South Entrance on Hwy 9 (called Zion Park Blvd) is packed to the gunwales with upscale lodges, good places to eat and interesting shops. The Canyon Super Market (☎ 435-772-3402), just south of the South Entrance at 65 Zion Park Blvd, has a good selection of groceries and camping supplies; open 8 am to 10 pm (9 am to 6 pm October to May). The Switchback C-Store (☎ 435-772-3700), next to the Switchback Grille at 1215 Zion Park Blvd, is the only place in the area to buy beer, wine and other alcohol.

The Zion Adventure Company (☎ 435-772-1001, 💻 www.zionadventures.com), at the north end of town on the west side of Zion Park Blvd, rents tents, bivvy sacks, stoves, sleeping bags and pads, and equipment for climbing and canyoneering; it also offers guided hikes. Zion Outdoor Downstairs (☎ 435-772-0630, 📧 zionoutdoor@zionadventures.com), 868 Zion Park Blvd, is the retail store, with clothes, gear, books and maps. On the first floor of the same building, photographer Michael Fatali has a beautiful gallery (☎ 435-772-2422) of amazing shots from around the Southwest.

Places to Stay & Eat The prices listed here are for peak season – mid-May to mid-September – when advanced reservations are recommended; prices usually drop 20% to 40% in fall and spring, and may be 50% less in winter.

There's undesignated camping (no water) along the North Fork of the Virgin River, 9mi south of Springdale on the east side of Hwy 9; look for a road leading down to the river and cars parked along the riverbank. In Springdale, the *Zion Canyon campground* (☎ 435-772-3237) takes reservations by mail only: PO Box 99, Springdale, UT 84767. Campsites are $16, cabins that sleep four people are $55, and showers (open to the public) are $3.

The older, less expensive spots in town are the *Terrace Brook Lodge* (☎ 435-772-3932, 800-342-6779, ☐ www.terracebrook lodge.com, 990 Zion Park Blvd), with $49 doubles and a small pool; the *El Rio Lodge* (☎ 435-772-3205, 888-772-3205, 995 Zion Park Blvd), with $49 doubles and rooms that sleep up to four for $52; and the *Canyon Ranch Motel* (☎ 435-772-3357, fax 772-3057, ☐ www.canyonranchmotel.com, 668 Zion Park Blvd), with a large lawn and $58/78 singles/doubles.

With highly designed architecture and decor, the *Desert Pearl Inn* (☎ 435-772-8888, 888-828-0898, fax 772-8889, ☐ www. desertpearl.com, 707 Zion Park Blvd) is arguably the best spot in town. It has a large pool and each room ($73/115 singles/doubles) has a microwave, refrigerator, TV and VCR.

The *Zion Pizza & Noodle Co* (☎ 435-772-3815, ☐ www.zionpizzanoodle.com, 868 Zion Park Blvd), is a great place for pizza ($13), pasta ($10) and micro-brewed beers. The *Bit & Spur Mexican Restaurant & Saloon* (☎ 435-772-3498, 1212 Zion Park Blvd) has healthy Mexican food ($7 to $11), good margaritas and live entertainment most nights. For standard coffee-shop fare, try the *Pioneer Restaurant* (☎ 435-772-3009, 828 Zion Park Blvd), which serves breakfast, lunch or dinner for less than $10.

Kanab

This is the largest town in the area, 80mi south of Bryce Canyon National Park via US 89 and 37mi southeast of Zion National Park's East Entrance via Hwy 9. The main intersection is where US 89 meets US 89A, named Center St in town. One block east of

the intersection is an IGA Supermarket, open 7 am to 10 pm Monday to Saturday, with groceries, bulk food, a deli and limited camping supplies. Adjacent to the IGA is a laundrette, open daily 8 am to 10 pm.

Places to Stay & Eat The *Parry Lodge* (☎ 435-644-2601, 800-748-4101, fax 644-2605, 89 E Center St) was built in 1929 to lodge movie stars who came to Kanab to shoot westerns; illustrious guests have included John Wayne, Tyrone Power, Henry Fonda, Barbara Stanwyck and Claudette Colbert. The historic, rather worn, rooms cost $47/67 for singles/doubles. The *dining room* makes great breakfasts (around $6); lunch and dinner are $7 to $14.

South of the US 89/US 89A intersection, the *K Motel* (☎ 435-644-2611) has a jacuzzi and nice rooms for $46/50.

A giant saguaro cactus and some associated wildlife, Arizona.

Chain motels such as **Shilo Inn**, **Quality 9**, **Super 8** and **Best Western** are at the north end of town, nearly a mile north of the intersection.

There are many fast food **restaurants** east of the US 89/US 89A intersection. **Nedra's Too**, at the intersection's southwest corner, has decent Mexican food. Chinese dishes at the **Wok Inn**, one block south of E Center St at 86 200 St W, are not terribly exciting, but many vegetarian dishes are available.

GETTING THERE & AWAY

I-15 connects the Zion area to Las Vegas, Nevada (158mi southwest), and Salt Lake City, Utah (325mi north). Flagstaff, Arizona, is 243mi south on US 89. It's about a $25 cab ride from St George, Utah (see Gateways), to the South Entrance of Zion National Park. During certain periods, the St George Shuttle (☎ 435-628-8320, 800-933-8320) makes this trip for about the same price.

Zion Narrows

Duration	1 or 2 days
Distance	16mi (25.8km)
Standard	medium-hard
Start	Chamberlain's Ranch
Finish	Temple of Sinawava (Zion Canyon)
Nearest Town	Springdale
Public Transport	yes

Summary This popular one-way hike through the narrow canyon of the North Fork of the Virgin River is as close to canyoneering as you can get without helmets and ropes.

The North Fork of the Virgin River flows toward Zion National Park from the east, then turns south and is joined by four tributary creeks – Crystal, Deep, Kolob and Goose – within an 8mi stretch. The force of these waterways coming together has carved a tremendous 16mi-long slot-canyon in the Navajo Sandstone found in this part of Zion National Park. While notorious for dangerous flash floods, the Narrows hike is a classic (and extremely popular) Southwest canyoneering experience, worthy of the time and effort it requires.

The Zion Adventure Company, in Springdale (see Nearest Towns, above), takes people through the narrows and provides a very good orientation and safety seminar the night before; footwear, a walking stick and drysuit (when needed) are included in the $30 price.

PLANNING
When to Hike

The best time to hike the Narrows is late June to early July and late September. The water is often cold enough to require full wetsuits. Shortened days are also an issue, as this hike normally takes 10 to 12 hours; early or late in the season you may need to camp overnight just to have enough daylight.

What to Bring

Be prepared to swim. Pack your things in waterproof bags (heavy-duty, sealable plastic bags, found in most grocery stores, are good) and stuff them into the smallest backpack possible. A walking stick (or sticks) is recommended for stabilizing yourself against the current. Sandals (even river-rafting ones) are not recommended, as they leave your feet

WARNING

Rarely does a year go by without at least one person getting caught in the Narrows during a flash flood. The NPS does its best to warn people against going into the Narrows when the weather is unstable or water is too high; play it safe and heed the warning, even if it seems over-cautious. Remember that the river drains a large watershed: it may be raining 50mi upstream, even if the sky is clear overhead. There are 3mi – between Big Springs and Orderville Canyon – without escape from the canyon; don't enter this stretch unless you're certain of safe weather and water levels. In most other parts of the Narrows, sand deposits and boulders offer high ground to escape to in case of a flash flood; never try to beat the flood out of the canyon. Water levels generally subside within 24 hours.

vulnerable to rocks and debris; better to hike in waterproof boots or an old pair of sneakers. Wear quick-drying synthetics as opposed to cotton; shorts with mesh pockets (or no pockets) will provide less drag in the water.

Permits & Regulations
The required permit ($5 per person, per day) is never issued more than 24 hours in advance. You must pick up the permit after 8:30 am the day before your trip at the Zion Canyon visitor center (☎ 435-772-0170). Maximum group size is 12 people; those under 12 years old or shorter than 56 inches are not allowed.

GETTING TO/FROM THE HIKE
The Zion Lodge Transportation Desk (☎ 435-772-3213) has a shuttle from Zion Lodge to Chamberlain's Ranch (the north end of the hike) at 6:30 and 9:30 am daily ($12). Reservations are a good idea – make them after buying your backcountry permit. A tram runs regularly between the Temple of Sinawava (the hike's terminus) and Zion Lodge and is free; the last one departs for the Lodge at 5:20 pm (if you miss this, it's a 3mi hike to Zion Lodge).

The Backcountry Desk at Zion Canyon visitor center has a ride board where people who need a ride or are willing to give one post messages. The road to Chamberlain's Ranch is occasionally closed (usually at some time December through March) due to snow or heavy rain.

To reach the trailhead in your own vehicle, drive east from the East Entrance on Hwy 9 for 2½mi, turn left and continue 18mi to a small wooden bridge. Cross the bridge, turn left and continue a half-mile to the gate of Chamberlian's Ranch (this is private property); you can drive another half-mile to where the dirt road crosses the river and a parking lot is marked by an NPS trail register. Please close all gates behind you and do not camp on this private land.

THE HIKE
There is no trail for this hike: the route is the river bed and the river. Strong hikers can usually hike the Narrows in a long day (10

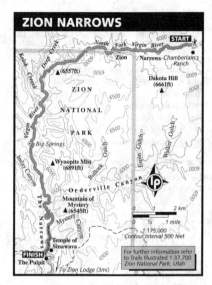

to 12 hours), though spending the night half-way is enjoyable and allows the exploration of side canyons; the obvious drawback to overnighting is having to carry a full pack through the river. Because the prospect of entering the Narrows depends so much on the weather, expect to be disappointed – that way if you can do the whole hike, it's even more of a pleasure.

For a day hike part-way into the Narrows, begin at the Temple of Sinawava and take the Riverside Walk Trail until it ends. Continue along the riverbed; three hours of hiking should bring you past the entrance (from the east) of Orderville Canyon and into the narrowest section of the Narrows.

Camping in the Narrows
There are 12 designated backcountry *campsites* (no water) in the Narrows, two of which are for groups of six or more. Sites are assigned when the hiking permit is issued and camping is limited to one night. The fee is $5 per person, per night (in addition to the permit fee). Water is usually available at Big Springs (no camping is allowed here), but needs to be filtered, as does any other water taken from the river or its tributaries.

Across Zion

Duration	4 days
Distance	35.5mi (57.2km)
Standard	medium
Start	Lee Pass
Finish	Grotto picnic area (Zion Canyon)
Nearest Town	Springdale
Public Transport	no

Summary This hike links several shorter segments to traverse Zion National Park, encountering a variety of terrain and scenery – but little traffic – along the way.

Starting in the relatively remote northwest corner of Zion National Park and traversing the park's multiple landscapes to reach the hub of activity at Zion Canyon is vastly satisfying. Not only do you have a chance to see several of the park's official 'highlights' – Kolob Arch, North and South Guardian Angel, the West Rim and Angels Landing – you also get to experience the unnamed cliffs and spires, lush valleys and sage plateaus in between.

The route is a series of day hikes linked together to form one, extended, backcountry trip. The trail crosses the Kolob Terrace Rd once and comes within 2mi of the campground and fire lookout at Lava Point; either of these places are good starting or ending points for a shorter trip. The first day's hike (Lee Pass Trailhead to Kolob Arch Trail) makes a good day hike or one-night trip.

PLANNING
When to Hike
May, June and September have comfortable night temperatures for the first part of the hike, though once you drop into Hop Valley and, at the end, Zion Canyon, it could be very warm. There are no flash-flood areas along the route, so the thunderstorms in July and August will just get you wet.

GETTING TO/FROM THE HIKE
The parking area for the Lee Pass Trailhead is 4½mi east of the Kolob Canyons visitor center via Kolob Canyons Rd; the end of the hike is near the Grotto picnic area in Zion Canyon, where there is ample parking. It's best to have a car at the end of the hike. Catching a ride from Zion Lodge or the Zion Canyon visitor center (check the ride board next to the Backcountry desk) to the Lee Pass Trailhead is usually not too difficult; in a pinch, try for a ride to the Kolob Canyons visitor center: most people who stop there are headed into the park along Kolob Canyons Rd.

THE HIKE
Day 1: Lee Pass Trailhead to Kolob Arch Trail
2½–3½ hours, 6.6mi (10.6km), 200ft (60m) ascent, 960ft (288m) descent
From the Lee Pass Trailhead, on the north end of the Lee Pass parking area, the trail heads south, undulating along a ridge on the east side of the valley carved by Timber Creek. After a mile of gradually descending, you'll reach the valley bottom and continue along the west side of the creek. Sage, juniper and pine are plentiful. Paria Point, Beatty Point and Nagunt Mesa are visible high above on the opposite (east) side of the valley.

Another mile of hiking brings you to the base of east-facing Shuntavi Butte. The trail continues south another mile below the terraced skirt of **Gregory Butte** to where there is a good *campsite* on the right (west) side of the trail. From here, the trail veers east and goes gently downward to meet La Verkin Willis Creek.

The creek runs clear here, over smooth Chinle Shale, and is an attractive place to pause or soak your feet. The trail skirts the north side of the creek for another 2½mi before the Kolob Arch Trail enters on the left at a clearly signed junction.

There are 11 *campsites* along La Verkin Willis Creek, west of the Kolob Arch Trail; the numbering system changes each year, so it's impossible to give concrete recommendations, but the ones at the west end of the valley are generally farther apart than those closer to the Kolob Arch Trail and the ones on the north side of the valley are, overall, more spacious than those on the south side.

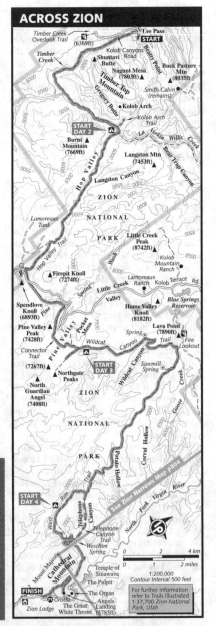

ACROSS ZION

Timber Creek Overlook Trail
Timber Creek
Lee Pass
(6369ft) START
Kolob Canyons Road
Shuntavi Butte
Nagunt Mesa (7803ft)
Buck Pasture Mtn (8035ft)
Timber Top Mountain
Smith Cabin (remains)
Gregory Butte
Kolob Arch
START DAY 2
Burnt Mountain (7669ft)
Kolob Arch Trail
La Verkin Willis Creek
Langston Mtn (7453ft)
Bear Trap Canyon
Hop Valley
Langston Canyon
ZION
Lamoreaux Tank
NATIONAL
Little Creek Peak (8742ft)
PARK
Kolob Mountain Ranch
Wash
Hop Valley Trail
Firepit Knoll (7274ft)
Lamoreaux Ranch Kolob Terrace Rd
Little Creek Valley
Spring
Blue Springs Reservoir
Spendlove Knoll (6893ft)
Pine
Home Valley Knoll (8182ft)
Pine Valley Peak (7428ft)
Pine Valley
Pocket Mesa
Spring
Lava Point (7890ft)
Fire Lookout
Connector Trail (7267ft)
Wildcat Canyon
Wildcat Canyon Trail
Sawmill Spring
START DAY 3
Northgate Peaks
North Guardian Angel (7408ft)
ZION
Potato Hollow
Corral Hollow
Goose Creek
NATIONAL
PARK
START DAY 4
Rim
West Rim Trail
Telephone Canyon
North Fork Virgin River
See Zion Narrows Map p304
Telephone Canyon Trail
WestRim Spring
0   2   4 km
0   1   2 miles
Mount Majestic
Cathedral Mountain
Temple of Sinawava
1:200,000
Contour Interval 500 feet
The Pulpit
FINISH
The Organ
For further information refer to Trails Illustrated 1:37,700 Zion National Park, Utah
Grotto
Zion Lodge
The Great White Throne
Angels Landing (5785ft)

The two **campsites** between the Kolob Arch Trail and the Hop Valley Trail (farther on) are not recommended, as they are brushy and don't receive much sun.

Alternative Campsites

There are five more **campsites** along La Verkin Willis Creek, east of the Hop Valley Trail junction where the canyon narrows between the escarpments of Langston Mountain and Herbs Butte; they receive less traffic but also less light.

Another prospect is one of the three **campsites** farther along the route in Hop Valley. The climb from La Verkin Willis Creek to Hop Valley is steep and arduous (see Day 2), so it's best to choose these sites if you plan on starting early in the day and visiting Kolob Arch as a side trip en route. The extra 3mi added to the route described above will make Day 1 quite long, but shorten Day 2.

Side Trip: Kolob Arch

1½–3 hours, 1.2mi (1.9km)

The graceful, red arch spanning 310ft at the end of this trail is a destination for many. Its proximity to the cliff from which it was carved makes Kolob Arch difficult to see in certain light: mid-morning or early afternoon are the best viewing periods.

From La Verkin Willis Creek, the Kolob Arch Trail ascends gently north along the creek bed, skirting the east side of the creek most of the way. At the trail's end is a small clearing where most people stop to gaze at the **arch** which is across the creek, high on the southern wall of the east-facing amphitheater. For a better view, don't go toward the arch but climb 40ft or so up the rock outcrop on the north side of the clearing. Here, above the oaks clustered around the creek, there is an unobstructed view.

Day 2: Kolob Arch Trail to Northgate Peaks

3½–5 hours, 11.7mi (18.8km), 1650ft (495m) ascent

From the Kolob Arch Trail junction, continue southeast, then sharply southwest (right) along La Verkin Willis Creek. Within 15 minutes the trail crosses the creek (wading may be necessary) and passes a fairly reliable spring (check with the Backcountry Desk) on the right.

From here the trail ascends for a quarter-mile to where it turns sharply south (right) and mounts a steep section of rocky, sandy switchbacks. As you climb the views become increasingly comprehensive: north is the amphitheater where Kolob Arch resides; the tree-topped toupee of Langston Mountain is visible in the east; and you can see the alcove-ridden sandstone of Burnt Mountain is in the west. At the top of the switchbacks is a table-like knob of Moenkopi Sandstone that has eroded in concentric circles to form an elliptical bullseye pattern – very cool.

The trail now levels out and begins a rhythm of traverse-climb, traverse-climb, over grass meadows where the trail becomes sandy underfoot), and up through brush where the hiking is quite rocky. After three-quarters of a mile of this you'll crest a knoll and leave the valley of La Verkin Willis Creek to descend 80ft into a wide, sandy plain that is the head of Hop Valley. Most of this valley is still private land, used for grazing cattle in summer.

The trail stays on the west bank of the creek for most of the next 2mi, though many prefer to stay on the flat mud of the creek bed itself, wading in the shallow water when necessary. Pay attention to the topography of the eastern wall of Hop Valley: after Langston Canyon enters from the east, there are three more recesses in the wall (the first and third of which are drainages) before the trail bears west (right) and begins its ascent out. Somewhere before this ascent you'll need to gather and filter water (from the creek) for the rest of the day and, if the creek near Northgate Peaks is dry (check with the Backcountry Desk before leaving), the night as well.

The steep ascent out of Hop Valley is on a wide, rocky road with little shade. After nearly a mile of climbing you'll gain the top of a ridge with a chorus of cross-bedded peaks to the left (east). The trail levels and turns briefly west to cross a grassy mesa where an old fence and primitive road are part of the Lamoreaux Ranch which is

northeast off Kolob Terrace Rd. Follow the trail sign toward the Hop Valley Trailhead.

The next 1½mi present a whole new landscape – views south and west take in Cave Valley, Smith Mesa and the entire drainage of the Virgin River, while the sculpted spires off Firepit Knoll loom nearby in the east (left). The trail climbs gradually to the Hop Valley Trailhead parking lot on Kolob Terrace Rd; there's a toilet here.

From the parking lot the trail (called the Connector Trail for the next 4mi) heads east for a half-mile, crosses Kolob Terrace Rd and continues east along the north end of Spendlove Knoll. Leaving the knoll behind, you'll begin a 1½mi traverse across open grassland littered with lava rocks at the head of Lee Valley. Sculpted sandstone knobs dominate the view south.

The trail bears north then climbs gradually south and east over a slickrock bench (marked with cairns) toward **Pine Valley Peak** – the graceful, white dome with a pink skirt that lies ahead on the right. Beavertail cacti and dark red manzanita are watered by seeps, some of which offer enough water to gather and filter if rain has recently fallen.

At the top of the slickrock the trail turns east (left) again to skirt the north side of Pine Valley Peak. Here is a close-up view of cross-bedded Navajo Sandstone whose vertical cracks cross the horizontal ones to give it a checkerboard appearance like that of Checkerboard Mesa, off Hwy 9 on the east side of the park.

From here the trail dips into Pine Valley then rises along the Left Fork of Little Creek to a lovely stand of pine and fir where there is a sign for the Connector Trail Trailhead; the trailhead is 1mi northwest, off Kolob Terrace Rd.

Turn northeast (right) at the sign; a quarter-mile further is the junction with the Northgate Peaks Trail, which is also the starting point for the popular hike to the Subway. Turn south (right) here; there is usually water in the small creek that parallels the trail just south of the turn-off. You're now 1mi from the Kolob Terrace Rd, so *camping* is permitted anywhere out of sight of the trail. There are some very nice level spots – on slickrock among ponderosa pine and manzanita – east of the trail about a half-mile from the turn-off.

Day 3: Northgate Peaks to West Rim
5–8 hours, 12.4–14.2mi (20–22.9km), 550ft (165m) ascent

This next leg is composed of the Wildcat Canyon Trail and the first two-thirds of the West Rim Trail; the two trails meet at an unimproved road (closed October to May) a half-mile from Lava Point where there's a fire lookout and six primitive *campsites* (no water, pit toilets, first-come, first-served).

From the Northgate Peaks Trail junction, the Wildcat Canyon Trail advances east atop the head of Russell Gulch and through a water-laden valley to where it climbs briefly and widens to nearly the breadth of a road. For the next 2½mi the trail saunters along a grainy, cream-colored slope of Navajo Sandstone – covered with sage, spruce and pine – that forms the west side of Wildcat Canyon. At the canyon's vortex, the trail crosses a crumbly section of lava rock; the views of the entire length of the canyon are spectacular. From here the trail twists around a section of cliffs between the canyon's two tributary creeks and mounts a plateau at the foot of Lava Point. The trail to Lava Point turns northwest (left) from here, marked by a trail sign and an old plow seat, used on the Lamoreaux Ranch.

The main trail (now the West Rim Trail) turns southeast (right) and begins its traverse of Horse Pasture. After three-quarters of a mile, a well-signed trail leads southwest (right) a quarter-mile to Sawmill Springs; this is an excellent water source (it's protected by a barrel lid) and scenic rest stop. There is one *campsite* here.

Two miles past the Sawmill Springs Trail is a rather obvious but unofficial point from which to view the Left Fork of North Creek. **Greatheart Mesa**, a white peak with red knobby terraces around its skirt, is directly ahead (south); the pyramid-like summits of North and South Guardian Angels are on the right; the flat, green top of Irvins Mountain is partially visible on the left; and in the

far distance stretches the expanse of the Virgin River Valley above which rises the Kaibab Plateau.

The views continue for another half-mile until the trail bears slightly east and descends into Potato Hollow, site of a lightning-caused fire in 1998. Follow the hollow bottom for a half-mile and a large pool of water on the left indicates the existence of Potato Hollow Spring, another reliable water source; there is a *campsite* on the east side of the pool.

From here the trail makes a relentlessly steep climb – over two false summits – out of the hollow to where it flattens briefly, then up and over a camel-back ridge. The climbing ends at a Y-junction where the West Rim Trail goes right (west) and the Telephone Canyon Trail goes left; the trails rejoin at the West Rim.

Which trail you take will largely depend on the campsite you've been assigned: the West Rim Trail, which skirts the scenic east edge of Phantom Valley, passes five *campsites*; the less scenic (but shorter) Telephone Canyon Trail gives access to the two spacious and well-situated *campsites* near Cabin Spring (also called West Rim Spring), close to the trail junction at the West Rim.

Day 4: West Rim to Grotto Picnic Area
2½–4 hours, 4.7mi (23.7km), 2450ft (735m) descent

Fill up with water at Cabin Spring, 250ft north (well marked) from the West Rim/Telephone Canyon Trail junction. Most of the trail between the West Rim and Zion Canyon is paved with large stones cut from the surrounding rocks. Because the West Rim is a popular day-hike destination, you may see more people along this last stretch of trail than on all the other days' routes combined – a reminder that this is the day you return to 'civilization'.

From the West Rim/Telephone Canyon Trail junction, the trail descends steeply via paved switchbacks through magnificent yellow sandstone streaked with iron oxide to the head of Behunin Canyon and down to a wide terrace at the base of the first cliffs you'll descend today.

Here, the trail bends east toward Zion Canyon, crosses a small bridge and makes three swift uphill turns to a wide slickrock bench where signs point the way east and south over its nose. Cathedral Mountain towers directly ahead on the right; the Great White Throne is across Zion Canyon on the left, with Red Arch Mountain (look for its gothic arch a third of the way down from its summit) and Mountain of the Sun to its south.

As you begin to descend the slickrock ridge between Refrigerator Canyon (on the right) and Zion Canyon, take time to stop at the sharp bends in the trail and look over the edge at the sheer, red walls of Zion Canyon: often you'll see climbers (look for the ropes and gear first, as they're easier to spot) ascending highly technical routes.

After half a mile of descending, the trail reaches a wide saddle across from the sheer eastern face of **Refrigerator Canyon**. Here, where the number of people gathered can be staggering, is the turn-off for Angels Landing (see the side trip at the end of this day's hike description). Beyond the saddle, the trail drops through a steep, curvy section – aptly named Walters Wiggles – into the cool, damp environment of Refrigerator Canyon. Water seeping down through the porous rock nourishes a lush variety of mosses and wildflowers.

You'll leave Refrigerator Canyon after a half-mile; descend the last set of switchbacks on this hike to near the bottom of Zion Canyon and head south, paralleling the North Fork of the Virgin River. In another half-mile the trail descends to river level; cross the footbridge (east) and follow the trail for the last quarter-mile to the Grotto picnic area parking lot.

Side Trip: Angels Landing
1mi (1.6km), 386ft (116m) ascent/descent
This is a fun, if crowded, day hike destination from the floor of Zion Canyon. From its junction with the West Rim Trail, the route to Angels Landing is well-marked and highly visible due to the line of people that are usually perched or moving gingerly along its edge.

Most of this south-facing promontory is narrow and extremely steep and rocky, with long drops on both sides. Chains have been put up along the route for added security, but even using these might not soothe people who are prone to vertigo. In any case, you'll be using your arms as much as your legs to climb and descend this half-mile trail. At the top of the trail is a wide, flat landing (maybe you'll see angels, maybe not) with spectacular views in all directions; the view south down the length of Zion Canyon is unique from this vantage point. Watching climbers ascend the north wall of **Angels Landing** might make you feel that, despite all the effort, you took the easy way up.

Capitol Reef National Park

Bigger than Bryce Canyon and Zion National Parks combined, Capitol Reef National Park is a rare 'diamond in the rough'. Hwy 24 cuts across the narrow width of the park, but most of its 77mi length has to be explored on dirt roads, which prevents most national park visitors from staying for more than a few hours. The Waterpocket district in the south is especially scenic and accessible; at the north end of the park, Cathedral Valley is known for its sandstone monoliths which are only accessible with a high-clearance vehicle.

Capitol Reef's backbone and its raison d'être is the 100mi-long Waterpocket Fold, a serpentine bulge in the earth's crust. Its west-facing edge has been heavily eroded into linked cliffs and domes resembling the teeth of a beast who has a firm dental grip on the earth. An especially magnificent segment of white Navajo Sandstone domes, said to look like the Capitol Building in Washington DC, is the hallmark of the park.

HISTORY
John Charles Fremont, part of Powell's expedition in the 1870s (see the boxed text on page 300), is said to have 'discovered' the headwaters of the river which crosses the

Waterpocket Fold in the north end of the park. It is here in the early 20th century that archaeologist Noel Moss first made a distinction between the people living on this river, which he called the Fremont Culture, and the Anasazi who lived to the south and east. The Fremont Culture, he observed, did not domesticate dogs and turkeys (as the Anasazi did), wore leather moccasins instead of woven sandals and lived in pithouse dwellings after the Anasazi had developed masonry structures. Both peoples left the area around 1300, but petroglyphs depicting mountain sheep and trapezoidal figures with elaborate headgear and earrings remain throughout the area.

Mormon settlers came through the area as early as 1871, as shown by carvings on a rock wall called the 'pioneer register' in Capitol Gorge, but settlement began in earnest in 1878 when Nels Johnson planted a fruit orchard near the confluence of Sulphur Creek and the Fremont River. Heat-absorbing cliffs and the valley's rich soil proved ideal orchard conditions and Fruita prospered as a fruit-growing Mormon community. The first wagon passed through Capitol Gorge in 1884, establishing a route that served as the main road across south-central Utah until the Fremont River Hwy (Hwy 12) was built in 1962. In 1971 Capitol Reef was 'upgraded' from a national monument (which it had been since 1937), absorbing Fruita as its national park headquarters in the process.

NATURAL HISTORY

The three layers of the Glen Canyon Group, formed during the Jurassic period, are the park's signature sights: the red cliffs along Scenic Dr are of Wingate Sandstone and the Kayenta Formation, and the many narrows, slot-canyons and domes along the fold are carved from creamy Navajo Sandstone.

Water pockets are a unique part of the park's ecosystem. Rainwater that collects in these bowl-like depressions supports organisms that are adapted to survive long periods of drought. The spadefoot toad, for example, lays eggs which hatch into tadpoles and mature to repeat the cycle before the water in a pocket dries up. On a totally different time scale, fairy- and tadpole-shrimp eggs can wait up to 25 years for water to come and bring them to life.

CLIMATE

May and September are ideal, with days that average 78°F, nights in the 50°s, and not much rain. April and October generally have even less rain, though there is a slight chance of snow in either month; temperatures usually stay below 70°F with nights in the 40°s. From November to March the nights are usually below freezing, while days can range from freezing to 60°F. July and August are the hottest months here, with daily temperatures above 90°F and night temperatures in the mid-60°s; August is also the wettest month – there is usually more than an inch of rain in the form of afternoon thundershowers.

INFORMATION
Maps & Books

A good selection of history books, guides and maps is available through the Capitol Reef Natural History Association (☎ 435-425-3791 ext 113, fax 425-3098, @ care_co operating association@nps.gov), HC 70 Box 15, Torrey, UT 84775, and the Capitol Reef visitor center (see Fruita under Nearest Towns). They also have a free *Common Wildflowers of Capitol Reef* handout.

The 1:62,500 Earthwalk Press *Hiking Map & Guide: Capitol Reef National Park*, available in paper ($4.95) and waterproof ($8.95) editions, is the best general map to the park and is detailed enough to be used for day hikes.

Permits & Regulations

Entrance to the park is $5, payable (on the honor system) at the visitor center or the Fruita campground. A backcountry permit (free), available at the visitor center, is required for all overnight trips. Day hiking does not require a permit. Maximum group size is 12 people.

Information Sources

The Wayne County Travel Council (☎ 435-425-3365, 800-858-7951, 🖳 www.capitol reef.org), PO Box 7, Teasdale, UT 84773, will send an abundance of tourist brochures to your home, free of charge. You can also contact the visitor center in Fruita for park-specific information.

NEAREST TOWNS
Boulder
See Nearest Towns in the Grand Staircase–Escalante National Monument section later in this chapter.

Fruita
This historic district is actually within the park. At the junction of Hwy 24 and Scenic Dr (the park's only paved roads), Fruita is home to the visitor center (☎ 435-425-3791, 💻 www.nps.gov/care/), open daily 8:30 am to 4:30 pm, some historic buildings and the *Fruita campground* (☎ 800-280-2267), a NPS campground with $10 sites, picnic tables, grills and running water. Sites can be reserved up to six months in advance, but half are saved as first-come, first-served. There's no place in the park to buy provisions.

Torrey
This is a rootsy little enclave that survives, primarily, on tourism. Most businesses close their doors from mid-October to mid-May, but enough stay open to serve winter visitors. People from outside the area notice a certain openness that is largely absent in other parts of Utah – could it have to do with the fact that nearly 70% of the town is from somewhere else (including Florida and California)?

Hwy 24 runs through Torrey as Main St, along which you'll find all its businesses including several gas stations and Austin's Chuckwagon General Store & Laundrette (☎ 435-425-3288), 12 W Main St, which has a reasonably good selection of groceries and camping supplies, and a coin-op laundrette. For a better choice of food go to the Red D Market (☎ 435-425-3521) on Hwy 24, 7mi west of Torrey in Bicknell.

Places to Stay & Eat *Sand Creek Hostel RV Park & Campground* (☎ 435-425-3577, 540 W Main St) is open April to October, with a lovely bunkhouse ($11 per person)

and 12 tent/RV sites for $9/18, plus laundry facilities and a terrific owner. *Austin's Chuckwagon RV Park & Campground* (☎ 435-425-3335, fax 425-3434, 12 W Main St) has a pool and spa, laundry facilities, RV sites ($15) and new motel rooms ($48).

Capitol Reef Inn & Café (☎ 435-425-3721, ✉ cri@capitolreefinn.com, 360 W Main St) has 10 motel rooms with handmade furniture, jacuzzi tubs and refrigerators ($40/44 for a single/double), and an excellent *restaurant* with healthy food for $6 to $11.

Outside of town, 1mi west of the Hwy 12/24 junction, the *Boulder View Inn* (☎ 435-425-3800, 800-444-3980, ✉ cptlreef @color-country.net) is open year-round. Motel rooms are $48/52 including a light breakfast. A mile farther south on Hwy 12, the *Cowboy Homestead & Country Cabins* (☎ 435-425-3414) is highly recommended ($65 to $85 for one to four people).

For a real treat, have dinner at *Café Diablo* (☎ 435-425-3070, 599 W Main St), where pumpkin-seed-crusted trout and chocolate double diablo are among the award-winning offerings.

Getting There & Away Torrey is 13mi west of the Capitol Reef visitor center and 2mi west of the junction of Hwys 12 and 24.

Upper Muley Twist Canyon

Duration	1–2 days
Distance	15mi (24.2km)
Standard	easy-medium
Start/Finish	Upper Muley Twist Canyon Trailhead
Nearest Towns	Fruita, Torrey
Public Transport	no
Summary	A loop hike with one section atop a ridge of the Waterpocket Fold and the other section in a scenic canyon with several natural arches.

The Upper portion of Muley Twist Canyon is slightly less dramatic than its lower counterpart (see next hike), but offers easier terrain

SOUTHWEST

and extensive views from the top of the Waterpocket Fold. Along the canyon bottom you'll pass several natural arches and sculpted sandstone narrows that occasionally hold enough water for a refreshing dip. Upper Muley can be done as a long dayhike, but is better split in two to enjoy the scenery. Most people set up camp near the Rim Trail junction, then do the rest of the trail (the Rim Trail Loop) without a pack. With a high clearance vehicle, you can drive the first 3mi of the hike (cutting it from a 15mi to a 9mi loop), to the Strike Valley Overlook Trailhead.

PLANNING
When to Hike
From mid-June to August, temperatures are usually too high for this nearly shadeless hike, and water sources are unreliable.

Maps
The trail is well marked with cairns and signs, so the Earthwalk Press map (see Maps & Books under Information earlier in this section) should be fine. The relevant USGS quads, *Bitter Creek Divide* and *Wagon Box Mesa*, are available at the visitor center.

GETTING TO/FROM THE HIKE
To/From Fruita
Drive 9mi east on Hwy 24 then turn south on the Notom-Bullfrog Rd. After 2mi the sealed road will end and a road will enter from the right (west) – continue south. After another 8mi a road enters from the right (east); again, continue south. Where a sign points (left) to the Bullfrog Marina, continue straight then turn right on the Burr Trail Rd toward Strike Valley Overlook. Mount the steep switchbacks, go 1mi and turn right on the road leading to Strike Valley Overlook. A wide clearing on the left (east) side of the road is where most hikers park; high-clearance vehicles can continue 3mi further to where a chain stretches across the road at the Strike Valley Overlook Trailhead.

To/From Boulder
From Hwy 12, turn east onto the Burr Trail Rd and drive 31mi to where the sealed road ends (this is the Capitol Reef National Park boundary). Continue 1½mi and turn left on the road toward Strike Valley Overlook.

THE HIKE
Day 1: Upper Muley Twist Canyon Trailhead to Rim Trail
2½–3 hours, 5.3mi (8.5km)
From the Upper Muley Twist Canyon Trailhead, follow the gravel wash east for a quarter-mile, then turn north (left) into the main body of Muley Twist Canyon. The canyon is relatively wide at this stage and the gravel wash provides level terrain for the 3mi hike to the Strike Valley Overlook Trailhead; here there is a chain across the wash, a 'no camping' sign and 'no vehicles past this point' sign. The well-signed jaunt (a half-mile roundtrip) up to **Strike Valley Overlook** is worth the energy, especially if you leave your pack at the trailhead.

Upper Muley Twist Canyon begins to narrow a half-mile past the Strike Valley Overlook Trailhead and red sandstone cliffs pull in close and high on the east (right) side. At 1¼mi, after the wash takes a deep bend west, a large arch – Saddle Arch – is visible near the top of the west canyon wall. A sign on the east side of the wash indicates the beginning of the Rim Trail. Follow the cairns up the east side of the canyon. After 10 to 15 minutes, you'll reach a broad bench with plenty of flat spots for *camping* among juniper trees. Choose your site carefully and resist the temptation to tread upon the crumbly, black cryptobiotic soil found in abundance here. (If you want to have a view, but little shade and a risk of high winds, *camp* at the saddle where the trail meets the top of the Waterpocket Fold.)

Day 2: Rim Trail Loop to Upper Muley Twist Canyon Trailhead
7½–10 hours, 10.4mi (16.7km)
From the campsite area, continue up the east canyon wall along the cairned route through the red and yellow-gray stripes of the Carmel Formation. At the top of the climb you'll be rewarded with spectacular views of what lies east: the Henry Mountains, Halls Creek, Oyster Shell Reef and Swamp Mesa. A sign

points down to 'Canyon Route' from where you just came, and several sandy sites hold potential for camping.

Follow the ridge north, hiking through patches of coarse sand and slickrock bordered by prickly pear and pineapple cactus, juniper, bristlecone pines and desert paintbrush. At a high-point on the ridge you can see north along the uplifted spine of the Waterpocket Fold to the white Navajo Sandstone domes near the visitor center (around 35mi away). After 1½mi of ridge-hiking, the trail turns from light gray to gold underfoot and a break in the Waterpocket Fold becomes visible up ahead. Just before reaching this break, the trail drops quite steeply toward the west side of the ridge then begins a steep descent down the east side of Muley Twist Canyon. There are many cairned routes here, each involving quite a bit of scrambling and all ending at the bottom of the canyon. A wooden sign near where the trail ends points to the 'Rim Route' from where you've just come.

Turn south, downcanyon and stay high, close to the east wall. About 300ft past some wonderful hat-shaped formations (on your right), sandstone slopes cut in from the west (right) and the trail swings up to the east (left) to avoid the narrows below. Deep potholes created by the narrows act as natural water-storage tanks.

After passing a gap in the west canyon wall and some beehive-shaped mounds of orange- and pink-circled rock, the trail descends back to the canyon bottom at a stand of cottonwood trees. A quarter-mile downcanyon the trail is cairned up the east wall again; you may be able to continue along the canyon bottom in dry periods. The high route ends at a double arc carved in the eastern wall, and swirled cushions of sandstone honeycombed with holes where softer rock has eroded away from the Wingate Sandstone walls.

Soon you'll pass **Saddle Arch**, high on the west (right) wall, and the sign for the 'Rim Route' (near the east edge of the canyon) which marks the end of your loop. From here the high, red canyon walls become low and golden and the hike retraces

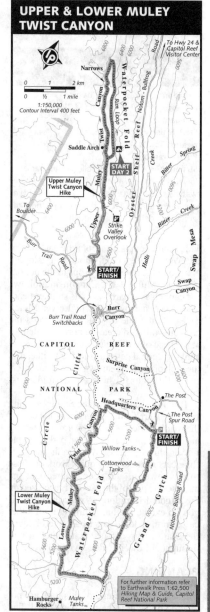

UPPER & LOWER MULEY TWIST CANYON

SOUTHWEST

the route out of the wash, past the Strike Valley Overlook Trailhead to the Upper Muley Twist Canyon Trailhead, 5mi away.

Lower Muley Twist Canyon

Duration	1–2 days
Distance	15mi (24.2km)
Standard	medium
Start/Finish	The Post
Nearest Towns	Fruita, Torrey
Public Transport	no

Summary This loop hike follows the dramatic lower section of Muley Twist Canyon, where water's erosive force has cut large alcoves from sheer, red canyon walls, then returns through grasslands dotted with colorful hills.

This scenic loop starts from the east side of the Waterpocket Fold, mounts its sloping Navajo Sandstone back, drops to the bottom of Lower Muley Twist Canyon and follows the canyon as it narrows to its southern end. The sheer, narrow walls of Lower Muley Twist tell the tale of water as it scours the canyon walls and creates enormous alcoves at the base of cliffs that rise 800ft above the canyon floor. The return to the trailhead is through open, sage-strewn grasslands interrupted by colorful hills on the fold's east side.

The hike can be extended 8mi by starting from the Burr Trail Rd a quarter-mile east of the road's switchbacks, or by 4mi by starting at this road and having a car parked at the Lower Muley Twist Canyon Trailhead. Shuffling cars is not exactly quick work on these roads, however, and people agree that the most scenic part of the canyon is accessed on the standard 15mi loop as described here. If you do extend the hike (turning it, in either case, from a long day to an overnighter), there are plenty of places to pitch a tent throughout Lower Muley Twist Canyon.

PLANNING
When to Hike
The narrows at the end of this hike are not where you want to be in a flash flood. The watershed that pours into this canyon is far reaching, so the entire region must be relatively dry when you undertake this hike. Check at the visitor center for current stream and weather conditions.

Maps
The Earthwalk Press maps (see Maps & Books under Information earlier in this section) should suffice for this straightforward hike. The relevant USGS quads are *Wagon Box Mesa* and *The Post*. In this book, see the map on page 313.

GETTING TO/FROM THE HIKE
Three miles south of the junction of the Notom-Bullfrog and Burr Trail roads (29mi south of Hwy 24) is a well-signed road that leads right toward The Post. This short spur road passes several fenced corrals and ends at a large, dirt parking lot where there is a pit toilet but no water. Lower Muley Twist Canyon Trailhead is at the southwest edge of the parking lot.

THE HIKE
It's not a bad idea to warm up or stretch a bit before beginning this hike, as the first mile is extremely steep. From the trailhead parking lot, follow the well-marked trail east through the grass to the red, sloping back of the Waterpocket Fold. Climb the steep, red switchbacks to where the trail turns white underfoot and continue climbing over white-rose-gray-yellow stripes of rock that characterizes the Moenkopi Formation. Passing an area where the rock is colored by yellow-green lichen and golden bands of iron-oxide, the trail bears northwest to views of the Henry Mountains, Oystershell Reef and Strike Valley.

After an hour or so of steady climbing, the trail hits sand and the red walls of Muley Twist Canyon become visible to the northeast. Here, the trail levels out and crosses a sandy area strewn with sage, dune evening primrose, Mormon tea, buffalo barberry, sand verbena, Spanish bayonette yucca and Harrison's milkvetch. A large, **wave-shaped alcove** streaked with black desert varnish and cut by a red diagonal stripe is an obvious and intriguing piece of rock; notice the honeycomb texture of the red member, where loose or softer stones have fallen away through erosion.

Leaving this wash, the trail bears south to meet the main body of Lower Muley Twist Canyon, staying high on the canyon's east side at first, then gently cutting to the canyon bottom. Already the dramatic scenery that typifies Lower Muley Twist is evident, as sheer red Wingate Sandstone walls tower 300ft on both sides.

Continue south along the canyon bottom and an enormous arc soon comes into view on the west (right) wall. Water that funnels through Lower Muley Twist hits the north-facing part of this alcove and is directed with force to the next canyon wall where it cuts into the second large alcove (on the east canyon wall) and is again redirected downcanyon. In this manner, water has formed the numerous and regular undercuts to the southern terminus of this canyon.

After passing two gaps in the western (right-hand) wall, a big side canyon cuts in from the northeast. Exploring this canyon reveals several good *campsites*.

Back in the main canyon, the trail soon turns from sand to sandstone and continues straight where the main canyon swings west. Mounting a sandy plain brings more *campsites*, among sage and junipers.

The hike continues in the same manner – from riverbed to high ground – as the canyon twists south. Each alcove seems bigger, deeper and more graceful than the last.

At length the trail reaches a cul-de-sac, with gradually stepped walls on all sides. The trail wraps around the east side of a low, sandy plain, where Mormon pioneers had to 'twist' their mules to get them through. In this, the **narrowest part of the canyon**, the walls are less than 10ft apart at points, and up to 800ft tall.

After a quarter-mile these narrows, and Muley Twist Canyon, end where Muley Twist's river flows into Strike Valley toward its final destination of Halls Creek. At this point, cairns mark the trail north to The Post. At first the trail is wide, resembling a jeep road, and startlingly red underfoot. As you continue north, below the west-facing escarpment of Big Thompson Mesa the red becomes streaked with green, purple and gray Moenkopi Shale. Strike Valley opens wider the further north you go, and soon it appears more like a meadow, covered with Mormon tea, sage and juniper. Ridges that resemble the back of a submerged dinosaur line the east side of the trail for its remaining length.

Navajo Knobs

Duration	4–6 hours
Distance	9mi (14.5km)
Standard	medium-hard
Start/Finish	Hickman Natural Bridge Trailhead
Nearest Towns	Fruita, Torrey
Public Transport	no

Summary A climb to the upper, west-facing edge of the Waterpocket Fold affords breathtaking views, unparalleled in the Southwest.

This hike is easily accessed and its lower part (to Hickman Bridge) is one of the most popular hikes in the park. Few people, however, make the entire 4½ mile (1649ft ascent) trip to the Navajo Knobs – two bumps of Navajo Sandstone perched high on the precipitous western edge of the Waterpocket Fold. Views from the Knobs are unsurpassed, and along the approach trail (mostly a slickrock route, well-marked with cairns) you'll pass the classic, white domes of Capitol Reef.

PLANNING
When to Hike

October to June is the best time for this hike: it's a steep climb with little shade, no water and no flash-flood danger.

Maps

This is a rare hike in that the entire hike fits on one USGS 7.5-minute series quadrangle: *Fruita, Utah*, available at the visitor center. The quad is not necessary, however, as the hike is well-marked and the route is rather obvious. If you do take the quad, be sure to have a smaller-scale map along, to identify distant features from atop the Knobs.

GETTING TO/FROM THE HIKE

The Hickman Natural Bridge Trailhead, from where this hike starts, is well signposted off the north side of Hwy 24, 5mi east of the visitor center. There is a pit toilet, but no water, at the trailhead parking lot.

THE HIKE

The beginning of the hike takes you along the Fremont River, under the gaze of Pectol's Pyramid – a massive block of Navajo Sandstone that rises above the south side of the trail, river and highway (as you mount the forthcoming switchbacks notice that this 'pyramid' is actually a triad of rock summits: one atop the Moenkopi cliff whose base meets the highway and two further south that are linked by a saddle).

After 585yd is a well signed junction where the Navajo Knobs trail turns north, away from the main Hickman Natural Bridge Trail, to climb across a draw littered with dark volcanic rocks. Following the

draw west (left), the trail skirts the bottom of magnificent, rounded white peaks. The **Hickman Bridge Overlook** is well signposted off the south (left) side of the trail, but the 133ft natural bridge can be hard to identify: it is at the same level as you (across a small canyon) and the same color as the walls from which it's been eroded.

From the overlook sign, the main trail swings west to views of Boulder Mountain (10,908ft) and the Circle Cliffs in the west and south, respectively. Here, ripple marks on the ground show evidence of ancient shallow seas that lapped upon the shore of tidal flats to deposit muddy layers that are now mudstone. Also on the ground are remnants of yellow 'footprints' that once guided people along this route; the yellow paint has chipped and faded so that it now looks like lichen.

The trail zig-zags through a south-facing side canyon, a rhythm which continues for most of the remainder of the hike. As you

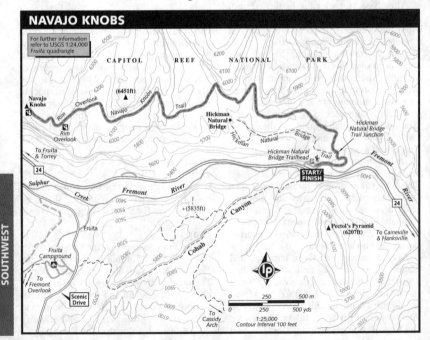

continue upward, the trail winds past the mouth of three more side canyons before reaching the **Rim Overlook**, 2¼mi from the trailhead. Views are really special from here: a profile of the Waterpocket Fold and its northern terminus, the canyon where the Fremont meets the Dirty Devil River, the Kaiparowits Plateau (west), Castle Dome (north) and, 1000ft below, the visitor center and Fruita campground. Some may be tempted to turn back at this point.

From the Rim Overlook, follow the sign pointing toward the Navajo Knobs Trail. After climbing two more sandstone pitches you'll swing north around a point, pass between the cliffs (on your right) and a weather tower, and find yourself on a tremendous ledge face-to-face with The Castle – a large chunk of the Waterpocket Fold that has been eroded away from the main fold (which you've probably noticed from Hwy 24 and the visitor center).

The trail rambles along this ledge to the northwest edge of a west-facing, W-shaped canyon. Following the cairns, mount the west edge of the 'W'. Soon your destination appears – the double bumps that mark the highest point on the next promontory are the Navajo Knobs. The trail winds around the eastern base of the knobs and up through some loose rock to the double summit.

Retrace your steps to the trailhead.

Grand Staircase–Escalante National Monument

In 1996 President Bill Clinton made a surprise wilderness designation which, among other things, set aside 1.7 million acres in southern Utah as Grand Staircase–Escalante National Monument. The enormous area spans the Kaiparowits Plateau, the Escalante River and its tributary canyons, and the Grand Staircase from which it takes its name.

The most remote and primitive of all national monuments (and the only one managed by the Bureau of Land Management),

Grand Staircase–Escalante has few of the hiker-friendly amenities found in other nationally designated areas: there are few maintained trails, even fewer trail signs and sparsely scattered campgrounds and visitor facilities. However, the hiking here is terrific for hikers who are self-sufficient and comfortable in the desert environment. Crowds are seldom a problem and the area is so vast that the terrain varies from lush, riparian waterways to stark, slickrock plateaus.

HISTORY

An abandoned Kayenta Anasazi village near Boulder is one of the few remnants of the Fremont and Anasazi cultures. Until the 16th century the Southern Paiutes were the main tribe in the area.

In the 1870s and 1890s stockmen established the area's two main communities, Boulder and Escalante. Most early exploration here, including that of the Hole in the Rock expedition of 1879, was undertaken to find a route across the canyons of the Escalante River, the most formidable barriers to east-west travel in southern Utah. Little by little, ranchers connected one trail to another, skirting the more precipitous canyons (which still remain inaccessible to anyone not on foot or horseback). Using wagon roads as a template, the CCC began construction of the current road between Boulder and Escalante in 1940. The final portion of this road was not paved until 1971.

NATURAL HISTORY

The Grand Staircase is a geologic sequence that begins at the north rim of the Grand Canyon and rises, via a set of cliffs and plateaus (the steps of the staircase), 5000ft to the Pink Cliffs at the southern edge of Bryce Canyon. The vertical risers, which are up to 2000ft high, are comprised of rock layers with differing erosion rates, while the horizontal treads are formed by homogenous rock plateaus up to 15mi wide.

On the east side of the Grand Staircase lies the Kaiparowits Plateau, a wedge-shaped region that fans out from the Aquarius Plateau in the north to man-made Lake Powell (which straddles the Utah-Arizona border) in the south. This plateau was the eastern contact point for the Fremont and Anasazi cultures, and is rich in undocumented Native American dwelling and ceremonial sites.

East of the Kaiparowits, a series of canyons that run east-west dump into the south-flowing Escalante River. This is one of the more popular hiking regions, as the river and its side canyons provide water (most of the year) and are easily navigated.

PLANNING
When to Hike
Like most Southwest destinations, Grand Staircase–Escalante hikes are best done in late spring/early summer and fall. Since crowds are not an issue, it's the weather that dictates comfort here: spring brings a risk of cool temperatures but almost always has plenty of water; if summer comes early, there's a risk of mosquitoes, gnats and black flies; the primary concern when hiking in the fall is a lack of water.

What to Bring
Wading shoes are imperative, as most hikes in the region (and all of those covered here) require that you wade through rivers and/or streams. A long-sleeved shirt and long pants are also recommended for protection against sun and insects and for making your way through slot canyons. If you don't have a 4WD vehicle, bring some blocks and a shovel for emergency situations: very few access roads are paved, and they turn to mud with the slightest precipitation.

Maps & Books
For maps and information, stop by the Escalante Interagency visitor center (☎ 435-826-5499, 🖳 www.ut.blm.monument/) at 755 West Main St.

The best map is the 1:70,500 National Geographic Trails Illustrated *Canyons of the Escalante (No 710)*, which covers the central part of the national monument, around Escalante and Boulder. The definitive book on hiking the area is Rudy Lambrechtse's *Hiking the Escalante* (1985), available widely ($9); it has an entire section on summer hikes.

Permits & Regulations
At the time of writing, free, self-registration backcountry permits are the only kind needed for hiking here, and these are only required on the busiest trails. If there is not a self-registration box and permits at the trailhead, there is no permit required. This may change in the near future, however, so ask at a ranger station or the visitor center to be sure.

NEAREST TOWNS
Escalante
Named for a Franciscan Padre who helped establish a route between Santa Fe, New Mexico, and Monterey, California, Escalante was primarily a ranching/farming town until surrounding lands became part of the national monument. It's now the main place to fuel up before heading into the wilds. Hwy 12 is the town's main street, and along it you'll find a post office, several gas stations, Julie's Laundrette (next to the Frosty Shop and Phillips 66 gas station; open daily 9 am to 7 pm) and Escalante Outfitters (☎ 435-826-4266, 🖳 www.aros.net/~), 310 W Main St, which sells maps, books, camping and backpacking supplies, has a message board out front and is a friendly source of information. The other store in town is Griffin Groceries & Hardware, one block west on the other side of the street, which is good for foodstuffs but not much else. Bryce Canyon National Park is 43mi west.

Places to Stay & Eat *Escalante Outfitters* has two-person cabins for $30, and serves espresso, bakery items, gourmet pizzas and draft beer, open 8 am to 7 pm daily. For in-town camping, the ***Broken Bow*** (☎ 435-826-4959, 495 W Main St) has very exposed tent sites for $11, RV sites for $17 and showers for $3 (free for paying guests). More scenic are the $7 campsites at ***Calf Creek campground***, 16mi northeast of Escalante on the west side of Hwy 12.

In town, the ***Circle D Motel*** (☎ 435-826-4297, 475 W Main St), has singles/doubles for $35/40. Across the street, the ***Moqui Lodge*** has comparable rooms and prices. A step up in quality is ***Escalante's Grand Staircase*** (☎ 435-826-4890, 280 W Main St), with rooms for $60/80, including breakfast. For local gossip and excellent American grub (pancakes, cheeseburgers, onion rings), the *Golden Loop Café* (☎ *435-826-4433, 215 W Main St)*, is open from 6 am to 8 pm daily.

Boulder

Until Hwy 12 between Escalante and Boulder was paved in 1971, Boulder had no paved access road. It is thus considered, and highly touted by local promoters, as one of the last towns to be reached by sealed road in the USA. It occupies a scenic hilltop on Hwy 12, 29mi northeast of Escalante and approximately half-way between Hwys 89 and 24.

Escalante Canyon Outfitters (☎ 435-335-7311, 🖳 www.gorp.com/escalante), PO Box 1330, Boulder, UT 84716, runs full-service, horse-supplied hiking trips in the Escalante canyons. You hike and the horse carries your gear – what a set up!

Places to Stay & Eat The best destination in the area is the *Boulder Mountain Lodge* (☎ *435-335-7460, reservations 800-556-3446, 🖳 www.boulder-utah.com)*, at the junction of Hwy 12 and Burr Trail Rd. It has a cozy lodge, gourmet *restaurant* and finely decorated rooms for $70 to $100.

Pole's Place (☎ *435-335-7422, 🖳 www .boulderutah.com/polesplace)*, also on Hwy 12, across from Anasazi State Park, has motel rooms for $44/52 for singles/doubles and a family style *restaurant*.

Rattlesnakes rarely bite unless confronted or annoyed – stand well back anyhow.

Boulder Mail Trail

Duration	2–3 days
Distance	16mi (25.8km)
Standard	hard
Start	Boulder landing strip
Finish	Upper Escalante Canyon Trailhead
Nearest Towns	Boulder, Escalante
Public Transport	no

Summary This historic trail, which requires route-finding and orienteering abilities, passes through the little-visited and very scenic watershed of the Escalante River.

This trail follows a route that was used to carry mail and supplies (mostly by mule) between Boulder and Escalante from 1902 to the mid-1950s. It's not a trail for beginners, as much of the route is unmarked and requires orienteering and path-finding skills. The scenery along the way is diverse, with pinyon and juniper benches meeting cracked sandstone plateaus and lush, steep-sided canyons that drain into the Escalante River. Most people do the one-way trip in two days, but a third day allows you to do some cross-country wandering and possibly explore Phipps Death Hollow Outstanding Natural Area.

PLANNING
When to Hike

There needs to be water flowing in Death Hollow (in normal years this is year-round) to do this hike. This will give you water at your overnight camp, but you'll still need to carry all your water for both days' hiking. For a really comfortable hike, where you can get water half-way through each day, water needs to be flowing in Sand and Maimie Creeks, which is usually the case from April to early July; ask in Escalante or Boulder before you go.

Maps

While the entire route is marked on the Trails Illustrated map mentioned in Maps & Books under Planning at the start of this section, you'll need larger-scale quadrangles to do

HUGH D'ANDRADE

SOUTHWEST

this hike. The necessary USGS 7.5-minute series quadrangles – *Boulder Town*, *Calf Creek* and *Escalante* – are available from Escalante Outfitters and the Interagency visitor center.

GETTING TO/FROM THE HIKE

Most people start the hike at the Boulder landing strip and end at the Escalante River Trailhead, just outside the town of Escalante. As it's a one-way hike, you'll need to arrange a shuttle to/from your car to the start/finish point.

To find the Boulder landing strip, turn northwest off Hwy 12 (24.8mi northeast of Escalante, 4.2mi south of Boulder) onto the signed Hells Backbone Rd. Take the first dirt road on your left (called McGath Bench Rd, but unsigned) and follow it south for half a mile to the Boulder landing strip, where there is a parking area on the left; with a high-clearance vehicle, you can continue across the airstrip and another quarter-mile to an unofficial parking area next to the trail register box.

The Upper Escalante Canyon Trailhead (the end of the hike) is well signposted off the north side of Hwy 12, three-quarters of a mile east of Escalante and just east of the high school and cemetery.

THE HIKE
Day 1: Boulder Landing Strip to Phipps Death Hollow
4–5 hours, 5½mi (8.9km)

The first leg of this hike takes you from the juniper and pinyon pine flats atop New Home Bench (at 6660ft) down to the sandy drainage of Sand Creek (at 6200ft), then back up to the Slickrock Saddle Bench (around 6600ft) before making the precipitous, 900ft drop into Death Hollow. Don't start too late in the day, as you'll want plenty of light to make this last descent.

From the landing strip, follow the jeep road a quarter-mile to the trail register box (on the left, usually flanked by several cars). Register your party here and attach a copy of the permit to your pack. Continue south for 1mi down the jeep road, toward the cream-colored mesa with a green toupee

of trees that is McGath Bench, and turn right (southwest) at the sign that marks the official start of the Boulder Mail Trail.

With red sand underfoot and pinyon pines and junipers all around, you'll make your way down the west side of New Home Bench. Cairns along the trail mark the way toward, then down, a sandstone ledge that ends on a sandy slope on the west side of a shallow draw. As the trail gets steeper and turns to solid slickrock, you get your fist unobstructed view of the Slickrock Saddle Bench, with Kings Bench in the foreground in the west. Follow the cairns across the slickrock to where the trail becomes sand again.

After a quarter-mile of sandy hiking you'll come to the edge of a beautiful slickrock bowl which descends over several ledges to where the smaller Sweetwater Creek meets Sand Creek. At the confluence, among swirled pockets of pink sandstone, are a few shade-giving cottonwood trees, Indian paintbrush and, when water is running upstream, pools from which you can take water.

Head downstream (left) along the west (right) side of the stream bed to where sandstone closes in on both sides and cairns mark the sharp turn up the west side of the bank and out of the wash. This is only a brief detour to high ground. The trail drops to creek-level again and continues for a quarter-mile before crossing a dry wash and ascending, via a cairn-marked slickrock route, around the north end of a whimsically capped butte. As you round the west side of this butte, look up for an old telephone wire. This is an old USFS line that gave service to 35 families in the Boulder area from 1910 until recently.

The line marks the beginning of a climb across a sandy section toward a break in the Slickrock Saddle Bench. With sufficient water, this could be a good *campsite*. Atop the pass, you'll be rewarded with views on all sides. Following the telephone line would take you over the brink of **Death Hollow** – a move you don't want to make. Instead, follow the cairned route slightly south from the telephone line, down a steep but wide draw and along a crack in the northeast

Three Faces of Paria Canyon, Grand Staircase–Escalante National Monument, Arizona. **Top:** Hollows and undercuts are the legacy of centuries of violent flash-flooding. **Bottom Left:** Each night's camp is spent beneath looming rock walls. **Bottom Right:** From little things, big things grow – the Paria River has carved the world's longest canyon.

Scenery of the Southwest. Clockwise from Top Left: Waterpocket Fold from Muley Twist Canyon, Capitol Reef National Park, Utah; the Grand Canyon's painted mesas from Yaqui Point, Grand Canyon National Park, Arizona; Lipan Point overlook, Grand Canyon; O'Neill Butte on the South Kaibab Trail, Grand Canyon; the Bright Angel Trail, the most popular in Grand Canyon National Park.

wall. At points, the trail looks like it goes right off the edge of the earth so people prone to vertigo need to beware. After the steep descent, you're rewarded with the gorgeous, riparian canyon that is Death Hollow (so named because of the many mules that were lost on the steep trip down).

There are plenty of *campsites* within a quarter-mile of where the trail meets the creek bed, both up- and downstream; some of the best are 300yd downstream (south).

Side Trip: Phipps Death Hollow Outstanding Natural Area
4–5 hours, 5¼mi (8.5km)

To extend this trip, spend a night in the **Phipps Death Hollow Outstanding Natural Area**, a world of gullies, grottoes, spires and other slickrock wonders perched on the eastern edge of Death Hollow. The area is named for early settler Washington Phipps, who was shot by his partner in a business brawl somewhere in the area.

From the edge of Death Hollow, where the route veers south from the telephone line (see Day 1), stay high and instead of dropping down into the canyon, continue south along the edge of Death Hollow and climb up and over Slickrock Saddle. From here you can usually see a faint trail, worn between low-growing sage and sand verbena, in the red sand. Follow this trail south for a half-mile to where it crosses some slickrock (look for cairns, though they are not reliable here) and continues making its way through the sand. After 1mi, the trail swings west and down over slickrock ledges to an area with numerous pockets, slopes and shallow draws, lone junipers and stands of pinyon and ponderosa pines.

There are few enough visitors here that *campsites* are not evident; find a flat patch of ground and make your own. Water is often available in pools along the cracks of slickrock draws. There are no real markers showing the extent of Phipps Death Hollow Outstanding Natural Area, but if you continue south you'll reach the edge of the cliffs above the Escalante River, and if you go too far east you'll find yourself perched on the edge of Death Hollow.

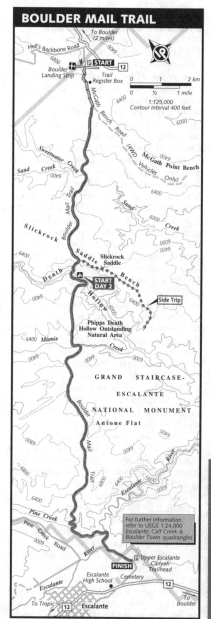

BOULDER MAIL TRAIL

To Boulder (2 miles)
Hell's Backbone Road
START 12
Boulder Landing Strip
Trail Register Box
0   1   2 km
0   ½   1 mile
1:125,000
Contour Interval 400 feet
McGath Bench Road
(4WD Vehicles Only)
McGath Point Bench
Sweetwater Creek
Sand Creek
Slickrock
Boulder Mail Trail
Sand Creek
Saddle Bench
Slickrock Saddle
Death Hollow
START DAY 2
Side Trip
Phipps Death Hollow Outstanding Natural Area
Mamie Creek
GRAND STAIRCASE-
ESCALANTE
NATIONAL MONUMENT
Antone Flat
Boulder Mail Trail
Escalante River
Pine Creek
Pine Creek Road
For further information refer to USGS 1:24,000 Escalante, Calf Creek & Boulder Town quadrangles
Upper Escalante Canyon Trailhead
FINISH
Escalante High School
Cemetery
12
Escalante
To Tropic   12   To Boulder

SOUTHWEST

Day 2: Death Hollow to Upper Escalante Canyon Trailhead

6–8 hours, 10½mi (16.9km)

The rhythm of slickrock–sand-flats, slickrock–sand-flats continues for the rest of the hike as you climb up, over and down several benches and draws created by tributaries of the Escalante River. The first climb of the day – the 800ft ascent out of Death Hollow – is matched only by the last descent of the day – the 900ft descent to Pine Creek and the Escalante River.

After descending into Death Hollow, your path will depend largely on the water line. When the water is low, there is usually dry land on one side or another, forcing you to cross the river many times via rocks and logs. When the water is high, you'll have to grab a walking stick and wade. In either case, the way out of Death Hollow is six bends (approximately a half-mile) downstream (south) from where the trail entered the hollow from above. Look for cairns on the west (right) side of the river at a southwest bend, amid a stand of tall, straight ponderosa pines.

Drink plenty of water (and filter enough for the rest of the way if Mamie Creek is dry), to prepare for the exceedingly strenuous climb out of Death Hollow. From the cairns at river level, the trail heads directly up the west side of the hollow before leveling out (slightly) along a sandstone draw at the base of three north-facing rock outcrops. Look for the telephone lines again, overhead on your right (west).

Follow the cairned route under the line and up to where it traverses a burned plateau dotted with sage, juniper and some healthy ponderosas. The trail remains sandy underfoot as it follows the telephone line to a slickrock plateau where it bears right (pay attention to the cairns here) and swings down to Mamie Creek. Upon reaching the creek bottom, turn left (south) and hike 200ft down the wash to where cairns lead you over a rock nose and up, bearing west (right) over a cracked sandstone formation that looks like a **giant cerebellum**.

Coming out of the 'brains', the next open country you encounter is Antone Flat, a sage and juniper meadow bordered by spectacular volcanic escarpments in the south and west. (The Trails Illustrated map puts Antone Flat slightly farther west than it actually is, so be careful if you are using that map.) A flat, sandy trail follows the old telephone line across the meadow, bearing slightly south around the east side of the butte which is prominent on the not-so-distant horizon (about a half-mile away).

At the west edge of Antone Flat you'll enter a chalky-white slickrock draw where water is often available in deep pockets. Head right (northwest) up the draw, following cairns past the northern point of the rock promontory on the left and over a mound of sandstone that was weathered in concentric circles from rain dropping on its rounded summit (imagine putting a jawbreaker under a dripping faucet – same effect). After a quarter-mile of steep climbing the route bears south (left) along the east side of a broad, hogback ridge to the last sandy, sage-juniper-pinyon flat of the hike. Where the trail turns west (right) and the trees thin out, you'll catch the first glimpse of 'civilization' – alfalfa fields, a few sheds and the town of Escalante.

But don't get too anxious – from here you have a terrifically steep descent, following cairns down the south, then north, side of a slickrock slope before swinging south (left) toward the rock island atop the hill on the left. Climb a final pitch over the saddle on the right side of the thumb sticking up from the island, and continue down over loose rock switchbacks to Pine Creek.

The west side of the creek is private land, so resist the temptation to cross and head straight into town via farm roads; instead, follow the east side of Pine Creek to where it meets the Escalante River. Head west (right) a quarter-mile until the canyon opens wide to a shallow wash where the trail swings south, through the brush, and meets a jeep road and the Upper Escalante Canyon Trailhead.

Paria Canyon

The longest and most flash-flood prone canyon in the world, Paria (pronounced Pa-ree-a) is a great feather in the cap of most

Southwest hikers. It is not a technical hike, but requires a significant amount of wading, weather observation and good judgment. While the threat of flash flood is real for part of the year, the hike can be made with little trouble when the weather is fine.

The highlights of the one-way hike described here, which starts in Utah and ends in Arizona where the Colorado River begins its descent through the Grand Canyon, are many. One of the most striking is the relaxation people associate with being in the canyon: once you've entered there is only one route to follow, eliminating the need for much navigation or thought of the outside world.

Politically, Paria is part of the Grand Staircase–Escalante National Monument (see previous hike) but is covered separately because it has its own history, permits and regulations, and access routes.

HISTORY

The area has been used for grazing sheep, cattle and goats since the mid-1880s, and you'll see old cabin sites and even an old pump along the hike. Before any permanent settlers arrived the area was explored by Mormon and military expeditions, and was inhabited by Southern Paiutes who left some pictographs on boulders in the lower part of the canyon.

At the end of the hike, the Lees Ferry area is rich with history. The Wilson Ranch dates from 1918, the Spencer Place (and its rusty old car) is from the 1920s, the Red Wing Mine is from a uranium boom in the 1950s, and the Lonely Dell Ranch (where there is now a museum and cemetery) was occupied from the 1870s to the 1940s. All were built, independently, by polygamous Mormon families who worked in conjunction with the Grand Canyon Cattle Company, housing cowboys and running a ferry service across the Colorado River.

The completion of Navajo Bridge in 1929 ended ferry services across the Colorado, and in 1964 Lees Ferry became part of Glen Canyon National Recreation Area. The surrounding ranch buildings are now owned by the NPS, which runs the Lees Ferry campground and ranger station.

Paria Canyon

Duration	5 days
Distance	37.5mi (60.4km)
Standard	medium-hard
Start	Whitehouse Trailhead
Finish	Lees Ferry
Nearest Towns	Page, Kanab
Public Transport	no

Summary This one-way, in-the-river hike takes you through a narrow canyon (known for its flash flooding) to historic Lees Ferry, where the Colorado River enters the Grand Canyon.

PLANNING
When to Hike

Mid-July to mid-September is flash-flood season and August, especially, should be avoided. Late April, May and October are probably the best months to hike, though the water (remember you'll be wading much of the time) can be chilly if the winter comes early or stays late. Mosquitoes and deer flies tend to arrive in early June and stay through July.

What to Bring

You'll definitely need a pair of wading shoes – old sneakers (worn without socks) work best – and a pair of boots or hiking shoes. In-camp footwear is optional, since your hiking shoes will be dry most of the time. A walking stick may be helpful if the water is running high, though most of the time the wading is relatively easy. If you plan to explore far into Buckskin Gulch you'll need a 30ft length of rope.

Maps

The best USGS maps for this hike are the 1:62,500 *Smoky Mountain* and *Glen Canyon Dam* quadrangles, which are no longer in print. If you can't find these, you'll need six 7.5-minute series quads: *West Clark Bench*, *Poverty Flat*, *Wrather Arch*, *Water Pockets*, *Ferry Swale* and *Lees Ferry*.

Many people forgo using USGS maps and instead rely on the BLM's *Hiker's Guide to Paria Canyon* booklet which has panels of USGS 7.5-minute quads that correspond specifically to this part of Paria Canyon. It's a handy (waterproof) booklet, with mileage markers, safety tips, permit information etc. Pick one up ($9) at the Paria information station near the White House Trailhead.

Permits & Regulations

A backcountry permit is required for day hikes or overnight trips and costs $5 per person, per day. There is a 10-person maximum for any group. Day hikers can self-register at the trailhead; backpackers can make reservations up to one year in advance online (🖳 paria.az.blm.gov), or by phone through the Arizona Strip Interpretive Association (☎ 435-688-3230) in St George, Utah. In both cases, they prefer to mail the permit to you, but you can pick it up at the Paria information station, on the south side of Hwy 89, 44mi from Kanab, Utah, and 30mi from Page, Arizona; open daily 8 am to 5 pm. Walk-in permits are often available and can be obtained from the information station up to seven days prior to an available date.

WARNING

There is no water at White House Trailhead; get water at the pump outside the Paria information station (2mi from the trailhead parking lot).

NEAREST TOWNS
Kanab

See Nearest Towns in the Zion National Park section earlier in this chapter.

Page

Carved out of the desert in the mid-1950s, this resort town owes its existence to John C Page, commissioner of the Bureau of Reclamation under President Franklin Roosevelt, and one of the strongest proponents of Glen Canyon Dam. The town sprawls across the hills around the southwest end of Lake Powell, and is known for its John Wesley Powell Museum and visitor center (on Lake Powell Blvd).

Places to Stay & Eat Most businesses are of the chain variety, and food is best had from one of the many family-style and fast-food restaurants along Hwy 89. For lodging, check-out *Canyon Colors B&B (☎ 520-645-5979, 800-536-2530, 225 South Navajo St)*, half a block off Navajo Loop Dr, which has rooms for $75 to $100 including breakfast; *Uncle Bill's Place (☎ 520-645-1224, 800-944-8270, 117 8th Ave)*, two blocks south of Hwy 89, which has 'guesthouse' rooms (with shared bath) for $36 to $44 and suites for $50 to $140; or the *Red Rock Motel (☎ 520-645-0062, 114 8th Ave)*, across from Uncle Bill's, which has old motel rooms ($42/54 for singles/doubles). If you want to indulge yourself, head to the *Best Western at Lake Powell (☎ 520-645-5988, 208 North Lake Powell Blvd)*, which has air conditioning, a pool, fitness center and in-room refrigerators for $70 to $105.

Getting There & Away Page is on Hwy 89, 30mi east of the Paria information station, 75mi east of Kanab and 115mi from Zion National Park. Sunrise Airlines (☎ 800-347-3962) provides daily flights to Phoenix.

GETTING TO/FROM THE HIKE

This hike presents one of the more difficult shuttle arrangements because it takes around two hours to drive from the finish (at Lees Ferry) to the start at the White House Trailhead parking lot. It's achievable, just time-consuming. An alternative is to take a taxi in one direction ($65 per person); Page Taxi (☎ 520-645-8540) is usually available for same-day service (you can call from a pay phone at either end of the hike), though it doesn't hurt to let them know which day you plan on using their services. Hikers have been known to hitchhike without trouble.

To reach the White House Trailhead, turn south off Hwy 89, between Miles 20 and 21; the Paria information station is on the right just off the highway, and the trailhead is 2mi further at the end of the road. There is a campground ($5 per car) with picnic tables, toilets and fire rings at the trailhead; water is available from a pump outside the Paria information station.

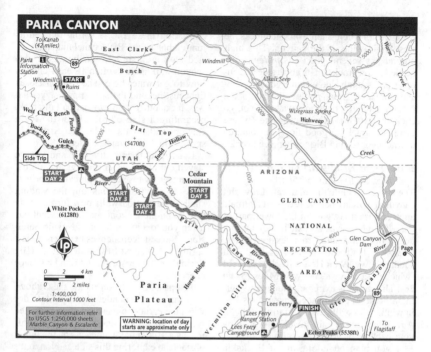

PARIA CANYON

THE HIKE
Day 1: White House Trailhead to Buckskin Gulch Confluence
4–5 hours, 7¼mi (11.7km)

A sign at the trailhead reading 'Trail' directs you into the dry riverbed which is, essentially, the trail. Follow the river's course south, past gothic-looking windows left by rocks which have dislodged from the Navajo Sandstone. After 2¼mi you pass under a set of power lines which mark the entrance to Paria Canyon–Vermilion Cliffs Wilderness. After another three-quarters of a mile, a lone cottonwood offers shade and marks the first *campsite* in the canyon.

From here, you may want to hike along the east (left) bank of the river, where the earth is a bit firmer and is strewn with sand verbena, sage and wild buckwheat. The bank eventually ends at a cliff, forcing you back into the main wash, near where a campsite is marked on the BLM panel map; this campsite is hard to find and offers no real attraction.

After 4mi, a section called **the Narrows** begins quite suddenly when the cliff pinches in from the east and the walls close together, obstructing sunlight except during midday. Large stripes of desert varnish drip down from the cliff rims, and horizontal bands mark different periods of deposition within the larger time frame over which the Navajo Sandstone was laid down. These narrows, which run for about 2mi, are where you do not want to be during a flash flood.

Out of the narrows, though still in a high-walled, narrow part of the canyon, you'll come to the much-photographed **Slide Rock Arch** which formed when a large chunk of cliff slid down from the east canyon wall and remained intact. The river continues to widen the arch as it flows around the base of the fallen rock.

Half a mile away, the narrow Buckskin Gulch (see Side Trip) makes a scenic, angled entry on the right, also marking the Utah-Arizona border. The river makes a deep southward bend, then sweeps into a north-ward U-turn where a large mound blocks the west (right) side of the canyon. This high ground has several good *campsites* – one nestled among rocks on its north side and another on its south side which is lower, sandy and more level. Small pools at the base of the mound may provide ample water; if not, go back to the Buckskin confluence (where there is normally a good flow) or continue downcanyon 2mi to Big Spring (see Day 2).

Side Trip: Buckskin Gulch
1–3 days, up to 32mi (51.5km)
The Buckskin Gulch is an ultra-narrow slot canyon that many people use as an alternate approach from Hwy 89 to the lower part of Paria Canyon, or as an exit if they are not doing the entire hike to Lees Ferry. The Buckskin Trailhead is just less than 5mi south of Hwy 89 on House Rock Valley Rd (which meets Hwy 89 between Miles 25 and 26). This gulch is extremely dangerous during a flood: one 13mi section averages 12ft in width, with walls from 50ft to 100ft high! A rope is necessary for lowering or hauling your pack up or down several rockfalls.

If you plan on hiking all of Buckskin Gulch, pick-up a copy of Michael Kelsey's *Hiking and Exploring the Paria River* ($12) at the Paria information station, or ask the BLM staff there for current information about the gulch. Sometimes water sits in pools through most of the gulch, turning a hike into a series of swim-wade-swims.

You needn't hike the entire gulch to make it a worthwhile side trip. The most spectacular part of the gulch is, arguably, near its confluence with Paria Canyon. Start in to Buckskin from its narrow mouth and continue along its high-walled, narrow path until you feel like turning back. A boulder jam, 1¼mi from the confluence is a good turning point, as is the Middle Route Exit 3½mi further up the gulch.

Day 2: Buckskin Gulch Confluence to Big Spring
3–5 hours, 4½mi (7.3km)
The scenery between the Buckskin Gulch confluence and the recommended camp-sites is representative also of the following 2mi. After these 2mi, a spring marked as 'unreliable' on the BLM panel map has created a low grotto of ferns on the west (right) canyon wall; there is often a steady enough flow to get water here. The canyon closes tight just beyond the spring and stays that way for another mile to where a tall crack, separating a slab of rock from the main canyon wall on the right, marks another spring which is covered by ferns.

Even if its been a dry year and you've stayed out of the water thus far, it's almost guaranteed that past this point you'll be getting wet. Time to break out the wading shoes! The canyon walls now turn a shade toward purple as your gradual descent has taken you to a lower layer of Navajo Sandstone. Several deep alcoves between the last spring and the next fresh water source (Big Spring) are precursors to the rich landscape ahead.

Just past Mile 11 you'll pass the **Oxbow**, an abandoned meander that was left dry when the Paria's course dramatically shifted west during a flash flood. Its final pour-off makes a 10ft chute which acts as the major obstacle to exploring this side canyon; once you've mounted the chute, it's a dry sandstone amphitheater that would be a good place to escape to during a flood.

Past the Oxbow the canyon makes a broad S-turn before coming to Big Spring which, in most years, flows from near the bottom of the canyon's west (right) wall. The mini-oasis created by the continual flow of water is refreshing, and a good *camping area* lies across the river on a sandy bench dotted with willow trees. There are other campsites about 1mi further downcanyon (see Day 3).

Day 3: Big Spring to Shower Spring
7½–10 hours, 9½mi (15.3km)
This is a long day that can be cut in half by camping at Judd Hollow.

From Big Spring, the canyon tends west and pushes relatively straight for about 1mi until it begins a beautiful sequence of curves which cut high, broad alcoves into the soaring red-and-gold cliffs. Numerous low rock shelves and tree-covered earthen mounds provide *campsites*, unmarked on the BLM panel map.

Near the end of this serpentine section, tight canyons cut in on both sides forming an angled crossroads. Soon after, the canyon walls broaden slightly to reveal a big patch of sky. A figure-eight shaped side canyon opens onto the west (right) side of the main canyon here, a good place to put your pack down and do some exploring. At the south end of the figure-eight, the main canyon makes a hard turn west and approaches a lofty, pink alcove swirled with dark red iron-oxide and white calcium carbonate. Opposite the alcove, a flat, grassy plain strewn with oak and cottonwood trees offers ample space for *campsites*.

South of here Paria Canyon really opens up and wide floodplains covered with rushes, willows and a variety of wildflowers offer land routes for those who are tired of wading. A mile further, just past Mile 16, large boulders block the river, creating several deep, jade-colored pools. Soon, you'll reach the rusty old **Judd Hollow pump** that sits below Judd Hollow on the east (left) river bank. The pump was brought into the canyon in 1939 to pump water to the grazing land atop the plateau to the north, then sold and moved (from 3mi upriver) to its present site in 1949. It rained the day after it was installed, eliminating the need to import water from river to rim, and then the new owner died before he got it running – it has never been used. A flat, sandy area and a big cottonwood tree make a lovely *campsite* which would be good for anyone who wants to explore Judd Hollow, an abandoned meander with relatively easy access.

Past the pump, the canyon opens very wide and its bottom spreads flat between towering red walls for 250yd. Shortly after the canyon narrows again and swings east (left), there is a small spring on the right, often marked by a cairn. There are actually a few places where water gurgles up from below the riverbed; look for rocks placed in circles around the springs and some low-growing ferns. There is a campsite marked on the BLM panel map here (between Miles

18 and 19), but it is not readily evident or attractive.

Also marked on the BLM map, and talked about in books, is **the Hole**. Apparently this was a 14ft opening in the west canyon wall that looked like an inverted keyhole. Hikers who explored the canyon before 1999 tell of being able to enter this feature and hike 120ft to its back wall where a water seep entered. At the time of writing, debris had blocked the lower part of the Hole, making it difficult to find and impossible to enter.

A mile south, around Mile 20, **Wrather Canyon** enters on the right (west). As you're hiking downcanyon (south) the entrance looks like a 15ft wave breaking toward you. A well-trodden path enters this narrow (around 8ft wide) mouth and swings right before heading up the side canyon.

Past Wrather Canyon, horizontal intrusions on the left mark the beginning of the Kayenta Formation. The transition from Navajo to Kayenta is not obvious, as both are part of the same sandstone grouping and differ very little in appearance. Half a mile further downcanyon, after a deep southwest bend, numerous seeps appear on the right wall accompanied by ferns hanging from ledges atop small alcoves. Shower Spring is a bit of a euphemism for the drizzle that seeps from the wall. A high bench opposite the spring requires some scrambling to mount but makes a scenic *campsite*.

Day 4: Shower Spring to Bush Head Canyon
3–4 hours, 4¾mi (7.7km)
South of Shower Spring, the river makes two deep bends before entering the Moenave Formation, obvious from its rich-colored stripes of chocolate-brown, jade-green and maroon. From here until the Last Reliable Spring at Mile 25, the canyon makes dramatic cuts through polished, multi-colored Moenave benches which have the fluid contours of the water that carved them. Plan on spending some time navigating through this beautiful terrain. If the river is running high, you may need to do a lot of wading, crossing from one side to the other and, possibly, route finding above the water line.

At Mile 25, where the canyon turns west and abuts a steep red slope, the **Last Reliable Spring** is on the south (left) wall about 10ft above the river bed. It is not always a strong flow, and a cup or collecting receptacle may be needed to gather enough water to filter. Filtering river water this low in the canyon is not recommended, as the high mineral content wreaks havoc on most filters – use chemical treatments instead.

Boulders and cottonwood trees line a wide, flat bench opposite the spring, allowing for several very good *campsites*. Due to unreliable water past this point, many people choose to stay here and hike the remaining 13½mi to Lees Ferry in one long day.

A quarter-mile past the spring, the colorful slopes of Chinle Shale begin. The colors of Chinle – aqua, gray and deep red – resemble those in the Moenave Formation, but Chinle is softer and thus forms mounds instead of polished cliffs and ledges. The canyon walls spread apart for the last time now and wide benches covered with sage, juniper and yucca lie between the river and the sheer canyon walls that top-out 2200ft above. A mile and a half farther on, a distinct cut in the wall on the right (west) makes obvious the entrance of **Bush Head Canyon**.

At the confluence of Bush Head and Paria Canyons is a *campsite* with big cottonwood trees and a few seats made from fallen logs. Exploring up Bush Head Canyon, which is less than 1mi from its mouth to the rim but over 2000ft high, is fun but should be done with caution. A herd of 18 bighorn sheep were released here in 1984, and are supposedly still in the area.

Day 5: Bush Head Canyon to Lees Ferry

8–10 hours, 11½mi (18.5km)

Beyond Bush Head you'll get your first river-to-rim views. These become increasingly impressive, as the river level drops and canyon walls appear taller and taller. Hiking is generally dry along the west (right) side of the canyon. In the next 1½mi, three smaller canyons cut their way down to the Paria. The third splits the high walls into two sub-canyons and marks the beginning of the High Water Route.

Though the BLM map indicates that 'hiking in the river bed is possible in low water', the High Water Route is very scenic since it takes you high above the river bed. The route is not officially maintained but it does cut a distinct path through low shrubs, a few boulder fields and across the benches that flatten out 250ft to 400ft above the river.

Nearly 2mi along the High Water Route a tremendous, orange sand dune descends from the right (west). This stuff, which looks and feels like powdered orange drink, is mostly Kayenta and Navajo Sandstone that has eroded from above. From here, the trail changes quite a bit from season to season, depending on how floods have re-formed the landscape. Generally, you'll continue along the west (right) side of the river until a sheer, maroon-colored cliff pinches in on the right. Find a crossing here and continue across the sandy plain. This rhythm continues for the rest of the hike. At no point is making your own trail necessary – crossing the river to the opposite side usually does the trick.

Past Mile 31, a wide section of white earth flanked by fallen red boulders appears on the east (left) side of the river. Take time to inspect these rocks closely – be sure to walk around the backs of them – and you'll see terrific **petroglyphs** of a scorpion, bighorn sheep and human-looking figures. Those that are upside down and covered with dark desert varnish (which makes the imprints stand out) are older, while the light ones that are upright are thought to be more recent. A good landmark to look for when searching for this site is a light-colored rock with a wide, flat top and narrow base (it looks like a precariously balanced table) – this rock is 100ft past (south of) the boulderglyphs.

About a mile past the rock art the river makes a sharp turn east then continues another half-mile to where remnants (a few foundations and a wooden shack) of the Wilson Ranch stand on the west (right) bank. It was built about 1920, occupied until the 1940s and acquired by the NPS, along with Lonely Dell, in 1974.

As the Paria approaches the Colorado River, it loses momentum, gains a few degrees in temperature and its canyon widens into a broad valley. At length you'll reach a wide spot in the river where you'll need to wade across. Just beyond this point, around Mile 37, you'll reach an old cabin and outhouse not marked on the BLM map and, about 300ft beyond, a BLM trail register. From here the progression into 'civilization' speeds up exponentially. Cross through the barbed-wire fence and onto the numbered trail that is part of a self-guided tour through Lonely Dell. Follow the dirt road past the shady oasis surrounding the ranch buildings and you'll soon be at the Colorado River.

Where the road splits, the left fork goes to the parking lot where river expeditions put in for trips into the Grand Canyon and fishermen launch their boats to explore up-river toward Glen Canyon Dam; go right along the paved road (and up what seems to be the most arduous hill of the hike) to reach the ranger station, its adjacent restroom (with running water) and the *Lees Ferry campground* which has artificial shelters (no trees), picnic tables, pit toilets and $11 sites.

Sierra Nevada

The Sierra Nevada is the longest continuous mountain range in the USA. Extending 430mi through eastern California from the southern end of the Cascade Range near Lassen Peak to the Mojave Desert, it is 40mi to 80mi wide and has an area roughly equivalent to that of the French, Swiss, and Italian Alps combined. First called '*una gran sierra nevada*' by 18th century Spanish missionaries, this great snowy range boasts 500 peaks over 10,000ft and 14 peaks over 14,000ft. Its characteristic rocky, lake-dotted wilderness above 9000ft, known as the High Sierra, is snow-covered for about two-thirds of the year.

Structurally the Sierra Nevada is a huge, tilted, rectangular block with a steep eastern side and a gentler western slope. Its distinctive, glacier-polished granite prompted naturalist and author John Muir to dub it the 'Range of Light'.

Eighty percent of the Sierra Nevada's wealth of natural beauty is protected by three world-renowned national parks (Yosemite, Sequoia and Kings Canyon), eight national forests, 17 wilderness areas, and 20 state parks and recreation areas; and offers hikers stretches of wilderness unbroken by roads for more than 200mi. It is a range of superlatives for the contiguous USA – the highest peak, the largest and deepest alpine lake, the highest alpine lake, the tallest waterfall, and what many call the finest mountain hiking. Approachable from either its western or eastern sides, and crossed by six highways, the Sierra is accessible and inviting for a trip of a day, a weekend, a week or longer.

In addition to the famous Pacific Crest National Scenic Trail (PCT), described in the Long-Distance Trails chapter, three impressive trails which range in length from 150mi to 218mi traverse key segments of the Sierra Nevada: the Tahoe Rim Trail encircles the Lake Tahoe Basin; the Tahoe-Yosemite Trail links Lake Tahoe to Yosemite National Park; and the John Muir Trail links Yosemite National Park to Mt Whitney. Each of these

HIGHLIGHTS

Campsite at Lower Monarch Lake, beneath Sawtooth Peak, Great Western Divide.

- Three world-renowned national parks featuring granite domes and spires, waterfalls and canyons, with 500 peaks over 10,000ft and groves of giant sequoia, the largest living organisms on earth
- Mt Whitney (14,496ft), the highest peak in the contiguous USA
- Lake Tahoe, one of the world's largest and deepest alpine lakes

extended trails is briefly outlined in a boxed text. In addition, many of the hikes in this chapter cross or follow a segment of one of these renowned trails.

HISTORY

Native Americans were traveling through the Sierra Nevada at least 7000 years ago. People living in the western foothills and those living in the eastern Sierra crossed

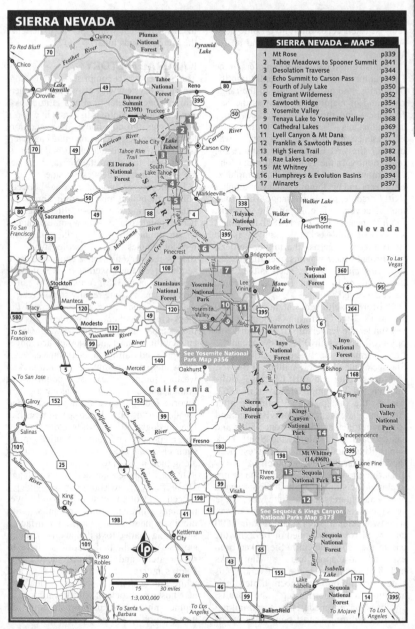

SIERRA NEVADA – MAPS

1 Mt Rose   p339
2 Tahoe Meadows to Spooner Summit   p341
3 Desolation Traverse   p344
4 Echo Summit to Carson Pass   p349
5 Fourth of July Lake   p350
6 Emigrant Wilderness   p352
7 Sawtooth Ridge   p354
8 Yosemite Valley   p361
9 Tenaya Lake to Yosemite Valley   p368
10 Cathedral Lakes   p369
11 Lyell Canyon & Mt Dana   p371
12 Franklin & Sawtooth Passes   p379
13 High Sierra Trail   p382
14 Rae Lakes Loop   p384
15 Mt Whitney   p390
16 Humphreys & Evolution Basins   p394
17 Minarets   p397

SIERRA NEVADA

the mountain passes in summer to trade, notably seashell beads and pinyon pine nuts. Arrowheads have even been found on Mt Whitney.

Spanish missionaries and explorers of the 18th century ventured infrequently into the mountains, and only the name of the range itself and of major rivers such as the San Joaquin – and the now-anglicized Kings and Stanislaus – bear witness to the Spanish presence. Jedediah Smith, a trapper, was in 1827 the first European to explore the high country. In the 1840s, Lieutenant John C Frémont of the US Army Topographical Engineers and his famous scout Christopher 'Kit' Carson explored the range. But it was the discovery of gold in the western foothills near Coloma in 1848 that brought a flood of gold-seekers – known as the 'forty-niners' – across the range. Settlers, too, brought their wagons over the passes, following pioneer routes such as the Overland Trail, or Emigrant Trail as the route was also called.

California achieved statehood in 1850 and in 1863 the California Geological Survey, under the leadership of Harvard geology professor Josiah D Whitney, began the first systematic scientific exploration of the Sierra Nevada. Whitney, William H Brewer, and topographer and artist Charles F Hoffman visited Tuolumne Meadows in 1863, naming the first peak they climbed after Hoffman. The next summer Brewer and Hoffman, together with Clarence King and James Gardiner, explored the South Fork Kings River and named the highest peak they saw after their absent chief.

During the latter part of the 19th century exploration continued, by both the surveyors and by adventurers such as John Muir. These activities brought recognition to the Sierra, with two national parks established in 1890 and the Sierra Club formed in 1892. By the end of the 1930s the entire Sierra had been explored and mapped and the major peaks had all been climbed. In the 1950s and 1960s a new generation of climbers turned their attention to the Sierra's big granite walls, and backpackers made High Sierra hiking one of California's most popular forms of recreation. Backpacking remains the mode of travel through which people experience the Sierra Nevada today.

NATURAL HISTORY
The Sierra Nevada comprises a single, continuous ecosystem whose diversity is evident with changes in elevation and latitude. Ascending into the Sierra is like traveling north; one passes through bands of vegetation, termed life zones, each containing characteristic, easily recognizable plants and animals. On the eastern side of the Sierra, the zones are higher than on the western side.

In the lower montane zone between 3500ft and 6000ft mixed conifers predominate, including the five-needled, jigsaw-barked ponderosa (or yellow) pine, Douglas fir, sugar pine – the world's tallest pine, with foot-long cones – silver-needled white fir, shaggy red-barked incense cedar and giant sequoia (see the boxed text 'Regal Redwoods' on page 375). Active, bushy-tailed Douglas squirrels are readily seen here.

Coyote, black bear, mule deer and the black-crested Steller's jay reside in this and in the upper montane zone, between 6000ft and 8500ft. In this zone, two-needled lodgepole pine and California red fir thrive. Western white pine is common, with red-barked western juniper on exposed, south-facing granite slopes and ridges. Quaking aspen, a favorite food of beavers, lines streams and meadows as do other broad-leafed trees like Pacific dogwood and white alder. Lodgepole chipmunks and golden-mantled ground squirrels – with black-bordered white stripes along their back – are common.

In the subalpine zone, between 8500ft and 10,500ft, trees are shorter, more widely-spaced, and often twisted by wind. Five-needled whitebark pine prevails, with mountain hemlock on moist, north-facing slopes and gnarled foxtail pine on dry, rocky slopes. Yellow-bellied marmots thrive in rocky areas and the loud-voiced, gray Clark's nutcracker, with black wings and white tail feathers, is common. Meadows here host a multitude of wildflowers such as lupine, phlox and paintbrush, and red heather forms profuse carpets.

Above treeline at over 10,500ft – the alpine zone – are grasses and wildflowers, lush in meadows where rusty-brown Belding's ground squirrel and gray-crowned rosy finch are characteristic. On rocky slopes dotted with cushion plants small, round-eared American pika live.

CLIMATE

The Sierra Nevada has the mildest, sunniest climate of any major US mountain range. Prevailing westerly winds bring moist Pacific air over the mountains between October and April, when 80% of the annual precipitation falls as snow. A 'rain shadow' effect leaves the eastern slopes comparatively drier. Snowfall also varies with elevation and latitude, with more snow falling between 6000ft and 8500ft and in the northern Sierra. Typically 100 inches of snow falls at 5000ft and as much as 450 inches in the High Sierra. Snow, however, can fall during any month and the weather generally changes rapidly.

Summer temperatures range from daytime highs of 80°F to nighttime lows of 50°F, but it can be 20°F cooler at high elevations. During summer, the Central Valley and eastern deserts that surround the Sierra Nevada are hot, with daytime temperatures reaching from 90°F to over 100°F. The warmest time in the mountains is from mid-July to mid-August, when daytime high temperatures range from 70°F to 90°F. Nighttime temperatures at the highest elevations drop to freezing even in midsummer.

INFORMATION
When to Hike

Hiking conditions depend upon the previous winter's accumulated snowpack and the rate of the annual spring thaw, which is determined by the amount of spring sunshine. The thaw begins in May, reaching the High Sierra in June and July. Hikers can contact ranger stations by April to ask if the snowpack is light, average, or heavy.

The hiking season, from June to October, has three parts. From June to July is early season, when snow remains in the high country, especially on north- and east-facing slopes. Rivers and streams are swollen

and mosquitos flourish at lower elevations. Occasionally unstable weather brings rain, or snow at higher elevations. By mid-season, from August to Labor Day (early September), most snow has melted except on the north faces of high passes. Days are warm and the weather is stable. Afternoon thunderstorms with lightning are common; though they rarely last more than an hour or two, it is a good idea to cross passes before noon. In late season, from Labor Day to mid-October, skies are generally clear and nights cold – often below freezing – and the mosquitos are gone. Pleasant days can alternate with days of light rain or snow. The first major snowstorm, producing a foot of snow over 10,000ft, usually arrives after mid-September, but typically melts off. By mid-October, however, snowfall no longer melts and winter accumulation begins.

What to Bring

In the Sierra, a three-season sleeping bag is more than adequate. A lightweight tent with netting is desirable, not so much for rain (summer rain is rare at night) as for mosquitos. A lightweight stove, fuel, and a pot or two for cooking are necessary as campfires are not allowed at or above treeline.

Maps

US Geological Survey (USGS) topographic quadrangles and privately published equivalents cover all Sierra Nevada trailheads and routes superbly. USGS 1:125,000 maps with 200ft contour intervals ($8) and 1:100,000 maps with 150ft contour intervals ($6) are useful planning and backpacking maps. USGS 1:24,000 (7.5 minute) series maps with 40ft contour intervals ($4 to $5) offer excellent detail – sometimes *too* much when a long route covers multiple quadrangles.

The predecessor to this series, the USGS 1:62,500 (15 minute) series with 80ft contour intervals, is discontinued after being used from 1954 to the mid-1980s. Random 15 minute series quadrangles ($1 to $6) can occasionally still be found in stores and ranger stations. Map Link (☎ 805-692-6777, fax 692-6788, ✆ custserv@maplink.com), 30 S La Patera Lane, Unit 5, Santa Barbara,

CA 93117, is the best source for reprints ($6) of many USGS 1:62,500 quadrangles. Wilderness Press (☎ 800-443-7227, fax 510-558-1696, ✉ mail@wildernesspress.com, 🖳 www.wildernesspress.com), 1200 5th St, Berkeley, CA 94710, has revised and reprinted some USGS 1:62,500 quadrangles and sells these and other maps ($5 to $7).

The US Forest Service (USFS) publishes nine maps of the Sierra's national forests ($4) and 14 1:63,360 topographic maps with 80ft contour intervals of its 17 wilderness areas ($4 to $8). To request a map list or order maps, contact and send payment to USFS Pacific Southwest Region (☎ 707-562-8737), 1323 Club Dr, Vallejo, CA 94592.

Tom Harrison Cartography (☎ 415-456-7940, 800-265-9090, 🖳 www.tomharrison maps.com), 2 Falmouth Cove, San Rafael, CA 94901-4465, publishes excellent six-color, shaded-relief topographic maps (waterproof) of various Sierra regions in scales ranging from 1:24,000 to 1:125,000.

For information on where to buy the maps covering the hikes in this chapter, see either Maps & Books under Information or Nearest Towns & Facilities for each region.

Books

Sierra North: 100 Back-country Trips and *Sierra South: 100 Back-country Trips in California's Sierra*, both by Thomas Winnett et al, are time-honored guidebooks. The pocket-sized *High Sierra Hiking Guide* series offers comprehensive detail, with each regional title containing a USGS 1:62,500 topographic map.

Gentle Wilderness: The Sierra Nevada by John Muir updates Muir's writings with modern photographs. *Yosemite and the High Sierra* by Ansel Adams, the most renowned photographer of the Sierra, offers a compilation of his finest images and most exuberant writings.

Information Sources

The three national parks in the Sierra Nevada – Yosemite, Sequoia and Kings Canyon – provide endless information about hiking and backcountry travel (see those sections later in this chapter).

WARNING

Black bears, active day and night through the Sierra Nevada, are notorious for breaking into vehicles in parking lots and into campgrounds and backcountry campsites in search of food. Everyone must take precautions to protect their food and scented personal items at all times by using metal food-storage boxes where provided at campgrounds and trailheads, by hanging these items in trees using the counter-balance method when feasible (see the boxed text in the Facts for the Hiker chapter), or by storing them in plastic, bear-resistant food canisters at backcountry campsites.

The USFS (🖳 www.fs.fed.us) provides trail information for national forests – and wilderness areas, which may overlap one or more national forests – and issues wilderness permits (see Permits & Regulations later in this section). These offices can also direct hikers to ranger stations close to trailheads. Administered as part of the USFS Pacific Southwest Region 5, except for the Toiyabe National Forest, the national forests in the Sierra Nevada and the wilderness areas they manage are:

Eldorado National Forest (☎ 530-622-5061) 100 Forni Rd, Placerville, CA 95667. Carson-Iceberg, Desolation and Mokelumne wilderness areas.

Inyo National Forest (☎ 760-873-2400) 873 N Main St, Bishop, CA 93514. Ansel Adams, Golden Trout, Hoover and John Muir wilderness areas.

Plumas National Forest (☎ 530-283-2050) 159 Lawrence St, Quincy, CA 95971. Bucks Lake Wilderness.

Sequoia National Forest (☎ 209-784-1500) 900 W Grand Ave, Porterville, CA 93257. Dome Land, Golden Trout, Monarch and Jennie Lakes wilderness areas.

Sierra National Forest (☎ 559-297-0706) 1600 Tollhouse Rd, Clovis, CA 93611. Ansel Adams, Dinkey Lakes, John Muir, Kaiser, Monarch and Jennie Lakes wilderness areas.

Stanislaus National Forest (☎ 209-532-3671) 19777 Greenley Rd, Sonora, CA 95370. Carson-Iceberg, Emigrant and Mokelumne wilderness areas.

Tahoe National Forest (☎ 530-265-4531) 631 Coyote St, Nevada City, CA 95959. Granite Chief wilderness area.

Toiyabe National Forest (☎ 775-331-6444) 1200 Franklin Way, Sparks, NV 89431. Carson-Iceberg, Hoover, Mokelumne and Mt Rose wilderness areas.

Permits & Regulations

Wilderness permits, also called backcountry use permits, are required for overnight trips in all national parks and most wilderness areas covered in this chapter. Permits are not required for day hikes, except where noted. Many regions have a trailhead quota system that limits the number of day hikers and/or backpackers who can begin from each trailhead on any day. A varying percentage of the available permits may be allocated by advance reservations – which guarantees the trailhead and entry date – with the remaining permits being issued on a daily first-come, first-served basis. Permits are free, although there is usually a nominal advance reservation fee. The federal agency with jurisdiction over the region where a hike starts issues a permit for the entire route. When a hike crosses from one jurisdiction into another, it is not necessary to obtain another permit.

The elevations above which fires are prohibited vary between jurisdictions; backpackers should plan on carrying their own stoves and fuel. In some regions, a free campfire permit is also required.

For detailed information requirements for each hike, see Permits & Regulations under Information for each region or Permits under Planning for the individual hikes.

WARNING

Eastern Sierra and trans-Sierra trailheads near passes typically begin above 8000ft and often over 9000ft. Hikers starting at these high elevations must be cautious of proper acclimatization. For example, if driving from sea level in the Los Angeles or San Francisco areas spend a night at an intermediate elevation before camping or hiking at high altitudes.

GATEWAYS

Approaching the Sierra Nevada from California's major coastal cities (Los Angeles, San Francisco) is likely to take you through Sacramento, Fresno or Bakersfield. In particular, if traveling by public transport you may find it necessary or convenient to spend the night in one of these places. Similarly, if approaching from the east, you may find yourself in Reno or Carson City, Nevada. All are major cities with a wide range of accommodations, large stores (including hiking-gear stores) and other facilities. See Lonely Planet's *California & Nevada* for detailed information.

Lake Tahoe Region

Brilliantly blue and surrounded by mountains, Lake Tahoe sits like a jewel along the California-Nevada state line; the western shore is in California, the eastern in Nevada. On the Sierra's western side, the well-watered forests extend down through California's gold country to the grasslands and towns of the Central Valley. On the eastern side, the Carson Range drops off to the Nevada desert. The Truckee River, whose headwaters are north of Carson Pass, flows into the lake's southern end and out from its northwest end. In the mountains encircling the lake are three national forests – Eldorado, Tahoe, and Toiyabe – and four wilderness areas – Desolation, Granite Chief, Mt Rose and Mokelumne – offering a multitude of trails. On a warm day the vanilla-like fragrance of the bark of Jeffrey pines drifts by hikers walking through Tahoe's eastern forests.

HISTORY

Native American Washoe lived in the Carson Valley in winter and migrated to Tahoe in summer. They revered the lake and called it Da Ow A Ga, meaning 'the edge of the lake'. Early explorers mispronounced 'Da Ow' as 'tahoe', and the name stuck. John C Frémont was the first European to record seeing Lake Tahoe when he reached the summit of Red Lake Peak north of Carson

SIERRA NEVADA

Lake Tahoe

The Tahoe Basin formed during a major Sierra Nevada uplift period about 65 million years ago. The lake itself began to form about 2.3 million years ago when lava produced a natural dam that blocked the basin's outflow. At least seven major lava flows over the next million years raised lake level to over 7000ft, but the Truckee River has since eroded through the lava to bring the lake to its present level (6229ft). Relatively recent glaciation (glaciers retreated only 13,000 years ago) left moraine features such as that forming the sides of Emerald Bay and that which impounds Fallen Leaf Lake.

Lake Tahoe is the Sierra Nevada's largest lake, North America's third-deepest and the world's 10th-deepest. The lake is 22mi long and 10mi wide with about 72mi of shoreline. Its greatest depth is 1685ft, while its average depth is 1000ft. The lake's bottom is lower than the Carson Valley at the base of the Carson Range.

Pass in 1844. In the same year came the first wagon train guided by a Piute known as Captain Truckee, after whom the emigrants named the river they followed. The pass over the Sierra along this route is named for the infamous Donner Party, some of whom survived the harsh winter of 1846–47 at Donner Lake only by eating the party's dead.

Deposits of gold and silver drew miners to Tahoe in the 1850s and 1860s, where they made roads and logged the hillsides surrounding the lake to supply the Comstock Lode mines of Nevada's Virginia City. The Central Pacific Railroad, built by Mark Hopkins and Leland Stanford in the 1860s, used Truckee as the main town on the transcontinental railroad between Sacramento and Ogden, Utah. By the beginning of the 20th century the mining and timber industries diminished, and the unique beauty of the lake and mountains shifted the area's emphasis to recreation.

NEAREST TOWNS & FACILITIES

For trailhead campgrounds, see Getting to/from the Hike for individual hikes.

Truckee

The Truckee-Donner chamber of commerce (☎ 530-587-2757, 🖳 www.truckee.com) at 10065 Donner Pass Rd is in the train depot at the west end of Commercial Row/Donner Pass Rd. Tahoe National Forest's Truckee ranger station (☎ 530-587-3558), 10342 Hwy 89 North, is at the east end of town. Commercial Row, north of and parallel to

the railroad tracks, is lined with restaurants and stores. The Sierra Mountaineer (☎ 530-587-2025), at Bridge and Jibboom Sts, is the best spot to buy gear.

Places to Stay & Eat The USFS *Granite Flat campground* ($14) is just south of town on Hwy 89. Donner Memorial State Park (☎ 800-444-7275 for reservations – $7.50 fee applies), 3mi west of downtown along Donner Pass Rd, has *campgrounds* ($12) along Donner Lake's southeast shore.

The *Truckee Hotel (☎ 530-587-4444, 800-659-6921, fax 587-1599, 10007 Bridge St)* is an historic Victorian place with rooms with shared bathrooms starting at $60 and an excellent restaurant. *Earthly Delights Bakery & Grocery (☎ 530-587-7873, 10087 W River St)* has gourmet take-out and rustic breads. *OB's Pub & Restaurant (☎ 530-587-4164, 10046 Commercial Row)* is a popular lunch and dinner spot.

Getting There & Away Truckee, which straddles I-80 and Hwy 89, is 13mi north of Lake Tahoe via Hwy 89 from Tahoe City or Hwy 267 from Kings Beach, and 35mi west of Reno and the region's only international airport.

Amtrak trains depart for Reno ($14) at 3:41 pm and for San Francisco ($36) at 4:35 and 7:55 am. Greyhound buses depart four times each day for Reno ($10/19 one way/roundtrip) and six times daily for San Francisco ($36/72). Both stop at the train depot.

Tahoe City

The North Lake Tahoe chamber of commerce (☎ 530-581-6900), 245 N Lake Blvd, at the Hwy 28/Hwy 89 junction, has useful information. Two miles south of Tahoe City, on the west side of Hwy 89, is the USFS William Kent visitor information station with helpful rangers. Alpenglow Sports (☎ 530-583-6917), 415 N Lake Blvd, sells maps and gear.

Places to Stay & Eat The USFS William Kent visitor information station has an adjacent *campground* ($14). Rooms at the *Tahoe City Inn* (☎ 800-800-8246, 790 N Lake Blvd) start at $60; the nearby *Pepper Tree Inn* (☎ 530-583-3711, 800-624-8590, 645 N Lake Blvd) has rooms from $74. *Java Stop* (☎ 530-583-4700, 274 N Lake Blvd) is a fine choice for a quick meal. *Tahoe House Restaurant & Backerei* (☎ 530-583-1377, 625 W Lake Blvd) serves Swiss and Californian cuisine and sells European-style breads in the bakery and deli.

Getting There & Away Tahoe City (6253ft) is on the lake's northwestern shore at the Hwy 89/Hwy 28 junction, 13mi south of Truckee and 29mi northwest of South Lake Tahoe. For transport links to other towns in the Lake Tahoe Region, see Getting Around later in this section.

South Lake Tahoe

The USFS Lake Tahoe visitor center (☎ 530-573-2674) is on Hwy 89, 3mi northwest of the Hwy 89/US 50 junction, about a mile west of Camp Richardson. It provides trail information, issues wilderness permits (☎ 530-573-2736), and sells books and maps. USFS Lake Tahoe Basin headquarters & visitor information center (☎ 530-573-2600 for information) is at 870 Emerald Bay Rd (Hwy 89) near the US 50 junction.

The Interagency visitor information station on US 50/Hwy 89 near Meyers is useful for a quick orientation, but has limited information. The Lake Tahoe Visitors Authority (☎ 530-544-5050, 800-288-2463, @ ltva@virtualtahoe.com, ☐ www.virtualtahoe.com) at 1156 Ski Run Blvd runs an invaluable free reservation service for South Lake Tahoe lodging. The South Lake Tahoe chamber of commerce (☎ 530-541-5255, ☐ www.tahoeinfo.com) at 3066 Lake Tahoe Blvd is another very useful resource. The Sportsman (☎ 530-542-3474), 2556 Lake Tahoe Blvd, sells maps and gear.

Places to Stay & Eat *Doug's Mellow Mountain Retreat* (☎ 530-544-8065, @ hostelguy@hotmail.com, 3787 Forest Rd), a hostel four blocks off US 50, has beds for $15. The city-run *Campground by the Lake* (☎ 530-542-6096), on US 50 at Rufus Allen Blvd near the chamber of commerce, starts at $16.50 and has showers. Hundreds of *motels*, the least expensive of which start at about $50, are mostly along US 50. It is easiest to contact the Lake Tahoe Visitors Authority for availability and rates.

Red Hut Waffle Shop (☎ 530-541-9024) at 2723 Lake Tahoe Blvd is a popular breakfast spot. *Sprouts Natural Food Cafe* (☎ 530-541-6969) at 3123 Harrison Ave serves inspired, healthy choices and tasty smoothies.

Getting There & Away South Lake Tahoe, as its name implies, wraps itself along the southern lakeshore on US 50. The regional Lake Tahoe airport, south of town on US 50, is served by Tahoe Air (☎ 888-824-6324) from San Jose and Los Angeles, and by Allegiant Air (☎ 877-202-6444) from Fresno, Burbank and Las Vegas. Greyhound buses depart for San Francisco ($27/52 one way/roundtrip) at 9:50 am and 6:40 pm from 1000 Emerald Bay Rd at the US 50/Hwy 89 junction. The Nifty 50 Trolley (☎ 530-541-7548) plies the shoreline.

GETTING AROUND

Tahoe Area Regional Transit (TART) (☎ 530-581-6365, 800-736-6365) operates a shuttle service between Truckee and Tahoe City ($1.25). Buses depart from the depot in Truckee at 8:30 and 10:30 am and 12:45, 2:45 and 4:45 pm.

TART buses ($1.25) ply 30mi of the lakeshore throughout the day from Tahoe City south on Hwy 89 along the west shore to Sugar Pine Point State Park near Tahoma,

SIERRA NEVADA

Long Hike – Tahoe Rim Trail

Duration	14–17 days
Distance	152.8mi (246km)
Standard	medium
Start/Finish	Any of nine trailheads
Nearest Towns	Tahoe City, South Lake Tahoe
Public Transport	no

Summary This unique ridge-top trail encircling enormous, azure Lake Tahoe offers the ultimate in lake vistas.

Circumambulating the Lake Tahoe Basin mostly along ridge tops, the 150mi Tahoe Rim Trail bestows inspirational views of Lake Tahoe, the snowcapped peaks of the Sierra crest to the west, and Nevada's Great Basin valleys to the east. Along the diverse glacial and volcanic terrain are subalpine meadows; aspen-lined creeks; thick conifer forests of the Crystal Range; sage- and Jeffrey pine- covered slopes of the Carson Range; crystalline lakes; and a delightful diversity of wildflower gardens clinging to windswept, rocky peaks.

Whether hiking one segment at a time (one to four days each) – the popular way to complete the trail – or becoming a '150-miler' at one go (10 to 15 days), this medium-standard trail crosses easy passes with the ultimate in Tahoe panoramas. Staying between 6300ft and 10,150ft and passing through three wilderness areas, state park and national forest lands, the Tahoe Rim Trail also joins segments of the Pacific Crest and Tahoe-Yosemite Trails.

The route is best done in eight segments: Tahoe City to Brockway Summit (18½mi, 1 to 2 days); Brockway Summit to Mt Rose Summit (16mi, 1 to 2 days); Ophir Creek to Spooner Summit North (22mi, 2 days); Spooner Summit South to Kingsbury North (11.8mi, 1 day); Kingsbury South to Big Meadow North (22.3mi, 2 days); Big Meadow South to Echo Summit (16mi, 2 days); Echo Summit to Barker

Pass (32.6mi, 4 days); and Barker Pass to Tahoe City (13.6mi, 1 day).

The Tahoe Rim Trail Association (☎ 775-588-0686, fax 588-8737, ☻ tahoerim@aol.com, 💻 www.tahoerimtrail.org, postal address: PO Box 4647, Stateline, NV 89449) at 298 Kingsbury Grade (Hwy 207), Stateline, is the best information source.

Several USGS 1:24,000 and 1:62,500 quadrangles are useful when hiking segments of the Tahoe Rim Trail. Tom Harrison Cartography's 1:71,280 *Recreation Map of Lake Tahoe* depicts the trail on one sheet.

The Tahoe Rim Trail traverses country typical of the Sierra Nevada's Lake Tahoe region, California.

and east on Hwy 28 along the north shore to Incline Village. TART also operates the Tahoe Trolley, a shuttle between Squaw Valley and Emerald Bay via Tahoe City.

Mt Rose

Duration	6–8 hours
Distance	11.8mi (19km)
Standard	medium-hard
Start/Finish	Hwy 431, Mt Rose Summit
Nearest Towns	Tahoe City, South Lake Tahoe
Public Transport	no

Summary Tahoe's best day hike reaches the summit of the region's third-highest peak with incomparable views and abundant wildflowers.

Mt Rose (10,776ft), in the Carson Range northeast of Lake Tahoe, is the third-highest peak in the Tahoe area and the only peak over 10,000ft with a trail to its summit. This day hike climbs 1876ft in almost 6mi (and descends by the same route), offering dramatic views and spectacular wildflowers. Blue and white lupine, bright-yellow mountain mule-ears and purple penstemons are common. Close to dry ground look for the broad, yellow, coconut-scented flowers of the unusual woody-fruited evening primrose, and on midsummer days inhale the minty fragrance of sagebrush and mountain pennyroyal.

PLANNING

Snow lingers along many north-facing aspects until early July, after which the trail is snow-free. The summit is notoriously windy and often very cold, so bring a jacket even on a hot, sunny day. No wilderness permit is required, even if one is inspired to spend the night on the summit or anywhere else in Mt Rose Wilderness.

Maps

The USGS 1:24,000 *Mt Rose* and 1:62,500 *Mt Rose* quadrangles cover the hike.

GETTING TO/FROM THE HIKE

The trail starts at a gated, unpaved service road on the north side of Hwy 431, 0.3mi

west of Mt Rose Summit (8900ft) – not to be confused with the summit of Mt Rose – and 7.7mi northeast of Incline Village. Parking is along Hwy 431's wide shoulder or in a paved lot with toilets at the Tahoe Meadows trailhead on the south side of Hwy 431, 0.4mi west of the Mt Rose trailhead. At Mt Rose Summit is the attractive USFS Mt Rose campground ($9).

THE HIKE

From the trailhead contour gently upwards along the service road through stands of lodgepole pine on the slopes above Tahoe Meadows. Lake Tahoe and the Crystal Range soon come into view, as does small Incline Lake in the forest beyond the southwest edge of Tahoe Meadows. The road bends north, with Third Creek below to the west and, after a fairly level 2.3mi, rolls on to a small, seasonal pond. Flowery meadows surround this pond, which is home to vocal tree frogs.

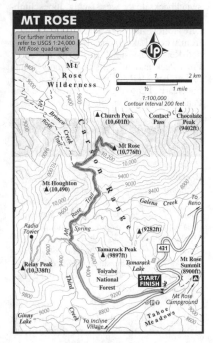

MT ROSE

The Mt Rose Trail leaves the road here, turning northeast (right) over a gentle saddle and passing through broad meadows at the head of Galena Creek, following an old dirt road across the head of the meadows. Passing among some trees at the meadow's far edge, the trail turns northeast and skirts a gushing spring, the source of Galena Creek. The trail rejoins the dirt road and follows power lines. Descending mostly open slopes, the way narrows to become a trail again and reaches another stream, the last year-round water source. The trail crosses the stream and traverses generally north across open slopes where lupine blooms profusely.

The trail rounds a corner to enter a gully – dry by mid-August – and ascends northwest. A steady climb, with some steep sections, brings you to Mt Rose Wilderness and a saddle and trail junction southwest of Mt Rose. The left fork goes to Davis and Big Meadows. The trail to the summit of Mt Rose, still 1.4mi away, follows the right fork and switchbacks up the west-facing slope, climbing above treeline to the summit ridge. From here, follow the ridge south to the summit, from where Lake Tahoe, Truckee Meadows and Reno are visible. To the distant south Freel Peak and Jobs Sister, the only points higher than Mt Rose in the Tahoe area, stand out clearly. Far to the north, volcanic Lassen Peak (10,457ft) is visible on a clear day.

Tahoe Meadows to Spooner Summit

Duration	2 days
Distance	22mi (35.4km)
Standard	easy-medium
Start	Hwy 431, Tahoe Meadows
Finish	US 50, Spooner Summit
Nearest Town	South Lake Tahoe
Public Transport	no

Summary Continuous breathtaking panoramas of Lake Tahoe and the surrounding peaks make this hike along the 8000ft to 9000ft crest of the Carson Range a delight.

Hiking the crest of the Carson Range, high above Lake Tahoe's eastern shore, offers continuously fine vistas of the entire Tahoe region. This well-signed segment of the Tahoe Rim Trail is best approached as a leisurely overnight trip, but can be done as a long, strenuous day hike. The trail crosses several unpaved service roads inside the Lake Tahoe Nevada State Park, which offer shorter, alternative ways to Hwy 28 along the lakeshore.

PLANNING
Weekdays have negligible mountain bike traffic (which is allowed only between Hwy 431 and Snow Valley Peak Rd) compared to weekends. No permit is required to camp in the state park.

Maps
The USGS 1:24,000 *Mt Rose*, *Marlette Lake* and *Glenbrook* quadrangles, and the 1:62,500 *Mt Rose* and *Carson City* quadrangles cover the hike.

GETTING TO/FROM THE HIKE
To the Start
The unsigned Ophir Creek trailhead is at the southern edge of Tahoe Meadows on the southeast side of Hwy 431, 6½mi northeast of Incline Village and opposite a private road leading west to Incline Lake. Parking is limited along the gravel shoulder of Hwy 431. A larger, paved parking area is 0.8mi further east on Hwy 431.

From the Finish
A Tahoe Rim Trail sign at Spooner Summit – on US 50, 0.8mi east of the US 50/Hwy 28 junction on Lake Tahoe's eastern shore and 9mi west of the US 50/US 395 junction in Carson City – easily identifies the trailhead. An unpaved parking area is along the road's north shoulder.

THE HIKE
Day 1: Tahoe Meadows to Marlette Peak
7–8 hours, 13mi (20.1km)
The Tahoe Rim Trail follows the Ophir Creek Trail, an abandoned dirt road, along the edge of **Tahoe Meadows** for 10 minutes, and then turns south (right) at a junction. The

trail rises slightly through forest and crosses a dirt road after another 30 minutes, with the first views of Lake Tahoe. It narrows and contours gently through open forest, coming to a small, year-round stream about 2½mi from the trailhead. (The next water is at Lower Twin Lake, 6mi farther.)

The trail traverses a ridge through Toiyabe National Forest with superlative views west to Lake Tahoe and east to Washoe Lake. About 2½mi from the stream it skirts the edge of the Diamond Peak ski area, with views east and west. The trail traverses the west side of the ridge, then descends the eastern slope on two long, moderate switchbacks to reach a long saddle across the ridge back to the west side – and more remarkable Tahoe views. Here the trail enters the Lake Tahoe Nevada State Park.

The trail drops to meet the unpaved Tunnel Creek Rd, which descends to Incline Village, 3½mi from the ski area. Walk east (left) on Tunnel Creek Rd for five minutes, then turn right onto another dirt road for five more minutes to a junction with another dirt road leading to Upper Twin Lake. The trail turns left off the road and 50yd further forks left and drops slightly to skirt the east shore of the small, shallow, grass-fringed Lower Twin Lake.

South of Lower Twin Lake, the trail climbs 750ft through open forest on long switchbacks, offering glimpses of Tahoe, Crystal Bay and Washoe Lake – the only serious climb on the hike. From the top, the trail drops to a level area and soon comes to the junction with the **Sand Harbor Overlook Trail**, 2½mi from Tunnel Creek Rd. This spur trail (0.6mi one way) crosses an 8840ft ridge to a viewpoint that is not to be missed, directly overlooking Sand Harbor, 2600ft below, and all of Lake Tahoe.

The main trail continues south through forest for 15 minutes to an open, meadowy ridge overlooking pretty **Marlette Lake** (7823ft). The trail now works down to a junction with the Marlette Peak Trail, which turns right and rejoins the Tahoe Rim Trail further ahead. Contouring around the eastern slopes of Marlette Peak (8780ft) through

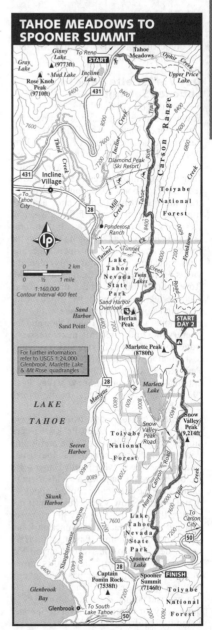

TAHOE MEADOWS TO SPOONER SUMMIT

1:160,000
Contour Interval 400 feet

For further information refer to USGS 1:24,000 Glenbrook, Marlette Lake & Mt Rose quadrangles

forest, and crossing a small, sparkling snowmelt stream, the trail soon arrives at the somewhat primitive but free *Marlette Peak campground*.

Day 2: Marlette Peak to Spooner Summit
5–6 hours, 9mi (14.5km)

Water is scarce between the campground and Spooner Summit. The Tahoe Rim Trail passes the southern end of the Marlette Peak Trail within five minutes, and in five more minutes crosses the unpaved North Canyon Rd, which descends 5.8mi via Marlette Lake to Spooner Lake on Hwy 28. The trail main continues south and, after 20 minutes, turns right and follows a set of jeep tracks for a few minutes. It then turns left at a signpost and winds up through the forest to emerge into an open sage and lupine meadow. As it climbs this ridge, the views open up to the north, including of Mt Rose, Slide Mountain and a distant Reno. Meandering up through flower-filled meadows high above Marlette Lake with truly exceptional views of all Lake Tahoe and the country beyond, the trail next crosses a ridge above Marlette Lake and drops gently to a junction with the unpaved Snow Valley Peak Rd, which goes 0.3mi southeast to the antenna-infested top of **Snow Valley Peak** (9214ft) and west down to the North Canyon Rd.

The trail narrows and traverses downwards across Snow Valley Peak's western slope through meadows of sage and lupine with outstanding, continuous Tahoe vistas. Contouring down, with North Canyon Rd visible below, the sagebrush yields to manzanita and the trail enters forest about 45 minutes from Snow Valley Peak Rd. It descends through the forest, with glimpses east and west, to reach a trail junction 4.2mi from Spooner Summit. Passing this trail, which descends to the North Canyon Rd, the Tahoe Rim Trail next rolls down steadily through forest, passing several wooden signposts directing the way to nearby vista points. Road noise from US 50 indicates your imminent arrival at Spooner Summit (7146ft).

Desolation Traverse

Duration	4 days
Distance	31.2mi (50.2km)
Standard	medium
Start	US 50, Lower Echo Lake
Finish	Hwy 89, Meeks Bay
Nearest Towns	Tahoe City, South Lake Tahoe
Public Transport	no

Summary This traverse of the lake-filled granite landscape of the highly popular Desolation Wilderness has abundant forested campsites, great swimming, and crosses two 9500ft passes en route to Lake Tahoe's western shore.

The glacier-polished granite landscape of 100-sq-mile Desolation Wilderness holds more than 100 lakes and many streams. With its dramatic, almost lunar appearance, splendid vistas, subalpine forest, flower-filled meadows, renowned fishing, good trails, easy access and close proximity to Lake Tahoe's southwestern shores, it is one of the most popular wilderness areas in the USA. This hike, part of the Tahoe-Yosemite Trail, also includes a segment of the combined Pacific Crest and Tahoe Rim Trails. This is the quintessential Desolation walk, crossing two passes and camping at beautiful lakes.

PLANNING
As the Crystal Range receives comparatively more snowfall than other Tahoe regions, the hike is better in mid- or late-season.

Maps
The USGS 1:24,000 *Echo Lake*, *Pyramid Peak*, *Rockbound Valley* and *Homewood* quadrangles, and the 1:62,500 *Fallen Leaf Lake* and *Tahoe* quadrangles cover the hike. Three maps cover Desolation Wilderness on one sheet: Tom Harrison Cartography's 1:42,240 *Desolation Wilderness Trail Map*; the Wilderness Press 1:62,500 *Fallen Leaf Lake*, revised from the USGS quadrangle of the same name; and the USFS 1:63,360 *Desolation Wilderness* map.

Permits & Regulations

Free wilderness permits are required for day- and overnight hikes. Day hikers can self-issue a free permit at most east-side trailheads. A trailhead quota system operates from June 15 to Labor Day owing to Desolation's popularity. The USFS accepts reservations no more than 90 days in advance and only during the quota period. It issues half the available permits by reservation and half on a first-come, first-served basis. To make a reservation, mail or fax the request with a $5 reservation fee to Eldorado National Forest (☎ 530-644-6048, fax 644-3034), 3070 Camino Heights Dr, Camino, CA 95709.

Everyone must pick up their permit in person from this office (5mi east of Placerville off US 50) or from the USFS Lake Tahoe visitor center (see South Lake Tahoe under Nearest Towns at the beginning of this section). Backpackers with a reservation and who have previously made arrangements may also pick up their permit at the USFS William Kent visitor information station (see Tahoe City under Nearest Towns at the beginning of this section). A camping fee of $5 per person for one night or a maximum of $10 per person for two or more nights must also be paid when picking up the permit.

GETTING TO/FROM THE HIKE
To the Start

A mile west of Echo Summit on US 50 is a paved road that heads east and then north for 1½mi to the southeast end of Lower Echo Lake. From here, a water taxi ($6) shuttles visitors from this hike's trailhead to Upper Echo Lake, saving the first 2.9mi of walking.

From the Finish

Meeks Bay, between Sugar Pine Point and DL Bliss State Parks, is on US 89 along Lake Tahoe's western shore, 19mi northwest of South Lake Tahoe and 11mi south of Tahoe City. The signed trailhead is west of the highway just north of Meeks Creek, across from the USFS Meeks Bay campground ($14). The Tahoe Trolley and Nifty 50 Trolley both service this trailhead (see Getting Around earlier in this section).

THE HIKE
Day 1: Lower Echo Lake to Lake Lucille

3½–4 hours, 6½mi (10.5km), 900ft (270m) ascent

From Echo Chalet (7414ft), the trail crosses the dam at the outlet stream and turns west to follow the rocky northern shore of Lower Echo Lake. It goes through forest along Upper Echo Lake, beyond which it ascends rocky switchbacks, passing a junction left to Tamarack Lake and reaching **Haypress Meadows** after 4.2mi. The trail levels and crosses a saddle, then passes a junction left to Lake of the Woods. A short distance beyond, a side trail turns right and descends to *campsites* along the northwest shore of pretty Lake Lucille (8200ft) beneath Keiths Dome, with beautiful views north of Mt Tallac (9735ft) and Dicks Peak (9974ft).

Day 2: Lake Lucille to Dicks Lake

5–6 hours, 9.8mi (15.8km), 1440ft (432m) ascent, 1220ft (366m) descent

Return to the main trail and turn north (right) onto the combined Tahoe Rim and Tahoe-Yosemite Trails, which descend to the artificial **Lake Aloha** (8116ft). The trail follows the rocky northeast shore of this large, blue lake dotted with many small, granite islands. Pyramid Peak and Mt Price rise dramatically above its southwest shore. At a junction near the eastern end of the lake's northern shore, the trail turns right and descends east to pass along the northern shore of pretty Heather Lake (7920ft) and continues down to popular Susie Lake (7760ft); there are *campsites* at both. After skirting Susie Lake's southern shore, the trail turns north, crosses the lake's outlet and, bending eastwards, winds down to the valley floor, passing a trail that descends to Fallen Leaf Lake.

The trail turns north and begins to ascend through forest, passing another right turn to Fallen Leaf Lake and a trail turning left to Half Moon Lake. The trail switchbacks up

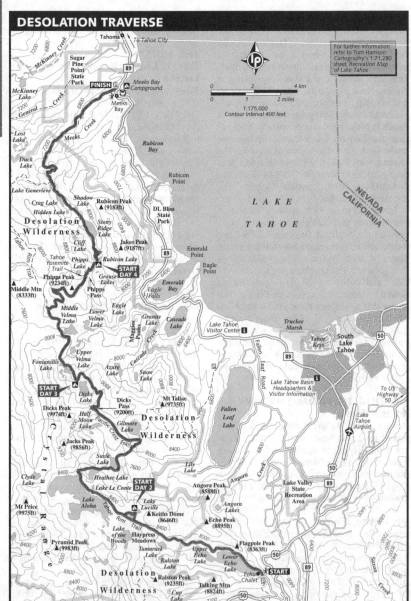

SIERRA NEVADA

DESOLATION TRAVERSE

For further information
refer to Tom Harrison
Cartography's 1:71,280
sheet *Recreation Map
of Lake Tahoe*

1:175,000
Contour Interval 400 feet

Tahoma
To Tahoe City

Sugar
Pine
Point
State
Park

McKinney Creek

FINISH

Meeks Bay
Campground

Meeks
Bay

McKinney
Lake

Lost
Lake

Duck
Lake

Lake Genevieve

Crag Lake

Hidden Lake

Shadow
Lake

Rubicon Peak
▲ (9183ft)

Desolation
Wilderness

Stony
Ridge
Lake

Jakes Peak
▲ (9187ft)

Cliff
Lake

Phipps
Lake

Rubicon Lake

START
DAY 4

Grouse
Lakes

Tahoe
Yosemite
Trail

Phipps Peak
(9234ft)

Phipps
Pass

Middle Mtn
(8333ft)

Middle
Velma
Lake

Eagle
Lake

Lower
Velma
Lake

Fontanillis
Lake

Upper
Velma
Lake

Azure
Lake

Maggies Peaks

Granite
Lake

Cascade
Creek

Snow
Lake

START
DAY 3

Dicks
Lake

Dicks Peak
(9974ft) ▲

Half
Moon
Lake

Dicks
Pass
(9200ft)

Pacific Crest Trail

Gilmore
Lake

Mt Tallac
▲ (9135ft)

Desolation
Wilderness

Jacks Peak
(9856ft) ▲

Crystal Range

Susie
Lake

Clyde
Lake

Mt Price
(9975ft) ▲

Heather Lake

Lake Le Conte

START
DAY 2

Lake
Aloha

Lake
Lucille

Keiths Dome
▲ (8646ft)

Tahoe Rim Trail

Pyramid Peak
▲ (9983ft)

Lake
of the
Woods

Haypress
Meadows

Tamarack
Lake

Ralston
Lake

Ralston Peak
▲ (9235ft)

Cup
Lake

Talking Mtn
▲ (8824ft)

Desolation
Wilderness

Angora Peak
(8588ft) ▲

Angora
Lakes

Lily
Lake

Upper
Echo
Lake

Lower
Echo
Lake

Echo Peak
▲ (8895ft)

Flagpole Peak
(8363ft) ▲

Echo
Chalet

START

To Sacramento

To Luther Pass

LAKE
TAHOE

Rubicon
Bay

Rubicon
Point

DL Bliss
State
Park

Emerald
Point

Eagle
Point

Emerald
Bay

Eagle
Falls

Cascade
Lake

Lake Tahoe
Visitor Center

Truckee
Marsh

Tahoe
Keys

South
Lake
Tahoe

Fallen
Leaf
Road

Lake Tahoe Basin
Headquarters &
Visitor Information

Lake
Tahoe
Airport

Fallen
Leaf
Lake

Angora
Creek

Lake Valley
State
Recreation
Area

To US
Highway
50

Saxon Creek

NEVADA
CALIFORNIA

open slopes and enters forest, working up along the outlet stream from Gilmore Lake. Shortly before reaching Gilmore Lake, the trail turns left and begins a steady climb towards Dicks Pass. (Ending the day at one of Gilmore Lake's *campsites* allows for a 3.6mi roundtrip excursion to the summit of Mt Tallac.)

With views of the impressive cliffs above Gilmore Lake to the right and inviting Half Moon Lake below to the left, the trail traverses open slopes and small meadows to reach **Dicks Pass** (9200ft) on the ridge between Dicks Peak and Mt Tallac. The pass is not the actual low point, but is a few hundred yards east and higher along the ridge. From the broad, grassy pass the trail descends through forest to a junction leading to Emerald Bay. Here the trail turns left and angles back to the abundant *campsites* on the north shore of Dicks Lake (8420ft).

Day 3: Dicks Lake to Rubicon Lake

3½–4½ hours, 6.8mi (11km), 510ft (153m) ascent, 1350ft (405m) descent
The trail heads north passing east of shallow Fontanillis Lake, then descends through forest west of Upper Velma Lake. The trail now turns left, passing south of Middle Velma Lake (7960ft), then turns north and descends into a marshy area west of that lake. Heading north, it rises through forest to a junction where the route leaves the combined Pacific Crest and Tahoe Rim Trails and turns right, following the Tahoe-Yosemite Trail towards Phipps Pass.

The trail rises steadily through forest, then switchbacks up open slopes to a hairpin turn, which offers sweeping views over Rockbound Valley, through which flows the Rubicon River. The trail turns back sharply southeast and begins a steadily rising traverse of the southern slopes of Phipps Peak (9234ft). Passing south of the peak, with views back down to the Velma Lakes, the trail bends northeast to reach **Phipps Pass** (8850ft) on the peak's shoulder. It traverses down steep, rocky slopes – passing high above the tiny Grouse Lakes – and switchbacks down into forest to **Rubicon Lake**

(8340ft). There are *campsites* along its western shore and under hemlocks at the southern end.

Day 4: Rubicon Lake to Meeks Bay

4 hours, 8.1mi (13km), 2040ft (612m) descent
After ascending above the northwest shore of Rubicon Lake, the trail switchbacks down through forest, crosses Meeks Creek and passes along the western shore of Stony Ridge Lake (*campsites*). From its outlet the trail follows the tumbling creek, passes above Shadow Lake and descends through forest to recross the creek and reach the eastern shore of Crag Lake. The trail rolls down beneath Rubicon Peak (9183ft) to the heavily used *campsites* at shallow Lake Genevieve, at the northern end of which it passes a trail junction leading to General Creek.

The main trail descends steadily along the well-shaded Meeks Creek, swinging east, then back west, to reach a crossing of the creek. From here, the sandy trail rolls through meadows and open forest and, leaving Desolation Wilderness, drops down to meet the unpaved, closed road that leads to Meeks Bay (6300ft).

Tahoe to Yosemite

Stretching from the southern end of Lake Tahoe to Yosemite National Park's northern boundary, this more lightly-used region of the northern and central Sierra Nevada encompasses four wilderness areas: Mokelumne, Carson-Iceberg, Emigrant and Hoover. Lightly-trafficked trans-Sierra highways provide easy access and, once away from trailheads, hikers find delightfully surprising solitude.

HISTORY

Native American Maidu and Miwok of the western Sierra, and Washoe and Piute of the eastern Sierra, traversed the region's passes to hunt and trade. Spanish missionaries entered the area at the beginning of the 19th century and one of the main rivers here, the Stanislaus, was named after Estanislao, a Native American who refused to stay at the mission. In 1844, John C Frémont and his scout Kit Carson surveyed the region. A river, a pass, a mountain range, and the Nevada state capital were later named in honor of this famous scout. During the California Gold Rush the Overland Trail served as the main route through the region, and traces of the original trail are found along Hwy 88. Ebbetts Pass on Hwy 4 was named for John Ebbetts, who led a party over the pass in 1850 and recommended it as a railroad route!

NATURAL HISTORY
Ancient lava once covered much of the area, but subsequent erosion exposed the underlying granite, leaving black basaltic and reddish volcanic summits in sharp contrast with white and grey granite outcrops. Rivers, lakes, meadows and a relatively dense forest cover further heighten the contrast, and give the region a colorful and distinctive flavor.

NEAREST TOWNS & FACILITIES
Markleeville
Settled by Jacob Marklee in 1861, this is the seat of remote Alpine County, California's least densely populated county.

The USFS and Alpine County chamber of commerce (☎ 530-694-2475, fax 694-2478, 🖳 alpinecounty.com) jointly run the visitor information center at the north end of town where hikers can self-issue free wilderness permits for the Carson-Iceberg and Mokelumne wilderness areas.

Places to Stay & Eat The *Alpine Hotel/Cutthroat Saloon (☎ 530-694-2150)* is the best place for hearty, inexpensive meals. Next door, the *Alpine Inn (☎ 530-694-2591)* has singles/doubles for $35/40. Nearby is *The J Marklee Town Station (☎ 530-694-2507)*, a comparably priced motel with a restaurant. Behind the saloon is *M's Coffee House*, a fine place for espresso and bagels. Grover's Corner and the Markleeville General Store sell groceries; the latter also sells some hiking gear.

A mile south of town on the east side of Hwy 89 is the USFS *Markleeville campground* ($9), open May to September. Year-round Grover Hot Springs State Park is 4mi west of town on Hot Springs Rd. The pleasant, forested *campground* ($16) has showers. Call ☎ 800-444-7275 for reservations; a $7.50 fee applies. Across the adjacent meadow is a well-known hot spring with two large pools ($4 entrance fee, $1 bathing suit and towel rental).

Getting There & Away Markleeville is on Hwy 89 between Hwy 88 and Hwy 4, 30mi southeast of South Lake Tahoe via Luther Pass and 63mi northwest of Bridgeport via spectacular Monitor Pass.

Bridgeport
Toiyabe National Forest's Bridgeport ranger station (☎ 760-932-7070) is on the east side of US 395 just south of town. As well as issuing free wilderness permits for Hoover Wilderness, it provides trail information and sells books and maps (mail order: HCR 1000, Bridgeport, CA 93517). Ziglar's Sporting Goods (☎ 760-932-7331) at 323 Main St sells hiking gear.

Places to Stay & Eat *Bridgeport Inn (☎ 760-932-7380, fax 932-1160, 🖳 www.the bridgeportinn.com)* on Main St has single/double hotel rooms for $45/50 above its restaurant, and motel rooms ($50/56) in back. *Silver Maple Inn (☎ 760-932-7383)* at 310 Main St has a pleasant, shaded garden and friendly owners ($55/65). *The Barn*, with outdoor patio tables only, is the best bet for hungry hikers in search of burgers, burritos, tacos and the like. *Rhino's Bar & Grille* is the choice for beer and pizza. The Bridgeport General Market and Busters Market are the only places to buy groceries.

Five desirable USFS *campgrounds* ($9 to $10) are along Twin Lakes Rd and at Lower Twin Lake.

Getting There & Away Bridgeport, the largest town along the 125mi stretch of US 395 between Carson City and Mammoth

Long Hike: Tahoe-Yosemite Trail

Duration	19–23 days
Distance	185.7mi (298.9km)
Standard	hard
Start	Hwy 89, Meeks Bay
Finish	Hwy 120, Tuolumne Meadows
Nearest Facilities	Tahoe City, Tuolumne Meadows
Public Transport	yes

Summary Connecting Lake Tahoe with Yosemite National Park, this classic trail contours the spine of the northern Sierra, crosses seven passes, and gets hikers deep into the wilderness away from crowds.

Linking two Sierra gems, Lake Tahoe and Yosemite National Park, the 185mi Tahoe-Yosemite Trail traverses four wilderness areas and crosses seven passes and is a more varied and less frequently used trail than its southern counterpart, the John Muir Trail, or the parallel

segment of the Pacific Crest Trail. Elevations range from a low point of 5200ft in the canyon of the Mokelumne River to a high of 10,440ft at St Mary's Pass.

Thru-hikers can easily cover the trail in one season, although it is more common for hikers to complete short segments over a few seasons. Hiking the trail by segments typically takes 19 to 23 days, a slower pace than that of thru-hikers, who might take as little as 11 days. Five trans-Sierra highways provide easy access to the trail.

The route is best done in five segments: Meeks Bay to Echo Summit (31.2mi, 4 days); Echo Summit to Carson Pass (13½mi, 1 to 2 days); Carson Pass to Lake Alpine (26mi, 3 to 4 days); Lake Alpine to Kennedy Meadow (44mi, 5 to 6 days); and Kennedy Meadow to Tuolumne Meadows (71mi, 6 to 7 days).

A string of USGS 1:62,500 quadrangles covers the trail. *The Tahoe-Yosemite Trail* by Thomas Winnett is the definitive guidebook.

Backpackers setting up a campsite in the backcountry of Yosemite National Park, Sierra Nevada. Meticulous camping habits are required to guard against the attentions of bears.

Lakes, is 25mi north of Lee Vining and 72mi south of Carson City.

Greyhound buses ply US 395 once daily in each direction between Los Angeles and Reno. The southbound bus to Los Angeles ($54/108 one-way/roundtrip) departs at 10:40 am, and the northbound bus to Reno ($29/57) departs at 2:35 am.

Inyo-Mono Dial-A-Ride (☎760-937-5976, 800-922-1930) operates a service ($6) from Bridgeport to Bishop (see the Eastern Sierra section later in this chapter), stopping at all towns in between including Lee Vining. The bus departs once a day on Monday and Wednesday at 8 am and arrives at 3 pm.

Lee Vining

The Mono Lake Committee information center and bookstore (☎ 760-647-6629, 647-6595) on US 395 at Third St has helpful staff. The Mono Basin National Forest Scenic Area visitor center (☎ 760-647-3044), a half-mile north of town on US 395, provides trail information, sells maps and issues free wilderness permits for Inyo National Forest. Bell's Sporting Goods (☎ 760-647-6406) sells hiking gear.

Places to Stay & Eat *El Mono Motel & Latte Da Coffee Caf'* (☎ 760-647-6310) on US 395 at Third St has single/double rooms for $55/75. At the north end of town, *Murphy's Motel* (☎ 760-647-6316) costs $78/83. *Nicely's Restaurant*, on US 395 at Fourth St, is a family-style restaurant. Next door is *Bodie Mike's Pizza*. The bright-red and unsigned Lee Vining Market sells various groceries.

Getting There & Away Lee Vining is on US 395 a half-mile north of its junction with Hwy 120, which leads to Yosemite National Park. It is 25mi south of Bridgeport and 26mi north of the Mammoth Lakes exit. The southbound Greyhound bus to Los Angeles ($57/114 one-way/roundtrip) departs at 11:15 am, and the northbound bus to Reno ($32/63) departs at 2 am. The Bridgeport to Bishop Inyo-Mono Dial-A-Ride bus stops in Lee Vining (see Bridgeport).

Echo Summit to Carson Pass

Duration	2 days
Distance	12.4mi (20km)
Standard	easy-medium
Start	US 50, Echo Summit
Finish	Hwy 88, Carson Pass
Nearest Towns	South Lake Tahoe, Markleeville
Public Transport	no

Summary Easy walking, beautiful wildflower gardens and remarkable solitude recommend this hike between two trans-Sierra highways as one of the best overnight trips close to Lake Tahoe.

The superb through-hike between Echo Summit and Carson Pass follows a lightly-used but interesting segment of the combined Pacific Crest and Tahoe-Yosemite Trails, and visits the scenic headwaters of the Truckee River.

PLANNING

No permit is required for this hike in the Eldorado National Forest.

Maps

The USGS 1:24,000 *Echo Lake*, *Caples Lake* and *Carson Pass* quadrangles cover the hike. The USFS 1:63,360 *Eldorado National Forest* map also does, but without topographic detail.

GETTING TO/FROM THE HIKE
To the Start

The trailhead is at the Echo Summit Sno-Park (7382ft) at the end of a short road that turns south off US 50 0.3mi west of Echo Summit.

From the Finish

The trailhead meets Hwy 88 0.3mi west of Carson Pass (8573ft). From the pass, Hwy 88 leads east to Pickett's Junction, from where Hwy 89 heads north over Luther Pass, joins US 50, and leads to South Lake Tahoe. Hwy 89 continues east and then south to Markleeville.

THE HIKE
Day 1: Echo Summit to Showers Lake
5–6 hours, 8mi (12.9km)

After heading south a mile to Benwood Meadow, the trail ascends southwest, crossing a forested ridge to reach the head of Bryan Meadow (*campsites*). Bearing south again, the trail follows the forested ridge between Sayles Canyon and the Upper Truckee River. It turns southeast to skirt Little Round Top (9590ft), where patches of snow lie late into the season. Passing through a gated fence, it descends into

beautiful meadows of wildflowers. As your near Showers Lake (8650ft), turn east onto a trail that circles its north shore to picturesque *campsites* near its outlet. Nearby Round, Dardanelles and Four Lakes are inviting across the open basin of the Upper Truckee Meadows.

Day 2: Showers Lake to Carson Pass
3–4 hours, 4.4mi (7.1km)

Circle the lake's south shore and rejoin the main trail, which rises slightly to the south, then turns southeast to descend into Upper Truckee Meadows. It crosses several small streams and comes to a junction with the Round Lake Trail after 2.2mi where the Tahoe Rim Trail turns northeast (left). Continuing south, the trail rolls upwards through beautiful meadows, crossing the nascent Truckee River and its feeders several times, with striking Red Lake Peak to the east providing a wildly colorful backdrop to the lush meadows. From the saddle (8800ft) at the head of the meadows that separates the Truckee and American River basins are views south to Round Top and back north to Freel Peak. The trail descends a steep, open slope, then passes under trees, crossing a small stream, and turns southeast to Carson Pass.

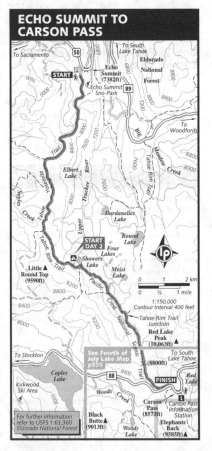

Fourth of July Lake

Duration	2 days
Distance	14mi (22.5km)
Standard	easy-medium
Start/Finish	Hwy 88, Carson Pass
Nearest Town	Markleeville
Public Transport	no

Summary This clockwise loop around an ancient, ochre-colored volcanic peak includes a night at a sparkling alpine lake.

The popular overnight circumambulation of volcanic Round Top (10,381ft), the highest summit in Mokelumne Wilderness, crosses the jagged Sierra crest at one of its lowest points and camps at the beautiful Fourth of July Lake.

PLANNING
Maps
The USGS 1:24,000 *Carson Pass* and *Caples Lake* quadrangles cover the hike, as does the USFS 1:63,360 *Mokelumne Wilderness* map.

Permits
The Eldorado, Stanislaus and Toiyabe National Forests (see Information Sources under Information at the beginning of this chapter) issue free wilderness permits for Mokelumne Wilderness. The closest place to get a permit is the USFS Carson Pass information station.

GETTING TO/FROM THE HIKE
The trailhead is 0.1mi east of Carson Pass on Hwy 88.

THE HIKE
Day 1: Carson Pass to Fourth of July Lake
6–7 hours, 9½mi (15.3km)
The trail climbs a ridge south into Mokelumne Wilderness for a mile to popular Frog Lake. At a junction beyond the lake, the trail forks. Follow the PCT – the left fork – and climb southeast, then east to pass north of old volcanic **Elephants Back**

(9585ft) – with fine views both east and west. Snow patches linger here late into the season. The trail descends to a northeast spur, then turns and descends south to traverse the upper Forestdale Creek basin high above Faith Valley. Climbing out of the basin, the trail passes above some small lakes and switchbacks to **Forestdale Divide** (9000ft), 4½mi from Carson Pass. Leaving the PCT, which forks left, follow the Summit City Trail which heads right and descends to Summit City Creek. Turn north (right) onto the Tahoe-Yosemite Trail 3½mi from Forestdale Divide, leaving the Summit City Trail, and ascend 1½mi to spectacular *campsites* along the east shore of Fourth of July Lake (8164ft).

Day 2: Fourth of July Lake to Carson Pass
3–4 hours, 4½mi (7.3km)
Head north from the lake on the Tahoe-Yosemite Trail, climbing over the ridge to Round Top Lake as the trail bends east. Continue east past Winnemucca Lake and turn north, passing west of Elephants Back, to Frog Lake and back to Carson Pass.

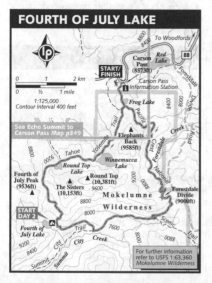

FOURTH OF JULY LAKE

Emigrant Wilderness

Duration	6 days
Distance	45.4mi (73.1km)
Standard	medium
Start/Finish	Hwy 108, Kennedy Meadow
Nearest Town	Bridgeport
Public Transport	no

Summary Following streams through big meadows, this pioneer route through Emigrant Wilderness crosses two easy passes, offering easy access to northern Yosemite National Park from the western Sierra Nevada.

Along the western slopes of the central Sierra Nevada, the gentle terrain of Emigrant Wilderness, shaped by glaciers and volcanoes, offers the easiest access to northern Yosemite National Park. Following a segment of the Tahoe-Yosemite Trail between 6400ft and 9700ft elevation, this hike visits expansive meadows and fine fishing lakes, and crosses two gentle passes to meet the PCT just inside the park.

HISTORY

In 1852, the Clark-Skidmore party, traveling on the West Walker route, were the first to cross Emigrant Pass. More parties crossed in 1853, but the route was soon abandoned as too difficult. The Kennedy brothers established Kennedy Meadows Resort in 1886, and the area has focused on recreation ever since. It first received protection as Emigrant Basin Primitive Area in 1931 and became a wilderness area in 1975.

PLANNING
Maps

The USGS 1:24,000 *Sonora Pass*, *Emigrant Lake* and *Tower Peak* quadrangles, and 1:62,500 *Sonora Pass* and *Tower Peak* maps cover the hike; as does the USFS 1:63,360 *Emigrant Wilderness* map, which includes northwestern Yosemite.

Permits

Stanislaus National Forest (see Information Sources under Information at the beginning of this chapter) issues free wilderness permits for Emigrant Wilderness. The nearest place to get one is the ranger station in Pinecrest.

GETTING TO/FROM THE HIKE

On Hwy 108, 9½mi west of Sonora Pass and 25.7mi east of Pinecrest, is the mile-long, paved Kennedy Meadows Rd that leads south to Kennedy Meadows Resort and the trailhead. Parking at the road's end is on private land and costs $5 per day, but trailhead parking is free along Kennedy Meadows Rd.

THE HIKE
Day 1: Kennedy Meadow to Sheep Camp

6–7 hours, 8½mi (13.7km), 2400ft (720m) ascent

From the gated trailhead (6400ft) on the Middle Fork Stanislaus River, the route follows the Huckleberry Trail on a wide track south over a saddle to skirt the east side of Kennedy Meadow and enter Emigrant Wilderness. It crosses the Stanislaus and follows its south bank to cross Summit Creek. Ascending past the Kennedy Lake Trail junction, it traverses above the east side of Relief Reservoir and crosses Grouse Creek. Ascending steadily, the trail rises southeast, passing an early emigrant's grave in Saucer Meadow and soon meets Summit Creek. Multicolored, volcanic Relief Peak (10,808ft) looms to the north as the trail crosses a forested ridge above a bend in the creek to reach the meadow known as *Sheep Camp* (8800ft), with sites along Summit Creek.

Day 2: Sheep Camp to Emigrant Meadow Lake

4–5 hours, 7½mi (12.1km), 1000ft (300m) ascent, 400ft (120m) descent

The trail follows Summit Creek east through Lunch Meadow, at the end of which is a junction with a trail that heads south to Emigrant Lake (see Days 4B to 6B). Continuing east, the trail rises to **Brown Bear Pass** (9765ft), the watershed between the Stanislaus and Tuolumne Rivers, and descends to expansive Emigrant Meadow and Emigrant Meadow Lake (9400ft), just west of Emigrant Pass, a mid-19th century pioneer route. There are *campsites* along the lake's west shore.

Day 3: Emigrant Meadow Lake to Grace Meadow

3–5 hours, 6.7mi (10.8km), 600ft (180m) ascent, 1280ft (384m) descent

The trail rises 300ft over a ridge to Grizzly Meadow and its two small lakes, then dips through the headwaters of East Fork Cherry Creek, passing the Horse Meadow road to Maxwell Lake (see Days 4B to 6B below) and arriving at Summit Meadow. Rising 300ft to gentle **Bond Pass** (9730ft), the boundary of Yosemite National Park, the trail descends to meet the PCT (9400ft). Hikers can turn north (left) to reach *campsites* along the west shore of beautiful Dorothy Lake (9400ft) after 0.9mi, or south (right) and continue 2.3mi to peaceful Grace Meadow (8720ft) and *campsites* along Falls Creek.

SIERRA NEVADA

EMIGRANT WILDERNESS

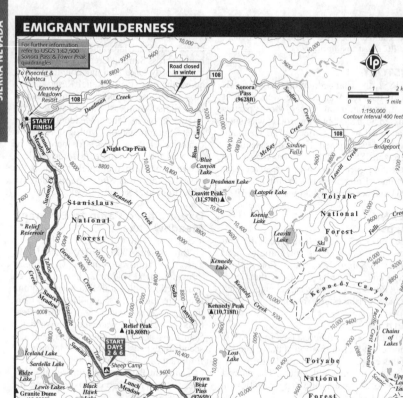

For further information refer to USGS 1:62,500 Sonora Pass & Tower Peak quadrangles

Sublime Sierra Nevada. Clockwise from Top Left: Shooting stars flank an alpine landscape, Franklin–Sawtooth Passes area, Sequoia National Park; Circle Meadow in the Giant Forest, Sequoia National Park; Gilmour Lake and the rocky peaks of the Crystal Range from Mt Tallac, Desolation Wilderness; wildflowers along South Fork Bishop Creek, John Muir Wilderness.

Top Left: Moro Rock, Sequoia National Park, California. **Top Right:** Mt Tallac towers above Lake Tahoe's southwestern shore, Desolation Wilderness. **Middle:** Hot Creek, world-class trout fishing in the Mammoth Lakes area. **Bottom Left:** Barney Lake in John Muir Wilderness, near Mammoth Lakes, eastern Sierra, California. **Bottom Right:** Some of the extraordinary giant sequoia trees of Sequoia National Park.

Days 4A to 6A: Grace Meadow to Kennedy Meadow
3 days, 22.7mi (36.6km))
Return along the same trails to Kennedy Meadow and the trailhead.

Days 4B to 6B: Grace Meadow to Kennedy Meadow via Maxwell Lake
3 days, 24.7mi (40km)
Alternatively, recross Bond Pass to Summit Meadow and turn south on the wide Horse Meadow road which follows the East Fork Cherry Creek for about 5mi to fine **campsites** on the north shore of Maxwell Lake (8700ft), beneath distinctive granite **Sachse Monument** (9405ft). Return to Sheep Camp by heading north for 6mi via Emigrant Lake and **Mosquito Pass** (9410ft), and on Day 6 retrace your steps from Day 1 to Kennedy Meadow.

Sawtooth Ridge

Duration	6 days
Distance	51mi (82.1km)
Standard	medium-hard
Start/Finish	Upper Twin Lake
Nearest Town	Bridgeport
Public Transport	no

Summary This loop follows forested rivers through spectacular, steep-walled granite canyons of remote northern Yosemite National Park, crossing three passes as it swings around the magnificent towers of Sawtooth Ridge.

The solid, white granite pinnacles and arêtes of Sawtooth Ridge, one of the Sierra Nevada's most interesting rock climbing areas, range from 11,400ft to 12,281ft in height and form the most dramatic portion of Yosemite National Park's northeastern boundary. With four small glaciers under the northeast face, the rocky summits rise abruptly more than 5000ft only 3mi or so from Twin Lakes. Passing through Hoover Wilderness into the park, this rewarding six-day hike skirts the ridge, following a segment of the PCT before returning via incomparable Matterhorn Canyon and isolated, tranquil

Upper Piute Creek. Crossing three passes and two minor saddles, this demanding route explores the exquisite canyons and relatively unvisited, superb high country of northern Yosemite.

PLANNING
Maps
The USGS 1:24,000 *Twin Lakes*, *Dunderberg Peak*, *Buckeye Ridge* and *Matterhorn Peak* quadrangles, and 1:62,500 *Matterhorn Peak* and *Tower Peak* quadrangles cover the hike. The USFS 1:63,360 *Hoover Wilderness* map covers the trail outside the national park.

Permits
Toiyabe National Forest issues free, first-come first-served wilderness permits for Hoover Wilderness, where a quota system is in effect from July 1 to September 15. Half of the available permits can be reserved by mail (see Information Sources under Information earlier in this chapter), with a $3 reservation fee per person, from March 1 to three weeks prior to the entry date. The other half are available from the ranger station in Bridgeport (see Nearest Towns & Facilities).

GETTING TO/FROM THE HIKE
Access is from the eastern Sierra via Hoover Wilderness from Bridgeport. From the western end of town, follow Twin Lakes Rd 14mi southwest to its terminus and the trailhead at **Annett's Mono Village** (☎ 760-932-7071, fax 932-7468), a resort at the northwestern end of Upper Twin Lake. Parking is available only on private land and costs $5 for any length of time.

THE HIKE
Day 1: Upper Twin Lake to Peeler Lake
6–7 hours, 8mi (12.9km), 2400ft (720m) ascent
From the trailhead (7092ft), the trail runs gently west until entering Hoover Wilderness north of Little Slide Canyon. From here, the trail ascends and turns south to the warm Barney Lake. Passing along its west shore, the trail traverses above the inlet area, then fords and refords Robinson Creek. After

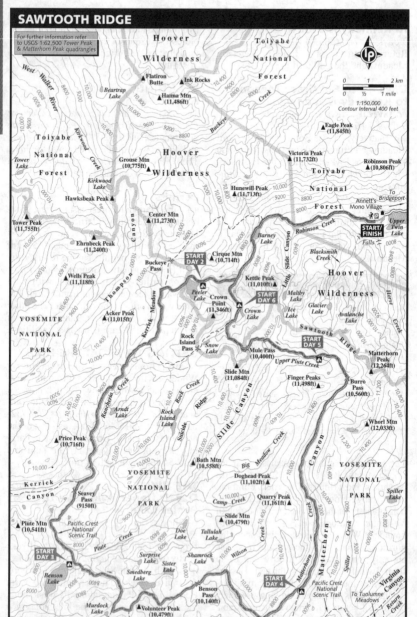

SIERRA NEVADA

SAWTOOTH RIDGE

For further information refer to USGS 1:62,500 *Tower Peak* & *Matterhorn Peak* quadrangles

Hoover Wilderness

Toiyabe National Forest

West Walker River

Flatiron Butte

Ink Rocks

Beartrap Lake

Hanna Mtn (11,486ft)

Buckeye Creek

Eagle Peak (11,845ft)

Toiyabe National Forest

Kirkwood Creek

Hoover Wilderness

Grouse Mtn (10,775ft)

Victoria Peak (11,732ft)

Robinson Peak (10,806ft)

Tower Lake

Kirkwood Lake

Hunewill Peak (11,713ft)

Toiyabe National Forest

To Bridgeport

Hawksbeak Peak

Annett's Mono Village

Tower Peak (11,755ft)

Center Mtn (11,273ft)

Robinson Creek

Upper Twin Lake

Ehrnbeck Peak (11,240ft)

Barney Lake

START/FINISH

Falls

Blacksmith Creek

Wells Peak (11,118ft)

Buckeye Pass

START DAY 2

Cirque Mtn (10,714ft)

Kettle Peak (11,010ft)

Hoover Wilderness

Peeler Lake

Crown Point (11,346ft)

Maltby Lake

Glacier Lake

Horse Creek

Acker Peak (11,015ft)

START DAY 6

Ice Lake

Avalanche Lake

YOSEMITE NATIONAL PARK

Rock Island Pass

Crown Lake

Sawtooth Ridge

Snow Lake

Mule Pass (10,400ft)

START DAY 5

Matterhorn Peak (12,264ft)

Rancheria Creek

Rock Creek

Slide Mtn (11,084ft)

Upper Piute Creek

Finger Peaks (11,498ft)

Burro Pass (10,560ft)

Arndt Lake

Rock Island Lake

Suicide Ridge

Slide Canyon

Whorl Mtn (12,033ft)

Price Peak (10,716ft)

Bath Mtn (10,558ft)

Big Meadow Creek

Doghead Peak (11,102ft)

YOSEMITE NATIONAL PARK

Matterhorn Canyon

Spiller Lake

Kerrick Canyon

Seavey Pass (9150ft)

YOSEMITE NATIONAL PARK

Quarry Peak (11,161ft)

Camp Creek

Piute Mtn (10,541ft)

Pacific Crest National Scenic Trail

Slide Mtn (10,479ft)

Spiller Creek

Piute Creek

Doe Lake

Tallulah Lake

Wilson Creek

START DAY 3

Surprise Lake

Sister Lake

Shamrock Lake

START DAY 4

Pacific Crest National Scenic Trail

To Tuolumne Meadows

Virginia Canyon

Return Creek

Benson Lake

Smedberg Lake

Benson Pass (10,140ft)

Matterhorn

Murdock Lake

Volunteer Peak (10,479ft)

0   1   2 km
0   ½   1 mile
1:150,000
Contour Interval 400 feet

crossing the stream from Peeler Lake, the trail ascends two long sets of steep switch-backs to a junction with the Crown Lake Trail. The trail to Peeler Lake turns right and ascends to large Peeler Lake (9500ft), with *campsites* on its east and north shores.

Day 2: Peeler Lake to Benson Lake

6–7 hours, 10mi (16.1km), 250ft (75m) ascent, 2150ft (645m) descent

Peeler Lake sits on a ridge crest, and its waters flow both east and west. The trail goes around the north end of the lake, and enters Yosemite National Park as it descends along its western outlet to Kerrick Meadow. Here it turns left onto the trail coming from Buckeye Pass and continues down Rancheria Creek through canyon and meadow to a junction with the PCT (8910ft), about 6½mi from Peeler Lake. Turning left onto the well-traveled PCT, the trail rises out of Kerrick Canyon 0.6mi to granite **Seavey Pass** (9150ft). Next it follows a rocky descent for 2½mi to the valley floor and the side trail that leads another 0.3mi to enormous blue Benson Lake (7590ft), with its popular sandy beach and *campsites* along its east shore.

Day 3: Benson Lake to Matterhorn Canyon

7–8 hours, 10.6mi (17.1km), 2550ft (765m) ascent, 1650ft (495m) descent

Return 0.3mi to the PCT and turn right. The trail rises along a stream and passes two side trails as it runs beneath Volunteer Peak's west face to reach Smedberg Lake (9220ft), with *campsites*, in 3.9mi. It is another 2.2mi of climbing to **Benson Pass** (10,140ft). Descending from the pass, the trail meets Wilson Creek and follows it down for 4.2mi to the forested Matterhorn Canyon (8490ft) where the trail fords Matterhorn Creek to reach well-used creekside *campsites*.

Day 4: Matterhorn Canyon to Upper Piute Creek

6–7 hours, 8½mi (13.7km), 2070ft (621m) ascent, 1000ft (300m) descent

On the east side of Matterhorn Creek the trail turns left, leaving the PCT, and heads up the granite-walled canyon. Crossing the creek three times, it finally runs along the west side to enter spectacular upper cirque meadows (with *campsites*) beneath Finger Peaks (11,498ft), Whorl Mountain (12,033ft) and Matterhorn Peak (12,264ft). Traversing up, the trail makes some final switchbacks to **Burro Pass** (10,560ft), 6.2mi up the canyon with jagged Sawtooth Ridge rising to the north. The trail descends past fine granite climbing walls for 2.3mi into the forest along Upper Piute Creek (9600ft), where deer often wander through *campsites*.

Day 5: Upper Piute Creek to Crown Lake

4–5 hours, 6mi (9.7km), 800ft (240m) ascent, 900ft (270m) descent

The trail traverses west through forest and crosses a side stream entering from the north. It works up open slopes to reach **Mule Pass** (10,400ft) and descends a series of benches beneath Slide Mountain (11,084ft) where snow often lingers. Crossing the stream from Snow Lake and passing the trail to Rock Island Pass, the route switchbacks down to the west side of Crown Lake (9500ft), with *campsites* along its outlet.

Day 6: Crown Lake to Upper Twin Lake

4–5 hours, 8mi (12.9km), 2400ft (720m) descent

Following Crown Lake's outflow stream, the trail passes between two small lakes and after about 2mi meets the Peeler Lake Trail tackled on Day 1, turns right and descends the switchbacks to Barney Lake, Robinson Creek and the trailhead.

Yosemite National Park

Yosemite National Park, with some of the USA's most exquisite scenery, draws visitors from around the world. Sheer, glacially-sculpted granite cliffs tower well over a half-mile above the meadow-carpeted Yosemite Valley, through which courses the

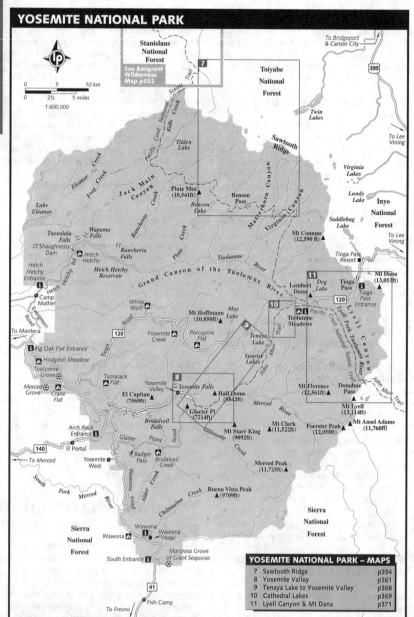

YOSEMITE NATIONAL PARK

0   5   10 km
0   2½   5 miles
1:600,000

Stanislaus
National
Forest

See Emigrant
Wilderness
Map p352

7

To Bridgeport
& Carson City

395

Toiyabe
National
Forest

Twin
Lakes

Sawtooth
Ridge

Tilden
Lake

To Lee
Vining

Virginia
Lakes

Piute Mtn
(10,541ft)

Benson
Pass

Lundy
Lake

Inyo

Benson
Lake

Jack Main Canyon

Saddlebag
Lake

National

Eleanor Creek

Frog Creek

Rancheria Creek

Matterhorn Canyon

Virginia Canyon

Mt Conness
(12,590 ft)

Forest

Lake
Eleanor

Wapama
Falls

Tueeulala
Falls

To Lee
Vining

O'Shaughnessy
Dam

Hetch Hetchy

Rancheria
Falls

Piute Creek

Tuolumne River

Tioga Pass
Resort

Mt Dana
(13,053ft)

11

Hetch Hetchy
Entrance

Hetch Hetchy
Reservoir

Grand Canyon of the Tuolumne River

Lembert
Dome

Dog
Lake

Tioga
Pass

120

Camp
Mather

White
Wolf

May
Lake

Tuolumne
Meadows

Tioga Pass
Entrance

Evergreen Road

Mt Hoffmann
(10,850ft)

Lyell Fork Tuolumne River

To Manteca

Big Oak Flat Entrance

Yosemite
Creek

Porcupine
Flat

9

Tenaya
Lake

10

Pacific Crest National Scenic Trail

Lyell Canyon

Hodgdon Meadow

120

Tuolumne
Grove

Tioga Road

Sunrise
Lakes

John Muir Trail

Merced
Grove

Tamarack
Flat

Crane
Flat

8

Yosemite
Valley

Yosemite Falls

Half Dome
(8842ft)

Mt Florence
(12,561ft)

Donahue
Pass

John Muir Trail

El Capitan
(7569ft)

Glacier Pt
(7214ft)

Merced River

Mt Lyell
(13,114ft)

Bridalveil
Falls

Illilouette Creek

Mt Starr King
(9092ft)

Mt Clark
(11,522ft)

Foerster Peak
(12,058ft)

Mt Ansel Adams
(11,760ft)

Arch Rock
Entrance

Glacier   Point

Road

Badger
Pass

Merced Peak
(11,725ft)

140

To Merced

El Portal

Yosemite
West

Bridalveil
Creek

South Fork Merced River

Alder Creek

Wawona Road

Chilnualna Creek

Buena Vista Peak
(9709ft)

Sierra
National
Forest

Wawona

Wawona
Hotel

Sierra
National
Forest

Mariposa Grove
of Giant Sequoias

41

South Entrance

To Fresno

Fish Camp

YOSEMITE NATIONAL PARK – MAPS

7	Sawtooth Ridge	p354
8	Yosemite Valley	p361
9	Tenaya Lake to Yosemite Valley	p368
10	Cathedral Lakes	p369
11	Lyell Canyon & Mt Dana	p371

Merced River. The incomparable granite monoliths of world-renowned El Capitan and Half Dome are instantly recognizable, and several of the world's highest waterfalls thunder over the rim to the valley floor. The dramatic scale of this 7mi long, half-mile wide valley dazzles hikers who take any of the trails from the valley floor to the rim.

Beyond Yosemite Valley itself, more than 800mi of trails through the park's nearly 1200 sq miles offer hikers an uncrowded backcountry experience. Yosemite's high country is an alpine wilderness with flower-filled meadows ringed by conifer forests and threaded by streams, where gem-like lakes shimmer beneath granite pinnacles. The 2½mi-long Tuolumne Meadows, the Sierra Nevada's largest subalpine meadow, lies beneath the Sierra crest and is the center of Yosemite backpacking. Here smooth, dome-like peaks once covered by glaciers stand opposite jagged peaks that rose above the ice.

HISTORY
Native American Ahwahneechee, a subtribe of the Southern or Sierra Miwok, knew of Yosemite Valley 5000 years ago and had settled there by 1000 BC, living on black oak acorns and fish, and occasionally deer and rabbits. They lived in the valley during fall and winter, and in spring headed to the high country where they traded with eastern Sierra Piutes.

Not until the mid-19th century did non-Native Americans visit the secluded valley. In 1833 a party of 58 fur trappers and hunters, led by Joseph Reddeford Walker, glimpsed Yosemite Valley as they crossed the Sierra Nevada from east to west, passing between the Tuolumne and Merced Rivers. Sixteen years later two lost gold miners stumbled briefly upon Yosemite Valley. Conflict between gold-country prospectors and Native Americans, who had raided the miners' camps, led to a military expedition in 1851 to 'punish' the Ahwahneechee. The Mariposa Battalion, led by Major James D Savage, entered the valley on March 27, 1851 via the route of present-day Wawona Rd, forcing the capitulation of Chief Tenaya and his tribe.

In 1855, San Franciscan publisher James Mason Hutchings and artist Thomas Ayres visited the valley. Through Hutchings' articles and Ayres' sketches, published nationwide, Yosemite's captivating beauty quickly drew other tourist parties. As the numbers of visitors increased Hutchings, conservationist Galen Clark, landscape architect Frederick Law Olmstead and others recognized the importance of protecting Yosemite Valley and the Big Tree Grove (ie, Mariposa Grove) of giant sequoias south of the valley. In 1864 the US Congress passed, and President Abraham Lincoln signed into law, the Yosemite Grant, a bill that transferred these two areas to California as a public trust and created Yosemite State Park.

Through the efforts of John Muir and editor Robert Underwood Johnson, the US Congress established Yosemite as the USA's third national park on October 1, 1890. In 1906 Congress approved the recession of the Yosemite Grant and incorporated Yosemite State Park into the national park.

The US Cavalry managed and administered the park from 1890 to 1914, when administration passed to the US Department of Interior. The first civilian park rangers were employed in 1898. The park currently operates according to a 1980 general management plan that emphasizes education through interpretation, and environment-first (as opposed to people-first) ethics. Yosemite became a UNESCO World Heritage Site in 1984.

Long Gone Grizzlies

Although the California state flag sports one, grizzly bears have long been extinct in the state. Common throughout California in the mid-19th century, the last grizzly was shot near Kings Canyon in the 1920s. Grizzlies were especially common in the Yosemite region, where the Native American Ahwahneechee people were known by the Miwok word *uzumati*, which means 'grizzly bear'. This word, incorrectly pronounced by soldiers, was anglicized into 'Yosemite'.

SIERRA NEVADA

John Muir (1838–1914)

Muir immigrated from Scotland to America with his father in 1849 and settled in Wisconsin. After studying botany and geology at the University of Wisconsin, Muir set out on what would become a never-ending journey through the wilds. His journeys took him all over the world – he is credited with discovering Alaska's Glacier Bay.

But more than anywhere else, Muir is synonymous with the Sierra Nevada. Muir first visited his special love, Yosemite, in 1868 and returned in 1869 to work as a carpenter and sheep herder. He wandered and studied for the next 10 years, discovering 75 glaciers and mapping much of the Sierra, almost always alone. He scouted the area between Yosemite Valley and Mt Whitney, where the John Muir Trail now pays him tribute.

Muir became an influential author and conservationist. His eloquent articles and determined lobbying efforts were instrumental in the establishment of Yosemite and Sequoia National Parks in 1890. In 1892, Muir founded the Sierra Club 'to do something for wildness and make the mountains glad'. Muir was the USA's most important conservationist and his legacy remains an inspiration today.

HUGH D'ANDRADE

NATURAL HISTORY

The park contains all the Sierra Nevada life zones from lower montane to alpine. The western part of the park is densely forested, while the eastern side of the park along the Sierra crest is a drier subalpine environment. Yosemite Valley, at 4000ft, is in the lower montane zone, where a mixed conifer forest of ponderosa pine, incense cedar and Douglas fir rises over an understory of flowering shrubs, and woodlands of black oak and California live oak.

INFORMATION
When to Hike

Yosemite Valley and the west of the park experience a mild climate. The best months are May, June, September and October, although the valley is enjoyable year-round. In summer, hikers escape from the valley heat to Tuolumne Meadows and Yosemite's high country, which is between 15°F and 20°F cooler. Snow can fall here in any month of the year, typically as late as June and as early as September. The meadows are at their peak in July, after the June snowmelt and before the first August frosts.

Maps & Books

The USGS 1:125,000 *Yosemite National Park and Vicinity* map with 200ft contour intervals covers the entire park. Tom Harrison Cartography's 1:125,000 *Yosemite National Park Recreation Map* and 1:24,000 *Yosemite Valley* are good. For information on the maps required for individual hikes, see Planning for each hike.

The Yosemite by John Muir, with photographs by Galen Rowell, is a beautiful coffee-table book. *Yosemite: Its Discovery, Its Wonders & Its People* by Margaret Sanborn is a fascinating and thorough account of the park and its history.

Maps and books are available from the Yosemite Association Bookstore (☎ 209-379-2648, fax 379-2486, ✆ yosemite.org), PO Box 230, El Portal, CA 95318, and at park visitor centers and stores. The Tuolumne Meadows Sport Shop, at the gas station, also sells maps.

Information Sources

For general information contact Yosemite National Park (☎ 209-372-0200 for recorded general information, 372-0745 for wilderness information, 900-454-9673 for an operator from 8 am to 4:30 pm weekdays, 🖳 www.nps.gov/yose), PO Box 577, Yosemite, CA 95389.

The National Park Reservation Service (☎ 800-436-7275, 301-722-1257 from overseas, 🖳 reservations.nps.gov), PO Box 1600, Cumberland, MD 21502, handles bookings for those campgrounds that accept reservations. Yosemite Concession Services (☎ 559-252-4848, fax 456-0542, 🖳 www.yosemitepark.com), 5410 East Home, Fresno, CA 93727, handles reservations for all lodging including tent cabins and High Sierra Camps (☎ 559-253-5674). See Nearest Towns & Facilities later in this section for campground and lodging details.

Permits & Regulations

The park entrance fee, valid for seven days, is $20 per vehicle or $10 per person for cyclists, walk-ins and bus passengers. An annual pass costs $40.

Free wilderness permits are required for all overnight backcountry trips, but not for day hikes. First-come, first-served permits are available from these permit stations: the Wilderness Center (next to the Ansel Adams Gallery) in Yosemite Valley; Wawona; Big Oak Flat; Hetch Hetchy; and the building in the parking lot in Tuolumne Meadows, east of the river along the south side of Tioga Rd and opposite Lembert Dome. Call the park or ask at any visitor center to verify when each permit station is open.

Permits are also available by reservation ($5 reservation fee per person, payable to the Yosemite Association; credit cards accepted) from six months to two days in advance of an entry date. Reservations are recommended for popular trailheads from May to September; contact Wilderness Permits (☎ 209-372-0740), PO Box 545, Yosemite, CA 95389. Wilderness permit reservation procedures were expected to change in 2000, but this information was not available at the time of writing.

GETTING THERE & AWAY

Yosemite National Park is six hours from Los Angeles and three-and-a-half hours from San Francisco by car. There are regional airports in Fresno (90mi from South Entrance) and Merced (73mi from Arch Rock Entrance).

VIA Adventures (☎ 209-384-1315, 800-369-7275) operates the Yosemite Gray Line deluxe bus service from Merced and Fresno to Yosemite Lodge and the Yosemite Valley visitor center. Several daily roundtrip buses depart from Merced's Greyhound bus terminal, Transpo and the Amtrak train station. The one-way/roundtrip Merced fares are $20/38 and include the $10 park entrance fee.

One daily bus departs Fresno's Amtrak station at 1:50 pm and airport at 2:15 pm, arriving in Yosemite Valley at 4:45 pm. Another daily bus departs the valley at 9 am for Fresno. The one-way/roundtrip Fresno fares are $25/48 and include the park entrance fee.

Amtrak (☎ 800-872-7245) serves Merced from Emeryville, across the bay from San Francisco; Fresno; and Bakersfield in southern California.

NEAREST TOWNS & FACILITIES
In Yosemite Valley

The Yosemite Valley visitor center and the nearby wilderness center provide information.

Places to Stay & Eat Wilderness permit holders are allowed to camp in the *Back-packers' Walk-in Camp* from April to October on the night before the permit entry date and the night of the permit exit date. Sites ($3 per person) are available on a first-come, first-served basis. Intentionally not marked on park maps, it is along the north bank of Tenaya Creek behind North Pines campground. See the Yosemite Valley map.

At the valley's west end is the usually crowded first-come, first-served *Sunnyside Walk-in campground* ($3 per person). Reservations are necessary at *North Pines*, *Upper Pines*, and *Lower Pines* campgrounds ($15) at the valley's eastern end.

Valley lodging ranges from *Housekeeping Camp* ($42.75), *Curry Village* ($39.75 tent cabin, $57.25/74.75 cabin without/with bath,

continued on page 366

YOSEMITE VALLEY – TWO CLASSIC HIKES

Yosemite Valley is the hub of activity in Yosemite National Park – although for most visitors this activity does not stretch beyond the immediate confines of the valley and its major attractions. Of the many hikes and climbs possible within Yosemite Valley, the two short routes described here can provide an excellent sampling of this fascinating place including two of its most famous features, Half Dome and Yosemite Falls.

For hikers with limited time, each can be done as a long day hike, although two days will make for a more pleasant experience.

Half Dome

Duration	2 days
Distance	17mi (27.4km)
Standard	hard
Start/Finish	Happy Isles, Yosemite Valley
Nearest Facilities	Yosemite Valley
Public Transport	yes

Summary It is an awesome hike to the summit of this world-famous granite dome towering above Yosemite Valley. If you only do one hike, make it this one.

Rising more than 4800ft above the eastern end of Yosemite Valley, the granite monolith of Half Dome (8842ft) has awed visitors since the park's inception. Its 2000ft vertical north face has attracted climbers from around the globe since the first ascent (of the northeast face) in 1875 by George Anderson, a Scottish sailor and gold prospector who worked as a valley blacksmith. Hikers, too, covet this imposing landmark. An 8½mi trail from Yosemite Valley past two dramatic waterfalls culminates in 360-degree panoramic views.

The rigorous hike is most enjoyable as a two-day trip, although fit hikers can attempt it as a demanding 10 to 12 hour day hike. Day hikers need to start by 6 am or 7 am in order to return by dark; carrying a flashlight is recommended.

WARNING

- No reliable drinking-water source exists above the Merced River at Little Yosemite Valley. To avoid dehydration, drink up before going above this point and carry at least one quart for a day hike and three quarts if camping on the northeast shoulder. Heed this warning – people have fainted while on the cables.
- Lightning strikes on Half Dome have been recorded during every month of the year, so do not proceed above the dome's northeast shoulder when storm clouds are visible on the horizon.

PLANNING

Hiking to the top of Half Dome is only allowed when the cable route to the summit is open. Depending upon snow conditions, the NPS puts up the cables in June and takes them down in mid-October.

Maps

The USGS 1:24,000 *Half Dome* and *Yosemite Falls* quadrangles, and 1:62,500 *Yosemite* quadrangle cover the trail.

GETTING TO/FROM THE HIKE

The trailhead is Happy Isles, near the south end of Upper Pines campground in Yosemite Valley, which is shuttle bus stop 16.

THE HIKE
Day 1: Happy Isles to Northeast Shoulder

4–5 hours, 8mi (12.9km), 3600ft (1080m) ascent

From Happy Isles (4035ft), ascend the paved pathway for 400ft to Vernal Fall bridge. Just beyond the bridge, turn right, staying on the John Muir Trail; the Mist Trail continues straight to Vernal Fall. Follow gentle switchbacks for about 2mi up to Nevada Fall (5907ft) and cross the bridge over the Merced River. Continue over a low rise and reach level **Little Yosemite Valley** where many people *camp* to avoid carrying their

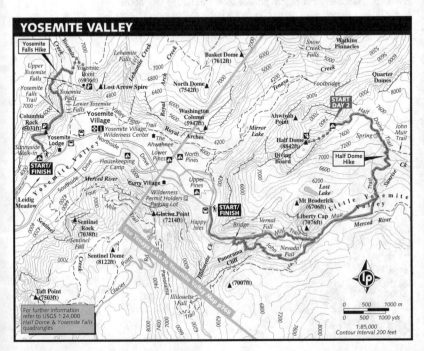

backpacks higher. At the east end of Little Yosemite Valley, the Merced Lake Trail heads east (right) along Merced River. Stay on the John Muir Trail, which turns north (left) and climbs steeply through forest for 1.3mi to the Half Dome Trail junction.

Turn west (left) onto the Half Dome Trail, where a signpost reads 2mi to Half Dome. A short distance beyond the junction on the left side of the trail is a seasonal spring. Continue up through forest, then up switchbacks to the northeast shoulder (7600ft). While a bear-free night is almost guaranteed, hang your food on the wire cable at all times to dissuade other hungry critters at this lightly-used and very pleasant *campsite* with spectacular views.

Side Trip: Half Dome Summit

1¾–3 hours, 1mi (1.61km), 1242ft (373m) ascent/descent

Backpackers who camp on the northeast shoulder can visit the top of Half Dome in the late afternoon for sunset and again the next morning for exquisite solitude when the top is all but deserted. However, the exposed route above the campsite keeps some hikers from going beyond this point.

A rocky trail snakes 650ft up two dozen switchbacks in 30 minutes to the top of the dome's shoulder and the base of the cables. From here, notch steel cables bolted to the granite provide handholds, and intermittent wooden cross-boards provide footholds for the final 600ft ascent up an exposed, 45-degree rock face. Grab a pair of gloves from the pile at the base (to protect your hands from the steel cables). A trip up uncrowded cables takes about 15 minutes, but on crowded cables or if intimidated it may take 30 minutes or longer.

From the relatively flat five-acre expanse on top, enjoy the amazing views of Yosemite Valley – especially from the overhanging northwest point – Mt Starr King, Cloud's Rest (9926ft), the Cathedral peaks, Unicorn Peak and the Sierra crest. Most people spend 30 minutes to an hour on top. Watch the time carefully to avoid having to descend in the dark.

NEIL WILSON

Left: A hiker on the trail to Half Dome, with Vernal Fall in the background, Yosemite Valley, California.

The Legend of Tisse'yak

Tisse'yak and her husband arrived in Yosemite Valley after a long journey across the mountains. Tisse'yak had carried a heavy conical basket, but her husband had only a light load. Tisse'yak arrived first and thirstily drank from Lake Awai'a (Mirror Lake), draining it dry. Her husband, angry that no water was left for him to drink, beat his wife. She became enraged and flung her basket at him. As they stood in anger, facing each other, they were transformed into stone for their wickedness. He is North Dome, the basket is Basket Dome, and she is Half Dome *(below)*, whose face is stained black from tears.

TOM DOWNS

Camping on top of Half Dome is prohibited for three reasons: to protect the habitat of the Mt Lyell salamander that was disturbed by people moving rocks to build wind shelters; to reduce human waste left on top; and to protect the last remaining tree – six of the summit's seven trees were illegally cut for campfires. Respect the camping ban and protect this fragile ecosystem.

Day 2: Northeast Shoulder to Happy Isles
4 hours, 8mi (12.9km), 3600ft (1080m) descent

Retrace your steps to Little Yosemite Valley. At the northeast brink of the 594ft Nevada Fall, turn right onto the Mist Trail just before the bridge and descend the 500-step rock staircase alongside **Nevada**

Fall. Cross the bridge above the vertical, 317ft **Vernal Fall** and continue to the fall on a more gentle trail. Descend another short rock staircase and follow the paved pathway from the Vernal Fall bridge back to Happy Isles.

Yosemite Falls

Duration	6–8 hours
Distance	7.2mi
Standard	medium–hard
Start/Finish	Sunnyside Walk-in, Yosemite Valley
Nearest Facilities	Yosemite Valley
Public Transport	yes

Summary The classic hike to the top of Yosemite's most extraordinary waterfall offers a close-up experience of the valley's sheer vertical wonder.

Cho'lok, or Yosemite Falls, plunges 2425ft in three cascades – the upper fall is 1430ft, the middle 675ft, and the lower 320ft – creating the world's fifth-highest free-leaping waterfall. An excellent 7.2mi roundtrip trail leads from the valley floor to its rim, but the stiff climb of 2610ft and equivalent descent makes this a particularly strenuous six- to eight-hour day hike.

PLANNING
When to Hike
This south-facing trail is free from snow earlier in the season than other trails to the valley rim, making it a desirable hike in May and June when the falls are most powerful. By August they can be just a trickle by comparison.

Maps
The USGS 1:24,000 *Half Dome* and *Yosemite Falls* quadrangles, and 1:62,500 *Yosemite* and *Hetch Hetchy Reservoir* quadrangles cover the hike.

GETTING TO/FROM THE HIKE
The nearest Yosemite Valley shuttle bus stops are Nos 7 (Lower Yosemite Falls) and 8 (Yosemite Lodge), from where a very short walk leads to the trailhead.

THE HIKE
From the east side of Sunnyside Walk-in campground (3990ft), go up-slope for a minute to the north-side Valley Floor Trail. Head west for a minute to the start of the Yosemite Falls Trail. The trail immediately ascends four dozen short switchbacks, climbing steeply up a talus slope through gold-cup oak. After three-quarters of a mile, the trail becomes more gradual and switchbacks east to reach **Columbia Rock** – a viewpoint of the valley floor 1000ft below and of Half Dome and Quarter Dome to the east – a mile from the trailhead.

After another 0.4mi the trail approaches Lower Yosemite Falls, beyond which are a few more switchbacks. The trail then traverses northeast and bends north for views of the upper fall. The switchbacks resume and lead steadily up a rocky cleft in the cliffs to the valley rim.

The trail tops out 3mi from the trailhead and bends east. Bearing right at the Eagle Peak Trail junction, the trail leads downhill to the bank of **Yosemite Creek** and the nearby brink of upper Yosemite Falls. At the broad crest are overused *campsites* in a forested area surrounding the creek. Follow the trail back to the valley.

Side Trip: Yosemite Point
1 hour, 1½mi (2.4km)

From the bridge over Yosemite Creek, a trail climbs three-quarters of a mile first north, then east up switchbacks, then south to the valley rim and **Yosemite Point** (6936ft), a fenced viewpoint. Here are spectacular views of Cloud's Rest, Half Dome, Glacier Point, Cathedral Rocks and a close-up view of **Lost Arrow Spire**.

Right: Upper Yosemite Falls, Yosemite Valley, California.

RICHARD I'ANSON

continued from page 359

$91.25 standard room) and *Yosemite Lodge* ($91.25 standard room, $114.75 lodge room), to the elegant *The Ahwahnee* (starting from $265.50). Showers are available ($2) at Housekeeping Camp and Curry Village.

Yosemite Village has three *restaurants* and a store with every imaginable item including groceries and hiking gear. Curry Village has a *cafeteria*, *snack stands* and a small grocery store. Yosemite Lodge has a *cafeteria*, two *restaurants* and a *bar* that offers snack service. A trip to the *Ahwahnee dining room* is unforgettable – but expensive and formal.

Getting There & Away Three park entrances on the western side of the Sierra lead to the valley: South Entrance on Hwy 41 (Wawona Rd) north of Fresno, convenient from southern California; Arch Rock Entrance on Hwy 140 (El Portal Rd) east of Merced, convenient from northern California; and Big Oak Flat Entrance on Hwy 120 (Big Oak Flat Rd) east of Manteca, also convenient from northern California. Gasoline is not available in Yosemite Valley.

Backpackers starting from Yosemite Valley park their vehicles in the Wilderness Permit Holders parking lot south of Curry Village near Upper Pines campground.

Getting Around The free Yosemite Valley shuttle bus stops at 19 consecutively numbered valley locations at 20-minute intervals every day.

Along Tioga Rd (Hwy 120)

There is an information station at Big Oak Flat Entrance on Hwy 120 and a visitor center in Tuolumne Meadows.

Places to Stay & Eat *Walk-in sites* ($3 per person) are available for backpackers on a first-come, first-served basis from June to September behind Tuolumne Meadows campground. Other first-come, first served campgrounds along the 39mi of Tioga Rd between Crane Flat and Tuolumne Meadows are *Tamarack Flat* ($6, 6315ft), *White Wolf* ($10, 8000ft), *Yosemite Creek* ($6,

7659ft) and *Porcupine Flat* ($6, 8100ft). Reservations are recommended at *Hodgdon Meadow* (4872ft), *Crane Flat* (6191ft) or *Tuolumne Meadows* (8600ft) campgrounds (all $15). All campgrounds are open only July to early September, except the year-round *Hodgdon Meadow*.

Tuolumne Meadows Lodge ($46) and *White Wolf Lodge* ($42) are summer-only canvas tent-cabins where everything is provided except sleeping sheets or bags. Both lodges serve simple, family-style meals and have public showers ($2).

Adjacent to Tuolumne Meadows campground is the *Meadow Grill* and a well-stocked grocery store geared towards backpackers. There is another grocery store at Crane Flat.

Getting There & Away East–west Hwy 120/Tioga Rd (closed in winter) is the only road to bisect the park and give access to Tuolumne Meadows. Visitors enter via Big Oak Flat Entrance east of Manteca off US 99 from the western Sierra or via Tioga Pass Entrance (9945ft), 8mi east of Tuolumne Meadows, from the eastern Sierra at Lee Vining.

In Tuolumne Meadows, the backpackers' parking lot at the wilderness permit station is along the paved road to Tuolumne Meadows Lodge that turns south off Hwy 120 east of the river near Lembert Dome.

Getting Around The Tuolumne Meadows Tour and Hikers' Bus plies the 56mi route between Yosemite Valley and Tuolumne Meadows from mid-July to early September. The bus departs Yosemite Valley once daily (Curry Village at 8:20 am, Yosemite Village at 8:25 am and Yosemite Lodge at 8:45 am), stops along Hwy 120 at Crane Flat, White Wolf, Yosemite Creek junction, May Lake junction and Tenaya Lake, and arrives at Tuolumne Meadows Lodge at 10:55 am. The daily return bus departs Tuolumne Meadows Lodge at 2:35 pm, returning to Curry Village at 4:30 pm. Hikers can flag down the bus at any trailhead along the route. Depending where you get on or off, one-way fares range from $2 to $14 and roundtrip fares from $9 to $22.

A free shuttle bus plies Tioga Rd between Tenaya Lake and Tioga Pass during summer.

Wawona

On Hwy 41 north of South Entrance is Wawona, with a seasonal information station (take Chilnualna Falls Rd to the first right turn after the stables), *Wawona campground* ($15, 4000ft) and European-style *Wawona Hotel* ($94/120.75 without/with bathroom) with a *restaurant* and nearby store.

Other Camping

In the backcountry of northern Yosemite are five enormously popular **High Sierra Camps** – dormitory-style canvas cabins ($45 including two meals) with beds, shower facilities and a central dining tent. Guests hike in and provide their own sleeping sheet or bag. The camps, all within a day's hike of one another, are *Glen Aulin*, *May Lake*, *Sunrise*, *Merced Lake* and *Vogelsang*. Reservations (☎ 559-253-5674) are mandatory and applications for a reservation lottery, held in mid-December, are accepted only between October 15 and November 30 for the following year.

There are eight USFS campgrounds outside the park along the 12mi of Hwy 120 between Tioga Pass and US 395, and the 2mi of Saddlebag Lake Rd. Those nearest to the park are *Tioga Lake* and *Ellery Lake*.

Tenaya Lake to Yosemite Valley

Duration	3 days
Distance	17.4mi (28km)
Standard	medium
Start	Hwy 120, Tenaya Lake
Finish	Happy Isles, Yosemite valley
Nearest Facilities	Tuolumne Meadows, Yosemite Valley
Public Transport	yes
Summary Traversing Yosemite's biggest chunk of granite, Clouds Rest, this mostly downhill hike is the most scenic approach to Yosemite Valley.	

Clouds Rest (9926ft), the largest granite expanse in Yosemite, rises 4500ft above Tenaya

Creek with spectacular views from the summit and along the trail. This generally downhill hike is perhaps the most scenic approach to Yosemite Valley from Tioga Rd, and can be combined with a trip to the top of Half Dome for an outstanding tour of Yosemite granite.

PLANNING
When to Hike

As its name implies, clouds often settle on Clouds Rest. Hikers should visit the summit only in clear weather.

Maps

The USGS 1:24,000 *Tenaya Lake*, *Yosemite Falls* and *Half Dome* quadrangles, and 1:62,500 *Tuolumne Meadows*, *Hetch Hetchy Reservoir* and *Yosemite* quadrangles cover the hike.

GETTING TO/FROM THE HIKE
To the Start

Tenaya Lake, west of Tuolumne Meadows on Tioga Rd/Hwy 120, is accessible by the Tuolumne Meadows Tour and Hikers' Bus (see Along Tioga Rd in Nearest Towns & Facilities).

From the Finish

Happy Isles, Yosemite Valley shuttle bus stop 16, is at the south end of Yosemite Valley's Upper Pines campground.

THE HIKE
Day 1: Tenaya Lake to Sunrise Lakes

3–4 hours, 4mi (6.4km), 1100ft (330m) ascent

The trail from the picnic area (8150ft) at the Tenaya Lake's west end crosses the lake's outlet and follows it southwest for less than a half-mile, then turns south, rising through meadow and forest to cross the outlet streams from Sunrise Lakes. The trail switchbacks up to a ridge and a junction with a trail that leads to *Sunrise High Sierra Camp* (see Other Camping under Nearest Towns & Facilities). Turn left onto this trail and go about a half-mile to the first of the Sunrise Lakes (9166ft), with secluded, peaceful *campsites*.

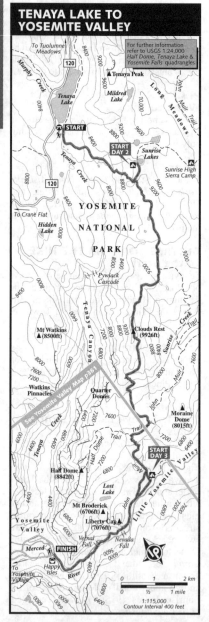

TENAYA LAKE TO YOSEMITE VALLEY

For further information refer to USGS 1:24,000 *Half Dome, Tenaya Lake & Yosemite Falls* quadrangles

Day 2: Sunrise Lakes to Little Yosemite Valley

4½–5 hours, 9mi (14.5km), 1100ft (330m) ascent, 4000ft (1200m) descent

Return to the junction and turn left, descending south towards Sunrise Creek. The trail passes a seasonal pond and crosses a small feeder of Tenaya Creek, then rises in about two-thirds of a mile to a junction (9100ft). Here the trail to Clouds Rest goes straight, while the trail to the left descends to Sunrise Creek where it meets the John Muir Trail. Continue for 1.3mi to Clouds Rest, then descend for about 5½mi to **Little Yosemite Valley** (6100ft), joining the John Muir Trail on the way, and meeting the trail coming from Half Dome 1.3mi above Little Yosemite Valley. Two-story, solar-composting latrines testify to this *campsite*'s popularity.

Day 3: Little Yosemite Valley to Happy Isles

2–2½ hours, 4.4mi (7km), 2065ft (620m) descent

See Day 2 of the Half Dome hike for a description of the route from Little Yosemite Valley to Happy Isles.

Cathedral Lakes

Duration	4–5 hours
Distance	7.6mi (12.2km)
Standard	easy-medium
Start/Finish	Hwy 120, Tuolumne Meadows
Nearest Facilities	Tuolumne Meadows
Public Transport	yes

Summary These gem-like lakes beneath the unique, white granite spires and fins of the Cathedral Range invite day hikers to picnic, swim or contemplate the peaks' reflections on the water.

The Cathedral Range runs northwest from the main Sierra crest, separating the Tuolumne and Merced Rivers. The striking granite pinnacles and cockscombs of the range give it a unique beauty, and the many lakes, streams and meadows among the high forests endow the range with a truly park-like atmosphere. Cathedral Lakes offers fine swimming. Camping is possible, but serious bear problems make a visit to the lakes more enjoyable as a four- to five-hour, 7.6mi roundtrip day hike.

PLANNING
Maps
The USGS 1:24,000 *Tenaya Lake* and 1:62,500 *Tuolumne Meadows* quadrangles cover the hike.

GETTING TO/FROM THE HIKE
The hike starts from a parking area on the south side of Hwy 120, 1.7mi west of Tuolumne Meadows visitor center. The Tuolumne Meadows Tour and Hikers' Bus passes the trailhead.

THE HIKE
Joining the John Muir Trail about 500ft from the trailhead, the trail rises steadily southwest, moving away from Budd Creek. It descends slightly, with views of Unicorn Peak, and crosses Cathedral Creek. Follow the trail as it ascends past a spring and skirts the west side of Cathedral Peak, reaching a junction after about 2¾mi. The right fork

leads after about a half-mile to Lower Cathedral Lake (9288ft), while the main John Muir Trail goes south for slightly more than a mile – passing Upper Cathedral Lake (9585ft), which beautifully reflects Cathedral Peak (10,940ft) – to **Cathedral Pass** (9700ft), with fine views of the peaks of the Cathedral Range including Tressider Peak, Echo Peaks and Matthes Crest. The are *campsites* at both the upper and lower lake. From the high point, return to Hwy 120 along the same trail.

Lyell Canyon

Duration	2 days
Distance	17.6mi (28.3km)
Standard	easy-medium
Start/Finish	Hwy 120, Tuolumne Meadows
Nearest Facilities	Tuolumne Meadows
Public Transport	yes

Summary Following the Lyell Fork Tuolumne River, this level segment of the John Muir Trail meanders through quintessential subalpine meadows and forest to the base of Mt Lyell, Yosemite's highest peak, from where an ascent is possible.

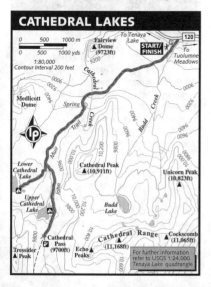

CATHEDRAL LAKES

The John Muir Trail along the Lyell Fork Tuolumne River is surely the most level stretch of trail anywhere in the Sierra Nevada, gaining only 200ft over 8mi. Strolling the lovely forested meadows along the winding Lyell Fork beneath the Sierra crest is an unforgettably scenic hike that also offers experienced hikers an opportunity to ascend Mt Lyell.

PLANNING
What to Bring
Bear-resistant canisters for food storage are recommended for this area as the counterbalance method (see the boxed text on page 87) is no longer effective.

Maps
The USGS 1:24,000 *Vogelsang Peak* and 1:62,500 *Tuolumne Meadows* quadrangles cover the hike. The USGS 1:24,000 *Mt Lyell*

and 1:62,500 *Merced Peak* quadrangles cover the optional side trip to Mt Lyell.

GETTING TO/FROM THE HIKE

The trailhead is near the backpackers' parking lot in Tuolumne Meadows. The Tuolumne Meadows Tour and Hikers' Bus links the trailhead to Yosemite Valley.

THE HIKE
Day 1: Tuolumne Meadows to Lyell Base Camp
5–6 hours, 8.8mi (14.2km)
The trail parallels the road to Tuolumne Meadows Lodge for a short distance, then turns south and follows the Lyell Fork Tuolumne River. The trail crosses it and heads south for about a half-mile to a set of bridges over the Lyell Fork Tuolumne River. Across the river, the route meets, and turns left onto, the John Muir Trail. Soon the trail crosses Rafferty Creek and turns southeast into Lyell Canyon, traversing the river's meadow-lined south bank. Passing the trail to Ireland and Evelyn Lakes and Tuolumne Pass, about 4mi from the trailhead, the trail crosses Ireland Creek, passes beneath Potter Point and continues to *Lyell Base Camp* (10,240ft) on a forested bench at the base of the John Muir Trail's climb to Donohue Pass.

Bubbly in the Back Country

No trip to Tuolumne is complete without a sip of the naturally carbonated mineral water issuing forth from Soda Springs in the heart of the Sierra's largest subalpine meadows. First described in 1863 by William H Brewer of the California Geological Survey as 'pungent and delightful to the taste,' these bubbly founts continue to delight and amaze travelers.

Bring your own cup to dip from the several pools inside a split-rail enclosure near McCauley Cabin, an early residence now used by the NPS, and Parsons Memorial Lodge, built by the Sierra Club in 1914. The level, 1.5mi stroll from the unpaved parking lot near Lembert Dome takes less than an hour.

Side Trip: Mt Lyell
5–7 hours
Mt Lyell (13,114ft), named for British geologist Sir Charles Lyell and first climbed in 1871, is Yosemite's highest peak. The easiest and most popular route is Class 2 to Class 3 (see Levels of Difficulty in the Facts for the Hiker chapter) over the north glacier and the north face, but requires prudence. The difficulty varies with snow conditions, and a rope should be carried for safety.

From Lyell Base Camp, head southeast across the upper basin, crossing talus and the west end of the Lyell Glacier to the saddle between Mts Lyell and Maclure. From here, sloping Class 2 ledges above the glacier lead toward the summit. A short, steep Class 3 crack with some exposure is the crux. Allow three to four hours for the ascent and two to three hours for the descent.

Day 2: Lyell Base Camp to Tuolumne Meadows
5 hours, 8.8mi (14.2km)
Follow the John Muir Trail along the Lyell Fork back to the trailhead.

Mt Dana

Duration	6–7 hours
Distance	5.8mi (9.3km)
Standard	hard
Start/Finish	Hwy 120, Tioga Pass
Nearest Facilities	Tuolumne Meadows
Public Transport	yes

Summary Experience unrivaled views of the Yosemite high country and distinctive Mono Lake from the rocky summit of Yosemite's second-highest peak, Mt Dana, on a short, but steep, classic day hike.

Mt Dana (13,053ft) is Yosemite's second-highest peak, named for American geologist Charles Dwight Dana. Only 5.8mi round-trip, but more than 3100 vertical feet above Tioga Pass (9945ft), this strenuous six- to seven-hour hike offers unrivaled views of Mono Lake, the Grand Canyon of the Tuolumne River and the rest of the Yosemite high country.

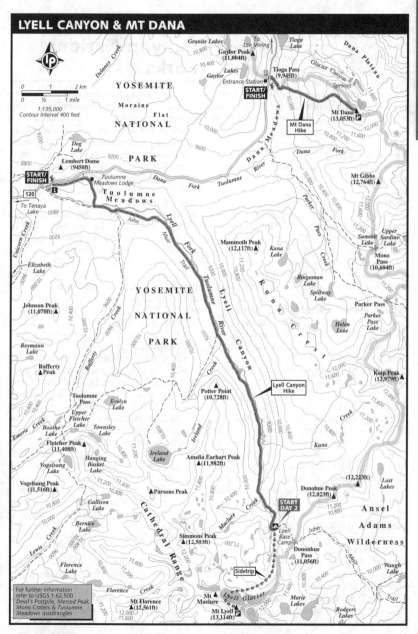

LYELL CANYON & MT DANA

0   1   2 km
0   ½   1 mile
1:135,000
Contour Interval 400 feet

YOSEMITE

Moraine

Flat

NATIONAL

PARK

Granite Lakes
10,800

To Lee Vining

Tioga Lake

Dana Plateau

Gaylor Peak
(11,004ft)

Tioga Pass
(9,945ft)

Glacier Canyon

Springs

Lakes
Gaylor

Entrance Station

START/FINISH

Mt Dana
Hike

Mt Dana
(13,053ft)

Dana Fork

Mt Gibbs
(12,764ft)

Dana Meadows

Delaney Creek

Dog Lake

Lembert Dome
(9450ft)

START/FINISH

120

To Tenaya Lake

Tuolumne Meadows Lodge

Tuolumne Meadows

Dana Fork
Tuolumne

Dana River

Parker Pass

Summit Lake

Upper Sardine Lake

Mono Pass
(10,604ft)

Unicorn Creek

Elizabeth Lake

Johnson Peak
(11,070ft)

John

Muir

Trail

Lyell

Fork

Tuolumne River

Mammoth Peak
(12,117ft)

Kuna Lake

Bingaman Lake

Spillway Lake

Helen Lake

Parker Pass Lake

YOSEMITE

NATIONAL

PARK

Reymann Lake

Rafferty Peak

Rafferty

Creek

Kuna Crest

Koip Peak
(12,979ft)

Tuolumne Pass

Evelyn Lake

Potter Point
(10,728ft)

Lyell Canyon Hike

Upper Fletcher Lake

Boothe Lake

Townsley Lake

Ireland Lake

Lyell River

Lyell Canyon

Creek

Kuna

Fletcher Peak
(11,408ft)

Vogelsang Lake

Hanging Basket Lake

Ireland

Amelia Earhart Peak
(11,982ft)

(12,223ft)

Lost Lakes

Vogelsang Peak
(11,516ft)

Gallison Lake

Parsons Peak

Donohue Peak
(12,023ft)

START
DAY 2

Ansel

Adams

Bernice Lake

Cathedral Range

Simmons Peak
(12,503ft)

Maclure

Creek

Lyell Base Camp

John

Dononhue Pass
(11,056ft)

Wilderness

Lewis Creek

Florence Lake

Emeric Creek

Sidetrip

Mt Maclure

Lyell Glacier

Marie Lakes

Muir

Waugh Lake

Trail

For further information
refer to USGS 1:62,500
Devil's Postpile, Merced Peak,
Mono Craters & Tuolumne
Meadows quadrangles

Florence Creek

Mt Florence
(12,561ft)

Mt Lyell
(13,114ft)

Rodgers Lakes

PLANNING

When to Hike

Snow may block the trail early in summer. The summit is always windy and often draws afternoon clouds, so start in the morning and carry a jacket. Do not attempt the hike if a storm threatens. In July beautiful, deep blue-violet flower clusters of sky pilot, with its sweet musky fragrance, bloom near the summit.

What to Bring

No water is available, so carry at least two quarts, along with lunch.

Maps

The USGS 1:24,000 *Tioga Pass* and *Mt Dana* quadrangles, and 1:62,500 *Tuolumne Meadows* and *Mono Craters* quadrangles best show the hike. A smaller-scale map (see Maps & Books under Information at the beginning of this section) will help to identify the peaks visible from the summit.

GETTING TO/FROM THE HIKE

The trail begins at Tioga Pass Entrance on Hwy 120, 8mi northeast of Tuolumne Meadows and 12mi west of Lee Vining. Parking areas are on either side of the entrance. The Tuolumne Meadows Tour and Hikers' Bus goes to the trailhead.

THE HIKE

The unsigned trailhead is on the east side of Tioga Pass. The trail heads east, passing between two broad, shallow pools, then begins ascending. The angle soon steepens and the trail passes through flower-filled meadows about half way up the 1700ft climb to a west-descending ridge – marked by a large, loose cairn – 1.8mi from Tioga Pass. From this cairn, several indistinct paths head up the rocky (Class 1) western slope to the summit, still 1.1mi and 1400 vertical feet away. Avoid the left-most path, through difficult talus blocks along the northwest ridge, in favor of paths to the right that offer easier footing. The views from **Mt Dana's summit** are so outstanding that some hikers spend the night on top where there are two small rock *windbreaks*.

Sequoia & Kings Canyon National Parks

Isolated groves of sequoia and deep granite gorges characterize Sequoia and Kings Canyon National Parks, adjacent to Yosemite but with their own unique character. These parks cover almost 1350 sq miles and showcase the splendor of the southern Sierra Nevada, offering limitless day hiking and backpacking opportunities.

The towering granite peaks of the Great Western Divide, a southern branch of the Sierra Nevada, bisect Sequoia National Park. To its west are the canyons created by four forks of the Kaweah River – the Marble, Middle, East and South. To its east is the north–south flowing Kern River, which descends from Forester Pass and the lofty peaks on the Kings-Kern Divide. The vast canyon created by the Kern River separates the Great Western Divide from the Sierra Nevada crest, which forms the park's eastern boundary and is crowned by glorious Mt Whitney.

Kings Canyon National Park consists of two discontiguous segments: a small, finger-like protrusion centered around Grant Grove (abutting its south end Sequoia National Park); and the vast Kings Canyon high country adjacent to the northern boundary of Sequoia National Park. Kings Canyon is the wildest and most rugged part of the Sierra Nevada, where the Middle and South Fork Kings Rivers, separated by the Monarch Divide, descend from the High Sierra to form the Kings River. The canyon through which the river flows, first cut by streams and enlarged by glaciers, is among the deepest in the USA, reaching a depth of 7891 ft from the summit of Spanish Mountain (10,051 ft) to the river.

Roads penetrate a tiny fraction of both parks only from the western side of the Sierra. No trans-Sierra roads cross either park, and access to the parks from the eastern Sierra is by foot only (see the Eastern Sierra section later in this chapter).

SEQUOIA & KINGS CANYON NATIONAL PARKS

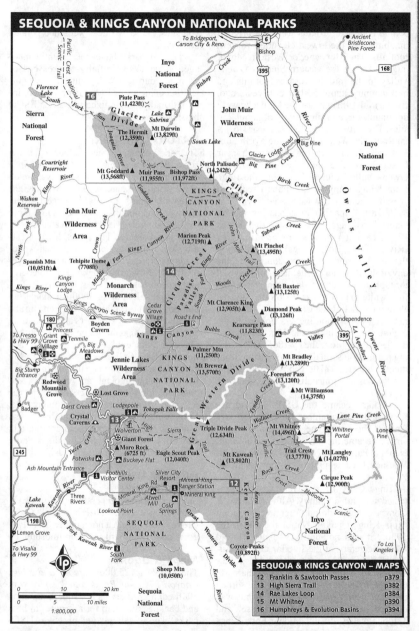

To Bridgeport,
Carson City & Reno

Bishop

Ancient
Bristlecone
Pine Forest

Inyo
National
Forest

Pacific Crest National Scenic Trail

Florence
Lake
South

Sierra
National
Forest

Piute Pass
(11,423ft)

Lake
Sabrina

Glacier Divide

The Hermit
(12,359ft)

Mt Darwin
(13,829ft)

South
Lake

John Muir
Wilderness
Area

Glacier Lodge Road

Big Pine

Inyo
National
Forest

Courtright
Reservoir

Mt Goddard
(13,568ft)

Muir Pass
(11,955ft)

Bishop Pass
(11,972ft)

North Palisade
(14,242ft)

Big Pine Creek

Birch Creek

Owens Valley

Wishon
Reservoir

John Muir
Wilderness
Area

KINGS
CANYON
NATIONAL
PARK

Marion Peak
(12,719ft)

Taboose Creek

Mt Pinchot
(13,495ft)

Spanish Mtn
(10,051ft)

Tehipite Dome
(7708ft)

Monarch
Wilderness
Area

Cedar
Grove
Village

Paradise Valley

Mt Clarence King
(12,905ft)

Woods Creek

Sawmill Creek

Mt Baxter
(13,125ft)

Diamond Peak
(13,126ft)

Kings
Canyon
Lodge

Boyden
Cavern

Kings Canyon Scenic Byway

Road's End

Kings Canyon

Bubbs Creek

Kearsarge Pass
(11,823ft)

Independence

Onion Valley

Princess

Grant
Grove
Village

Tenmile

Big
Meadows

Jennie Lakes
Wilderness
Area

Palmer Mtn
(11,250ft)

Mt Brewer
(13,570ft)

KINGS
CANYON
NATIONAL
PARK

Mt Bradley
(13,289ft)

Forester Pass
(13,120ft)

Big Stump
Entrance

Redwood
Mountain
Grove

Lost Grove

Mt Williamson
(14,375ft)

Badger

Dorst Creek

Lodgepole

Tokopah Falls

Tyndall Creek

Wallace Creek

Lone Pine Creek

Crystal
Caverns

Wolverton

High Sierra Trail

Triple Divide Peak
(12,634ft)

Mt Whitney
(14,496ft)

Whitney
Portal

Lone
Pine

Giant Forest

Moro Rock
(6725 ft)

Eagle Scout Peak
(12,040ft)

Trail Crest
(13,777ft)

Mt Langley
(14,027ft)

Buckeye Flat

Mt Kaweah
(13,802ft)

Cirque Peak
(12,900ft)

Potwisha

Foothills
Visitor Center

Ash Mountain Entrance

Silver City
Resort

Mineral King
Ranger Station

Three
Rivers

Mineral King Rd

Atwell
Mill

Mineral King

Lake
Kaweah

Lookout Point

Cold
Springs

Lemon Grove

SEQUOIA
NATIONAL
PARK

Coyote Peaks
(10,892ft)

Inyo
National
Forest

To Los
Angeles

To Visalia
& Hwy 99

South Fork Kaweah River

South
Fork

Sheep Mtn
(10,050ft)

Sequoia
National
Forest

| 0 | 10 | 20 km |
| 0 | 5 | 10 miles |

1:800,000

SEQUOIA & KINGS CANYON – MAPS

12	Franklin & Sawtooth Passes	p379
13	High Sierra Trail	p382
14	Rae Lakes Loop	p384
15	Mt Whitney	p390
16	Humphreys & Evolution Basins	p394

HISTORY

Native American Yokuts were the original inhabitants of the lowest-elevation western foothills. The Monache, or Western Mono, migrated from the eastern Sierra's Owens Valley to the middle western foothills and high country about 500 or 600 years ago. By the mid-19th century, the Monache were dominant, three groups living at about 250 sites. The Potwisha group lived near Hospital Rock, the Wuksachi near the North Fork Kaweah River, and the Wobonuch near Grant Grove. The Monache traded with the Owens Valley Piutes, following the route from Kings Canyon up Bubbs Creek and crossing the Sierra at Kearsarge Pass.

In 1805, Spanish missionaries led by Gabriel Moraga discovered the Kings River, calling it *Río de los Santos Reyes* (River of the Holy Kings), an indication that they camped there on January 6, the day of the Epiphany. Jedediah Smith passed through in 1827 on a failed attempt to be the first white man to cross the Sierra Nevada. With the onset of the California Gold Rush, ranchers, miners and loggers flocked to the region, settling it in the mid-19th century and displacing the Monache by 1865. The growing population soon devastated the environment and by the 1870s a conservation effort led by Visalia journalist George Stewart began.

Sequoia became the USA's second national park on September 25, 1890. Six days later, at the same time as Yosemite, Grant Grove became the 4-sq-mile General Grant National Park. In 1926, Kern Canyon and Mt Whitney became part of Sequoia National Park.

Kings Canyon, however, was not protected for half a century. Although the US Congress considered creating a John Muir–Kings Canyon National Park in the 1930s, it was not until 1940 that Harold Ickes, Secretary of the Interior under President Franklin Roosevelt, succeeded in persuading the Congress to establish the park. Grant Grove National Park was absorbed into the new park, but Muir's name was omitted – as were Kings Canyon itself and Tehipite Valley on the Middle Fork Kings River, which were viewed as potential reservoir sites. These two areas were incorporated in 1965.

The two parks have been jointly managed since 1943, initially for reasons of economy during WWII – an effective policy that endures. In 1976 the parks were internationally recognized as a UNESCO biosphere reserve.

NATURAL HISTORY

The parks contain the Sierra's four vegetation zones from lower montane to alpine. In a 60mi stretch south of the Kings River are 68 of the world's 75 giant sequoia groves. Kings Canyon contains the world's largest grove, Redwood Mountain, which contains more than 15,000 trees with trunks greater than 12 inches in diameter. The parks' lower western slopes also have extensive open woodlands where oak and digger pine rise over profusely flowering buckeye, coffeeberry and poison oak.

Also prevalent up to 5000ft is chaparral, composed of aromatic evergreen shrubs adapted to hot, dry summers and cool, rainy winters. This vegetation, unique to California and adjacent southern Oregon and northern Baja California, is adapted to fire and most seeds germinate only with intense heat. Its common plants are white-flowered chamise, blue-flowering ceanothus, scrub oak and smooth, red-barked manzanita. Early summer visitors to Sequoia via Ash Mountain Entrance spot the dramatic, tall, flowering stalk of Our Lord's Candle (*Yucca whipplei*) along the roadside.

INFORMATION
When to Hike

Summer daytime temperatures at low elevations often exceed 100°F, although Cedar Grove rarely gets that hot. Higher Giant Forest is cooler, but still warm in midsummer.

Maps & Books

The USGS 1:125,000 *Sequoia and Kings Canyon National Parks and Vicinity* with 200ft contour intervals is a superb planning and backpacking map for all routes in both parks. The excellent, yet massive, USFS

1:63,360 series John Muir Wilderness (Inyo and Sierra National Forests) and National Parks Backcountry (Sequoia and Kings Canyon National Parks) includes three sheets: *North Section*, areas north from Evolution Basin in northern Kings Canyon National Park; *Central Section*, all of Kings Canyon National Park except areas south of the South Fork Kings River; and *South Section*, areas of Kings Canyon National Park south of the South Fork Kings River and all of Sequoia National Park.

Tom Harrison Cartography's 1:125,000 *Sequoia & Kings Canyon National Parks Recreation Map* covers the parks and their eastern Sierra approaches; and the 1:63,360 *Mt Whitney High Country Trail Map* provides greater detail of the region between Kings Canyon's Roads End and Sequoia's Mineral King.

The Sequoia National History Association (SNHA) publishes 1:9500 *Cedar Grove*, *Lodgepole*, *Giant Forest* and *Mineral King* maps that show most day hikes in these areas.

Sequoia & Kings Canyon: The Story Behind the Scenery by William C Tweed is a fine reference for nature lovers.

Maps and books are available by mail order from SNHA (☎ 559-784-1500, 🖳 www.sequoiahistory.org), HCR 89 Box 10, Three Rivers, CA 93271; and also from park visitor centers and ranger stations.

Information Sources

Sequoia and Kings Canyon National Parks (☎ 559-565-3341 for recorded information, 559-565-3134 for an operator from 8 am to 4:30 pm, 🖳 www.nps.gov/seki, 47050 Generals Hwy, Three Rivers, CA 93271-9651, are jointly administered.

Permits

An entrance fee, valid for seven days for both parks, is $10 per vehicle or $5 per person for cyclists and walk-ins. An annual pass for both parks costs $20.

Free wilderness permits are required for all overnight backcountry trips; permits are not required for day hikes. First-come, first-served permits are available year-round from Sequoia's Foothill and Lodgepole visitor

Regal Redwoods

The giant redwood (*Sequoiadendron giganteum*), commonly called giant sequoia, is an ancient species more than 50 million years old. Once widespread, climatic changes have altered its distribution and it now survives only in 75 isolated groves in the western Sierra Nevada between 4500ft and 8000ft. These towering red giants are the largest living single organisms on earth. A giant sequoia typically reaches between 250ft and 300ft in height and 40ft in diameter, and lives as long as 3000 years. (The oldest is estimated to be 3500 years old.) Impervious to fire and resistant to disease and insects, it is their immense mass that eventually causes the trees to topple when their shallow root system can no longer support their great weight. Related to the taller coast redwood (*Sequoia sempervirens*) and dawn redwood (*Metasequoia gylptostrobides*) of China, protected groves of these majestic trees stand in Sequoia, Kings Canyon and Yosemite National Parks.

HAYDEN FOELL

Giant sequoias (right) are stockier than their cousins, the coast redwoods (left).

centers, and from Kings Canyon's Grant Grove visitor center. First-come, first-served permits are also available in hiking season from Sequoia's South Fork and Mineral King ranger stations, and from Kings Canyon's Roads End (7:15 am to 2:45 pm, but after 1 pm for next-day permits) and Cedar Grove ranger station (after 2:45 pm). Some trailheads have self-issuing permits.

Reservations are recommended between May 22 and mid-September, particularly for weekend entry dates. To make a reservation, mail or fax after March 1 and no later than three weeks before a desired entry date ($10 reservation fee per permit) to Wilderness Permit Reservations (fax 559-565-4239), HCR 89 Box 60, Three Rivers, CA 93271. The Backcountry Wilderness Office (☎ 559-565-3708) is open from 8 am to 4:30 pm and provides general information.

GETTING THERE & AWAY

Los Angeles is a four-hour drive from Kings Canyon National Park; San Francisco is a five-hour drive. The nearest regional airport is in Fresno.

From Fresno, Hwy 180 leads 53mi east to Kings Canyon's Big Stump Entrance. Just beyond the entrance, the 45.8mi Generals Hwy (Hwy 198) branches southeast to Sequoia National Park's Ash Mountain Entrance, 36mi from Visalia. Hwy 180 continues for 2mi beyond the Big Stump Entrance to Grant Grove Village, then plummets 3200ft along South Fork Kings River into an impressive canyon. There is no public transport between Fresno or Visalia and these national parks.

Beyond Grant Grove Village Hwy 180 (known as Kings Canyon Scenic Byway) is open only mid-April to mid-November. It leads 30mi to Cedar Grove Village and 5½mi further to its terminus at Roads End.

GETTING AROUND

In Sequoia National Park from late June through Labor Day a free shuttle bus operates every 30 minutes from 9 am to 6 pm between Wuksachi Village and the Crescent Meadow trailhead, stopping at Lodgepole, Wolverton, Giant Forest and Moro Rock.

NEAREST FACILITIES
In Kings Canyon National Park

Visitor centers are at Grant Grove (☎ 559-565-4307) and Cedar Grove in the ranger station adjacent to Sentinel campground, a quarter-mile south of Cedar Grove Village.

Places to Stay & Eat *Sunset*, *Azalea* and *Crystal Springs campgrounds* are near Grant Grove Village (6589ft). Near Cedar Grove Village (4635ft) are *Sheep Creek*, *Sentinel*, *Canyon View*, and *Moraine campgrounds*. All cost $14.

Year-round *John Muir Lodge* in Grant Grove has $125 rooms, $210 suites, cabins ($85–$90/55 with/without bathrooms) and summer-only tent cabins ($35 to $45). *Cedar Grove Lodge (☎ 559-335-5500)*, open May to October, has basic rooms ($85) above the market and a counter-service *restaurant*, and a few kitchenettes on the ground floor. Showers ($3) are available at Grant Grove Village (11 am to 4 pm, go to Lodging Information–Registration) and at Cedar Grove Village.

To make campground or lodging reservations, contact Kings Canyon Park Services (☎ 559-335-5500, fax 335-2498), PO Box 909, Kings Canyon National Park, CA 93633.

In Sequoia National Park

Foothills visitor center is beyond Ash Mountain Entrance and Lodgepole visitor center is at Lodgepole Village.

Places to Stay & Eat Along Mineral King Rd are *Atwell Mill* (6540ft) and *Cold Springs* (7580ft) *campgrounds* ($8). The low-elevation and often too-hot *Potwisha* (2080ft) and *Buckeye Flat* (2820ft) *campgrounds* ($14) are along Generals Hwy northeast of Ash Mountain Entrance. *Lodgepole campground* (6720ft), along the Marble Fork Kaweah River, is 4mi north of Giant Forest. *Dorst Creek* (6720ft) *campground*, also along Generals Hwy west of Lodgepole, is near the Lost Grove. Dorst Creek and Lodgepole are the only campgrounds ($16) for which reservations are accepted; contact the National Park Reservation Service (☎ 800-365-2267, 301-722-1257 from overseas,

🖥 reservations.nps.gov). There are showers ($3) and a laundromat at Lodgepole Village, adjacent to a grocery store and **snack bar**.

Wuksachi Village & Lodge (☎ 888-252-5757, 559-253-2199 from overseas) at 7200ft is 2mi west of Lodgepole and sits above Generals Hwy with spectacular views of Tokopah Valley. Rooms range from $110 (economy) and $125 (standard) to $155 (deluxe).

Other Campgrounds

Six campgrounds in Sequoia National Forest offer excellent alternatives when the national park campgrounds are full. Of these, the most attractive choices are: **Stony Creek** ($14) on Generals Hwy near Sequoia's Lost Grove; **Tenmile**, 5½mi north of the Kings Canyon's Redwood Mountain Overlook off Generals Hwy; and **Princess** ($12) along Hwy 180 north of Kings Canyon's Grant Grove.

Franklin & Sawtooth Passes

Duration	4 days
Distance	30mi (48.3km)
Standard	medium-hard
Start/Finish	Mineral King
Nearest Facilities	Silver City Resort
Public Transport	no

Summary Two scenic passes over the Great Western Divide, forested canyons and beautiful lakes with excellent fishing make this Sequoia National Park's most popular loop from Mineral King.

Mineral King Valley is surrounded by half a dozen valleys, each with lakes in alpine basins and passes leading to more distant backcountry. Hiking anywhere from Mineral King entails a steep climb out of the valley along strenuous trails. The most popular loop from Mineral King crosses two passes – Franklin and Sawtooth – along the Great Western Divide. For some backpackers, the beginning of this route offers an alternative, western, approach to Mt Whitney via direct access to the Kern River basin.

HISTORY

Mineral King, as the name invokes, was a mining center that rose to prominence in the late 1870s. Prospectors built the first road into the valley and established a small town, but hopes of endless silver ore faded after just a few years. In 1893 Mineral King became part of the Sierra Forest Preserve, and soon afterwards the USFS leased the land to summer vacationers. By 1926 expansion of Sequoia National Park encircled Mineral King. In the ensuing years developers fought to turn it into a large-scale ski resort. Fortunately, Mineral King was saved when the US Congress made it part of Sequoia National Park in 1978.

PLANNING
Maps

The USGS 1:24,000 *Mineral King* and *Chagoopa Falls* quadrangles, and 1:62,500 *Mineral King* and *Kern Peak* quadrangles cover the hike.

Permits

A wilderness permit is required. See Permits & Regulations under Information at the beginning of this section.

NEAREST FACILITIES

Mineral King has no services, but the private **Silver City Resort** about 3mi west of the ranger station on Mineral King Rd has a

---

WARNING

An abundant population of yellow-bellied marmots in Mineral King is creating havoc for some unsuspecting motorists. From early spring through mid-July, these largest members of the ground squirrel family (*Marmota flaviventris*) chew on the hoses, belts and wiring of parked vehicles to get the salt (sodium) they crave before their winter hibernation. The only known technique to protect vehicles parked at all Mineral King trailheads is to physically enclose the vehicle in chicken wire (1-inch or 2-inch hex netting 36 or 48 inches high and 50ft long costs $15 to $20), weighted down with rocks.

small *restaurant* and store. Drinking water and a food-storage hut are opposite the ranger station.

GETTING TO/FROM THE HIKE

The 25mi Mineral King Rd begins at Hwy 198, 4mi north of Three Rivers and 2mi south of Sequoia's Ash Mountain Entrance. The first 17mi of this steep, narrow, winding road are open year-round, but the last 8mi are closed during winter and reopen Memorial Day weekend. The drive takes 1½ hours one way.

THE HIKE
Day 1: Mineral King to Franklin Lakes
4–5 hours, 6mi (9.7km), 2480ft (744m) ascent

From the Eagle-Mosquito parking area (7840ft), walk back over the bridge and follow the road south for a few minutes past the pack station where the pavement ends. The trail soon narrows and after a mile fords Crystal Creek. Rising gently above the green valley, the trail fords Franklin Creek, then rises in a series of switchbacks and long traverses through meadows to the junction with the Farewell Gap Trail after 2½mi. Follow the left fork, which heads north and then east, climbing to a second ford of Franklin Creek. Passing through contrasting dark, multicolored metamorphic rock and pale granite, the trail switchbacks above the north bank of Franklin Creek to cross a granite shoulder above dammed **Lower Franklin Lake** (10,320ft). Attractive *campsites* are above the northeast shore.

Day 2: Franklin Lakes to Little Claire Lake
4–6 hours, 7mi (11.3km), 1480ft (444m) ascent, 1350ft (405m) descent

The trail rises through the last bit of forest, then makes a series of well-graded switchbacks up the pulverized granite slope as it climbs out of the Franklin Lakes cirque. It crosses two tiny, year-round, flower-lined streams and rises steadily upwards to a long traverse to panoramic **Franklin Pass** (11,800ft), 2½mi from the lake.

Descending switchbacks from the pass into forested upper Rattlesnake Canyon, the trail soon comes to the junction with the Shotgun Pass Trail. A quarter-mile below (beyond) this junction, the trail forks. The right fork crosses Rattlesnake Creek and descends along the creek to the Kern River (the alternative route to Mt Whitney). Follow the left fork, which goes a mile to Forester Lake. Beyond Forester Lake, ascend through forest, over a ridge, and down into the Soda Creek drainage to Little Claire Lake (10,450ft), with good *campsites* along its outlet.

Day 3: Little Claire Lake to Upper Lost Canyon
5–6 hours, 9mi (14.5km), 1200ft (360m) ascent, 1400ft (420m) descent

The trail descends switchbacks west of the outlet stream from Little Claire Lake down a steep, forested slope to a ford of Soda Creek. Keeping north of Soda Creek, the trail descends through forest to a trail junction, about 5mi from Little Claire Lake. The right fork descends to Big Arroyo Canyon. Take the left fork, which climbs through open brush and enters Lost Canyon, crossing Lost Canyon Creek to its north side. The trail then rises steadily for more than a mile to a junction with the Big Five Lakes Trail. Just beyond the junction, the Lost Canyon Trail fords the creek, which it recrosses within another mile. The trail then climbs steeply through meadows and mixed forest to grassy *campsites* amid scattered pines (10,200ft), with Needham Mountain rising to the south.

Day 4: Upper Lost Canyon to Mineral King
5–6 hours, 8mi (12.9km), 1400ft (420m) ascent, 3760ft (1128m) descent

The trail rises above timberline and ascends a rocky slope. Crossing this low saddle, the trail drops to dramatic Columbine Lake beneath Sawtooth Peak and crosses its outlet. It is possible to *camp* here. Circling the northern lakeshore, the trail climbs steeply to **Sawtooth Pass** (11,600ft). From the pass, marked by a small cairn, the trail descends northwest towards Glacier Pass. Many paths head steeply down over loose, pulverized

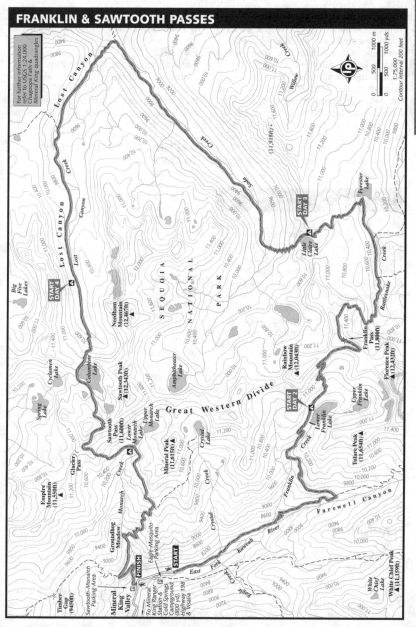

granite, but the best route stays high, aiming northwest towards a saddle with a few trees several hundred yards south of Glacier Pass. From above the saddle, the route works down a grassy gully between granite outcrops, then makes a level traverse to Lower Monarch Lake (10,380ft) with popular *campsites*, sweeping vistas west over Mineral King and the chance to view a spectacular sunset. A good trail descends to Sawtooth-Monarch parking area, visible more than 3700ft below (see Lower Monarch Lake in Other Hikes at the end of this chapter).

High Sierra Trail

Duration	8 days
Distance	72.2mi (116.2km)
Standard	hard
Start	Crescent Meadow
Finish	Whitney Portal
Nearest Towns	Lodgepole, Lone Pine
Public Transport	no

Summary A classic journey across Sequoia National Park from west to east, which crosses two passes and traverses the Kern River canyon, linking the sequoias of Giant Forest to Mt Whitney.

This 72mi trail traverses the very heart of the High Sierra across Sequoia National Park. Starting from giant sequoia groves, this varied hike crosses the Great Western Divide at its lowest pass, skirts the multicolored Kaweah peaks, ascends the Kern River canyon, crosses a high plateau and reaches Mt Whitney's summit, before descending to the eastern side of the Sierra. Backpackers should be in top shape to enjoy the splendors of this long and strenuous route.

PLANNING
Maps
The USGS 1:24,000 *Lodgepole, Triple Divide Peak, Mt Kaweah, Chagoopa Falls* and *Mt Whitney* quadrangles, and 1:62,500 *Triple Divide Peak, Kern Peak* and *Mt Whitney* quadrangles cover the trail. The USGS 1:100,000 *Mt Whitney* sheet and

Tom Harrison Cartography's 1:63,360 *Mt Whitney High Country Trail Map* do it in one.

Permits
The trail enters the Whitney Zone and requires a special endorsement in addition to a wilderness permit (see the Mt Whitney hike in the Eastern Sierra section for details). Sequoia National Park issues this with the permit.

GETTING TO/FROM THE HIKE
To the Start
From Generals Hwy in Giant Forest, drive 3½mi east on Crescent Meadow Rd to its end at the trailhead.

From the Finish
From Whitney Portal, a road leads 13mi east to Lone Pine (see the Eastern Sierra section).

THE HIKE
Day 1: Crescent Meadow to Bearpaw Meadow
6–7 hours, 11mi (17.7km), 1100ft (330m) ascent

Skirting Crescent and Log Meadows (6700ft), passing some giant sequoias and swinging by Eagle View Overlook, the High Sierra Trail begins an undulating traverse high along the forested north side of the canyon of the Middle Fork Kaweah River. Crossing numerous streams, many with small *campsites*, it presents a continuous panorama of the Kaweah Basin and the peaks of the Great Western Divide. Shortly after crossing Mehrten Creek the trail passes a spur trail leading north to the Alta Trail and continues to the bridge over Buck Creek. From here it ascends to **Bearpaw Meadow** (7800ft) and intersects a trail leading north to Elizabeth Pass and descending south to Little Bearpaw and Redwood Meadows. Heavily used *campsites* lie a few yards ahead and south of the trail in the forest. A ranger station and Bearpaw Meadow Camp are on either side of the trail a short distance ahead. ***Bearpaw Meadow Camp*** (☎ 888-252-5757, 559-253-2199 *from overseas*), open mid-June to mid-September, is a tent 'hotel' ($150 per person including two daily meals) that offers complete bedding and showers; reservations are required.

Day 2: Bearpaw Meadow to Big Arroyo Creek Junction

6–7 hours, 11mi (17.7km), 2900ft (870m) ascent, 1100ft (330m) descent

Continue east and swing northeast to cross Lone Pine Creek and pass the trail junction for Tamarack Lake (which has *campsites*) after 2mi. The trail begins ascending towards fantastic, granite-walled Hamilton Lakes and Kaweah Gap, contouring the cliff face and switchbacking up to cross Hamilton Creek below the smaller, lower Hamilton Lake and recrossing it below the larger upper **Hamilton Lake** (8200ft). There are overused *campsites* northwest of the lake.

Rising steeply out of the cirque, the trail, engineered by blasting, passes tunnel-like across the cliff face. Climbing past Precipice Lake, which lies beneath towering Eagle Scout Peak, the trail emerges at **Kaweah Gap** (10,700ft) on the Great Western Divide, to face Nine Lake Basin and the jagged, black-and-red spires of the Kaweah peaks. Descending first along the west side of Big Arroyo Creek, then crossing to its east side, the trail enters forest and crosses side streams coming from Black Kaweah and Red Kaweah. It arrives at *campsites* (9600ft) several hundred yards before the junction with the Big Arroyo Creek and Little Five Lakes Trails, 2mi from Kaweah Gap.

Day 3: Big Arroyo Creek Junction to Moraine Lake

5–6 hours, 8mi (12.9km), 1040ft (312m) ascent, 1340ft (402m) descent

Pass the trail junction and climb east along the northern slopes of Big Arroyo Creek to emerge on broad **Chagoopa Plateau**, south of the Kaweah peaks. Descending gradually along this tableland, the trail crosses a branch of Chagoopa Creek and comes to a junction. The left fork continues 3.3mi to Sky Parlor Meadow beyond Moraine Lake, where it rejoins the right fork. Follow the right fork down to *campsites* along the southern shore of Moraine Lake (9300ft).

Day 4: Moraine Lake to Kern Hot Spring

4–5 hours, 7mi (11.3km), 2500ft (250m) descent

Heading east through Sky Parlor Meadow and fording Funston Creek, the trail rejoins the High Sierra Trail in a mile. Continuing east, it begins an ever-steepening descent into **Kern Canyon**, paralleling Funston Creek, to meet the Kern River Trail 3.7mi from the junction. Turning left, it heads north up the deep canyon through meadows and forest. The trail crosses a bridge to the east side of the Kern River and passes opposite **Chagoopa Falls**, tumbling down the canyon's west wall. Just beyond the crossing of South Fork Rock Creek lies Kern Hot Spring (6880ft), where a *campsite* is just north and east of the hot spring near the Kern River.

Day 5: Kern Hot Spring to Junction Meadow

4–6 hours, 8mi (12.9km), 1156ft (347m) ascent

Ascending steadily north along the east side of the Kern River beneath impressive high granite cliffs, the trail crosses the Guyot Flat stream and Whitney and Wallace Creeks to arrive at Junction Meadow (8036ft), with heavily used *campsites* along the river.

Day 6: Junction Meadow to Crabtree Ranger Station

5–6 hours, 9mi (14.5km), 2664ft (799m) ascent

Ascending north along the Kern River for a mile, the trail comes to a junction where it turns sharply right, leaving the Kern River Trail. Working southeast, the High Sierra Trail rises into the Wallace Creek canyon and parallels the creek for 3½mi to a junction (10,390ft) with the combined Pacific Crest and John Muir Trails. Turning right onto this, the High Sierra Trail crosses Wallace Creek (*campsites*), rolls over the saddle west of Mt Young and skirts Sandy Meadow. Three-and-a-half miles from the junction the High Sierra and John Muir Trails turn east (left), leaving the PCT. The trail reaches Crabtree ranger station after just less than a mile, with *campsites* (10,700ft) just south of Whitney Creek.

HIGH SIERRA TRAIL

Day 7: Crabtree Ranger Station to Trail Camp

7–8 hours, 12.2mi (19.6km), 3077ft (923m) ascent, 1777ft (533m) descent

Staying north of Whitney Creek, the trail climbs above treeline, passing Timberline and Guitar Lakes. It crosses the outlet stream from Arctic Lake, traverses a meadow and begins a long series of switchbacks up the western slopes of Mt Whitney. The junction with the trail to the summit of Mt Whitney (see the Mt Whitney hike in the Eastern Sierra section) is reached about 5½mi from Crabtree ranger station. Many hikers leave their backpacks here and turn north along the spectacular ridge crest, continuing for 2mi to **Mt Whitney's summit**. Returning from this breathtaking high point to **Trail Crest**, the trail turns east, leaving Sequoia National Park, and descends many short, steep switchbacks to heavily-used *Trail Camp* (12,000ft), among the boulders above Consultation Lake.

Day 8: Trail Camp to Whitney Portal

3–4 hours, 6mi (9.7km)

Follow the busy trail down to Whitney Portal (see Day 1 of the Mt Whitney hike in the Eastern Sierra section).

Rae Lakes Loop

Duration	5 days
Distance	43.5mi (70km)
Standard	medium
Start/Finish	Roads End
Nearest Facilities	Cedar Grove Village
Public Transport	no

Summary The best loop in Kings Canyon National Park tours forests, meadows, a pass and passes a chain of lakes. The first section of Day 1, to Mist Falls, makes an excellent day hike.

Deservedly Kings Canyon's most popular hike, this 43½mi clockwise circuit of King

HIGH SIERRA TRAIL

Spur, a cluster of high peaks, offers access to many less-frequently-visited parts of the park. It traverses the Rae Lakes and Glen Pass segments of the combined Pacific Crest and John Muir Trails. Planning a layover day allows time to explore this beautiful region, but camping at Rae Lakes is limited to one day at each lake.

Alternatively, Mist Falls – Kings Canyon's largest and most impressive waterfall, passed on Day 1 – makes a great, easy, 9.2mi, four- to five-hour (roundtrip) day hike. This section of the trail is most spectacular in early summer when the South Fork Kings River and the falls are at their peak.

PLANNING
When to Hike

Early in the season, streams and rivers may be uncrossable. Especially difficult is the South Fork crossing on the Woods Creek Trail.

Maps

The USGS 1:24,000 *The Sphinx* and *Mt Clarence King* quadrangles, and 1:62,500 *Marion Peak* and *Mt Pinchot* quadrangles cover the hike, as does the USGS 1:100,000 *Mt Whitney* sheet.

GETTING TO/FROM THE HIKE

The trail begins and ends at Roads End (5030ft), 5½mi east of the turnoff to Cedar Grove Village.

THE HIKE
Day 1: Roads End to Middle Paradise Valley

5–6 hours, 8mi (12.9km), 1610ft (483m) ascent

The hike begins on the Woods Creek Trail to Mist Falls. This quickly crosses Copper Creek over a bridge and traverses level, sandy ground through stands of open forest for about 1½mi. It then enters a shaded, fern-filled area and after a half-mile passes

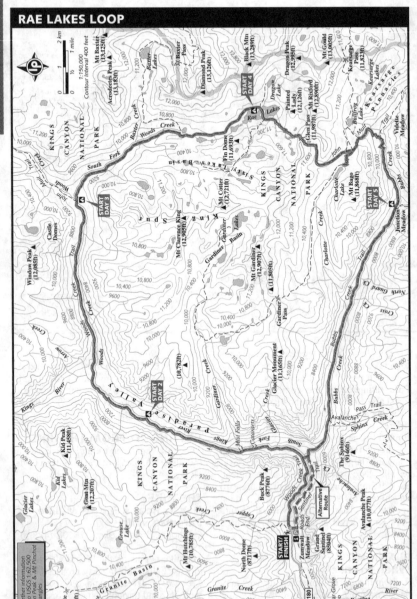

the Bubbs Creek Trail (which crosses the South Fork Kings River over a Bailey bridge). The trail to Mist Falls turns left at this junction and begins a steady, gradual 1½ to two hour ascent along the river. After a mile, the trail approaches a series of dramatic cataracts, then surmounts a granite hillside. Back down the valley are striking views of Avalanche Peak and **The Sphinx** (9146ft), high above Bubbs Creek. The trail continues through forest to reach **Mist Falls** (5663ft), named for the remarkable plume of mist that rises like a specter from its base. (The series of falls 20 to 30 minutes below Mist Falls is also formidable, but Mist Falls proper is easily identified by a signpost.)

Day hikers can make a leisurely return to Roads End via the same trail, or try a pleasant alternative between the Bailey bridge and Roads End. Cross the Bailey bridge onto the Bubbs Creek Trail and turn right shortly after the bridge onto the **Sentinel Trail**. This less-frequently used, level, 2.6mi trail hugs the true left bank of the South Fork Kings River, recrossing the river downstream on a sturdy bridge near Roads End.

Beyond Mist Falls, the Rae Lakes loop ascends steadily to the level Paradise Valley, where the South Fork Kings River flows placidly through forest and meadows. The first *campsites* are at **Lower Paradise Valley** (6600ft), 7mi from the trailhead, with those at Middle Paradise Valley (6640ft) a mile further.

Day 2: Middle Paradise Valley to Woods Creek

5–7 hours, 9mi (14.5km), 1860ft (558m) ascent

Leaving Middle Paradise Valley, the trail rises past the confluence with Woods Creek and crosses the river to reach **Upper Paradise Valley** after 2.2mi. Following the north side of Woods Creek, the trail crosses two tributaries and meets the combined Pacific Crest and John Muir Trails. Turning right onto that trail, it crosses Woods Creek (8500ft), with *campsites* near the crossing, just below its confluence with the South Fork Woods Creek.

Day 3: Woods Creek to Middle Rae Lake

3–4 hours, 6mi (9.7km), 2050ft (615m) ascent

The trail stays west of the creek as it ascends, crossing several tributaries. Near the north end of Dollar Lake, a faint trail branches east (left) to Baxter Pass. Continue south as the main trail recrosses the creek below Arrowhead Lake (10,300ft). Ascending past *campsites* east of **Lower Rae Lake**, beneath striking Fin Dome, the trail reaches **Middle Rae Lake** (10,550ft) with *campsites* near its south end.

Day 4: Middle Rae Lake to Junction Meadow

5–6 hours, 8½mi (13.7km), 1437ft (431m) ascent, 3787ft (1136m) descent

Just beyond Middle Rae Lake, the trail turns west and crosses the stream connecting Middle and Upper Rae lakes, passing a trail that branches east to Dragon Lake. Another side trail climbs west to secluded **Sixty Lakes Basin**. The main trail turns south, rising above the west side of Upper Rae Lake. The steep trail climbs switchbacks, with dramatic views back to the north, and soon arrives at narrow **Glen Pass** (11,987ft), 2½mi from Middle Rae Lake.

Descending steeply south past small pothole lakes, the trail turns west, then heads south contouring well above attractive Charlotte Lake. Passing an eastbound trail to Kearsarge Pass, the trail arrives at a four-way junction about 2mi from Glen Pass, where the west (right) fork leads down to Charlotte Lake and the east (left) fork is the Kearsarge Pass Trail (see Kearsarge Pass under Eastern Sierra in Other Hikes). Continuing south, the main trail makes a scenic descent into the Bubbs Creek canyon, twice crossing the outlet from Bullfrog Lake, to reach Lower Vidette Meadow (9550ft), which has *campsites*, and another junction about 2mi from the Kearsarge Pass Trail junction. Leaving the John Muir Trail, which continues southeast, the trail down Bubbs Creek back to Roads End turns right (west). Descending west on switchbacks above cascading Bubbs Creek, the trail arrives after another 2mi at *campsites* at the western end of Junction Meadow (8200ft), where a side trail to East Lake and Lake Reflection ascends south along East Creek.

Day 5: Junction Meadow to Roads End
6–7 hours, 12mi (19.3km), 3170ft (951m) descent

The trail passes more *campsites* at the west end of Junction Meadow, descending steadily to more *campsites* just east of **Charlotte Creek**, about 3mi from Junction Meadow. Crossing Charlotte Creek, the trail continues west down Bubbs Creek and comes to Sphinx Creek (6240ft), with *campsites*, where the trail to Avalanche Pass crosses Bubbs Creek on a wooden bridge. The main trail descends steeply on switchbacks, with sweeping views into Kings Canyon, and the granite pinnacle of **The Sphinx** towering above Bubbs Creek. Reaching the valley floor, the trail crosses Bubbs Creek and then a Bailey bridge over the South Fork Kings River to join the Woods Creek Trail. Turning left, it retraces level ground back to Roads End.

Eastern Sierra

The eastern Sierra is for many backpackers the Sierra Nevada's most appealing region. It spans more than 250mi of six nearly contiguous wilderness areas – Hoover, Ansel Adams, John Muir, Golden Trout, South Sierra and Dome Land – from north to south. Here the jagged Sierra crest rises abruptly almost 2mi above the high desert, with 14 peaks over 14,000ft and Mt Whitney as the crown jewel. Most trails access one of these wilderness areas and many cross passes over the crest into Sequoia and Kings Canyon National Parks.

US 395, which connects Los Angeles to Reno, follows the length of the eastern Sierra through the Owens Valley between Deadmans Pass and Hwy 178. Paved roads lead west from US 395 several thousand feet up steep canyons to popular trailheads at high elevations offering quick access to the high country. In most of these inviting canyons, where creeks and rivers tumble from formidably steep granite pinnacles, are USFS recreation areas with convenient campgrounds, as well as an occasional small private resort or store.

The Owens Valley lies between the Sierra Nevada and the ancient White Mountains. Volcanic activity is evident, especially around Mammoth Mountain, a relatively recent volcano on the rim of a huge 760,000 year old caldera. Volcanic activity last occurred as recently as 500 years ago, and the Mammoth region today is California's most active seismic zone.

HISTORY
Native American Piute and Shoshone thrived in the Owens Valley, calling it *Inyo*, a Piute word for 'dwelling place of the great spirit'. John C Frémont named it Owens Valley after his cartographer Richard Owens. Towns began as mining settlements in the 1860s and later became ranching centers. Basque emigrants from the Spanish Pyrenees won fame as sheep herders. The Owens Valley was once a productive agricultural region watered by Sierra streams, but since the early 20th century, water from the Owens River has been drained away by the Los Angeles Aqueduct, reducing the valley to a desert-like wasteland. Owens Dry Lake, once 30ft deep, is a notable casualty of these 'water wars'. Hollywood discovered the area in the 1920s, and visitors to Whitney Portal pass the Alabama Hills, location of such famous TV westerns as *The Lone Ranger*, *Rawhide* and *Maverick*. Recreation is now the main focus of this high desert region.

INFORMATION
Maps
See Maps under Information in the Sequoia & Kings Canyon National Parks section for recommended maps for the eastern approaches to the parks. The USFS 1:126,720 *Inyo National Forest* map is also useful for secondary roads, campgrounds and some trails. For where to buy maps locally, see Nearest Towns later in this section.

Silence of the Lambs

Sierra Nevada bighorn sheep (*Ovis canadensis*) are unique to the steep, rugged crest and eastern escarpment of the Sierra. Historically, bighorn were found from the Sonora Pass to the southern end of today's Sequoia National Park. Disease and competition from huge flocks of domestic sheep in the 19th and 20th centuries decimated the once abundant bighorn population. In 1971 the USFS created two Bighorn Sheep Zoological Areas, north and south of Kearsarge Pass, to protect the sheep and in 1972 California listed the bighorn as threatened. Bighorn were reintroduced to the Lee Vining canyon east of Yosemite National Park in 1985.

Since 1986, bighorn populations have dropped by two thirds and little more than 100 sheep remain. The main factor driving the decline is predation by mountain lions and the sheep's subsequent abandonment of its low-elevation winter range. A Californian law protecting mountain lions from hunting has helped increase their population, but with the ironic consequence that bighorns are dying from poor nutrition. California upgraded the bighorn's status from threatened to endangered in March 1999. The USFS plans to use prescribed burning to reduce hiding cover for mountain lions, which should improve the habitat of the bighorn and its chance for survival.

HUGH D'ANDRADE

Permits

Inyo National Forest, which extends along 175mi of the eastern Sierra from Lundy Canyon north of Mono Lake to the southern end of the Owens Valley, issues free wilderness permits for all hikes in this section. From March 1 to the end of hiking season it accepts reservations up to 10 days before the entry date – recommended for weekend entry dates from late June to mid-September. Permits are 60% reservable and 40% first-come, first-served, except for the Whitney Zone for which they are 100% reservable.

Reservations are accepted by mail (addressed to Inyo National Forest, Wilderness Reservation Office, 873 N Main St, Bishop, CA 93514, or by fax to 760-873-2484) but not by telephone. Reservation forms can be downloaded from the Internet at 🖳 www.r5.fs.fed.us/inyo. Permits are free, but a $5 reservation fee per person applies for all trails except those in the Whitney Zone, for which the reservation fee is $15. Permits must be collected in person from one of the ranger stations in Lone Pine, Bishop or Mammoth Lakes (see Nearest Towns later in this

section) or Lee Vining (see Nearest Towns & Facilities in the Tahoe to Yosemite section).

For information on Whitney Zone endorsements, see Permits under the Mt Whitney hike.

NEAREST TOWNS

For information on transport between these towns and from these towns to the trailheads, see Getting Around later in this section and Getting To/From the Hike for individual hikes.

Lone Pine

The Inter Agency visitor center (☎ 760-876-6222), 1½mi south of town at the US 395/Hwy 136 junction, offers a plethora of information and sells books and maps. The Lone Pine chamber of commerce (☎ 760-876-4444, fax 876-9205, ✉ info@lone-pine.com, 🖳 www.lone-pine.com, PO Box 749, Lone Pine, CA 93545) at 126 S Main St is also helpful. The Mt Whitney ranger station (☎ 760-876-6200, PO Box 8, Lone Pine, CA 93545) is on US 395 at Inyo St at the south end of town.

Places to Stay & Eat *Historic Dow Hotel* (☎ 768-876-5521, 800-824-9317), at the southeast corner of US 395 and Post St, has $38 rooms without bathroom or telephone and $50 rooms with bathroom. Adjacent to it is *Motel Dow Villa* (☎ 760-876-5521, 800-824-9317, fax 876-5643 @ dowvilla@qnet.com, 🖳 www.dow villamotel.com), with singles/doubles for $75/85. *Alabama Hills Inn* (☎ 760-876-8700, 800-800-6468, fax 876-8704) at 120 Main St is a clean, friendly place on the southern outskirts of town ($58/68).

The Mt Whitney Restaurant (☎ 760-876-5751, 227 S Main) is proud of its Hollywood memorabilia display and boasts the best burgers, including buffalo and venison ones. Joseph's Bi-Rite Market, 119 S Main St, is a convenient place to buy groceries.

Getting There & Away Lone Pine is about 200mi north of Los Angeles and 59mi south of Bishop. Greyhound buses ply US 395 once daily in each direction between Los Angeles and Reno, stopping in Lone Pine, Independence, Big Pine, Bishop, and Mammoth Lakes. The southbound bus to Los Angeles ($37/74 one way/roundtrip), which stops at 126 W Post St, departs at 2:43 pm, and the northbound bus to Reno ($49/97) departs at 11:05 pm. See also Getting Around later in this section.

Bishop

White Mountain ranger station (☎ 760-873-2500), 798 N Main St (US 395) at Yaney St at the north end of town, sells books and maps. The Bishop Area chamber of commerce & visitor bureau (☎ 760-873-8405, @ info@bishopvisitor.com, 🖳 www.bish opvisitor.com), 690 N Main St, is nearby, next to the city park. Wilson's Eastside Sports, 224 N Main St, and Sierra Sherpas, 115 W Line St, sell maps and hiking gear.

Places to Stay & Eat *The Trees Motel* (☎ 760-873-6391, fax 872-1843, 796 W Line St), owned by very accommodating and friendly folks, has quiet, clean rooms ($40, all non-smoking). *Mountain View Motel* (☎ 760-873-4242, fax 873-3409, 730

W Line St) has rooms starting at $57; it is clean and has a pool. Rooms at the *Village Motel* (☎ 760-872-8155, 286 W Elm St at N Warren St), at the north end of town, start at $39; it also has a pool.

Brown's Town (☎ 760-873-8522), a half-mile south of town at US 395 and Schober Lane, is a nicely shaded campground ($12) with guest-only shower facilities ($0.50), a grocery store and *deli*.

Ardi's Deli Cafe, on Academy St at N Warren St, has gourmet foods, homemade pies and cappuccino. *Erick Schat's Bakery* at 763 N Main St is a local favorite. Joseph's Bi-Rite Market at 211 N Main St is a convenient grocery store.

Getting There & Away Bishop (4140ft) is on US 395, 39mi southeast of Mammoth Lakes and 15mi north of Big Pine. A southbound Greyhound bus to Los Angeles ($42/84 one way/roundtrip), which stops at 201 S Warren St, departs at 1:35 pm, and a northbound bus to Reno ($46/91) departs at 12:15 am. See also Getting Around later in this section.

Mammoth Lakes

The Mammoth visitor center, on Hwy 203/Main St, houses Mammoth Lakes visitor bureau (☎ 760-934-2712, 800-367-6572, fax 934-7066, @ mmthvisit@qnet .com, 🖳 www.visitmammoth.com) and the USFS ranger station (☎ 760-924-5500). The visitor bureau offers 24-hour lodging information and referrals (☎ 888-466-2666). The ranger station provides trail information, reserves campgrounds, issues free wilderness permits for Ansel Adams Wilderness, and sells books and maps.

Mammoth Mountain Inn has public shower facilities ($4). Kittredge Sports (☎ 760-934-7566), 3218 Main St, and Sandy's Ski & Sport (☎ 760-934-7518), also on Main St, sell hiking gear.

Places to Stay & Eat Lodging is expensive, so it helps to use the visitor bureau service. Try *Alpenhof Lodge* (☎ 760-934-6330, 800-828-0371, 6080 Minaret Rd) with its European ambience, starting at $62; or

Econo Lodge (☎ 760-934-6855, 800-845-8764, 3626 Main St), starting at $69.

The Looney Bean (☎ 760-934-1345, 3280 Main St) is a fine choice for breakfast. *Anything Goes (☎ 760-934-2424)* on Old Mammoth Rd serves very creative breakfasts, good soups and salads and has a reasonable dinner menu with good vegetarian options.

Getting There & Away Mammoth Lakes, on Hwy 203, is 3mi west of US 395, 307mi north of Los Angeles, 168mi south of Reno and 320mi east of San Francisco.

The southbound Greyhound bus to Los Angeles ($49/97 one way/roundtrip) departs at 12:30 pm, and the northbound bus to Reno ($37/74) departs at 1:15 am. For other transport options, see also Getting Around later in this section.

GETTING AROUND
There are a number of shuttle services which transport hikers between Owens Valley towns and all Inyo National Forest trailheads. Services include: Inyo Trailhead Transportation (call ☎ 760-876-5518 or 760-876-0035 for shuttles from Lone Pine, or ☎ 760-872-1901 for shuttles from Bishop), which is affiliated with Inyo-Mono Dial-A-Ride; Kountry Korners Enterprises (☎ 760-872-4411, 800-872-0316, ✉ williams@qnet.com); and Backpacker Shuttle Service (inquire at the Greyhound bus station in Bishop ☎ 760-872-2721 for shuttles from Bishop). Rates tend to vary widely depending on itineraries and number of passengers.

Inyo-Mono Dial-A-Ride (☎ 800-922-1930) operates two daily Lone Pine–Bishop roundtrip buses every weekday, departing Lone Pine at 6:30 am and 12:30 pm (one hour, $4) and stopping at Independence and Big Pine. The return service leaves Bishop at noon and 5:30 pm. It also operates a service ($6) from Bishop to Bridgeport, stopping at all towns in between including Mammoth Lakes, departing Bishop at 10:45 am on Monday and Wednesday and arriving at Bridgeport at 5:30 pm. Call to verify pick-up locations.

Mt Whitney

Duration	3 days
Distance	21.4mi (34.5km)
Standard	hard
Start/Finish	Whitney Portal
Nearest Town	Lone Pine
Public Transport	yes

Summary This hugely popular trail rises more than 6000ft in 10.7mi to the top of Mt Whitney, the highest peak in the contiguous USA.

Mt Whitney (14,496ft) is named for Josiah Dwight Whitney, who headed the California State Geological Survey from 1860 to 1874, and is the Sierra Nevada's highest peak. Nearby, five other southern Sierra peaks tower over 14,000ft. The well-marked and maintained trail to the summit gains a challenging 6000ft over 10.7mi. Hikers in good physical condition can reach the summit, but only superbly conditioned and previously acclimatized hikers should attempt this as a gargantuan day hike. (If you go for it, bring a flashlight in case you don't make it all the way down by sunset.) With more than 200 permits issued daily during summer (50 for backpackers and 150 for day hikers), no one is likely to be alone making their way to Mt Whitney's summit.

PLANNING
When to Hike
The trail is usually snow-free from July to September, although patchy ice remains above Trail Camp year-round. Early in the season an ice axe and crampons are useful.

Maps
The USGS 1:24,000 *Mt Whitney* and *Mt Langley* quadrangles and 1:62,500 *Mt Whitney* and *Lone Pine* quadrangles cover the hike, as does Tom Harrison Cartography's 1:63,360 *Mt Whitney High Country Trail Map*.

Permits
Wilderness permits (see Permits under Information earlier in this section) for the Whitney Zone – a designated region jointly

managed by Inyo National Forest and Sequoia and Kings Canyon National Parks – are 100% reservable and in great demand. The permit is free, but a special $15 reservation fee applies.

As well as a wilderness permit, an endorsement (stamp) for the Whitney Zone is required for day hikers and backpackers from May 22 to October 15. The Whitney Zone endorsement is free, but a reservation fee of $2.25 per day hiker and $1.25 per backpacker applies. Self-issue wilderness permits only are required from October 16 to May 21 and can be obtained from any ranger station.

Approaching from Whitney Portal, the Whitney Zone starts above Lone Pine Lake.

NEAREST FACILITIES

Two campgrounds are west of Lone Pine's Alabama Hills. The BLM *Tuttle Creek campground* (by donation) is 1mi south of Whitney Portal Rd off Horseshoe Meadow Rd. The USFS *Lone Pine campground* ($10, 6000ft) is along the south side of Whitney Portal Rd 7mi west of Lone Pine.

Within the USFS Whitney Portal Recreation Area, west of Lone Pine, are two attractive campgrounds tucked in a pine forest along Lone Pine Creek: *Whitney Portal Family campground* ($12, 8000ft), and the first-come, first-served, walk-in only *Hiker Overnight Camp* ($6, 8300ft), which is at the Whitney Portal trailhead. The nearby *Whitney Portal Store* has a good selection of groceries and snacks as well as shower facilities.

GETTING TO/FROM THE HIKE

From Lone Pine's only intersection with a traffic light, drive west from US 395 on Whitney Portal Rd for 13mi to the dramatic granite canyon at Whitney Portal where the road ends. For details of hikers' shuttle services see Getting Around earlier in this section.

THE HIKE
Day 1: Whitney Portal to Trail Camp
4–5 hours, 6mi (9.7km), 3640ft (1092m) ascent

Start early and carry water, as the trail faces east and gets hot by mid-morning. From Whitney Portal (8360ft), the Mt Whitney Trail switchbacks up through forest to cross North Fork Lone Pine Creek and enter John Muir Wilderness after a half-mile. It continues steeply up open switchbacks, then

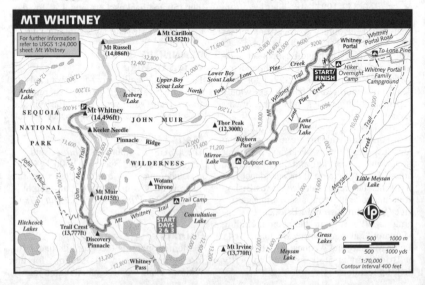

Long Hike – John Muir Trail

Duration	19–20 days
Distance	218mi (351km)
Standard	hard
Start	Happy Isles, Yosemite Valley
Finish	Whitney Portal
Nearest Facilities	Yosemite Valley, Lone Pine
Public Transport	yes

Summary Traversing the roadless crest of Muir's 'Range of Light' through three national parks and two wilderness areas is an unforgettable adventure and the ultimate Sierra Nevada experience.

Offering what many consider to be the USA's very best mountain hiking, the 218mi John Muir Trail links Yosemite Valley and Mt Whitney. Uncrossed by roads, the trail goes through a continual wilderness comprised of Yosemite National Park, the Ansel Adams and John Muir wilderness areas, and Kings Canyon and Sequoia National Parks. Crossing 11 passes, half of which are over 12,000ft and all but one of which are over 10,000ft, the trail traverses the timberline country of the High Sierra and passes thousands of lakes and many granite peaks between 13,000ft and 14,000ft high. The trail frequently descends from the Sierra's crest into forested areas of the western Sierra, with 5000ft deep canyons.

Because of its length, substantial elevation changes and remoteness, completing the John Muir Trail requires top physical fitness, prior backpacking experience and advance planning. It can be hiked in either direction. As a thru-hike, it is both the Sierra's most difficult and rewarding – and a once-in-a-lifetime adventure. To enrich the experience, many hikers choose to divide it into shorter, more manageable, but equally exhilarating, segments with layover days. An average thru-hiker covering 12mi per day would take 19 or 20 days to complete the trail. Faster backpackers might take as few as 12 days.

The route is best covered in six segments: Yosemite Valley to Tuolumne Meadows (24mi, 2 to 3 days); Tuolumne Meadows to Reds Meadow (33mi, 3 days); Reds Meadow to South Fork San Joaquin River (50mi, 4 days); South Fork San Joaquin River to LeConte Canyon (26mi, 3 days); LeConte Canyon to Lower Vidette Meadow (46mi, 4 days); and Lower Vidette Meadow to Whitney Portal (39mi, 3 days).

Most thru-hikers go from north to south rather than beginning with the trail's steepest climb to its highest elevation, the summit of Mt Whitney. In a typical year most of the trail and its passes are not free of snow until mid-July; by late August hikers should be aiming to finish the trail, for although sometimes it is possible to hike into early September, by mid-September storms close the trail for the year.

Several USGS 1:24,000 and 1:62,500 quadrangles cover the John Muir Trail, but not all of the trails leading to and from it. Tom Harrison Cartography's 1:63,360 *Map Pack of the John Muir Trail* consists of 13 maps, each covering a typical day's hike. *Guide to the John Muir Trail* by Thomas Winnett & Kathy Morey is the definitive guidebook.

Backpacking in the Yosemite National Park high country, Cathedral Peak in the background.

eases off to pass through stands of forest and open fields of flowers en route to a crossing of Lone Pine Creek, 2mi from the trailhead. Beyond the creek, a side trail leads east to Lone Pine Lake.

The main trail heads west and ascends to a boggy meadow. Beyond *Outpost Camp* (10,365ft), at the west end of this meadow (labeled Bighorn Park on most maps) 3½mi from the trailhead, the trail crosses Lone Pine Creek and switchbacks up to ford the outlet of Mirror Lake (10,640ft), which lies in a cirque beneath Thor Peak. The trail climbs out of the cirque and leaves the last trees behind as it follows the creek beside huge boulders and granite outcrops. A final ascent up concrete steps leads to *Trail Camp* (12,000ft), beneath Wotans Throne and above the large **Consultation Lake**, with the last reliable water.

Day 2: Trail Camp to Mt Whitney Summit and Return
6–7 hours, 9.4mi (15.1km), 2496ft (749m) ascent/descent
The trail switchbacks relentlessly for 2.2mi up the talus slope to **Trail Crest** (13,777ft), the pass marking Sequoia National Park's eastern boundary. To the west, the Kern River canyon and the distant Great Western Divide come into view with the two large Hitchcock Lakes close below. From the pass, the trail descends north along the ridge line for a half-mile to meet the John Muir Trail. Many hikers leave their backpacks here and continue the 2mi to the summit with day-packs.

The trail zigzags through granite blocks with occasional exposure and sweeping eastern views, and finally reaches the several-acre **summit plateau** and metal-roofed stone hut. Retrace your steps to Trail Camp, Outpost Camp or, if time and your legs allow, all the way back to Whitney Portal.

Day 3: Trail Camp to Whitney Portal
3–4 hours, 6mi (9.7km), 3640ft (1092m) descent
Follow the trail back down, enjoying the views and memory of your ascent.

Humphreys & Evolution Basins

Duration	7 days
Distance	53.8mi (86.6km)
Standard	hard
Start	North Lake
Finish	South Lake
Nearest Town	Bishop
Public Transport	no

Summary This superb circuit through the High Sierra of northern Kings Canyon National Park features the famous Muir Pass and Evolution Valley and crosses three passes, entering and exiting steeply from the eastern Sierra over the range's crest.

This one-week hike includes a circuit of the Glacier Divide and is one of the most impressive longer hikes in the High Sierra. The trail crosses three high passes, visits alpine basins and traverses northern Kings Canyon National Park. Demanding and beautiful, the route ranges between 8000ft and 12,000ft. Hikers should be in top shape to enjoy it.

PLANNING
Maps
The USGS 1:24,000 *Mt Thompson*, *Mt Darwin*, *Mt Tom*, *Mt Hilgard*, *Mt Henry*, *Mt Goddard* and *North Palisade* quadrangles; 1:62,500 *Mt Tom*, *Mt Abbot*, *Blackcap Mountain* and *Mt Goddard* quadrangles; and 1:100,000 *Bishop* sheet cover the hike.

NEAREST FACILITIES
Almost a dozen campgrounds ($12) between 7500ft and 9500ft, most with very few sites, are in the USFS Bishop Creek Recreation Area west of Bishop. Beyond the South Lake Rd turnoff on the way to Lake Sabrina are *three campgrounds*, and beyond North Lake is *North Lake campground* at the Piute Pass trailhead. *Four campgrounds* are along South Lake Rd. The largest is *Four Jeffrey*, although *Willow* is closest to the Bishop Pass trailhead at the end of the hike. Two small stores and two signed public shower facilities are also along South Lake Rd.

GETTING TO/FROM THE HIKE

The North Lake and South Lake trailheads are 12mi apart, which necessitates prearranging a vehicle shuttle or planning to hitchhike or walk on the road between the trailheads. A hikers' shuttle service can drop your vehicle at the finishing trailhead and drive you to the starting trailhead for about $60. (See Getting Around earlier in this section for information on shuttle services.) It is also worth inquiring about arranging shuttles from the pack stations near the trailheads – Bishop Pack Outfitters (☎ 760-873-4785) at North Lake and Parcher's Resort (☎ 760-873-4177) at South Lake.

From downtown Bishop, drive west for 14mi on Hwy 168 (W Line St) to the South Lake Rd junction. To reach North Lake and the beginning of the hike, continue straight for three more miles, beyond Aspendell towards Lake Sabrina, and turn onto the single-lane, 2mi-long, partly paved road to the North Lake trailhead parking lot. Walk for 0.6mi along the road to North Lake campground from where the Piute Pass Trail begins.

To reach South Lake, turn left onto South Lake Rd at its junction with Hwy 168 and go 7mi to its end at the Bishop Pass trailhead.

THE HIKE
Day 1: North Lake to Upper Golden Trout Lake

5–6 hours, 8mi (12.9km), 2063ft (619m) ascent, 570ft (171m) descent

The Piute Pass Trail, heavily used by pack strings (horse trains), is dusty and rutted as it climbs through aspens along North Fork Bishop Creek. It soon enters John Muir Wilderness and crosses the creek twice in quick succession. After switchbacking up a small granite bench, the trail levels off through forest, then works its way up the north slope across red rock beneath Piute Crags. Turning back towards the cascading creek, the well-engineered trail surmounts an enormous granite bench to emerge at Loch Leven (10,700ft), which lies in a broad, glacially formed granite valley, with Piute Pass visible ahead. The walking is easy up this meadow-dotted bowl with impressive granite peaks on either side. Passing a few *campsites* at the east end of Loch Leven, the trail rolls upwards north of the splashing stream to Piute Lake (10,985ft), with more *campsites*, 3½mi from the trailhead. The trail rises over grassy benches and switchbacks up a final granite rib to **Piute Pass** (11,423ft), 1½mi from the lake. The broad vista sweeps from the Glacier Divide to the distant Pinnacles and across the Humphreys Basin to Mt Humphreys (13,986ft), rising north of the pass.

The trail swings north of grass-lined Summit Lake as it descends over alpine terrain, crossing several streams and passing a trail leading north to Desolation Lake. Where the trail crosses the outlet from Desolation Lake, head south about a half-mile to the *campsites* around Upper Golden Trout Lake (10,850ft), about 3½mi from the pass.

Day 2: Upper Golden Trout Lake to Piute Creek

5–6 hours, 9mi (14.5km), 2800ft (840m) descent

The trail descends into forest and passes through many meadows as it follows Piute Creek to Hutchinson Meadow (9438ft), just west of the confluence with French Canyon Creek and about 4½mi from Upper Golden Trout Lake. From this lovely meadow (with *campsites*), the trail stays along the north side of Piute Creek and crosses East Pinnacle Creek, the last reliable water until reaching the South Fork San Joaquin River. Soon it leaves the forest and descends rocky slopes into the narrowing Piute Canyon, staying high above the creek. A series of dry switchbacks brings the trail to seasonal Turret Creek. It then descends to meet the combined Pacific Crest and John Muir Trails and turns southeast (left) to cross Piute Creek over a steel bridge (8080ft) which marks the boundary of Kings Canyon National Park. *Campsites* are along the creek beyond the bridge.

Day 3: Piute Creek to McClure Meadow

4–5 hours, 7.3mi (11.8km), 1200ft (360m) ascent

The trail ascends along the north side of the South Fork San Joaquin River, passing level

SIERRA NEVADA

HUMPHREYS & EVOLUTION BASINS

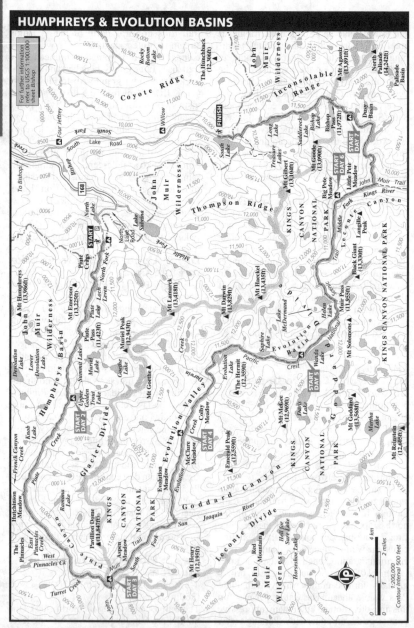

Aspen Meadow. Continuing up the canyon, the trail ascends over rock and crosses the river on a bridge to its south side. As the canyon opens, the trail crosses meadows and passes a trail that leads south up Goddard Canyon. Turning east, the trail crosses the South Fork San Joaquin River and begins a series of switchbacks that brings it to a crossing of Evolution Creek and into Evolution Meadow (9280ft). There are *campsites* here, or follow the forested trail along the north side of the Evolution Valley to soon arrive at large McClure Meadow (9600ft), with abundant, popular *campsites*.

Day 4: McClure Meadow to Wanda Lake
5–6 hours, 8mi (12.9km), 1800ft (540m) ascent

The trail continues for about 1½mi to Colby Meadow (9840ft), the highest meadow in the picturesque valley and a good alternative place to *camp*. It rises to cross Darwin Creek, then switchbacks up out of forest and turns southeast to the northern shore of exquisite **Evolution Lake** (10,850ft), another possible *camp*. Continuing along the eastern lakeshore, the trail fords the lake's inlet, then rises to pass west of beautiful Sapphire Lake and switchbacks up to cross the outlet of dramatically barren Wanda Lake (11,426ft) in the midst of Evolution Basin. Stark *campsites* near the lake's outlet afford spectacular views.

Day 5: Wanda Lake to Big Pete Meadow
5–6 hours, 8½mi (13.7km), 530ft (159m) ascent, 2755ft (827m) descent

Tracing the eastern lakeshore, the trail rises to pass southeast of Lake McDermand and then continues up to **Muir Pass** (11,955ft), crossing the Goddard Divide, with outstanding views and a stone hut erected by the Sierra Club as a memorial to John Muir, 2.2mi from Wanda Lake. Stony switchbacks bring the trail to the southern end of barren Helen Lake to cross its inflow stream, the source of Middle Fork Kings River. After skirting Helen Lake's southeast shore, the trail descends along its outflow stream to an unnamed lake, fords its inlet and outlet and continues down to a meadow at the inlet of a second unnamed rocky lake east of Helen Lake. The trail skirts its south shore and fords its outlet, then turns south and descends steep talus into forested **Leconte Canyon** to reach Big Pete Meadow (9200ft), with plentiful *campsites* amid the trees.

Day 6: Big Pete Meadow to Dusy Basin
4–5 hours, 6mi (9.7km), 2600ft (780m) ascent, 480ft (144m) descent

The trail heads south to the alternative *campsites* at Little Pete Meadow (8880ft), then descends to a junction with the Bishop Pass Trail (8710ft). Here, the trail to Bishop Pass leaves the combined Pacific Crest and John Muir Trails and turns east (left) and switchbacks up two steep sections through forest along Dusy Branch Creek – which it crosses twice – to the sparsely forested Dusy Basin. Passing north of the lowest lake, it turns north and ascends to *campsites* at the west end of the northernmost large lake (11,350ft) in the stark alpine basin.

Day 7: Dusy Basin to South Lake
5–6 hours, 7mi (11.3km), 625ft (188m) ascent, 2200ft (660m) descent

The trail continues up over granite and sand and swings east to broad **Bishop Pass** (11,972ft), from where it descends between Thompson Ridge and the Inconsolable Range past the headwaters of South Fork Bishop Creek and its chain of lakes. From the pass, the good trail begins switchbacking down a granite buttress and across talus blocks to pass northeast of Bishop Lake and then along the east shore of Saddlerock Lake. After it crosses the lake's outlet it descends along the tumbling stream past pretty Timberline Tarns. Crossing their outlet, the trail traverses down a rocky slope high above Spearhead Lake to the south end of Long Lake, a desirable *campsite*. Running along the east shore of this aptly named lake, it passes the junction with the Ruwau Lake Trail, and continues down, passing a side trail to Bull and Chocolate

Lakes. The trail drops past two granite ribs and switchbacks down to more level forest and past the side trail to Treasure Lakes, then descends above the east side of South Lake to the trailhead.

Minarets

Duration	3 or 4 days
Distance	15.2mi (24.5km)
Standard	hard
Start	Agnew Meadows
Finish	Devil's Postpile
Nearest Town	Mammoth Lakes
Public Transport	yes

Summary The lakes nestled at the base of the magnificent Minarets may be the most beautiful in the Sierra Nevada, as well as some of the most accessible, making them a photographer's delight.

The many pinnacles of the knife-edged Minarets ridge are part of the Ritter Range – hard, dark metamorphosed mountains more than 100 million years older than the Sierra's granite peaks. The twin summits of Mt Ritter (13,157ft) and Banner Peak (12,945ft) are the highest of the central Sierra and this range. The lakes along the eastern base of the range are renowned for their charm. Both the Pacific Crest and John Muir Trails pass nearby and, with the added attraction of Devil's Postpile National Monument, this hike through Ansel Adams Wilderness is extremely popular.

PLANNING
When to Hike
Snow does not melt off the rugged trail between Iceberg and Minaret Lakes until mid-August.

What to Bring
Bear-resistant canisters for food storage are recommended as the counter-balance method has not been successful in this area.

Maps
The USGS 1:24,000 *Mammoth Mountain* and *Mt Ritter* quadrangles and 1:62,500 *Devils Postpile* quadrangles cover the hike, as do Tom Harrison Cartography's 1:63,360 *Mammoth High Country Trail Map* and the USFS 1:63,360 *Ansel Adams Wilderness* map.

Permits
A free wilderness permit is required for hikes in the Ansel Adams Wilderness. These can be arranged at the Mammoth Lakes USFS ranger station (see Mammoth Lakes under Nearest Towns earlier in this section).

NEAREST FACILITIES
For information on Mammoth Lakes, see Nearest Towns earlier in this section. On Hwy 203 in the USFS Mammoth Lakes Recreation Area west of Mammoth Lakes are six campgrounds ($12). The USFS campgrounds (from north to south) are: *Agnew Meadows* (at the trailhead), *Upper Soda Springs*, *Pumice Flat*, *Minaret Falls* and *Red's Meadow*, which has a natural hot spring and shower facilities. Nearby is the NPS *Devil's Postpile campground*.

GETTING TO/FROM THE HIKE
Agnew Meadows and Devil's Postpile are on Minaret Summit Rd west of Mammoth Lakes and Mammoth Mountain (11,053ft). In Mammoth Lakes, Hwy 203 follows Main St and turns north onto Minaret Rd. The road then climbs to Minaret Summit (9175ft), a pass beyond which the road is closed to private vehicles from 7:30 am to 5:30 pm daily from mid-June to mid-September.

During these hours everyone must use the Red's Meadow/Devil's Postpile shuttle service, except those with confirmed campground reservations. (A wilderness permit on its own does not entitle backpackers to drive their own vehicles to trailheads.) The shuttle operates every 20 to 30 minutes and makes 10 stops, including the six campgrounds. The first daily shuttle departs from *Mammoth Mountain Inn* (☎ 760-934-0686) on Minaret Rd at 8 am; the last departs at 5:30 pm. The last bus departs Red's Meadow at 6:15 pm. The one-way/round-trip fare is $5/9.

THE HIKE
Day 1: Agnew Meadows to Ediza Lake

4–5 hours, 6mi (9.7km), 965ft (290m) ascent

From the Agnew Meadows campground (8335ft) the trail leads northwest, descending to meet Middle Fork San Joaquin River and the combined Pacific Crest and River Trails. After passing Olaine Lake, the trail turns west (left), leaving the River Trail, and switchbacks up the canyon wall towards the cascading outlet of Shadow Lake, 3mi from the trailhead. The trail skirts the northern shore to meet the John Muir Trail on the north side of Shadow Creek, which it follows upstream for a mile to a junction where the John Muir Trail heads north. The trail to Ediza Lake continues west along lovely Shadow Creek, passing the trail north to Nydiver Lakes, arriving after 1½mi at Ediza Lake (9300ft), where *camping* is restricted to the south shore.

Day 2: Ediza Lake to Minaret Lake

3–4 hours, 3mi (4.8km), 980ft (294m) ascent, 480ft (144m) descent

From the lake's southeast end, the faint trail switchbacks up, paralleling the willow-lined stream for a mile to **Iceberg Lake** (9800ft), close under the Minarets. Beyond Iceberg Lake the Class 2 route is cross-country, steep, often snow-covered and is recommended only for experienced backpackers; others can retrace their steps to Agnew Meadows via Ediza Lake.

The route works around Iceberg Lake's eastern shore, then ascends along the outlet of Cecile Lake over often snow-covered steep, difficult talus to **Cecile Lake** (10,280ft) with unsurpassed views and reflections of the Minarets. Skirt its east shore and descend steeply over rock and talus to splendid Minaret Lake (9800ft), with *campsites* along the north, east and south shores.

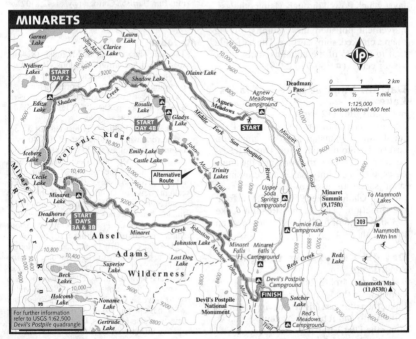

Day 3A: Minaret Lake to Devil's Postpile

4–5 hours, 6.2mi (10km), 1240ft (372m) descent

A good trail descends switchbacks, following the outflow stream to Minaret Lake into more level forest and meadow along the creek, after which it descends rocky switchbacks into forest. Following the creek, the trail descends through Johnston Meadow. Just before the two small Johnston Lakes is another junction with the John Muir Trail, which is followed south past **Minaret Falls** for 2mi to *Devil's Postpile campground* (7560ft).

Side Trip: Devil's Postpile National Monument

30 minutes, 1mi (1.61km)

This monument's 60ft, four- to seven-sided columns of blue-gray basalt are the most conspicuous and interesting product of the area's volcanic activity. The columns formed more than 100,000 years ago when lava, which flowed through Mammoth Pass, cooled and fractured vertically. Later glacial movement polished the columns, giving them a cracked, shiny surface. The half-mile trail to the top of the columns starts at the visitor center (☎ 760-934-2289).

Day 3B: Minaret Lake to Gladys Lake

5–6 hours, 8mi (12.9km)

Follow the trail down from Minaret Lake for 4.2mi to Johnston Meadow, then turn east (left) onto the John Muir Trail. The ascending trail soon turns north and the angle eases, passing Trinity Lakes and crossing a small saddle to less-crowded *campsites* at pleasant **Gladys Lake** (9580ft), 3.8mi from the junction. The larger **Rosalie Lake** (9350ft) is 0.6mi further, with *campsites* on the east shore.

Day 4B: Gladys Lake to Agnew Meadows

3–4 hours, 5.1mi (8.2km)

Continue on the John Muir Trail to Shadow Lake, then turn east (right), leaving the John Muir Trail, and return to Agnew Meadows along the Day 1 trail.

Other Hikes

LAKE TAHOE REGION

Mt Tallac

Hiking 4½mi (7.3km) to the top of Mt Tallac (9735ft) above Tahoe's southwestern lakeshore rewards strenuous hiking with majestic views of Fallen Leaf Lake, Desolation Wilderness and Lake Tahoe. A wilderness permit is required for this six- to seven-hour day hike (see the Desolation Traverse hike for details.)

The trailhead parking area (6480ft) is at the end of a paved road south and directly opposite the entrance to Baldwin Beach, 0.7mi west of the USFS Lake Tahoe visitor center (see South Lake Tahoe under Nearest Towns & Facilities in the Lake Tahoe Area section). The first 2½mi past Floating Island Lake to Cathedral Lake rises gradually above Fallen Leaf Lake, beyond which the trail climbs steeply to the rocky summit.

An alternative, longer, route starts from the Glen Alpine trailhead (6560ft) beyond the south end of Fallen Leaf Lake, and goes 4.2mi to Gilmore Lake (8300ft), then 1.8mi to the summit. Tom Harrison Cartography's 1:42,240 *Desolation Wilderness Trail Map* covers the hike.

Mt Judah

The accessible summit of Mt Judah (8243ft), west of Truckee, affords fabulous views of the northern Sierra's lakes and peaks in and surrounding Tahoe National Forest. This well-used, easy, 4½mi (7.3km) trail is a three- to 3½-hour roundtrip. The USGS 1:24,000 *Norden* quadrangle covers the hike.

The signed trailhead is just east of an unpaved road which leads south off US 40 from Donner Pass. Follow the PCT south to its junction with the Mt Judah Loop. The trail soon turns east, before the chairlifts, to climb along a forested trail to Donner Peak (8019ft) and excellent views of Donner Lake. It then turns south along a ridge to the broad summit of Mt Judah, then descends south through hemlock forest to rejoin the PCT. A five-minute detour south leads to historic Roller Pass.

The hike can easily be extended into a longer day hike or overnight trip by continuing south on the PCT to Mt Lincoln, Anderson Peak, Tinker Knob and beyond. Two excellent alternatives are to continue for one or two days to Squaw Valley or to traverse Granite Chief Wilderness (no wilderness permit required) over two or three days to Alpine Meadows, both on the west side of Hwy 89 between Truckee and Tahoe City.

TAHOE TO YOSEMITE
Carson Pass to Ebbetts Pass

South of Carson Pass (8573ft) on Hwy 88, the PCT continues to Ebbetts Pass (8730ft) on Hwy 4. This four-day, 28mi (45.1km) long segment passes through two portions of Mokelumne Wilderness in the middle of which is Blue Lakes, a popular recreation area. The USFS 1:63,360 *Mokelumne Wilderness* map covers the hike, which is best done between mid-June to mid-August, after which bow-hunting season begins near Blue Lakes.

See Day 1 of the Fourth of July Lake hike for a description from Carson Pass to Forestdale Divide. Leaving Mokelumne Wilderness, the PCT crosses the unpaved Blue Lakes Rd from Hope Valley and parallels it southeast past Lost Lakes and the open western slopes of the Nipple, well above Upper Blue Lake. Descending to recross Blue Lakes Rd, the trail crosses Pleasant Valley Creek and an outlet of Tamarack Lake, passes several lakes and reservoirs, goes over a saddle south of a small knob and re-enters Mokelumne Wilderness.

The PCT then switchbacks up a ridge to a junction with the short spur trail to Raymond Lake beneath Raymond Peak (10,014ft). The PCT then heads southeast, south and then east around Reynolds Peak, crossing Eagle Creek and Raymond Meadows, then goes over a saddle to Upper Kinney Lake. It next swings south of the lake, rises over a ridge and descends to Ebbetts Pass.

Green Creek & Virginia Canyon

This excellent three-day loop through Hoover Wilderness and upper Virginia Canyon in northeastern Yosemite National Park offers plenty of solitude and scenic splendor. The Green Creek trailhead (8100ft) is at the end of bumpy, unpaved Green Lakes Rd, which turns southwest off US 395 4½mi south of Bridgeport. The USFS 1:63,360 *Hoover Wilderness* map depicts the region.

The route goes southwest along West Fork Green Creek to Green Lake, then turns south to East Lake and the beautiful, smaller Gilman Lake beneath the imposing Dunderberg Peak (12,374ft). The second day it ascends southwest past Hoover Lakes to Summit Lake (10,240ft), then descends to a junction with the Virginia Canyon Trail, 4mi north of its junction with the PCT. To the right an indistinct trail leads up along the Return Creek canyon to fine campsites on a bench between the confluence of two streams in Upper Virginia Canyon. Great day hikes can be made from

this campsite beneath Stanton, Virginia and Twin Peaks. Return east over nearby Virginia Pass (10,400ft) on a good trail down Glines Canyon to Green Lake and the trailhead.

YOSEMITE NATIONAL PARK
Glacier Point & Panorama Cliff

This strenuous 12.6mi (20.3km), six- to seven-hour hike, which climbs out of Yosemite Valley and traverses its south rim before descending to the valley floor, is a visual feast of cascades, granite domes and walls. Passing alongside three of the valley's major waterfalls, the trail has 7800ft of elevation gain and descent, making it a grueling yet rewarding experience. The USGS 1:24,000 *Half Dome* quadrangle covers the trail, which is best tackled between July and October.

Beginning from Leidig Meadow along Southside Dr at Yosemite Valley's western end, the Four Mile Trail (actually more like 4.6mi) climbs steadily to Glacier Point (7214ft), a 3200ft cliff overlooking Yosemite Valley. At Glacier Point are unique perspectives of Royal Arches, Washington Column and North and Half Domes. From Glacier Point the Panorama Trail descends south to cross Illilouette Creek with views of 370ft Illilouette Fall and climbs east along Panorama Cliff, with amazing views. The trail descends to join the John Muir Trail a short distance before Nevada Fall, then descends either the Mist Trail via Vernal Fall or the longer and more gentle John Muir Trail to Happy Isles at the valley's eastern end.

Mt Hoffman

Mt Hoffman (10,850ft) rises in the park's geographical center and commands outstanding views of the entire high country, with more than 50 peaks visible. The first peak climbed in Yosemite, it remains one of the park's most frequently visited summits. The 6mi (9.7km), easy-medium hike takes four to five hours. Start from the May Lake trailhead on Old Tioga Rd, which turns north off Tioga Rd (Hwy 120) 2.2mi west of Olmsted Point and 3.2mi east of Porcupine Flat campground. The USGS 1:24,000 *Tenaya Lake* and *Yosemite Falls* quadrangles cover the hike, which is best done between July and October.

The easy 2.1mi trail to May Lake has fine views of Cathedral Peak, Mt Clark, Clouds Rest and Half Dome. At May Lake the trail forks; the left fork runs along the lake's southern shore through attractive campsites to the lake's southwest corner. From there, the trail turns south and ascends through a talus field where it is indistinct (although the route is obvious). Following the left side of a small stream, the trail soon reaches a small meadow, beyond which it heads southwest and angles upwards for about 0.1mi before turning back sharply northwest directly towards Mt Hoffman's eastern summit. Several paths marked with cairns lead up this open, rocky slope – they all converge above and angle northwest though a broad, sloping meadow towards the western, highest summit, reached by a short, easy, Class 2 scramble. Camping is possible on the vast plateau near the eastern summit although water must be carried from May Lake or snow lying in the north-facing couloirs melted. The 360-degree views from the summit plateau are outstanding.

SEQUOIA & KINGS CANYON NATIONAL PARKS
Moro Rock
This exfoliating granite feature rises 4000ft above the Middle Fork Kaweah River. A quarter-mile trail climbs 300ft up 400 steps to the summit (6725ft) with commanding views of much of Sequoia National Park. A quick trip to the top and a glimpse of the peaks of the Great Western Divide may inspire the hiker to head straight to Mineral King for a backpack. From Generals Hwy in Giant Forest, drive 1½mi southeast on Crescent Meadow Rd to the trailhead.

Congress Trail
A 2.1mi (3.4km) paved loop in the heart of Giant Forest, the Congress Trail is the star attraction of Sequoia National Park. Understandably popular, it offers the best introduction to what John Muir called 'the most beautiful and majestic woods on earth.' Beginning from the 2300–2700 year old General Sherman Tree – the largest of the giant sequoias – the easy trail passes the giant President and Chief Sequoyah trees, the imposing House and Senate groups, and the General Lee and McKinley trees. A pamphlet for this impressive, self-guided nature trail is available at the trailhead. To spend more time hiking in Giant Forest, combine this hike with the Trail of the Sequoias to make a 7.2mi loop.

Trail of The Sequoias
This is an easy, 5.1mi (8.2km) hike past open meadows and along streams through some of the finest stands of sequoias. It follows the Congress Trail clockwise for its first 0.8mi, leaving the paved pathway just past the Chief Sequoyah tree. The trail ascends a small ridge, then descends to Crescent Creek and parallels it to Log

Meadow and historic Tharp's Log – a huge hollow log that served as the summer home of Hale Tharp, Giant Forest's first settler. The trail continues through Crescent Meadow and loops around to pass the smaller, more intimate Circle Meadow before rejoining the Congress Trail at the Senate Group. Alternatively, start the Trail of the Sequoias from the parking lot at the end of Crescent Meadow Rd, 3½mi southeast of Generals Hwy from Giant Forest.

Lower Monarch Lake
This lake lies in a rocky bowl above treeline beneath jagged Sawtooth Peak (12,393ft), which dominates Mineral King Valley, and between colorful Empire and Rainbow Mountains. This popular 10mi (16.1km) roundtrip, a steep and strenuous day hike from Mineral King, rewards overnight backpackers with photogenic views. The USGS 1:24,000 *Mineral King* quadrangle covers the hike.

From the Sawtooth-Monarch parking area (7840ft), follow the dusty Sawtooth Pass Trail on a long traverse through sagebrush to its junction with the Timber Gap Trail after about a mile. Bear east (right) at the junction and continue up the open slope into the Monarch Creek canyon and Groundhog Meadow in another mile. Cross the creek into forest and switchback relentlessly up the ridge to the Crystal Lake Trail junction in 2.2mi. Follow the Sawtooth Pass Trail north across the shoulder of the ridge to regain the Monarch Creek drainage, with glimpses of Sawtooth Peak and nearby Glacier Pass. Passing through a rocky area, the trail crosses Monarch Creek twice and arrives at the west end of Lower Monarch Lake (10,380ft) with campsites above the lake's north shore.

A three-hour, 2.4mi side trip to Sawtooth Pass (11,600ft) on the Great Western Divide follows a difficult and faint trail over pulverized granite, but rewards with views of the Kaweah Peaks and the Whitney crest.

Little Five Lakes Loop
Another popular hike from Mineral King in Sequoia National Park, this strenuous, 31mi (49.9km), four-day loop crosses three passes, one of which is on the Great Western Divide, and visits fine fishing lakes.

From the Sawtooth-Monarch parking area, the trail ascends north to Timber Gap, then drops steeply through flower gardens at the head of Timber Creek to a crossing of Cliff Creek. North of the creek are campsites and a trail junction.

The trail turns east, follows the north side of Cliff Creek past some falls and climbs to cross the outlet from Pinto Lake. A short spur (right) leads to Pinto Lake and a campsite, 8½mi from the trailhead. The main trail continues east and switchbacks steadily to Black Rock Pass (11,650ft) with immense views of Little Five Lakes, Big Five Lakes, Kaweah peaks and the distant Sierra crest. The trail descends southeast, turns northeast to pass Little Five Lakes, then crosses the outlet of the main lake to descend through forest for a mile before rising to a ridge above the Big Five Lakes. At the ridge a side trail forks right to upper Big Five Lakes, while the main trail continues down switchbacks past (east of) the lowest lake with campsites near the outlet. A rocky ascent then leads to the ridge south of the Big Five Lakes and north of a small, unnamed lake. The trail then switchbacks down to join the Lost Canyon Trail before ascending west into upper Lost Canyon. Continuing west, it crosses Sawtooth Pass and returns via Monarch Lake to Mineral King.

Sierra High Route
Traversing along the axis of the Sierra Nevada, the 195mi (314km) Sierra High Route is a rugged and extreme alternative to the classic John Muir Trail. With many sections of Class 2 hiking, the route is recommended only for experienced and adventurous backpackers who enjoy the challenge of route finding through isolated, rigorous terrain and commitment to a difficult route. Never dropping below 9000ft, the route is best hiked between August and Labor Day. *The Sierra High Route: Traversing Timberline Country* by Steve Roper, who conceived this route, is the definitive guidebook.

Starting from Roads End in Kings Canyon National Park, the High Sierra Route stays close to timberline and avoids major trails en route to its terminus at Twin Lakes near Bridgeport via Yosemite National Park. It is best done in five roughly week-long segments, which can be done independently or consecutively: Kings Canyon to Dusy Basin; Dusy Basin to Lake Italy; Lake Italy to Devil's Postpile (the easiest segment); Devil's Postpile to Tuolumne Meadows; and Tuolumne Meadows to Twin Lakes.

EASTERN SIERRA
Palisade Crest
Rising almost 2mi above the Owens Valley town of Big Pine, the granite Palisades in John Muir Wilderness are the Sierra Nevada's second highest group of peaks and the most ruggedly alpine in character, with six summits which are over 14,000ft. Glaciers lie at their eastern base; Palisade Glacier is the largest in the Sierra (2½mi long and almost 1mi wide) and the southernmost in the contiguous USA. It is possible to see the Palisade Crest up close on either an 18mi (29km) day hike or an overnight trip.

From Big Pine (4000ft), drive west on Crocker St, which becomes Glacier Lodge Rd, 10mi to the trailhead. Hike along North Fork Big Pine Creek past small First Falls walk-in campground and continue 5½mi past the first three of seven turquoise lakes in a numbered chain. Half a mile beyond Third Lake the trail forks. The left fork heads south through Sam Mack Meadow to the snout of Palisade Glacier (3mi one way). The right fork continues to a campsite above the west shore of Fourth Lake (10,750ft). About 1½mi further is Sixth Lake (11,100ft). From Fourth Lake, continue on the trail past Black Lake to the trailhead. The USGS 1:24,000 *Split Mountain* quadrangle covers the trail.

Kearsarge Pass
This pass (11,823ft), one of the easiest passes in the eastern Sierra, is just 4.8mi (7.7km) and three to four hours from the trailhead (9200ft) in Onion Valley. The pleasant day hike to the pass offers spectacular views of the Kearsarge Pinnacles and quick access to the John Muir Trail and Rae Lakes Loop. From the junction of US 395 (Edwards St) and Market St in Independence, drive 13mi west on Onion Valley Rd. Onion Valley campground, open June to mid-September, is at the trailhead. The national forest requires backpackers to use bear-resistant food canisters when camping east of the pass; rent them from the campground host for $5 per day from 7:30 am to 11:30 am. The USGS 1:24,000 *Kearsarge Pass* quadrangle is adequate for this hike.

The trail ascends past Little Pothole Lake and the attractive Gilmore and Flower Lakes. It climbs past pretty Heart Lake to the top of a large granite wall and passes above Big Pothole Lake to Kearsarge Pass. From here the trail descends past the Kearsarge and Bullfrog Lakes to meet the John Muir Trail.

Pacific Northwest

PACIFIC NORTHWEST

Avid hikers living in the mountainous and heavily-timbered states of Oregon and Washington spend most of their lives hiking to places they've never been before. Wild, scenic and remarkably diverse, the Pacific Northwest offers unlimited hiking on more than 20,000mi of trails.

At the heart of the Northwest is the Cascade Range, a queue of snow-topped volcanoes preserved in a patchwork of wilderness areas and national parks. Headliners include Mt Rainier National Park and Alpine Lakes Wilderness, both in Washington. Jet-setters and mountaineers love this state, which shoulders the highest and most glaciered Cascade peaks. While Oregon certainly has its own big mountains, its backyard splendors are more varied and offer more solitude. Exquisite volcanos, an abundance of waterfalls and a 362mi ocean coastline preserved as a public park are the signatures of this state.

Backpacking in this region is not for the comfort-oriented. Mountain hikes involve steep climbs, there are no lodges (the Rogue River Trail being the only exception) and hikers must constantly gamble against rain, though river valleys and the ocean coast offer longer hiking seasons and kinder terrain.

HISTORY

Native Americans inhabited the Pacific Northwest 10,000 years before the arrival of the first European settlers, who walked to Oregon on a 2000mi, six-month journey from Missouri. It was one of the last regions of the contiguous USA to be settled by Europeans, and was first pioneered by fur trappers.

Explorers such as Lewis & Clark and Canadian David Thompson set out to the region in canoes and on foot in the early 19th century in search of a waterway to the Pacific Ocean. But it wasn't until Methodist missionaries from New England traveled to Oregon in the 1830s that this unclaimed territory finally attracted settlers. More than 53,000 Midwest farmers and homesteaders poured into the Willamette Valley over the

HIGHLIGHTS

JOHN ELK III

Mt Rainier towers over hikers in the Paradise area, Cascade Range, Washington.

- A cold night at the toe of a glacier in North Cascades National Park
- Vaulting off a 500ft sand dune near the seashore in the Oregon Dunes National Recreation Area
- Emerging from dark forest to a dazzling wildflower meadow on a snow-topped Cascade Range volcano
- Contemplating Native American rock carvings on a wilderness beach in Olympic National Park
- A cooling plunge down a natural rock waterslide along the Rogue River Trail

Oregon Trail in the 1840s and 1850s. Oregon attained statehood in 1848, and Washington in 1889.

NATURAL HISTORY

Pressures built up by the subduction of the ocean floor beneath the North American

PACIFIC NORTHWEST

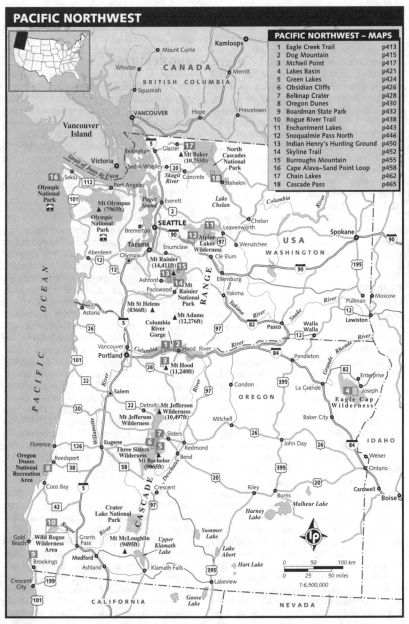

PACIFIC NORTHWEST

PACIFIC NORTHWEST – MAPS

1	Eagle Creek Trail	p413
2	Dog Mountain	p415
3	McNeil Point	p417
4	Lakes Basin	p421
5	Green Lakes	p424
6	Obsidian Cliffs	p426
7	Belknap Crater	p428
8	Oregon Dunes	p430
9	Boardman State Park	p432
10	Rogue River Trail	p438
11	Enchantment Lakes	p443
12	Snoqualmie Pass North	p446
13	Indian Henry's Hunting Ground	p450
14	Skyline Trail	p452
15	Burroughs Mountain	p455
16	Cape Alava–Sand Point Loop	p458
17	Chain Lakes	p462
18	Cascade Pass	p465

PACIFIC NORTHWEST

continent have been shaping the landscape with lava flows and volcanic eruptions for 40 million years. Today's Cascade mountains are relatively recent, formed by successive lava flows that occurred during the intense volcanic activity of the last 1 to 7 million years. Ice ages recurring over the last 2 million years scooped out straits and basins and sharpened peaks. An explosive eruption that obliterated the summit of Mt St Helens in 1980 shows that many of these seemingly quiet volcanoes are still active.

Northwest forests are distinguished by tall stands of fir, pine and cedar. Some, like the Douglas fir, easily reach heights of 300ft. Bears, elk, cougars and deer all make tracks here. Chinook salmon, a migratory fish revered by Native Americans and sport fisherman alike, still run in the region's rivers but are threatened with extinction by hydroelectric dams and logging. Offshore, in the Pacific Ocean, gray whales migrate.

CLIMATE

Oregon's and Washington's diverse geographies are subject to a variety of weather patterns. Cold and wet winters are the norm for the entire region, making summer the most favorable time to hike.

The Cascades divide the Northwest into two primary climates. West of the Cascades the Pacific Ocean generates rainfall that gets dumped over the coast and western valleys. Spring tends to be prolonged and rainy; summers pleasantly sunny and warm with temperatures from 60° to 90°F. The coast is cooler and gets more rain and less sun – expect foggy mornings, windy afternoons and summer temperatures in the 60°s or 70°sF.

Clouds disperse as they pass over the Cascades, casting a rain shadow over the eastern regions. Land east of the Cascade crest is dry and desert-like, with hotter summers and colder, snowy winters. Hot temperatures in the mid-90°sF are the norm in the summer.

Snow reaches the lower elevations of the Cascades from November to June. Upper elevation trails (5000ft and higher) often don't thaw until mid-July or August. Hikers on alpine trails in good weather can expect hot days and cold nights. Mosquitoes are

unbearable for the first month after snowmelt and are present at all hours near mountain forests, lakes and meadows. Mid-August and September are usually the best months for an overnight trip.

A winter of heavy winds and precipitation brings landslides, washouts and blowdowns to western forests, which can close trails during the following season. Hot, dry summers threaten deadly forest fires in the eastern regions, often caused by lightning. The United States Forest Service (USFS) monitors fire danger in all regions, and will close trails in conditions of extreme danger.

INFORMATION
Maps

Widely available Green Trails 1:69,500 maps are ideal for hikers and have ranger station and campground information printed on the back. Unfortunately, this Washington-based company produces only a few maps for Oregon. Topographic hiking maps by other publishers are available only for Oregon's most popular wilderness areas. United States Geological Survey (USGS) 7½ minute series topographic maps and forest service maps are widely available, though these are often too cumbersome for trail use.

Free state highway maps can be ordered from the Oregon Tourism Commission (☎ 800-547-7842) and the Washington State Tourism Division (☎ 800-544-1800 x800). DeLorme's *Oregon Atlas & Gazetteer* and *Washington Atlas & Gazetteer* ($16.95) are both large books of comprehensive 1:150,000 and 1:300,000 scale topographic maps that detail backroads, campgrounds and recreation facilities.

Books

William Sullivan's regional titles in the 100 Hikes in Oregon series weave ecology, geology, history and folklore with straightforward trail descriptions and hand-drawn maps. These books set the standard for Oregon trail guides and it's rare to pull up to a trailhead without spotting a worn-out copy on the front seat of the next car. *100 Hikes in Northwest Oregon* and *100 Hikes in the Central Oregon Cascades* cover the most popular areas. Oregon's wilderness areas are inventoried in *Exploring Oregon's Wild Areas*, also by Sullivan.

The conservationist duo Ira Spring & Harvey Manning author the 100 Hikes in Washington series published by the Mountaineers; these guides seem intended to lead hikers to every glacier in Washington's Cascades. Marge & Ted Muller's *Exploring Washington's Wild Areas*, is a good source for those itching to strike out to other parts of the state.

National Audubon Society's *Field Guide to the Pacific Northwest* succinctly describes Oregon's and Washington's ecology in more than 400 compact, color pages. *Plants & Animals of the Pacific Northwest* by Eugene N Kozloff provides deeper insight into the western regions of these states. *Trees To Know in Oregon* (published by OSU Extension Service) contains useful clues for making sense out of the Northwest's diverse forests, and is a good $4 investment regardless of which state you visit. Peterson Field Guides' *Pacific States Wildflowers* identifies hundreds of wildflowers.

For travel carry Lonely Planet's *Pacific Northwest* and/or *Seattle*.

Information Sources

The USFS, National Park Service (NPS), Bureau of Land Management (BLM) and Oregon and Washington state parks departments are the main administrative agencies for the parks, forests and wilderness areas mentioned in this chapter. If you're camping, bear in mind that there may be state or county park campgrounds that don't appear in USFS or NPS references.

One of the Northwest's best centralized information sources is the Portland-based Nature of the Northwest visitor center (☎ 503-872-2750, 🖳 www.naturenw.org), which specializes in providing outdoor recreation information for national forests, state parks and other agencies (*except* national parks) in both Oregon and Washington. It carries a full line of maps by the major publishers and has an excellent selection of books for purchase in person or online. You can pick up Northwest Forest Passes here (see the boxed text

on page 406), or order them by phone or online. There are also brochures on general tourism. Ask nicely and they'll even give you a free highway map. It's open 9 am to 5 pm Monday to Friday.

Ranger Stations Oregon and Washington have 19 national forests, each divided into smaller districts. Individual USFS district ranger stations provide the most up-to-date trail and campground conditions. Supervisors' offices coordinate districts within each forest and can provide you with general planning information and direct you to the right district station.

National park headquarters provide little beyond general tourist information. Even in the planning stages it's better to skip directly to an NPS ranger station or wilderness information center.

Many national forests and parks publish annual newspaper tabloids that list direct telephone extensions and addresses for ranger stations, campground information, user fees and closures. If you call or write to request planning information you can often receive one by mail.

Tourist Information Contact the Oregon Tourism Commission (☎ 800-547-7842), 775 Summer St NE, Salem, OR 97310, to order an official highway map, a copy of *Where to Stay in Oregon* and *The Official Oregon Travel Guide*. The all-in-one Washington version is called the *Washington State Travel & Lodging Guide*, available from the Washington State Tourism Division (☎ 800-544-1800 x800), 101 General Administration Bldg, AX-13, Olympia, WA 98504-1800.

Websites The following are some of the most useful websites for planning a hike. USFS and NPS websites are updated frequently and generally contain useful information. Some even have trail conditions and maps, though the level of detail varies widely. Always confirm information with a ranger before setting out.

Nature of the Northwest Visitor Center A helpful virtual visitor center for Oregon and

PACIFIC NORTHWEST

Northwest Forest Passes – How Your Trail Fees Really Work

The practice of having to pay before stepping onto a USFS trail is both new and controversial in the Northwest. In 1996 the US Congress authorized the USFS Recreation Fee Demonstration Program (which took effect in 1997) to allow national forests to collect money from hikers and other users to fund back-logged repairs. Many environmental groups feel the Northwest Forest Pass program (trail fees) is poor public policy given the agency has long subsidized logging operations by footing the bill to build expensive logging roads. With coffers emptied by decades of money-losing timber sales that obliterated forests, critical voices question whether the tax-funded agency should collect extra money from hikers to maintain trails.

Law-abiding hikers not wanting to get fined and hoping to find a bridge in place when they need one consider $3 a small price. But where does this money go? One has to wonder after clambering over blowdowns with a full pack, negotiating a smashed bridge or finding a glossy USFS publication that extols the virtues of 'your fees at work'.

Some fees obviously pay to administer the program itself. And a hefty chunk of the money really does go toward trail maintenance – at a cost of a reported $200 to $500 per mile (and that's in a dry, low-maintenance forest). Want a footbridge replaced? That'll run to $55,000. A new two-seat toilet (a pit toilet, mind you) is a steal at $24,000.

Congress has extended this experimental program through 2001, after which trail fees are likely to become permanent. The public can send comments to the Recreation Trail Park Coordinator, USDA Forest Service, Pacific Northwest Region, PO Box 3623, Portland OR 97208.

Jennifer Snarski

Washington; contains phone numbers and addresses to USFS ranger stations and information on USFS campground reservations and Northwest Forest Passes. Links to individual USFS and NPS websites. Books and Northwest Forest Passes can be ordered online.
www.naturenw.org

USFS Pacific Northwest Region Links to homepages for all 19 of Oregon and Washington's national forests. Has a national forest locater map.
www.fs.fed.us/r6/

National Parks A locater homepage with links to individual national parks.
www.nps.gov

Oregon State Parks Informative profiles of nearly every Oregon state park. Links to online campground reservations; shows site maps.
www.prd.state.or.us/home.html

Washington State Parks Information about Washington state parks. Links to online campground reservations.
www.parks.wa.gov

Oregon Tourism Commission Travel information about Oregon.
www.traveloregon.com

Washington State Tourism Division Travel information about Washington.
www.tourism.wa.gov/

Permits

USFS Permits To use the most popular USFS trails hikers must pay a trailhead parking fee, done by purchasing a *Northwest Forest Pass* ($3/30 for a daily/annual pass good for a year from the month of purchase). Passes are valid in any national forest participating in the USFS Pacific Northwest Region Recreation Fee Demonstration Program. Forests include:

Oregon
- Columbia Gorge National Scenic Area
- Deschutes National Forest
- Mt Hood National Forest
- Rogue River National Forest
- Siskiyou National Forest
- Siuslaw National Forest
- Wallowa-Whitman National Forest
- Willamette National Forest
- Umatilla National Forest

Washington
- Gifford-Pinchot National Forest
- Mt Baker–Snoqualmie National Forest
- North Cascades National Park
- Okanogan National Forest
- Olympic National Forest
- Wenatchee National Forest

Not all trails require a pass and since they're rarely sold at the trailhead it's important to know whether you need one *before* embarking on that 20mi, bone-jolting drive down a dirt road. Ranger stations, information centers and designated businesses all sell them. You'll save time by ordering an annual pass or several day passes in advance by phone (☎ 800-270-7504) or online through the Nature of the Northwest visitor center website (see Information Sources).

Display passes on the driver's side dashboard of your car, but *don't* use the adhesive strip to affix your daily pass to the windshield – the sun will cement it to the glass. The program is still evolving, so contact each national forest directly for the latest regulations and list of trails which require a pass. If you're using daily passes on an overnight trip you'll need to buy one for each day your car is parked at the trailhead. See the boxed text for some background.

Travel through a designated wilderness usually requires a free, self-issuing *wilderness permit* – see Hiking Permits under Visas & Documents in the Facts for the Hiker chapter and Planning for individual hikes.

For certain places you may need a *special-use permit* (also called a limited-entry permit) which restricts the number of visitors to overused areas. Permits are limited in number and must be obtained from a designated ranger station; they may be free, or there may be a charge. The Obsidian area in Three Sisters Wilderness (see the section later in this chapter) and the Pamelia area in Mt Jefferson Wilderness are currently the only places in Oregon to require one. In Washington, thousands participate in a yearly lottery for special-use permits to the Enchantment Lakes region of Alpine Lakes Wilderness (see the section later in this chapter). Special-use permits should be carried with you when you hike. Rangers patrol special-permit areas and can both fine and turn back violators.

NPS Backcountry Permits Backpackers must obtain a backcountry permit for overnight camping in national parks. These

---

Bears

The shy black bears that roam the forests of Oregon and Washington are not normally aggressive, and are feared more than they are dangerous. Hand-to-claw bear attacks that play in the subconscious of hikers are uncommon, but because bears *can* cause serious harm they should always be avoided and treated with respect.

A typical black bear diet includes tree bark, plants and berries, insects, fish and small mammals. However, their exceptionally keen sense of smell makes them adept at pilfering other food sources. A bear that learns to associate backpacks with food can become aggressive and endanger both hikers and itself. Avoid attracting bears: hang food *and garbage* in scent-proof containers and keep a clean camp. Always ask about recent bear-sightings at a ranger station before heading out overnight. See the Health & Safety chapter for more advice.

---

permits are limited by the number of campsites available and require hikers to adhere to a planned itinerary. Specific regulations vary; a fee may or may not be charged. Backcountry permits are issued from designated wilderness information centers, and may be reserved for Rainier and Olympic National Parks. See the individual hikes for specific information.

Place Names

State highways in Washington are often called *state routes*, spoken and written as the abbreviation SR. Thus SR 14 means the same as Hwy 14.

Exchanging Money

Seattle and Portland are the only convenient Northwest cities with foreign exchange services. If you're heading out on a trip straight from the airport be sure to stop by the foreign exchange counter.

GETTING AROUND

A car or motorcycle is necessary to reach nearly all the trails in this chapter. Sometimes

WARNING

- Use caution when crossing any patch of permanent or lingering snow. Aside from the obvious danger of a deadly fall down a rocky slope, hikers can break through soft spots in snow that has melted from underneath. Snowfields also obscure the trail and can cause you to become lost.
- Glaciers are extremely unstable rivers of ice. Never venture onto a glacier unless properly trained and equipped for mountain climbing.

a taxi could be hired if a trailhead isn't too far, though some cab drivers may be reluctant to drive out to a trailhead to pick you up (where they'll have to decide what to do if you aren't there). In the long run the cost of a cab may be comparable to renting a car. A few trailheads are accessible to cycling tourists.

GATEWAYS

Seattle and Portland are the Pacific Northwest's principal transportation hubs. Seattle-Tacoma International (Sea-Tac) is the region's largest airport, and is served by most national and international airlines. Portland international airport has connections to most domestic cities and direct service to Asia. From San Francisco there are also direct flights to Eugene, Medford and Redmond in Oregon. Eugene also has direct connections to Denver and Phoenix.

Greyhound (☎ 800-231-2222) and Amtrak (☎ 800-872-7245) provide frequent bus and train services between Vancouver, Canada, and San Francisco, California, and link major cities along the I-5 freeway in western Oregon and Washington. Service to smaller cities is often on other bus lines coordinated with Greyhound. Amtrak's *Empire Builder* line runs east-west from Seattle and Portland to Minneapolis, Minnesota, and Chicago, Illinois. Travel between Seattle and Northwest cities such as Portland is often faster, cheaper and easier by rail than by air.

The legendary Green Tortoise (☎ 800-867-8647, 🖳 www.greentortoise.com) makes a fun alternative to Greyhound for those

traveling between Seattle and San Francisco. (See Alternative Carriers under Bus in the Getting Around chapter.) Twice-weekly buses stop in Ashland, Eugene, Portland and Seattle, though stops anywhere along I-5 can be arranged with advance notice. Reservations are required.

The Fred Meyer chain of oversized grocery and variety stores carries white gas (Coleman) stove fuel, butane/propane cartridges and basic camping supplies. These stores are prevalent in most larger towns throughout the Northwest.

Seattle

Centrally located along the Puget Sound on the western edge of Washington, Seattle provides easy access to trails in the Cascades (and contributes heavily to their overuse).

Information Meet all your needs for information, equipment, books, maps and Northwest Forest Passes at impressive REI (☎ 206-323-8333), 222 Yale Ave N, convenient to I-5 exits 166 or 167, and downtown. This warehouse-like flagship store also rents backpacks, sleeping bags, tents and stoves and does repairs.

Upstairs is the busy Outdoor Recreation Information Center (☎ 206-220-7450), which provides USFS and NPS information for Washington. ORIC is staffed 10:30 am to 7 pm Tuesday to Friday, 9 am to 6 pm Saturday, and 10 am to 6 pm Sunday; after-hours visitors may flip through information binders on their own.

Places to Stay & Eat *Hostelling International Seattle* (☎ 206-622-5443, 888-622-5443, *❷ reserve@hiseattle.org, 84 Union St*), downtown near Pike Place, has dorm beds ($16 to $18), a few private rooms ($47), a kitchen and a laundry. If that's full try the nearby *Green Tortoise Backpacker's Guesthouse* (☎ 206-322-1222, 1525 2nd Ave) where dorm beds are $17 and private rooms are $40; come prepared to pay a refundable $20 key deposit (cash only). Don't count on rolling into either without a reservation (made at least two weeks in advance). Both are well-connected to public transport.

The Seattle Center area, just north of downtown, has the best value hotels. The *Seattle Inn* (☎ *206-728-7666, 225 Aurora Ave N)* has basic rooms and an indoor pool from $63. There are also cheap motel rooms near the airport along Pacific Hwy S (Hwy 99) in the city of Sea-Tac, between I-5 exits 152 and 154.

Cheap food stalls and cafes abound at Pike Place Market and trendy Capitol Hill. *Marco's Supper Club* (☎ *206-441-7801, 2510 1st Ave)* offers multiethnic eating in Belltown. Unbearably hip *Café Septieme* (☎ *206-860-8858, 214 Broadway E)* on Capitol Hill serves up sophisticated homemade meals that make Martha Stewart proud.

Getting There & Away Sea-Tac International Airport (☎ 206-433-5288, 800-544-1965) is 13mi south of Seattle off I-5. Horizon Air and United Express connect Seattle with Bellingham, Port Angeles and Wenatchee. When returning to the airport avoid Airport Way, which leads to the Boeing airfield. Northbound travelers should get off at I-5 exit 152, southbound travelers at exit 154.

Metro Transit (☎ 206-553-3000) bus No 194 provides express service between Sea-Tac and Westlake Center downtown. A Gray Line Airport Express (☎ 206-626-6088) shuttle runs every 15 minutes between 5 am and midnight between Sea-Tac and downtown hotels ($7.50/13 one-way/roundtrip).

Seattle's bus and train stations are right downtown. Amtrak's (☎ 800-872-7245) King Street Station is at 303 S Jackson St. The *Empire Builder* travels east to Spokane and Chicago. Several Amtrak trains and buses connect Seattle to Portland and San Francisco.

Greyhound (☎ 206-628-5526) buses arrive and depart from the station at 811 Stewart St. From Seattle there are buses north to Bellingham ($13 one-way), south to Portland ($20), west to Port Angeles ($29), and east to Leavenworth ($22), Wenatchee ($23) and La Grande, Oregon ($61 via Pasco). Some buses link directly to the airport.

Green Tortoise (☎ 800-867-8647) buses arrive and depart to Portland ($15 one-

way), Eugene ($25), and San Francisco ($59) twice weekly from 9th Ave and Stewart St (behind Greyhound Package Express, downtown).

For a taxi call Yellow Cabs at ☎ 206-622-6500.

Portland

Oregon's largest city sits at the north end of the state, at the confluence of the Willamette and Columbia Rivers in the Willamette Valley. Portland has easy access to the Cascades and the Columbia Gorge, but the rest of the state is still pretty remote. Eugene, a smaller city at the south end of the Willamette Valley, is a better gateway to southern and central Oregon.

Information The Nature of the Northwest visitor center (☎ 503-872-2750), at 800 NE Oregon St on the ground floor of the State Office Building, offers one-stop shopping for books, maps, Northwest Forest Passes, and trail and travel information. It operates cooperatively between the USFS and several state bureaus to help visitors plan outdoor activities in Oregon and Washington. It's convenient to I-5, I-84 and the MAX light-rail line and is open 9 am to 5 pm Monday to Friday.

REI (☎ 503-283-1300), at Jantzen Beach Center, north of Portland at I-5 exit 308, has

---

Hypothermia

Hypothermia is the greatest threat to hikers in the Northwest, and is most often caused by rain rather than extreme cold. Be familiar with the causes, symptoms and treatment of hypothermia as outlined in the Health & Safety chapter.

Because weather at higher elevations may suddenly turn cold and rainy without warning, rain gear, a watertight tent and extra clothing should be standard equipment for any overnight trip. Wool and quick-drying, synthetic fabrics are the best choices for cold or wet conditions. Breathable, water-repellant fabrics like Gore-Tex are ideal for outerwear.

gear and supplies. It also carries books and maps, rents gear (packs, sleeping bags, tents and stoves) and does repairs. Oregon Mountain Community (OMC; ☎ 503-227-1038), 60 NW Davis St, downtown, has gear and also rents internal-frame packs. An infectious weirdness makes Andy & Bax (☎ 503-234-7538), 324 SE Grand Ave, a fun place to shop for freeze-dried meals and army surplus treasures. It's open late Friday night and is convenient to I-84 and I-5.

Places to Stay & Eat *McMenamins Edgefield (☎ 503-669-8610, 800-669-8610, ❸ edge@mcmenamins.com, 2126 SW Halsey in Troutdale)*, a historic poor farm turned classy European-style hotel, offers one of the best lodging values in the Northwest with comfortable hostel beds for $20. Dorms are clean and spacious, all bedding is provided and large hardwood lockers easily accommodate backpacks. On site are several *restaurants* and *pubs*, a movie theater (free to guests), winery and garden. Located 15mi east of Portland off I-84 (exit 16), it is conveniently en route to the Columbia Gorge and Mt Hood, and well past I-84's daily traffic jams. Private rooms start at $50/85 for a single/double and include breakfast.

Downtown there's the *Hostelling International Northwest Portland (☎ 503-241-2783, ❸ hinwp@transport.com, 1818 NW Glisan St)*, a full-service hostel in a renovated house with dorm beds ($14 to $15) and private rooms ($43 and up) conveniently located just 12 blocks from the bus and train stations. Ask about van tours to popular hiking destinations.

Budget *eateries* crowd Southeast Portland's youth-oriented Hawthorne district on SE Hawthorne Blvd. *Restaurants* lining NW 23rd and NW 21st Aves in Portland's Northwest district are more upscale. Cajun food dominates a huge menu at *Montage (☎ 503-234-1324, 301 SE Morrison St)* under the Morrison St Bridge, open until at least 1 am every day. *Esparza's Tex Mex Cafe (☎ 503-234-7909, 2725 SE Ankeny St)* is a local favorite for exotic Mexican and smile-provoking Western kitsch. Closed Monday.

Getting There & Away Portland International Airport (☎ 503-460-4234, 877-739-4636) is in Northeast Portland near the Columbia River. Horizon and United Express connect Portland with Pendleton, Redmond (Bend), Eugene, Coos Bay and Medford. From downtown take I-84 east to I-205 north and get off at exit 24A. Tri-Met bus No 12 to downtown Portland departs two to four times an hour from the south end of the upper-level passenger island ($1.10). Gray Line of Portland (☎ 503-285-9845) shuttle buses travel to downtown hotels twice an hour from outside the baggage claim area ($12/22 one-way/roundtrip). MAX light-rail service to downtown is scheduled to begin in the fall of 2001.

The bus and train stations are right next to each other, downtown. Buses depart the Greyhound station (☎ 503-243-2310), 550 NW 6th Ave, north to Seattle ($20 one-way), south to Eugene ($13) and Grants Pass ($40), and east to La Grande ($40) and Bend ($24). Green Tortoise (☎ 800-867-8647) buses arrive and depart twice weekly for Eugene ($10), Seattle ($15) and San Francisco ($49) from in front of Union Station.

Amtrak buses and trains traveling between Seattle and San Francisco stop at Union Station (☎ 503-241-4290), NW 6th Ave and Irving St. The *Empire Builder* travels east to Spokane and Chicago.

Eugene

A better gateway to hikes in southern and central Oregon, 110mi south of Portland on I-5, is Eugene – centrally located along the western part of Oregon.

Information Find books, maps, supplies and Northwest Forest Passes at REI (☎ 541-465-1800), 306 Lawrence, or at McKenzie Outfitters (☎ 541-485-5946), 79 W Broadway, in the downtown pedestrian mall.

Places to Stay & Eat *Eugene International Hostel (☎ 541-349-0589, 2352 Willamette St)*, near the university, has clean, quiet dorm beds ($13 to $16), private rooms ($34) and locked storage. *Timbers Motel (☎ 541-343-3345, 800-643-4167, 1015 Pearl St)* next to the bus station is Eugene's favorite budget hotel ($46). Barbecued ribs overshadow an ethnic vegetarian menu at *West Brothers Bar-B-Que* (☎ 541-345-8498, 844 Olive St) next to the adjoining *Eugene City Brewery*.

Getting There & Away Horizon and United Express link Eugene's Mahlon Sweet Airport to Portland, San Francisco and Denver. America West (☎ 800-235-9292) flies direct from Phoenix.

Amtrak's *Coast Starlight* stops at the train station (☎ 541-687-1383), E 4th and Willamette St, on its run between Portland and Sacramento, California. There are also express services to Portland and Seattle on the *Cascadia*.

Buses depart the Greyhound station (☎ 541-344-6265) at 987 Pearl St for Bend, Portland and Grants Pass. A coast bus travels Hwy 101 south via Florence to Brookings. The Green Tortoise also stops here (☎ 800-867-8647) between San Francisco and Seattle.

Rent cars from the airport or from Enterprise (☎ 541-344-2020), 810 W 6th, downtown. Call Emerald Taxi (☎ 541-686-2010) for a lift.

Columbia Gorge

The mighty Columbia River, the nation's second largest, parts the Cascade mountains at the Columbia Gorge, an 80mi canyon dividing Oregon and Washington. A 13,000-year succession of massive ice-age floods carved this broad, U-shaped valley from solid basalt – a hard rock formed by fluid lava that flooded the region 12 million to 18 million years ago. The area's many dramatic changes in elevation and the influence of converging east and west ecologies produce fantastic scenes of plunging waterfalls, verdant chasms and windswept grasslands.

As an ancient transportation corridor, the gorge facilitated Native American trade and migration between the inland plains and the west coast for 10,000 years. Explorers

Lewis and Clark (see the boxed text on page 20) coursed the river in windblown canoes in 1805. The river was later a conduit for Oregon Trail settlers who opted to float and portage their wagons around the Cascades in the 1840s. Popularity as a favorite hiking destination helped champion construction of Oregon's historic Columbia Gorge Hwy in the 1910s, fragments of which still exist as a worthwhile scenic byway. Interstate traffic streams through the gorge today on a busy freeway.

The federally protected Columbia River Gorge National Scenic Area preserves the gorge for recreation.

INFORMATION

The Columbia River Gorge National Scenic Area (☎ 541-386-2333), a special unit of the USFS, has its headquarters at 902 Wasco Ave, Suite 200, Hood River, OR 97031 (💻 www.fs.fed.us/r6/columbia).

Maps & Books

Hikes to other waterfalls and viewpoints are detailed in William Sullivan's *100 Hikes in Northwest Oregon*. The 1:65,000 Geo-Graphics *Trails of the Columbia Gorge* shows the most popular trails on one handy map.

Eagle Creek Trail

Duration	6–8 hours or 2 days
Distance	12mi (19.3km)
Standard	medium to medium-hard
Start/Finish	Eagle Creek Trailhead
Nearest Town	Cascade Locks
Public Transport	no

Summary This historic trail on the Oregon side of the Columbia Gorge visits 11 waterfalls along a narrow canyon. Makes a satisfying day hike of any length or can be extended into a multiday trip.

Known for North America's highest concentration of waterfalls, the Oregon side of the Columbia Gorge contains 77 falls within 420 sq miles. The Eagle Creek Trail passes 11 of these as it meanders up wooded

> **WARNING**
>
> Gorge trailheads have a reputation for car break-ins, so be sure to lock your car and stow all belongings in the trunk. Take any valuables with you.

slopes and sheer rock walls through a narrow basalt canyon. Early gorge promoters engineered this scenic trail in 1910 to coincide with the opening of the Columbia Gorge Hwy, and blasted some segments into cliff walls that hang high above Eagle Creek. These perilous ledges have no guardrails and can be dangerous for children and dogs.

It is a classic 12mi, down-and-back hike to Tunnel Falls which passes a swimmable pool at the foot of a cliff, and crosses a dizzying bridge over a 150ft chasm before reaching a tunnel carved behind a waterfall. An overnight at 7½ Mile Camp (1½mi past Tunnel Falls) turns a tiring day hike into an easy two-day trip. Punchbowl Falls (4.2mi roundtrip) and High Bridge (7mi roundtrip) are turning points for shorter hikes.

The trail continues past Tunnel Falls for longer backcountry loops to viewpoints at Wahtum Lake and Benson Plateau, accessible via connections with the Pacific Crest Trail, Wy'East Trail No 434 and Ruckel Creek Trail No 405.

Camping is permitted along the Eagle Creek Trail, but only at one of seven designated campsites.

PLANNING

Blowdowns and landslides often close the trail in the winter and spring – check conditions before setting out. A USFS visitor center at the Multnomah Falls Lodge is convenient to I-84 exit 31. Purchase the necessary Northwest Forest Pass for this hike at the gift shop next door, from the Bonneville Dam visitor center (exit 40), or from the Port of Cascade Locks gift shop or the Charburger restaurant in Cascade Locks (exit 44).

Trailside camping is allowed only at one of seven designated (but not always signed or named) camps, each with two or three

sites. The first is just past High Bridge. Campfires are banned in Mark O Hatfield Wilderness in the summer.

When to Hike

Summer and fall are the best times to hike. Waterfalls, mossy rocks and shady trees cool the trail on hot days. The trail and its camps are packed out on weekends.

What to Bring

Bring a bathing suit and an extra pair of shoes that can get wet for the rocky swimming beach at Punchbowl Falls. Backpackers should bring a camp stove.

Maps

The up-and-back day hike is easy enough to follow without a map. Backpackers should carry Green Trails 1:69,500 map *Bonneville Dam (No 429)*, which shows the extensive trail network along the Eagle Creek watershed.

NEAREST TOWN & FACILITIES

Eagle Creek is usually hiked as a day trip from Portland (see Gateways at the beginning of this chapter). Cascade Locks, 3mi east, has the closest *restaurant* and *hotel*.

Eagle Creek campground near the trailhead was established in the same year as the trail, and is the oldest campground in the national forest system. A handful of the 20 forested sites ($10) have gorge views (and wire fences to protect sleepwalking campers).

GETTING TO/FROM THE HIKE

Eagle Creek is right off I-84, 41mi east of Portland. Drive straight past the fish hatchery to the end of a paved road along Eagle Creek to reach the trailhead. There's no

> **WARNING**
>
> Avoid poison oak, a shrubby plant which grows in rocky soil along lower elevation trails throughout the gorge. Spindly-looking, rash-producing leaves resemble oak leaves, and are green in the spring and turn yellow and red in the fall. It's often found near oak trees.

westbound freeway access, so to get back to Portland you have to take I-84 east to exit 44 and turn around.

THE HIKE

The trail picks up from the left side of the parking lot and climbs the canyon's east wall through treetops of bigleaf maple, cedar and Douglas fir on a narrow ledge above the creek. This cliff-faced trail gives way to a forested slope in about a mile. At 1½mi a shrubby path leads to a view of **Metlako Falls,** a graceful, 150ft white wisp named after a Native American salmon goddess. A half-mile ahead is another side trail, which drops into a mossy grotto to reach Eagle Creek at a tranquil green pool. **Punchbowl Falls** pours over a 15ft ledge just upstream. (To return to the trailhead from here makes an easy, two- to three-hour, 4.2mi day hike.)

Climb back to the main trail and in the next mile pass an upper viewpoint for Punchbowl Falls and an overlook for another waterfall. Streaming down the opposite bank at a flat clearing is **Loowit Falls**, named for a beautiful sorceress of ancient Native American lore.

Eagle Creek next dives down a 150ft fissure, spanned at 3½mi by the intimidating **High Bridge**. (To turn back here makes a medium-level, three- to four-hour, 7mi day hike.) Travel the west bank past the first campsites at *Tenas Camp*, before crossing back over the creek on 4½ Mile Bridge after 1mi. About 100yd up is a nice riverside *camp* with two large, forested sites fronting a twin waterfall across the creek. A wooden footbridge precedes the next sites at *Wy'East Camp*, where a stand of uncannily straight Douglas fir attests to a forest fire in 1902. Here the trail enters Mark O Hatfield Wilderness, crosses a stream on wooden slats beneath another waterfall, and passes a junction for the left-leading Eagle-Benson Trail to the Benson Plateau. *Blue Grouse Camp* is 0.2mi ahead.

At 6mi the trail inches up a precipice to meet 120ft-high **Tunnel Falls** at a sheer cliff – a dead end, if it weren't for an eerie tunnel passing through solid rock behind the thundering falls. Suck in your breath and venture

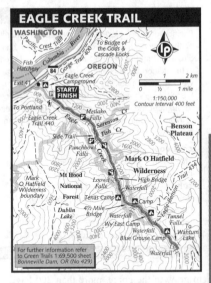

slightly further along this precarious, cable-clutching ledge to view one last waterfall before turning back. *7½ Mile Camp* is another 1½mi ahead, but day hikers should turn back here for the trailhead.

For a more leisurely experience, camp at Wy'East, Blue Grouse or 7½ Mile Camps and return to the trailhead the next day.

Dog Mountain

Duration	5–6 hours
Distance	6.2mi (10km)
Standard	medium-hard
Start/Finish	Dog Mountain Trailhead
Nearest Town	Stevenson
Public Transport	no

Summary A difficult climb to the top of a grassy bluff overlooking the Columbia Gorge. Famous for a fantastic variety and abundance of spring wildflowers. Gains 2900ft (870m) in 3mi.

Brilliant springtime wildflowers and sweeping views of the Columbia are the payback for this strenuous hike up a grassy bluff on the Washington side of the river. Of the 800 species of flowering plants known

Chinook Jargon

Pacific Northwest place names recall the frontier impressions of white explorers and settlers and the Native Americans they displaced. Cities like Yakima, Wenatchee and Spokane, and rivers like the Siuslaw, Umpqua, Umatilla and Nisqually, all speak names of tribes that once inhabited the region.

In addition to indigenous place names, natural features in Oregon and Washington also contain words from Chinook jargon, a makeshift trade language of only a few hundred words borrowed from French, English and several tribal languages. Developed in the 18th century, the jargon was used throughout the region for communication between Native American tribes, trappers and settlers.

Words in Chinook jargon crop up regularly on trail maps throughout the Northwest. Here are a few to watch for:

chetwoot - black bear (Chetwoot Trail)
chikamin - metal, money (Chikamin Peak)
chuck - water (White Chuck River)
cultus - worthless (Cultus Lake)
delate - straight, direct (Delate Meadow)
illahee - land (Illahee)
lolo - to carry (Lolo Pass)
mowich - deer (Mowich Lake)

olallie - berry (Olallie Lake)
polallie - sand, gunpowder (Polallie Canyon)
shahalie - upper (Shahalie Falls)
skookum - strong, powerful (Skookum Lake)
tamolitch - barrel, tub (Tamolitch Pool)
tenas - small (Tenas Camp)
tyee - chief (Tyee Rapids)

---

to grow in the gorge, more than 200 have been found here, including several that are endemic. Those intimidated by the prospect of climbing nearly 3000ft in 3mi can expend half this effort to reach a fulfilling wildflower meadow at a lower viewpoint.

PLANNING

Maps, permits, books and information are available at the USFS's full-service information booth inside the Skamania Lodge in Stevenson (☎ 503-427-2528), 1131 SW Skamania Lodge Dr, open 9 am to 8 pm Thursday to Sunday and 9 am to 7 pm Monday to Wednesday.

When to Hike

Wildflower seasons determine the best time to hike, usually March to mid-May. Sunflower-like balsam root, one of the boldest steppe flowers, paints the meadows in deep tawny hues from late April to late May. Flowers continue to bloom throughout the summer, and the view is still nice even after the most spectacular displays have faded.

What to Bring

Bring a plant identification guide, even if you're only going to the first viewpoint.

Inexpensive books and pamphlets illustrating the area's wildflowers are available from the USFS information booth at the Skamania Lodge. Carry water.

Maps & Books

The Green Trails 1:69,500 map *Hood River (No 430)* is a fine map, though hikers aren't likely to have much trouble navigating this well-trodden route.

Wildflowers of the Columbia Gorge by Russ Jolley (Oregon Historical Society Press) contains color photos and characteristics to help identify the hundreds of wildflowers found here.

Permits & Regulations

A Northwest Forest Pass is required, available from the USFS information booth at Skamania Lodge or from the Skamania County chamber of commerce, 167 NW 2nd Ave, in downtown Stevenson.

NEAREST TOWNS & FACILITIES

Most people visit Dog Mountain as a day trip from Portland (see Gateways at the beginning of this chapter). *Home Valley Park*, 3½mi west of the trailhead on Hwy 14 in Home Valley, offers the closest camping ($12) and a night of constant freight trains. For quieter sites head 9mi north of the timber community of Carson to the wooded *Panther Creek campground,* in the Gifford-Pinchot National Forest ($11). Follow the Wind River Rd through Carson and turn right at Panther Rd after Mile 5. Turn left immediately onto paved USFS Rd No 65 and follow the signs.

While not everyone can afford one of the craftsman-style rooms at the upscale *Skamania Lodge (☎ 509-427-7700, 800-221-7117, 1131 SW Skamania Lodge Dr)* anyone is welcome to enjoy a post-hike burger and beer at the *pub* and *restaurant.*

GETTING TO/FROM THE HIKE
From Portland drive 44mi east on I-84 to exit 44 (Cascade Locks), pay the 75c toll to cross the Bridge of the Gods and turn right onto Hwy 14 in Washington. The trailhead is 12½mi east, past the communities of Stevenson, Carson and Home Valley.

THE HIKE
Signs at the east (right) end of the parking lot welcome hikers to the start of two routes up Dog Mountain. Ignore the left-leading Augsperger Trail and continue straight ahead to the sign for 'Dog Mountain Trail, Top of the Mountain'. In a few feet another sign warns of poison oak and describes the wildflowers that lie ahead.

The trail begins a tireless climb through a hot, shrubby forest of Garry oak and Douglas fir. Wild strawberry, pink star flower, sweet pea, desert parsley and blue, broadleaf lupine line switchbacks up the mountain's sunny south face. Be wary of vandalized trail signage at a flat trail junction a half-mile up. Fork right regardless of which way the arrows point and hike another mile through shady fir to the first viewpoint, a yellow-hued meadow of balsam root, buttercup and cream-colored death camas. Indian paintbrush and Douglas' tretelia supply flecks of red and blue.

If the grassy temple of Dog Mountain still seems attainable, continue up the meadow and back into forest, where good eyes can catch the first heads of chocolate lily (also called checker lily or rice root). A sign points

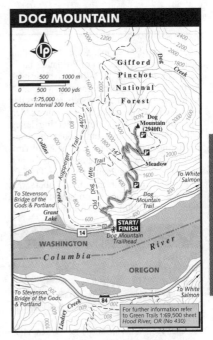

up a troublesome grade at a junction that meets up with the old Dog Mountain route bypassed below. After a painful half-mile the trail breaks out of the woods at another big wildflower meadow – larkspur and spreading phlox adding violet to a vibrant palate.

Proceed left at the loop junction after taking in views down both sides of the gorge. The trail climbs open meadow and rounds a basalt outcropping for a head-on **view of Mt St Helens.** Continue right another 0.1mi past the junction for Augsperger Mountain to reach the **summit,** which is profuse with wildflowers. A left-leading spur achieves a humble summit at a grassy patch in front of some trees. Barges and old-fashioned sternwheelers ply the river below, and the snowy crest of Mt Hood peeks over the shoulder of Mt Defiance.

The trail loops east to hook up with the main trail below, but the wooded route is so dull you may as well just climb down the way you came.

Mt Hood

The tallest of Oregon's Cascade mountain peaks, Mt Hood rises out of Portland's backyard to a height of 11,240ft, exacting itself on the skyline in a perfect snowy wedge. On its forested slopes a trail system provides day hikers with easy access to a scenic wilderness of waterfalls, quiet reflecting lakes, wildflower meadows and mountain vistas. Circumnavigating the peak is the 38mi Timberline Trail, which shares its route for part of the way with the Pacific Crest Trail (PCT). Immensely popular among climbers, Mt Hood is the world's second-most climbed peak over 10,000ft after Mt Fuji.

McNeil Point

Duration	5–6 hours
Distance	7.5mi (12.1km)
Standard	medium
Start/Finish	Top Spur Trailhead
Nearest Towns	Zig Zag, Welches, Wemme
Public Transport	no

Summary Breathtaking alpine scenery featuring outstanding views of Mt Hood. The Timberline and Pacific Crest Trails join to provide this partial-loop day hike through forest and wildflower meadows.

This hike along a ridgeline portion of Mt Hood's Timberline Trail to two ponds rimmed with wildflowers offers the Mt Hood area's most photogenic scenery. Giant views of Mt Hood at the end of the Muddy Fork valley fill the sky and offer deliverance to anyone who has admired the mountain from below. Portlanders come here with out-of-state guests when they want to show off, knowing it's only a short distance and a moderate climb to the first breathtaking viewpoint at Bald Mountain, from where it's possible to make an abbreviated 2.3mi loop back to the car.

PLANNING

See Gateways earlier in this chapter for information sources in Portland. The USFS Mt Hood information center (☎ 503-622-7674, 888-622-4822), 68260 E Welches Rd, offers a place to purchase maps and the required Northwest Forest Pass en route. It shares space with a large RV Park in Welches, just west of Lolo Pass Rd, and is open every day from 8 am to 6 pm year-round.

When to Hike

The short loop around Bald Mountain opens in June, but the trail to the ponds at McNeil Point isn't completely snow-free until mid-July. Bank on wildflowers all summer long – displays at McNeil Point are richest in early August. In September and October the valleys flanking Mt Hood are painted in deep veins of yellow and gold. The hike is pleasant on cloudy days, though if it's too cloudy you may lose the view of the mountain completely.

Parking is crowded, so go early and avoid weekends.

Maps

Call around to find who carries the Green Trails 1:69,500 maps *Government Camp (No 461)* and *Mt Hood (No 462)*. These maps are hot items and stores often sell out. Geo-Graphics's *Mt Hood Wilderness Map* presents the mountain on a single page for those who don't mind fine print.

NEAREST TOWNS & FACILITIES

Mt Hood is typically done as a day trip from Portland (see Gateways). *Riley* and *McNeil USFS campgrounds* on USFS Rd No 1825 are about a mile off Lolo Pass Rd en route to the trailhead, near the junction with USFS Rd No 1828. Riley, a horse campground on Lost Creek, is the nicer of the two ($10). Camping is free at McNeil, across the street, but there's no water.

GETTING TO/FROM THE HIKE

From Portland drive 42mi east on Hwy 26 to Zig Zag and turn left onto the paved Lolo Pass Rd (USFS Rd No 18). Bear right after 4.2mi onto USFS Rd No 1825, continuing straight after a mile onto USFS Rd No 1828, a gravel road which follows a ridge on Mt Hood's northwest slope. After 6.3mi fork

Highlights of Yosemite National Park, Sierra Nevada. Top Left: Sparkling May Lake nestled among glacier-scoured rock-slabs. **Top Right:** The Merced River wends beneath cloud-covered Half Dome. **Middle:** The Tuolumne River valley beyond Glen Aulin. **Bottom Left:** Sky pilot on Mt Dana's rocky summit. **Bottom Right:** The Cathedral Range beckons beyond Dana Meadows.

Wildflowers on Paradise Meadow, Mt Rainier National Park, Washington. Behind looms Mt Rainier, the 'great snowy peak'. Clothed by 25 glaciers, it is the highest mountain in the Cascades.

right and continue for another three-quarters of a mile to an unsigned parking pullout for Top Spur Trail No 785.

THE HIKE

Find the sign for Top Spur Trail No 785 on the south side of the road. The trail climbs steeply at first into dark, cool forest and then settles into a more moderate grade, passing through a quiet stand of hemlock and huckleberry for the next half-mile. Make a right at the junction with the PCT and continue uphill for 0.1mi to a well-tromped, four-way trail hub, where a large signboard proclaims the Mt Hood Wilderness boundary. Steer to the right of this sign onto Timberline Trail No 600/PCT (Hiker Route), following the sign for the viewpoint. The trail levels out over the next 0.8mi as it rounds Bald Mountain, curves east and breaks out onto cliffs of steep wildflower meadows. Linger here along Bald Mountain's sunny, south slope to take in the first huge, eye-to-eye views of Mt Hood, and to watch Sandy Glacier trickle into the Muddy Fork below.

The trail dips and weaves through more meadow and passes a smaller vista before ducking into a forest clearing after about a half-mile. Here the bare forest floor makes it difficult to spot a faint, unmarked shortcut leading up a small slope between lean firs. Follow this path left over a ridge to intercept the Timberline Trail and complete the loop around Bald Mountain. (Miss this cut and the PCT leads down to the valley to the bridgeless Muddy Fork and Ramona Falls).

Head right on the Timberline Trail to continue toward McNeil Point (turn left to finish early and head back to the trailhead) and climb steadily through more forest, ignoring the McGee Creek Trail on the left. Dainty carpets of white glacier lily cover the forest floor early in the season. Cascade lily, freckled-orange tiger lily and cream-colored wands of bear grass line the trail as it emerges above timberline and marches up the shin of Mt Hood to another viewpoint in 1.4mi. **Majestic views** of the mountain and down the valley from this rocky slope are prime, and many are content to head back from here. But meadows of Indian paintbrush, lupine, purple shooting star, and fuzzy-headed western pasqueflower are less than a mile away at the ponds beneath McNeil Point. From here a

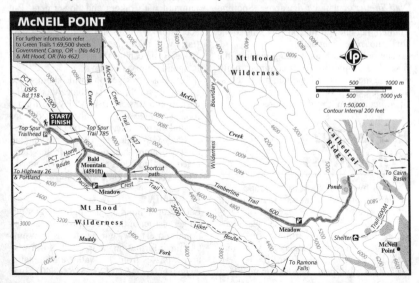

Common Northwest Wildflowers

Alpine meadows painted with vibrant wildflowers are one of the splendors of hiking the Cascade mountains. While studied wildflower aficionados can probably name one for every hue, you don't need a field major in biology to identify the most common:

avalanche lily - small, white lily
bear grass - tall, bulbous wand of cream-colored flowers
glacier lily - small, yellow lily
Indian paintbrush - short with red or orange tips
lupine - tapered wand of blue-violet flowers
shooting star - small, with five lavender petals pulled back to a black tip
tiger lily - small, orange lily
western pasqueflower - bears a funny-looking, hairy seedhead on a single stalk; five-petaled flowers are butter-yellow and cup-like

---

forsaken path leads to the CCC-built *McNeil Shelter* on a high ridge above. Spotting this stony bump from the ponds below is challenging enough for most. Hiking to the top is not recommended.

The ponds mark the turning point of the hike. The Timberline Trail continues north to more meadows and another, more accessible CCC-built *shelter* at Cairn Basin, on the other side of a bridgeless creek.

Eagle Cap Wilderness

The Northwest's highest trails scrape skies in the Wallowa Mountains, a region of tall granite peaks and alpine lakes that is Oregon's largest wilderness. An ice sheet blanketing the Wallowas a million years ago raked this range with steep canyons that lead in all directions from Eagle Cap (9572ft), a snow-heaped mountain visible at

the end of nearly every valley. These non-volcanic 'Alps of Oregon' rise from lonely northeast Oregon ranchland to heights just short of 10,000ft.

The Nez Perce people occupied the region until 1877, when they fled the US Army in a famed four-month, 1170mi chase to escape relocation to western Idaho.

Lakes Basin

Duration	4–5 days
Distance	31mi (49.9km)
Standard	medium
Start/Finish	Two Pan campground
Nearest Town	Enterprise
Public Transport	no

Summary Sweeping views highlight this loop hike on the Lostine River to a popular cluster of lakes in northeast Oregon's high Wallowa Mountains. Hikers establish a base camp at Mirror Lake and explore the Lakes Basin on side trips.

Rivers and valleys converge at the Lakes Basin, a pocket of high alpine lakes surrounded by 9000ft peaks. As the busy hub of wilderness traffic, the basin is often jammed with hikers and horseriders. But the scenery is spectacular and remarkably accessible – climbs are evenly graded and trails well maintained. Taken in stride, the Lakes Basin can be a warmly sociable place to spend four or five days.

The Lostine River offers the shortest and easiest approach, and combines the parallel eastern and western river valleys to form a loop. This hike allots two days for side trips around Mirror Lake, a reflecting pool cradled by Eagle Cap. Wilderness purists not wanting to spend more than one night in the same place will find it less crowded on a more rigorous loop beginning from Wallowa Lake.

PLANNING

Eagle Cap Wilderness lies in the Eagle Cap ranger district of the Wallowa-Whitman National Forest (💻 www.fs.fed.us/r6/w-w). Obtain information, maps and Northwest Forest Passes from the Wallowa Mountains visitor center (☎ 541-426-5546), 88401 Hwy

82, Enterprise, OR 97828, open 8 am to 5 pm Monday to Friday, 8 am to 5 pm on Saturday and 12 to 5 pm Sunday only in summer. Several routes lead to the Lakes Basin, so be prepared to provide the names of the trails and passes you'll be using when calling about trail conditions.

Stove fuel and groceries are readily available, but specialized backpacking supplies are not. There's no drinking water at the trailhead, nor at any campgrounds along the way. Fill up at the faucet across from the Lostine guard station, 12mi up Lostine River Rd.

Camping is dispersed and there are no toilets.

When to Hike
Trails and passes are usually snow-free from August to October. Sudden rain and thunderstorms are inevitable in August. Don't even think about going on a weekend or Friday, when crowds are worst.

Maps & Books
Hikers should carry Imus Geographics' 1:100,000 *Wallowa Mountains: Eagle Cap Wilderness, Oregon* ($6.95). For other routes to the Lakes Basin see *50 Hikes in Hells Canyon & Oregon's Wallowas* by Rhonda & George Ostertag.

Permits & Regulations
A Northwest Forest Pass is required – buy a daily pass for each day of your hike. Don't forget to fill out a wilderness permit at the trailhead. Special restrictions apply to all the lakes on this hike. Camping is prohibited within 100ft of water (even though some sites are right on the lakes), fires are not permitted within a quarter-mile of the lakes (even though most sites have fire rings) and group size is limited to six. Rangers patrol the area and can fine violators.

NEAREST TOWNS & FACILITIES
Pendleton
Flights on Horizon (☎ 800-547-9308) connect Portland with Pendleton municipal airport, 52mi northwest of La Grande on I-84. If you're taking the bus, Pendleton is also the most convenient place to rent a car for

the drive to the trailhead. Buses from Portland, Pasco and Boise, Idaho, all stop at the Greyhound station (☎ 541-276-1551) at 320 SW Court Ave, downtown. Rent a car at the airport.

Enterprise & Joseph
These towns – 10mi and 16mi east of the turn-off at Lostine, respectively – have *motels* and *restaurants*. Rooms at Joseph's *Indian Lodge Motel* (☎ 541-432-2651, 201 S Main St) are the area's least expensive ($47) and fill quickly. *The Wilderness Inn* (☎ 541-426-4535, 800-965-1205, 301 W North St) in Enterprise offers more comfort ($61).

Tourist-savvy Joseph has better restaurants. *Magnoni's Marketplace* (☎ 541-432-3663, 403 N Main St) serves a different pasta entree every day except Sunday, when there's an Italian buffet. *Old Town Café* (☎ 541-432-9898, 8 S Main St) is the best place for breakfast or lunch.

Camping
Primitive USFS campgrounds provide riverside camping right at the trailhead. *Two Pan campground* at the end of the road is more a congested parking lot. *Shady campground* a mile back is quieter and much nicer. Plenty of other campgrounds line the Lostine River Rd so there's need to worry about not finding a site. There's no drinking water and no fee.

GETTING TO/FROM THE HIKE
The Two Pan Trailhead in northeast Oregon's Eagle Cap Wilderness is a 6½-hour drive east of Portland. Exit I-84 at La Grande and follow Hwy 82 55mi north and east to Lostine. Fork right onto Lostine River Rd (USFS Rd No 8210) at a sign for 'Lostine Campgrounds.' The trailhead is 17mi south, at the end of the road. The last 10mi are gravel.

THE HIKE
Day 1: Two Pan Campground to Minam Lake
4–5½ hours, 6.1mi (9.8km), 1800ft (540m) ascent
Long before there was even a road to it, this camp bustled with sheep ranchers, who hung

PACIFIC NORTHWEST

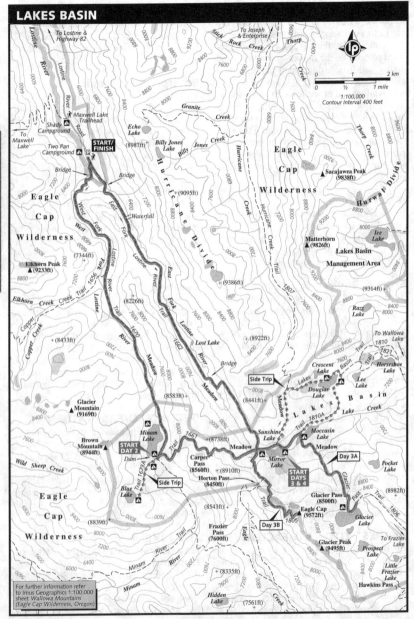

LAKES BASIN

For further information refer to Imus Geographics 1:100,000 sheet *Wallowa Mountains (Eagle Cap Wilderness, Oregon)*

two frying pans on a tree for public use. Take up the forested East Fork Lostine River Trail (No 1662) at the end of the road, and after a brief climb turn right at a sign for the West Fork Lostine River. Trail No 1670 abandons the East Fork at a footbridge and leads upward on moderate switchbacks through a deadfall forest of Engelmann spruce, mountain hemlock, Douglas fir and alder. Join the lively West Fork Lostine River a mile later and head south along a high canyon through shrubby meadow alternating with pine to a gushing waterfall. A talus slope opens to Elkhorn Peak (9233ft) on the right before reaching calmer waters at a flat junction with Cooper Creek Trail (No 1656) at 2.6mi.

Glacier Peak (9169ft) and Brown Mountain (8944ft) gain gradual prominence as the main trail veers left and rises more steeply into the woods, until ultimately the canyon splays into a broad, meadowed valley bordered by high divides. At 4.1mi hikers meet a shallow crossing over the river, which unravels to its swampy origins at **Minam Lake**, 2mi ahead. Turn right upon arrival for picturesque *campsites* on the west shore, or continue straight to reach more accessible *campsites* near the trail junction at the lake's south end.

Side Trip: Blue Lake
1–1½ hours, 2mi (3.2km), 500ft (150m) ascent

Many end the day with a trip up to Blue Lake, a tiny jewel-like tarn hedged against jagged granite peaks. Fork right at the trail junction to round the south end of Minam Lake over a low dike. The trail leads southwest up the forested mountainside on rocky switchbacks, yielding to eastern views of Eagle Cap and Glacier Peak before ending at the lake. Few people camp at this wild and rugged hideaway, and those equipped for wind and cooler temperatures can have it all to themselves.

Day 2: Minam Lake to Mirror Lake
2–3½ hours, 3.7mi (6km), 1100ft (330m) ascent

Begin the day with a short, brisk climb over Carper Pass (8560ft) to arrive at the Lakes Basin just in time for lunch. From the south end of Minam Lake find a sign for Mirror Lake and fork left to head northeast into the woods, climbing steeply to views of Brown and Glacier Mountains. The forest thins to a sparse, windblown scattering of bushy whitebark and limber pines. Up ahead the trail turns east to confront boulders, and scrambles up the pass on rocky switchbacks to meet a skyline crowded with tall peaks and divides.

Drop down a rocky meadow to **Mirror Lake**, continuing straight at the intersection for Eagle Cap, Horton Pass and the East Fork Lostine River to start looking for *campsites*. A spectacular view of Eagle Cap compels many to pitch a tent at the west end of the lake. In another mile Glacier Pass Trail leads right to more choice sites between Mirror and Moccasin Lakes. Wooded Crescent and Douglas Lakes offer *quieter camping* in another vicinity, though you'll be settling for less scenery.

Side Trip: Lakes Basin Loop
3½–4 hours, 5mi (8km), 500ft (150m) ascent

Spend the rest of the afternoon touring the basin's quiet forest lakes. Pick up the trail for Hurricane Creek at a dusty fork just 0.2mi east of the intersection for Eagle Cap. A level trail leads 1.1mi north through a strange canyon bog, and glimpses the blunt Matterhorn (9826ft) before dipping down a meadowed valley to a junction for the Lakes Basin Trail.

Turn right (east) onto trail No 1810, which sinks through forest and Cascades azalea to bottom out in another bog confined by high, chiseled peaks. Paths to *campsites* and fishing holes frequent the shores of marshy Crescent, Douglas and Craig Lakes. Keep on the flat main trail to round the east end of Douglas Lake and in 1.4mi intercept the return trail to Mirror Lake. A hard right at a sign for Glacier Pass leaves Douglas Lake on wooded switchbacks. After a short climb south the trail emerges from forest and continues west, high above Moccasin Lake. It's another 0.7mi back to the east end of Mirror Lake.

Day 3A: Glacier Lake

3–4½ hours, 6.4mi (10.3km), 1300ft (390m) ascent

The first of two recommended day hikes beginning at Mirror Lake (the other is described as Day 3B). This exposed climb over Glacier Pass (8450ft) to a desolate, lake-filled cirque beneath Eagle Cap and Glacier Peak (9495ft) offers the finest alpine spectacle in the Wallowas. Follow signs for Glacier Pass to leave Mirror and Moccasin Lakes and head south up a damp, forested slope. The trail dips through a meadow basin and rises to views of Moccasin Lake, the Matterhorn and bronze, scrabbly peaks fronting the Hurwal Divide. Rocky switchbacks glance the cliff-lined edge of a deep chute and rise alongside a roaring cascade that peters out up ahead to a trickle crossed with one or two steps.

A narrower, rockier path edges up the barren slope past whitebark pine to gain an ominous saddle beneath Eagle Cap. Pause at the pass to take in a stunning view of Glacier and Frazier Lakes, Cusick Mountain (9518ft) and Hawkins Pass before dropping 300ft to granite-studded Glacier Lake. It's easy to tarry a few solitary hours gazing at the crystal-clear lake against the ripped ridge of Glacier Peak. Head back over the pass to return to camp.

Day 3B: Eagle Cap

4–5 hours, 5mi (8km), 2000ft (600m) ascent

It's not often that hikers of average fitness get a chance to summit a 9572ft mountain on a 2½mi hiking trail. While Eagle Cap isn't the tallest peak in the Wallowas, the view is superb. From the west end of Mirror Lake follow signs south for Eagle Cap, forking left past the trail to Horton Pass to reach the top.

Day 4: Mirror Lake to Two Pan Campground

4–5½ hours, 7.3mi (11.8km), 2100ft (630m) descent

Depart the Lakes Basin from the west end of Mirror Lake, turning right (north) at the trail junction to enter a broad, glacier-cut

passage for the East Fork Lostine River. In 1½mi a gradual, timbered descent touches down in open meadow and cuts left to an easy river crossing. Proceed down the west side of the valley past burn and boulder field before entering dry pine forest. Here the Lostine drains into Lost Lake, where it quietly collects momentum for a tumultuous course that is heard, but scarcely seen, over the next 3mi.

Leave the lake at a short waterfall and head back into forest. After a series of steep, rocky switchbacks the trail drops past views of the Hurricane Divide and bottoms out at a small cascade. A dusty half-mile further, the trail crosses the Lostine on a high log. Another mile returns you to Two Pan campground.

Three Sisters Wilderness

The North, Middle and South Sisters – all glacier-topped peaks over 10,000ft – form the heart of central Oregon's Cascades. These three volcanoes at the center of Three Sisters Wilderness at one time exploded, spat blobs of lava and fumed ash with as much spite and malice as real siblings, leaving jagged lava flows as the marks of an unsettled geologic feud. Most Cascade mountains formed just as fitfully, but nowhere else are the forces that shaped them more evident. Open, arid meadows littered with rocky pumice and shards of obsidian are the hallmark of the Three Sisters; the Cascades to the north, in contrast, are blanketed beneath vast meadows of wildflowers.

Conservationists worked to preserve the Three Sisters long before it became a national wilderness in 1964. Oregon's most popular wilderness, it contains the state's third-largest and most climbable mountain, largest glacier, more than a hundred lakes, and 52 scenic miles of the Pacific Crest Trail (PCT). With boundaries that straddle both sides of the Cascades and reach lower-elevation forests, the Three Sisters is one of the state's most biologically diverse regions, with dusty forests of lodgepole pine, damp groves of hemlock and old-growth fir, swampy lake basins and high alpine plains.

Green Lakes

Duration	4½–5 hours
Distance	8.8m (14.2km)
Standard	medium
Start/Finish	Green Lakes Trailhead
Nearest Town	Bend
Public Transport	no

Summary A down-and-back day hike in the central Oregon Cascades through dry, east-slope forest to emerald-hued lakes at the foot of volcanic South Sister. A popular gateway to multiday trips in the Three Sisters Wilderness.

This hike to the eastern portion of the wilderness leads from Oregon's most popular trailhead. Quiet forests of lodgepole pine, obsidian cliffs and wildflower meadows are openers for big views from a glacial lake at a rocky, alpine plain between South Sister (10,358ft) and Broken Top (9175ft).

South Sister is the one that wins our attention the most – it's the third-highest mountain in Oregon and can be climbed without any technical equipment. The shapely slopes of this fuming stratavolcano are heaped with pumice and ash, while Broken Top's serrated profile was carved by retreating glaciers.

For an easy two-day loop spend a night at Green Lakes and return the next morning via the Broken Top and Soda Creek Trails. A 7mi, down-and-back side trip north to Park Meadows adds an extra day.

PLANNING

Friendly volunteers dispense maps, brochures and Northwest Forest Passes (required) from the guard station at the trailhead, open 9 am to 6 pm every day from Memorial Day to Labor Day, and then only on weekends through late fall. For more information contact Deschutes National Forest's Bend/Fort Rock district ranger station

(☎ 541-388-5664), 1230 NE 3rd St, Suite A-262, Bend, OR 97701 (💻 www.fs.fed .us/r6/deschutes).

Backpackers may camp at Green Lakes, but only at one of 28 designated (and very popular) campsites; pick up a site map at the trailhead.

When to Hike

The trail is snow-free from early to mid-July through October. Central Oregon afternoons can be tremendously hot. Parking is competitive on weekends.

What to Bring

Wear waterproof boots for crossing early-season streams. Muted colors are preferred over brightly colored clothes, which may startle horses along the trail. Expect to be fending off mosquitoes in July.

Maps

Geo-Graphics' *Three Sisters Wilderness Map* ($6.95) features 1:26,966 and 1: 83,000 scale maps on either side, spans both the Deschutes and Willamette National Forests and extends north to include Mt Washington Wilderness. Be aware that some features are outdated.

NEAREST TOWN & FACILITIES
Bend

There are motels and restaurants in nearby Bend, central Oregon's largest city. The **Bend Cascade Hostel** *(☎ 541-389-3813, 14 SW Century Dr)*, a modern building southwest of town, has hostel beds for $14. There's pizza and pasta at **Hans** *(☎ 541-389-9700, 915 NW Wall St)* downtown. Mountain Supply (☎ 541-388-0688), 834 Colorado Ave, in Bend carries hiking and backpacking supplies including maps, freeze-dried meals and Northwest Forest Passes.

Getting There & Away Flights on Horizon (☎ 800-547-9308) and United Express (☎ 800-241-6522) connect the Bend/Redmond airport (18mi north of Bend) to Portland, Seattle and San Francisco. Greyhound has two daily buses to Bend from Eugene and Portland ($24 one-way). The station (☎ 541-382-2151), at 63076 N Hwy 97, is on the north end of town opposite the visitor center.

Rent automobiles at the airport from Hertz, or in Bend from Enterprise (☎ 541-383-1717), 315 NE Clay Ave. For a cab call Owl Taxi Service (☎ 541-382-3311).

Camping

Elk Lake campground, 6mi past the trailhead on Cascade Lakes Hwy, has 23 sites in a quiet pine grove near a clear lake ($10). The closer *Devil's Lake campground*, 3mi past Sparks Lake at the South Sister trailhead, has walk-up tent sites but no running water. There's no camping fee, but a Northwest Forest Pass is required to use the parking lot.

Hungry hikers can feed on burgers, ice cream and milkshakes at the family-oriented *Elk Lake Resort* (☎ 541-317-2994) on Cascade Lakes Hwy, 7mi past the trailhead. Long-distance PCT hikers use this lodge as a supply point. The resort also rents rustic lakeside cabins. The Mt Bachelor ski resort's *Sunrise Lodge* is open summer afternoons for lunch.

GETTING TO/FROM THE HIKE

The Green Lakes Trailhead near Sparks Lake is 25mi west of Bend on the Cascade Lakes Hwy. From Bend take Century Dr southwest out of town, following signs for the Cascades Lakes Hwy and Mt Bachelor. Bypass a left-leading fork for Mt Bachelor and continue another 4½mi to the trailhead.

THE HIKE

No sight sinks hearts faster than the foreboding sea of cars encountered at the trailhead parking lot. Trails to several other wilderness destinations make this Oregon's busiest trailhead. In addition to Green Lakes the 150 people who pass through here daily disperse to Moraine Lake, South Sister, the PCT and up the Soda Creek Trail to Soda Springs and Broken Top.

To start, head for the tiny log-hewn guard station and follow a path past signs for Green Lakes. Next, veer left across a footbridge

PACIFIC NORTHWEST

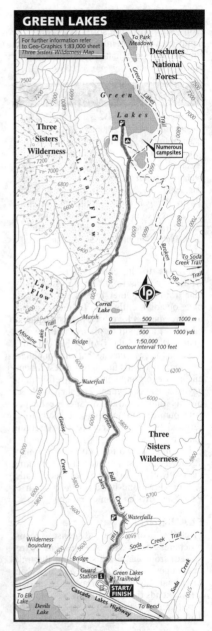

which crosses Fall Creek. The path enters a soothing forest of pine and mountain hemlock. A prattling stream is the only source of commotion as Fall Creek makes a spirited course over the many rocks and boulders. A short waterfall punctuates the creek after a half-mile, and a quick switchback leads up to an even lovelier two-tiered cascade which swirls into a fascinating bowl-like pool. The trail sustains this easy, streamside pace to another tumbling waterfall before leaving the creek behind and climbing through forest to a junction for Moraine Lake in another 1½mi.

Bypass this cut-off and cross two bridges to rejoin a subdued Fall Creek and hike along the east side of this drainage for the next 2.2mi. Patches of alpine grass, intermittent blocks of obsidian cliff, and glimpses of South Sister through gnarled pine mark the transition from forest to alpine meadow. After four steep switchbacks the trail opens out into meadows in earnest, and flecks of Indian paintbrush, lupine, shooting star and composites paint the trail in shades of red, blue, purple and yellow. Green whorls of hellebore flank the creek below. Heaps of dull-glinting rock on the opposite bank mark the edge of a massive obsidian flow that once seeped from the snow-splotched South Sister, damming Fall Creek and creating the original, unbroken Green Lake.

Upstream the valley widens at the foot of a short basin wall, where – on the other side – the churning action of retreating glaciers littered a broad meadow with crumbled pumice and glacial till. Unobstructed views of South Sister to the left and Broken Top to the right greet hikers at the top. Ignore the sign for Green Lakes Meadow and chug straight across the dusty plain to an island of trees along the largest Green Lake. Stands of lodgepole pine like this thrive in the pumice soils and grow in pure stands girdling South Sister and Broken Top. This shady oasis is a fine point for admiring the lake's emerald hue, produced by suspended bits of glacial till from the Lewis Glacier. The lake marks the turning point of the hike.

Obsidian Cliffs

Duration	6–7½ hours
Distance	12mi (19.3km)
Standard	medium-hard
Start/Finish	Obsidian Trailhead
Nearest Towns	McKenzie Bridge, Sisters
Public Transport	no

Summary A long, partial-loop day hike near McKenzie Pass to an obsidian plateau beneath North Sister. Encounters forest, lava and alpine meadow and views several central Oregon volcanoes.

Rivers of fresh lava that oozed from Yapoah, Collier and Four-in-One cones – a cluster of cinder cones near North Sister (10,085ft) – form stirring volcanics at the north edge of the wilderness near McKenzie Pass. A waterfall over an obsidian cliff is the main destination of this long, partial-loop hike through forest, lava and alpine meadows to a plateau beneath North Sister. Native Americans summered here to gather huckleberries and collect the black, glass-like obsidian for making arrowheads and knives. This much-loved corner is now a limited-entry area requiring special-use permits.

Add a day or two to explore Collier Cone and Linton Meadows, north and south along the Pacific Crest Trail. Sunshine Meadow is being restored after years of overuse. Camping here should be avoided.

PLANNING

Wilderness lands near McKenzie Pass fall under the jurisdiction of the McKenzie ranger district of the Willamette National Forest (💻 www.fs.fed.us/r6/willamette).

When to Hike

By mid-July the trail is mostly snow-free (with a few lingering patches on the shady Glacier Way Trail) and stays that way into October. Start early to beat the afternoon heat (pick up your permit the day before).

Maps

Ambiguous geography makes the portion of the PCT across the plateau above Obsidian

Falls tricky to navigate. Hikers should carry the 1:26,966 and 1:83,000 *Three Sisters Wilderness Map* ($6.95) by Geo-Graphics, and a compass. You'll receive an enlarged photocopy of this map with the limited-entry area marked on it with your permit. It's a good idea to carry both.

Permits & Regulations

Special-use permits restrict the number of visitors to 40 day hikers and 50 backpackers. Permits are issued exclusively from the McKenzie district ranger station (☎ 541-822-3381), 57600 McKenzie Hwy, McKenzie

Bridge, OR 97413, and can be reserved by phone or by mail up to 30 days in advance. Permits are free, but you'll still need to purchase a Northwest Forest Pass. The district ranger station is open daily 8 am to 4:30 pm. Allow at least 50 minutes to drive from the ranger station to the trailhead.

Backpackers should check restrictions before heading out; camping is prohibited within 100ft of water or trails.

NEAREST TOWNS & FACILITIES

Motels and *restaurants* can be found on either side of the pass in dinky McKenzie

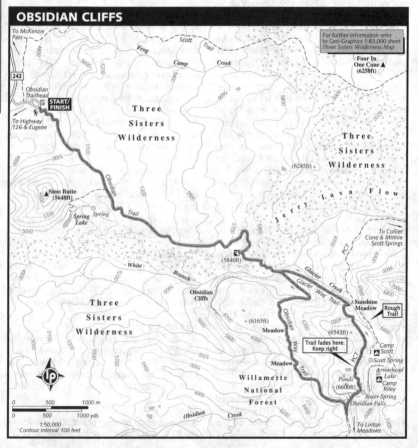

OBSIDIAN CLIFFS

Bridge or touristy Sisters. The hike is also a reasonable day trip from Eugene (see Gateways at the beginning of this chapter) or Bend (see Nearest Town & Facilities for the Green Lakes hike).

Camping

Swampy *Scott Lake campground*, 1½mi west of the trailhead near McKenzie Pass offers no running water, no fee and no mercy from bloodthirsty mosquitoes. Nearby *Lava Camp Lake campground*, another small wilderness campground a mile east of the pass near the PCT, has water.

A better base camp may be *Paradise campground*, which shelters 64 riverside sites ($10) in a grove of old-growth fir. It's 4½mi east of McKenzie Bridge near the junction for Hwy 242, and convenient to the ranger station for those needing to pick up permits the next morning.

GETTING TO/FROM THE HIKE

The Obsidian Trailhead is 7mi west of the Dee Wright Observatory at McKenzie Pass, between Miles 70 and 71 on Hwy 242 (the Old McKenzie Hwy). From Eugene travel Hwy 126 50mi east to the community of McKenzie Bridge and continue another 5mi to a junction for Hwy 242 – a slow, winding byway over McKenzie Pass (trailer travel prohibited). A sign for the trailhead appears after about 15mi. Parking is in one of the gravel slots at an old campground loop.

From Bend take Hwy 20 north to Sisters; the trailhead is 30mi west on Hwy 242.

THE HIKE

The trail makes a straightforward start from the east edge of the parking loop, and leads right onto Obsidian Trail past a sign for White Branch creek to gain 1000ft through quiet timber and huckleberry over the next 4mi. Lanky lodgepole pine gives way to shadier mountain hemlock and banners of lichen before the forest abuts the humped up **Jerry Lava Flow**. Mount a switchback up the black lava and contemplate how this fresh flow spilled from Collier Cone only 500 to 1600 years ago. Top out at views of North and South Sisters, Mt Washington

and Belknap Crater, and drop down the other side to rock-hop over the White Branch at a small meadow.

At a sign for Linton Meadow at a wooded trail junction, continue straight for a steeper mile of forest and lupine. Underfoot is a concealed obsidian flow that reveals itself in small flashes of black rock along the dusty trail. A meadow opens to Middle Sister (10,047ft) along a drainage for Obsidian Falls as the trail rounds a butte to a cool creek crossing a few hundred feet from a signed junction with the PCT. Take the sharp switchback up to the left, pausing to admire the ladder-like **Obsidian Falls** before easing up the obsidian cliff to an absorbing view of North Sister. An elusive PCT leads over a rocky plateau strewn with glinting shards of black obsidian. Stick to the edge of a talus slope near Sister Spring to stay on course, passing to the right of a small lake.

Continue down forested switchbacks and intermittent patches of snow to intercept the Glacier Way Trail at a scenic trail junction known as **Sunshine Meadow**. The PCT continues straight to Collier Cone and Minnie Scott Springs, and a right trail leads to a camp along a climber's route to North and Middle Sisters. Bear left onto the Glacier Way Trail and hike along Glacier Creek to finish the loop, which returns to the Obsidian Trail at the lava flow in 0.6mi.

Belknap Crater

Duration	2½–3 hours
Distance	5.2mi (8.4km)
Standard	easy-medium
Start/Finish	McKenzie Pass (PCT Trailhead)
Nearest Towns	McKenzie Bridge, Sisters
Public Transport	no

Summary This short hike on the PCT leads through a massive lava field to a panoramic view of the central Oregon Cascades from a volcanic crater. Easily accessible from Hwy 242 at McKenzie Pass.

This hike follows a stretch of the Pacific Crest Trail (PCT) into a desolate moonscape of jagged lava, and ends at a dramatic panorama of Mt Washington and the Three Sisters from the crater of a cinder cone volcano. The lava flows between these two peaks at McKenzie Pass are geologically fresh, and seeped from vents around Mt Belknap and Yapoah Cone 1500 to 3000 years ago. Although this foray north from McKenzie Pass technically leads into Mt Washington Wilderness, the flows here are identical to the ones that spill over from Three Sisters Wilderness on the other side of the highway.

The loose, sharp lava is hazardous for dogs, children or anyone with weak ankles.

PLANNING

The trail is open from mid-July to October. The treeless, heat-absorbing lava beds are too hot to enjoy on sunny afternoons. Mornings, cloudy days, and cool autumn afternoons are the best times to hike. Carry water.

Maps

The 1:83,000 Geo-Graphics *Three Sisters Wilderness Map* ($6.95) is helpful for identifying surrounding mountains, but useless for finding your way on the trail. There are no other appropriate maps.

Permits

A Northwest Forest Pass is required, available from the McKenzie ranger station (see Planning for the Obsidian Cliffs hike) and at most stores in McKenzie Bridge. In the town of Sisters, the passes are available at Sisters district ranger station at the Hwy 242 & US 20 junction on the west end of town (open mornings-only on Saturday), or from Sisters Oil.

NEAREST TOWNS & FACILITIES

See Nearest Towns & Facilities for the Obsidian Cliffs hike.

GETTING TO/FROM THE HIKE

Follow the directions for the Obsidian Cliffs hike to McKenzie Pass. The trailhead is a half-mile west of the Dee Wright Observatory on Hwy 242 (the Old McKenzie Hwy). A brown hiker symbol points left to an unsigned parking pullout near a clump of trees 76mi east of Eugene, just beyond the Linn County line. From Sisters the trailhead is 23mi west.

THE HIKE

Brown, bald and unimpressive-looking Belknap Crater directly north is the primary source of all this lava. Your final destination is the red-peaked Little Belknap, a small volcanic vent just downslope.

The hike begins in dust at the east edge of the parking lot, passes a sign for the PCT and Mt Washington Wilderness, then veers left toward lodgepole pine to climb north along an island of trees. After a short hop over a finger of lava the trail levels out, rounds the north side of a second tree-island and loops to the east to end at the foot of the lava beds. Here the trail makes a sharp switchback and ascends into mounds of black rock to wind its way north.

Like a desert, the landscape at first glance appears lifeless and sterile. Gnarled, white-washed trees marooned in lava are the haunting remains of a forest Pompeii. Here life demands a different perspective – look closely and you'll find lichen-covered rock,

BELKNAP CRATER

insect communities and an occasional hopeful shrub. The sound of crunching rock gives over to a timeless silence, as frozen currents of lava ebb in every direction for miles around. Long, hollow lava tubes can be seen closer to Little Belknap, and a good eye can pick out small caves.

Between Belknap Crater and Little Belknap watch for a small, unsigned trail to the right which leads up a lava tube to the base of Little Belknap. Don't mistake the short summit in the crater for the end. Carefully scale the red lava to reach the very top, where there are expansive views of the PCT trailing off past Mt Washington to the north and eye-to-eye views of the Three Sisters to the south. There isn't really anywhere to stop and sit along the way, and most people welcome the flat summit as a place to relax before heading back to the trailhead via the same route.

Southern Oregon Coast

Oregon's coastline of rocky, forested capes and windswept beaches stretches uninterrupted for 362 scenic miles. The entire length of this spectacular shore is preserved for recreation as public land, with access provided mainly by more than 70 state parks. Visions of an end-to-end coastline hike have evolved into the Oregon Coast Trail, which holds potential as a long-distance trail but is still mostly a series of poorly connected beach hikes.

Willamette Valley residents accustomed to getaways in north-coast resort towns often neglect the south coast's quiet coves and deserted beaches. Pristine, untamed landscapes in this remote, southwest corner of Oregon remain close to wilderness and offer hikers a sense of solitude lacking on popular mountain trails in the Cascades. The coast – cooler and wetter than the western valleys – is a good place to escape the inland heat in summer. The trails are also open all winter, which is the best time to watch the off-shore migration of gray whales.

Oregon Dunes

Duration	2½–3 hours
Distance	5mi (8.1km)
Standard	easy
Start/Finish	Eel Creek campground
Nearest Town	Lakeside, Reedsport
Public Transport	yes

Summary Cross lonely 400ft to 500ft mountains of sand on the way to a deserted ocean beach.

Mountains of sand up to 500ft tall highlight this short hike across restless, shifting dunes to a deserted ocean beach in the Oregon Dunes National Recreation Area, the nation's largest dunes area. Wind and water sculpt this 50mi abstraction by sweeping piles of offshore sand through a flat opening in Oregon's rocky coastline. Oceanfront forests, lakes, rivers and wetlands comprise a unique, highly transitional ecology defined by the perpetually changing dunes.

While more than 400,000 people come here each year to tear around the sand on dune buggies and dirt bikes, some portions are closed to off-road vehicles. These undisturbed areas provide habitat for the threatened western snowy plover.

PLANNING

The Oregon Dunes National Recreation Area headquarters, 855 Highway Ave, is at the junction of Hwys 38 & 101 in Reedsport, OR 97467. It's open daily 9 am to 5 pm Memorial Day to Labor Day, and the rest of the year 8 am to 4:30 pm Monday to Friday and 10 am to 4 pm Saturday. After hours visit the lobby to get brochures, free maps and local tourist info.

Most visit during the drier summer season, though the dunes may be hiked year-round. Sunny, summer afternoons sometimes bring strong winds and unpleasant hiking conditions. Wind carves the wet sand into interesting sculptures in the winter.

What to Bring

Bring as little as possible, relying on zippered pockets or a fanny pack. A full backpack is a real nuisance and after climbing and leaping

PACIFIC NORTHWEST

over the first couple of dunes you'll long to get rid of it. Anything you *do* bring is only going to get covered in sand. Lightweight shoes or sandals are best for hiking on sand. Blowing sand can sting bare skin, so wear pants and long sleeves on windy days, as well as a snug-fitting hat or bandanna. A pair of binoculars in the winter and early spring can aid in spotting gray whales off the coast.

Maps & Books
This hike and others are mapped in *Hiking Trails in the Oregon Dunes National Recreation Area*, a free booklet available from the Oregon Dunes National Recreation Area headquarters in Reedsport.

Permits & Regulations
A Northwest Forest Pass is required, but waived if you've paid to camp overnight in Siuslaw National Forest, or if you've purchased a Coastal Access Pass ($10, good for five days), which provides admission to 16 designated recreation sites along the coast.

Passes are available from the national recreation area headquarters in Reedsport or the Hauser KOA campground on Hwy 101, 7mi south of Coos Bay.

NEAREST TOWNS & FACILITIES
The clean and comfortable *Salty Seagull* (☎ 541-271-3729, 1806 Hwy 101) in Reedsport has three-room units with full kitchens for $45. *Don's Diner* (☎ 541-271-2032, 2115 Winchester Ave) is the local favorite for hearty burgers and homemade soups. *Bayfront Bistro* (☎ 541-271-9463, 208 Bayfront Loop) in Winchester Bay has classier dining centered around seafood, pasta and microbrews.

There are more *hotels* and *restaurants* in Coos Bay, 15mi south of the trailhead.

Camping
Eel Creek campground, 10mi south of Reedsport on Hwy 101, is a peaceably shrubby and well-sheltered USFS campground right at the trailhead.

GETTING TO/FROM THE HIKE
The trailhead at Eel Creek campground is 10½mi south of Reedsport on Hwy 101. Make a left immediately after turning into the campground and follow signs to the trailhead. To reach Reedsport from Eugene, take I-5 south and exit onto Hwy 38; Reedsport is reached after 64mi.

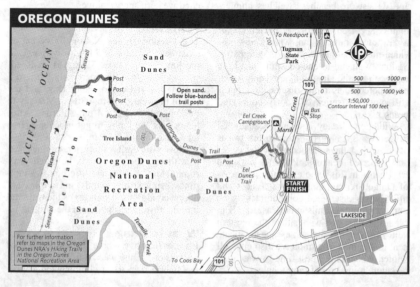

Porter Stage and Greyhound buses from Eugene and the south coast via Florence and Coos Bay stop in Lakeside in front of the Tree Acres Mini-Mart, 10980 Hwy 101. From here it's a quarter-mile walk to the trailhead. Call Coastal Cab (☎ 541-271-2696) for a taxi.

THE HIKE

The trail starts as a gravel path that meanders through the campground for the first half-mile. From the west edge of the parking lot head right (north) along a fence and cross a bridge over Eel Creek. Keep right at the next fork and continue through a shrubby forest past a small, lily-pad covered lake. Silvery, crone-like manzanita trees, pink-flowering rhododendron, and salal with its edible purple berries (watch for bugs) are all skinny plants which speak of poor soil and hint at the mountains of sand ahead.

Cross a service road toward a sign for the Umpqua Dunes Trail and start climbing through a forest of Douglas fir, bypassing a right-leading path to the campground. The trail ends in a sandy hump. On the other side are long lines of oblique dunes, spreading out for miles, and the beach, heaving and sighing 2mi away.

Weathered gray posts topped by blue bands are the only trail markers for the next 1¼mi, so be sure to get your bearings before charging out onto the open sand. A massive, 500ft oblique dune rises to the south, extending a long, sandy finger past a tree-island toward the beach. Trail posts run west in the basin beneath it, but most hikers surrender all guidance and scramble up the dune's steep, sandy face to walk along the ridge.

Either approach delivers you to a trail post at the edge of the deflation plain – a swampy, low-lying strip of vegetation between the foredune and open sand. Follow the direction of a faded hiker symbol and head north along this fringe, side-stepping sporadic clumps of yellow coast monkey flower and stunted blue seashore lupine. The trail cuts left across the deflation plain after a quarter-mile at a sign for the beach, and continues through grassy flats and maze-like corridors of salal and huckleberry for the last half-mile.

The trail ends abruptly at an 8ft to 10ft seawall on the west side of the foredune. Scout along the edge for an easy place to climb down the soft, sandy cliff to the deserted beach, noting first where you left the trail.

After crossing back over the dunes, vary the return route slightly by following the straight arrow at a sign for the Umpqua Dunes Trailhead near the edge of the forest. Trail posts lead south and east along a sandy route that traverses a few forested parabola dunes before dropping back to the trailhead. Turn right at the next junction and cross the Eel Creek footbridge to the parking lot.

Boardman State Park

Duration	3–4 hours
Distance	5.4mi (8.7km)
Standard	easy-medium
Start/Finish	Natural Bridges viewpoint
Nearest Towns	Brookings, Gold Beach
Public Transport	no

Summary The dramatic sea-stacks, arches and offshore islands seen on this short, down-and-back day hike on the Oregon Coast Trail are one of Oregon's best-kept secrets. A good place to watch whales in the winter and spring.

A rugged preserve of seaside prairies, secluded beaches and craggy headlands hemmed by coastal islands honors Samuel H Boardman, Oregon's first state park superintendent. Established in 1950, this coastline park contains 12mi of Oregon's most dramatic coastal scenery in tribute to the man who spent 20 years acquiring scenic lands and wilderness for the state parks system. Winding through this forested corridor is the scenic Oregon Coast Trail (OCT), which plunges down hidden coves and scales clifftop vistas at every turn.

This down-and-back hike, from the Natural Bridge viewpoint to the Arch Rock picnic area at the north end of the park, visits a place where caves and vents formed by past volcanic activity have collapsed into a garden of rock arches, islands and sea stacks.

PLANNING

Campground staff at neighboring Harris Beach State Park (☎ 521-469-2021) oversee the park's general maintenance but know little about day-to-day trail conditions. Visit the Oregon State Parks website (💻 www.prd.state.or.us) for more information.

Summer is the most pleasant time to hike, though the trail is open year-round. Binoculars can help spot seals and island bird life. The headlands are also good place to watch for gray whales in the winter or spring.

There are no permits or fees required and no appropriate/up-to-date maps.

NEAREST TOWNS & FACILITIES

For a budget motel try the *Pacific Sunset Inn* (☎ 541-469-2141, 800-469-2141, 1144 Chetco Ave) in Brookings ($45). Food is good at the *Hog Wild Cafe* (☎ 541-469-8869, 16158 S Hwy 101) in Harbor, open for breakfast and lunch. The *Wharfside Restaurant* (☎ 541-469-7316, 16362 Lower Harbor Rd) is the local favorite for fish and chips.

Camping

Harris Beach State Park (☎ 541-469-2021), on the beach between the south park boundary and Brookings on Hwy 101, is the closest campground ($17). Smaller and quieter *Alfred Loeb State Park* is 10mi northeast of Brookings up Chetco River Rd, on the river in a redwood grove ($16). Both have showers, flush toilets and RV hookups (powered sites); Harris Beach also has yurts ($27) and takes reservations (☎ 800-452-5687). Alfred Loeb also has cabins ($35).

GETTING TO/FROM THE HIKE

Boardman State Park is on Hwy 101 between Gold Beach and Brookings, just north of the California border. The trailhead at Natural Bridge viewpoint is 17mi south of Gold Beach, just 2mi from the northern park boundary. Inland travelers can pick up Hwy 199 (the Redwood Hwy) from Grants Pass and follow it south to Crescent City, California, then continue 15mi north on Hwy 101 to Brookings.

Medford's Rogue Valley International–Medford airport, 29mi south of Grants Pass, is the closest airport. Greyhound buses pass through Brookings en route to both Portland and San Francisco twice daily. There is no local transit to the park – rent a car in Brookings at Coast Rent-A-Car (☎ 541-469-5321), 530 Chetco Ave, or call Bob's Taxi (☎ 541-469-7007) for a cab.

THE HIKE

Weathered cedar posts carved with a peace-symbol likeness mark the OCT as it weaves around headlands and crosses gravel parking lots. Two such posts stand ready to guide at either end of the parking area. The wooden viewing platform for the **Natural Bridges** is 0.1mi from the left corner of the parking lot, in the opposite direction of the trail to Arch Rock. Views of ocean waves rolling under pairs of eroded rock arches are just the beginning of some truly impressive ocean scenery in the next 2.6mi.

From the viewpoint, backtrack to the parking lot and find the northbound trail to start hiking toward Arch Rock. Continue through woods below Hwy 101 for 0.3mi to a pullout for **Thunder Rock Cove.** Across the

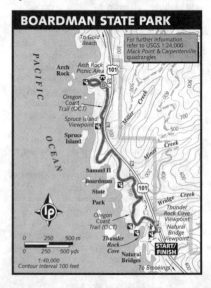

parking lot the trail makes a sharp left and dives toward the ocean on steep switchbacks through a dense grove of 300-year-old sitka spruce. A trail post marks a fork where a spur trail leads straight down a bluff to several spectacular views of rock arches and sea stacks at a secluded cove. The right path continues north around the headland, and climbs more switchbacks through shrubby salal to reach a trail junction just below the highway.

Turn left here, hike below Hwy 101 for a short distance and bypass an abandoned construction road that leads up to a parking pullout north of Miner Creek. The trail plunges down the wooded flanks of another cape and reaches another fork with more great views along a left-leading trail. Short paths dead end at clifftop vistas over another cove. Find the best views up and down the coast at the tip of a grassy headland.

Return to the main trail and take the right fork to ascend a slope and emerge from the woods at Miller Creek, on Hwy 101. The trail picks up to the left, on the other end of the guardrail. Views of **Spruce Island** peek through the trees as the trail leads around yet another headland to the Spruce Island viewpoint on Hwy 101. Spruce Island, an unmistakably long and flat island topped by a wiry mop of spruce trees, lies directly offshore.

The OCT disappears into the woods at the end of the parking lot for one last haul before reaching the developed **Arch Rock** picnic area. Walk to the end of the drive and past the toilets to follow a paved path to picnic tables and dramatic views of rock arches and offshore wildlife. The point is a good place to sit, eat lunch and gaze out over the ocean before heading back to the car by the same route.

Wild Rogue Wilderness

A river famous for its turbulent class IV rapids, southern Oregon's Rogue River winds through a remote, basalt canyon strewn with artefacts of pioneer life. Takelma and Tutuni people living along the river fished for salmon, hunted deer and bear, and

collected acorns and camas root for more than 8000 years before white settlers drove them out to claim the region's gold, which ran out in the early part of the 20th century. Only a handful of riverside homesteads remain, disconnected from roads and modern life.

In a region preoccupied with rafting and fishing, hiking is a secondary activity. More than 9000 people float the canyon every year, yet few ever set foot on the scenic 40mi trail that parallels this segment of federally designated Wild and Scenic River, which has no road access to its banks. The Rogue River Trail is the Northwest's only wilderness trail to feature commercial lodges.

GATEWAY
Medford

Medford's Rogue Valley International–Medford Airport, 29 miles south of Grants Pass on I-5, links southern Oregon directly to Portland, Seattle, San Francisco and Los Angeles on Horizon (☎ 800-547-9308) and United Express (☎ 800-241-6522). Hertz (☎ 541-773-4293, 800-654-3131) and Avis (☎ 541-773-3003, 800-331-1212) rent cars right at the airport. For a taxi call Yellow Cab (☎ 541-772-6288).

McKenzie Outfitters (☎ 541-773-5145), 130 E 8th St, downtown, is the only place in these parts to buy specialized equipment and supplies.

PACIFIC NORTHWEST

Rogue River Trail

Duration	5 days
Distance	40mi (64.4km)
Standard	medium
Start	Foster Bar Trailhead
Finish	Grave Creek boat ramp
Nearest Towns	Galice, Illahe, Agness
Public Transport	no

Summary Hike a roadless canyon end-to-end along a wild, twisting river famed for its white water. Follows a relatively easy grade through scrub oak and laurel past historic homesteads and cabins, some of which offer lodging.

Rich in history, this 40mi trail from Illahe to Grave Creek visits mining claims and homesteads on a pack trail once used to transport mail and supplies from Gold Beach. Episodes in natural and human history unfold with every mile, taking in waterfalls and river rapids, battle sites, pioneer cabins and open-air museums.

This hike takes five days, and presumes arriving at the trailhead too late to put in a full day. A settlement at Marial divides the trail between Wild Rogue Wilderness and rugged BLM land. Camps and lodges line the way, so it's easy to adjust your itinerary for a shorter or longer trip. While hikers can expect to cover 10mi a day, it's difficult to divide the trail into exact 10mi intervals.

Hiking west to east (as written here) puts the sun behind the hiker during the hottest part of the afternoon and affords a better view of rafters crashing over rapids. The BLM's trail guide (see Maps & Books under Planning) is written from east to west (Grave Creek to Illahe). Many who recommend the east–west option think the descent from 700ft to 475ft makes it easier. In truth it's the other way around – the Grave Creek Trailhead in the east starts off with two days of steep, hilly terrain (and a full pack), whereas the Illahe Trailhead begins with a few gentle hills and quickly levels off.

WARNING

Black bears and poison oak are serious hazards on what is otherwise a relaxing and relatively easy trail. Use common sense to avoid both.

HISTORY

The river takes its name from local Native Americans, whom French trappers called *coquins* (rogues) after being assaulted in an attack that sparked a bloody war in 1885–86.

NATURAL HISTORY

Ancient seafloor and volcanic rock comprise the Klamath Mountains, which joined the subcontinent around 100 million years ago to form Oregon's oldest mountains. This rocky canyon is distinguished by deciduous forests of Garry oak, red-skinned madrone and camphor-scented California laurel (myrtlewood).

PLANNING

The Rogue River Trail traverses Wild Rogue Wilderness, Siskiyou National Forest and BLM land. Staffed by USFS rangers, the Rand visitor center (☎ 541-479-3735), 14335 Galice Rd, Merlin, OR 97532, 5mi south of the Grave Creek Trailhead, is the best source of information and the most convenient place to buy Northwest Forest Passes. It's open daily 7 am to 4 pm May 5 to October 15.

Get information and permits in Gold Beach at the Gold Beach district ranger station (☎ 541-247-6651), 1225 S Ellensburg Ave, Gold Beach, OR 97444. It's open 7:30 am to 5 pm Monday to Friday year-round, and on weekends 8 am to 4 pm Memorial Day to Labor Day. The Medford district BLM (☎ 541-770-2200), 3040 Biddle Rd, Medford, OR 97504, open 7:30 am to 4:30 pm Monday to Friday, has information year-round. The Siskiyou National Forest website is at 🖳 www.fs.fed.us/r6/siskiyou.

When to Hike

Temperatures in the 90°s and 100°sF make the canyon too hot for hiking in the summer. The best months are May, early June, September and October. Spring hikers will enjoy blooming azaleas and wildflowers. In the fall, trails are drier and strewn with acorns. Spring and fall are the river's shoulder seasons, and while that shouldn't stop you, expect some facilities to be closed.

What to Bring

You'll need a tent and stove for at least one night. Pack a swimsuit to take advantage of a water slide and several swimming holes. There may not be water at Illahe campground, so fill up before driving to the trailhead.

Maps & Books

Hikers should carry the BLM's *Rogue River Trail: Grave Creek to Illahe*, a free booklet containing a mile-by-mile narrative and centerfold map of campsites, lodges and historic landmarks. Obtain a copy from one of the ranger stations listed earlier in this section.

If you can find it, the BLM's free 1:250,000 *Southwestern Oregon Recreation*

Map shows the trail through the region in shaded relief. Otherwise, there are no suitable topographic maps for this hike.

Permits & Regulations

Northwest Forest Passes are required. Some shuttle companies store cars on private property until the last day of your hike, so a permit may not be necessary for each day you're on the trail. Overnight parking at the Grave Creek Trailhead is not permitted. In addition to the visitor centers and ranger stations listed earlier in this section, permits can also be purchased at the Galice Resort in Galice or the Cougar Lane Lodge in Agness.

Fires are allowed, but the restrictions for building them make them impractical.

Camping & Lodges

Camps along the trail are rarely signed and not always obvious. Many are accessed by steep climbs down the riverbank, and most are convenient to water from streams (the river is not a recommended water source). A toilet indicates a nearby camp. Expect to share larger riverside camps with boaters.

Camp-raiding bears are a nuisance mostly from Flora Dell Creek and Paradise, though you should exercise faultless bear-proofing at every camp. A few camps have hoists and electric fences. (See the Health & Safety chapter for more information on bears.)

Trailside homesteads make it possible to hike lodge-to-lodge for most of the way. Meals are included with a night's stay, which costs about $80 per person. Rooms are rustic and bathrooms may be private or shared. There's only one lodge from Marial to Grave Creek, on the opposite side of the river (hikers can arrange to stay on either bank). Reservations are required and should be made well in advance.

Lodges along the way (from west to east) include:

Illahe Lodge (☎ 541-247-6111) 33709 Agness-Illahe Rd, Agness, OR 97406. $70 per person includes three meals.
Clay Hill Lodge (☎ 800-228-3198 x8235) 06373 Rogue River, Agness, OR 97406. $80 per person includes three meals.
Paradise Lodge (☎ 800-525-2161) PO Box 456, Gold Beach, OR 97444. $77 per person includes two meals.
Half Moon Bar Lodge (☎ 541-247-6968) PO Box 455, Gold Beach, OR 97444. $85 per person includes two meals. South bank.
Marial Lodge (☎ 541-474-2057, 479-4923 x7718) PO Box 1395, Grants Pass, OR 97526. $60 per person includes two meals and a sack lunch. Open May to November 15.
Black Bar Lodge (☎ 541-479-6507) PO Box 510, Merlin, OR 97532. $70 per person includes three meals. South bank. Open May to November.

NEAREST TOWNS & FACILITIES

Grants Pass on I-5 or Gold Beach on the coast are the closest major towns, depending on your approach. Grants Pass is better linked to public transport. Campgrounds and general stores comprise the small settlements of Agness and Galice near the start and finish, respectively. McKenzie Outfitters (☎ 541-773-5145), 130 E 8th St, in Medford is the closest place for specialized equipment and supplies.

Grants Pass Area

Places to Stay & Eat *Budget Inn* (☎ 541-479-2952, NE 1253 6th St) has decent rooms from $35. An eclectic seafood and vegetarian menu at *The Laughing Clam* (☎ 541-479-0551, 121 SW G St) makes a perfect end to five days of trail food.

If you're arriving from the north, a stop at the historic *Wolf Creek Inn* (☎ 541-866-2474) off I-5 exit 76 may save you a trip to Grants Pass. The inn serves lunch and dinner and has farmhouse-style rooms from $65. Back roads lead from here to Galice.

Getting There & Away Horizon (☎ 800-547-9308) and United Express (☎ 800-241-6522) fly direct from Portland, San Francisco and Los Angeles to Medford's Rogue Valley International-Medford Airport. Buses traveling I-5 between Portland and San Francisco stop in Grants Pass at the Greyhound bus station (☎ 541-471-6311) at 460 NE Agness Ave.

Rent cars from Budget Rent-A-Car (☎ 541-471-6311), 825 NE F St, in Grants

Pass, or at Medford airport call Hertz (☎ 541-773-4293, 800-654-3131) or Avis (☎ 541-773-3003, 800-331-1212). Call Grants Pass Cab Co (☎ 541-476-6444) for a taxi.

Agness Area

Agness, on USFS Rd No 33, is 6mi from the trailhead at Illahe, the start of the hike. *Cougar Lane Lodge (☎ 541-247-7233, 4219 Agness Rd)* has a store, *restaurant* and motel near the junction of the road to Galice.

Illahe campground, 2mi south of the trailhead on USFS Rd No 33, has pleasant riverside sites ($6) and drinking water (May 1 to October 31). An unappealing campground at *Foster Bar boat ramp* is a mile closer to the trailhead (no water).

Illahe Lodge (see Camping & Lodges under Planning) offers basic rooms and meals at the trailhead. *Singing Springs Resort (☎ 541-247-6162)*, on USFS Rd No 33 between Illahe and Agness (on the north bank), serves sandwiches and salmon dinners on an outdoor deck. Rustic cabins, some with kitchens, cost $40 to $65.

Galice Area

Galice is 7mi from the Grave Creek Trailhead at the end of the hike, at the junction for the road leading to Agness. The *Galice Resort (☎ 541-476-3818, 11744 Merlin-Galice Rd)* sells groceries and burgers and is pretty much the extent of the town.

The campground at *Alameda Park* on Merlin-Galice Rd is an unlikely place to spend the night ($12) given that the first trail camp is only 3mi in. However, it does have the nearest pay phone and is the closest place to park a car overnight ($5); it's 4mi south of the trailhead.

Gold Beach

The Rogue empties into the ocean at Gold Beach, the turn-off for Agness. Basic rooms at the *City Center Motel (☎ 541-247-6675, 94200 Harlow St)* cost $45. *Rod'n Reel (☎ 541-247-6823, 94321 Wedderburn Loop Rd)* at Jot's Resort is a steak and seafood place. It's also open for breakfast.

Although Greyhound buses stop in Gold Beach, Coos Bay and Brookings are the closest towns for car rentals. The station (☎ 541-247-7710) is at 310 Colvin St.

GETTING TO/FROM THE HIKE

The western trailhead at Illahe, near Agness, is in southern Oregon between Grants Pass on I-5 and Gold Beach on Hwy 101. From Grants Pass take the I-5 Merlin exit north of town and follow the Merlin-Galice Rd 15mi to Galice. Or, from Wolf Creek (I-5 exit 76) go right past the inn, duck under a railroad bridge and turn left onto Lower Wolf Creek Rd to reach Galice in 22mi.

BLM Rd 34-8-36, Galice Access Rd and Bear Camp Rd are all names for the 44mi, mostly paved road leading west over the mountains from Galice to Agness (where the road emerges as USFS Rd No 23). Keep left near the summit at a sign for the coast, and at the end turn right onto USFS Rd No 33. A gravel road to the trailhead leads right a mile past the Foster Bar boat ramp. It's 1½ to two hours to the trailhead from Galice.

From Gold Beach, Jerry's Flat Rd (USFS Rd 33) leads 55mi to Illahe from Hwy 101.

The trail ends at Grave Creek boat ramp, 7mi north of Galice near the end of Merlin-Galice Rd. Lower Grave Creek Rd leads north on back roads to I-5 at Wolf Creek.

Jet Boat

Flat-bottomed jet boats carrying tourists and mail from Gold Beach to Blossom Bar make it possible for shorter (two- or three-day) hikes on the trail below Marial. Although few use the boats to hike the trail end-to-end, a night bus arrives in Gold Beach at 6 am in time for boats leaving at 8 am for Foster Bar ($40 one-way). From the Grave Creek trailhead it's another 4mi south to the dam at Alameda Park where you'll have to arrange a cab to Grants Pass ($40), 18mi away.

Boats run from May 1 to October 31. Call Rogue River Mail Boat Trips (☎ 541-247-7033, 800-458-3511, 💻 www.mailboat.com) for reservations.

Shuttle Service

It costs $50 to have a shuttle service pick your car up from the starting point and deliver it to the trailhead at the end. Unless you can arrange your own shuttle or have friends pick you up this service is largely unavoidable. Rogue-Agness Shuttle Service (☎ 541-247-6778, 800-207-7886), in Agness, and Lower Rogue Shuttles (☎ 541-479-4477), in Merlin, are just a few of the companies that serve hikers. The ranger station (see Planning) has a complete list.

Washouts on the road from Galice to Agness can cause flat tires, so be sure your car has a jack and a spare. And because things don't always go as planned, be sure to carry the name and number of your shuttle company, some extra money and coins for a pay phone (or a phone card), and your own car key (leave the driver a duplicate). You'll be glad you did.

Most companies shuttle cars only and won't take passengers, so count on driving to the trailhead on your own and having your car picked up later. Drivers pick up most cars from the Foster Bar boat ramp, the pullout for rafters, although the actual trailhead is another mile east. You won't necessarily be meeting your driver, so make sure you agree on where to leave the car!

THE HIKE
Day 1: Illahe to Tate Creek
3–4½ hours, 6.1mi (9.8km)
If you're leaving the car at Foster Bar boat ramp you'll need to hike an extra mile up the road to the trailhead. Take a right at a sign for the Rogue River Trail and follow a gravel road through a field for a half-mile. The trail starts from the left side of the parking lot and leads away from the river and up through pasture. A place of significant beginnings and endings, the trailhead here at Big Bend was the site of a decisive battle in an Indian war that lasted from 1855 to 1856. In the end, Takelma and Tutuni people, who had occupied this canyon for more than 8000 years, were relocated to a reservation at Alsea, opening the Rogue to settlement by gold prospectors.

After passing *Illahe Lodge* the trail crosses a dirt road to enter a fragrant forest of Garry oak and California laurel (myrtlewood), and after a couple of hills, settles into an easy grade high above the river. The *Wild River*

Lodge appears through trees on the opposite bank at 3.9mi, and a wooden footbridge over Hicks Creek follows before too long.

It's another mile to the next bridge and a 30ft **waterfall** at Flora Dell Creek, named after Flora Dell Thomas, the wife of Hathaway Jones (1870-1937). Jones made a living along the canyon as a packer and mail carrier, but is mostly remembered as an imaginative storyteller who spun improbable tales about pioneer life. If you were unable to begin the hike in the morning, you may wish to climb down a steep bank west of the bridge to reach a sandy *camp* along the river (mind the poison oak). There's water from a lower pool along the creek. The toilet is off the trail, back toward Hicks Creek.

Hikers departing the trailhead before noon can probably cover the full 6.1mi from the trailhead to Tate Creek, where they can look forward to a 25ft water slide at the end of a hot afternoon. From Flora Dell Creek continue above the river canyon along an exposed trail for 1.6mi to the forested *Clay Hill Lodge*, bypass a left-leading trail to an old home site (private) and head downhill to cross Clay Hill Creek.

The trail flattens at a grassy clearing for *Camp Tacoma,* crosses Camp Tacoma Creek and continues back into the woods for 0.1mi to the Tate Creek bridge. A shady clearing on the east bank makes an inviting spot to relax and draw water. From here it's 200yd upstream past big boulders to the **Tate Creek Slide,** a natural rock chute ending in a deep pool.

Campsites are down along the river, on both sides of Tate Creek. A path leads left up to a toilet from the west end of the bridge.

Alternative Campsites
Camp Tacoma This large riverside camp 0.1mi west of Tate Creek has a trailside toilet and access to water along the creek. Sites along the beach get heavy use by rafters and are frequented by bears. Store food and packs inside the electric fence.

Brushy Bar Those forging ahead will find pleasant riverside sites near the Brushy Bar guard station, 1.7mi past Tate Creek. The

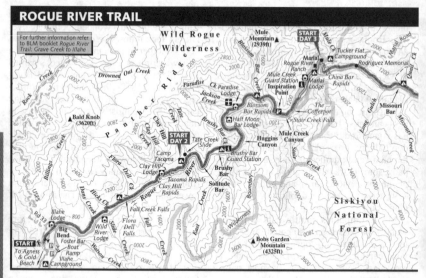

ROGUE RIVER TRAIL

toilet is on the trail in the woods. Creek water piped through a faucet at the guard station must be treated before drinking. Signs point the way to bear hoists and there's also an electric fence.

Day 2: Tate Creek to Marial
6–8 hours, 9.4mi (15.1km)
If you made it only as far as Flora Dell Creek on Day 1, complete the extra 1 to 1½ hours (1.9mi) to Tate Creek.

The trail leaves Tate Creek and in 1.7mi arrives at Brushy Bar, shrouded in a dark stand of fir. Volunteers at the parklike Brushy Bar guard station don't get much company, and will gladly fill your ear with tales of bear sightings and rafting mishaps. Water from the outdoor faucet must be treated before drinking.

The next 3mi are action-packed, and start through Huggins Canyon on a narrow ledge lined with poison oak. The worst is over by Half Moon Bar, where the trail overlooks a cairn on a rocky beach. What follows is an apparition – neat cabins lining a long green airstrip (mind the planes) to *Paradise Lodge*, the turning point for jet boats. Meals are served to lodgers only, but hikers can

still get soda and beer, use the bathroom and relax on the riverside balcony in the main lodge. Rather than hike back up the airstrip, turn right at the gate to pick up the trail in the woods east of the lodge.

Wind through gentle, forested hills for 1.2mi to Blossom Bar, the river's most difficult rapids (see *Alternative Campsite* at the end of this day). Next, the Rogue quickens through narrow **Mule Creek Canyon**, vaulting rafters through dramatic whitewater pitfalls. In 1.4mi the trail reaches Inspiration Point for a view of plunging **Stair Creek Falls** across the river. Just 0.2mi farther the churning **Coffeepot** spits boats out of a tricky whirlpool. Mules and horses once carried mail along this high canyon trail, which leaves Wild Rogue Wilderness and turns inland up Mule Creek at the end of Marial Rd. Follow this road downhill 1½mi through fragrant laurel forest, past the Mule Creek guard station and *Marial Lodge* to a bridge at Mule Creek.

From the west end of the bridge a path leads down to sandy *campsites* along the river; a more popular camp on the creek's east bank is reached by hiking across the Rogue River Ranch (see Day 3). For a

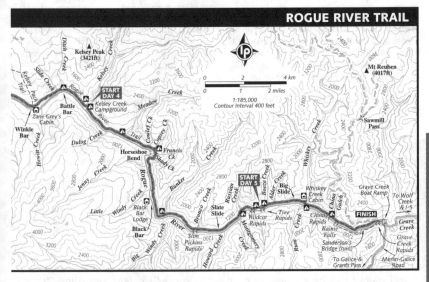

ROGUE RIVER TRAIL

change of pace, cross the bridge and turn left up a short road to the developed *Tucker Flat campground*, a pleasant wooded spot with picnic tables and trash cans. The tap water here must be treated.

Alternative Campsite
Blossom Bar Stop here to save the last 3.6mi to Marial for tomorrow. Shrubby sites lie right off the trail amid a makeshift table and tall poison oak. There's a bear hoist, and water from a pleasant creek pool. A trailside toilet is 100yd west.

Day 3: Marial to Kelsey Creek
6–8 hours, 8.1mi (13km)
Start the day on Marial Rd by walking 0.2mi to the **Rogue River Ranch**. The farmhouse at this idyllic homestead-turned-museum contains interesting pioneer artefacts (a butter churn hollowed out of a wood stump), and tells about a permanent Native American village once at this site. Allow at least an hour to explore the estate.

The trail picks up from the end of the field in the left (east) corner of the property near the river (opposite the toilets). Avoid the beach unless you're here to *camp*. Instead

turn left at the fence to head up a dirt road toward the ranch. A trail sign points up into the woods 10yd on the right.

It seems odd for a trail leaving a designated wilderness to become more primitive. But the 23mi segment from Marial to Grave Creek does just that, and becomes progressively more rugged as it rises and falls on steep, rocky slopes through grass and oak forest. The trail reaches a bronze plaque at the **Rodriguez Memorial** in about 2mi, and a barren *campsite* at the Quail Creek bridge in another 1.6mi. Stop for water before continuing another 2.7mi to Slide Creek. A **cabin** passed at Winkle Bar was once the home of Western writer Zane Grey. It's now private property, but respectful visitors are welcome.

In a mile the trail rolls out of an oak grove and into a scenic meadow near Ditch Creek across from Battle Bar, site of a skirmish between US soldiers and Takelma. Slightly further is a riverside *camp* in a narrow canyon at Kelsey Creek, one of the Rogue's most beautiful spots. A steep path from the west bank leads right to sandy sites and perfect swimming holes along a basalt flat. The toilet is just upslope, and there's easy access to water from the creek.

Alternative Campsite

Kelsey Creek Campground Cross Kelsey Creek and continue up two switchbacks to reach a small, wooded site on the east bank. A trail leads down at a sign to a picnic table and bench next to the creek. No toilet.

Day 4: Kelsey Creek to Tyee Rapids

6–8 hours, 10.6mi (17.1km)

The trail crosses the wooded Kelsey Creek Bridge, climbs out the watershed on two steep switchbacks past *Kelsey Creek campground* and leads back into canyon country. Poison oak is thick along this stretch, and sticks straight out onto the trail at a washout in 1½mi. It's still profuse a half-mile later around Meadow Creek, where the trail flattens at a green oasis of grass and shade. There's a small *campsite* on the west bank.

The preceding hilly terrain is just a warm-up for even steeper slopes ahead. After Cowley Creek the trail makes a sharp left and descends into **Horseshoe Bend**. A shaded picnic table and *campsite* on Copsey Creek at the end of this forested glen, 1.3mi from Meadow Creek, makes a good goal for an early lunch. Good canyon views highlight 3.2 strenuous miles to the next water at Bunker Creek. A steep trail down to a pick-up point for *Black Bar Lodge*, across the river, is signed along the trail.

Relax at Bunker Creek's **suspension bridge** before hiking the last 4.6mi to Tyee Rapids. Views of the canyon to Bronco Creek are some of the most spectacular. The winding and climbing gets pretty monotonous, and you'll be tempted to camp at Russian Creek. But refreshing riverside campsites below Tyee Rapids are just a mile away. Watch for a narrow rock path that intercepts the trail on a grassy hillside and leads straight down to a rocky beach. Remember to fill up on water at Russian Creek, or fetch some at Booze Creek, a hilly 0.1mi east of the *Tyee Rapids campsite*.

Alternative Campsites

Booze Creek Continue 0.1mi to sheltered sites at a small, wooded camp on Booze Creek. No toilet.

Big Slide A park-like campground at Big Slide a mile ahead has serene, forested sites on a bench overlooking the river. There's a toilet off the trail to the left in the woods, but no water.

Day 5: Tyee Rapids to Grave Creek Trailhead

3–4 hours, 4.8mi (7.7km)

The trail from Tyee Rapids continues through the Booze Creek watershed. Mining activity was particularly heavy along this final stretch, though attempts to mine gold from Booze and Alder Creeks were unsuccessful. In a mile the trail opens to great views of the river at a flat grove of trees at **Big Slide**, where the Rogue once backed up 15mi behind a massive landslide.

In another half-mile fork left and hike a quarter-mile up Whiskey Creek to the **Whiskey Creek Cabin**, an 1880s mining cabin and one of the best-preserved relics of the Rogue River gold rush. Allow 20 minutes to explore various innovations at the site, which is maintained by the BLM and listed on the National Historic Register.

Head back along Whiskey Creek to return to the trail, which soon reaches another scenic *camp* near the river. Steep, slippery rock ledges line the narrow canyon ahead. A trail leading down to a secluded riverside *campsite* at China Gulch precedes 20ft **Rainie Falls**, which is better viewed from a short trail on the opposite bank. Concrete piers a half-mile ahead mark Sanderson's Bridge, destroyed by a flood in 1927. A sign commemorates the high water mark.

A strenuous last half-mile and big canyon views end the hike at **Grave Creek Rapids** and the east trailhead at the Grave Creek boat ramp.

Alpine Lakes Wilderness

Cirque, tarn and moraine are stock phrases of Washington's legendary Alpine Lakes Wilderness, a patchwork of old mining claims and railroad grants that sprawls over the Cascade Crest between Snoqualmie and Stevens Passes. Its towering spires, razor-sharp ridges and nearly 700 lakes are the special obsession of Seattle-area hikers, who inundate this 614-sq-mile wilderness every weekend for three- and four-day backpacking trips. Rows of granite mountains, chiseled and polished by glaciers, distinguish these peaks from the symmetrical volcanoes that typify the Cascades. The 67mi of Pacific Crest Trail (PCT) that traverse these mountains on high, exposed ledges are among the most scenic in the Pacific Northwest.

Enchantment Lakes

Duration	3–4 days
Distance	20mi (32.2km)
Standard	hard
Start/Finish	Snow Lake Trailhead
Nearest Town	Leavenworth
Public Transport	no

Summary A grueling climb up granite mountains in the southeast corner of Alpine Lakes Wilderness pays off at a famous alpine-lake basin. One of the most magnificent backpacking trips in the Northwest.

A lifetime of backpacking culminates at the Enchantment Lakes, an otherworldly realm of granite slabs, jewel-like tarns, lofty spires and mythical names lodged in the crescent of central Washington's Stuart Range. As with any path destined for greatness the going is tedious and discouraging, the viewless Snow Lake Trail demanding tremendous strength and endurance as it transcends a strand of steep lake basins partitioned by high granite walls.

The 5900ft (1770m), 10mi climb to the Lower Enchantments (Lake Viviane to Inspiration Lake) is ambitious enough for experienced backpackers, the last 3½mi attained most sensibly as a side trip from Snow Lakes. A trail-less crescendo to the often snow-filled Upper Enchantments (Perfection Lake to Aasgard Pass) takes magic powers and at least two days. Special-use permits for this popular protected area present the greatest

barrier to this hike, and thwart thousands before they ever set foot on the trail.

PLANNING
When to Hike
The trail is open late July to October. The chance of getting a permit is better with a midweek departure. October brings fabulous displays of fall color when the coniferous subalpine larch turns bright yellow and loses its needles like leaf-bearing trees.

What to Bring
A walking stick or trekking poles earn their weight in several places along this steep trail. Those camping at the Enchantment Lakes will need cold-weather gear and a three-season tent suited for high wind and rocky terrain.

Maps
The Green Trails 1:44,500 map *The Enchantments, WA (No 209S)* is the only map you'll need.

Permits & Regulations
Special-use permits for the Enchantments Lakes region are difficult to obtain, and available only from the Leavenworth ranger station (☎ 509-548-6977), 600 Sherbourne, Leavenworth, WA 98862, open 7:45 am to 4:30 pm daily. Most permits are divvyed out in the spring by reservation, requests for which are taken only by mail. Applications are processed randomly beginning March 1. Follow instructions carefully and be sure to include the fee for the entire trip – $3 per person, per day. Applications sent too soon are rejected. Cancelled reservations are nonrefundable. Call or write for an application form, or get one from the Wenatchee National Forest website at 🖳 www.fs.fed.us/r6/wenatchee. Start planning in January.

If you don't have a reservation you can try for the limited number of same-day permits, distributed in a daily lottery held promptly at 7:45 am. While suspenseful, the success rate for a mid-week departure is pretty good.

Maximum group size is eight and campfires are not allowed. A Northwest Forest Pass is provided at no cost.

NEAREST TOWNS & FACILITIES
Leavenworth & Wenatchee

Leavenworth is a faux-Bavarian 'village' in central Washington a mere 4mi from the trailhead. Tourists really do jam this resurrected timber town to stroll past Bavarian-themed gift shops staffed by clerks wearing lederhosen and dirndls. Avoid downtown if you're in a rush. Inflated room prices are considerably discounted on weekdays. Hotels in Wenatchee, 21mi east on Hwys 2 & 97, aren't any cheaper than in Leavenworth. However, Wenatchee does have the nearest train station and airport as well as car rentals.

Der Sportsmann (☎ 509-548-5623, 800-548-4145), 837 Front St, Leavenworth, has maps, freeze-dried meals, fuel and gear.

Places to Stay & Eat Pine-paneled rooms at the *Evergreen Inn* (☎ 509-548-5515, 800-327-7212, 1117 Front St) cost $45 on weekdays and go up to $60 on weekends.

Leavenworth's *Bavarian restaurants* do a heavy trade in schnitzel, sausages and sauerkraut. *Los Camperos* (☎ 509-548-3314, 200 8th St) serves good Mexican food on an outdoor terrace. *Leavenworth Pizza Company* (☎ 509-548-7766, 894 Hwy 2) is open every day for dinner, and for lunch on weekends.

Getting There & Away Northwestern Trailways (☎ 509-662-2183, 800-366-3830) buses stop in Leavenworth en route to Seattle and Wenatchee twice daily ($22 one-way); one of the buses travels via Everett. In Leavenworth, call Mountain View Taxi (☎ 509-782-3346) for a cab.

Trains from Seattle and Spokane stop daily at the combined rail and bus station at Wenatchee Ave and Kittitas St, downtown Wenatchee. Rent cars at the Pangborn Airport, across the river in East Wenatchee, or from U-Save Auto Rentals (☎ 509-663-0587), 908 S Wenatchee. For a lift call Courtesy Cab (☎ 509-662-2126). The free Link bus No 22 connects Wenatchee to Leavenworth; no Sunday service.

Camping

Eightmile campground, 7mi southwest of Leavenworth up Icicle Rd, is close to the trailhead and has pleasant sites along Icicle Creek ($9). There are more *campgrounds* further up the road.

GETTING TO/FROM THE HIKE

The Snow Lake Trailhead is 4mi southwest of Leavenworth on Icicle Creek Rd at a signed, gravel parking area along Icicle Creek. Two routes, Hwy 2 and I-90, connect Leavenworth to Seattle and the Puget Sound. It's about 120mi from Seattle either way. I-90 travelers should exit at Cle Elum and continue north on Hwy 97 over Blewett Pass to Hwy 2.

THE HIKE
Day 1: Snow Creek Trailhead to Snow Lakes

6½–8 hours, 6½mi (10.5km) 4200ft (1260m) ascent

An ugly hillside charred by fire in 1994 anticipates the first punishing mile of hot, dusty switchbacks through blackened pine. To start, follow Snow Lake Trail down the left edge of the parking lot and turn right for a bridge over Icicle Creek. Speck-sized climbers scaling the **Snow Creek Wall** come into view on the right as the trail enters the Snow Creek canyon and crosses the wilderness boundary on a kinder grade through greener timber. At 2mi hikers have already earned a rest at a shady grove of creekside cedar. A few raucous waterfalls and a second clearing at Toketie Creek are the last landmarks until the next water at the Snow Creek Bridge, a dogged 2½mi away.

The 2mi, 1200ft climb that follows is the most toilsome yet. The trail drifts out of the canyon and pulls out of the woods to find footing over granite boulders, and then flattens for a short stroll along forested **Nada Lake**. Snow Lakes, the next flight up, are the source for an artificial geyser that discharges from a rock-heaped slope at the opposite end of the lake. Rock cairns lead a boulder-hopping climb to the crest. A short, gentle descent levels, at last, across a small dam to **Upper Snow Lake**, its deep, clear waters and granite-lined shore a solace for weary hikers.

Signs point to designated *campsites* along the forested east shore. Or, turn left

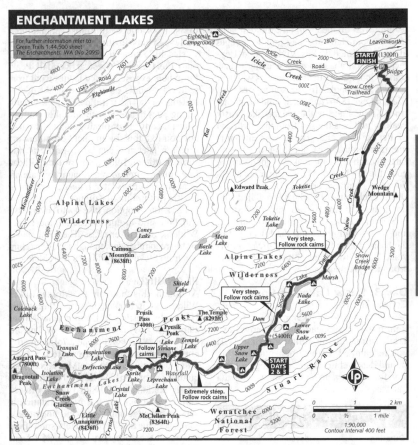

ENCHANTMENT LAKES

For further information refer to
Green Trails 1:44,500 sheet
The Enchantments, WA (No 209S)

PACIFIC NORTHWEST

before the dam for secluded sites along marshy Lower Snow Lake. Water is from the lakes; toilets are nearby.

Day 2: Lower Enchantment Lakes Return

6½–8 hours, 7mi (11.3km), 1700ft (510m) ascent

While shorter than Day 1's hike, the climb to the Lower Enchantments is more severe and in several places you'll need all four limbs to haul yourself up the rocks. If this sounds too much with a full pack, cache your gear and make it a 7mi, up-and-back day hike.

Warm up with a flat, forested walk to the lake's log-jammed west end. A sharp left follows the lake inlet to ascend the basin wall on a trail runged with steep, short switchbacks. A view of Upper Snow Lake is the only good thing about an exposed boulder field that impedes the final grasp for the top. The climb ends 1400ft above the lake, beneath a snaggle-toothed peak named **The Temple** (8292ft), at the threshold of the Lower Enchantments. To enter, hikers must summon courage for a perilous log crossing over a waterfall that spills from the sheer-faced rim of Lake Viviane.

Cairns pick up where the trail leaves off, leading west up the basin past the first larch over smooth slabs of white granite. Ledges along cliff-lined Lakes Viviane and Leprechaun soon abate to easy walking over a stark, windswept plain that sparkles with tiny rivulets and pools. To the south rises McClellan Peak (8364ft), and around the corner from Sprite Lake is the wedge-like **Prusik Peak**, which jabs the sky from the north end of Perfection Lake. The **Lower Enchantments** conclude just ahead at Inspiration Lake, which at 3½mi makes a good turning point for day hikers. Those with more ambition can continue up a rocky pass to the **Upper Enchantments**, which is puddled with tiny pools like Gnome Tarn and Troll Sink.

Sheltered *campsites* are hard to come by, and found mainly around the lower end of the basin. Many favor a rocky *niche* on Viviane Lake. Toilets are clustered here and around Leprechaun Lake.

Day 3: Snow Lakes to Snow Creek Trailhead

4–5½ hours, 6½mi (10.5km)
Return to the trailhead via the Snow Lake Trail, retracing the route for Day 1. If you're camped at the Enchantments you should descend in stages, allowing an extra day for a return to either Snow or Nada Lakes.

Snoqualmie Pass North

Duration	4 days
Distance	33.2mi (53.5km)
Standard	medium
Start/Finish	Snoqualmie Pass
Nearest Town	North Bend
Public Transport	yes

Summary Four days of ridgeline hiking on exposed, rocky ledges past jagged peaks and shimmering lakes to a stunning viewpoint of Spectacle Lake. One of the Northwest's most scenic Pacific Crest Trail hikes.

Travelers with four days and little forethought can experience the very essence of the PCT on this superb, up-and-back ridge-line hike north from Snoqualmie Pass. As the start of one of the most mountainous PCT segments in the Northwest, the trail wastes little time in forest before busting onto the Cascade Crest at Kendall Peak. From here exposed, rocky ledges wind from saddle to saddle past jagged peaks, shimmering lakes and wildflowers to a breathtaking pass above Spectacle Lake. But this is just a convenient turning point – the trail goes on like this for another 236mi, ending a month later in Canada. A short bus ride from Seattle on I-90 arrives at the trailhead in plenty of time to reach camp by late afternoon. Four days later, hikers can return to Seattle just in time for dinner.

For a longer option, take six to seven days and hike end-to-end across Alpine Lakes Wilderness to Stevens Pass. The 67mi hike is highly recommended, though lack of a return bus from Stevens Pass makes it problematic.

PLANNING

Although this portion of Alpine Lakes Wilderness is managed by the Wenatchee National Forest's Cle Elum district ranger station (☎ 509-674-4411), 803 W 2nd St, Cle Elum, WA 98922 (open 7:45 am to 5 pm Monday to Friday and 8 am to 2 pm Saturday), it's the job of the Mt Baker–Snoqualmie National Forest's North Bend ranger station (☎ 360-888-1421) to maintain the PCT. As a result neither station is very knowledgeable about trail conditions. Make sure the trail is completely snow-free; ask about the conditions for the PCT from Snoqualmie Pass north to Spectacle Lake. The trail is usually open from late July to October. Avoid weekends.

Purchase Northwest Forest Passes (required), maps and supplies in Seattle (see Gateways at the beginning of this chapter). Passes can also be purchased en route at the North Bend ranger station, 42404 SE North Bend Way, in North Bend, or near the trailhead at the Snoqualmie Pass visitor center at I-90 exit 52, open 8:30 am to 4 pm Thursday to Sunday only.

Fires are not allowed and hikers must camp at established campsites at Ridge Lake and Park Lakes Basin.

Maps
The Green Trails 1:69,500 map *Snoqualmie Pass, WA (No 207)* shows the PCT to Spectacle Lake. The Trading Post store at Snoqualmie Pass sells them.

NEAREST TOWN & FACILITIES
Snoqualmie Pass
This ski area (I-90 exit 52) has a *motel*, *restaurant* and a few convenience stores. Unless you're camping it's best to come straight from Seattle (see Gateways at the beginning of this chapter).

Camping
Lushly forested *Denny Creek campground* offers close camping with flush toilets, warm water and RV hook-ups ($12), 3mi west of the trailhead. Turn left across the freeway at I-90 exit 47, and then right onto paved Denny Creek Rd (USFS Rd No 58) to reach the campground in 2mi. Continue east on this road the next morning to reach the trail. The next closest camping is at the more primitive *Tinkham campground,* 1½mi down USFS Rd No 55, off I-90 exit 42; sites cost $12.

GETTING TO/FROM THE HIKE
The PCT intercepts I-90 near the Snoqualmie Pass ski area, 52mi east of Seattle at exit 52. Turn left onto Alpental Rd and right at a sign for the PCT to reach the northbound trailhead, on the north side of the freeway.

The 7:20 am Greyhound bus from Seattle stops at the Trading Post (☎ 509-434-6300) store at Snoqualmie Pass; the last bus back leaves at 6:50 pm. The one-way fare is $9. Cross the road and walk a quarter-mile north to find a signed path for the PCT that leads up a grassy embankment on the opposite side of the freeway underpass.

THE HIKE
Day 1: Snoqualmie Pass to Ridge Lake
4½–6 hours, 7.3mi (11.8km), 2400ft (720m) ascent
A prominent gravel path at the end of the North Snoqualmie Pass PCT parking lot draws hikers into an old-growth forest of hemlock and Douglas fir. After 30ft fork left

onto the PCT at a signed junction for Stevens Pass to begin hastening up the Commonwealth Valley on long, gentle switchbacks (bus travelers enter here on the right-leading trail). Shade-loving vanilla leaf, queen's cup lily, bunchberry and Cascades blueberry give way to columbine, bleeding heart, larkspur and fuzzy, pink-flowered spiraea as the trail nears a rock field for a view of Guye Peak (left) and triangular Red Mountain (ahead). At 2.5mi continue up past the Commonwealth Basin Trail. A sharp right doubles back into forest to cross a refreshing stream and a brief clearing before resuming a northbound course up Kendall Ridge a mile later.

Indian paintbrush, lupine, tiger lily and pentsemon paint the way up a bouldery slope as the trail breaks onto a rocky ledge and curves east around Kendall Peak to meet a skyline crowded by Red Mountain, Lundin Peak and Snoqualmie Mountain. At 5.7mi and 5400ft altitude a steep, narrow cliff crests a flat ridge for a stunning panorama that takes in Kendall Peak, Alta Mountain and host of peaks bordering the Gold Creek Valley. Up ahead the **Kendall Katwalk** leads a rolling descent past Red Mountain on a landmark ledge of solid granite. A final spectacular mile alternates boulders and open meadow to a rocky saddle between **Ridge** and **Gravel Lakes**, the last camps and sure water for 7mi. A path on the right leads to established *campsites* on Ridge Lake; and a steep climb left, down heather meadows, accesses secluded sites on the west end of talus-heaped Gravel Lake. Water is from the lake; there are no toilets.

Day 2: Ridge Lake to Park Lakes Meadow
5–6½ hours, 7.9mi (12.7km), 2300ft (690m) ascent
The hike continues to Park Lakes on a sunny, south-facing ridge that travels the perimeter of the bowl-like Gold Valley. If the scenery doesn't take your breath away the trail surely will, as it constantly rises and falls up steep, rocky slopes. Water is scarce, so start with full bottles.

A boulder field leads the first 2mi on a hilly traverse around Alaska Mountain that

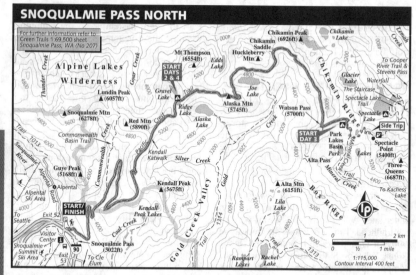

SNOQUALMIE PASS NORTH

For further information refer to
Green Trails 1:69,500 sheet
Snoqualmie Pass, WA (No 207)

ambles high above Alaska Lake amid views of Mt Rainier. The trail eases onto a point at 5700ft, where it ducks around the north side of Alaska Mountain and plunges 600ft down the next cirque to a marshy saddle between Joe and Edds Lakes. A brisk eastward ascent through forest begins the next 4.4mi to Watson Pass as the trail rounds the rocky face of Huckleberry Mountain above Joe Lake. Pause from climbing at the meadowed Chikamin Saddle on the shoulder of pointy Chikamin Peak (6926ft) to rest and draw water from small ponds that may be present early in the season.

The trail rises higher up Chikamin Peak to approach a long, cliff-like traverse on Chikamin Ridge. The Chinook name Chikamin (see the boxed text on page 414) recalls a time when the region's mineral-rich mountains were mined for silver, copper and gold. Slippery switchbacks over loose rock and washouts meet at a difficult ascent to Watson Pass (5700ft), where Alta Mountain and Gold Creek are left behind for a fresh horizon featuring Box Ridge and Three Queens mountain. A small stream passed on the descent of the Park Lakes Basin reappears near the signed *hiker-stock camp* at Park Lakes

Meadow, halfway down the slope. There are more sites at the bottom on stagnant Upper Park Lake.

Side Trip: Spectacle Point
1½–2 hours, 2.4mi (3.9km), 500ft (150m) ascent
The hike culminates with an easy climb up Chikamin Ridge to a magnificent view over Spectacle Lake, a tarn hemmed by sheer cliffs and glacier-topped Lemah Mountain. Leave the packs at camp, descend a shrubby meadow to Upper Park Lake and keep left at the junction with Mineral Creek Trail. Moderate switchbacks rise up open forest slope to reach the pass viewpoint in about a mile.

Although spectacular, *campsites* on Spectacle Lake are beyond the scope of a relaxed, four-day trip – the 2.5mi-long descent would add an extra 1000 vertical feet and 3.7mi to Day 3's climb back to Ridge Lake.

Day 3: Park Lakes Meadow to Ridge Lake
4½–6 hours, 7.9mi (12.7km) 1800ft (540m) ascent
Return to Ridge Lake via the PCT, following the route of Day 2's hike.

Day 4: Ridge Lake to Snoqualmie Pass
4–5 hours, 7.3mi (11.8km), 400ft (120m) ascent
Return to the trailhead via the PCT, following route of Day 1's hike.

Mt Rainier National Park

Northwest Native American tribes called 14,411ft Mt Rainier *Tahoma, Takhoma* or *Taco-bet*, and believed it was the dwelling place of an ill-tempered god responsible for hurling fire, rocks and snow onto their lowland villages. Translated as 'great snowy peak', the word is a succinct title for a mountain covered by 25 glaciers and the highest mountain in the Cascades. Like neighboring Mts St Helens and Adams, Mt Rainier was formed by a series of violent volcanic eruptions. Explosive forces that reduced the mountain from 16,000ft to its present height some 5800 years ago slumber deep inside this volcano, believed to be not entirely extinct.

Rainier's extensive trail system features waterfalls, glaciers, wildflower meadows and stately old-growth forests, making it an extremely popular place to hike. At the heart of the network is the 93mi Wonderland Trail, which takes hikers for a scenic spin around the entire mountain (see Other Hikes at the end of this chapter). Most opt for day hikes, leaving overnight trips to those with the time and patience to compete for hard-to-get backcountry permits. A reservation system established in 1999 ends a legacy of ranger-dictated itineraries and wasted days waiting around for a permit, and should make backpacking in the area more accessible.

Hoary marmot, pika mouse, mountain goat and the lunch-snatching gray jay are the animals most encountered by visitors. Cougar (mountain lion) sightings are on the rise.

HISTORY
British explorer Captain George Vancouver named the mountain after colleague Rear Admirable Peter Rainier in 1792. James Longmire brought commercial tourism to Mt Rainier in 1890, when he built a mineral hot springs lodge at present-day Longmire and engineered an access road to ferry visitors there and up the mountain to Paradise. Mt Rainier was established as a national park only nine years later, becoming the fifth national park in the USA.

PLANNING
Request a park road map and a copy of *Tahoma News* from Mt Rainier National Park, Tahoma Woods, Star Route, Ashford, WA 98304 (☎ 360-569-2211, ✉ morainfo @nps.gov). The Mt Rainier homepage is at 🖥 www.nps.gov/mora.

When to Hike
Alpine trails are typically snow-free by late July or early August. The park is unbearably crowded during these months on weekends and Fridays. Plan early to obtain rooms, campsites and backcountry camping permits by reservation (see Permits & Regulations).

What to Bring
Mt Rainier is notorious for generating bad weather and because conditions can change without warning it's important to carry rain gear and warm clothing on any hike. On any given summer afternoon you're likely to experience temperatures ranging from 40°F to 90°F, even in August.

Permanent snowfields on some trails make waterproof boots the footwear of choice. A combination of strong insect repellent and a long-sleeved shirt is the best defense against the biting flies that linger around high-elevation meadows and forests.

Maps & Books
The best maps for day hikers are often the free, photocopied trail maps distributed at ranger stations and visitor centers. The Northwest Interpretative Association's (NWIA) Hiking Guide to Mount Rainier National Park series of pocket-sized, topographic hiking maps are good for some hikes, but are sometimes hard to read. Green Trails maps, scarce at park visitor centers, are another alternative.

Two 1:50,000 maps, Trails Illustrated's *Mount Rainier National Park* ($9) and Earthwalk Press' *Mt Rainier* ($7.95) show trails for the entire park. Both are printed on durable plastic. The Earthwalk Press map has insets of congested trail areas and an index of backcountry campgrounds. The Trails Illustrated map, however, is easier to read.

Books and maps about Mt Rainier sold at park visitor centers can also be purchased by mail or online. Contact NWIA (☎ 360-569-2211 x3320, ✉ morainfo@ups.gov), Mt Rainier National Park, Longmire, WA 98397, for a catalog. Ira Spring & Harvey Manning's *50 Hikes in Mount Rainier National Park* contains more day hikes and overnight trips.

Permits & Regulations
For any overnight trip, a backcountry permit must be picked up in person from one of the wilderness information centers at Longmire or White River Entrance, or from the Paradise ranger station. The number of permits is limited by the number of campsites available and is greatly exceeded by demand. A nonrefundable $20 fee reserves permits up to two months in advance, although reservations are usually unnecessary for midweek travel. The conditions allow for one penalty-free itinerary change, which should be saved for bad weather. Reservation requests can be made by phone, fax, mail or email (☎ 360-569-4453, fax 569-2255, ✉ mora_longmire_wic_@nps.gov).

The $10 park entry fee is valid for seven consecutive days. Keep your receipt – you may need it to get in at other park entrances. Dogs are not allowed on any trails. Fires are prohibited at backcountry camps.

GATEWAYS
Seattle
See the Gateways section at the beginning of this chapter.

Tacoma
Tacoma, 30mi south of Seattle, has the closest bus and train station. The Amtrak depot (☎ 253-627-8141) is at 1001 Puyallup, and the Greyhound station (☎ 253-383-4621) is at 1319 Pacific Ave. Car rentals are available downtown from Enterprise (☎ 253-566-6480), 455 St Helens St. For a taxi call Yellow Cab (☎ 253-472-3303).

Indian Henry's Hunting Ground

Duration	7–8 hours or 2 days
Distance	13mi (20.9km)
Standard	hard
Start/Finish	Kautz Creek Trailhead
Nearest Town	Ashford
Public Transport	no

Summary A vibrant field of wildflowers and a spectacular mountain view caps this long day hike in the southwest corner of Mt Rainier National Park.

This long forest hike travels the oldest-known route to Indian Henry's Hunting Ground, where Mt Rainier makes an unforgettable backdrop to a technicolor display of wildflowers. Anyone making this tiresome ascent leaves dazzled by an impression that lingers long after the meadows are whitened by snow. Some of the park's most famous images originate here including a 1934 postage stamp of the mountain reflected in nearby Mirror Lake.

The hike can be made into a two-day trip with an overnight at Devil's Dream Camp, a mile south of Indian Henry's Hunting Ground on the Wonderland Trail (backcountry permit required). A car shuttle would make it possible to loop via the Wonderland Trail to end at Longmire.

PLANNING
For trail conditions contact the Longmire wilderness information center (☎ 360-569-2211 x3317), open 6:30 am to 9 pm Friday to Saturday and 7 am to 8 pm Sunday to Thursday. Books, maps and information are available here, or at the handy Longmire Museum (☎ 360-569-2111 x3314), near the lodge across the street.

Carry at least three quarts of water. If you happen to have a water purifier by all means bring it along.

Clockwise from Top Left: Natural Bridges Cove, Samuel H Boardman State Park, Oregon. **Top Right:** A hiker heads toward the summit of Mt Baker, the northernmost peak in the Cascades, Washington. **Middle Right:** Mt Baker's neighbor, Mt Shuksan, reflected in the waters of Picture Lake. **Bottom:** Oregon Dunes National Recreation Area, Oregon, contains the largest expanse of coastal dunes in the USA.

JOHN ELK III

Three Moments on the USA's Long-Distance Trails.
Top Left: Admiring Mt Freemont, Wind River Range, Wyoming, on the Continental Divide Trail.
Top Right: Alpine meadows flank the Pacific Crest Trail in Yosemite National Park, Sierra Nevada.
Bottom: The Continental Divide Trail joins the Highline Trail in Glacier National Park, Montana.

CLEM LINDENMAYER

WOODS WHEATCROFT

CLEM LINDENMAYER

Maps

NWIA's pocket-sized *Southwest Hiking Guide to Mount Rainier National Park* ($1.25) is an ideal map for this hike.

NEAREST TOWNS & FACILITIES

Mt Rainier National Park's Nisqually Entrance on Hwy 706 in the park's busy southwest corner gives access to hikes to Indian Henry's Hunting Ground and Paradise. There are convenient places to stay and eat both in and outside the park. Ashford is the last place to buy gas.

Paradise

Paradise, 18mi east of the Nisqually Entrance, is the highest road-accessible point on the mountain's south side and Mt Rainier's most popular destination. Rooms at the cedar-built *Paradise Inn (☎ 360-569-2400, 569-2275 for reservations)* cost $69 to $98 (with or without a private bathroom) and are booked out a year in advance. Northwest-inspired breakfast, lunch, and dinner is served limited hours in the busy *dining room* (closed at 8:30 pm). Trail lunches can be ordered for hikes the next day.

The turn-off to Paradise closes temporarily once the parking lot is full, which in peak season usually means every weekend afternoon.

Longmire Area

Quiet Longmire, midway between Paradise and the Nisqually Entrance, is little more than a lodge and a wide spot in the road. Beautifully wooded *Cougar Rock campground,* Rainier's most popular, is 2½mi east of Longmire on Hwy 706. The 200 sites cost $14 and are virtually unobtainable without a reservation from the National Park Reservations Service (see Accommodations in the Facts for the Hiker chapter), which can be made up to three months in advance. You can also write for information and an application at PO Box 1600, Cumberland, MD 21502.

Longmire's pleasant *National Park Inn (☎ 360-569-2400, 569-2275 for reservations)* is a lower-key version of the lodge at Paradise. Rooms cost $66 to $91 and book

out three to four months in advance. Burgers, steak, chicken and trout comprise a limited lunch and dinner menu. Ice cream is served from a hidden *snack window* at the back of the lodge.

A small store stocks limited grocery items, including beer and stove fuel.

Ashford Area

Ashford, 5mi west of the Nisqually Entrance on Hwy 706, is the closest real town. The 18 grassy sites ($10) at *Sunshine Point campground,* a mile past the park entrance, attract Washington's hugest RVs. Few know about the quiet, wooded sites ($11) at *Big Creek campground* in nearby Gifford-Pinchot National Forest. Turn south onto Kernahan Rd (USFS Rd No 52) between Ashford and the park entrance and follow signs for Packwood to reach the campground in 2mi.

Whittaker's Bunkhouse (☎ 360-569-2439, 3025 Hwy 706 E) caters to climbers and adventure travelers and is a congenial place to book a bunk with a shared bathroom ($25). Private rooms start at $65.

Wild Berry Restaurant (☎ 360-569-2628) is an easy-going cafe with pizza, burritos, sandwiches, trout and pasta.

GETTING AROUND

Rainier Shuttle (☎ 360-569-2331) has a twice-daily service from Sea-Tac Airport to Paradise ($34 one-way), with scheduled stops at Ashford ($26 one-way), Longmire and Cougar Rock campground. The service is geared mainly to climbers headed straight to Paradise, and doesn't provide the means to see any other parts of the park. Reservations are required.

GETTING TO/FROM THE HIKE

The Nisqually Entrance on Hwy 706 is 60mi southeast of Tacoma. Hwy 7 leads south from Tacoma to the junction for Hwy 706 at Elbe. To reach Elbe from Portland, take I-5 north to Hwy 12, drive east to Morton, and turn north onto Hwy 7.

The trailhead at Kautz Creek is between Ashford and Longmire on Hwy 706, about 3mi from the park entrance on the right side of the road.

Glacial Debris Flows

Debris flows like the one at Kautz Creek happen when hot weather or heavy rain causes water to suddenly burst from the base of a glacier in what geologists call an outburst flood. As the flood travels down a stream valley it accumulates rock, sediment and vegetation in a bouldery mass that reaches heights of 30ft to 60ft and speeds of 10 to 20 miles per hour. Although glacier-caused flows are Mt Rainier's smallest type of debris flow, they happen with the most frequency and are a living example of how glaciers work to carve the Northwest landscape. Repeated debris flows on neighboring Tahoma Creek have caused the closure of nearby Westside Rd, buried several times since 1988.

Hikers should always be alert to the possibility of debris flows. A sudden rise in water level, accompanied by a deafening roar and shaking ground, is the signal to immediately abandon any stream channel by climbing upslope to higher ground.

THE HIKE

Cross the highway to begin the hike on a boardwalk, turning right after 20yd at a sign for the Kautz Creek Trail. A gravel path ascends gently for 1mi to a log-and-cable crossing over gray Kautz Creek. Leave the creek here for good, but not without first noticing a displaced streambed left behind by the largest debris flow in park history. The 1947 flow swept down Kautz Creek to bury the highway under 28ft of mud, and accounts for the big boulders and giant logs strewn at odd angles in the forest ahead.

The trail rises quickly on steady switchbacks through picturesque old-growth cedar, hemlock and Douglas fir, and crosses a footbridge over a refreshing stream. Trailside tufts of bear grass and a short forest meadow mark advances through vegetation zones. The trail increases in pitch, succumbing at last to a series of steep, scrabbly stair steps that continue to the first sighting of Mt Rainier since Kautz Creek, 3mi back.

Level out briefly to pass through a meadow of lupine and avalanche lily before continuing upward to top out at a stony outcropping on **Mt Ararat**, named in Ben Longmire's overeager discovery of what he believed was Noah's Ark. The trail rises and falls through meadows and subalpine fir for another half-mile, unfolding to a brilliant plain of red and blue beneath the snowy dome of Mt Rainier. Indian paintbrush, lupine, avalanche lily and bear grass are familiar flowers by the time one arrives here at **Indian Henry's Hunting Ground**, 5.7mi from the trailhead. Drop your pack and admire the

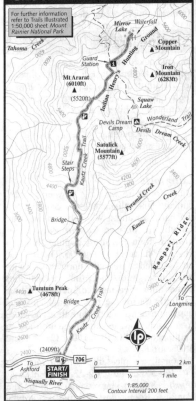

INDIAN HENRY'S HUNTING GROUND

meadow from the nearby guard station, just north of the junction with the Wonderland Trail.

Many follow a restful lunch with a 1.8mi roundtrip hike to **Mirror Lakes**. Proceed 0.2mi north along the Wonderland Trail and turn right at a sign to follow a meandering stream past a small waterfall. Rowdy hiking groups often blur the mountain's picture-perfect reflection on weekends, but the spot is still scenic.

Head back to the Kautz Creek Trail junction and return to the trailhead the way you came. If you wish to camp for the night and make the return hike in the morning, continue a mile south on the Wonderland Trail to camp at *Devil's Dream* (backcountry permit required – see Permits & Regulations at the beginning of this section).

Skyline Trail

Duration	3–4½ hours
Distance	5.5mi (8.9km)
Standard	medium
Start/Finish	Paradise
Nearest Town	Ashford
Public Transport	yes

Summary A glacier, mountain vistas, wildflowers and waterfalls are all strung together on this scenic loop hike over a rocky meadow on Mt Rainier. The most popular trail in the park.

Alpine scenes typical of those from all over the park are collected here in condensed form on this short, showcase hike over open meadow to wildflowers, waterfalls and a glacier. The Skyline Trail at Paradise, the most-visited place in the park, is one of the most accessible (and the most crowded) above-timberline trails of its kind. Listen carefully for the whistles of the hoary marmot, a rodent-like animal that lives on rocky slopes and eats the very wildflowers children are chided against picking.

The immediacy of Mt Rainier at Paradise is enough to compel hikers to hop out of the car and saunter straight up the summit. Many climbers do just that, and depart from here on the most popular climbing route up to

Columbia Crest, a tough technical challenge with a success rate of 50%.

PLANNING

The Paradise ranger station (☎ 360-569-2211 x2313) is open 6:30 am to 8 pm Friday to Sunday and 7:30 am to 7 pm Monday to Thursday. Books and maps are for sale at the round Henry M Jackson Memorial visitor center (☎ 360-569-2211 x2328), open 9 am to 7 pm daily.

Waterproof boots, while not required, are preferred for hiking over snowfields. Flowers are most vibrant from mid- to late June. Start early to avoid the crowds.

Maps

No map makes better sense of Paradise's tangled trails than the simple tourist map *Paradise Area Trails*, free at the ranger station or any NPS information desk. The 1:17,500 Green Trails map *Paradise, WA (No 270S)* is the best topographic map, though most would rather use the free map and save the $3.50 for ice cream and postcards.

NEAREST TOWNS

Paradise is reached via the park's southwest Nisqually Entrance. See Nearest Towns & Facilities in the Indian Henry's Hunting Ground hike for information on Paradise and Ashford.

GETTING TO/FROM THE HIKE

Follow directions for the Indian Henry's Hunting Ground hike to reach the Nisqually Entrance. Paradise is another 18mi east, past Longmire off Hwy 706. The turn-off closes temporarily once parking reaches capacity, usually on weekend afternoons.

THE HIKE

Signs along the first half of the Skyline Trail point frequently to side trails and destinations, but hardly ever name the trail you're actually walking on. The route strays off the Skyline Trail only once, when it follows the High Skyline Trail on a half-mile detour around an often impassable patch of snow.

Start up the mountain as climbers do, by mounting a paved path for the Skyline Trail

SKYLINE TRAIL

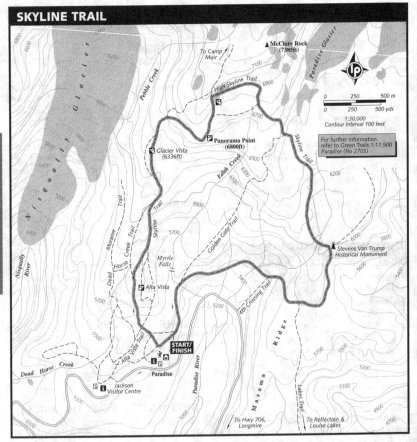

near the ranger station or behind the Paradise Inn. The trail rises stiffly up a rocky meadow past turn-offs for Alta Vista (right) and Dead Horse Creek (left), and encounters a trail junction at Alta Vista. From here the trail moderates to gravel switchbacks and sidles alongside the mighty **Nisqually Glacier,** bypassing lower trails to Dead Horse Creek and Glacier Vista.

Part company with the glacier and traverse a slope to southward views of Mts Adams, St Helens and Hood, passing a trail for Camp Muir. The trail levels to a junction for **Panorama Point**, where people attempting to eat lunch spend most of their time fighting chipmunks. Turn left up the High Skyline Trail for better viewpoints. A ledge behind a shaded rock near a second junction for Camp Muir puts the Nisqually Glacier beneath your boots. It's also a good place to watch humanity's greatest parade of overexertion, as out-of-shape tourists in flip flops and sneakers take on the snowfield to 10,000ft Camp Muir (a camp for climbers).

Begin the second half of the hike by following a sign east (right) for 'Golden Gate, High Lakes Trail.' After a quarter-mile the Skyline Trail begins a rocky descent over talus and snow, and passes the Golden Gate Trail to arrive at the first lupine and Indian paintbrush near a climbing memorial at the junction for Paradise Glacier. Spreading phlox (pink or white), bear grass and western pasqueflower appear later in a colorful wildflower display that lasts all the way back to the lodge. A picturesque footbridge beneath Mt Rainier tops off the green mountain meadows and meandering streams that lie between turn-offs for the Lakes and Fourth Crossing Trails.

Hikers eventually spot a high waterfall and drop down a small valley to a bridge over the Paradise River. An easy climb past **Myrtle Falls** near the Golden Gate Trail takes you to the end of the hike behind the Paradise Inn.

Burroughs Mountain

Duration	3½–4 hours
Distance	7mi (11.3km)
Standard	medium
Start/Finish	Sunrise
Nearest Towns	Enumclaw, Packwood
Public Transport	no

Summary Mountain goats frequent the tundra on this short, ridgeline loop hike near Sunrise in the east corner of Mt Rainier National Park. Overlooks the largest glacier in the contiguous USA from the highest trail in the park.

A mountain of sheer ice and rock confronts hikers from a viewpoint at Burroughs Mountain (7400ft), an early lava flow whose ridgeline plateau provides the highest hiking trail in the park. Rainier's famed wildflowers are noticeably absent at this elevation, the landscape a monochrome of barren tundra, mountain goats and gritty glacial till. Rainier's east slope crowds the sky for most of the way, overwhelmed by the 4mi long Emmons Glacier, the largest in the Lower 48 states.

The trail leaves from Sunrise on Rainier's east side in a quieter and drier section of the park. Temperatures are cooler here, and on a cloudy day it can be downright cold.

PLANNING
Call the White River wilderness information center (☎ 360-569-2211 x2356, 360-663-2273) for trail conditions. Sunrise visitor center at the trailhead has information and is open 9 am to 6 pm daily.

Trails are mostly snow-free from early August to September. Ask at the ranger station for the best time to view mountain goats.

Maps
Go with NPS's free *Hiking Trails in the Sunrise Area*. If trail distances and contour lines are important to you take the Green Trails 1:69,500 map *Mount Rainier East, WA (No 270)*.

NEAREST TOWNS & FACILITIES
The closest places to stay and eat are scattered around the vicinity of the White River Entrance in the park's northeast corner. Enumclaw and Packwood are the nearest towns for groceries and gas, while snacks and breakfast are available at the trailhead from the *Sunrise Lodge,* open from 10 am to 7 pm.

Enumclaw
Enumclaw, at the junction for Hwy 410 which leads to the park's east entrances, is the last real town between Seattle and the trailhead. Rooms at the business-class *Best Western Park Center Hotel (☎ 360-825-4490, 1000 Griffin Ave)* cost $70. *Baumgartner's Deli (☎ 360-825-1067, 1008 E Roosevelt)*, on the highway, is a local favorite for sandwiches and desserts.

Packwood
Packwood, east of I-5 on Hwy 12 at the end of the Cowlitz Valley, is the closest town for visitors coming from Portland. *Mountain View Lodge Motel (☎ 360-494-5555)* on Hwy 12 is a standard motor lodge with rooms from $37. *Club Cafe (☎ 360-494-5977)* serves hot meals in a town not noted for dining.

Hotels & Lodges
Northeast of the park entrance off Hwy 410 there's a hotel complex at *Crystal Mountain*

Resort (☎ *360-663-2262, 888-754-2262,* @ *reservations@crystalhotels.com).* Among many lodging choices is the ***Alpine Inn Hotel***, which has bunkbeds with shared bathrooms for $50 and private rooms from $75. The resort's sluggish ***Alpine Inn*** is the closest place for a sit-down dinner, and serves seafood and pastas a la carte ($13 to $18). It's also open for breakfast.

Camping
The 117 wooded sites at ***White River campground*** offer the closest camping, 5mi west of the White River Entrance ($10). If that's full try ***Silver Springs campground*** in the Mt Baker–Snoqualmie National Forest, 9mi north of Cayuse Pass on Hwy 410 (just north of the road to Crystal Mountain). Or head 10mi east of Cayuse Pass through ongoing construction to reach ***Lodgepole campground*** in the Wenatchee National Forest ($10). Check road closures before camping here.

GETTING TO/FROM THE HIKE
The trailhead at Sunrise, in the northeastern corner of the park, is at the end of a paved park road that winds 16mi up the east side of Mt Rainier via the White River Entrance. From Enumclaw follow Hwy 410 37mi southeast to the White River Entrance.

Hwys 169, 167 and 164 all lead southeast from Seattle to Enumclaw. The White River Entrance is also reached on Hwys 12 and 123 via Packwood.

To reach Sunrise from Paradise, drive Hwy 706 east to exit the park at the Ohanapecosh Entrance and turn left at the junction for Hwy 123.

THE HIKE
Turn your back on the ranger station and head for a simple dirt trail that points down a glacier-cut valley from the lower edge of the parking lot. Whitebark pine and subalpine fir, hardy trees that thrive at high altitudes, line a meadowed descent to a junction

A hiker in the Sunrise area takes in the spectacular view of Washington's Mt Rainier, the highest peak in the Cascade Range.

JOHN ELK III

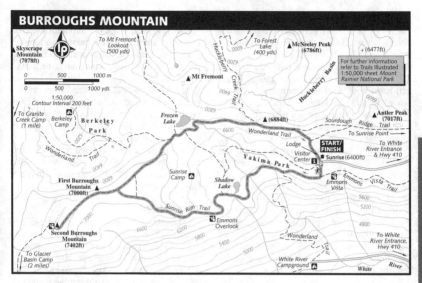

BURROUGHS MOUNTAIN

To Mt Fremont Lookout (500 yds)

To Forest Lake (400 yds)

McNeeley Peak (6786ft)

+(6477ft)

Skyscrape Mountain (7078ft)

Mt Fremont

Huckleberry Creek Trail

Huckleberry Basin

For further information refer to Trails Illustrated 1:50,000 sheet Mount Rainier National Park

0   500   1000 m
0   500   1000 yds
1:50,000
Contour Interval 200 feet

To Granite Creek Camp (1 mile)

Berkeley Camp

Berkeley Park

Frozen Lake

(6884ft)

Wonderland Trail

Sourdough Ridge

Antler Peak (7017ft)

Trail

To Sunrise Point

Wonderland Trail

Lodge

Visitor Center

START/ FINISH

Sunrise (6400ft)

To White River Entrance & Hwy 410

Yakima Park

First Burroughs Mountain (7000ft)

Sunrise Camp

Shadow Lake

Emmons Vista

Emmons Vista Trail

Sunrise Rim Trail

Emmons Overlook

Second Burroughs Mountain (7402ft)

Wonderland Trail

To White River Entrance, Hwy 410

To Glacier Basin Camp (2 miles)

White River Campground

White River

PACIFIC NORTHWEST

for the dusty Sunrise Rim Trail. Fork right, keeping straight past the Wonderland Trail and several glimpses of the Emmons Glacier as the trail skirts a slope to **Shadow Lake** and comes upon a rocky lava flow at a flat restoration area near Sunrise Camp. A steep climb opens to a clear vista of the glacier snaking down the mountain at the **Emmons Overlook**, 0.2mi ahead.

Climb steadily on to reach First Burroughs (7000ft), a trail junction on the barren Burroughs Mountain plateau. Turn left and ascend into sky over a colorless landscape to Second Burroughs (7402ft), a stony bump which gazes straight onto the snowy face of Mt Rainier. Park volunteers are often at hand to point out mountain goats and to keep stray hikers from damaging the tundra's fragile plants.

Backtrack to First Burroughs and continue left along the rocky ridge to **Frozen Lake**. Several trails converge at this saddle; the Wonderland Trail can be seen winding up the green meadows of Berkeley Park to the left. Go right and keep straight at a turn for Sunrise Camp to return via Sourdough Ridge, an extension of the same lava flow that forms Burroughs Mountain. A short

climb levels at a meadow for a pleasant view north down the Huckleberry Basin before arriving at a turn for the Wonderland Trail, which leads back to the ranger station.

Olympic National Park

Three parks in one, the 2344-sq-mile Olympic National Park contains snowy mountains, 63mi of rugged wilderness beach, and the continent's only stands of temperate rainforest. The Puget Sound separates the Olympic Peninsula from mainland Washington. At the core are the Olympic Mountains, which once rose from the ocean floor and fed the ice-age glaciers that carved the Puget Sound and Strait of Juan de Fuca. Heavy rains – 133 inches annually – fill the west-facing valleys with thick-canopied rainforests, gothic forests of giant spruce, hemlock and cedar dripping with moss and littered with rotting logs. Fog shrouds the park's shoreline of sea stacks, arches and off-shore islands through most of the summer.

Initially established as a national monument in 1909, the Olympics were put under federal protection to stop the harvesting of Roosevelt elk incisors for men's apparel. The area was declared a national park in 1938 in response to reckless logging. Western rainforests and northern beaches were added in 1953 and 1976. Roads and highways touch only the park's perimeter, leaving most of the wilderness and beaches accessible only on foot.

Flora and fauna is similar to that of the western Cascades, though some species, such as the golden marmot and Flett's violet, are found only here. The park's most famous animal is the threatened northern spotted owl, which in the late 1980s and early 1990s became plaintiff to a successful environmental lawsuit to halt the logging of old-growth forests. Hikers are most likely to encounter the banana slug, found in obscene lengths on the wet forest floor.

Cape Alava–Sand Point Loop

Duration	4–5½ hours
Distance	9.3mi (15km)
Standard	medium
Start/Finish	Ozette Trailhead
Nearest Towns	Sekiu, Clallam Bay
Public Transport	no

Summary A flat loop hike through temperate rainforest to Native American petroglyphs at a rocky wilderness beach in Washington's Olympic National Park. Visits the northwesternmost corner of the contiguous USA.

Ancient petroglyphs hidden on a rocky coastal headland are the main highlight of this flat hike through rainforest to a wilderness beach. The rock carvings hint at the pastimes of the Makah people who flourished in this northwesternmost corner of the USA for more than 2000 years. Traditional Native Americans of this region weathered the cruel coastal climate in large, one-roomed longhouses and hunted whales in the Pacific Ocean from long canoes carved from a single cedar log. The Makah, who live on reservation land around the town of Neah Bay, recently generated national controversy when granted permission to resume traditional whale hunting. The hunt, conducted in 1999, was the tribe's first since the 1920s.

A lot is known about early tribes from a wealth of artefacts unearthed at Ozette, an ancient village discovered just north of Cape Alava in 1970. Archeologists spent a decade excavating homes at the site, preserved under a 500-year old mudslide. Exhibits about the dig are displayed at the Makah museum (☎ 206-645-2711) in Neah Bay.

PLANNING

The Ozette ranger station (☎ 360-963-2725) at the trailhead is open every day 8 am to 4:30 pm. For general park information contact Olympic National Park (☎ 360-452-4501), 600 East Park Ave, Port Angeles, WA 98362. The park's website is at 🖥 www.nps.gov/olympic.

The coast is least rainy from July to September. Certain headlands along the beach cannot be passed at tides above 5½ft – check tide tables in advance before setting out. Trails are open year-round; dogs are not allowed. The boardwalk can be slippery in wet weather. Wear lightweight shoes with rubber soles.

There's a $1 parking fee, paid using one of the self-serve envelopes at the parking lot pay station.

Reservations are required to stay overnight at Sand Point or Cape Alava beach camps. Both of these camps are immensely popular with families. All food must be protected from raccoons in a heavy pail with a tight-fitting lid (available from the Lost Resort store). Reservation requests are handled by the Wilderness Information Center (☎ 360-422-0300) and the park's website.

Maps

The Green Trails 1:69,500 map *Ozette, WA (No 130S)* shows the route. There's also a 1:24,000 Custom Correct Map, *Ozette Beach Loop, WA*, with slightly more detail.

NEAREST TOWNS & FACILITIES

Sekiu and neighboring Clallam Bay, near the turn-off for Hoko-Ozette Rd, offer only a few places to stay or eat – expect full campgrounds and motels in summer. Many places close for winter, so call ahead before visiting in the off-season. Grocery stores and gas stations are scarce, so buy fuel and most of your food in Port Angeles or Aberdeen.

Port Angeles

Port Angeles, on the northern coast of the Olympic Peninsula, has the nearest airport, bus station and car rentals. Olympic Bus Service (☎ 360-417-0700) links Port Angeles to the downtown Seattle bus station ($29 one-way) and Sea-Tac airport ($43). Four buses arrive and depart daily from the Double Tree Hotel near the Port Angeles ferry dock at 221 N Lincoln. Reservations required. Budget Rent-A-Car (☎ 360-452-4774), 111 E Front St, is just a block away.

Sekiu & Clallam Bay

Sekiu and neighboring Clallam Bay, the towns closest to the trailhead, are 51mi west of Port Angeles on the Strait of Juan de Fuca in the northwest corner of the Olympic Peninsula.

The *Bay Motel* (☎ *360-963-2444)* in Clallam Bay has clean, no-frills rooms with kitchenettes for $44. (There are more *motels* at nearby Sekiu's boat basin.)

Start looking for a good restaurant and you'll quickly discover why all the motels have kitchenettes. You'll be wise to take the hint and cook your own food. The *Breakwater Restaurant*, next to the Bay Motel in Clallam Bay, is a decent enough diner with burgers and pork chops.

Camping

Lake Ozette campground at the trailhead offers 15 primitive lakeside sites ($10) that fill every day before noon. Reservations are not taken for this campground (confusingly, reservations *are* required for Ozette's popular backcountry beach camps – see Planning). In a pinch try the tent sites 8mi west of Sekiu at *Tretteviks RV Park* (☎ *360-963-2688, 6850 Hwy 112)*, right on the bay.

Sandwiches, ice cream, espresso and beer are available from the store at the *Lost Resort* (☎ *360-963-2899)*, a quarter-mile from the Ozette ranger station and trailhead.

GETTING TO/FROM THE HIKE

The trailhead at Lake Ozette is 24mi southwest of Sekiu on the Olympic Coast. To reach it, continue 3mi past Sekiu and turn left off Hwy 112 onto Hoko-Ozette Rd. Allow at least 45 minutes for the 21mi drive to the end.

Sekiu is 51mi west of Port Angeles on Hwy 112, or 140mi north of Aberdeen via Hwys 101 and 113. It's a four- to five-hour drive from Seattle and six to seven hours from Portland.

From Seattle Getting to the Olympic Peninsula from Seattle involves taking a ferry across the Puget Sound. The Edmonds-Kingston and Seattle-Bainbridge routes are the most direct and sail approximately once an hour; waits are longest for summer departures from 2 to 7 pm. For fares and schedules contact Washington State Ferries (☎ 206-464-6400, ☎ 800-843-3779, ▯ www.wsdot.wa.gov/ferries/. Once across the sound continue on Hwy 104 and follow it northwest to pick up Hwy 101, which leads to Port Angeles. Beyond the town, take Hwy 112 (right) to Clallam Bay and Sekiu.

From Portland Head west on Hwy 12 at I-5 exit 88 and pick up Hwy 101 in Aberdeen. At Sappho, take Hwy 113 (left) to Hwy 112 and Sekiu.

THE HIKE

The trail leaves a busy ranger station from a kiosk that offers an interpretive brochure on forest ecology. Bridge the first currents of the Ozette River and fork left at a sign for Sand Point. Cedar planks bear hikers on a 3mi boardwalk through a damp forest of bulging hemlock, cedar and Douglas fir. Watch for nurselogs along the way – partially decomposed trees that host new seedlings and are the best demonstrators of an insatiable rainforest lifecycle. The seedlings spurt hastily into tall trees with

PACIFIC NORTHWEST

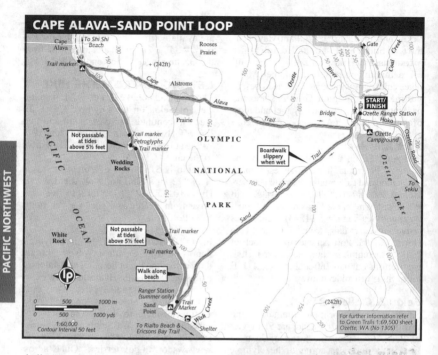

CAPE ALAVA–SAND POINT LOOP

shallow root structures, which topple prematurely to feed a barrage of forest organisms living on the nutrient-rich forest floor.

Campsites in a forest clearing greet hikers to Sand Point. Emerge from the woods to gray skies, casting a backwards glance to notice a prominent orange and black trail marker along treeline. These round symbols indicate alternate routes over headlands and mark the return trail at Cape Alava, 3mi north. Clamber over driftwood logs and resume hiking north (right) along the beach. Rocky shoreline reefs stretch toward the ocean and at low tide imprison hermit crabs, sea anemone and starfish for prodding by excited children (and some adults). A sluggish walk over dark, gravelly sand splotched with seaweed reaches a headland in 1mi. If the bluff can't be rounded (due to high tide) grab the rope dangling down a steep path and climb over.

Continue another mile past sea stacks and off-shore islands to reach the next headland near Wedding Rocks. It takes a careful eye to find **Native American petroglyphs** on the rocks below treeline. Orca whales, an old-fashioned sailing ship and human figures are just a few of the carvings to look for. The mysterious oval shape is believed to represent a vulva. Some carvings, like a cross, were added by vandals.

Ozette Island marks your arrival at Cape Alava. Turn inland past well-established ***campsites*** at a grassy prairie, leaving the beach behind for an easy climb back into the woods. The boardwalk alternates rainforest, bog and edible salal on a 3.3mi loop back to the ranger station.

Mt Baker

The northernmost mountain in the Cascade Range, Mt Baker (10,755ft) is known first and foremost as a ski destination popular for deep piles of dry, powdery snow. As an off-season hiking area it's flanked on all sides by trails that offer a wide variety of terrain. Short, parklike trails at Heather Meadows are favored for moderate day hikes through scenes of high meadowed lakes and hanging glaciers. A number of trailside camps provide memorable backpacking destinations for beginners and families with children. The area makes a beautiful, low-key alternative to crowded alpine trails at Mt Rainier.

One of the Cascades' youngest stratavolcanoes, Mt Baker steamed hot sulfurous gases as recently as 1975. A fault along the eastern wilderness boundary separates Mt Baker's shapely volcanic form from neighboring Mt Shuksan (9127ft), which was born of a buckled seafloor belonging to the North Cascades. Miners and loggers first settled the region in the 1900s in a rush to find fortunes in natural resources. The area today is given over mainly to recreation. Tracts of virgin forest that became part of the designated wilderness area in 1984 are reputedly home to Bigfoot (see the boxed text on page 460).

Chain Lakes

Duration	4–5 hours
Distance	6.5mi (10.5km)
Standard	medium
Start/Finish	Heather Meadows visitor center
Nearest Town	Glacier
Public Transport	no

Summary Tour two alpine-lake basins past huge views of Mt Baker and Mt Shuksan on this short loop hike in Mt Baker's popular Heather Meadows Recreation Area.

This alpine loop hike from the Heather Meadows visitor center begins with a steep climb past Mt Shuksan to Artist Point, and then proceeds to nearly continuous views of Mt Baker on an easy wilderness stroll through meadows dotted with small lakes. Finish by dropping down a rocky basin to small pools beneath a basalt plateau. Total ascent is 1500ft (450m).

Under snow this trail around Table Mountain is one of the most popular routes in Washington with cross-country skiers. In the summertime reflections of Mt Baker shimmer in wildflower-rimmed ponds, and sculpted ice bobs in spectacular Iceberg Lake.

PLANNING
Mt Baker is comprised of wilderness, national forest and national recreation area lands, and managed collectively with the North Cascades National Park under a combined headquarters. The *North Cascades Challenger* contains information for both places. Contact the Mt Baker district office, Mt Baker–Snoqualmie National Forest (☎ 360-856-5700, 🖳 www.fs.fed.us/r6/mbs), 2105 Hwy 20, Sedro Woolley, WA 98284, open 8 am to 4:30 pm Monday to Thursday (and weekends in summer) and 8 am to 6 pm on Friday.

Contact the Glacier public service center (☎ 360-599-2714) on Hwy 542 in Glacier for the latest trail conditions, open 8:30 am to 4:30 pm daily mid-May to mid-October.

When to Hike
The trail is usually hikeable from late July to October, though a few snowfields linger late into the season. In the first weeks after snowmelt the meadows are carpeted with pink-flowering heather.

Maps & Books
The Green Trails 1:69,500 map *Mt Shuksan, WA (No 14)* shows all the trails at Heather Meadows. *100 Hikes in the North Cascades* by Ira Spring & Harvey Manning includes descriptions of more hikes in the Mt Baker area.

Permits & Regulations
A Northwest Forest Pass is required to park in the Heather Meadows Recreation Area. Rangers check cars for permits and make on-the-spot sales at a checkpoint below the visitor center. Permits can also be purchased in advance at the Glacier public service center. Fires are not allowed at any of the wilderness camps.

Bigfoot Territory

Bigfoot (or Sasquatch) is a legendary resident of the Pacific Northwest. While sightings have been reported all over North America, this area seems to be the creature's favorite stomping ground. Tales of Bigfoot abound, especially among loggers and hunters, but several Native American legends also contain a *Sasquatch* or *Omah* – a similar 'wild man of the woods'. The creature is actually pursued by some scientists and wildlife biologists who take Bigfoot research seriously.

Could the animal be a link in the evolutionary process?

Commonly described as looking like a large ape, Bigfoot stands about 7½ feet tall and walks upright while swinging its arms; it weighs 400lb to 500lb, is covered in hair (from gray to reddish-brown or black), has dark brown or yellow eyes and possesses a foul, overpowering odor. Photos and plaster casts of its tracks show human-like, five-toed footprints averaging 16 inches in length.

MICK WELDON

According to most reports, Bigfoot is non-aggressive and usually flees when sighted, but he's also been said to occasionally throw rocks, shake cars or chase people. In general, Bigfoot seems to stick to the woods, but he has been spotted crossing highways and wandering through campgrounds, backyards and other unlikely places.

Despite a variety of 'evidence' – blurred photos and video footage, hair samples, plaster casts of footprints and audio recordings of Bigfoot's call (a loud roaring or growling sound) – the creature's existence has never been confirmed. To catch a virtual glimpse of the big guy (and hear an audio file), check out the Washington State Sasquatch Homepage at 💻 www.angelfire.com/wa/sasquatchsearch.

NEAREST TOWNS & FACILITIES
Bellingham

The old port city of Bellingham, 89mi north of Seattle off I-5, is the closest link to public transport. Hosteling International's *Bellingham Hostel (☎ 360-671-1750, 107 Chuckanut Dr)* in Fairhaven has bunkbeds ($16) and one small private room ($20). Budget and mid-priced hotels along Samish Way are convenient to I-5 exit 252; reservations are advised on weekends. The *Coachman Inn (☎ 360-671-9000, 800-962-6641, 120 Samish Way)* has a pool and rooms from $45.

Bellingham's collegiate counter-culture meets for lunch at the *Old Town Cafe (☎ 360-671-4431, 316 Holly St)*. For dinner try the *Orchard Street Brewery (☎ 360-676-9136, 709 W Orchard Dr)* off I-5 exit 256.

Getting There & Away Greyhound buses from Seattle ($13) stop at the bus depot (☎ 360-733-5251), 1329 N State St, eight times daily. Trains arrive at the Amtrak station (☎ 360-734-8851) at the end of Harris Ave near the ferry terminal. For car rental call Bellingham Enterprise (☎ 360-733-4363). For a taxi call Yellow Cab (☎ 800-734-8294).

Glacier Area

Glacier is the last town on Hwy 542. Mt Baker has two forested USFS campgrounds east of Glacier on Hwy 542. *Silver Fir campground*, 12mi east, has 21 sites ($12) along the North Fork Nooksack River and is the closest to the trailhead. The 30 sites at *Douglas Fir campground*, 2mi east of Glacier, usually fill first. Reservations are highly recommended for weekend travelers or late arrivals (☎ 877-444-6777, 🖥 www .reserveusa.com).

The **Snowline Inn** (☎ *206-599-2788, 800-228-0119, 10433 Mt Baker Hwy*) in Glacier has one-bedroom units with full kitchens from $65.

Expect a line out the door at **Milano's** (☎ *360-599-2863, 9990 Mt Baker Hwy*) in Glacier, a bustling Italian bistro with huge portions of fresh pasta (well worth the wait). Open for breakfast on weekends.

Maple Falls and Kendall, back towards Bellingham and Sedro Woolley on Hwy 542, are the last places to buy gas.

GETTING TO/FROM THE HIKE
Mt Baker's Heather Meadows Recreation Area is east of Bellingham near the end of Hwy 542, just south of the Canadian border. The trailhead, at the Heather Meadows visitor center, is 18mi east of Glacier, a mile below Austin Pass.

From the north end of downtown Bellingham, Broadway leads northeast and becomes Sunset Dr before continuing as Hwy 542. (From I-5 take exit 255.) If you're driving north from Seattle you can bypass Bellingham by following Hwy 9 north to Hwy 542 from Sedro Woolley, 5mi east of I-5 exit 230. Follow Hwy 542 to Glacier and continue to the trailhead.

THE HIKE
Disregard the maze of nature trails near the visitor center and head up to a gravel path for the Wild Goose Trail near the road. Gray-and-white goose symbols mark a trail that ascends left of Terminal Lake and begins climbing stair steps, gaining 900ft in 1mi. Give pause to admire **Mt Shuksan** at Austin Pass, and then push on to cross the highway near an overflow parking area and emerge near a toilet at busy Artist Point (5100ft).

Head straight across the parking lot to find the Chain Lakes Loop Trail under the shadow of Table Mountain's basalt plateau. The trail dips through trees and passes a right turn for Table Mountain to take aim at beaming Mt Baker. Traverse the south side

A hiker makes her way along the Chain Lakes Loop Trail high above Bagley Lakes. Mt Shuksan looms above the Mt Baker ski area (invisible behind Panorama Dome).

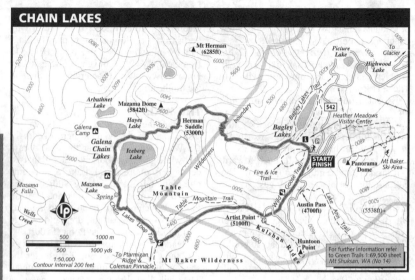

CHAIN LAKES

of Table Mountain on a gentle route through a glacier-carved valley to enter Mt Baker Wilderness, arriving at a trail junction a mile closer to Baker's snowy foot. The mountain's busiest climbing route stretches south from this stunning viewpoint along Ptarmigan Ridge.

Keep right to resume a northbound course around Table Mountain to the Galena Chain Lakes. Forested *campsites* and a small waterfall at signed Mazama Lake head the first wildflower meadows after less than a mile. Over the next ridge is **Iceberg Lake**, a shaded niche beneath Table Mountain where the snow sometimes never melts through summer. Bear right between Iceberg and Hayes Lakes, passing a side trail on the left to *Galena Camp* and Arbuthnet Lake.

Over-the-shoulder scenes of Mt Baker reflected in Iceberg Lake are continuous for the next 1½mi of increasingly rocky switchbacks to Herman Saddle. Snowfields often linger in the ominous passage between Mt Herman and Table Mountain. Level out at the last great views of Mt Baker before heading east across a rockfield to breach the saddle and drop back into the Bagley Lakes basin.

The trail loses 1000ft to a steep wall, and bottoms out in a rock basin at Bagley Lakes. Turn right across a clear pool on a stone-arch bridge to end the hike beneath the visitor center. Go straight to continue a tour of the lower Bagley Lake on a flat loop that adds an extra mile.

North Cascades National Park

A region of ice and avalanches, this jumble of 7000ft to 9000ft glacier-clad peaks east of Mt Baker is a haven for seasoned mountaineers and offers hundreds of miles of trails that traverse a rugged alpine wilderness through deep valleys and sheer cliffs. The mountains of the North Cascades are nonvolcanic, and formed from the buckled seafloor of an ancient micro-continent. Ice age glaciers sharpened the upheaval into a crowded range of broken peaks that press south from Canada into central Washington, supplying the Cascades with its most jagged terrain.

The Skagit River cuts a narrow valley across the North Cascades, dividing the 789-

sq-mile park into north and south units patched together by boating-oriented Ross Lake and Lake Chelan National Recreation Areas. Collectively these lands comprise what is often called a 'national park complex'. Limited road access preserves the North Cascades National Park as one of the nation's least-visited.

Cascade Pass

Duration	2 days
Distance	9.4mi (15.1km)
Standard	medium
Start/Finish	Cascade Pass Trailhead
Nearest Towns	Marblemount, Stehekin
Public Transport	no

Summary A spectacular view down the Stehekin Valley at an ancient mountain pass in Washington's North Cascades National Park. A strenuous trip up Sahale Arm (optional) leads to a 7600ft camp at the foot of a glacier.

This short overnight to Cascade Pass at the west end of the Stehekin Valley samples a popular route to the isolated village of Stehekin, a town of about 76 people accessible only by foot or by a long, 50mi boat trip across central Washington's Lake Chelan. Icefalls crack and thunder through this awe-inspiring passage, carved by ice-age glaciers and hemmed on all sides by sheer, craggy peaks. A grueling (optional) path up Sahale Arm offers hardened backpackers a chance to view the valley from the perspective of a glacier. The entire trip to the top enatils a total climb of 4000ft in 6mi, but reaps the greatest rewards for the most work. Cascade Pass return also makes a medium day hike.

Those with time for a longer trip should continue down the valley from Pelton Basin Camp to Stehekin (route not described here). The number of days it takes to get there from Cascade River Rd varies with road and trail conditions – it's been several years since the NPS shuttle van has been able to reach Cottonwood campground at the very end of 23mi Stehekin Valley Rd to pick up hikers. The road is usually clear to High Bridge, 11mi up, by late June. Maintained campgrounds line the road and there's lodging in rustic log cabins closer to town. Using the shuttle, the trip takes four to six days.

PLANNING

The North Cascades National Park wilderness information center (☎ 360-873-4500, x39) in Marblemount issues backcountry permits and answers questions about trail conditions; it's open daily May to September. Peak season hours (July and August) are 7 am to 8 pm Friday to Sunday, and 7 am to 6 pm Monday to Thursday. Washouts have been known to close Cascade River Rd for the whole season, so be sure to call ahead.

Grizzly bears are known to occasionally visit the park, so don't forget to ask about sightings.

To request general park information contact North Cascades National Park (☎ 360-856-5700), 2105 Hwy 20, Sedro Woolley, WA 98284.

When to Hike

The trails are open from late July to October. Show up early a day before departure to get permits for a weekend trip.

What to Bring

Although bears prowl camps around Cascade Pass, marmots pose a bigger threat to food supplies. Consider leaving room in your pack for a bear-proof canister, available on loan from the wilderness information center with a credit card imprint. The canisters are especially recommended for Sahale Glacier Camp, where there are lots of marmots and no trees.

Those headed up Sahale Arm will also need a three-season tent suitable for pitching in a rock cairn, waterproof hiking boots and cold-weather gear. Crampons and an ice-axe are minimum requirements for climbers heading beyond here up the ice to Sahale Mountain.

Water is scarce along the way. Carry enough to get to camp.

Maps & Books

Carry Green Trails 1:69,500 maps *Cascade Pass (No 80)* and *McGregor Mt (No 81)*.

For more hikes pick up a copy of *100 Hikes in the North Cascades* by Ira Spring & Harvey Manning.

Permits & Regulations
NPS backcountry permits, required for overnight camping, need to be picked up from the Marblemount wilderness center. The permits are free, but limited to the number of available campsites. Only three groups are allowed at Pelton Basin, and five at Sahale Arm. Six groups may camp at Basin Creek 2mi downhill from Pelton Basin. Use backcountry toilets where provided.

NEAREST TOWNS & FACILITIES
Along Hwy 20
Spent logging and construction towns of Concrete, Rockport and Marblemount along Hwy 20 in the Upper Skagit River valley offer only rudimentary services. Marblemount, at the junction for Cascade Pass Rd, is closest to the trailhead, while Concrete offers better motels and restaurants. Tourist traffic often overwhelms Concrete's only gas station and grocery store, making Sedro Woolley a better place to buy supplies.

Places to Stay & Eat Flush toilets, showers and RV hook-ups offer comfort at *Rockport State Park* (☎ *360-853-8461*), 6mi east of Concrete on Hwy 20, a campground in a lush, old-growth forest ($15).

Eagles Nest Motel (☎ *360-853-8662, 46346 Hwy 20*) in Concrete, has clean, spacious rooms with refrigerators and ceiling fans from $48. *Annie's Pizza Station* (☎ *206-853-7227, 44568 Hwy 20*) in a strip mall next to Concrete's grocery store turns out delicious pizzas, salads, calzone and lasagne, and offers a lot for vegetarians; closed Monday.

Marblemount's *Buffalo Run Restaurant* (☎ *360-873-2461, 5860 Hwy 20*) is the place to go if you've ever wanted to try burgers made of venison, buffalo or ostrich. Hearty logger's breakfasts appeal at the *Log House Inn* (☎ *360-873-4311*) just across the street.

Organic berry shakes from the *Cascadian Farms* (☎ *360-853-8173*) roadside stand are just 3mi east of Rockport.

Other Camping
Those gunning for an early start can camp along Cascade River Rd on the way to the trailhead at *Marble Creek campground*, a small USFS campground with no water and no fee, 8mi east of Marblemount.

GETTING TO/FROM THE HIKE
The trailhead is 23mi up Cascade River Rd, which leads west off Hwy 20 in Marblemount. The road becomes steep at the end, and while it's not the worst gravel road there is quite a bit of bumpy washboard. Hwy 20 leads west from I-5 at Burlington.

THE HIKE
Day 1: Cascade River Rd to Pelton Basin Camp
3–4 hours, 4.7mi (7.6km), 1800ft (540m) ascent

There are 35 switchbacks, or so they say, on the first 3.1mi of the Cascade Pass Trail. Find the trailhead on the left side of the gravel parking loop and start counting. Walking is relatively easy on a steady uphill grade through a dark forest of hemlock and Douglas fir. At 1400ft, and with less than a mile to go, the trail emerges from the woods and straightens for a gentle ridgeline ascent to a breathtaking vista at Cascade Pass. The deeply gouged Stehekin Valley trails off to the east, guarded by Johannesburg Mountain (8200ft), Cascade Peak (7428ft), the Triplets, Mix-up Peak and Magic Mountain (7610ft) to the south; and Sahale Mountain (8484ft) and Buckner Mountain (9080ft) to the north.

A sign for Stehekin on the left draws hikers to follow the footsteps of Native Americans and early fur trappers who used this ancient trade route to travel between the Columbia Basin and the Puget Sound. Dip into the valley to reach forested *Pelton Basin Camp* in 1mi. Water is from Pelton Creek. A toilet is nearby.

Alternative Campsites
Basin Creek Camp If permits are unavailable for Pelton Basin, rangers are likely to recommend the camp at *Basin Creek*, 2mi further. The steep descent from Pelton

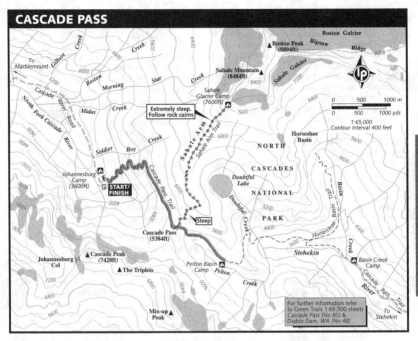

CASCADE PASS

Basin and Horseshoe Creek adds 1600ft to tomorrow's climb back to Cascade Pass.

Side Trip: Sahale Arm
4–6 hours, 4.4mi (7km),
2200ft (660m) ascent/descent
From Cascade Pass head left toward a sign for Stehekin to find a narrow path ascending a steep slope of Cascade blueberry. Slippery switchbacks achieve the ridgeline meadows of Sahale Arm at around 6200ft, the trail leveling out just long enough to allow hikers to catch their breath and admire Doubtful Lake below. The meadow maintains a steady uphill pitch and peters out at a tiny creek at the base of the first rockfield. Hikers must negotiate rocks and boulders the rest of the way on a steep route marked by cairns and muddled by stray paths.

Several crests yield to bigger boulders as the grueling rockfield continues endlessly skyward. Sahale Glacier remains out of sight

the whole time, hovering in clouds well above the next ridge. A sign for the toilet provides an unexpected thrill as one finally arrives at *Sahale Glacier Camp* (7600ft), a notch beneath the Sahale Mountain summit. Bear right across a snowfield to one last ridge to make camp in one of the large rock cairns. Streams of snowmelt provide water.

Retrace your steps to Pelton Basin Camp.

Day 2: Pelton Basin Camp to Cascade River Rd
2–4 hours, 4.7mi/600ft gain
Return to the trailhead via the Cascade Pass Trail, following the route of Day 1's hike.

Other Hikes

COLUMBIA GORGE
Multnomah Falls
   Scenic, 620ft Multnomah Falls – 31mi east of Portland in the Columbia Gorge – is Oregon's

tallest waterfall and the state's most popular tourist destination. The 1.1mi trail to the top was closed after falling boulders stranded a honeymooning bride (still in her gown) and bonked a Japanese tourist on the noggin. An alternate route from the Wahkeena Falls Trailhead (I-84 exit 28) on trails Nos 420 and 441 gets you there and back in 7.4mi via a 2200ft elevation gain. No permits required. See Information in the Columbia Gorge section for information sources.

MT JEFFERSON WILDERNESS
Mt Jefferson

Portland's favorite weekend backpacking destination is Jefferson Park, a wildflower meadow on the west face of Mt Jefferson (10,497ft). The Pacific Crest Trail links South Breitenbush Trail with Craig Trail for a popular, two-day, 14mi loop that departs from the South Breitenbush Trailhead on USFS Rd No 4685 (past Breitenbush Hot Springs). The Green Trails 1:69,500 map *Mt Jefferson (No 557)* shows the trails. Detroit, east of Salem on Hwy 22, is the nearest town. A Northwest Forest Pass is required.

Mt Jefferson Wilderness is administered by the Willamette National Forest. For more information contact the Detroit district ranger station (☎ 503-854-3366), a mile west of Detroit on Hwy 22.

MT RAINIER NATIONAL PARK
Wonderland Trail

The Northwest's ultimate hike is this challenging, 93mi trail that rings Mt Rainier mostly above timberline. Longmire, Paradise and Sunrise are the main starting points for this 10- to 14-day hike. Stash extra supplies in cars and at ranger stations at Sunrise and Paradise (ranger stations won't store fuel).

One of the most stunning shorter trips to be made along this trail is the 14mi to 17mi, two-to four-day hike to Indian Bar via Summerland that starts from the Fryingpan Creek Trailhead near the White River Entrance. Return via the same route, or continue on for a cross-park hike ending at Box Canyon (car shuttle required).

See Planning in the Mt Rainier National Park section for information sources and how to obtain backcountry permits. A midweek start is strongly advised.

OLYMPIC NATIONAL PARK
Hoh Rainforest

Visitors flock to Hoh Rainforest to admire giant, mossy trees and rotting logs. Many never leave the short nature trail and visitor center; but the Hoh Trail probes deep into the park's interior, ending in 18mi at a glaciered Mt Olympus (7965ft). An easy down-and-back hike of any length can be made of the flat

Majestic Mt Rainier. Sprawling down the mountain's northeast slope is the Emmons Glacier; note the black stripe of an arete and medial moraine slicing down its middle.

lower portion, which tours some of the world's only temperate rainforest. Happy Four Camp is a good goal for a 11½mi day hike. Turn east off Hwy 101 9mi south of Forks to reach the trailhead, on the west side of the Olympic Peninsula.

There is $10 park entrance fee. Backcountry permits are required to camp overnight. See Planning for the Cape Alava–Sand Point Loop hike for information sources.

MT ST HELENS NATIONAL VOLCANIC MONUMENT
Loowit Trail

Mt St Helens, whose top was blown off in a volcanic eruption in 1980, is visited on the 27mi Loowit Trail, a shadeless and arid three- to four-day hike around the crater over pumice and ash. Truman Trail, which leads from USFS Rd No 99 at Windy Ridge in the monument's northeast corner, is one of several possible starting points. Most hike counterclockwise. There is an $8 per person monument fee. Randle on Hwy 12 in southwest Washington is the closest town.

A popular, non-technical climb to the crater's rim on the mountain's south side starts on Ptarmigan Trail at the end of USFS Rd No 830, accessed via Cougar on Hwy 503. Fit hikers routinely take on this mostly trailless 5mi, 4500ft climb; obtaining a climbing permit ($15) takes foresight and planning. Call the Mt St Helens climbing information line (☎ 360-247-3961) for specifics.

The Green Trails 1:40,500 map *Mt St Helens NW, Wash (No 364S)* serves for either hike. For information contact the Mt St Helens National Volcanic Monument (☎ 360-247-3900, ⌨ www.fs.fed.us/gpnf/mshnvm), 42218 NE Yale Bridge Rd, Amboy, WA 98601.

Long-Distance Trails

The USA spans more than 3.5 million sq miles – plenty of room for some really long hiking trails. The eight trails featured in this chapter traverse more than 15,000 trail miles, and range in length from 700mi to 4400mi. These routes take weeks and months to complete and relatively few hikers complete a trail in its entirety. The majority enjoy segments of a trail on day hikes or shorter backpacking trips.

For hikes in this book traversing segments of these trails, see the entries for each long-distance trail in the book's index.

Three trails – the Appalachian, Continental Divide and Pacific Crest Trails – follow the crests of major mountain chains. The other five each follows a theme: the Florida Trail explores subtropical lowlands; the Natchez Trace Trail wends along a historic route; the Potomac Heritage Trail follows the Potomac River from the ocean into the mountains; the Ice Age Trail traces the imprints of ancient glaciers; and the North Country Trail traverses the Great Lakes landscape.

The terrain and difficulty vary widely – some segments are remote and extremely challenging, others are easily accessible, broad paths – but all take hikers through arguably the finest scenery in the USA.

HISTORY

Trails leading to a land where a person can be free are an integral part of the American Dream. The pioneer trails of the mid-19th century carried the dream from east to west to build a nation out of a wilderness. The great obstacles on those pioneer trails were the mighty mountain ranges running north to south. Today, those mountains retain some of the USA's last bits of wilderness and recall the frontier spirit of self-reliance.

As the wilderness receded in the early 20th century, outdoor enthusiasts in New England and the Pacific states began to build trails through the remaining patches in the mountains. The Long Trail in Vermont's Green Mountains, begun in 1910, was the

first, followed by the Appalachian Trail in the 1920s and the Pacific Crest Trail in the 1930s.

The popularity of these routes led President Lyndon B Johnson to propose a national system of backcountry trails. In October 1968 Johnson signed the National Trails System Act, establishing 'a nationwide system of scenic, recreational, and historic trails'. Of these, national scenic trails are the only continuous, protected, scenic

LONG-DISTANCE TRAILS

Pacific Crest NST

Appalachian NST

North Country NST

Ice Age NST

Continental Divide NST

Natchez Trace NST

Potomac Heritage NST

Florida NST

CANADA

MEXICO

WA · OR · MT · ND · MN · WI · MI · ME · VT · NH · MA · CT · RI · NY · PA · NJ · DE · MD · ID · WY · SD · IA · OH · IN · WV · VA · NV · UT · CO · NE · IL · KY · CA · AZ · NM · KS · MO · TN · NC · SC · OK · AR · AL · GA · TX · LA · MS · FL

0   500   1000 km
0   250   500 mi
1:43,000,000

NST National Scenic Trail

corridors designed solely for hiking and prohibiting motorized vehicles.

The act leaves acquisition of land and construction of trails to nonprofit partnership organizations, but it is the National Park Service (NPS) that certifies segments and places official national scenic trail emblems along the trail to indicate it conforms to the approved national trail plans. Colored paint blazes supplement these emblems to mark the way. Other segments that have not yet received certification are similarly blazed along the trail, but lack the official emblem. Some segments have not yet been built, and may appear on official maps as proposed segments. Hikers typically divert onto roads through these stretches.

INFORMATION
Maps & Books
Most national scenic trails can be followed easily in good weather, but adverse weather, snow pack, ongoing trail construction, and the impermanence of blazes and trail markers make maps and a guidebook essential for hiking.

See Maps & Navigation in the Facts for the Hiker chapter for information on US Geological Survey (USGS), US Forestry Service (USFS) and third-party maps. See also the regional hikes chapters.

Information Sources
The NPS (🖳 www.nps.gov/trails), under the US Department of the Interior, and the USFS (🖳 www.fs.fed.us), under the US Department of Agriculture (🖳 www.usda.gov), are responsible for the overall administration of the eight national scenic trails. Five are administered by the NPS, and three by the USFS. Direct any inquiries to the National Trails System Branch (☎ 202-343-3780), NPS (782), PO Box 37127, Washington, DC 20013-7127.

The trails are managed and maintained by various federal, state and local agencies as

The Trails	Length (mi)	Standard	States Traversed
Appalachian	2158	medium	Georgia, North Carolina, Tennessee, Virginia, West Virginia, Maryland, Pennsylvania, New Jersey, New York, Connecticut, Massachusetts, Vermont, New Hampshire, Maine
Continental Divide	3100	hard	New Mexico, Colorado, Wyoming, Idaho, Montana
Pacific Crest	2638	hard	California, Oregon, Washington
Florida Trail	1300	easy	Florida
Natchez Trace	694	easy	Mississippi, Alabama, Tennessee
Potomac Heritage	704	easy	Virginia, Maryland, Pennsylvania
Ice Age	1000	easy	Wisconsin
North Country	4400	easy-medium	New York, Pennsylvania, Ohio, Michigan, Wisconsin, Minnesota, North Dakota

For hikes traversing segments of these trails, see the entries for each long-distance trail in the book's index.

well as private, nonprofit partnership organizations and individual volunteers. The partnership organizations work with these agencies to promote and protect the trail, and to provide resource information, trail updates and maps. The Partnership for the National Trails System, 214 North Henry St, Suite 201, Madison, WI 53703, comprises 16 trail associations and works with US Congress to support the national trails system.

Permits & Fees
See Hiking Permits in the Facts for the Hiker chapter.

What to Bring
Long-distance hikers need backpacking gear (see What to Bring under Planning in the Facts for the Hiker chapter for a list), but should bear in mind that the more one carries, the easier the camping, but the less one carries, the easier the hiking. The weight of food and fuel makes resupply a necessity beyond about two weeks; most long-distance hikers resupply every seven to 10 days.

Warnings
The national scenic trails are generally safe, but hikers should be most cautious near towns and roads. Hiking on mountainous trails carries all the inherent risks of travel in remote and rugged terrain where weather, isolation and physical hazards are

unpredictable. Campfire restrictions apply in many areas and in all national forests, so hikers should plan to cook over a stove.

See the Health & Safety chapter for important information on environmental and other natural hazards.

TOWNS & FACILITIES
No accommodations other than primitive campsites exist along most trails, so backpackers sleep in the tents they carry. Where trails cross roads, and at trailheads, hikers can detour to post offices, to collect mail drops, and to towns where accommodations and supplies are available. Contact each trail's partnership organization for details (see Planning under the individual hike descriptions).

Appalachian National Scenic Trail

Duration	145 days (5 months)
Distance	2158mi (3474km)
Start	Springer Mountain, Georgia
Finish	Mt Katahdin, Maine

Summary The original national scenic trail, this ribbon of wilderness unwinds along the length of the Appalachian Mountains, which flank USA's eastern seaboard.

Known to thru-hikers as the 'long green tunnel', the Appalachian National Scenic

Elevation Range (ft)	Terrain	When to Hike	Page
124 to 6642	mountains	April to October	470
4200 to 14,230	mountains	June to September	474
140 to 13,200	mountains	April to October	477
0 to less than 325	swamps, plains	October to March	480
0 to less than 800	plains, rolling hills	March to April, October to November	483
0 to 2000	rolling hills	April to November	485
500 to 1875	rolling hills	May to October	487
less than 300	plains, rolling hills	April to November	490

Trail (AT) stretches 2158mi from Springer Mountain in Georgia to Mt Katahdin in Maine, passing through 14 states and within a day's drive of about two-thirds of the US population. The AT runs along the crest of the Appalachian Mountains parallel to the Atlantic coast, much of it through protected areas, including two national parks, two national recreation areas and 60 state parks.

Easy access draws more than three million people a year to the AT, most of whom are day hikers or weekend backpackers. Each year, more than 2000 hardy souls set out to hike the entire AT, but fewer than 200 actually complete the trail in one season.

The Georgia, North Carolina–Tennessee, southern Virginia, Vermont, New Hampshire and Maine segments are generally more strenuous. The segments north of Waynesboro, VA, to the Massachusetts-Vermont state line are generally better for moderate overnight trips.

HISTORY
Benton MacKaye in 1921 proposed an interstate wilderness trail along the ridge of the Appalachian Mountains from North Carolina to New Hampshire, and in 1925 local hiking clubs organized the Appalachian Trail Conference (ATC) to link existing trails along MacKaye's route. The trail, a collaboration of the NPS, USFS, state and local governments and the Depression-era Civilian Conservation Corps (CCC), reached its approximate present length by 1937. Thus, it became the first continuously marked recreational hiking trail in North America and the first national scenic trail designated by the US Congress in 1968.

NATURAL HISTORY & CLIMATE
See the New England & Adirondacks and Southern Appalachia chapters.

PLANNING
When to Hike
The hiking season is longer in the south than the north. Thru-hikers, whose preferred route is south to north, usually start in mid-April and finish in mid-October.

Maps & Books
The ATC publishes 11 official *Appalachian Trail Guides*, which are updated every three to five years, and are organized roughly by state. Each guide contains detachable water-resistant topographic maps that range in scale from 1:38,750 to 1:100,000. These map sets can be purchased separately.

The indispensable *Appalachian Trail Data Book*, a pocket-sized handbook detailing mileages between features and facilities, is updated annually and lists all water sources, shelters, campsites, hostels and lodging, restaurants, stores and post offices within 5mi of AT road crossings. The *Appalachian Trail*

LONG-DISTANCE TRAILS

Thru-Hikers

Thru-hikers, also known as end-to-enders, set out to hike the entire length of a national scenic trail. Some complete a trail in one season, averaging from 15mi to 20mi per day for weeks and months at a time. Others complete a trail by hiking it in segments over several years. The continuous physical and mental effort makes a single-season thru-trip not recommended for those who want to appreciate a trail more fully. Thru-hikers carefully plan the logistics of a season on the trail, mailing their food and supplies to post offices along the way. Specialty guidebooks and even cookbooks discuss the myriad of details.

Few without previous backpacking and first-aid experience commit to a thru-hike, which is the most demanding approach to a long-distance trail. Of those who try, only about 10% achieve their goal. Thru-hikers form a distinctive part of the culture of the long-distance trails, embodying the mythos of the rugged, self-contained hiker. They even have their own associations, and completing the 'big three' mountain trails – the Appalachian, Continental Divide, and Pacific Crest – is referred to as the 'Triple Crown'. For more information, contact the Appalachian Long Distance Hikers Association (🖳 www.aldha.org), 10 Benning St, Box 224, West Lebanon, NH 03784, or the American Long Distance Hikers Association West (🖳 www.gorp.com/nonprof/aldhaw), PO Box 651, Vancouver, WA 98666-0651.

Workbook for Planning Thru-Hikes has detachable pages listing all details of food, equipment, money, weather, shelter and towns.

The Best of the Appalachian Trail: Day Hikes and *The Best of the Appalachian Trail: Overnight Hikes*, both by Frank and Victoria Logue, help to select and plan shorter hikes.

A Walk in the Woods: Rediscovering America on the Appalachian Trail by Bill Bryson is a best-selling narrative told with wit and dry humor.

Information Sources

The NPS (☎ 304-535-6278) administers the trail from the Appalachian Trail Project Office, c/o Harpers Ferry Center, Harpers Ferry, WV 25425. The partnership organization is the ATC (☎ 304-535-6331, ✉ info@atconf.org, 🖳 www.atconf.org), PO Box 807, 799 Washington St, Harpers Ferry, WV 25425-0807; ask for its free *Walking the Appalachian Trail Step by Step* booklet.

TOWNS & FACILITIES

More than 250 three-sided shelters, most about 10mi apart, are available on a first-come, first-served basis. Along many segments, camping is not permitted between shelters. In Shenandoah National Park, the Potomac Appalachian Trail Club operates shelters on a self-regulated basis.

THE HIKE
Georgia

The southern terminus of the AT, at the summit of **Springer Mountain** (3782ft), is reached by an 8.7mi hike from Amicalola Falls State Park. From Springer Mountain, the trail runs 75mi through the rugged **Chattahoochee National Forest** and Springer Mountain National Recreation Area northeast to the Georgia–North Carolina state line.

North Carolina & Tennessee

The AT heads north and west through **Nantahala National Forest**, the most rugged of the southern segments, to the Little Tennessee River, where it enters the **Great Smoky Mountains National Park**. For 70mi it follows the ridge along the North Carolina–Tennessee state line through the park's hardwood forests; this section of the trail is a hiker's delight. **Clingmans Dome** (6642ft), the highest point on the AT, is 5mi south of Newfound Gap on US 441, the only road through the park. The AT continues northeast through the Pisgah and Cherokee

National Forests, to the Tennessee-Virginia state line, 371mi from the Georgia–North Carolina state line.

Virginia & West Virginia

About one quarter, or 544mi, of the Appalachian Trail is in Virginia. From the **Mt Rogers National Recreation Area** near the Tennessee-Virginia state line, the AT runs northeast through the Jefferson and George Washington National Forests, passing just north of Roanoke and following the Blue Ridge of the Appalachians, parallel to the Blue Ridge Parkway, for about 100mi. Entering the **Shenandoah National Park**, the AT continues another 100mi adjacent to Skyline Dr, which affords easy access for day hikes and shorter backpacking trips. Along the last 20mi, the trail parallels the Virginia–West Virginia state line along the crest, then descends to the confluence of the Shenandoah and Potomac Rivers at historic **Harpers Ferry**. Here, where three states meet, is the ATC headquarters, with its visitor center and bookstore.

Maryland & Pennsylvania

The AT's 41 miles through Maryland start along the **C&O Canal**, then ascend and follow the South Mountain ridge north to the Maryland-Pennsylvania state line, passing through four state parks along the way. Convenient access and attractive vistas make this a popular segment for short backpacking trips. The AT then crosses the Mason-Dixon Line, which separates the North from the South, staying along South Mountain ridge, and descends into the Cumberland Valley, crossing the Susquehanna River north of Harrisburg, Pennsylvania. Turning east, it follows the Blue Mountains through coal country before descending to the Delaware River and the picturesque **Delaware Water Gap National Recreation Area**, 232mi from the Maryland-Pennsylvania state line.

New Jersey & New York

The trail heads north along remote Kittatinny Ridge, parallel to the Delaware River, then passes through three state parks on its 71 New Jersey miles. New York City is only a one-hour drive from the AT as it traverses **Harriman–Bear Mountain State Park**, where the first trail segment was built in 1923. After dipping to 124ft to cross the Hudson River, the trail angles northeast to complete its 88 New York miles.

Connecticut & Massachusetts

The trail follows a scenic ridge above the Housatonic River valley in the extreme western part of Connecticut, crossing Bear Mountain to exit the state after 52mi. Continuing north through Massachusetts' **Berkshire Mountains**, it climbs the state's highest peak, Mt Greylock (3491ft) and, passing near Williamstown, reaches the Massachusetts-Vermont state line, a total of 90mi.

Vermont & New Hampshire

Vermont has 146 trail miles. For about 100mi, the trail joins Vermont's **Long Trail** through the Green Mountain National Forest. After crossing Killington Peak (4241ft), the trail turns east, crosses the Connecticut River, and enters New Hampshire near Hanover. Through valleys and across mountains, the trail heads into the **White Mountain National Forest**, with its windswept granite peaks. Much of the trail is above timberline, and the highest point is **Mt Washington** (6288ft), where weather can be stormy at any time. The trail then follows the rugged Mahoosuc Range and, after 161mi in New Hampshire, reaches the New Hampshire–Maine state line.

Maine

The trail traverses 281mi of Maine wilderness to reach its northern terminus in **Baxter State Park**. From the granite-strewn Mahoosuc Notch in western Maine, the trail winds up and down steep mountains to reach the broad Kennebec River, where the Maine Appalachian Trail Club and the ATC operate a free ferry service. Continuing through Maine among spruce and fir forest and then past lakes and bogs, the AT climbs above treeline to end at its famous terminus, **Mt Katahdin** (5267ft).

Continental Divide National Scenic Trail

Duration	205 days (7 months)
Distance	3100mi (4991km)
Start	Antelope Wells, New Mexico
Finish	Waterton Lakes National Park, Alberta, Canada

Summary Clinging to the Rocky Mountains crest, the USA's most rugged and challenging national scenic trail visits some spectacular national parks.

The Continental Divide National Scenic Trail (CDT) follows the Continental Divide from Mexico's Sonora-Chihuahua border to Canada's British Columbia–Alberta border for 3100mi through five states: New Mexico, Colorado, Wyoming, Idaho and Montana. The CDT takes hikers across sprawling reaches of semidesert, fertile mountain valleys, plunging canyons and high alpine plateaus, and within reach of peaks towering over 14,000ft. It passes through three spectacular national parks: Rocky Mountain, in north-central Colorado; Yellowstone, in northwestern Wyoming; and Glacier, in northwestern Montana. Ninety percent of the trail stays within 5mi of the Continental Divide, making this route the most rugged and challenging national scenic trail.

HISTORY
The US Congress designated the CDT in 1978, establishing a 50mi corridor on both sides of the Continental Divide in which to build the trail. As of early 2000 the trail was 70% complete, with about 1000mi still to go. Many segments in New Mexico and Wyoming have yet to be designated, and hikers there plan their own routes over existing trails and backcountry roads.

The trail through most of Colorado and the 795mi certified segment between Yellowstone and Glacier National Parks is a continuous, high-quality backcountry trail, with the exception of 60mi in Montana. The CDT crosses 25 national forests, 12 wilderness areas, three national parks, one national monument, eight Bureau of Land Management (BLM) resource areas, and private land.

NATURAL HISTORY & CLIMATE
See the Rocky Mountains chapter.

PLANNING
When to Hike
Very few hikers attempt to complete the entire trail in one season. Those that do usually complete the New Mexico and southern Wyoming segments during May and June, and wait for July to begin the remaining mountain segments. Most hikers recommend completing the CDT in two or more seasons. Hikers traveling south to north may find snow at high elevations in Colorado through June, while snowfall can block trails in Glacier National Park in September. Hikers traveling north to south typically find snow and high water from snowmelt in Montana's Scapegoat, Bob Marshall and Great Bear wilderness areas and Glacier National Park.

Maps & Books
The Continental Divide Trail Society (CDTS) publishes a series of guides called Guide to the Continental Divide Trail by James R Wolf, each of which describes the preliminary route and identifies the relevant USGS maps. The titles are: *Northern Montana Vol 1*; *Southern Montana and Idaho Vol 2*; *Wyoming Vol 3*; *Northern Colorado Vol 4*; *Southern Colorado Vol 5*; and *Northern New Mexico Vol 6*. Separate supplements to volumes 2 and 3 reflect new trail construction. Each volume (except volume 6) includes overview maps at a scale of 1:126,720. Separate map packs corresponding to volumes 1, 3, 4 and 5 – containing maps ranging in scale from 1:25,000 to 1:100,000 – are also available.

Where the Waters Divide: A Walk Along America's Continental Divide by Karen Berger and Daniel R Smith is the best account of a thru-hike.

Information Sources
The USFS administers the trail from two offices: USFS Rocky Mountain Region (☎

303-275-5350), 740 Simms St, Box 25127, Lakewood, CO 80225, for New Mexico, Colorado, and Wyoming; and USFS Northern Region (☎ 406-329-3150), Federal Building, PO Box 7669, Missoula, MT 59807, for Idaho and Montana.

The two relevent partnership organizations are the Continental Divide Trail Alliance (☎ 303-838-3760, 888-909-2382, fax 838-3960, ✉ cdnst@aol.com, 🖳 www.cd trail.org), Park-view Plaza Offices, 13700 Hwy 285, Unit C, PO Box 628, Pine, CO 80470-0628; and the CDTS (☎ 410-235-9610, ✉ cdtsociety@aol.com, 🖳 www.gorp .com/cdts), 3704 N Charles St, Suite 601, Baltimore, MD 21218-2300.

THE HIKE
New Mexico
New Mexico has the fewest established segments of the CDT. The Continental Divide passes through Native American land, private land and traditional-use areas where easements, cultural sensitivity and ownership issues divert the CDT away from the actual mountain range, making the 'true' route of the CDT a contentious issue. Following the CDT through New Mexico is an exercise in route-finding and preparation, and advance permission is often needed to cross some segments. Other segments, such as through the Gila National Forest, are well established.

The southern terminus is in the Chihuahua desert near the tiny outpost of Antelope Wells on the Mexican border. From here the trail tracks through the Big Hatchet Mountains before crossing I-10 en route to the Gila National Forest. Skirting Silver City, the CDT runs south of Gila Wilderness into the Black Range, passing Diamond Peak (9850ft) in **Aldo Leopold Wilderness**, and following the divide. Beyond the national forest and BLM land, the presence of private land holdings diverts the CDT onto public roads to Pie Town and onto the badlands and lava beds at **El Malpais National Monument**, where it follows a short segment of the ancient Zuni-Acoma trail. Crossing I-40, the CDT runs through Cibola National Forest near Mt Taylor (11,301ft),

then near Cabezon Peak (7785ft) and over public roads to the town of Cuba on US 550. The CDT enters the Santa Fe National Forest and crosses beautiful **San Pedro Wilderness** near San Pedro Mountain (10,610ft). A system of trails and forest roads continues north through the Carson National Forest.

Colorado
The CDT enters the Rio Grande and San Juan National Forests south of Cumbres Pass, then travels through wild **South San Juan Wilderness**, where the trail can be hard to follow. Crossing US 160 at Wolf Creek Pass (10,550ft), the CDT traverses the popular **Weminuche Wilderness**, rising to 12,956ft through the San Juan Mountains. East of Silverton the CDT turns east and, joining the Colorado Trail, crosses Hwy 149 at Spring Creek Pass (10,901ft) to traverse La Garita Wilderness, continuing with the Colorado Trail until just south of Monarch Pass (11,312ft) on US 50. North of US 50, the CDT rises to its highest point (14,230ft) as it travels along the flanks of Colorado's highest mountains, traversing the **Collegiate Peaks**, Mt Massive and Holy Cross wilderness areas.

Passing north of Leadville, the CDT crosses US 24 at Tennessee Pass (10,424ft) and continues past Copper Mountain and Breckenridge ski resorts. A recently designated segment passes near the summit of Grays Peak, then crosses I-70 and – passing Ptarmigan Peak and Vasquez Peak wilderness areas – continues north to Rollins Pass on USFS Rd 149. The CDT heads north through Indian Peaks Wilderness to enter **Rocky Mountain National Park**. A recently designated 30mi segment through the park takes hikers along Lake Granby, through the town of Grand Lake, then across high country along the Continental Divide. It crosses US 34 and the Colorado River, leaves the park and enters **Never Summer Wilderness**. The CDT then heads west through national forest to Arapaho Pass beyond which a 10mi segment of private land diverts the trail onto public roads until Muddy Pass (8722ft), where Hwy 14 meets US 40. (The landowners are working to eliminate this block.)

From Rabbit Ears Pass (9426ft) on US 40 the CDT heads north through Buffalo Pass, on Hwy 60 east of Steamboat Springs, into the splendid **Mt Zirkel Wilderness** and on to the Colorado-Wyoming state line.

Wyoming

Entering southern Wyoming, the CDT follows the crest of the Sierra Madre through the **Medicine Bow–Routt National Forest**, crossing Battle Pass.

There is no formal route for the CDT between the national forest and Yellowstone National Park. The CDT descends the forested slopes of the Sierra Madre to the desolate **Great Divide Basin**, a 90mi wide expanse of high desert. At Bridger Pass, the Continental Divide physically splits in two, encompassing the basin. (All precipitation in the basin stays there – water neither flows east nor west to the oceans.) Water sources are infrequent across the basin. I-80 skirts the basin's southern edge with Rawlins on the east and Rock Springs on the west. Hikers can either follow the Continental Divide itself or traverse the arid basin. The route around the eastern rim of the Great Divide Basin, partly along 4WD roads, is being developed as the official trail. It passes west of Rawlins through sagebrush country and skirts the southern flanks of the Seminoe and Ferris Mountains and forested Green Mountain. This region, also called the Red Desert after the color of its soil, is rich in natural beauty and teems with pronghorn antelope, wild horses and other wildlife.

The routes converge near the Oregon Buttes and the isolated Sweetwater Canyon, southeast of Hwy 28 near the South Pass National Historic Landmark. **South Pass** (7550ft), the gentlest route across the Continental Divide, was used by more than 500,000 emigrants, miners and trappers on the Oregon and Mormon Pioneer trails between 1843 and 1912. Nearby are the former mining communities of Atlantic City and South Pass City, now preserved as a state historical site.

The CDT heads northwest into the glacier-carved, granite **Wind River Range**, Wyoming's highest. For more than 100mi,

the trail wends beneath rugged peaks flanked by the largest glaciers in the Lower 48 states, through the Bridger-Teton National Forest and the Bridger Wilderness, with their innumerable lakes and streams. The CDT passes Three Waters Mountain and Triple Divide, where the waters of the Mississippi, Colorado, and Columbia Rivers diverge. A permanent route for the CDT through the Winds has not yet been established.

Leaving the Winds, the CDT passes through the northern Gros Ventre Mountains. Hikers are rewarded with impressive views of the Teton Range looming large to the west above the valley of Jackson Hole. Early in the season many rushing streams cross this segment. The CDT crosses US 26/US 287 near Togwotee Pass (9658ft). Continuing north, the trail bisects the heavily forested **Teton Wilderness**. At Two Ocean Pass, a national natural landmark, Two Ocean Creek divides into two branches, one of which flows into the Atlantic, and the other into the Pacific Ocean.

Forested slopes beneath the volcanic Absaroka Range dominate the northeastern views as the trail enters the southeast corner of internationally renowned **Yellowstone National Park**, the world's first national park.

The CDT contours south of Yellowstone Lake, one of the earth's largest alpine lakes, through prime bird and wildlife habitat as it drops into the 28mi segment along 47mi Yellowstone Caldera. It continues past Shoshone Lake and, near Craig Pass (8262ft), enters the park's southwest corner. Here 21 of Yellowstone's 110 waterfalls and most of its geothermal features are concentrated, including the famous Old Faithful geyser. Following the Summit Lake Trail across the drier Madison Plateau, the CDT exits Wyoming via the park's western boundary.

Idaho & Montana

Entering eastern Idaho in the Targhee National Forest, the CDT currently descends to Macks Inn, traversing a forested plateau where the **Henrys Fork**, known for its quintessential fishing, hurries through meadows and stands of lodgepole pine. US 20 provides access to this region of alpine lakes and meadows, where the rugged western faces of the Teton Range soar to the southeast. The designated route of the CDT will eventually stay closer to the divide, first crossing Targhee Pass (7072ft) at US 20 between Idaho's Henrys Lake and Montana's Hebgen Lake and then recrossing the divide at Raynolds Pass (6836ft).

The CDT crisscrosses west-northwest through the Beaverhead and Bitterroot Ranges along the Idaho-Montana state line for the next 80mi. From the Henrys Lake region, it winds west along the crest of the Centennial Mountains above Montana's **Red Rock Lakes National Wildlife Refuge**. Crossing Monida Pass (6823ft) at I-15, the trail enters the Beaverhead Mountains and National Forest. This higher elevation segment is predominantly an arid grassland, and crestline segments offer broad vistas and excellent wildlife-viewing opportunities, reaching the highest trail-point in Montana near Eighteenmile Peak (11,141ft). The trail continues north through Idaho's Salmon National Forest and crosses Lemhi Pass (7373ft), the headwaters of the Missouri River. Nearby is a memorial called the Sacajawea Historic Area. The CDT crosses back into Montana for good at Lost Trail Pass (6995ft) on US 93, where Lewis and Clark's Corps of Discovery passed in 1805 (see the boxed text on page 20).

The trail stays high above the Big Hole Valley as it passes through the rugged Pioneer Mountains, where valleys above 6000ft in elevation are dotted with lakes. Heading northeast, the CDT crisscrosses the divide for 30mi through **Anaconda-Pintler Wilderness**, then passes through the Deer Lodge National Forest, staying south of Butte, and traveling temporarily along roads. The trail turns north and crosses US 20 at MacDonald Pass (6325ft) west of Helena. This less rugged, mostly forested segment follows some roads.

North of Helena, the CDT crosses Hwy 200 at Rogers Pass (5610ft) and enters 2344 sq miles of the contiguous **Scapegoat**, **Bob Marshall** (the 'Bob'), and **Great Bear** wilderness areas, with an additional 1563 sq miles of adjacent national forests. The CDT follows both ridge tops and valleys through Scapegoat Wilderness before entering Bob Marshall Wilderness, staying east of the main divide and west of the Rocky Mountain Front that rises out of the prairie in a 100mi-long, 1000ft-high swoop. The backbone of the divide, and the highlight of the 'Bob', is the 13mi-long Chinese Wall, whose east side is a sheer, 1000ft-high limestone escarpment.

Entering the southern boundary of **Glacier National Park**, the CDT meanders north through glacial valleys beneath jagged, snowy peaks. After crossing the Going-to-the-Sun Rd (Hwy 2) east of Logan Pass (6646ft) at Siyeh Bend, it joins the popular Highline Trail along the Garden Wall, hugging the Continental Divide as it enters Canada's **Waterton Lakes National Park**. Hikers usually boat across Wateron Lake (4200ft), the trail's lowest point and its northern terminus.

Pacific Crest National Scenic Trail

Duration	175 days (6 months)
Distance	2638mi (4247km)
Start	Campo, California
Finish	Manning Provincial Park, British Columbia, Canada

Summary The USA's finest alpine hiking travels through the Sierra Nevada and Cascade mountain ranges and crosses seven national parks in a continuous wilderness experience.

The Pacific Crest National Scenic Trail (PCT), a high wilderness route along the Pacific Rim mountains, stretches 2638mi from Campo, on the California-Mexico border, to British Columbia, Canada. It hugs the crest of the glacier-carved Sierra Nevada in California and the volcanic Cascade Range in northern California, Oregon and Washington, crossing seven national parks – three in the Sierra and four in the Cascades – that showcase these mountains' splendor.

Although the PCT passes through the Sonoran and Mojave Deserts and reaches a low point of 140ft along the Columbia River, average trail elevations exceed 6000ft in California, 5000ft in Oregon and 4500ft in Washington, peaking at 13,200ft, 7560ft, and 7620ft in each state, respectively. Most of this mountainous terrain lies within 24 national forests and 33 roadless wilderness areas, with the longest unbroken stretch extending for more than 200mi. The solitude of wilderness and the extremes of altitude give the PCT a more rugged and exuberant character than its eastern counterpart, the Appalachian Trail.

The majority of hikers tackle just a short segment of the PCT, but longer segments such as the John Muir Trail from Mt Whitney to Yosemite National Park in California, Mt Jefferson Wilderness in Oregon, or Alpine Lakes Wilderness in Washington are all popular.

HISTORY

Credit the idea of a border-to-border mountain trail to Clinton C Clarke of Pasadena, who formed the Pacific Crest Trail Conference in 1932. This group of hiking and riding clubs worked to link existing trails, such as the John Muir Trail (185mi), the Oregon Skyline Trail (442mi) and Washington's Cascade Crest Trail (445mi), into a continuous wilderness trail. In 1948, the US Congress put the USFS in charge of the project. The PCT was designated a national scenic trail in 1968, and had its first thru-hiker in 1972. The trail through Oregon and Washington was completed in 1987, and in 1993 the PCT was formally declared complete. Today only about 30mi in California remains unprotected; a few segments still follow roads or detour around private land.

NATURAL HISTORY & CLIMATE

See the Natural History sections of (from south to north) the Southwest, Sierra Nevada and Pacific Northwest chapters.

PLANNING
When to Hike

Thru-hikers attempting to complete the trail in one year usually begin in Campo by mid-April and reach Canada by mid-October. Many complete the trail over two years; in the first year, they depart Canada in July,

cross Washington and Oregon, and reach Lassen Volcanic National Park in northern California by mid-September. In the second year, hikers begin in early July at the point where they left off the previous year, cross the high Sierra in late July and August, and reach Mexico by mid-October.

The trail is also frequently divided into five roughly month-long segments hiked during the optimal season over five years: southern California (33 days); central California (44 days); northern California (30 days); Oregon (30 days); and Washington (31 days).

Careful planning is needed in southern California, where it can be days between water in the Sonoran and Mojave Deserts.

See the Southwest, Sierra Nevada and Pacific Northwest chapters for information on the best times to hike various segments of the PCT.

Maps & Books

The USFS sells 1:63,360 topographic maps of the PCT (three for Oregon, two for Washington, but none for California) from its Pacific Northwest Region 6 office. The only accurate and comprehensive PCT guide is the highly recommended *The Pacific Crest Trail – Volume 1: California* and *The Pacific Crest Trail – Volume 2: Oregon & Washington* by Jeffrey P Schaffer et al, which contains black-and-white reproductions of 1:50,000 USGS topographic trail maps. *The PCT Data Book* by Ben Go, a concise handbook detailing mileages, elevation profiles, water sources, nearby facilities and post offices, is available from the Pacific Crest Trail Association (PCTA). *The PCT Hiker's Handbook* by Ray Jardine presents Jardine's ultralight approach to long-distance hiking. Sometimes controversial, and always thought-provoking, anyone considering a long hike should read this.

Information Sources

The USFS administers the trail and provides information from two offices: USFS Pacific Southwest Region 5 (☎ 707-562-8737), 1323 Club Dr, Vallejo, CA 94592, for California; and USFS Pacific Northwest Region 6 at the Nature of the Northwest Visitor

Center (☎ 503-872-2750, fax 731-4066, 🖂 info@naturenw.org, 💻 www.naturenw.org), 800 NE Oregon St, Room 177, Portland, OR 97232, for Oregon and Washington.

The PCTA (☎ 916-349-2109, 888-728-7245, fax 349-1268, 🖂 pctrail@compuserve.com, 💻 www.gorp.com/pcta), 5325 Elkhorn Blvd 256, Sacramento, CA 95842, is the partnership organization.

THE HIKE
Southern California

Starting 50mi east of San Diego at the Mexican border near Campo (east of Tecate) on Hwy 94, the trail winds through chaparral into oak woodland of the Laguna Mountains, skirting the edge of Anza Borrego Desert State Park. Reaching 9000ft in the **San Jacinto Mountains** west of Palm Springs, the trail turns west in the **San Bernardino Mountains** above Los Angeles, where Mt Baden Powell (9399ft) marks the southern high point. The pine-forested mountains east of Los Angeles offer a quick getaway from urban sprawl, so day hikes and overnight trips are popular here. The trail parallels the San Andreas Fault, then turns north to skirt the Mojave Desert along the Tehachapi Range, crossing Hwy 58, and enters the southern Sierra. In the Sonoran and Mojave Deserts it can be days between water.

Central & Northern California

The high Sierra wilderness is crossed by only five roads between Walker Pass at Hwy 178 and Donner Summit at I-80, a distance of more than 275mi as the crow flies, and more than 500mi hiking. Many consider the high Sierra offers the finest mountain hiking in the USA: it boasts 13,000ft and 14,000ft granite peaks, sparkling lakes and streams, and near-perfect weather from June to September. Though popular, the PCT is rarely crowded and apart from sections close to trailheads and in the national parks, hikers experience the vistas and flower-filled meadows in solitude.

The PCT joins the **John Muir Trail** in Sequoia National Park, just west of Mt Whitney (14,496ft), the highest peak in the USA outside Alaska. The trail leaves the park via Forester Pass (13,200ft), the trail's highest point, and enters **Kings Canyon National Park**, where imposing peaks rise above the deep canyons of the Kings River. Heading north, it passes **Devils Postpile National Monument** and enters **Yosemite National Park**, leaving the John Muir Trail at Tuolumne Meadows on Hwy 120. Running north out of the park and over Sonora Pass (9628ft) on Hwy 108, the trail then crosses Ebbetts Pass (8730ft) on narrow Hwy 4, Carson Pass (8573ft) on Hwy 88 and Echo Summit (7382ft) on Hwy 50. Entering popular **Desolation Wilderness** west of Lake Tahoe, the trail passes Alpine Meadows and Squaw Valley ski resorts en route to Donner Summit (7239ft) on I-80.

The trail undulates through deep river valleys in the northern Sierra, whose granite outcrops and domes end a few miles north of Hwy 70. The PCT continues through **Lassen Volcanic National Park**, with its geysers, fumaroles, mud pots and hot springs, and passes east of Lassen Peak (10,457ft), a recently active volcano that marks the southern extent of the Cascade Range. Swinging west, the PCT crosses I-5 south of massive Mt Shasta (14,162ft), traverses the rugged **Trinity Alps** and then turns north through the Marble and Siskiyou Mountains to enter Oregon and recross I-5 south of Ashland.

Oregon

In southern Oregon, the trail is dry and somewhat dreary, but it enters lake-filled wilderness after crossing Hwy 140 en route to **Crater Lake National Park**, where a clear, blue lake – the deepest in the USA – lies in an extinct volcano. Following the Cascade crest north, the PCT crosses Hwy 58 near Willamette Pass (5128ft) and passes glacier-clad extinct volcanoes as it heads north, crossing Hwy 242 and US 20 into Mt Jefferson Wilderness. Continuing north, it crosses US 26 and Hwy 35 and then skirts **Mt Hood** (11,235ft), Oregon's highest summit, en route to the Columbia River, 35mi east of Portland.

Washington

Crossing the Bridge of the Gods in the Columbia River Gorge National Recreation

Area, the PCT climbs out of the damp forest along the river to again attain the Cascade crest. Passing lakes, the trail circles quiescent **Mt Adams** (12,276ft), as massive Mt Rainier (14,408ft) – the range's highest summit – comes into view. After crossing US 12, the trail touches the eastern edge of **Mt Rainier National Park**, passing lakes and meadows. The forested crest east of Seattle is crossed by I-90, which intersects the PCT at Snoqualmie Pass (3022ft). The trail traverses the classic Alpine Lakes Wilderness en route to Stevens Pass (4061ft) on Hwy 2. Entering the rugged Glacier Peak Wilderness, the PCT works north past Glacier Peak (10,568ft). The storm-swept northern Cascades contain more than 750 glaciers; the trail crosses the southeastern corner of **North Cascades National Park** en route to Rainy Pass (4855ft) on Hwy 12. Continuing north along the crest, the PCT reaches the Canadian border and **Manning Provincial Park** and comes to its northern terminus (3800ft) 7.2mi farther on, at Hwy 3.

Florida National Scenic Trail

Duration	85 days (3 months)
Distance	1300mi (2093km)
Start	Big Cypress National Preserve
Finish	Gulf Islands National Seashore

Summary Exploring the USA's subtropical ecosystem, where remarkable wildlife lives amid cypress swamps, pine forests, springs and pools, the trail spans the length of the sunshine state.

Florida, the USA's southernmost state, evokes images of Disney World, Miami, citrus groves, beaches and sunshine. Hiking may not be at the top of the what-do-to-in-Florida list for most travelers, but the near-sea-level, 1300mi-long Florida National Scenic Trail (FT) offers a unique experience that won't disappoint the adventurous hiker.

Designed to showcase Florida's tropical and subtropical ecosystems, the trail begins in south Florida's Big Cypress National Preserve, passes through three national forests and ends at the Gulf Islands National Seashore in Florida's panhandle. Naturalists and birdwatchers will be kept busy as the trail journeys through swamps and forests, crosses rivers and prairie, and passes sandy beaches and fresh springs. Side trails lead to nearby historic sites and other points of interest.

HISTORY

James A Kern, a wildlife photographer and real estate broker, envisioned the Florida Trail in 1964 while hiking along the Appalachian Trail. Soon thereafter, Kern formed the Florida Trail Association (FTA), establishing the framework for today's trail. The US Congress designated it a national scenic trail in 1983 and the first segment was certified in 1986. About 1100mi of the 1300 trail miles are currently open.

NATURAL HISTORY

Florida supports North America's only subtropical landscape and the flora and fauna of Florida's ecosystems are unique to any national scenic trail. Big Cypress National Preserve, characteristic of south Florida, is a pristine swamp where hummocks of orchid- and bromeliad-draped cypress mixed with sabal palm tower above air plants and sawgrass marsh.

Central Florida's lakes and rolling prairie (which stretches from Lake Okeechobee to north of Orlando) support sand pine, sabal palm, and moss-covered live oak trees. One of the world's largest remaining continuous sand pine forests survives in the dry, sandy soil of Ocala National Forest, which also supports palm, live and scrub oak, pond pine, and loblolly bay, an evergreen member of the tea family that bears fragrant, white flowers. The spread and height of the forest canopy and sizable trunk diameter of the slash pine and buckeye trees are impressive.

Low-lying woodlands with little drainage, called flatwoods, are interspersed by marshy terrain and swamps throughout Osceola National Forest. Remnants of old-growth cypress and black gum, bay, and maple are among the hardwood hummocks and pine-covered ridges.

In the flood plains of the Big Bend region, the deep woods of bald cypress, water hickory, American elm, river birch and sweetgum are cleaved by rivers. Turkey oak, post oak, live oak and longleaf pine grow in the drier areas.

Park-like stands of slash- and longleaf pines with their grassy understory cover the flatwoods and sandhills of Apalachicola National Forest. Thickets of titi shrub – with its glossy leaves and elongated clusters of fragrant, white flowers – tupelo-gum swamps, virgin pine- and cypress forests dominate Bradwell Bay Wilderness. In other forested, wet lowlands, cypress, live oak, swamp bay and magnolia thrive. At Apalachicola's western end are wildflower-covered savannas with the largest remaining blocks of natural longleaf pine and wiregrass.

Florida's best known creature, the broadsnouted alligator *(Alligator mississippiensis)*, grows up to 17ft in length. This aquatic predator has no natural enemies and preys on everything from feral hog, dog, cattle and deer to muskrat, beaver, turtle, egret, and fish; attacks on humans are rare. During the day, hikers may spot the nocturnal alligator basking in the sun on a sandy beach or resting in warm waters.

An array of migratory birds visit Florida between November and March. Florida has the world's largest population of red-cockaded woodpeckers and sizable populations of bald eagle, osprey, egret, bobwhite quail, and countless songbirds. Around Lake Okeechobee live two endangered species: the Everglades kite, and the Florida panther (of which only 30 to 50 remain). More commonly seen wildlife include white-tailed deer, wild turkey, bobcat, otter, beaver, black bear, tortoise and armadillo. Florida's swamps are also home to reptiles such as the eastern diamondback and pine and coral snakes.

CLIMATE

Known for its sunshine, Florida has a hot, humid, tropical climate year-round. The hottest, most humid, and rainiest months are from May to September when most of the region's 50-plus inches of annual rainfall occurs. From October to early April temperatures are pleasant, rainfall is low and the insects are least active.

PLANNING
When to Hike

The FT has the advantage of being the only national scenic trail open year-round, but the most pleasant time for hiking is from October to March.

Maps & Books

The *Hiking Guide to the Florida Trail* by N Gildersleeve, only available through the FTA, has trail data and maps for segments on private and public land. The national forests provide good trail maps.

Information Sources

The USFS (☎ 850-942-9300), Woodcrest Office Park, 325 John Knox Rd, Suite F100, Tallahassee, FL 32303-4160, administers the trail and provides information on national forest segments. Contact the Florida Division of Forestry (☎ 850-488-6611, fax 921-6724), 3125 Conner Blvd, Tallahassee, FL 32399-1650, for information about state forest segments – ask for the brochure *A Guide to Your Florida National Scenic Trail*, which has a useful map. The Department of Environmental Protection (☎ 850-488-9872, 🖳 www.dep.state.fl.us/parks), Division of Parks & Recreation, 3900 Commonwealth Blvd, Tallahassee, FL 32399, provides useful information about state parks.

The partnership organization is the FTA (☎ 352-378-8823, 800-343-1882, fax 378-4550), PO Box 13708, Gainesville, FL 32604-1708 and 5415 SW 13 St, Gainesville, FL 32608-5037.

Permits & Fees

Some segments that cross private property (eg, near the Suwannee River, and between US 192 and Hwy 520 near Orlando) are only open to FTA members.

THE HIKE
South Florida

Adjacent to the northern boundary of the 5000-sq-mile Everglades National Park along Florida's gulf coast is the **Big Cypress National Preserve**, the trail's southern terminus. A discontinuous segment of the trail explores these swamps.

The trail resumes farther north at 30mi-wide **Lake Okeechobee**, which it circumnavigates along levees built in the 1940s by US Army Corps of Engineers to control flooding and drain the Everglades. Leaving the lake's northwest shore, this segment follows the banks of the Kissimmee River for just a few miles before ending.

Central Florida

The trail resumes several miles north, following the Kissimmee River to Lake Kissimmee. Near here, the trail divides into eastern and western routes. The main, continuous, eastern route passes east of heavily populated Orlando, where much of the trail is on public land, and then north through Tosohatchee State Reserve, Seminole Ranch Wildlife Management Area, and Little Big Econ and Seminole State Forests. The alternative, western route has discontinuous segments through the Green Swamp Wildlife Management Area, a rail-to-trail project, and through the Withlacoochee State Forest along the old Cross Florida Barge Canal land. The two routes converge at the **Ocala National Forest**, east of the city of Ocala.

Semitropical Ocala, the oldest national forest east of the Mississippi River, is the most heavily used trail segment. The FT wends 65mi around Ocala's rivers, lakes, ponds, springs and sinkholes. Entering Ocala's southern boundary at Clearwater Lake near Paisley Woods, the trail follows the southern boundary of **Billie's Bay Wilderness**. The headwaters of warm Alexander Springs Creek flow east from this marshy area. Passing several lakes, the trail traverses **Juniper Prairie Wilderness** and Hopkins Prairie west of Lake George, with the Salt Springs Spur Trail to the eastern shore of Lake Kerr an easy diversion. The FT continues around the southern and western shores of Lake Kerr, passing well west of Little Lake George Wilderness, and exits the northern boundary of the national forest at Lake Ocklawaha.

North of Ocala National Forest, the trail passes colonial rice plantations. This segment ends northwest of Gainesville near Starke.

Northern Florida

Named for the 19th-century Seminole chief, **Osceola National Forest** contains a marshy 21mi segment. The trail enters the national forest along its southern boundary at Olustee Battlefield, the site of Florida's 1864 Civil War battles. Skirting the northeast shore of Ocean Pond, the trail crosses I-10 and passes by the southwestern boundary of **Big Gum Swamp Wilderness**. Cypress flourish in this riverine wetland where a thick, spongy mat of organic material floats on the restored swamp's surface. The trail leaves the national forest at its western boundary near the Suwannee River.

Several major rivers cut through northern Florida on their way into the Gulf of Mexico. The 240mi-long **Suwannee River**, which flows southwest from its headwaters in southeast Georgia, creates the easternmost boundary of a region known as Big Bend, in reference to the way Florida curves around the gulf's northeasternmost extent. The Big Bend region extends west to the 90mi-long Apalachicola River, whose headwaters are in northwest Florida. Following the Suwannee for many miles, the trail passes spring-fed tributaries, cypress swamps, sandhills and limestone bluffs.

Leaving the Suwannee south of **Twin Rivers State Forest** near the confluence of the Suwannee and Withlocoochee Rivers, the trail runs west across the Aucilla River, sections of which disappear and reappear in the limestone, and reaches the **Aucilla Wildlife Management Area**. An abandoned railroad bed serves as the trail for most of the 41mi along Apalachee Bay through St Marks, one of six national wildlife refuges in the Big Bend region.

As the trail continues west across northern Florida it traverses 66mi of the **Apalachicola National Forest**, southwest of Tallahassee. Within the national forest is **Bradwell Bay Wilderness**, one of the East's largest wilderness areas. The 'trail' here is less about walking and more about wading through waist-deep water. Those who make the effort can see one of the last remaining first-growth cypress forests. North of the FT, a side trip to the Leon Sinks Geological Area reveals a labyrinth of sinkholes, caverns, natural bridges, underground streams and ravines formed by water dissolving the underlying limestone bedrock. At the west end of Bradwell Bay Wilderness, the FT crosses the Ochlockonee River. It continues west, passing north of **Mud Swamp–New River Wilderness**, and crosses the Apalachicola River just beyond the national forest's western boundary.

Steamboats once hauled cotton on the Apalachicola, and artifacts of this era are on display at the **Fort Gadsden Historic Site**, off Hwy 65 near the southwest corner of the national forest. On a plateau above the riverbank, key battles of the First Seminole War and the American acquisition of Florida from Spain were fought, and one of first communities of free African-Americans was formed.

West of Apalachicola, the FT exists only in discontinuous segments. Northwest of Panama City a segment leads through **Pine Log State Forest** to the Choctawhatchee River. Farther northwest, another segment traverses the **Blackwater State Forest**. The final certified segment is in **Gulf Islands National Seashore** on Santa Rosa Island. Stretches of white sand beaches on offshore islands bring hikers to the western terminus at Fort Pickens.

Natchez Trace National Scenic Trail

Duration	30 days
Distance	694mi (1117km)
Start	Natchez, Mississippi
Finish	Nashville, Tennessee

Summary An ancient footpath between the Mississippi and Tennessee river valleys, the trace explores a history older than the USA.

Animal tracks and human footprints formed an ancient *trace* (path) between the lower Mississippi River and the valley of the Tennessee River. The trace was named after the town of Natchez, which in turn was named after a Muskogean tribe that once lived along the lower Mississippi. Centuries of use by Native Americans, explorers, merchants, settlers and soldiers made the trace the most-traveled wilderness route of its time. This rich historic tradition is preserved along the Natchez Trace National Scenic Trail, which traverses three states – Mississippi, Alabama and Tennessee.

The trace arose from the historic necessity of long-distance walking, but today's national scenic trail is better suited to the history buff who likes shorter hikes, rather than the serious hiker looking for a physical challenge or a wilderness experience. The 'deep south' is not known for its hiking. Even so, the notion of thru-hiking has taken hold – with positive reports – despite the fact that much of the trail will remain along roads indefinitely. Numerous short side trails lead to museums, restored buildings, battle sites, ancient burial mounds and other interesting attractions. The hiking is easy and the highest elevation along the trail is only 800ft.

HISTORY

The trace began with Native Americans following animal tracks. The first European to record the trace was Hernando DeSoto, who spent the winter of 1540–41 near present-day Tupelo, Mississippi. French and Spanish settlers first mapped the trace in 1733, and by 1785 it had become a major route. Ohio, Kentucky and Tennessee settlers and traders (called *kaintuck*) floated crops and goods down the Ohio and Mississippi Rivers on flatboats for sale at Natchez and New Orleans, where they dismantled their flatboats, sold them for lumber, and returned home by foot along the trace. For the first 500mi the trace passed through the Choctaw and Chickasaw nations of Mississippi.

The US Army began improvements in 1800, by which time the trace became an official post road. It also served as the route to St Louis, the capital of upper Louisiana, which the USA purchased from France in

1803. Records showed that 10,000 people traveled the trace at its peak in 1810, and the road was used by General Andrew Jackson after his 1815 victory in the Battle of New Orleans. By 1820, almost two dozen *stands* (inns) provided travelers with food and shelter. It was the original road to Texas, and was used by men who died at the Alamo. But the arrival in 1812 of the steamboat on inland waterways ushered in a new era. The steamboats journeyed upriver as far as Nashville, Louisville and St Louis and quickly became the preferred mode of transportation, leading to the trace's decline by the 1830s.

The trace was important in the process of building America and had far-reaching effects. Early explorers passed this way. It was the key to reaching Indiana and the Northwest Territory. And it was the route used to transport slaves – and the road some slaves used to escape. With all this traffic, the trace was known as a dangerous route where robbers prospered.

In the 1900s, the Daughters of the American Revolution and the Daughters of the War of 1812 began marking the vanishing trace with boulders. In 1934, US Congressman Thomas Jefferson (Jeff) Busby of Mississippi introduced a resolution to survey the trail 'with a view to constructing a national road...to be known as the Natchez Trace Parkway', which Franklin D Roosevelt designated as the Natchez Trace National Parkway in 1938.

The 445mi-long Natchez Trace Parkway, a paved road, roughly parallels the historic route. Mileposts line the parkway, indicating its attractions and trailheads. The Natchez Trace National Scenic Trail was designated in 1983, with an initial 694mi authorized as national scenic trail, but the trail is far from complete. In 1987, 110mi were identified for construction, but only 62mi had been built by early 2000. The completed trail segments, all within the boundaries of the Natchez Trace Parkway, are near Rocky Springs, Jackson, and Tupelo in Mississippi, and Nashville in Tennessee. Until more trail segments are built, hikers have to walk along parkway shoulders and pleasant county and state roads.

NATURAL HISTORY

The trace passes through pine and hardwood forests, across rolling hills and meadows, and crosses steep ravines and creeks. Swamps of bald cypress and tupelo are found north of Jackson (Mile 122) and south of Jeff Busby (Mile 175.6). A lovely valley of dogwood trees is at Mile 275. White-tailed deer are abundant in this largely rural and agricultural region.

CLIMATE

From June to September temperatures are hot, often exceeding 100°F, with high humidity. The frequent heavy rain showers during these months can make the trail muddy and wet.

PLANNING
When to Hike

Hiking is most enjoyable during March, April, May, October and November, avoiding the hot, insect- and tick-filled summer.

Maps & Books

The Natchez Trace Parkway is the best source for detailed maps of the completed trail segments. *The Devil's Backbone: The Story of the Natchez Trace* by Jonathan Daniels gives a comprehensive historic account filled with interesting anecdotes. *Traveling the Trace*, a guidebook by Cathy and Vernon Summerlin, helps readers choose the most interesting historical sites.

Information Sources

The NPS (☎ 601-680-402, 800-305-7417) administers the trail from the Natchez Trace Parkway, 2680 Natchez Trace Parkway, RR 1 NT-143, Tupelo, MS 38801. The partnership organization is the Natchez Trace Trail Conference (☎ 601-373-1447), PO Box 1236, Jackson, MS 39215.

THE HIKE
Mississippi

The trail's southern terminus is in **Natchez** along the eastern shore of the Mississippi River, which forms the Mississippi-Louisiana state line. Natchez began as a French trading post in 1714 and grew into

End of an Explorer

In 1803 President Thomas Jefferson picked Meriwether Lewis to lead an expedition called the Corps of Discovery, to search for the Northwest Passage, a water route to the Pacific Ocean (see the boxed text on page 20). In 1806 Lewis, with his co-captain William Clark and other expedition members, returned to St Louis from their successful 8000mi expedition. In 1808, Lewis was appointed governor of the Louisiana Territory. One of the most famous travelers along the Natchez Trace, he died in 1809 of gunshot wounds at Grinder's Stand, 60mi southwest of Nashville. The circumstances of his death – whether it was a murder or suicide – remain a mystery. Lewis is buried next to the Natchez Trace.

the center of the 18th- and 19th-century cotton growing in the deep south. The Natchez National Historic Park in Natchez recalls this rich history.

Between Natchez and Rocky Springs the trace parallels the Mississippi River. A 10mi-long certified segment north of Port Gibson (Mile 40) runs between Russell Rd (Mile 50.8) and Regantown Rd (Mile 59), passing through **Rocky Springs**. The trace continues northeast to Jackson, Mississippi's capital. North of Jackson, a 20½mi-long segment runs along the western shore of Ross Barnett Reservoir between the West Florida Boundary (Mile 108), near Ridgeland, and the Upper Choctaw Boundary (Mile 128½).

Continuing north, the trace passes through the **Jeff Busby** site, where the Little Mountain Overlook is one of Mississippi's highest elevations (603ft). At the western end of Tupelo, a 7mi-long certified segment runs between Chickasaw Village (Mile 261.8) and the Beech Springs parking area (Mile 266). The trail passes through Tishomingo State Park and reaches Buzzard Roost at the Mississippi-Alabama state line.

Alabama & Tennessee

The trace cuts across the northwest corner of Alabama for about 30mi. After Freedom

Hills Overlook (800ft), the trail's high point, the trace crosses the Tennessee River at **Colbert Ferry** and continues to Tennessee. The trace passes the **Meriwether Lewis** grave site and crosses the Duck River at Gordons Ferry west of Columbia. A 24mi-long certified segment between Hwy 50 (Mile 408) and Garrison Creek parking area (Mile 427.6), southwest of Franklin, crosses the Tennessee Valley Divide (Mile 423.9). This formed the boundary between the USA and the Chickasaw Nation to the south when Tennessee became a state in 1796. The trail's northern terminus is southwest of **Nashville** (beyond Mile 440) at Hwy 100.

Potomac Heritage National Scenic Trail

Duration	20 days
Distance	704mi (1133km)
Start	Mt Vernon, Virginia
Finish	Johnstown, Pennsylvania

Summary This gentle trail traces the historic Potomac River route from the nation's capital to the highlands of western Pennsylvania.

The Potomac River and its tributaries flow southeast nearly 400mi from the Allegheny Mountains of West Virginia, Maryland and Pennsylvania into Chesapeake Bay, the USA's largest bay on the Atlantic Ocean. The Potomac, which forms the Virginia-Maryland state line, has served as a corridor into the mountains from colonial times. The 704mi Potomac Heritage National Scenic Trail (PHT) was proposed 'to trace outstanding natural and cultural features of the Potomac River Basin in Virginia, Maryland, Pennsylvania and the District of Columbia'.

The trail, however, is very much a work in progress and its entire route has yet to be designated. The northern half – almost 300mi from Washington, DC, to Johnstown, Pennsylvania – has three major segments in place, but the southern half – envisioned as running along both the Maryland and Virginia banks of the broad Potomac River from Washington, DC, to the river's confluence with the Chesapeake Bay – has yet to be laid out.

The PHT offers hiking within shouting distance of the nation's capital. It follows an almost level path more than 200mi into western Maryland, mostly along the Chesapeake & Ohio (C&O) Canal towpath, which is part of the Chesapeake & Ohio Canal National Historic Park.

HISTORY
President Lyndon B Johnson first proposed the idea of a Potomac trail. The US Congress finally designated it as a national scenic trail in 1983. But the history of its major component, the C&O Canal, begins with the first president, George Washington, who envisioned a water route to transport natural resources from the mountains to the sea ports down the Potomac River. His 'Patowmack Company', organized in 1785, built short 'skirting' canals to bypass rapids on the river, but never achieved substantial success. The 19th century brought a new vision of a continuous canal linking the Chesapeake Bay with the Ohio River. Work began in 1828 and the canal was completed to Cumberland in 1850, but no additional work was done. The C&O Canal operated commercially until 1924, but by then railroads had replaced canals as the movers of freight. The C&O Canal languished and in the 1950s there was talk of paving the towpath to make a superhighway into the mountains. But outdoor enthusiast and Supreme Court Justice William O Douglas organized efforts to save the canal, leading a hike of its entire length in 1954. The canal was proclaimed a national monument in 1961 and named a national historic park in 1971.

NATURAL HISTORY
The tidal Potomac estuary supports cat-tail marshes, where muskrat and hundreds of bird species live. Deciduous poplar, oak, sycamore, beech, blackgum, maple and dogwood provide summer shade and autumn color along the C&O Canal. Deer, partridge and grouse live in the piedmont areas of Maryland and in the Allegheny Mountains, where a few black bears also live. Fragrant laurel blossoms in early June and colorful rhododendron flowers in late June and July decorate the mountains, which burst out in color again in fall.

CLIMATE
July and August tend to be hot and muggy. Rains fall from March to June, with thunderstorms in July and August. September and October have cool, clear days and crisp nights. In the mountains, snow makes foot travel difficult from December to April.

PLANNING
When to Hike
From April to June and from September to November are the most pleasant hiking times. The Laurel Highlands, however, offer respite from the coastal heat and humidity during July and August. Along the C&O Canal, hiking is pleasant on any clear day, even in December.

Maps & Books
The C&O Canal Companion by Mike High covers the PHT's longest segment. *A Hiker's Guide to the Laurel Highlands Trail* is available from the Sierra Club, PO Box 8241, Pittsburgh, PA 15217.

Information Sources
The NPS (☎ 202-619-7027), National Capital Region, Land Use Coordinator, 1100 Ohio Dr SW, Washington, DC 20242, administers the trail from the Mt Vernon Trail/George Washington Memorial Parkway (☎ 703-285-2600, fax 285-2398), Turkey Run Park, McLean, VA 22101. It also manages the Chesapeake & Ohio Canal National Historic Park (☎ 301-739-4200), Box 4, Sharpsburg, MD 21782.

The partnership organization for this trail is the Potomac Heritage Partnership (☎ 202-338-1118), 1623 28th St NW, Washington, DC 20007. Contact the Allegheny Trail Alliance (🖳 www.atatrail.org/ata-info/aboutata.htm) for information about the trail between Cumberland and the Laurel Highlands Trail. Laurel Ridge State Park (☎ 724-455-3744, 🖳 www.parec.com/state_parks/lrlstpk.htm), RD 3, Box 246 Rockwood, PA 15557, provides information about the Laurel Highlands Hiking Trail.

THE HIKE
Virginia & Washington, DC
Beginning at Mt Vernon, George Washington's stately Virginia home on the Potomac River, a paved riverside trail leads 17mi to Theodore Roosevelt Island, passing parks, historic sites, and the Dyke Marsh wetlands. This segment, the **Mt Vernon Trail**, runs through the streets of historic Alexandria and within sight of the Jefferson and Lincoln memorials and the Washington Monument. A footbridge crosses to the island, from where the PHT crosses Key Bridge and descends to the C&O Canal towpath.

Maryland
The approximately 12ft-wide, unpaved **C&O Canal towpath** rises only about 600ft over its 185mi between Georgetown and Cumberland. The first 14mi to the **Great Falls of the Potomac** receive heavy daily usage year-round. Beyond the falls, the trail brings quiet and solitude most of the year. The canal holds water only as far as Violettes Lock (Mile 22), with some short, isolated, watered segments thereafter. At Mile 60, the Appalachian National Scenic Trail joins the towpath for a short segment south of Harpers Ferry. At about Mile 155, the Paw Paw Tunnel carries the canal and towpath 3118ft through the hillside; an alternative hiking trail leads over the top of the tunnel.

Western Maryland & Pennsylvania
Between the C&O Canal and the Laurel Highlands Hiking Trail, the PHT has yet to be designated. The following description follows the PHT corridor, and state and local agencies have endorsed its inclusion into the PHT. From Cumberland, a proposed segment parallels the Western Maryland Scenic Railroad line to Frostburg. From Frostburg, the **Allegheny Highlands Trail** will run north to the Maryland-Pennsylvania state line, then through the 3300ft-long Big Savage Tunnel, passing into the Ohio River watershed. From Meyersdale, Pennsylvania, this rail-to-trail conversion follows the Casselman River, which it crosses via the 1908ft-long Salisbury Viaduct. From Garrett, the rail-to-trail conversion is completed through Rockwood and Markleton, stopping just short of Fort Hill. From Confluence, where the Casselman joins the Youghiogheny River, the completed Youghiogheny Trail leads 10mi through Ohiopyle State Park to Ohiopyle.

The 70mi-long, year-round **Laurel Highlands Hiking Trail** along Laurel Mountain, a scenic ridge of the Allegheny Mountains, passes through state parks and forests, and the well-maintained trail itself is part of Laurel Ridge State Park. The trail rises steeply from Ohiopyle and stays above 2000ft in elevation for most of its length, descending to its northern terminus near Seward, along the Conemaugh River about 8mi northwest of Johnstown.

Ice Age National Scenic Trail

Duration	65 days (2 months)
Distance	1000mi (1610km)
Start	Potawatomi State Park, Wisconsin
Finish	Interstate State Park, Wisconsin

Summary The imprints of North America's great glacial past are revealed through the farms and rolling hills of Wisconsin's dairy country.

Over the last two million years, glaciers advanced and retreated from the Arctic as the earth's climate warmed and cooled. During the last ice age, glaciers covered much of North America, reaching their maximum extent 25,000 to 10,000 years ago. The topography of the Great Lakes state of Wisconsin showcases the imprint of these glaciers. Only Wisconsin's rugged southwest corner, called the Driftless Area, escaped the glacial onslaught.

The Ice Age National Scenic Trail (IAT) traces this glacial history across 1000mi of Wisconsin's rolling plains from the shores of Lake Michigan to the Saint Croix River at the Wisconsin-Minnesota state line. It follows the southernmost extent of the once vast ice sheet along the terminal moraines left behind by the retreating glaciers. More

LONG-DISTANCE TRAILS

than 14,000 glacier-formed lakes and thousands of other recognizable glacial features form an impressive topographic narrative of the ice age. (See the boxed text 'Glaciers & Glacial Landforms' on page 214.)

The trail also meets Wisconsin's four largest rivers – the Wisconsin, Black, Chippewa and Saint Croix – which flow southwest into the Mississippi River. Elevations along the trail range from about 500ft to 1875ft, with a maximum elevation gain of only 800ft, making it one of the more gentle national scenic trails.

HISTORY

In the 1950s, Ray Zillmer of Milwaukee conceived of a trail following the terminal moraines of Wisconsin's last glaciation and proposed the Ice Age Glacier National Forest Park. Activists formed the Ice Age Park and Trail Foundation in 1958, and shortly thereafter volunteers built the first trail segment in Kettle Moraine State Forest. These activists drew US Congressional attention, leading to the creation of the Ice Age National Scientific Reserve in 1971. Administered by the Wisconsin Department of Natural Resources, the nine units of the reserve are spread across the state: Two Creeks Buried Forest; Kettle Moraine State Forest – Northern Unit; Campbellsport Drumlins; Horicon Marsh Wildlife Area; Cross Plains; Devils Lake State Park; Mill Bluff State Park; Chippewa Moraine Recreation Area; and Interstate State Park.

In 1975, the Ice Age Trail Council was formed, accelerating trail-building efforts, and in 1980 the US Congress designated the route a national scenic trail. The state legislature designated it as Wisconsin's first state scenic trail in 1987, and by 1990 the Ice Age Park and Trail Foundation merged with the Ice Age Trail Council. Today 225mi of the trail are certified and an additional 250mi are open.

NATURAL HISTORY

Prairie oak, hickory and maple are predominant in the central and eastern part of the state. In the northwoods, sugar and red maple, basswood, aspen, ash, oak, white birch, red pine, white pine, white spruce and balsam fir predominate, with hemlock in minor amounts. Chequamegon-Nicolet is largely a forest of second-growth red pine planted in the 1930s by the CCC in logged areas.

Black bear, white-tailed deer, bobcat, red fox, showshoe hare, coyote, wild turkey, fisher and pine marten are some of the mammals found in Wisconsin's backcountry. A herd of introduced Rocky Mountain elk thrive in the Chequamegon-Nicolet National Forest. About 150 endangered Great Plains wolves also roam the national forest in 13 packs. Moose herds from neighboring Minnesota and Michigan are occasionally spotted in the northwoods. Beaver and river otter frequent rivers that teem with walleye, perch, bass and trout. Large waterfowl populations include ducks and blue-winged teal, swans, and Canada geese. Wisconsin has the largest population of sandhill cranes in the Great Lakes states. Other notable birds include 200 trumpeter swans and 645 nesting pairs of bald eagles.

CLIMATE

Wisconsin has a continental climate modified by Lakes Superior and Michigan. It is warm and humid from June to August, when it gets about two-thirds of its annual precipitation, frequently as thunderstorms. From November to March it is very cold and snowy.

PLANNING
When to Hike

The eastern ridges are most pleasant from May to mid-October. The central plains and northwoods have a shorter season, from June to late August or early September, before or after which hikers can expect to encounter freezing temperatures.

Maps & Books

On the Trail of the Ice Age: A Guide for Wisconsin Hikers, Bikers, and Motorists by Henry S Reuss, a former US Congressman, is a comprehensive guidebook to the Ice Age National Scientific Reserve and Ice Age National Scenic Trail.

Information Sources

The NPS (☎ 608-264-5610), 700 Rayovac Dr, Suite 100, Madison, WI 53711-2476, administers the trail. The Department of Natural Resources (☎ 608-266-2181, 💻 www.dnr.state.wi.us), Box 7921, Madison, WI 53707, provides information about trail segments on state land and the Ice Age National Scientific Reserve. The Ice Age Park and Trail Foundation (☎ 414-278-8518, 800-227-0046, fax 278-8665, ✉ iat@exec pc.com; 💻 www.iceagetrail.org), 207 E Buffalo St, Suite 505, Milwaukee, WI 53202-5712, is the partnership organization. The Chequamegon-Nicolet National Forest (☎ 715-748-4875), 850 N 8th St, Hwy 13, Medford, WI 54451, provides information about national forest segments.

THE HIKE
Eastern Ridges

The eastern ridges run between the trail's eastern terminus in Potawatomi State Park on the prominent **Door County** peninsula to Janesville in southern Wisconsin. Also known as the Interlobate Moraine, these ridges were formed between the Green Bay and Lake Michigan lobes of the main Wisconsin glacial mass. This coastal area along Lake Michigan is the state's most densely populated farming and industrial region where the trail is at its lowest elevation (about 600ft).

From the shores of Sturgeon Bay, an inlet of Green Bay, the IAT heads south, following the Ahnapee Trail. North of Point Beach State Forest on Lake Michigan, the trail passes through **Two Creeks Buried Forest**. Here, layers of twigs, needles, pine cones and other forest matter are sandwiched between layers of glacial till (rubble), testimony to the glaciers' regular fluctuations.

Continuing through southeastern Fond du Lac County, the trail goes through the Campbellsport Drumlins and the rolling wooded hills of **Kettle Moraine State Forest**. The forest's Northern Unit displays classic examples of *kames* (conical hills formed as debris washed through holes in glacial ice) and *eskers* (mounds of debris deposited by sub-ice streams within a glacier's heart) in

addition to the *kettle holes* (depressions in the ground formed by melting ice blocks) and the *moraines* (piles of glacial till) for which it is named. The trail stays several miles east of Horicon marsh and national wildlife refuge, a reserve unit that is a remnant of the glacial Lake Oshkosh. The trail passes west of Milwaukee, crossing I-94, and enters the Kettle Moraine State Forest's Southern Unit. Swinging southwest, the trail follows railroad corridors to its southernmost point, in quaint **Janesville**.

Central Plains

From Janesville at the eastern edge of the Driftless Area, the trail turns northward towards **Madison**, the state capital. Passing 10mi west of the city, the trail touches a terminal moraine at Cross Plains where glacial meltwater cut a gorge through the bedrock of the Driftless Area.

After crossing the Wisconsin River, the trail rises about 800ft into the quartzite hills of the Baraboo Range and enters the popular **Devils Lake State Park**. Here, a gorge cut by glacial meltwater was dammed by a terminal moraine to form Devils Lake, which is surrounded by wooded hills and nearly 5mi of 500ft bluffs.

To the north, the trail divides. The western branch goes through Mirror Lake and Rocky Arbor State Parks, crossing the Wisconsin River at the gorge known as the **Wisconsin Dells**, and continues north across the flat bed of what was glacial Lake Wisconsin. The eastern branch follows a moraine north to rejoin the western branch southeast of Coloma near US 51. Staying east of US 51 and Stevens Point and Wausau, the trail then meanders along streams, past kettle holes, *drumlins* (elongated whale-back or teardrop-shaped mounds of glacial mud) and lakes, and across an outwash plain.

Northwoods

In the northwoods, a plateau that extends across northern Wisconsin and has the state's highest elevations and greatest concentration of lakes, the trail enjoys several long segments through the Chequamegon-Nicolet National Forest. Passing through an area filled with lakes and bogs, the trail turns 90 degrees westward into the northwoods. In the **Harrison Hills**, the trail reaches its highest point (1875ft) on the shoulder of Lookout Mountain. Crossing US 51 north of where I-39 ends, between Council Grounds and Tomahawk, the trail passes south of **Timms Hill** (1952ft), Wisconsin's highest point; the 10mi-long Timms Hill National Trail makes a good side trip.

Continuing along the crests of eskers, the trail passes through forest and crosses **Brunet Island State Park** along the Chippewa River. The adjacent Chippewa Moraine Recreation Area displays many glacial remnants. Beyond the forested **Blue Hills** is the northernmost point of the trail, along the Tuscobia State Trail at the Red Cedar River.

The trail continues west through dairy country to its western terminus in **Interstate State Park**, Wisconsin's oldest state park, along the Lower Saint Croix, a national scenic riverway forming the Wisconsin-Minnesota state line. Here, a deep gorge was cut by glacial meltwater from Lake Superior.

North Country National Scenic Trail

Duration	295 days (10 months)
Distance	4400mi (7084km)
Start	Crown Point State Park, New York
Finish	Lake Sakakawea, North Dakota

Summary Following the shores of the Great Lakes, the longest of the national scenic trails offers diversity of landscape through the USA's heartland.

The USA's northern border with Canada along the Great Lakes – Ontario, Erie, Huron, Michigan and Superior – is the setting for the North Country National Scenic Trail (NCT). The longest of the eight national scenic trails, it crosses seven states – New York, Pennsylvania, Ohio, Michigan, Wisconsin, Minnesota and North Dakota.

The NCT takes hikers through a glacier-carved landscape from the northeastern mountains and hardwood forests, past Midwestern farms, along the shores of the Great Lakes, by the streams and lakes of Wisconsin and Minnesota, and across the grasslands of the Great Plains to the Missouri River in North Dakota. The diverse landscape includes nine national forests and several state parks and forests that offer wilderness and near-wilderness experiences.

HISTORY

The USFS conceived the trail in the mid-1960s for hikers to experience the Great Lakes landscape, and the 1968 National Trails System Act proposed its inclusion in the system. In 1980, the US Congress designated it a national scenic trail. Originally estimated at 3200mi, it now stretches almost 4400mi, with about 1400mi certified and more than another 1000mi hikable.

NATURAL HISTORY

Across the north country, stream-cut gorges in the glacial landscape offer cool, moist habitats where hemlock thrives, including some of the few remaining stands of tall old-growth hemlock in Allegheny National Forest and Michigan's upper peninsula. Beaver flourish in the area's abundant lakes, streams and wetlands, where bass, pike, perch and muskellunge draw both fishermen and fish-eating ospreys and bald eagles. Relatively warmer Ohio has oak and hickory forests where deer, turkey, grouse, opossum and raccoon thrive. Northern Michigan is famous for summer blueberries, and the trail traverses hemlock and cedar forests and maple and ash woodlands across Michigan, Wisconsin and Minnesota. Black bears live in these woods, where timber wolves once again roam. In North Dakota, occasional stands of bur oak dot the tall grass prairie where greater prairie chickens and sandhill cranes nest.

CLIMATE

Despite its great length, most of the trail lies in the same climate zone. Winters from December to March are cold and snowy. May brings warmer and longer days, and during July and August days are hot and often humid. September and October bring cooler days and chilly nights, but clear skies. By November, early storms can feature snow, but days are clear and crisp.

PLANNING
When to Hike
July and August are the peak hiking months, although the trail carries hikers from April to November. In June and early July, however, swarms of mosquitos and biting deer flies descend.

The weather rules out a single-season thru-hike, so thru-hikers usually complete the trail over two years by hiking five months each year. To actually hike every inch of the trail, one must participate in the annual Labor Day Mackinac Bridge walk – every other day of the year the bridge is closed to pedestrian traffic and hikers have to ride in a vehicle.

Maps & Books
North Country Trail Association (NCTA) is the best source for maps and books, such as *Following the North Country National Scenic Trail* by Wes Boyd – although not a guidebook, this describes the entire trail; and *Certified Segments of the North Country Trail* by Byron and Margaret Hutchins – this features detailed information and maps in loose-leaf form.

Information Sources
The NPS (☎ 608-264-5610), 700 Rayovac Dr, Suite 100, Madison, WI 53711, administers the trail. The NCTA (☎ 616-454-5506, 888-454-6282, fax 454-7139, ✉ nct assoc@aol.com, 🖥 www.northcountry trail.org), 49 Monroe Center NW, Suite 200B, Grand Rapids, MI 49503, is the partnership organization. The NCT is more than 1000mi longer than the next-longest national scenic trail, so it is necessary to contact state-specific information sources in addition to the NPS and NCTA; the most useful sources follow.

For New York segments, the Finger Lakes Trail Conference (☎ 716-288-7191, ✉ fltc@axsnet.com), PO Box 18048, Rochester, NY 14618-0048, is the best source. For Ohio segments, contact the Buckeye Trail Association (🖥 www.neohio .net/bta), PO Box 254, Worthington, OH 43085.

These national forests, listed by name, provide indispensable information:

Allegheny
(☎ 814-723-5150) 222 Liberty St, PO Box 847, Warren, PA 16365
Wayne
(☎ 740-592-6644) 219 Columbus Rd, Athens, OH 45701-1399
Manistee
(☎ 616-775-2421, 800-821-6263) 1755 S Mitchell St, Cadillac, MI 49601
Hiawatha
(☎ 906-786-4062) 2727 N Lincoln Rd, Escanaba, MI 49829
Ottawa
(☎ 906-932-1330) 2100 E Cloverland Dr, Ironwood, MI 49938
Chequamegon-Nicolet
(☎ 715-762-2461) 1170 Fourth Ave S, Park Falls, WI 54552
Chippewa
(☎ 218-335-8632) Route 3, Box 244, Cass Lake, MN 56633
Custer
(☎ 701-683-4342) Box 946, Lisbon, ND 58054

The following state Department of Natural Resources (DNR) or Parks and Recreation offices provide information on segments in state parks and forests:

New York State Office of Parks, Recreation and Historic Preservation
(☎ 518-474-0456) Attn Trails Coordinator, Empire State Plaza, Agency Building 1, Albany, NY 12238-0001
DNR Harrisburg
(☎ 717-787-6640, 888-727-2757, 🖥 www.dcnr.state.pa.us) Bureau of State Parks, Trails Program, PO Box 8551, Harrisburg, PA 17105-8551
DNR Columbus
(☎ 614-265-6561, 🖥 www.dnr.state.oh.us/odnr/parks) 1952 Belcher Dr C-3, Columbus, OH 43224-1386
DNR Lansing
(☎ 517-373-9900, 🖥 www.dnr.state.mi.us) PO Box 30028, Lansing, MI 48909-7528
DNR Spooner
(☎ 715-635-4121, 🖥 www.dnr.state.wi.us) 810 W Maple St, Spooner, WI 54801

DNR St Paul
(☎ 651-296-6157) 500 Lafayette Rd, St Paul, MN 55155-4052

North Dakota Parks & Recreation Department
(☎ 701-328 5357, 🖳 www.state.nd.us/nd parks) 1835 Bismark Expressway, Bismark, ND 58504

THE HIKE
New York
The eastern terminus is at Crown Point State Historic Site on Lake Champlain in northeastern New York. Extension plans call for a link with Vermont's Long Trail, which links with the Appalachian National Scenic Trail. The NCT's route westward through the huge **Adirondack Park**, a forested mountain wilderness, has not been formally designated. Leaving the west side of the park near Boonville, the NCT picks up the Old Black River Canal towpath to Rome, then heads west along the Old Erie Canal towpath to Canastota, where the trail turns south along an abandoned rail line to Cazenovia. The NCT then joins the **Finger Lakes Trail** for about 390mi, passing sweeping views and numerous gorges and waterfalls, to Allegany State Park. Of New York's 625 trail miles, 550mi are continuously marked, mostly off-road.

Pennsylvania
The first 100mi of Pennsylvania's 300 trail miles traverse the rolling, forested hills of the state's northwestern Allegheny National Forest, passing old-growth hemlock in the **Tionesta National Scenic Area** and into Cook Forest State Park. A long, non-certified segment of NCT continues southwest to a certified segment through **Moraine** and **McConnell's Mill State Parks** and the Slippery Rock Gorge, north of Pittsburgh on I-79. The NCT picks up Little Beaver Creek and follows it to the Pennsylvania-Ohio state line west of the town of Beaver Falls.

Ohio
Paralleling Little Beaver Creek – a national scenic river – westward, the proposed NCT joins the **Buckeye Trail** south of Canton at Bolivar. This travels for 600mi through a series of state parks and a long segment of **Wayne National Forest** in the rolling hills of southern Ohio. East of Cincinnati, the NCT turns north and follows the Little Miami National Scenic River. The NCT skirts east of Dayton to Troy, where it rejoins the Buckeye Trail, which runs through Dayton. Continuing north, the NCT follows a segment of the old **Miami and Erie Canal**, then leaves the Buckeye Trail and follows a short stretch of the Wabash Cannonball Trail west of Toledo before heading north into Michigan. About half of Ohio's 1050mi are along roads.

Michigan
Michigan has 1150mi of NCT and more certified trail than any other state. Running northwest from the Michigan-Ohio state line, the NCT passes Hillsdale and Battle Creek, then turns north – passing east of Grand Rapids – to reach the **Manistee National Forest** along Lake Michigan's eastern shore, where there is more than 170mi of attractive, sandy trail. Continuing north through Pere Marquette and Mackinaw State Forests, the NCT crosses the Straits of Mackinac via a 5mi-long bridge to Michigan's scenic upper peninsula. Crossing the peninsula through the Hiawatha National Forest, the trail reaches Lake Superior, then runs 44mi through **Pictured Rocks National Lakeshore** – one of the most beautiful segments, where colorful sandstone cliffs afford vistas over the deep-blue lake. Heading west, the NCT crosses rivers and gorges through wilderness segments of the **Porcupine Mountains** and Ottawa National Forest to reach the Michigan-Wisconsin state line near Ironwood on US 2.

Wisconsin
The NCT dips into Wisconsin's remote northwoods for 220mi, meandering through the quartzite hills of the Penokee Mountains. The trail follows a westerly course, first visiting **Copper Falls State Park** with its many beautiful waterfalls. At nearby Mellen on Hwy 13, the trail enters the lake-dotted **Chequamegon-Nicolet National Forest**, where a 60mi-long segment passes through

the mixed hardwood and conifer forests of the Porcupine and Rainbow Lake wilderness areas. It exits the national forest at County Rd A, 5mi south of the town of Iron River on US 2. The trail continues west on county land, and then through **Brule River State Forest**. It crosses US 53 at Solon Springs and heads southwest, following the **Saint Croix National Scenic Riverway** for several miles. Turning north, the trail goes about 40mi through wetlands and over wooded ridges en route to the Wisconsin-Minnesota state line just south of Duluth, Minnesota.

Minnesota

The trail traverses 375mi of forested north-central Minnesota from east to west, past a myriad of lakes and rivers. Crossing the St Louis River on a suspension bridge, the NCT enters Jay Cooke State Park near Lake Superior's western tip. It meanders north-west to the Chippewa National Forest, where a 68mi-long segment along the forest's southern boundary skirts Leech Lake, one of the forest's 1321 lakes. The trail continues west through Paul Bunyan, Itasca and White Earth State Forests; a detour to the source of the Mississippi River, at Lake Itasca, is possible from Itasca State Forest. Turning southwest, the trail passes through the Tamarac National Wildlife Refuge and Maplewood State Forest before heading west again to the Minnesota–North Dakota state line.

North Dakota

North Dakota's 475mi of NCT begin at Fort Abercrombie State Historic Site in the agricultural Red River valley, south of Fargo in the state's southeastern corner. The fort once guarded merchants traveling the river to Canada and prospectors traveling to Montana's gold mines. From here, a 25mi-long segment cuts west through the **Sheyenne National Grassland**, one of the state's three national grasslands.

The trail then follows the heavily-wooded **Sheyenne River valley** through Sheyenne State Forest and Fort Ransom State Park, both near Lisbon. Continuing north along the river, the trail meanders through rolling hills and prairie and reaches the Devils Lake Sioux Indian Reservation. Along the southern shore of Devils Lake within the reservation is Fort Totten State Historic Site.

Rejoining the course of the Sheyenne River, a long, continuous segment heads southwest and then follows canals west to Audubon Lake. Along the lake's southern shore is the Audubon National Wildlife Refuge, which protects more than 220 bird species. The western terminus of the NCT is at nearby **Lake Sakakawea**, a 180mi-long dammed lake on the Missouri River. I-83 runs between the two lakes, and leads south to Bismark at I-94. From Lake Sakakawea, the Lewis and Clark National Historic Trail follows the Missouri River west.

Glossary

AAA – American Automobile Association, usually called 'triple-A'
Amtrak – national, government-owned railroad company
AT – Appalachian National Scenic Trail
ATM – Automated Teller Machine; electronic means for extracting cash from banks
avalanche slope – a steep slope kept largely treeless by the action of winter avalanches

backcountry – anywhere away from roads or other major infrastructure
bald – 'natural' clearing below treeline
basalt – a hard, dense and very common volcanic rock; solidified lava
bench – a naturally occurring terrace of rock or earth
bivouac or **bivvy** – basic shelter under a rock ledge; tent-like bag for one person
blaze – stripe of paint on a tree or rock, serving as a trail marker
BLM – Bureau of Land Management.
blowdown – also *falldown*; tree felled by a storm
bouldering – hopping from one rock to the next; climbing rocks without ropes or protection
branch – creek or stream (southern states)
butte – a prominent hill or mountain standing separate from surrounding ranges

cairn – pile or stack of rocks used to indicate the route or a trail or a trail junction, usually in treeless country
cascade – small waterfall
CCC – Civilian Conservation Corps, a federal program established in 1933 to employ single, unskilled men, usually in conservation or construction projects in national parks and wilderness lands.
CDT – Continental Divide National Scenic Trail
chamber of commerce – association of businesses that commonly provides a tourist information service
chinook – dry, warm, westerly wind on the east side of the Continental Divide

cirque – rounded, high ridge or bowl formed by past glacial action
clear-cutting – a destructive logging practice in which every tree over a large area is felled, regardless of size, species or usefulness as marketable timber
col – mountain pass
contiguous USA – see *Lower 48*
Continental Divide – major watershed separating east-flowing (to the Atlantic) from west-flowing (to the Pacific) streams
contour – to sidle around a hill at approximately the same altitude (or contour level)
creek – small stream; pronounced 'crick' in the Rocky Mountains; see also *branch*
cutoff – a shortcut trail

destination hike – hiking route finishing somewhere other than the starting point
diapensia – alpine tundra plants adapted to survive in severe climates
DMV – Department of Motor Vehicles
DNR – Department of Natural Resources
dogleg – a very long switchback
downvalley – towards the valley foot
draw – a desert watercourse, usually dry but subject to flash flooding; also called a *wash*
dropoff – an abrupt cliff
drumlin – a hill of glacial rubble (or 'till') with a streamlined or teardrop profile, shaped by the effect of advancing glacial ice
dude ranch – a ranch or farm that caters for paying guests

East, the – generally, states east of the Mississippi River
erratic – a boulder carried by glacial ice and deposited some distance from its place of origin
esker – serpentine ridge of gravel and sand, formed by streams under or in glacial ice

falldown – also *blowdown*; a tree that has fallen down in a forest, often as the result of a severe storm
flip-flops – rubber sandals; thongs

foot – base of a mountain; lower end of a valley or lake; see also *head*

ford – to cross a river by wading

fork – a branch or tributary of a stream or river

forty-niner – a prospector who came to California for the gold rush of 1849

14er, 14-thousander – a peak of 14,000ft or more; also, 13er

frontcountry – opposite of *backcountry*

FT – Florida National Scenic Trail

gap – mountain pass or saddle; also called a notch

glacial till – also glacial drift; gravel, sand or clay transported and deposited by a glacier or glacial meltwater

gorp – acronym for 'good ol' raisins and peanuts', commonly used when referring to *trail mix*

GPS – global positioning system; an electronic, satellite-based network that allows for the calculation of position and elevation using a hand-held receiver/decoder

graded – leveled road or trail

granite – coarse-grained, often grey, rock formed by the slow cooling of molten rock ('magma') deep within the earth

guard station – USFS post

gulch – narrow ravine cut by a river or stream

head – the uppermost part of a valley, or the upvalley end of a lake; see also *foot*

headwall – the often very precipitous rocky *cirque* at the uppermost end of a valley

HI/AYH – Hostelling International/American Youth Hostels

hoodoo – fantastically shaped rock formation produced by weathering

hookup – facility at a campsite for giving an *RV* water and/or electricity

IAT – Ice Age National Scenic Trail

isthmus – narrow stretch of land connecting two larger land masses

kame – conical ridge or mound formed as debris washed through holes in retreating glacial ice

kettle hole – deep, kettle-shaped depression in glacial drift

KOA – Kampgrounds of America; a private chain of campgrounds throughout the USA

krummholz – wind-twisted, stunted trees found near treeline

lean-to – simple shelter, usually without walls, windows or doors, with a steeply slanting roof that touches the ground on one side

limestone – sedimentary rock composed mainly of calcium carbonate

loop – a hiking route that returns to its starting point without backtracking; a circuit

Lower 48 – the 48 states of the continental (or 'contiguous') USA, ie, not including Alaska or Hawaii

mesa – Spanish word for elevated tableland or plateau

midden – domestic 'rubbish heap', often of shells or bones, marking a prehistoric Native American settlement

monkeywrenching – the sabotaging of logging or other equipment to prevent its use in environmentally sensitive areas

moraine – ridge, mound or irregular mass (mostly boulders, gravel, sand and clay) deposited at the snout or along the flanks of a glacier

morteros – hollows in rocks used by Native Americans for grinding corn, acorns and seeds; also called metates

narrows – a section of trail through high, narrow canyon walls

NCT – North County National Scenic Trail

no-see-um – a biting midge or sand-fly

NPS – National Park Service

NRA – National Recreation Area. Similar to a wilderness area, but allows some controlled development and motorized use; also National Rifle Association.

NTT – Natchez Trace National Scenic Trail

obsidian – a black, glassy volcanic rock commonly used by Native Americans to make cutting tools.

one-way – of a hike, having widely separated start and finish points; also called point-to-point

out-and-back – of a hike, a route that backtracks to its starting point from its destination

outfitter – business supplying guides, equipment and/or transport for fishing, canoeing, hiking, rafting or horseback trips
overlook – a lookout (above a scenic feature)

park – a valley clearing
PCT – Pacific Crest National Scenic Trail
petroglyph – a type of rock-art in which the design is pecked, chipped or abraded into the surface of the rock
PHT – Potomac Heritage National Scenic Trail
pictograph – a work of rock-art in which the design is painted or dyed onto the surface of the rock
point-to-point hike – see *destination hike*
privy – pit toilet at a campsite
pullout – a short roadside loop; a layby

quad – short for 'quadrangle'; generally, a topographical map in the USGS 1:24,000 series
quartzite – white or grey sandstone composed primarily of quartz grains

ridgeline – crest of a ridge, often used for travel through alpine areas
route – feasible passage from one place to another
RV – recreational vehicle, also called a motor home or camper

saddle – low place in a ridge
sandstone – sedimentary rock composed of sand grains
scramble – to climb a steep slope with the help of your hands
scree – weathered rock fragments at the foot of a cliff or on a hillside; also called *talus*
scrub – thick, low vegetation difficult to walk through
shuttle – hiker transportation to a trailhead
shuttle hike – a *destination hike* where it is necessary to leave a vehicle at both trailheads
sidle – to move across a slope; to *contour*
sign – (in animal tracking) evidence of the presence of a species in an area, especially scat but including tracks, hair etc
slack-packing – an AT term for a hiker who is having their pack transported from point to point by someone else (usually in a car)

slickrock – large expanse of exposed rock that has been sculpted and smoothed by erosion
snowline – level below which snow seldom falls and does not remain on the ground
South, the – generally, the states of Louisiana, Alabama, Mississippi, Tennessee, Kentucky and Georgia
spur – small ridge that leads up from a valley to a main ridge; small branch of a main trail
stage – individual section of a long walk
switchback – route that follows a zigzag course up or down a steep grade

talus – see *scree*
tarn – a small mountain lake
thru-hiker – anyone who hikes the entire length of a long-distance trail (generally in one season)
timberline – upper limit of forest; also *treeline*
topo – (contoured) topographical map
towpath – a path along the bank of a canal or river, primarily for use in towing boats
trail mix – snack-food mixture of nuts, dried fruit, seeds and/or chocolate
trapper – a fur-trader or hunter such as those who opened up much of the West
traverse – to move horizontally across a slope
treeline – uppermost (natural) level to which tree cover extends on a mountainside
triple-A – American Automobile Association (AAA)
tundra – stunted alpine vegetation found at the uppermost level above timberline

upvalley – towards the valley head
USFS – United States Forest Service, which manages the nation's system of national forests
USGS – United States Geological Survey, the national cartographic organization

wash – a watercourse in the desert, usually dry but subject to flash flooding; also called a *draw*
West, the – generally, states west of the Rocky Mountains
wilderness – an (officially designated) primitive area
wildfire – an out-of-control forest fire

LONELY PLANET

You already know that Lonely Planet produces more than this one guidebook, but you might not be aware of the other products we have on this region. Here is a selection of titles which you may want to check out as well:

USA
Alaska
California & Nevada
Deep South
Florida
New England
Hawaii
New York, New Jersey &
  Pennsylvania
Pacific Northwest
Rocky Mountains
Southwest USA
Texas
Virginia & the Capital Region
Chicago
Las Vegas
Los Angeles
Miami
New Orleans
New York City
San Francisco
Seattle
California condensed
New York City condensed
Boston city map
Chicago city map
Los Angeles city map
Miami city map
New York city map
San Francisco city map
World Food Deep South, USA
Diving & Snorkeling California's
  Central Coast
D & S Florida Keys
D & S Hawaii
D & S Monterey Peninsula &
  Northern California
D & S Southern California
Diving & Snorkeling Texas
Hiking in Alaska
Caught Inside
Drive Thru America
USA phrasebook

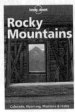

LONELY PLANET

Guides by Region

Lonely Planet is known worldwide for publishing practical, reliable and no-nonsense travel information in our guides and on our web site. The Lonely Planet list covers just about every accessible part of the world. Currently there are fifteen series: travel guides, Shoestrings, Condensed, Phrasebooks, Read This First, Healthy Travel, Walking guides, Cycling guides, Pisces Diving & Snorkeling guides, City Maps, Travel Atlases, Out to Eat, World Food, Journeys travel literature and Pictorials.

AFRICA Africa on a shoestring • Africa – the South • Arabic (Egyptian) phrasebook • Arabic (Moroccan) phrasebook • Cairo • Cape Town • Cape Town city map • Central Africa • East Africa • Egypt • Egypt travel atlas • Ethiopian (Amharic) phrasebook • The Gambia & Senegal • Healthy Travel Africa • Kenya • Kenya travel atlas • Malawi, Mozambique & Zambia • Morocco • North Africa • Read This First Africa • South Africa, Lesotho & Swaziland • South Africa, Lesotho & Swaziland travel atlas • Swahili phrasebook • Tanzania, Zanzibar & Pemba • Trekking in East Africa • Tunisia • West Africa • Zimbabwe, Botswana & Namibia • Zimbabwe, Botswana & Nambia Travel Atlas • World Food Morocco**Travel Literature:** The Rainbird: A Central African Journey • Songs to an African Sunset: A Zimbabwean Story • Mali Blues: Traveling to an African Beat

AUSTRALIA & THE PACIFIC Auckland • Australia • Australian phrasebook • Bushwalking in Australia • Bushwalking in Papua New Guinea • Fiji • Fijian phrasebook • Healthy Travel Australia, NZ and the Pacific • Islands of Australia's Great Barrier Reef • Melbourne • Melbourne city map • Micronesia • New Caledonia • New South Wales & the ACT • New Zealand • Northern Territory • Outback Australia • Out To Eat – Melbourne • Out to Eat – Sydney • Papua New Guinea • Pidgin phrasebook • Queensland • Rarotonga & the Cook Islands • Samoa • Solomon Islands • South Australia • South Pacific • South Pacific Languages phrasebook • Sydney • Sydney city map • Sydney Condensed • Tahiti & French Polynesia • Tasmania • Tonga • Tramping in New Zealand • Vanuatu • Victoria • Western Australia
Travel Literature: Islands in the Clouds • Kiwi Tracks: A New Zealand Journey • Sean & David's Long Drive

CENTRAL AMERICA & THE CARIBBEAN Bahamas, Turks & Caicos • Bermuda • Central America on a shoestring • Costa Rica • Cuba • Dominican Republic & Haiti • Eastern Caribbean • Guatemala, Belize & Yucatán: La Ruta Maya • Jamaica • Mexico • Mexico City • Panama • Puerto Rico • Read This First Central & South America • World Food Mexico
Travel Literature: Green Dreams: Travels in Central America

EUROPE Amsterdam • Amsterdam city map • Andalucía • Austria • Baltic States phrasebook • Barcelona • Berlin • Berlin city map • Britain • British phrasebook • Brussels, Bruges & Antwerp • Budapest city map • Canary Islands • Central Europe • Central Europe phrasebook • Corfu & Ionians • Corsica • Crete • Crete Condensed • Croatia • Cyprus • Czech & Slovak Republics • Denmark • Dublin • Eastern Europe • Eastern Europe phrasebook • Edinburgh • Estonia, Latvia & Lithuania • Europe on a shoestring • Finland • Florence • France • French phrasebook • Germany • German phrasebook • Greece • Greek Islands • Greek phrasebook • Hungary • Iceland, Greenland & the Faroe Islands • Ireland • Italian phrasebook • Italy • Krakow • Lisbon • The Loire • London • London city map • London Condensed • Mediterranean Europe • Mediterranean Europe phrasebook • Munich • Norway • Paris • Paris city map • Paris Condensed • Poland • Portugal • Portugese phrasebook • Portugal travel atlas • Prague • Prague city map • Provence & the Côte d'Azur • Read This First Europe • Romania & Moldova • Rome • Russia, Ukraine & Belarus • Russian phrasebook • Scandinavia & Baltic Europe • Scandinavian Europe phrasebook • Scotland • Slovenia • Spain • Spanish phrasebook • St Petersburg • Sweden • Switzerland • Trekking in Spain • Tuscany • Ukrainian phrasebook • Venice • Vienna • Walking in Britain • Walking in Ireland • Walking in Italy • Walking in Spain • Walking in Switzerland • Western Europe • Western Europe phrasebook • World Food Ireland • World Food Italy • World Food Spain
Travel Literature: The Olive Grove: Travels in Greece

INDIAN SUBCONTINENT Bangladesh • Bengali phrasebook • Bhutan • Delhi • Goa • Hindi & Urdu phrasebook • India • India & Bangladesh travel atlas • Indian Himalaya • Karakoram Highway • Kerala • Mumbai (Bombay) • Nepal • Nepali phrasebook • Pakistan • Rajasthan • Read This First: Asia & India • South India • Sri Lanka • Sri Lanka phrasebook • Trekking in the Indian Himalaya • Trekking in the Karakoram & Hindukush • Trekking in the Nepal Himalaya
Travel Literature: In Rajasthan • Shopping for Buddhas • The Age Of Kali

Mail Order

Lonely Planet products are distributed worldwide. They are also available by mail order from Lonely Planet, so if you have difficulty finding a title please write to us. North and South American residents should write to 150 Linden St, Oakland CA 94607, USA; European and African residents should write to 10a Spring Place, London, NW5 3BH; and residents of other countries to PO Box 617, Hawthorn, Victoria 3122, Australia.

ISLANDS OF THE INDIAN OCEAN Madagascar & Comoros • Maldives • Mauritius, Réunion & Seychelles

MIDDLE EAST & CENTRAL ASIA Bahrain, Kuwait & Qatar • Central Asia • Central Asia phrasebook • Dubai • Hebrew phrasebook • Iran • Israel & the Palestinian Territories • Israel & the Palestinian Territories travel atlas • Istanbul • Istanbul City Map • Istanbul to Cairo on a shoestring • Jerusalem • Jerusalem City Map • Jordan • Jordan, Syria & Lebanon travel atlas • Lebanon • Middle East • Oman & the United Arab Emirates • Syria • Turkey • Turkey travel atlas • Turkish phrasebook • World Food Turkey • Yemen
Travel Literature: The Gates of Damascus • Kingdom of the Film Stars: Journey into Jordan • Black on Black: Iran Revisited

NORTH AMERICA Alaska • Backpacking in Alaska • Baja California • California & Nevada • California Condensed • Canada • Chicago • Chicago city map • Deep South • Florida • Hawaii • Honolulu • Las Vegas • Los Angeles • Miami • New England • New Orleans • New York City • New York city map • New York Condensed • New York, New Jersey & Pennsylvania • Oahu • Pacific Northwest USA • Puerto Rico • Rocky Mountain • San Francisco • San Francisco city map • Seattle • Southwest USA • Texas • USA • USA phrasebook • Vancouver • Washington, DC & the Capital Region • Washington DC city map
Travel Literature: Drive Thru America

NORTH-EAST ASIA Beijing • Cantonese phrasebook • China • Hong Kong • Hong Kong city map • Hong Kong, Macau & Guangzhou • Japan • Japanese phrasebook • Japanese audio pack • Korea • Korean phrasebook • Kyoto • Mandarin phrasebook • Mongolia • Mongolian phrasebook • North-East Asia on a shoestring • Seoul • South-West China • Taiwan • Tibet • Tibetan phrasebook • Tokyo
Travel Literature: Lost Japan • In Xanadu

SOUTH AMERICA Argentina, Uruguay & Paraguay • Bolivia • Brazil • Brazilian phrasebook • Buenos Aires • Chile & Easter Island • Chile & Easter Island travel atlas • Colombia • Ecuador & the Galapagos Islands • Healthy Travel Central & South America • Latin American Spanish phrasebook • Peru • Quechua phrasebook • Rio de Janeiro • Rio de Janeiro city map • South America on a shoestring • Trekking in the Patagonian Andes • Venezuela
Travel Literature: Full Circle: A South American Journey

SOUTH-EAST ASIA Bali & Lombok • Bangkok • Bangkok city map • Burmese phrasebook • Cambodia • Hanoi • Healthy Travel Asia & India • Hill Tribes phrasebook • Ho Chi Minh City • Indonesia • Indonesia's Eastern Islands • Indonesian phrasebook • Indonesian audio pack • Jakarta • Java • Laos • Lao phrasebook • Laos travel atlas • Malay phrasebook • Malaysia, Singapore & Brunei • Myanmar (Burma) • Philippines • Pilipino (Tagalog) phrasebook • Read This First Asia & India • Singapore • South-East Asia on a shoestring • South-East Asia phrasebook • Thailand • Thailand's Islands & Beaches • Thailand travel atlas • Thai phrasebook • Thai audio pack • Vietnam • Vietnamese phrasebook • Vietnam travel atlas • World Food Thailand • World Food Vietnam

---

ALSO AVAILABLE: Antarctica • The Arctic • Brief Encounters: Stories of Love, Sex & Travel • Chasing Rickshaws • Lonely Planet Unpacked • Not the Only Planet: Travel Stories from Science Fiction • Sacred India • Travel with Children • Traveller's Tales

Index

Text

A

access issues 63
acclimatization, *see* altitude
  problems
accommodations 83-5
Acute Mountain Sickness
  (AMS) 93
Adams, Ansel 334
African-Americans 18, 50, 51,
  483
Agness 435, 436
Agnew Meadows 397
air travel
  airports 103
  baggage 105-6
  buying tickets 103-5, 107-
    10, 111-12
  domestic airlines 111
  fares 103-5, 107-10, 111-12
  international airlines 104
  to/from the USA 103-10
  travel passes 105, 112
  within the USA 105, 111-13
Alaska Basin 246-7
Alexandria 487
altitude problems 59-60, 90, 93
Alum Cave 173-7, **175**
American Discovery Trail 22
Anderson, George 360
Angels Landing 309
Antelope Wells 475
Apalachee Bay 482
Apgar 209
Appalachian Trail 21, 22, 170,
  468, 470-3, 492
  in Maine 124-32, 160-1
  in Maryland 487
  in New Hampshire 160-1
  in North Carolina 176-7,
    177-81
  in Tennessee 176-7, 177-81
  in Vermont 152-5
  in Virginia 181-4, 184-9, 198
Arapaho Pass 264-5
archeology 483
  industrial & agricultural 125,
    170-3, 189, 265, 271-2,
    288, 320, 323, 327, 328,
    483
  marine 157
  Native American 456
area codes 75

Artist Point 461
Ashford 451
Ashland 408
Aspen 265-6
Augusta 219
Avalanche Divide 246
Ayres, Thomas 357

B

backpacking, *see* hiking
banana slug 456
Bar Harbor 133-4
Bearpaw Meadow 380-1
bears 38, 64, 87, 100-1, 168,
  205, 208, 209, 212, 213,
  216, 219, 220, 225, 231,
  234, 235, 236, 241, 249,
  252, 275, 276, 334, 357,
  369, 401, 407, 434, 435,
  437, 438, 439, 463, 486,
  490, *see also* safe hiking
bedbugs 99
Beech Springs 485
bees 99
Behunin, Isaac 300
Belknap Crater 427-9, **428**
Bellingham 409, 460
Benchmark 219, 220
Bend 410, 411, 423-4, 427
Bennington 153
Beston, Henry 159
bicycle travel 121, *see also*
  outdoor activities
Bierstadt, Albert 251
Big Bend 481, 482
Big Cataloochee,
  see Cataloochee
Big Hole Valley 477
Big Meadows 257
Big Pine 401
Big Sandy Pass 249
Bigfoot 459, 460
Bighorn Flats 256
Bird Woman Falls 212
birds 40-2, *see also*
  birdwatching
birdwatching 157, 173, 219,
  237, 241, 256, 432, 480, *see*
  also birds, wildlife spotting
Bishop 388, 392

blisters 92
Blue Hills 490
body temperature 94
Bolivar 492
books 77-9
Boring, William 170
Boulder (Colorado) 207
Boulder (Utah) 311, 312, 317,
  319
Boulder Mail Trail 319-22, **321**
Boulder Pass 273
Bozeman 206
breathing rate 94
Brewer, William H 332
Bridgeport 346-8
Bridger, Jim 17
Brookings 411, 432
Brower, David 47, 282
Bryce 295
Bryce, Ebenezer & Mary 294
Buckskin Gulch 325-6
bus travel
  baggage 113
  bus stations 114
  buying tickets 113-14
  fares 113-14
  to/from the USA 110
  tours 115
  travel passes 105, 114, 115
  within the USA 105, 113-15
Busby, Thomas Jefferson (Jeff)
  484
business hours 81-2
Buzzard Roost 485

C

C&O Canal 473, 486
Cabot, John 17, 18
Cades Cove 162, 167, 168
Campo 477, 479
campsites & campgrounds 83,
  85
Canastota 492
canoeing, *see* outdoor activities
Canyon (town) 234
canyons
  Black Canyon of the
    Yellowstone 275
  Blodgett Canyon 270
  Bryce Canyon 293-9, 317

Bush Head Canyon 328
Grand Canyon 24, 278,
    281-93, 317
Grand Canyon of the
    Yellowstone 234-6
Granite Canyon 247
Huggins Canyon 438
Kern Canyon 374, 381
Kings Canyon 401
Lost Canyon 378
Lyell Canyon 369-70, **371**
Marble Canyon 283
Matterhorn Canyon 353, 355
Mule Creek Canyon 438
Muley Twist Canyon (Upper
    & Lower) 311-15, **313**
Paintbrush Canyon 243
Paria Canyon 322-9, **325**
Piute Canyon 393
Refrigerator Canyon 309
Sweetwater Canyon 476
Tapeats Canyon 292-3
Trampas Canyon 273
Virginia Canyon 399
Whiteoak Canyon 196-8
Wildcat Canyon 308
Zion Canyon 300-9, **306**
canyoneering see outdoor
    activities
Cape Alava 456-8, **458**
Cape Cod 18, 156-60, 161
Capitol Gorge 310
Capitol Reef 309-17
Captain Truckee 336
car travel
    car rentals 119-20
    car sharing 120
    drive-away cars 120-1
    driver's licenses 120
    driving distances & times
    118
    highway numbers 117
    insurance 110, 119-20
    road rules 117-19
    to/from the USA 110
    within the USA 117-21
Carrington expedition 241
Carson 415
Carson, Christopher 'Kit' 17,
    332, 346
Carson Pass 348-9, **349**, 350,
    399, 479
Carson, Rachel 46
Cartier, Jaques 18

Cascade Locks 412
Cascade Pass 463-5, **465**
Cataloochee 170-3, **172**
Cathedral Peak 369
Cathedral Valley 309
Cazenovia 492
Cedar Grove 376
Cedar Run 196-8
cell phones 102
Chamberlain's Ranch 304
Charlies Bunion 177
Cherokee 166-7
Chesapeake Bay 485
Chicago Basin 272
Chickasaw Village 485
Chief Tenaya 357
Chihuahuan Desert 24
children
    hiking with 64-5
    traveling with 106
Chinese Wall 219-25, **222**, 477
Cirque of the Towers 248-51,
    250
Clallam Bay 457
Clark, Galen 357
Clark-Skidmore party 351
Clark, William, see Lewis &
    Clark expedition
Clarke, Clinton C 22, 478
climate 24
    climate charts 25-6
Clinton, Bill 19, 22, 47, 317
clubs, hiking 65-6
Colbert, Edwin H 22
Colbert Ferry 485
Colter Bay 242
Colter, John 17, 232
Columbia Gorge 411-15, 465,
    479-80
Columbus 17, 18
Concrete 464
Confluence 487
Congress Trail 400
conservation, see ecology &
    environment
conservation movement 28-47,
    history of 21
consulates 70-1
Continental Divide Trail 468,
    474-7
    in Colorado 272
Cook, Dan 171
Cook, James 18
Cooke City 225
Coos Bay 410, 430
Cornando 281
Cortés 17

counter-balance method 87
Crabtree Falls 181-4
Craggy Gardens 201
Cross Florida Barge Canal 482
Cuba (New Mexico) 475
Cumberland 486, 487
customs regulations 71-2, 106

D

Damascus 185-6
Dana, Charles Dwight 370
Dawson Pass 274
de Cabrillo, Juan Rodríguez 18
de Cárdenas, García López 281
de Champlain, Samuel 132, 147
de Coronado, Francisco 17, 18
Death Canyon Shelf 246
Death Hollow 319
dehydration 94
Denver 206
DeSoto, Hernando 483
Detroit 466-7
Devil's Postpile 396, 398, 401
diarrhea 95-6
discounts, student 70
diseases, see health
documents 67-70
Donner party 336
Douglas, William O 486
Drake, Francis 18
Driftless Area 487, 489
drinks 87-8
Dunraven, Lord 251
Dutton, Clarence 281

E

Eagle Creek Trail 411-13, **413**
East Glacier (town) 209
Eastham 158
Ebbets, John 346
ecology & environment 26-47
electricity 80
Elk Park 179
email, see also Internet
    access 76-7
embassies 70-1
emergencies, see safe hiking
emergency transponders 102
endangered species 42-5
Enterprise 419
Enumclaw 453
environmental concerns, see
    ecology & environment,
    endangered species
equipment 55-9
Escalante 317, 318-19

Bold indicates maps.

Estanislao 346
Estes Park 252
Estes, Joel 251
Eugene 408, 410-411, 427
Evolution Basin 392-6, **394**

F
fauna 36-45
fax services 76
first aid 89, 97-8
fishing, see outdoor activities
fitness 59-60
Flagstaff 281
flora 30-6
Florida Trail 468, 480-3
food 85-7, 91, 92
Forks 466-7
Fort Pickens 483
fossils 282, 287
Four Lakes Basin 271
Franklin Pass 377-80, **379**
Franklin, Ben 51
Frémont, John Charles 309
    332, 335, 346, 386
Fresno 359
frostbite 95
Frostburg 487
Fruita 310, 311, 312
fungal infections 96

G
Galice 435, 436
Gardiner 231, 275
Gardiner, James 332
Garrett 487
Gatlinburg 166
geography 22-4
geology 23, 24, 133, 282, 317,
    483
geothermal areas,
    see volcanoes & hot springs
Glacier (town) 459, 460-1
Glacier Gorge 258-9
Glacier Point 399
glaciers 24, 133, 137, 156,
    213, 214, 217-19, 226,
    240, 241, 247, 249, 260,
    269, 273, 336, 350, 353,
    358, 398, 401, 402, 408,
    423, 446, 447, 450, 451,
    455, 459, 462, 463, 466-7,
    476, 477, 479, 480, 487-90
    Ahern 213
    Andrews 258
    Arapaho 264-5
    Castle Rock 228-9

Emmons 453-5, 466
    Grinnell 216-17
    Isabelle 262
    Jackson 218
    Lewis 425
    Lyell 370
    Nisqually 452
    Palisade 401
    Sahale 465
    Sandy 417
    Schoolroom 246
    Sperry 218-19
    Swiftcurrent 211, 274
    Teton 276
    Tyndall 256
global positioning system 55,
    102
Gold Beach 432, 434, 435, 436
gold rushes 19, 21, 332, 336,
    346, 357, 374, 433, 440,
    446, 493
Gold Valley 445-6
Gordons Ferry 485
government departments 65
GPS 55, 102
Grace Meadow 351-3
Grand Canyon, see canyons,
    national parks & reserves
Grand Lake (town) 252-3, 475
Grand Staircase, see national
    parks & reserves
Granite Pass 259-60
Grant Grove 372, 376
Grant Village 234
Grants Pass 410, 411, 432,
    435-6
Great Basin Desert 24
Great Divide Basin 476
Great Falls 206
Gregory Bald 168-70, **169**
Grey, Zane 439
Grinnell, George Bird 207
guidebooks
    health 90
    hiking 77-8
guided hikes 61-2

H
Half Dome, see mountains &
    peaks
Hampton 179
Hance, John 281
Harbor 432
Harpers Ferry 473, 487
Harrison Hills 490
Hayden, Ferdinand 233

health 59-60, 89-102
heat exhaustion 94
Heather Meadows 459, 461
heatstroke 94-5
helicopters 102
hepatitis 96-7
Hermitage Point 276
Hickman Natural Bridge 315-17
High Sierra Trail 380-82, **382**
hiking
    access issues 63
    clubs 65-6
    environmental
        considerations 62-3
    equipment 55-9
    guidebooks 77-8
    guided hikes 61-2
    itineraries 52-3
    permits 69
    route descriptions 60
    safety, see safe hiking
    seasons 53
    standards 60-1
    with children 64-5
    women 63-4
hiking festivals
    National Trails Day 82
Hill, Julia 46
history, US 17-22
hitchhiking 63, 121
Hoffman, Charles F 332
Hoh Rainforest 466-7
holidays
    hiking 61-2
    public 82-3
Hopkins, Mark 336
hot springs, see volcanoes &
    hot springs
hours, business 81-2
Hudson, Henry 147
Humphrey, JW 294
Humphreys Basin 392-6, **394**
100 Mile Wilderness 124-32,
    160-1
hunting 101
Hutchings, James Mason 357
hygiene 91
hypothermia 95

I
Ice Age Trail 468, 487-90
Ickes, Harold 374
Idaho Falls 206
immunizations 89
Indian Garden 289

Indian Henry's Hunting Ground 448-51, **450**
Indian Point Meadows 220, 221, 224, 225
insurance
  health 89
  travel 69-70, 89
  vehicle 110, 119-20
Internet 77, *see also* online resources
  access 76-7
itineraries 52-3
Ives, Joseph 281

J

Jackson 137-8, 242, 484, 485
Jackson, Andrew 484
Jackson Hole 241, 476
Jackson, William 233
Jamestown 18
Janesville 489
Jefferson, Thomas 17, 20, 202, 485
Jenny Lake (town) 242
Jewel Basin 269-70
John Muir Trail 330, 368-9, 369-70, 381-2, 382-6, 392, 396, 397, 398, 399, 401, 361-2, 478, 479
Johnson, Lyndon B 468, 486
Johnson, Noel 310
Johnson, Robert Underwood 357
Johnstown 485
Jones, Hathaway 437
Joseph 419
Joyce Kilmer Memorial Forest 201
Judy Springs 192
Junction Meadow 385-6

K

Kaibab Trail 286-9, **287**
Kalispell 206
Kanab 302-3, 324
kayaking, *see* outdoor activities
Kearsarge Pass 401
Kennedy brothers 351
Kennedy Meadow 351, 353
Kennedy, John F 19, 47
Kennedy, Robert 19
Kern, James A 480
King, Clarence 332

Bold indicates maps.

King, Martin Luther Jr 19
Kings Canyon 401
Kittatinny Ridge 473
Kolob Arch 305-7

L

La Grande 409, 410
La Salle 18
Lake Placid (town) 148
Lake Plateau 275
lakes
  Atsina Lake 215
  Audubon Lake 493
  Avalanche Lake 151
  Bagley Lakes 461, 462
  Basin Lakes 246
  Bear Lake 253, 255-8
  Becker Lake 226
  Benson Lake 355
  Bierstadt Lake 255
  Big Sandy Lake 249-51
  Black Lake 258
  Blue Lake 421
  Blue Lakes 399
  Bluebird Lake 276
  Bowman Lake 273
  Brainard Lake 262
  Caribou Lake 264, 265
  Cathedral Lakes 368-9, **369**
  Chain Lakes 459-62, **462**
  Clearwater Lake 482
  Cold Lakes 270
  Columbine Lake 378
  Consultation Lake 382, 392
  Cosley Lake 215
  Cracker Lake 273
  Crater Lake (Indian Peaks) 262
  Crater Lake (Maroon Bells) 268
  Crown Lake 355
  Devils Lake 489, 493
  Dicks Lake 343-5
  Donner Lake 336
  Dorothy Lake 351
  Echo Lake 342
  Ediza Lake 397
  Elizabeth Lake 215, 216
  Emerald Lake 256
  Emigrant Meadow Lake 351
  Enchantment Lakes 441-4, **443**
  Evolution Lake 395
  Fallen Leaf Lake 336
  Fern Lake 255
  Fourth of July Lake 349-50, **350**, 399

Franklin Lakes 378
Galena Chain Lakes, *see* Chain Lakes
Glacier Lake 422
Gladys Lake 398
Glass Lake 258
Glenns Lake 215
Grand Lake 252-3, 255-8
Green Lake 399
Green Lakes 423-5, **424**
Grinnell Lake 217
Gunsight Lake 218
Hamilton Lake 381
Heart Lake (New England & Adirondacks) 149, 151
Heart Lake (Rockies) 236-7, **237**
Helen Lake 216
Henrys Lake 477
Hidden Lake 219
Holly Lake 243
Iceberg Lake 273, 462
Inspiration Lake 444
Island Lake (Beartooths) 226, 229
Island Lake (Wind River Range) 276
Jackson Lake 241, 242, 276
Jenny Lake 242, 245
Kinta Lake 273
Lake Champlain 148, 492
Lake Chelan 463
Lake Colden 150
Lake Ellen Wilson 218
Lake Erie 490
Lake Granby 475
Lake Helene 253
Lake Huron 17, 490
Lake Isabelle 262
Lake Itasca 493
Lake Josephine 216, 217
Lake Katherine 273
Lake Kerr 482
Lake Kissimmee 482
Lake Lucille 343
Lake McDonald 218
Lake Michigan 487, 488, 489, 490, 492
Lake Nanita 257
Lake Ocklawaha 482
Lake Okeechobee 480, 481, 482
Lake Ontario 490
Lake Oshkosh 489
Lake Powell 282, 317, 324
Lake Sakakawea 493
Lake Superior 488, 490, 492, 493

lakes *(cont)*
  Lake Tahoe 330, 335-45, 398-401, 479
  Lakes of the Clouds 140-1
  Lawn Lake 276
  Leech Lake 493
  Little Claire Lake 378
  Little Five Lakes 400-1
  Loch, the 258
  Loch Leven 393
  Lonesome Lake 251
  Lost Twin Lakes 270
  Lower Monarch Lake 330, 380, 400
  Marion Lake 247
  Maroon Lake 266
  Martin Lake 228
  Maxwell Lake 353
  May Lake 399
  McDonald Lake 270
  Mills Lake 258
  Minam Lake 419-21
  Minaret Lake 397-8
  Mirror Lake 392 (Pacific Northwest), 418-22
  Mirror Lake (Sierra Nevada) 392
  Mirror Lakes 451
  Mistymoon Lake 270
  Mokowanis Lake 215
  Mollman Lakes 270
  Monarch Lake 261-2, 264
  Mono Lake 370
  Moraine Lake 381
  My Lake 223
  Nahmakanta Lake 126-7
  North Lake (Rockies) 249
  North Lake (Sierra Nevada) 393
  Odessa Lake 253-5
  Ouzel Lake 276
  Park Lakes 445-6
  Pawnee Lake 262
  Peeler Lake 353-5
  Pinto Lake (Rockies) 271
  Pinto Lake (Pacific Northwest) 401
  Piute Lake 393
  Ptarmigan Lake 216
  Rae Lakes 382-6, 401, **384**
  Rainbow Lake 128-9
  Rainbow Lakes (Indian Peaks) 265
  Rainbow Lakes (Absaroka-Beartooth) 275
  Ridge Lake 445-6, 446-7
  Rosalie Lake 398
  Rubicon Lake 345
  San Leonardo Lakes 273
  Sawtooth Lake 271
  Shoshone Lake 476
  Showers Lake 349
  Siberia Lake 269
  Snow Lakes 442-3
  Snowmass Lake 269
  Snyder Lakes 218
  South Lake 393, 395-396
  Sparks Lake 424
  Spectacle Lake 446
  Stoney Indian Lake 213, 215
  String Lake 243, 245
  Sue Lake 213
  Sunburst Lake 274-5
  Sunrise Lakes 367, 368
  Sunset Lake 246
  Swiftcurrent Lake 216, 217
  Tenaya Lake 367-8, **368**
  The Loch 258
  Trampas Lakes 273
  Two Medicine Lake 274
  Upper Golden Trout Lake 393
  Upper Twin Lake 353, 355
  Wallowa Lake 418
  Wanda Lake 395
  Waterton Lake (Canada) 273, 477
  West Ten Sleep Lake 270
  Williams Lake 273
  Wood Lake 219
  Wright Lake 228, 229
  Yellowstone Lake 476
Lakes Basin 418-22, **420**
Lakeside 429
language 50-1
  Chinook 414
  Native American 50, 51, 441
Las Vegas 280
laundry 81
Laurel Highlands 486
Leavenworth 409, 441, 442
Lee Vining 348, 387
Lees Ferry 323, 328-9
Leopold, Aldo 46
Lewis & Clark expedition 17, 18, 20, 202, 232, 402, 411, 477
Lewis, Merriweather, *see* Lewis & Clark expedition
lice 99
lightning 102
Lincoln, Abraham 19, 357
Little Cataloochee, *see* Cataloochee
Loch, the 258

Loch Leven 393
Loch Vale 258-9
logging, *see* ecology & environment
Lone Pine 380, 387-8, 390
Lonely Dell 329
Long Trail **154**, 468, 473, 492
Long, Stephen 202, 251
long-distance trails 22, 48, 468-493, **469**, *see also* names of individual trails
  history of 22
  thru-hiking 131, 152, 185, 471, 472, 478, 483
Longmire 447, 449, 466-7
Longmire, James 447
Loowit Trail 467
Lyme disease 97

M

MacKaye, Benton 21, 471
McKenzie Bridge 426-7
Mackinac Bridge walk 491
McNeil Point 416-18, **417**
McNichol, Gracie 175
magazines 79
mail, *see* postal services
Mammoth 234
Mammoth Lakes (town) 388-9, 396
Manchester 124
Many Glacier (town) 208-9, 216
maps 54-5, 61
Marblemount 463, 464
Marcy Dam 151
Marial 438-9
Markleeville 346
Markleton 487
Maroon Bells 266-9, **267**
Marshall, Robert 46, 219
Mason-Dixon Line 473
Mather, Stephen P 300
Mayflower 18, 156
measures 80-1, 82
Medford 408, 410, 432, 433, 435
medical kit 90
medical problems, *see* health
Mellen 492
Meyersdale 487
Millinocket 126
Mills, Enos 251
Minarets, the 396-8, **397**
Mineral King 377, 378-80, 400
minimum-impact hiking 62-3

Missoula 206
Mist Falls 382-5
mobile phones 102
Mojave Desert 24, 478, 479
money 72-4, 407
    taxes 74, 107
Montebello 181
Moose (town) 242
Moraga, Gabriel 374
Moran, Thomas 233
Moss, Noel 310
motorcycle travel 121, *see also*
    car travel
mountain bark beetle 236
mountain building, *see* geology
mountain ranges
    Absaroka 225-9, 275, 476
    Adirondack 22, 24, 122-61,
        150, 492
    Allegheny 22, 189-95, 201,
        485, 486, 487
    Appalachian 22, 23, 24, 28,
        162-201, 470-3
    Baldface 143-7, **145**
    Baraboo 489
    Barren Chairback 160
    Beartooth 24, 225-9, **227**,
        275
    Beaverhead 477
    Berkshire 473
    Big Hatchet 475
    Bighorn 23
    Bitterroot 23, 270, 477
    Black 475
    Blue 473
    Blue Ridge 22, 177-84, 201,
        473
    Carson 335, 339-40, 340-2,
        346
    Carter-Moriah 143-147,
        145
    Cascade 23, 24, 48, 402,
        404, 411-15, 416-18,
        422-9, 440-7, 447-55,
        458-62, 477, 479-80
    Cathedral 368-9
    Catskill 22
    Centennial 477
    Coastal 24
    Collegiate 271, 475
    Crystal 342-5
    Elk 265-9
    Ferris 476
    Franconia 160-1

Front 252, 260-5
Great Smoky 22, 165-77,
    201
Great Western Divide 330,
    372, 377-80, 380-2, 400
Green 22, 122, 152-5, 160-
    1, 468
Gros Ventre 476
Inconsolable 395
Kinsman 160-1
Klamath 434
Laguna 479
Lewis 212-16, 217-19, 274
Mahoosuc 473
Marble 479
Medicine Bow 23
Minarets, the 396-8, **397**
Mission 270
North Cascade 462-5
Olympic 24, 455-8, 466-7
Penokee 492
Pioneer 477
Porcupine 492
Presidential 136-43, **139**
Red 236
Ritter 396-8
Rocky 17, 22-3, 28, 48, 50,
    202-77, **203**, 468, 474-7
San Bernardino 479
San Jacinto 479
San Juan 23, 271-2, 475
Sangre de Cristo 272-3
Sawtooth 23, 271
Seminole 476
Sierra Madre 22, 476
Sierra Nevada 21, 23, 24,
    28, 330-401, **331**, 477,
    479
Siskiyou 479
Smoky, *see* Great Smoky
Stuart 441-4
Swan 269-70
Tehachapi 479
Teton 23, 240-7, 276, 476,
    477
Trinity Alps 479
Wallowa 418-22
White 136-47, 160-1, 386
Wind River 23, 247-51,
    276, 476
mountains & peaks
    Ahern Mountain 274
    Alaska Mountain 445-6
    Alta Mountain 445
    Anderson Peak 398
    Bald Mountain 155, 416-18
    Banner Peak 396

Baxter Peak (Mt Katahdin),
    127, 132
Bear Mountain 215-16, 473
Blackbird Knob 192-5, **194**
Blackfoot Mountain 218
Broken Top 423
Burroughs Mountain 453-5,
    455
Buzzard Rock 188
Cabezon Peak 475
Cadillac Mountain 135-6
Camel's Hump 160-1
Carter Dome 146
Castle Rock Mountain 229
Cathedral Mountain 309
Cathedral Peak 213
Champlain Mountain 134
Chikamin Peak 446
Citadel Mountain 218
Cliff Mountain 221
Clingmans Dome 176, 472
Cloud Peak 270-1
Clouds Rest 367-8
Craggy Pinnacle 201
Diamond Peak 475
Dog Mountain 413-15, **415**
Donner Peak 398
Dorr Mountain 135-6
Eagle Cap 418
Echo Summit 348-9, **349**,
    479
Eighteenmile Peak 477
El Capitan 357
Electric Peak 275
Elephants Back 350
Fairchild Mountain 276
Fifty Mountain 213
Flattop Mountain 253, 255-8
Flinsch Peak 274
Fremont Peak 276
Froze-to-Death Mountain
    275
Fusillade Mountain 218
Gauley Mountain 201
Glacier Peak 421, 422, 480
Glastenbury Mountain 154
Granite Peak 275
Grays Peak 475
Greatheart Mesa 308
Gulf Hagas Mountain 160
Gunsight Mountain 218
Half Dome 23, 357, 360-5,
    367, 368,
Hallet Peak 256
Haystack Mountain 224-5
Hump Mountain 180
Iroquois Peak 150

mountains & peaks *(cont)*
Kendall Peak 445
Killington Peak 473
Kings Peak 271
Lassen Peak 479
Laurel Mountain 487
Lemah Mountain 446
Lincoln Peak 218
Little Mountain 485
Livingston Range 211
Lizard Head Peak 251
Lonesome Mountain 228
Longs Peak 258, 259-60
Lookout Mountain 490
Mammoth Mountain 386, 396
Marlette Peak 340-2
Maroon Bells 266-9, **267**
Mary Mountain 275-6
Middle Sister 422, 427
Moro Rock 400
Mt Adams 447, 480
Mt Ararat 450
Mt Baden Powell 479
Mt Belford 271
Mt Dana 370-2, **371**
Mt Eisenhower 140
Mt Franklin 140
Mt Greylock 473
Mt Grinnell 211
Mt Hight 146
Mt Hoffman 399-401
Mt Hood 416-18, 479
Mt Jackson 218
Mt Jefferson 141, 466-7
Mt Judah 398-401
Mt Katahdin 124-32, **127**, 471, 473
Mt Leconte 173-7
Mt Lincoln 398
Mt Lyell 369-70
Mt Maclure 370
Mt Madison 141
Mt Marcy **150**, 151
Mt Marshall 150
Mt Mitchell 201
Mt Monroe 140
Mt Moran 243
Mt Morgan 274
Mt Olympus 466-7
Mt Oxford 271
Mt Pierce 139
Mt Rainier 402, 447, 448, 451, 454, 466-7, 480
Mt Ritter 396
Mt Rogers 184-9, **186**

Mt Rose 339-40, **339**
Mt St Helens 404, 415, 447, 467
Mt Shasta 479
Mt Sheridan 236, 237
Mt Shuksan 459, 461
Mt Tallac 345, 398
Mt Taylor 475
Mt Washburn 234-6, **235**
Mt Washington 136, 427, 428, 473
Mt Whitney 330, 358, 374, 377, 378, 380-2, 386, 389-92, **390**, 478, 479
Mt Woodring 243
Mt Wuh 253
Mt Yale 271
Nesuntabunt Mountain 128
Nipple, the 399
North Baldface 147
North Sister 422, 425-7
Northgate Peaks 306-8
Old Rag 198-201
Owl Mountain 132
Palisade Crest 401
Pawnee Peak 262
Peaks of Otter 201
Pectol's Pyramid 316
Peregrine Peak 175
Pine Mountain 187
Pine Valley Peak 307
Pingora Peak 251
Prairie Reef 220-1
Priest, the 183
Rainbow Mountain 129
Red Arch Mountain 309
Red Mountain 445
Relief Peak 351
Rendezvous Mountain 242, 247
Roan Mountain 177-81, **180**
Rockchuck Peak 243
Rocky Mountain 251-60
Round Top 349-50
Sahale Mountain 465
Salt Mountain 222
San Pedro Mountain 475
Sawtooth Peak 330, 400
Snow Valley Peak 342
South Baldface 147
South Mountain 473
South Sister 422, 423-5
Spooner Summit 340-2, **341**
Springer Mountain 471, 472
Spruce Knob 190-2, **191**
Stone Mountain 187

Straight Mountain 189
Swan Peak 274-5
Swiftcurrent Mountain 209-11, 274
Table Mountain 459-62
Tea Creek Mountain 201
Tempest Mountain 275
Temple, the 443
Tinker Knob 398
Trapper Peaks 270
Triple Divide Peak 273-4
Wahcheechee Mountain 213
Wheeler Peak 272-3
White Cap Mountain 160
Whitetop Mountain 187-8
Mt Leconte Lodge 174, 176
Muir Pass 392-6
Muir, John 28, 47, 330, 332, 334, 357, 358, 395, 400, *see also* John Muir Trail
Multnomah Falls 465-7
Murkowski, Frank 22
Murray, Stan 180

N

Nashville 484, 485
Natchez 483, 484, 485
Natchez Trace Trail 468, 483-5
national forests 48
Allegheny 490, 491, 492
Apalachicola 481, 482
Arapaho 260
Big Horn 270-1
Bridger-Teton 476
Carson 272, 475
Chattahoochee 472
Chequamegon-Nicolet 488, 489-90, 491, 492
Cherokee 472-3
Chippewa 491, 493
Cibola 475
Custer 225, 491
Deer Lodge 477
Deschutes 406, 423
Dixie 299
Eldorado 334, 335, 348-9, 350
Flathead 270
Gallatin 225
George Washington 181-4, 473
Gifford-Pinchot 406, 415, 449
Gila 475
Green Mountain 152-5, 473
Gunnison 265
Hiawatha 491, 492

Inyo 334, 348, 387, 389
Jefferson 473
Kaibab 285, 290
Manistee 491, 492
Medicine Bow–Routt 476
Mono Basin 348
Monongahela 189-95, 201
Mt Baker–Snoqualmie 406, 444, 454, 459
Mt Hood 406
Nantahala 201, 472
Ocala 480, 482
Okanogan 406
Olympic 406
Osceola 480, 482
Ottawa 491, 492
Pisgah 472-3
Plumas 334
Rio Grande 475
Rogue River 406
Roosevelt 260
Salmon 477
San Juan 475
Santa Fe 475
Sequoia 334, 377
Shoshone 225
Sierra 334
Siskiyou 406, 434
Siuslaw 430
Stanislaus 334, 350, 351
Tahoe 335, 336
Targhee 240, 476
Toiyabe 335, 341, 346, 350, 353, 398-401
Umatilla 406
Wallowa-Whitman 406, 418-22
Wasatch 271
Wayne 491, 492
Wenatchee 406, 441, 444, 454
White Mountain 136-43, 143-7, 473
White River 265
Willamette 406, 423, 425, 466-7
national parks & reserves 47-9
Acadia National Park 132-6, **135**
Arapaho National Recreation Area 262
Arches NP 278
Audubon National Wildlife Refuge 493

Big Cypress National Preserve 480, 482
Bryce Canyon NP 293-9
Canyonlands NP 278
Cape Cod National Seashore 156-60, **159**, 161
Capitol Reef NP 309-17
Chesapeake & Ohio Canal National Historic Park 486
Columbia Gorge National Scenic Area 406, 479-80
Columbia River Gorge NRA 479-80
Crater Lake NP 479
Delaware Water Gap NRA 473
Devil's Postpile National Monument 398, 479
Dinosaur NM 46
El Malpais NM 475
Everglades NP 481-2
Glacier NP 21, 24, 48, 207-19, **210**, 273-4, 474, 477
Glen Canyon NRA 323
Grand Canyon NP 281-93
Grand Staircase–Escalante NM 47, 317-22, 323
Grand Teton NP 24, 240-7, **244**, 276
Great Smoky Mountains NP 162, 165-77
Gulf Islands NS 480, 483
Horicon NWR 489
Ice Age National Scientific Reserve 488-90
Kings Canyon NP 372-86, **373**, 400-1, 479
Lake Chelan NRA 463
Lassen Volcanic NP 478, 479
Mt Rainier NP 21, 402, 447-55, 466-7, 480
Mt Rogers NRA 184-9, 473
Mt St Helens National Volcanic Monument 467
Natchez NHP 485
North Cascades NP 406, 459, 462-5, 480
Olympic NP 455-8, 466-7
Oregon Dunes NRA 429-31
Pictured Rocks National Lakeshore 492
Red Rock Lakes NWR 477
Rocky Mountain NP 24, 251-60, **254**, 276, 474, 475
Ross Lake NRA 463
St Marks NWR 482
Sawtooth NRA 271

Sequoia NP 330, 358, 372-86, **373**, 387, 392, 400-1, 479
Shenandoah NP 195-201, **198**, 472, 473
Sheyenne National Grassland 493
South Pass National Historic Landmark 476
Springer Mountain NRA 472
Spruce Knob–Seneca Rocks NRA 190-2
Tamarac NWR 493
Tionesta National Scenic Area 492
Waterton Lakes NP (Canada) 207, 477
Yellowstone NP 19, 21, 47, 48, 229-40, 275, 474, 476
Yosemite NP 47, 48, 345, 353-5, 355-72, **356**, 387, 399-401, 360-5, 478, 479
Zion NP 48, 280, 300-9
National Scenic Trails, see individual trail names, long-distance trails
National Trails Day 82
Native Americans 17, 18, 20, 21, 50
language 50, 51, 414
rock-art 18, 310, 323, 328, 456
stories 125, 293, 300, 363, 413, 447, 460
Naturalist Basin 271
nature tours 133
Navajo Knobs 315-17, **316**
Neah Bay 456
Nederland 261
Needle Falls 224
Nevada Trail 361, 363
New England & Adirondacks 122-61, **123**
New York 17, 18
Nixon, Richard 19
North Bend 444
North Conway 144
North Country Trail 468, 490-3
North Rim 285
northern spotted owl 27, 456

O
Obsidian Cliffs 425-7, **426**
Obsidian Falls 427
Ohiopyle 487

Bold indicates maps.

Old Faithful (town) 234
Olmstead, Frederick Law 357
Olympic Games 19, 148
100 Mile Wilderness 124-32, 160-1
O'Neill, Buck 286
online resources 77, *see also* Internet
   health 90-1
   hiking equipment 59-60
   rental cars 119
   travel agencies 103, 104-5
   weather 79
   women hikers 64
opening hours 81-2
Oregon Coast Trail 429, 431-3
Oregon Dunes 429-1, **430**
Oregon Trail 21, 204, 402, 411, 476
organizations, useful 65-6
organized tours, *see* tours
outdoor activities
   canyoneering 301, 303
   cycling & mountain biking 47, 133, 185, *see also* bicycle travel
   fishing 65, 144, 157, 224, 225, 231, 236, 238, 240, 248, 257, 270, 274, 275, 329, 404, 421, 433, 476, 490
   kayaking & canoeing 329, 433-40
   mountaineering 219, 247, 276, 462
   rafting 433-40
   rock climbing 190, 247, 301, 309, 332, 353, 360, 442, 449
   sea kayaking 133
   skiing 47, 140, 294, 458, 459
Owens Valley 386
Owens, Richard 386
Ozette 456

P
Pacific Crest Trail 22, 69, 330, 468, 477-80
   in California 342, 348-9, 351, 353, 381, 382-6, 393-5, 396, 397, 398, 399
   in Oregon 412, 416, 417, 422, 424, 425, 427-9, 441, 444-7, 466-7

Pacific Northwest 402-67, **403**
Packwood 453
Page 324
Page, John C 324
Paintbrush Divide 243-5
Panguitch 295
Panorama Cliff 399
Paradise 402, 449, 451, 466-7
Paradise Valley 385
Paria Canyon 322-9, **325**
Pawnee Pass 261-2
Pendleton 410, 419
permits 69
   Northwest Forest Pass 406
Petersburg 193
Phantom Ranch 287
Phipps, Washington 321
photography 50, 79-80
Pie Town 475
Pike, Zebulon 202
Pinedale 248
Pink Cliffs 296-9, 317
pirates 157
place names 61
Plateau Point 289
Pollock, George 198
population & people 49-50
Port Angeles 409, 457
Portland 408, 409-10, 411, 465
Post, the 314
postal services 74-5
Potomac Heritage Trail 468, 485-7
Powell, John Wesley 22, 281, 294, 300, 309, 324
prickly heat 94
private land, *see* access issues
Provincetown 156, 157, 159
Ptarmigan Tunnel 212-16
Ptarmigan Wall 215, 216
public transport, *see* bus travel, rail travel etc
pulse rate 94
Punchbowl Falls 413

R
rabies 97
rafting, *see* outdoor activities
rail passes, *see* train travel
Rainier, Peter 447
Raleigh, Walter 17, 18
Randle 467
Reagan, Ronald 19
Red Lodge 225
Redmond 408, 410
redwood, coast 375

redwood, giant 21, 28, 46, 375
   General Sherman Tree 400
   Trail of the Sequoias 400
Reedsport 429, 430
rescue 102
respiration 94
responsible hiking 62-3
Ribbon Falls 288
river crossings 101
rivers
   Apalachicola 482, 483
   Aucilla 482
   Bechler 238-40, **239**
   Belly 215
   Big Sandy 249-51
   Big Thompson 255
   Black 488
   Casselman 487
   Chippewa 488, 490
   Choctawhatchee 483
   Colorado 23, 27, 278, 281-93, 323, 329, 475, 476
   Columbia 27, 409, 411-15, 465-7, 476, 479
   Conemaugh 487
   Connecticut 473
   Crystal (North Fork) 268
   Cuyahoga 28
   Delaware 473
   Duck 485
   Escalante 317, 318, 319-22
   Firehole 238, 239
   Fremont 310, 316
   Henrys 476
   Housatonic 473
   Hudson 17, 18, 473
   Kaweah 372, 380, 400
   Kennebec 473
   Kern 372, 377, 378, 380-2
   Kings 332, 372, 374, 383-5, 395, 479
   Kissimmee 482
   Laird (Canada) 23
   Little Beaver Creek 492
   Little Miami 492
   Lostine 418-22
   Merced 357, 361-2
   Mississippi 17, 18, 22, 476, 483, 484, 485, 493
   Missouri 21, 22, 27, 477, 490, 493
   Mokowanis 215
   Ochlockonee 483
   Ohio 22, 483, 486, 487
   Opalescent 150
   Owens 386
   Penobscot 130

Potomac 473, 485-7
Red Cedar 490
Red 493
Rogue 433-40, **438**
Saint Croix 487, 488, 490, 493
St Lawrence 18
St Louis 493
St Mary 218
San Joaquin 393-5, 397
Shenandoah 473
Sheyenne 493
Skagit 462
Snake 27, 241
Stanislaus (Middle Fork) 351
Sun 220, 221, 224-5
Susquehana 473
Suwannee 481, 482
Tennessee 27, 483, 485
Thunder 289-3, **291**
Trukee 335, 348-9
Tuolumne (Lyell Fork) 369-70
Tye 183-4
Virgin (North Fork) 302, 303-4
Waterton 213
White 221-3, 224
Wild 145
Willamette 409
Wisconsin 488, 489
Withlocoochee 482
Yellowstone 234-6, 275
Youghiogheny 487
road travel, see car travel
Roan Mountain (town) 178
Roanoke 18
rock climbing, see outdoor activities
Rockefeller, John D 165
Rockefeller, John D Jr 241
Rockport 464
Rockwood 487
Rocky Springs 484, 485
Roller Pass 398
Rome (New York) 492
Roosevelt, Franklin D 19, 46, 177, 195, 324, 374, 484
Roosevelt, Theodore 21, 281
Roper, Steve 401

S
Sacagawea 20
Saddle Arch 312-14

Bold indicates maps.

safe hiking 63-4, 89-102
Sahale Arm 465
Saint Augustine 18
St George 280-1
St Louis 483
St Mary 209
Salt Lake City 206
San Diego 18
Santa Fe 207
Santa Rosa Island 483
Savage, James D 357
Sawtooth Pass 377-80, **379**
Sawtooth Ridge 353-5, **354**
scorpions 99-100
sea travel
   to/from the USA 110
search & rescue organizations 102
Seattle 408-9, 410, 411
Sekiu 457
Seneca Rocks 190-1
sequoia tree, see redwood
Serra, Padre Jun'pero 18
Sevenmile Hole 234-6, **235**
shipwrecks 156-7
Silvercord Cascade 235
Silverton 271-2
Sisters 427
skiing, see outdoor activities
Sky Pond 258-9
Skyline Trail 451-3, **452**
Slide Rock Arch 325
Slippery Rock Gorge 492
Smith, Jedediah 18, 332, 374
snakes 99-100
Snoqualmie Pass 444-7, **446**, 480
snowblindness 94
Soda Springs 370
Solon Springs 493
Sonoran Desert 24, 478, 479
South Lake Tahoe 337
South Rim 284-5
Southern Appalachia 162-201, **163**
Southwest 278-329, **279**
special events 82-3
spiders 100
Springdale 301-2
Spruce Island 433
Spruce Knob 190-2, **191**
Stanford, Leland 336
Stanley, FO 251
state parks & reserves 49
   Adirondack 147-51, 160-1
   Alfred Loeb 432
   Allegheny 492

Amicalola Falls 472
Anza Borrego Desert 479
Baxter 125-32, 473
Boardman 431-3, **432**
Brunet Island 490
Cook Forest 492
Copper Falls 492
Crawford Notch 138
Devils Lake 488, 489
DL Bliss 342
Donner Memorial 336
Fort Ransom 493
Franconia Notch 160-1
Grayson Highlands 185, 187
Grover Hot Springs 346
Harriman–Bear Mountain 473
Harris Beach 432
Interstate 488, 490
Jay Cooke 493
Lake Tahoe Nevada 340, 341
Laurel Ridge 486, 487
McConnell's Mill 492
Manning Provincial Park (Canada) 480
Mill Bluff 488
Mirror Lake 489
Moraine 492
Ohiopyle 487
Potawatomi 489
Roan Mountain 177-81
Rockport 464
Rocky Arbor 489
Samuel H Boardman 431-3, **432**
Sugar Pine Point 337, 342
Tosohatchee 482
Stehekin 463
Stevenson 414
Stewart, George 374
student discounts 70
Sturgeon Bay 489
Sunrise 453, 454, 466-7
Surprise Valley 292
Syrett, Ruben C 294

T
Tacoma 448
Tahoe City 337
Tahoe Meadows 340-2, **341**
Tahoe Rim Trail 330, 340-2, 348-9
Tahoe-Yosemite Trail 330, 342-5, 348-9, 350-3
taxes, see money
telephone services 75-6
temperature (body) 94

Temple of Sinawava 304
Temple Pass 249
tetanus 97
Teton Village 242
Texas Pass 248
Tharp, Hale 400
Thomas, Flora Dell 437
Thompson, David 17, 402
Thoreau, Henry David 130, 156-60
Thoreau's Walk 156-60, **159**
Three Ridges 181-4, **183**
thru-hiking, see long-distance trails
ticks 97, 100
time 80
time zones, **81**
Titcomb Basin 276
Torrey 311
tourist offices 66-7
tours, see also guided hikes
  bus 115
  motorcycle 121
  nature 133
Townsend 167
Trail of the Sequoias 400
train travel
  buying tickets 116
  fares 116
  to/from the USA 110
  travel passes 105, 116-17
  within the USA 105, 115-17
travel agencies 107-10, 111-12
  online 103, 104-5
travel passes, see each form of transport, eg, air travel
'Triple Crown' 472
Triple Divide Pass 273-4, 476
Tropic 295-6
Troy 492
Truckee 336, 337
Trudeau, Edward Livingston 147
Tuckerman's Ravine 140-1
Tunnel Falls 413
Tuolumne Meadows 332, 358, 366, 369, 370, 401, 479
Tupelo 484
Tusayan 285

U
Under the Rim Trail 296-9, **297**
useful organizations 65-6

V
Vancouver, George 447
Vernal Fall 361, 362

Vikings (Norse) 18
visas 67-70
volcanoes & hot springs 23, 24, 232-3, 234, 235, 236-7, 275, 277, 346, 350, 381, 386, 396, 398, 402, 404, 415, 422-9, 447, 458-62, 467, 476, 479

W
Walker, Joseph Reddeford 357
walking, see hiking
Wallface Ponds 149
Walters Wiggles 309
Washington, DC 18, 485, 487
Washington, George 18, 486, 487
wasps 99
water purification 91-2, 95
Waterpocket Fold 309-17
Wawona 367
Waynesboro 181-2
weather, see also climate
  information 79
  when to hike 53
Webster, Noah 51
weights & measures 80-1, 82
Wellfleet 158
Wenatchee 409, 442
West Glacier (town) 209
West Yellowstone 231-4
Whitney, Josiah D 332
Whydah 157
wilderness areas 49
  Absaroka-Beartooth 225-9, 275
  Aldo Leopold 475
  Alpine Lakes 402, 440-7, 478, 480
  Anaconda-Pintler 477
  Ansel Adams 386, 396-8
  Beaverhead 477
  Big Gum Swamp 482
  Billie's Bay 482
  Bob Marshall 219-25, 274-5, 474, 477
  Bradwell Bay 481, 482, 483
  Bridger 247, 476
  Bucks Lake 334
  Carson-Iceberg 334, 335, 345, 346
  Cloud Peak 270-1
  Collegiate Peaks 271
  Cranberry 201
  Desolation 334, 342-5, **344**, 398, 479
  Dinkey Lakes 334

Dolly Sods 192-5
Dome Land 334, 386
Eagle Cap 418-22
Emigrant 334, 345, 350-3, **352**
Fitzpatrick 247
Gila 475
Glacier Peak 480
Golden Trout 334, 386
Granite Chief 335, 398
Great Bear 219, 474, 477
Great Gulf 136-43
High Uinta 271
Holy Cross 475
Hoover 334, 335, 345, 346, 353, 386, 399
Indian Peaks 260-5, **263**, 475
Jedediah Smith 240, 245, 276
Jennie Lakes 334
John Muir 334, 386, 389-92, 393, 401
Juniper Prairie 482
Kaiser 334
La Garita 475
Lewis Fork 188
Little Lake George 482
Little Wilson Creek 187
Mark O Hatfield 412-13
Maroon Bells–Snowmass 265-9, 277
Mokelumne 334, 335, 345, 346, 349-50, 399
Monarch 334
Mt Baker 462
Mt Hood 417
Mt Jefferson 466-7, 478, 479
Mt Massive 475
Mt Rose 335, 339-40
Mt Washington 423, 428
Mt Zirkel 476
Mud Swamp–New River 483
Never Summer 475
Paria Canyon–Vermilion Cliffs 325-6
Pecos 273
Pemigewasset 160-1
Popo Agie 247, 251
Porcupine 493
Ptarmigan Peak 475
Rainbow Lake 493
San Pedro 475
Sawtooth 271
Scapegoat 219, 474, 477
Selway-Bitterroot 270

Slickrock 201
South San Juan 475
South Sierra 386
Teton 476
Three Sisters 422-9
Vasquez Peak 475
Weminuche 271-2, 468, 475
Wheeler Peak 272
Wild Rogue 433-40
wildflowers 35-6, *see also* flora
wildlife, *see* fauna
wildlife spotting 36, 65, *see also* birdwatching
Absaroka-Beartooth Wilderness 225
Allegheny Mountains 189, 201
Beaverhead National Forest 477
Blue Ridge Mountains 177
Bob Marshall Wilderness 224
Florida 481

Glacier National Park 208, 213, 217
Grand Teton National Park 246, 247
Great Smoky Mountains National Park 162-4, 171
Maroon Bells–Snowmass Wilderness 268
Mt Rainier National Park 447, 451, 453
Mt Rogers National Recreation Area 184
Paria Canyon 328
Rocky Mountain National Park 252
Southern Oregon Coast 429, 432
Wind River Range 247-8, 251
Yellowstone National Park 235, 236
Wilson, Woodrow 132, 282, 300

Winchester Bay 430
Wind River Roadless Area 247
Wisconsin Dells 489
women hikers 63-4
women's health 100
Wonderland Trail 447, 466-7
Woodford 153, 155
woolly adelgid 174, 176
wound cleaning 99

Y
York 20
Yosemite Decimal System 61
Yosemite Valley 21, 23, 24, 28, 355, 357, 358, 359, 360-5, 367-8, **368**, 399

Z
Zillmer, Ray 488
Zion Canyon 300-9, **306**
Zion Narrows 303-4, **304**

Boxed Text

150 Years of 'Improvements' 138
Airlines 104
Bears 407
Bigfoot Territory 460
Bubbly in the Back Country 370
Cape Cod Pirates 157
Chinook Jargon 414
Choosing Gear 56
Chronology of US History 18-19
Common Northwest Wildflowers 418
Doing Tucks 140
Driving by Numbers 117
End of an Explorer 485
Equipment Check List 56-7
Everyday Health 94
Excess of Elk, An 241
Extreme Hike in the Presidentials, An 142
Glacial Debris Flows 450
Glaciers & Glacial Landforms 214

Grizzly & Black Bears 231
Highlights 52
Hike Safety – Basic Rules 101
Hypothermia 409
John Muir (1838–1914) 358
John Wesley Powell 300
Lake Tahoe 336
Long Gone Grizzlies 357
Long Hike – John Muir Trail 391
Long Hike – Tahoe Rim Trail 338
Long Hike – Tahoe-Yosemite Trail 347
Medical Kit Check List 90
Metrication in the USA 82
Mexican Food 86
Northwest Forest Passes – How Your Trail Fees Really Work 406
Paiute Legend of Bryce's Hoodoos 293
Regal Redwoods 375
Silence of the Lambs 387

Struggling Upward 131
Balds of Roan Mountain, The 178
Carving Colorado River, The 283
Counter-Balance Method, The 87
Layering Principle, The 58
Legend of Tisse'yak, The 363
Lewis & Clark Expedition, The 20
Lodge on Mt Leconte, The 174
Peregrine Falcon, The 173
Thru-Hikers 472
Traveling with Stoves 106
Two Years in a Tree 46
What's Happening to the trees? 176
Where Do Mountains Come From? 23
Women & Bears 64
Women on the Trail 63
Wound Cleaning 99

MAP LEGEND

BOUNDARIES

............International
............Regional
............Disputed

HYDROGRAPHY

............Coastline
............River, Creek
............Lake
............Intermittent Lake
............Salt Lake
............Canal
............Spring, Rapids
............Waterfalls
............Swamp

ROUTES & TRANSPORT

............Freeway
............Highway
............Major Road
............Minor Road
............Unsealed Highway
............Unsealed Major Road
............Unsealed Minor Road
............Track
............Lane

............Tunnel
............Train Route & Station
............Cable Car or Chairlift

............Described Hike
............Alternative Route
............Side Trip
............Walking Tour
............Ferry Route

AREA FEATURES

............Park (Regional Maps)
............Park (Hike Maps)
............Glacier

ROUTE SHIELDS

90 ....Interstate Freeway
84 ....US Highway
101 ....State Highway

MAP SYMBOLS

✪ **CAPITAL** ....National Capital
◉ **CAPITAL** ....Regional Capital
● **CITY** ....City
● **Town** ....Town
○ **Village** ....Village

............Camping Area
............Hut
............Lookout
▼ ....Place to Eat
● ....Place to Stay
● ....Point of Interest
............Shelter
🚶 ....Trailhead

✈ ....Airport
🏄 ....Beach
🚏 ....Bus Stop
............Cave
✚ ....Church
............Cliff or Escarpment
500 ....Contour
❀ ....Gardens
............Gate
✛ ....Hospital
☆ ....Lighthouse
▲ ....Mountain or Hill
............Museum
............National Park

............Parking
)(............Pass
............Picnic Area
............Police Station
✉ ....Post Office
............Restroom
............Shopping Centre
............Ski Area
+(ft) ....Spot Height
............Telephone
............Tourist Information
● ....Transport
△ ....Trigonometric Point
............Zoo

Note: not all symbols displayed above appear in this book

LONELY PLANET OFFICES

Australia
PO Box 617, Hawthorn, Victoria 3122
☎ 03 9819 1877 fax 03 9819 6459
✉ talk2us@lonelyplanet.com.au

USA
150 Linden St, Oakland, CA 94607
☎ 510 893 8555 or ☎ 800 275 8555 (toll free)
fax 510 893 8572
✉ info@lonelyplanet.com

UK
10a Spring Place, London NW5 3BH
☎ 020 7428 4800 fax 020 7428 4828
✉ go@lonelyplanet.co.uk

France
1 rue du Dahomey, 75011 Paris
☎ 01 55 25 33 00 fax 01 55 25 33 01
✉ bip@lonelyplanet.fr
🖥 www.lonelyplanet.fr

World Wide Web: 🖥 www.lonelyplanet.com *or* AOL keyword: lp
Lonely Planet Images: ✉ lpi@lonelyplanet.com.au